THE AMERICAN BAR ASSOCIATION

The Complete Personal Legal Guide

The Essential Reference for Every Household

RANDOM HOUSE
REFERENCE

Copyright © 2008, 2004, 1994, 1990 by the American Bar Association

All rights reserved. No part of this book may be reproduced in any form or by any means, electronic or mechanical, including photocopying, recording, or by any information storage and retrieval system, without the written permission of the publisher. Published in the United States by Random House Reference, an imprint of The Random House Information Group, a division of Random House, Inc., New York, and simultaneously in Canada by Random House of Canada Limited, Toronto.

RANDOM HOUSE is a registered trademark of Random House, Inc.

The first edition of the *American Bar Association Family Legal Guide* published in 1990 by Times Books, a division of Random House, Inc. A second edition, also published by Times Books, a division of Random House, was published in 1994. The third edition was published in 2004 by Random House Reference, an imprint of the Random House Information Group, a division of Random House, Inc. This revised and updated edition is based on the third edition of the work.

Please address inquiries about electronic licensing of any products for use on a network, in software, or on CD-ROM to the Subsidiary Rights Department, Random House Information Group, fax 212-572-6003.

This book is available at special discounts for bulk purchases for sales promotions or premiums. Special editions, including personalized covers, excerpts of existing books, and corporate imprints, can be created in large quantities for special needs. For more information, write to Random House, Inc., Special Markets/Premium Sales, 1745 Broadway, MD 6-2, New York, NY, 10019 or e-mail specialmarkets@randomhouse.com.

Visit the Random House Reference Web site: www.randomwords.com

Printed in the United States of America

10 9 8 7 6 5 4 3 2 1

Library of Congress Cataloging in Publication Data TK.

ISBN: 978-0-375-72302-5

Fourth Edition

CONTENTS

Every day, Americans are faced with situations that raise significant legal issues—from home purchases and rentals to shopping online or driving a car. Even the most mundane activities can implicate the law, and chances are that you or someone in your family needs or will need practical, easy-to-understand information. This book is designed to meet that need. It will quickly become your "go to" source for a very wide range of legal situations.

Legal problems are all different. Some require immediate action so that you can protect your rights, while others might be solved through negotiation or other means. Many potential legal problems can be avoided altogether with good planning.

It's important that you know and understand your rights and options. It's also important that you understand the language of the law and the rights of others. This book, developed by the ABA's Division for Public Education, provides you with the benefit of the ABA's network of hundreds of thousands of lawyers. It was written with the aid of ABA members from all over the country who are experts in the many areas of law it covers, including judges and professors of law, as well as lawyers who practice in these areas and cope with these issues every day. Because of all the lawyers who worked on this book, you can be sure that the information it provides is useful, helpful, unbiased, and reader-friendly. And since ABA members practice in all jurisdictions, you can be sure that it reflects a national picture that is relevant to your legal needs.

Preserving the rule of law and helping people understand and appreciate the law are central to the mission of the American Bar Association. The ABA is the nation's premier source of legal information. With more than 413,000 members representing every specialty and every type of legal practice, the ABA is uniquely able to deliver accurate, up-to-date legal information to its members, the media, and the general public. Besides its commitment to public education, the ABA provides programs to assist lawyers and judges in their work. It pursues initiatives aimed at improving the legal system for the public, including the promotion of fast, affordable alternatives to lawsuits, such as mediation, arbitration, conciliation, and, in appropriate cases, small-claims courts. Through its support for lawyer referral programs and pro bono services (to which lawyers donate their time), the ABA has helped people find the best lawyers for their particular cases and receive quality legal help within their budgets.

We hope that this book provides you with a broader understanding of the role of law in our society. The law isn't just for lawyers; on the contrary, it touches every single American every single day in every single way. It is the cornerstone of our democracy and the glue that holds us together as a society. The county courthouse is a powerful symbol of our belief in the rule of law, because it is the place where anyone, regardless of income or social standing, can seek justice in an impartial court, under rules that assure fairness. The law is the best means we have devised to resolve disputes by reason instead of force. It is our best chance of achieving justice.

Henry F. White Jr., a retired Rear Admiral in the U.S. Navy Reserve, is the Executive Di-rector of the American Bar Association. He practiced law for over thirty years in the private, corporate, and public sectors and served as an arbitrator for maritime disputes.

How do you get your legal information? Today many of us surf the Web, moving from site to site as we search for the best information. The Web can be a great place to get information fast, but it can also be frustrating. If you're not using the right search terms, you can spend lots of time finding little information. And even if you're on the right track in your search, you might easily encounter the problem of information overload. Often you may find yourself sifting through multiple sites that provide conflicting information, trying to figure out who is responsible for providing that information, when it was last updated, or if it was even accurate in the first place. That's why this book is so important: It is an authoritative reference you can count on. It has the resources of the nation's premier legal organization—the American Bar Association—solidly behind it. The authors and editors are experts in their fields. They know the kinds of legal issues and problems you are apt to face. With their help, we've fashioned a book that answers the questions you are likely to ask, in language you can understand.

How This Book Can Help You

This book addresses those aspects of the law that affect us every day. In an easy-to-understand, question-and-answer format, it will help you

- buy or rent a home;
- get a mortgage, refinance your home, or find the best deal possible on a credit card;
- order products online, over the phone, or from a catalog;
- buy or lease a car;
- understand your rights in the workplace;
- understand your rights to Social Security, Medicare, Medicaid, and other benefits; and
- devise an estate plan that will provide for your family, protect you if you become incapacitated, and save you as much as possible in taxes.

You may still need to talk to a lawyer after reading this book, but you'll have the advantage of acting as an informed consumer. We provide guidance that will help you decide whether you need a lawyer and, if so, how to find one that's right for you and your budget. We give you tips on what to ask in your first interview with a prospective lawyer, and information about various fee structures and your rights as a legal client. We also explain how the legal system works, how a case moves through the system, and how you can protect your rights at every stage in the process.

Legal issues can pop up at all points in your life. The law affects everything from getting married to having a child, from buying your first home to purchasing a car to planning your estate. For each of these milestones, this book seeks to help you navigate the legal terrain. It explains your options, discusses how to evaluate your situation, and, if necessary, helps you find an attorney specializing in the area of law applicable to your situation.

New Topics

In the years since the first edition of this book was published, the world has changed greatly. That's why the authors and editors have reviewed and updated every entry, so that you'll have the latest and best information. We've also added new features, including an entire chapter on the law and special-needs children, a topic that is increasingly important to many families. As this legal specialty grows and more children are identified as needing additional services, this area of law is becoming more important—and, in many cases, more complex. This book now outlines the federal laws regulating special education and disabilities services and defines important rights and terms as they apply to families. Additionally, it provides you with tips and checklists for ensuring that your child receives the best education possible.

We are also proud to offer new sections on international family law issues, such as international kidnapping and child custody disputes, and discussions on disaster readiness to ensure that, in the event of a disaster, you and your family can focus on everyone's safety and not on your legal concerns.

Written with You in Mind

In writing this book, we sought to take the mystery out of the law. We begin each chapter with anecdotes drawn from real life, and then follow with a question-and-answer section. The answers are concrete—they try to point out how the law affects us every day, and what practical steps we can take to assure that our rights are protected. You won't find legal jargon or technicalities here—just concise, straightforward discussions of your options under the law. Within chapters, special sidebars also provide practical tips, warnings about potential pitfalls, and clear, plain-English definitions of legal terms.

As a new feature, this edition also provides checklists of key points from each section. Look for the features titled "Remember This"—at a glance, they provide key information that can help you navigate a variety of legal issues.

Finally, we've listed additional resources and Internet references in an appendix at the conclusion of this book. "The World at Your Fingertips" tells you where to find free or inexpensive materials providing more information about the topics covered throughout the book. Most of these resources can be found on the Internet, and point you to information you can trust for further research and education.

How to Use This Book

As the table of contents shows, each chapter in this book explains the way in which the law affects a major segment of everyday life. The family law chapter, for example, covers marriage (the requirements for getting married, who owns what property, and so forth) and separation and divorce (who gets what property, issues relating to support, and so on). This chapter also explains how the law affects children—from adoption to parental obligations relating to child custody and support.

If material in one chapter relates to information provided in other chapters—issues relating to home ownership, for example, can often arise during a divorce—this book cross-references the applicable topics and directs you to the exact chapter that covers each one in-depth. The book's index also helps you to research a topic by listing all of the pages where it is discussed.

This book was developed by the Division for Public Education. For more than thirty years, the Division for Public Education has been a national leader in helping students and the public learn about our rights and responsibilities under the law. This book is the result of a unique collaboration with ABA members from all over the country working together to provide you with the most accurate, up-to-date information possible.

The information included in this book is an excellent introduction to the law in a variety of important areas. Armed with your attorney's advice and the knowledge and insights provided by this book, you can be confident that the legal decisions you make will be in your best interests.

Dwight L. Smith is chair of the ABA's Standing Committee on Public Education and is an attorney in private practice in Tulsa, Oklahoma. His practice focuses on the areas of general business, commercial litigation, dispute resolution, banking, and probate.

CHAPTER ONE

When and How to Use a Lawyer

Simon has decided to buy a car. Julie and Sam are getting married. Annette thinks she might have been discriminated against when applying for a job. Do these people need to talk to lawyers? If so, how do they find one? What do they say? The law affects almost everything you do—from making a purchase, to driving a car, to interacting with others. There are many situations that you can handle on your own, without the assistance of a lawyer. However, when circumstances and laws are complex—for example, if you're injured, or if you might lose valuable rights—you may need a lawyer's guidance.

    When do you need a lawyer? How can you find one? How do you work with one? This chapter helps you find the answers to these and other critical questions.

LAWYER BASICS

This section outlines the basics of the legal profession and explains the role of a lawyer. It also helps you to determine when you need a lawyer's help, and explains the various types and specialties of lawyers.

What Is a Lawyer?

Q. What exactly is a lawyer?

A. A **lawyer** (also called an **attorney, counsel,** or a **counselor**) is a licensed professional who advises and represents people in legal matters. Today's lawyer can be young or old, male or female. Nearly one-third of all lawyers are under thirty-five years old.

Q. I come from another country, and I need to hire a lawyer. Are notaries public also lawyers?

A. A person with the title "notary public," "accountant," or "certified public accountant" is not necessarily a lawyer. Do not assume that such titles have the same meaning as in your native country. In some countries, a lawyer is called a "barrister" or a "solicitor."

Q. What are a lawyer's main duties?

A. A lawyer has two main duties: to uphold the law and to protect a client's rights. To carry out these duties, a lawyer should understand the law and be an effective communicator.

Q. Is most of a lawyer's time spent in court?

A. No. Most lawyers normally spend more time in an office than in a courtroom. The practice of law most often involves researching legal developments, investigating facts, writing and preparing legal documents, giving advice, and settling disputes. What we consider to be the "law" generally derives from three sources: the Constitution (the U.S. Constitution and the constitutions drafted by various states), statutes, and case decisions. The law changes constantly as new laws are enacted and existing laws are amended or repealed. In addition, decisions in court cases regularly alter what the law currently means, as judges interpret and apply the U.S. Constitution, state constitutions, federal or state statutes, and federal, state, and local codes and regulations. For these reasons, a lawyer must devote time to keeping current on changes in the law, and how those changes affect his or her practice.

Q. What are the professional requirements for becoming a lawyer?

A. To understand how laws and the legal system work, lawyers require special schooling. Each state has standards that a person must meet before obtaining a license to practice law there. Before being allowed to practice law in most states, a person must

- have a bachelor's degree or its equivalent;
- complete three years at an ABA-accredited law school;
- pass a state bar examination, which usually lasts for two or three days and tests knowledge in selected areas of law;
- pass required tests on professional ethics and responsibility;
- be approved by a committee that investigates character and background;
- swear an oath, usually to uphold the state and federal law and constitutions; and
- obtain a license from the highest court in the state, usually the state supreme court.

Q. Once licensed in one state, is a lawyer allowed to practice law in all states?

A. Not automatically. To become licensed in more than one state, a lawyer must usually comply with each state's bar admission requirements. However, some states permit licensed out-of-state lawyers to practice law if they have done so in another state for several years and the new state's highest court approves them. Many states also have provisions for lawyers to participate in specific cases in states where they are not licensed. The lawyer in such a case is said to be appearing pro hac vice, which means "for this one particular occasion."

Q. If I have a legal problem, do I have to hire a lawyer?

A. Not necessarily—you may represent yourself. Nonlawyers or paralegals may also be qualified to represent you in certain situations, such as in the bringing of a complaint before a government agency—for example, in a dispute over Social Security or Medicare benefits. (**Paralegals** are nonlawyers who have received training that enables them to assist lawyers in a number of tasks, though they typically cannot represent clients in court.) If you find yourself in this type of situation, ask the applicable government agency what types of representation are acceptable.

There are many matters you can handle yourself, if you know how to go about it. For example, you can represent yourself in traffic or small-claims court, or engage in negotiations and enter into contracts on your own. But if you are not sure about the consequences of your actions or are uncertain about how to proceed, getting some quick legal advice from a lawyer could be very helpful in preventing problems down the road.

Q. Why do lawyers seem to speak and write in a totally different language?

A. Lawyers and others trained in the law often use legal terms as shorthand to express complicated ideas or principles. These words and phrases, many derived from Latin, are often jokingly referred to as a foreign language—**legalese.** Although some legalese may be necessary in order to communicate certain ideas precisely, a document that is understood by very few of its readers is just plain poor communication.

Since 1978, the law has required that federal regulations be "written in plain English and understandable to those who must comply" with them. Many states also have laws requiring that insurance policies, leases, and consumer contracts be written in plain English. Of particular importance is a trend in law schools to discourage the use of legalese and to encourage the use of plain, comprehensible English.

When Do You Need a Lawyer?

Q. I think I might benefit from speaking to a lawyer, but I'm not actually involved in a legal dispute. Does this mean I shouldn't get an attorney?

A. No. In fact, lawyers often help clients in matters that are not legal disputes. For example, a person might consult a lawyer when starting a business or entering into a partnership, when buying or selling a home, or for information and advice on tax matters or estate planning. Some clients receive regular legal checkups that, like medical checkups, are designed to catch problems early or prevent them altogether.

Q. *I understand that consulting a lawyer may sometimes be unnecessary. But are there specific situations in which I should always consult a lawyer?*

A. Yes, some matters are best handled by a lawyer. While such matters are sometimes difficult to recognize, nearly everyone agrees that you should talk with a lawyer about major life events or changes, which might include

- being arrested for a crime;
- being served with legal papers in a civil lawsuit;
- being involved in a serious accident that causes personal injury or property damage;
- a change in family status such as divorce, adoption, or death; or
- a change in financial status such as obtaining or losing valuable personal property or real estate, starting a business, or filing for bankruptcy.

▶ TIME IS RUNNING OUT

Be aware that your right to initiate a legal action will not last forever. Every state has a time limit within which a lawsuit must be filed. The time limits vary for different types of claims. The logic behind such limits, called **statutes of limitations,** is that lawsuits are most easily and fairly resolved when memories are fresh and while evidence still exists. Therefore, it is important to act as soon as you suspect that you may have a valid legal claim.

Help from Nonlawyers

Q. *If I do not use a lawyer, who else can help me?*

A. There are many ways to solve a grievance without resorting to lawyers. For example, if you believe a business has cheated you, you may get help from a consumer protection agency run by your city, county, state, or fed-

---

▶ GET HELP EARLY

Don't just ignore those invoices or letters threatening legal action. Legal problems won't just go away. When dealing with legal issues, an ounce of prevention is worth many dollars and anxious hours of cure. Contacting a lawyer only after a legal problem has escalated to crisis proportions can lead to unnecessary anxiety, and may make the problem more difficult and expensive to solve. Lawyers should be thought of as preventers of legal problems, not just solvers.

If you call a lawyer as a last resort, it may already be too late. A lawyer may not be able to protect you if you have already lost your rights.

eral government. Many businesses, stores, and utility companies have their own departments to help resolve consumer complaints. In addition, some communities have an **ombudsman,** a government official whose job is to mediate and resolve minor landlord/tenant, consumer, employment, or other issues. Local television and radio stations may also have programs aimed at resolving consumer-related disputes.

Most states also have **dispute resolution centers.** These centers, which may be known as neighborhood justice centers or citizens' dispute settlement programs, specialize in helping people with common problems and disputes. Their services are often available for a small fee, or even at no cost.

Q. Can counseling solve some problems?

A. Yes. Sometimes problems that seem to be legal in nature may actually be solved or prevented by other means. Many groups offer guidance and counseling for personal problems relating to marriage, child rearing, or financial management. Private counselors or members of the clergy also may provide such help.

Q. What is a small-claims court?

A. A **small-claims court** is a streamlined forum in which people can air a dispute and have a judge decide it promptly. Most states allow people to represent themselves in small-claims court if the total amount of their claim does not exceed a certain dollar amount, such as $2,500. The cost of small-claims court is minimal, the procedures involved are relatively simple, and the resolution of a case is usually prompt. Keep small-claims courts in mind if your problem is not very complicated and your losses are relatively small. Chapter

---

▶ **REPRESENTING YOURSELF IN A LEGAL MATTER**

People without legal training may be able to handle some simple legal matters themselves—this is called proceeding **pro se** or **pro per.** Taking on a legal matter yourself is risky, because each step may involve consequences that you may not think about. Doing it yourself also requires a lot of time and energy. Moreover, a degree of objectivity is needed in most legal situations, and it may be difficult for you to stay objective when closely involved in your own case. But sometimes people feel that they can't afford legal representation or they just want to do it themselves.

A number of local courts or nonprofit organizations provide guidance to people who want to handle legal matters pro se. They assist people in selecting and completing court forms, understanding court procedures, and filing cases.

2, "How the Legal System Works," provides guidance on how to file and proceed with a small-claims lawsuit.

Q. A friend recommended that I try a local dispute resolution center. What does this type of center have to offer?

A. For the right kind of case, dispute resolution centers can be a quick, low-cost (or free) alternative to formal legal proceedings. These centers will be discussed further in the next chapter.

Q. Can the other party and I settle a dispute without lawyers?

A. Yes, although you might want a lawyer's help to put your agreement in writing. When attempting to resolve your dispute, always be open to possible solutions and listen to the other person's side of the story. Remember that, with or without the help of lawyers, most people resolve their civil disputes out of court.

Settlement of cases is discussed in more detail in Chapter 2, "How the Legal System Works."

Types of Lawyers

Q. Do lawyers normally work alone, or do most of them work for companies or the government?

A. About two-thirds of all lawyers are in private practice, usually employed by firms of various sizes. Almost half of the lawyers in private practice are sole practitioners who work alone. Others practice with one or more other lawyers.

Q. What are the different areas of law?

A. The answer to that question could be never-ending. The law affects virtually every aspect of life, and specialized areas of law exist in virtually every type of subject area. Most lawyers concentrate in one or a few specific areas, such as domestic relations, criminal law, personal injury, estate planning and administration, real estate, taxation, immigration, or intellectual property law.

REMEMBER THIS

- If you have a dispute, you don't automatically need a lawyer—keep an open mind and be aware of all your options. If you're not sure, then seek legal advice.

- Having said that, if your dispute is serious, if someone has commenced legal action against you, or if you're injured, you should see a lawyer without delay. Getting advice early could save you time and money.

CHOOSING A LAWYER

You've thought about it carefully, you've spoken to friends, and you've decided that you need to contact a lawyer. The big problem is—how to find one? This section gives you some tips on what to look for when choosing a lawyer, and leads you through some questions you can ask a lawyer when you first meet. If you do your homework, you can hire a lawyer who has the experience and expertise to help you with your problem.

Looking for a Lawyer

Q. What should I look for when choosing a lawyer?

A. The lawyer will be helping you solve your problems, so the first requirement is that you feel comfortable enough to tell him or her, honestly and completely, all the facts necessary to resolve your situation. When selecting your lawyer, don't rely on what you hear or read. Judge the lawyer for yourself—only you can determine which lawyer is best for your situation.

Q. What practical considerations should I keep in mind when choosing a lawyer?

A. Yes. A lawyer's area of expertise and prior experience are both important. Many states have specialization programs that certify lawyers as specialists in certain types of law. These states include Alabama, Arizona, California, Connecticut, Florida, Georgia, Idaho, Indiana, Louisiana, Maine, Minnesota, New Jersey, New Mexico, North Carolina, Ohio, Pennsylvania, South Carolina, Tennessee, and Texas. Some legal specialties also have their own certification programs, such as the National Association of Estate Planners and Councils and the National Elder Law Foundation. In states without certification programs, ask the attorney about his or her areas of specialization. You may also wish to ask about the types of cases the lawyer generally handles. Keep in mind that most lawyers are not certified in a specialty, but this does not necessarily mean that a lawyer is not an expert in a specific field.

When selecting a lawyer, other considerations include the location of the lawyer's office, the fees he or she charges, and the length of time required to resolve your case.

Q. Where should I start to look for a lawyer?

A. There are many ways to find a reliable lawyer. One of the best ways is to ask for recommendations from a trusted friend, relative, or business associate. However, be aware that each legal case is different and that a lawyer who is right for someone else may not suit you or your legal problem.

Q. Are advertisements useful for finding a lawyer?

A. In some ways, yes. However, always be careful not to believe everything you read and hear—especially with advertisements. Newspaper, telephone directory, radio, and television ads, along with direct mail, can familiarize you with lawyers who may be ap-

propriate for your legal needs. Some ads also will help you determine a lawyer's area of expertise. Other ads will quote a fee or price range for handling a specific type of "simple" case. But keep in mind that your case may not have a simple solution. If a lawyer quotes a fee, be certain you know exactly what services and expenses the charge does and does not include.

Q. What about a local referral service?

A. Most communities have referral services to help people find lawyers. You might be able to find them under "Lawyer Referral Service" or some similar heading in your yellow pages. These services usually recommend a lawyer in the area to evaluate a situation. Several services offer help to groups with unique characteristics, such as the elderly, immigrants, victims of domestic violence, or persons with a disability.

Bar associations in most communities make referrals according to specific areas of law, helping you find a lawyer with the right experience and practice concentration. Many referral services also have competency requirements for lawyers who wish to receive referrals in a particular area of law. You can find your local bar association in the phone book's white pages either under your community's name ("Centerville Bar Association") or under your county's name ("Cass County Bar Association"). You can also find your bar's website through your favorite search engine, or through the ABA's website (see The World at Your Fingertips, page 722 for all website references).

Still, these services are not a surefire way to find the best lawyer or the right lawyer for you. Some services make referrals without concern for the lawyer's type or level of experience. You may want to seek out a lawyer referral service that participates in the ABA-sponsored certification program, which uses a logo to identify lawyer referral programs that comply with certain quality standards developed by the ABA.

Q. My new job offers a prepaid legal services plan. What can I expect?

A. Legal services, like many other things, are often less expensive when bought in bulk. Some employers, labor and credit unions, and other groups have formed "legal insurance" plans. These plans vary. Many cover most, if not all, of the cost of legal consultations, document preparation, and court representation in routine legal matters. Other programs cover only advice and consultation with a lawyer. Before joining a legal plan, make sure you are familiar with its coverage and know whether you will be required to make out-of-pocket contributions. These group plans follow the same pattern as group or cooperative medical insurance plans. Employers or unions set up a fund to pay their employees' legal fees, with the employee sometimes contributing a small co-payment. Legal group plans have become much more widespread in recent years.

Q. I want to hire a lawyer, but I do not have much money. Where can I find low-cost legal help?

A. Many legal-assistance programs offer inexpensive or free legal services to those in need. Look in the yellow pages under topics such as "legal clinics," "legal aid," or "legal advice," or search online. Most legal-aid programs have special guidelines for eligibility, often based on where you live, the size of your family, and your income. Some legal-aid offices have their own staff lawyers, and others operate with volunteer lawyers. Note that

people do not have the right to a free lawyer in civil legal matters.

Q. I have been accused of a crime, and I cannot afford a lawyer. What can I do?

A. If you are accused of a crime, the U.S. Constitution guarantees you the right to be represented by a lawyer in any case for which you could be incarcerated for six months or more. State constitutions may guarantee your right to a lawyer for lesser crimes. If you cannot afford a lawyer, either the judge hearing the case will appoint a private lawyer to represent you free of charge or the government's public defender will handle your case, also at no charge. See Chapter 2, "How the Legal System Works," for more information about criminal trials and your right to an attorney.

Q. Besides court-appointed defenders, is there any other form of government assistance available?

A. Departments and agencies of both the state and federal governments often have staff lawyers who can help the general public in limited situations, without charge. Consider contacting the relevant agency if you have specific concerns, such as environmental protection problems or discrimination in employment or housing.

Your state's attorney general also may provide free guidance to the public regarding state laws. For example, some states maintain consumer protection departments as a function of the attorney general's office.

Similarly, counties, cities, and townships often employ government lawyers in their legal departments who may provide the public with guidance about local laws. Some of these local offices also offer consumer protection assistance.

To find such agencies, check the government listings in your phone book.

Questions to Ask a Lawyer

Q. *Can I meet with a lawyer before deciding to hire him or her?*

A. A lawyer will usually meet with you briefly or talk with you by phone so the two of you can get acquainted. This meeting is a chance to talk with the lawyer before making a final hiring decision. In many cases, there is no fee charged for an initial consultation. However, to be on the safe side, ask about fees before setting up your first appointment.

During this meeting, you can decide whether you want to hire the lawyer. Many people feel nervous or intimidated when meeting lawyers, but remember that you're the one

---

▶ **AREAS OF LEGAL PRACTICE**

Here are just a few examples of the different areas in which lawyers specialize, and the types of services they provide within each specialty:

- **Business law.** Advising about starting a new business (such as a corporation or partnership), general corporate matters, business taxation, and mergers and acquisitions.
- **Criminal law.** Defending or prosecuting those accused of committing crimes.
- **Domestic relations.** Representing individuals in matters relating to separation, annulment, divorce, child custody, and child support.
- **Estate planning.** Advising clients in drawing up wills, probate matters, and managing their estates.
- **Immigration.** Representing parties in proceedings relating to naturalization and citizenship.
- **Intellectual property.** Dealing with issues concerning trademarks, copyright regulations, and patents.
- **Labor and employment.** Advising and representing employers, unions, or employees regarding issues of union organization, workplace safety, job protection, and compliance with government regulations.
- **Personal injury.** Representing clients injured intentionally or negligently, and those with workers' compensation claims.
- **Real estate.** Assisting clients in developing property, rezoning, and buying, selling, or renting homes or other property.
- **Taxation.** Counseling businesses and individuals in local, state, and federal tax matters.

doing the hiring, and what's most important is that you're satisfied with what you're getting for your money. Before you make any hiring decisions, you might want to ask certain questions to aid in your evaluation.

Q. What sort of questions should I ask a lawyer?

A. Ask about the lawyer's experience and areas of practice. How long has the lawyer been practicing law? What kinds of legal problems does the lawyer handle most often? Are most of his or her clients individuals or businesses?

Q. Is it proper to ask the lawyer if anyone else will be working on my case?

A. Since you are the one paying the bill, this is well within your rights. Ask if staff such as paralegals or law clerks will be used in researching or preparing your case. If so, will there be separate charges for their services? Who will be consulted if the lawyer is unsure about some aspects of your case? Will the lawyer recommend another lawyer or firm if he or she is unable to handle your case?

Q. I met with a lawyer who referred me to another lawyer. Should I be angry?

A. Probably not. Occasionally, a lawyer will suggest that someone else in the same firm or an outside lawyer handle your problem. Perhaps the original lawyer is too busy to give your case the full attention it deserves. Maybe your problem requires another lawyer's expertise. No one likes to feel that a lawyer is shifting him or her to another lawyer. However, most reassignments and referrals occur for a good reason. Do not hesitate to request a meeting with the new lawyer to make sure you are comfortable with him or her.

> ▶ **HAVE FAITH**
>
> It is important that you trust the lawyer you hire, believing that he or she will do the best job possible in protecting your legal rights. However, remember that lawyers cannot work magic. No lawyer can be expected to win every case, and even the best legal advice may turn out to be not exactly what you wanted to hear.

Q. What, in particular, should I ask about fees and costs?

A. How are fees charged: by the hour, by the case, or by the amount won? About how much money will be required to handle the case from start to finish? When must you pay the bill? Can you pay it in installments? Ask for a written statement explaining how and what fees will be charged, and a monthly statement showing specific services rendered and the charge for each.

Q. When I first meet with my prospective lawyer, should I ask about the possible outcome of my case?

A. Certainly, but beware of any lawyer who guarantees a big settlement or assures a victory in court. Remember that there are at least two sides to every legal issue and that many factors can affect its resolution. Ask for the lawyer's opinion of your case's strengths and weaknesses. Will the lawyer most likely settle your case out of court, or is it likely that the case will go to trial? What are the advantages and disadvantages of settlement? Of going to trial? What kind of experience does the lawyer have in trial work? If you lose at the trial, will the lawyer be willing to appeal the decision?

Q. Should I ask if and how I can help with my case?

A. Yes. It is often in your best interest to participate actively in your case. When you hire a lawyer, you are paying for legal advice. Therefore, your lawyer should make no major decision about whether or how to proceed with your case without your permission. Pay special attention to whether the lawyer seems willing and able to explain the case to you and answers your questions clearly and completely. Also ask what information will be supplied to you. How, and how often, will the lawyer keep you informed about the progress of your case? Will the lawyer send you copies of any documents pertaining to your case? Can you help minimize fees by gathering documents or otherwise assisting in the effort?

Q. During our first meeting, should I ask what will happen if the lawyer and I disagree?

A. Yes. Your first meeting is the best time to establish how you and your lawyer will resolve potential problems. You should consider getting in writing any decisions you reach about how you will handle disagreements.

Q. Should I interview several lawyers before settling on one?

A. Yes. Your decision will be more informed if you consider several lawyers. Even if you think that you will be satisfied with the first lawyer you interview, you will feel better about your choice if you talk to several lawyers.

▶ **WHAT TO REMEMBER WHEN SELECTING AND HIRING AN ATTORNEY**

- **Get referrals.** Talk to people you know and trust to get referrals and recommendations for an attorney. Also consider contacting a referral program as offered by your local bar association.

- **Set up an initial meeting.** Make sure to ask the attorney if you will be charged for this meeting—and if so, how much.

- **Ask questions.** Make sure all your questions are answered at the initial meeting, including
  - How long has the attorney been practicing?
  - What types of cases does the attorney usually handle?
  - Does the attorney usually represent individuals or businesses?
  - Who in the firm will be handling the case?
  - How are fees determined? How and when are payments made?

- **Find out if you can help.**

- **Stay organized and aware of developments with your case.**

Q. Can I find out about problems or complaints that previous clients have had with a given lawyer?

A. Sometimes, yes. Some states make reports of lawyer grievances available to the general public, especially if such grievances resulted in disciplinary action being taken against the lawyer. If you are worried, contact the organization that licenses attorneys in your state to see if this option is available.

REMEMBER THIS

- It's worth spending some time finding a lawyer who is appropriately qualified and right for you. You may have to interview more than one lawyer to find the right match.
- Don't be afraid to ask your prospective lawyer questions—your lawyer is there to help you!

LEGAL FEES AND EXPENSES

Lawyers can be expensive. We all know that. But you can take a few steps to ensure that you avoid any surprises when the bill arrives in the mail. Talk to your lawyer about fees and expenses, and make sure that you understand all the information that your lawyer gives you regarding fees and costs. It's best to ask for this information in writing before legal work starts.

Q. What billing method do most lawyers use?

A. The most common billing method is to charge a set amount for each hour or fraction of an hour that a lawyer works on your case. What constitutes a "reasonable" hourly fee depends on several things. More experienced lawyers tend to charge more per hour than those with less experience—but they also may take less time to do the same legal work. In addition, the same lawyer will sometimes charge more for time spent in the courtroom than for hours spent in the office or library.

Q. How can I be sure that my lawyer will not overcharge me?

A. The fee charged by a lawyer should be reasonable from an objective point of view. The fee should be tied to specific services rendered, time invested, the level of expertise

---

▶ **TALK ABOUT FEES**

Although money is often a touchy subject, fees and other charges should be discussed with your lawyer early. You can avoid future problems by having a clear understanding of the fees to be charged, and by getting that understanding in writing before any legal work has started. If the fee is to be charged on an hourly basis, insist on a complete itemized list and an explanation of charges each time the lawyer bills you.

Legal advice is not cheap. A bill from a lawyer for preparing a one-page legal document or providing basic advice may surprise some clients. Remember that when you hire a lawyer, you are paying for his or her expertise and time.

provided, and the difficulty of the matter. However, the fee may also be a percentage of the amount recovered on your behalf, called a contingent fee, which is discussed below.

Here are some factors to consider when deciding whether a particular fee is reasonable:

- The time and work required by the lawyer and any assistants
- The difficulty of the legal issues presented
- The fee charged by other lawyers in the area for similar work
- The total value of the claim or settlement and the results of the case
- Whether the lawyer has previously worked for the same client
- The lawyer's experience, reputation, and ability
- The amount of other work the lawyer turned down to take on a particular case

Types of Fees

Q. Someone said that I should ask my lawyer to represent me on a "contingent fee" basis. What does this mean?

A. A **contingent fee** is a fee that is payable only if your case is successful. Lawyers and clients use this arrangement only in cases where money is being claimed—most often in cases involving personal injury or workers' compensation. Many states strictly forbid this billing method in criminal cases and in most cases involving domestic relations.

In a contingent fee arrangement, the lawyer agrees to accept a fixed percentage (often one-third to 40 percent) of the amount recovered. If you win the case, the lawyer's fee comes out of the money awarded to you. If you lose, neither you nor the lawyer will get any money.

On the other hand, win or lose, you prob-

> ▶ **UNDERSTAND FEES AND EXPENSES**
>
> The method used to charge fees is one factor to consider when deciding if a fee is reasonable. You should understand the different charging methods before you make any hiring decision. At your first meeting, the lawyer should estimate how much the total case will cost and inform you of the method he or she will use to charge for the work. As with any bill, you should not pay without first getting an explanation for any charges you do not understand. Remember, because unforeseen developments may occur during the course of your case, not all expenses can be estimated accurately.

ably will have to pay court filing charges, the costs related to deposing witnesses, and similar expenses. By entering into a contingent fee agreement, both you and your lawyer expect to collect some unknown amount of money. Because many personal injury actions involve considerable and often complicated investigation and work by a lawyer, this may be less expensive than paying an hourly rate. It also gives the client the option of defraying the up-front costs of litigation unless, and until, there is a settlement or money award. You should clearly understand your options before entering into a contingent fee agreement.

Q. Are all contingent fee arrangements the same?

A. No. An important consideration is whether the lawyer deducts costs and expenses from the amount won before or after you pay the lawyer's contingent fee. An example will illustrate this point.

Example: Joe hires Ernie Attorney to represent him, agreeing that Ernie will receive one-third of the final amount as a contingent fee. In this case, the final amount recovered is $12,000.

If Joe pays Ernie his contingent fee before deducting expenses, the fee will be calculated as follows:

$12,000	Total amount recovered in case
−4,000	One-third for Ernie Attorney
$8,000	Balance
−2,100	Payment for expenses and costs
$5,900	Amount that Joe recovers

However, if Joe pays Ernie his contingent fee after first deducting other legal expenses and costs, the fee will be calculated as follows:

$12,000	Total amount recovered in case
−2,100	Payment for expenses and costs
$9,900	Balance
−3,300	One-third for Ernie Attorney
$6,600	Amount that Joe recovers

This example illustrates that Joe will collect an additional $700 if Ernie Attorney agrees to collect his contingent fee after Joe pays the other legal expenses relating to his case. Many lawyers prefer to be paid before they subtract expenses, but this point is often negotiable. Of course, these matters should be settled before you hire a lawyer. If you agree to pay a contingent fee, your lawyer should provide a written explanation of the agreement, clearly stating how he or she will deduct costs.

Q. Why do some lawyers use contingent fee arrangements? Isn't there a chance they won't get paid at all?

A. Under a contingent arrangement, there is a chance that the lawyer won't get paid at all. However, there is also a chance that, if you end up recovering a large amount, the lawyer will earn more than under a traditional fee arrangement. The legal field has approved of contingent fees in most cases because they allow clients without much money to access the legal system. However, most states restrict the types of cases for which payment can be made on a contingent basis, and limit the attorney's fee to a "reasonable" percentage of the total amount recovered.

Q. If my lawyer and I agree to a contingent fee arrangement, should the method of settling my case affect the amount of my lawyer's fee?

A. Yes, but only if both of you agree beforehand. If the lawyer settles the case before

---

▶ WHAT IS "UNBUNDLING"?

Imagine that your case requires your lawyer to provide a "bundle" of legal services. Many lawyers are increasingly willing to open up this "bundle" and share some of the work with you. For example, maybe you could write the letter laying out your side of the case, and the lawyer could simply review it (thus taking up less of the lawyer's time and as a result, costing you less money). Often lawyers will provide advice in a matter but will become heavily involved only if the matter goes to court.

going to trial, less legal work may be required. On the other hand, the lawyer may have to prepare for trial, with all its costs and expenses, before a settlement can be negotiated.

You can try to negotiate an agreement in which the lawyer accepts a lower percentage if he or she settles the case easily and quickly or before a lawsuit is filed in court. However, many lawyers might not agree to those terms.

Q. A friend suggested that I might want to have a lawyer "on retainer." What does this mean?

A. If you pay a set amount of money regularly to make sure that a lawyer will be available for any necessary legal service you might require, then you have a lawyer **on retainer.** Businesses and people who routinely have a lot of legal work use retainers. By paying a retainer, a client receives routine consultations and general legal advice whenever needed. If a legal matter requires courtroom time or many hours of work, the client may need to pay more than the retainer amount. Retainer agreements should always be in writing.

Prepaid legal services plans, which were discussed earlier, are similar in effect to retainer agreements: a small fee paid periodically ensures that a lawyer will be available to provide legal services at any time.

Most people do not see a lawyer regularly enough to need a lawyer on retainer.

Q. Is having a lawyer "on retainer" the same thing as paying a "retainer fee"?

A. No. A retainer fee is something quite different. Sometimes a lawyer will ask the client to pay some money in advance before any legal work will be done. This money is referred to as a **retainer fee,** and is in effect a down payment that will be applied toward the total fee billed.

Q. I saw an advertisement for a law firm that charges fixed fees for specific types of work. What does this involve?

A. A **fixed fee** is a set amount charged for routine legal work. In some situations, this

---

▶ SOME TIPS FOR KEEPING DOWN FEES

- Be organized. Make sure you bring all relevant documents to any meeting with your lawyer, so that your lawyer's time isn't wasted.

- Be brief. If your lawyer is charging you by the hour, you don't want to waste time with irrelevant conversation or long-winded explanations.

- If your lawyer is working on something for you, don't call every time you have a minor question. Instead, save up a few questions to ask at the same time.

- Ask your lawyer if there is anything you can do to help. For example, can you write some letters, make some phone calls, or change the title of some assets?

- Ask your lawyer to let you know if the cost of your case starts to escalate beyond the cost discussed.

- Ask for an itemized bill—that way you can see the cost or fees for each service.

amount may be set by law or by the judge handling the case. Since advertising by lawyers is becoming more popular, you are likely to see ads making such promises as "Simple Divorce—$150" or "Bankruptcy—from $250." However, do not assume that these prices will be the total amount charged in your final bill. Advertised prices often do not include court costs and other expenses.

Q. Does the lawyer's billing method influence the other costs and expenses that I might have to pay?

A. No. Some costs and expenses will be charged regardless of the billing method. For example, the court clerk's office charges a fee for filing the complaint or petition that begins a legal action. The sheriff's office charges a fee for serving a legal summons. Your lawyer must pay for postage, copying documents, telephone calls, and the advice or testimony of some expert witnesses, such as doctors. These expenses may not be included in your legal fee, and you may have to pay them regardless of the fee arrangement you use. Your lawyer will usually pay these costs as needed, billing you at regular intervals or at the close of your case.

Q. What are referral fees?

A. If you go to Lawyer A, he or she may be unable to help, but might refer you instead to Lawyer B at another law firm, who has more experience handling your kind of case. In return for the referral, Lawyer A will sometimes be paid part of the total fee you pay to Lawyer B. The law may prohibit this type of fee, especially if it increases the final amount to be paid by a client. The ethics rules for lawyers in most states specify that lawyers in different firms may not divide a client's fee unless

1. the client knows about and agrees to the arrangement;
2. they divide the fee in a way that reflects how much work each lawyer did, or both lawyers are fully responsible for the case; and
3. the total bill is reasonable.

If one lawyer refers you to another, you have a right to know if there will be a referral fee. If there is, then ask about the specifics of the agreement between the lawyers.

Cost-Cutting Options

Q. Is there anything I can do to reduce my legal costs?

A. Yes, there are several cost-cutting methods available to you. First, answer all your lawyer's questions fully and honestly. Not only will you feel better, but you also will save on legal fees. If you tell your lawyer all the facts as you know them, you will save time that might be spent on the case and will help your lawyer do a better job.

Remember that the ethics of the profession require your lawyer to maintain in the strictest confidence almost anything you reveal during your private discussions. You should feel free to tell your lawyer the complete details of your case, even those that embarrass you. It is particularly important to tell your lawyer facts about your case that reflect poorly on you. These will almost certainly come out if your case goes to trial.

Q. Can I reduce my legal costs if I get more involved in my case?

A. Sometimes. Stay informed and ask for copies of important documents related to your case. Let your lawyer know if you are willing to help out, such as by picking up or delivering documents or making a few phone calls.

You should not interfere with your lawyer's work. However, you might be able to move your case more quickly, reduce your legal costs, and keep yourself better informed by doing some of the work yourself. Discuss this with your lawyer.

REMEMBER THIS

- Talk to your lawyer about fees. Make sure you understand how fees are going to be charged, and get a fee agreement in writing before legal work starts.
- Lawyers' services can be expensive. Make sure you have a good idea of what your case is likely to cost and be aware of ways you can reduce your fees.

WHEN THINGS GO WRONG

When you agree to hire a lawyer and that lawyer agrees to represent you, a two-way relationship begins in which you both have the same goal: to achieve a satisfactory resolution of a legal matter. To this end, each of you must act responsibly toward the other. In a lawyer-client relationship, acting responsibly involves duties on both sides—and often involves some hard work.

You have a right to expect competent representation from your lawyer. However, every case has at least two sides. You cannot always blame your lawyer if your case does not turn out the way you thought it would. If you are unhappy with your lawyer, it is important to determine the reasons. After a

▶ SOME TIPS ON TALKING TO YOUR LAWYER

- Before your first meeting with your lawyer, think about your legal problem, how you would like it resolved, and your ideal outcome.
- If your case involves other people, write down their names, addresses, and telephone numbers. Also jot down any specific facts or dates you think might be important and any questions you want answered. By being organized, you will save time and money.
- Bring all relevant information and documents with you to any meeting with your lawyer, including contracts, leases, or any documents with which you have been served.
- If there has been a development in your case, don't wait until your next scheduled meeting to tell your lawyer about it. Tell your lawyer immediately of any changes that might be important. It might mean that the lawyer will have to take a totally different action—or no action at all—in your case.
- Let your lawyer know if and why you are unhappy with his or her work.
- Don't wait for your lawyer to ask you about something—volunteer information that you think may be useful.

realistic look at your situation, if you still believe that you have a genuine complaint about your legal representation, there are several things you can do. This section outlines those options and some issues relating to disagreements over your legal representation.

Q. I lost my case, and I still had to pay my lawyer's bill along with costs and expenses. I am not very happy with my lawyer. What can I do?

A. First, talk with your lawyer. A lack of communication causes many problems. If your lawyer appears to have acted improperly, or did not do something that you think he or she should have done, talk with your lawyer about it. You may be satisfied once you understand the circumstances better.

Q. I have tried to discuss my complaints with my lawyer. However, my lawyer will not discuss them. Do I have any alternatives?

A. Yes. If your lawyer is unwilling to address your complaints, consider taking your legal affairs to another lawyer. You can decide whom to hire (and fire) as your lawyer. However, remember that when you fire a lawyer, you may be charged a reasonable amount for any work that he or she has already completed.

Most documents held by your lawyer that relate to the case are yours—ask for them. However, in some states a lawyer may have some rights to a file until the client pays a reasonable amount for work done on the case.

Q. What if I feel that my lawyer has acted unethically?

A. How a lawyer should act, in both professional and private life, is controlled by the rules of professional conduct in the state or states in which he or she is licensed to practice. These rules are usually administered by the state's highest court through its disciplinary board.

These rules describe generally how lawyers should strive to improve the legal profession and uphold the law. They also give more detailed rules of conduct for specific situations. If a lawyer's conduct falls below the standards set out in the rules, he or she can be disciplined by being **censured** or **reprimanded** (publicly or privately criticized); **suspended** (having the license to practice law taken away for a certain amount of time); or **disbarred** (having the license to practice law taken away indefinitely).

The law sets out punishments for anyone who breaks civil and criminal laws, including lawyers. But because of the special position of trust and confidence involved in a lawyer-client relationship, lawyers may also be punished for things that are unethical, even if not unlawful—such as telling others confidential information about a client or representing clients whose interests are in conflict.

Q. What are some specific examples of the ethical duties of lawyers?

A. Among the highest responsibilities a lawyer has is his or her obligation to a client. A number of strict rules and common-sense guidelines define these responsibilities.

Competence
Every lawyer must aim to provide high-quality work. This requires lawyers to analyze legal issues, to research and study changing laws and legal trends, and otherwise to represent clients effectively and professionally.

Following the Client's Instructions
A lawyer should advise a client of possible actions to be taken in a case and then act ac-

cording to the client's choice of action—even if the lawyer might have picked a different route. One of the few exceptions occurs when a client asks for a lawyer's help in doing something illegal, such as lying in court or in a legal document. In these cases, the lawyer is required to inform the client of the legal effect of any planned wrongdoing and to refuse to assist with it.

Diligence

Every lawyer must act carefully and in a timely manner in handling a client's legal problem. Unnecessary delays can often damage a case. If a lawyer is unable to spend the required time and energy on a case, whether because of overwork or for any other reason, the lawyer should refuse from the beginning to take that case.

Communication

A lawyer must be able to communicate effectively with a client. When a client asks for an explanation, the lawyer must provide it within a reasonable time. A lawyer must also keep the client informed about any changes relating to his or her case.

Fees

The amount the lawyer charges for legal work must be reasonable, and the client should be told the specifics of all charges.

Confidentiality

With few exceptions, a lawyer generally may not tell anyone else what a client reveals about a case. This strict rule enables a client to discuss case details openly and honestly with a lawyer, even if those details reveal embarrassing, damaging, or commercially sensitive information about the client. A rule called **attorney-client privilege** helps protect confidential information from being disclosed.

Conflicts of Interest

A lawyer must be loyal to his or her client. This means that a lawyer cannot represent two clients on opposite sides of the same lawsuit or related lawsuits. Ordinarily, there also can be no representation of a client whose interests conflict with the lawyer's interests. For example, a lawyer may not be involved in writing a will for a client who leaves the lawyer substantial money or property in that will.

Keeping Clients' Property

If a lawyer is holding a client's money or property, it must be kept safely and separately from the lawyer's own funds and belongings. When a client asks for the property, the lawyer must return it immediately and in good condition. The lawyer must also keep careful records of money received for a client and, if asked, report the amount of that money amount promptly and accurately.

Q. How can I file a complaint against my lawyer?

A. If you believe you have a valid complaint about how your lawyer has handled your case, inform the organization that governs law licenses in your state. Usually this is the disciplinary board of the highest court in your state. In some states, the state bar association is responsible for disciplining lawyers.

The board or the bar will either investigate the complaint or refer you to someone who can help. If your complaint concerns the amount your lawyer charged, you may be referred to a state or local bar association's fee arbitration service.

Filing a disciplinary complaint accusing your lawyer of unethical conduct is a serious matter. Try to resolve any differences or disputes directly with the lawyer before filing a complaint. Be aware that making a complaint of this sort may punish the lawyer for misconduct, but it will probably not help you recover any money.

If you have a case pending that your lawyer has mishandled, be sure to also protect your rights by taking steps to see that your case is now properly handled.

Q. My lawyer's incompetence meant that I lost my case. What can I do?

A. If you believe that your lawyer has been negligent in handling your case—and that negligence has ended up costing you money or injuring you or your legal rights—you may be able to bring a **malpractice** suit against your lawyer. Chapter 6, "Personal Injury," can provide you with more information.

Q. My lawyer settled my case out of court and refuses to pay me my share of the settlement. What can I do about it?

A. If you believe that your lawyer has taken or improperly kept money or property that be-

---

▶ A CLIENT'S RESPONSIBILITIES

As in any successful relationship, a good lawyer-client relationship involves cooperation on both sides. As a client, you should do all you can to make sure you get the best possible legal help. This includes

- **Being honest.** Be honest in telling all the facts to your lawyer. Remind yourself of important points or questions by writing them down before talking with your lawyer.

- **Notifying the lawyer of changes.** Tell the lawyer promptly about any changes or new information you learn that may affect your case. And let your lawyer know if you change your address or telephone number.

- **Asking for clarification.** If you have any questions or are confused about something in your case, ask the lawyer for an explanation. This may go a long way toward putting your mind at ease—and will also help your lawyer do a better job of handling your case.

- **Being realistic.** A lawyer can only handle your legal affairs. You may need the help of another professional—a banker, a family counselor, an accountant, or a psychologist, for example—for problems that have no "legal" solution. After you have hired a lawyer you trust, do not forget about that trust. The lawyer's judgments are based on experience and training. Also, keep in mind that most legal matters cannot be resolved overnight. Give the system time to work.

- **Paying.** A client has the duty to promptly pay a fair and reasonable price for legal services. In fact, when a client fails to pay, in some situations the lawyer may have the right to stop working on the case. Still, the lawyer must then do whatever is reasonably possible to prevent the client's case from being harmed.

longs to you, contact the state **client security fund, client indemnity fund,** or **client assistance fund.** Your local bar association or the state disciplinary board can tell you how to contact the correct fund. These funds may reimburse clients if a court finds that their lawyer has defrauded them. Lawyers pay fees to maintain such funds. Be aware, however, that most states' programs divide up the money that is available in a given period of time among all the clients who have valid claims. As a result, there is rarely enough money to pay 100 percent of every claim.

Q. If I am having a problem with my lawyer, is there any reason that I would want to call the police?

A. Yes. If you believe that your lawyer has committed a crime, such as stealing your money or property, you should report that crime. This is a last resort, and you should involve the police only when you feel certain that it is necessary. Do not feel intimidated because your complaint is against a lawyer.

REMEMBER THIS

- If things don't turn out the way you'd hoped, discuss your concerns with your lawyer. He or she might be able to explain what happened in a way that makes sense to you.

- If you have serious concerns about your lawyer's conduct, don't be afraid to pursue the matter through your state disciplinary authority.

- Don't forget that you have responsibilities as a client, too!

CHAPTER TWO

How the Legal System Works: Civil and Criminal Trials

Claire suffered an injury after she slipped and fell on a greasy floor at a local restaurant. After making some preliminary investigations, her lawyer advised her to file a civil suit against the restaurant owners. What does this mean? Which court will handle the case? What happens in a trial? Will there be a jury? How can Claire be sure the trial will be fair?

When one of Julie's suppliers failed to come through with an order, her little business lost thousands of dollars and lots of goodwill. Negotiation has failed, and the only way to get the money is to go to court. But what will that process be like? Will it be tense? Confusing? What are the likely results?

Eric and Kevin went to a local bar for a drink after work on Friday. Kevin had a bit too much to drink and ended up getting in a fight with the bouncer. He was arrested and taken to the police station. While answering questions about the bar incident, he also admitted to having been involved in a car accident the week before that resulted in another person's death. Did the police have the right to arrest Kevin or to start asking him questions? Should his attorney have been present? What will happen at Kevin's trial for the fight? And what about the death—can he be charged for that? Will Eric be called to testify against his friend?

With its complex procedures and technical language, the legal system can be confusing and frightening to a person without legal training who is caught up in it for the first time. As a result, having a good grasp of the system's structure and the way it functions is particularly important. Understanding the legal system will be useful if you ever need to go to court yourself. The courts also play an important part in American democracy, and understanding how they work might give you a deeper insight into our political process. And the more you know about how our legal system works, the more likely you are to respect the rights of others and demand that your own rights be respected.

Remember, federal laws and procedures differ from those of the states, and state laws and procedures differ among themselves. Because of the many differences between each system, this chapter can't convey all the variations that exist. If you want to pursue a lawsuit, are being sued, or are being criminally prosecuted, you should talk to a lawyer about the laws that apply in your jurisdiction.

INTRODUCTION TO THE LEGAL SYSTEM AND THE STRUCTURE OF THE COURT SYSTEM

In cities and small towns across the country, the courthouse is both a symbol of the rule of law and the place where the law is put into action. In the courthouse, criminal defendants have their day in court, and the government faces the challenge of proving them guilty beyond a reasonable doubt. Meanwhile, private parties seek resolution in civil cases ranging from disputes over car collisions to multimillion-dollar lawsuits between companies. In some communities, there may also be a federal courthouse in which federal judges hear criminal and civil cases under jurisdiction granted by the Constitution and federal law.

This section is an introduction to the legal system and the difference between civil and criminal suits. Additionally, this section gives you a broad overview of the structure of the courts, including a discussion of the meaning and significance of separation of powers and judicial independence.

Q. What is the idea behind our legal system?

A. We have what is known as an adversarial legal system, named for the belief that the truth in a matter can best be determined by giving two sides an equal chance to make their cases before an impartial judge or jury.

Our adversarial system has several essential features. Each side has a right to be represented by a lawyer, whose job it is to argue why the court should apply the law to the facts in a particular way. Each lawyer is bound by the same statutes, case law, and rules of procedure as his or her adversary. The judge is neutral and impartial, and ensures that the presentation of evidence and questioning of witnesses are carried out according to the rules of procedure. The trial procedure is based on rules, statutes, and historical precedent, modified as necessary by the changing needs of the justice system, and based on the experience of lawyers, judges, and litigants.

This is the basic pattern for both **civil** cases (in which a private person or business sues another person or business, typically to seek damages for noncriminal conduct, such as a broken contract or a personal injury) and **criminal** cases (in which the government accuses someone of violating a criminal law and the defendant may face a fine or jail time). Civil and criminal cases may not overlap, but sometimes a single action can result in both civil and criminal prosecutions. Later sections of this chapter will explain the similarities and differences between the two types of cases.

State and Federal Courts

Q. Why isn't there just one court system?

A. A judicial system is an essential component of both national and state governments.

▶ **WHAT'S IN A NAME?**

With more than fifty legal jurisdictions, America is full of courts that have different names but perform almost exactly the same function. For example, courts of general jurisdiction exist almost everywhere, but they are variously called circuit courts, district courts, superior courts, and courts of common pleas. In New York, the state court of general jurisdiction is called the supreme court. Whatever their name, these courts generally hear serious criminal and civil cases.

The U.S. Constitution provides for a dual system of government, with both state and federal powers and responsibilities. Article III of the U.S. Constitution calls for a **federal judiciary** operating as a coequal branch of our national government. Federal courts may only decide certain kinds of cases as provided by Congress or specified in the Constitution. Each state has a **state judiciary,** which is empowered to interpret the laws made by the state legislature. States also have their own constitutions, which can provide rights to the public in addition to those rights provided by the federal Constitution.

This dual court system is a consequence of our organization as a union of states. Such a system makes sense philosophically because it respects a state's right to establish and enforce the law with respect to its unique local problems and concerns. It also makes sense practically because, as a general rule, a state's own courts are more familiar with state and local laws. Federal courts are qualified to interpret and apply federal laws and ensure that federal laws are applied uniformly in the different states.

Q. How is the court system structured?

A. The courts of this country are organized as hierarchies. Higher courts have the power to review the decisions of lower courts. Basically, the courts of this country are divided into three layers:

- **trial courts,** where cases start;
- **intermediate (appellate) courts,** where most appeals are first heard; and
- **courts of last resort** (usually called **supreme courts**), which hear further appeals and have final authority in the cases they hear.

> ▶ **TALKING ABOUT COURTS**
>
> We really have fifty-two court systems in this country—one for each state and the District of Columbia, and a federal system. Because of the differences in the procedures each system uses, this chapter can't explain all the variations that exist between the different courts. But in focusing on the federal system and state courts in general, it should provide a good basic road map of the structure of the court system.

This division is generally true of both state courts and federal courts, although eleven states do not have an intermediate appellate court, and some states have more than one level of intermediate appellate review. Two states, Oklahoma and Texas, have separate courts of last resort for civil and criminal cases.

Q. What kinds of cases can federal courts decide?

A. Article III of the U.S. Constitution limits the kinds of cases federal courts can hear to the following:

- Cases involving issues of federal law. This so-called **federal question jurisdiction** authorizes federal district courts to decide both civil and criminal cases in which federal law must be interpreted or applied. The federal law at issue may have arisen out of a federal statute or regulation, a treaty, or a provision of the Constitution itself.
- Cases involving diversity jurisdiction over controversies:

- between citizens of different states;
- between two or more states; or
- between citizens of the same state claiming land under grants of different states.
- Cases in which the U.S. government or one of its officers is a party.
- Cases that might affect the United States's relations with other countries, including cases that involve ambassadors, consuls, and other public ministers.
- Cases involving laws relating to navigable waters (the oceans, the Great Lakes, and most rivers) and commerce on those waters.

A party to a federal lawsuit will have an opportunity to proceed through two levels of decision: the U.S. district court or other specialized trial court and a court of appeals. In rare cases, a party may receive a third level of decision from the U.S. Supreme Court.

Q. I have heard about a federal Tax Court. Is this different from the general federal courts?

A. There are several specialized federal courts that are part of the larger federal system—Tax Court, the Court of Federal Claims, the Court of Veterans Appeals, courts of criminal appeals for each branch of the armed forces, and the Court of International Trade. Each U.S. district court also has a U.S. bankruptcy court unit, as well as one or more magistrates.

In addition, using its Article I powers, Congress has created other courts to serve the U.S. territories of Guam, the U.S. Virgin Islands, and the Northern Mariana Islands. These are called **legislative courts** because they are authorized by Congress to serve U.S. territories, in contrast to courts authorized

under Article III of the Constitution to serve in the United States. Legislative courts operate much like Article III courts, but their presiding officers do not enjoy the constitutional protections accorded to Article III judges, such as life tenure and the prohibition against reducing judicial salaries.

Q. What sorts of cases do state courts decide?

A. The state courts handle the vast majority—over 98 percent—of all cases today. Forty-five states have two or more levels of trial courts—**special jurisdiction courts** with jurisdiction limited to specific types of cases, and **general jurisdiction courts** with jurisdiction over all other cases.

Special, or limited, jurisdiction courts have names that vary from state to state; depending on their location, they may be known as district courts, mayor's courts, city courts, justice courts, justice of the peace courts, magistrate's courts, county courts, municipal courts, or police courts. They hear relatively minor civil and criminal disputes, and are typically dominated by traffic cases. They often have exclusive jurisdiction over juvenile cases.

Courts of general jurisdiction hear most serious criminal and civil cases, and sometimes handle specific subject areas such as domestic relations or state and local tax. These courts have different names in different states (see the "What's in a Name?" sidebar on page 24). Five states now have unified trial courts, in which all types of cases are heard.

Q. Do I have a choice whether to sue in state or federal court?

A. Sometimes. Although some cases are exclusively within the jurisdiction of a particular court system (for example, divorces are handled by state courts, and all bankruptcies are filed in federal bankruptcy courts), the state and federal courts have **concurrent jurisdiction** over many cases. This means that these cases may be filed and heard in either state or federal court. A typical example would involve a state law that is being litigated by a plaintiff from one state and a defendant from another state. The state courts would have jurisdiction because of the state law issues. But if the case involves an **amount in controversy** of more than $75,000, the federal courts would also have jurisdiction, because the parties are citizens of different states. This type of federal jurisdiction is known as **diversity jurisdiction,** because the parties are citizens of different states. Plaintiffs can choose the type of court—state or federal—in which they wish to file suit.

It is occasionally possible to commence an action in both state and federal court. For example, in the Rodney King case, in which Los Angeles police officers were accused of beating a motorist, the officers were acquitted of state criminal charges but later convicted in federal court for depriving the victim of his civil rights.

Separation of Powers

Q. What does "separation of powers" mean?

A. Besides applying the law in individual cases, courts have an important role in the structure of American government. Just about any eighth grader can tell you that we have a system of separation of powers. But exactly what does that mean?

The framers of the Constitution created a federal government of divided power. There's an **executive branch** (the president and most government agencies), a **legislative branch** (Congress), and a **judicial branch** (the courts). The same three branches exist in every state government.

We have this structure because the framers were deeply suspicious of unchecked executive power. They had just emerged from a revolution against a powerful king, and they wanted to ensure that the American people would never have to face a homegrown dictatorship.

Setting up three interdependent yet separate branches of government meant that there would be a **balance of powers** (meaning that each branch keeps an eye on the others) and a **separation of powers** (meaning that none can unduly influence the others, because each branch is authorized to do different things). Think of it as a three-legged stool. No one leg can stand on its own.

Q. I have read that courts can overturn laws. Is this true? How does it work?

A. When the government makes laws that are at odds with the Constitution, a court can declare the law unconstitutional. The Constitution and the Bill of Rights enshrine certain rights, which cannot be abridged by our government. These rights include the right to worship freely, to speak and write freely, and to have fair and impartial trials. In our system, it often falls to courts to enforce these constitutional rights. This means that courts must sometimes ignore common beliefs or the clamor of the moment, and uphold positions that are unpopular.

The courts uphold the Constitution when they strike down a law that, under the Constitution, is impermissible. This practice of **judicial review** is often unpopular—after all, any law that got passed in the first place arguably had popular support. But judicial review is absolutely necessary if we are to live under a limited government, and if citizens are to have certain unalienable rights. A law contrary to the Constitution cannot stand. In matters of constitutional interpretation, courts have the final word—except on those very rare occasions when court decisions are overturned by a constitutional amendment.

Q. Are there limits on the power of the courts?

A. Obviously, the ability to strike down laws contrary to the Constitution gives courts enormous power. But several things keep the judicial branch from reigning supreme.

For one thing, judges can't strike down laws willy-nilly; courts can rule only on the controversies that come before them. This means that, unlike the other two branches, they can't shape their own agenda. They have no power to act on their own—only to act in response to legal cases on which they are asked to rule. Courts are generally careful to use their power of judicial review sparingly. Often judges will decide cases on narrow grounds to avoid sweeping pronouncements. As a result, declaring laws unconstitutional is much rarer than you might think. In fact, since its inception, the United States Supreme Court has declared fewer than 150 federal statutes unconstitutional.

It is often said that we are a government of laws and not of men. This adage is a reference to the cornerstone of our legal system: the rule of law. It means that, individually or collectively, judges or juries cannot simply do what they think is right in a particular case. They must follow the law as enacted by the Congress or a state legislature, or as defined in case law by the U.S. Supreme Court or the

> ▶ **THE CONSTITUTION IN ACTION**
>
> Cases in which the U.S. Supreme Court struck down laws that violated the Constitution include
>
> - *Brown v. Board of Education* (1954): struck down public school segregation;
> - *Baker v. Carr* (1962): struck down state reapportionment that gave more influence to certain voters than to others;
> - *Roe v. Wade* (1973): struck down some state laws illegalizing abortion;
> - *U.S. v. Eichman* (1990): struck down a federal law making it a crime to burn an American flag; and
> - *U.S. v. Lopez* (1995): struck down the federal Gun-Free Schools Act on the grounds that Congress had exceeded its authority by enacting it.

highest applicable state court. The rule of law is a type of discipline we have imposed on ourselves to ensure that all are treated equally under the law.

Judges

Q. What is a judge's role in court?

A. Judges are like umpires in baseball or referees in football or basketball. Their role is to see that both sides follow the rules of procedure. Like an umpire, judges call 'em as they see 'em—according to the facts and law, without regard to which side is popular (no home-field advantage); without regard to

▶ JUDICIAL INDEPENDENCE

By enabling judges to strike down actions of the legislative and executive branches without fear of reprisal, an independent judiciary makes possible a system of impartial, evenhanded justice.

Origins

The founders had firsthand experience being brought before courts they felt were unfair, so the Constitution created a system that guaranteed an independent federal judiciary.

Courts in the colonies were seen as instruments of oppression. Juries could be locked up until they reached the "right" decision. Judges were seen as puppets of the king. In fact, the Declaration of Independence criticized King George III for making "judges dependent upon his will alone for the tenure of their offices and the amount and payment of their salaries."

This experience convinced the founders that Americans needed independent courts to protect them from acts of overreaching government power, such as unreasonable searches and rigged trials.

Constitutional Protections

To guarantee rights such as freedom of speech and freedom of worship, and to make the rule of law a reality, the founders knew that courts had to be independent of politics. Judges had to be servants of law and the Constitution, not of political bosses, the media, or special-interest groups. In the Constitution, the founders protected federal judges from political and public pressure by:

- Specifying that they hold their office "during good behaviour." This means that their appointments are for life, unless they are removed for misbehavior.

- Specifying that their salaries cannot be diminished during their tenure. This prevents Congress from retaliating against judges by cutting their pay.

- Making the removal process difficult. (The only grounds for removal of a federal judge are "impeachment for, and conviction of, treason, bribery, or other high crimes and misdemeanors.")

After more than two hundred years, only thirteen attempts have been made to formally impeach federal judges, and only seven judges have been convicted and removed from office—for example, because of grave misconduct in office. None of the convictions were made because Congress disagreed with a judge's judicial philosophy or with a particular decision the judge rendered.

Throughout American history, the independence of the judiciary has protected individual liberties and prevented a tyranny of the majority—by extending voting rights, ending segregation, and protecting the average citizen from unwarranted government intrusion, to name just a few examples.

which side is "favored" to win; without regard for what the spectators want; and without regard to whether the judge personally agrees with the position taken by either party.

REMEMBER THIS

- The rationale for the adversarial system is that it provides the best way to find the truth of a matter. Each side has the right to a lawyer, and must argue its case before an impartial judge.

- State and federal courts hear different kinds of cases, are differently structured, and have different names—so you should always find out which court has jurisdiction over your case, and check the law in your state!

- Courts have specific powers granted to them under our system of separation of powers. One of the most important is their ability to invalidate a law on the grounds that it violates the Constitution.

THE CIVIL TRIAL: STEP BY STEP

It is difficult to make generalizations about trials because so much depends on the facts of your case and the court that conducts the trial. Nonetheless, this section gives you some general information about the steps you can expect to take in a civil trial. It leads you step by step through a civil trial. If you want to know how a jury is selected, or what happens during cross-examination of a witness, then this section helps you understand those processes.

> ### ▶ MEET THE PLAYERS
>
> The parties in a civil case are the plaintiff and the defendant. The **plaintiff** is the party filing the lawsuit and complaining of a wrong that has been done. The **defendant** is simply the other side of the coin, so to speak—the party alleged to have caused the grievance and obliged to defend himself or herself against the charge.

Proceedings and Procedures before Trial

Q. How much time does one have to decide whether to file a civil lawsuit?

A. It varies depending on the nature of the suit. Each state, and the federal government, has **statutes of limitations.** These govern the amount of time you have in which to sue after the incident takes place on which the suit is based; depending on the kind of suit involved, the amount of time allowed will be longer or shorter. The justification for imposing these time limits is that it is unfair to require a defendant to provide a defense long after an incident occurs, when memories may no longer be fresh and evidence may no longer be available. Thus, after the time limit set forth in the applicable statute of limitations has run out, you can no longer bring the suit—no matter how meritorious the case. Some limitation periods are very short, so you should determine early how long you have to bring your case.

Q. What begins a lawsuit?

A. A lawsuit begins when the plaintiff files a document called a **complaint** with the court.

▸ SERVICE

Service is the delivery of a legal document—such as a complaint, a summons, or a subpoena. The person receiving the document is said to have been **served.**

The complaint recounts what happened to the plaintiff, what the plaintiff wants the court to do about it, and the legal reasons why the court ought to do what the plaintiff asks. The various wrongs the plaintiff claims to have suffered are listed in separate **counts** of the complaint. The complaint also sets forth the remedy the plaintiff is seeking from the court.

Q. How does a defendant find out that he or she is being sued?

A. The lawyer for the plaintiff or the clerk of the court will draft a paper called a **summons.** The summons tells the defendant that a suit has been filed against him or her, who filed it, and the time and place at which the defendant must appear in court. This summons, along with the complaint, must then be given to the defendant. A sheriff or marshal may deliver the documents, or a private process server may be hired, or the documents might be mailed by registered mail. You should be sure to use whatever method of service is required for your case. These documents provide defendants with the first official notice that they are being sued.

Q. What are the defendant's options after being served with a complaint and summons?

A. At this point, most defendants hire a lawyer to prepare their defense. The defendant's lawyer will determine when the defendant needs to respond to the complaint, discuss the details of the complaint with the defendant, and review the complaint and summons to be certain that they meet all legal requirements. If the complaint appears defective, legally or factually, the defendant may file a motion with the court.

▸ MOTION

A **motion** is a formal written or oral request to the court asking that it take some specific action. Typical pretrial motions might include a defense motion to remove certain allegations from a complaint, or to dismiss all or part of the complaint for specific legal reasons. If the service of the summons and complaint was improper (because, for example, the server delivered the documents to the wrong address), the defendant may file a **motion to quash** service. Or a defendant might file a **motion to dismiss** based on the complainant's failure to state a valid claim upon which relief can be granted. The parties may be required to attend a hearing on a motion to resolve the issues raised.

Q. How much information should the defendant include in the answer?

A. Essentially, the defendant's answer must make the plaintiff and the court aware of the defendant's response to each allegation in the complaint, by stating whether he or she is contesting or admitting each allegation, or is unable to contest or admit because of insufficient information. A failure to respond can be interpreted as an admission by the defendant that the plaintiff's allegation is true. In addition, the answer may raise any affirmative defenses the defendant may have. An **affirmative defense** is a defense that goes beyond simple denial. In making an affirmative defense, the defendant attempts to counter, defeat, or remove all or part of the plaintiff's contentions. The defendant is essentially saying, "even if I did what you are claiming, I am still not legally responsible." Common examples of affirmative defenses include self-defense and mistake of fact. If a defendant raises an affirmative defense, the defendant will be required to prove that defense if the case goes to trial.

If the defendant has reason to believe that the court lacks jurisdiction to hear the case, the defendant should raise that issue at the earliest possible opportunity.

Q. What if the defendant believes that the plaintiff has caused damage to the defendant?

A. In that case, in addition to answering the plaintiff's complaint, the defendant in a civil case may file a claim against the plaintiff. This action is known as a **counterclaim.** If a counterclaim is filed, the plaintiff becomes a defendant and will be called on to file an answer to the allegations and counts contained in the counterclaim.

Q. I am being sued, but I think there are other claims or parties that should also be involved. What can I do?

A. If the defendant believes that others not named as defendants in the plaintiff's suit are responsible, in whole or in part, for the plaintiff's injury or loss, he or she may seek to bring those third parties into the case as additional defendants. This is known as an **action to implead** those parties. If a person who was not named in the original suit has interests that are affected by the lawsuit, and believes that he or she should be involved in order to defend those interests, that person may seek to join the suit as either an additional plaintiff or defendant. Such a party is said to **intervene** in the lawsuit. Finally, in suits that already involve multiple plaintiffs or defendants, parties may file **cross-claims,** which are actions by one named party against another. For example, one defendant could file a cross-claim against another defendant. These kinds of pretrial procedures are intended to encourage plaintiffs and defendants to resolve all related disputes in a single case, rather than in piecemeal litigation.

▶ VENUE

The **venue** is the county or district within a state or the United States where a lawsuit is to be tried. It is usually the place where the incident at issue in the lawsuit took place—for example, the place where an accident occurred, a contract was signed, or a crime was committed.

Q. How does a court determine whether it has jurisdiction to hear a case?

A. In federal court, the plaintiff bears the burden of proving, through relevant statutes and case law, that the court has jurisdiction to hear his or her case under Article III of the U.S. Constitution. In most state courts, by contrast, it is up to the defendant to prove that the court does *not* have jurisdiction to hear the case under applicable state jurisdictional laws.

Q. What is a motion for change of venue?

A. In addition to deciding whether it has jurisdiction to hear a case, a trial court may also be asked to determine whether the case should be heard where it was filed or in a court in some other city, county, or state. If the court determines that it would be more convenient for the parties if the trial were held somewhere else, or if the court determines that there is so much publicity about the case in one community that it should be heard elsewhere to assure a fair trial, the court will permit the case to be heard in a different location. This is called a **change of venue.** Congress (or, in the case of state courts, the state legislature) determines the rules regarding venue, which are generally designed to ensure that neither party is prejudiced by the trial's location.

Q. My lawyer is talking about filing a motion for summary judgment. What is this? How will it impact my case?

A. **Summary judgment** may be appropriate if the relevant facts are not in dispute and the only question is how the law should be applied to those facts. In such cases, there is no need for a jury or judge to hear witnesses or view evidence regarding what happened. All that is left for the court to do is to apply the law to the undisputed facts, without a trial.

In considering whether to grant a party's motion for summary judgment, the trial court will review the parties' **affidavits** (written statements made under oath) and discovery materials to determine whether, when viewed in the light most favorable to the party not bringing the motion, there is no genuine dispute regarding an important fact.

If the court is uncertain whether a genuine factual issue exists, it will deny the summary judgment motion and the case will proceed to trial. If, on the other hand, the court is convinced that there is no such factual dispute, it will consider the parties' written arguments on the legal issues and then rule on the motion for summary judgment, disposing of the case in favor of one of the parties.

Exchange of Information

Q. My case is getting ready for trial, but I think it would be really helpful if I at least knew the name of the other side's witnesses. Is there any way to make my opponent disclose information or witness names before trial?

A. Yes. The process of finding out information from the other side before a trial begins is called **discovery.** This is a vital step in any civil litigation, and a reminder that the goal of our legal system is to do justice rather than to reward the clever lawyer or secretive litigant. Surprise witnesses and secret evidence often show up on television or in the movies, but rarely in a real courtroom.

The advantage of exchanging information is that it becomes clear early what facts are at issue between the parties. As a result, the parties might need to spend less time presenting evidence at trial, or may even be able to resolve their dispute. Discovery may also make it clear that summary judgment is an appropriate option.

Some of the many available pretrial discovery tools include:

- **Depositions.** The lawyers for each side in a lawsuit may require potential witnesses to answer oral questions under oath before the trial.
- **Interrogatories.** Each party can submit a list of written questions to the other party, which again must be answered under oath.
- **Motion to produce.** For the purpose of inspecting, copying, or photographing, each party can ask the court to require the other party to produce relevant documents or physical evidence in the other party's possession.
- **Request to admit.** Each party can ask the other to agree that certain facts are true, thus sparing both parties the trouble, expense, and delay of having to prove those facts at trial.

Q. What if my opponent and I agree on some but not all of the facts in my case?

A. If the parties agree on certain facts, they can **stipulate** that those facts are undisputed, and thereby forgo the need to introduce evidence at trial to prove those facts. If they don't agree about some facts, then each side will have the opportunity to introduce evidence establishing those facts.

Trials

Q. My case will be tried before a jury. What does this involve?

A. Jury trials begin with **opening statements** presented to the jury by the lawyer for each party. The opening statement introduces the jurors to each side's theory of the case, and outlines what each side plans to prove during the trial. For example, in a personal injury case, the plaintiff will explain that the defendant was negligent and that, as a result, the plaintiff suffered a financial loss or other injury. The plaintiff will need to prove the elements of negligence: that the defendant owed the plaintiff a legal duty, that he or she breached that duty, and that the duty caused damage to the plaintiff. The defense, meanwhile, will explain why there is reason to doubt one or more of those elements of the plaintiff's case.

Q. How do parties present their cases?

A. The heart of the case is the presentation of evidence. In a civil case, the plaintiff begins the presentation of a case by calling witnesses. The witnesses may testify to matters of fact. They may also be called to identify documents, pictures, or other items introduced into evidence. The defense may cross-examine the plaintiff's witnesses.

After the plaintiff has finished calling witnesses, the defense puts on its case by calling witnesses, and the plaintiff will have the opportunity to cross-examine them.

Q. How does a direct examination differ from a cross-examination?

A. **Direct examination** is conducted by the party calling the witness, and is intended to establish that party's case. The witnesses may be **cross-examined** by the lawyer for the opposing party. In a cross-examination, the opposing party's lawyer attempts to undermine the testimony given by a witness under direct examination by bringing forth facts favorable to the cross-examining party or by discrediting that witness. Cross-examination is generally limited to questioning on matters raised in direct examination.

Q. Can my attorney present any document or can a witness testify to anything so long as it helps my case?

A. No. The rules of evidence require fact-finding judges or juries to base their decisions solely on relevant evidence that is reliable. Some evidentiary rules are fashioned to further other important policies, such as protecting civil liberties. There are several important rules of evidence.

- Witnesses generally cannot state opinions or conclusions unless they are experts or specially qualified to do so.
- Lawyers generally may not ask leading questions of their own witnesses. **Leading questions** are questions that suggest the answers desired, in effect prompting the witness. If a lawyer sought to establish certain whereabouts of a defendant, the lawyer likely could not specifically reference those whereabouts in a question to his own witness—for example, "Isn't it true that you saw John waiting across the street before his wife came home?" However, it is permissible for lawyers to ask leading questions during cross-examination.
- There is a prohibition on hearsay. **Hearsay** is information that a witness claims to

have heard from another person, with the witness trying to assert the truth of what that other person said. The witness is repeating a statement made by someone else, not what the witness actually saw or heard personally. There are complex exceptions to the rule against hearsay.

Q. How does a judge rule on objections?

A. One of your lawyer's duties is to make an appropriate **objection** to any violation of the rules of evidence by the opposing party.

Most courts require that a specific legal reason be stated for an objection. Usually, the judge will immediately either sustain or overrule the objection. If the objection is **sustained,** the lawyer must rephrase the question in a proper form or ask another question. If the witness has already given an answer, that answer is not to be considered evidence, and the judge will instruct the jury to disregard it. If the objection is **overruled,** the witness can answer the question, and that answer becomes evidence that may be considered by the jury.

Even if the court overrules your lawyer's objection, the objection will appear in the written record of your trial and can be raised again on appeal if you should lose at trial. In many instances, a failure to object at trial means that you **waive** (give up) your right to complain about the matter later.

Verdicts

Q. What happens after each side has presented all its evidence?

A. Each side will be given the opportunity to address the jury directly and to summarize what he or she believes was proven during the trial. At the conclusion of these arguments, called **closing statements** or **closing arguments,** the judge will consider each side's suggestions about how to instruct the jury on the law governing the case. In some state and federal courts, judges give the jury instructions on the law prior to the closing statements to assist them in understanding those statements better. The judge's instructions will specify the issues the jury must decide, and the law it must apply to the facts that were developed in the case. Then the jury will retire to the jury room to reach a decision. In a typical case, the jury will be asked to render a **general verdict** and to determine a winner on an all-or-nothing basis. Alternatively, the judge may ask for a **special verdict,** which requires the jury to enter separate written findings on each of several issues.

Q. So after each side has finished presenting its case, the jury will deliberate. Right?

A. Not necessarily. Sometimes, before turning a case over to the jury, the judge will consider either side's **motion to direct a verdict** in its favor. A directed verdict removes the need for the jury to determine whether a defendant is liable. However, such a ruling is appropriate only when the court is persuaded that a reasonable jury could decide the case in only one way. The court may grant, deny, or, more likely, **reserve** (postpone) ruling on such a motion until after the jury has rendered a verdict. If the jury rules against the party who requested the directed verdict, the judge can still overrule the jury's decision by granting a motion for **judgment notwithstanding the verdict.**

Q. Does a verdict consist simply of a guilty or not-guilty decision?

A. No. There can be more to a verdict than a simple determination of guilt or non-guilt. If the jury concludes that one of the parties is liable to the other, it must go on to decide the appropriate remedy. In most ordinary personal injury suits, this remedy will take the form of money **damages.** If a jury finds that the defendant should pay damages to the plaintiff, the court will direct the defendant to pay. The judge may decide to separate this portion of the trial from the liability portion. This is known as a **bifurcated trial.** A bifurcated trial can simplify the issues because it saves the jury from listening to instructions and arguments about damages until after it has determined whether the plaintiff is entitled to any damages in the first place.

Damages are supposed to restore plaintiffs financially to the position they would have been in if they hadn't been wronged in the first place. Of course, it is more difficult to calculate a proper award when the defendant's wrongful act caused more than out-of-pocket expenses—after all, how much money does it take to compensate a person for pain, suffering, loss of life's enjoyment, or damages to one's reputation?

In some circumstances, when the defendant's behavior is thought to be especially outrageous, the plaintiff may ask the jury to award **punitive damages** in addition to compensatory damages. For example, in the O. J. Simpson civil case, the jury awarded the Brown and Goldman families millions of dollars in punitive damages because they found that Simpson had caused the deaths of their family members. Punitive damages are designed to punish the defendant and to discourage others from engaging in similar conduct.

Procedures After Trial

Q. If the plaintiff wins, what happens next?

A. After the court enters judgment in favor of the plaintiff, it typically makes a formal judicial order that the defendant pay the compensation awarded. But winning a verdict may only be the beginning of a plaintiff's efforts to secure a remedy.

If a defendant against whom a judgment has been entered does not pay, the plaintiff will have to initiate collection proceedings. The plaintiff may have to seek orders from a judge that the defendant's property be sold, or that an amount be deducted periodically from the defendant's wages in order to satisfy the judgment.

Q. What options does the losing party have?

A. A losing party has two options. First, the losing party can ask the court to throw out the verdict and order a new trial if it can show the court that:

- the verdict was contrary to the weight of the evidence;
- serious errors or other misconduct were committed by the judge;
- there was serious misconduct on the part of a juror, lawyer, witness, or party;
- the damages awarded are significantly disproportionate to the harm caused; or
- vitally important evidence that could not have been discovered before the end of the trial has only now been discovered.

Alternatively, or if these new trial motions do not succeed, the party may appeal the judgment to an appellate court.

▶ APPEALS

A popular misconception is that cases are always appealed. In fact, a losing party does not always have an automatic right of appeal—on the contrary, the appeal must usually have a legal basis. The fact that the losing party did not like the verdict is not sufficient grounds for an appeal.

Q. How does a party appeal?

A. The losing party (or a prevailing party contending that the damages were insufficient) may ask for review of the trial court's decision in an appellate court. In the federal system, the party must appeal to the court of appeals in the appropriate circuit.

In those states that have two levels of appellate courts, parties challenging trial court decisions generally must bring their appeals to the intermediate court first. However, because intermediate appellate courts often have some limited discretion to determine which civil cases they will hear, not all civil appeals will necessarily be accepted, in which case the lower court's verdict will stand.

Q. How do appeals work?

A. Appeals courts review the procedures of lower courts and ensure that the law was properly applied. As a general rule, they do not retry cases. They don't hear witnesses or weigh evidence. Instead, in an appeal, the appellant must persuade the court to reverse the trial court's judgment because of significant legal errors that occurred during the trial, such as the improper admission or exclusion of evidence, or erroneous instructions on the law given by the judge to the jury that are likely to have affected the result. The appellee, on the other hand, will seek to persuade the court that no error was made in the lower court—or that, if there was an error, it was harmless because it did not affect the outcome. A printed transcript of the trial court proceedings, together with the original papers and exhibits, may be forwarded to the court for consideration in deciding the appeal.

Q. Are appeals only conducted in writing, or will there be a courtroom proceeding?

A. Some appeals involve only written briefs, while others involve an oral argument in which each side presents its argument to the court. Appellate courts generally schedule oral arguments in appeals cases, though they are not required to do so. If a case is before an intermediate appellate court, a panel of judges will hear the argument. However, in certain important cases before an intermediate court, the oral argument will be heard **en banc**—that is, heard by all the judges of the court. Oral arguments before the U.S. Supreme Court and the highest state courts are also en banc.

Prior to oral argument, the judges who will hear the appeal read the briefs and examine the record compiled in the trial court. At oral argument, the judges listen to the arguments of the lawyers for the parties and may question the lawyers about the case and how the law should be applied to the case. Typically each side is allotted a limited period of time in which to present its case orally. However, an appellate court is free to grant more or less time, based on the significance or complexity of the case. After oral argument, each judge votes on whether to uphold or reverse the trial court's judgment, in whole or in part. The court then issues a written opinion explaining its decision. As a general rule, the parties will not know the outcome of the case until the written opinion is released.

Q. Must an appellate court reach a unanimous decision?

A. No, only a majority must agree. If a judge or judges disagree with the majority's result, they may write a **dissent** to explain their disagreement. If a judge agrees with the result reached by the majority but disagrees with its reasoning, he or she may write a separate opinion **concurring** in the judgment.

Q. What recourse is there for the party who loses at the intermediate appellate level?

A. The party can seek review in the highest court in the system. In the federal system, that court is the Supreme Court of the United

---

▶ **APPELLANT AND APPELLEE**

The **appellant** is the party who appeals—that is, the party who carries his or her case to a higher court after receiving an adverse order in the lower court. The **appellee** is the party against whom an appeal is filed, and the one who must answer allegations of the appellant in the appeal. Appellees are sometimes referred to as **respondents,** because they must respond to the appellant's case on appeal.

States. In addition to reviewing decisions of the U.S. courts of appeal, the U.S. Supreme Court has the jurisdiction, but not the obligation, to review the final decisions of the highest state courts (or even of lower state courts, if the party was unable to secure additional review within the state court system) so long as the case is of the type described in Article III of the U.S. Constitution and was not decided on "adequate and independent state grounds." When the U.S. Supreme Court declines to hear a case, as it does in the vast majority of cases, the decision of the lower federal or state court becomes the final decision.

Q. How does the U.S. Supreme Court decide whether to hear a case?

A. In the usual course, a party seeking review in the U.S. Supreme Court will file a petition asking the Court to issue a **writ of certiorari.** This is simply a request to review the case. This petition will include a copy of the lower court's opinion and a **brief.** A brief is a document explaining why the Court should agree to review the lower court's decision. The other party may file a brief in opposition to the petition. The Court will then either deny the petition (which is what happens in most cases) or grant it. If the petition is granted, the Court will require the federal or state court to transmit the record of the case for its review.

Q. What is the effect of granting a request for review?

A. If a request for review is granted, the case will be set for briefing and oral argument in much the same way as it was in lower appellate court. If the Court makes a decision on the merits of the case (that is, based on the legal issues at stake), its decision will be binding and final, and becomes the law of the land. However, sometimes the Court will **remand,** or return, a case to the lower court. In this case, the Court will provide clarification about how the relevant constitutional or statutory provisions should be applied and interpreted, and will instruct the lower court to reconsider its earlier opinion in light of those clarifications.

REMEMBER THIS

- After the time limit set forth in the applicable statute of limitations has run out, the plaintiff is barred from bringing suit—no matter how meritorious the case.

- A lawsuit starts with a complaint. After being served with a complaint and summons, the defendant may file a defense with the court. Either party may file motions or seek summary judgment. Both parties participate in discovery before the trial.

- There is no right to a jury trial in every case.

- The losing party may be able to seek review of the trial court's decision in an appellate court. Remember that there is no automatic right to an appeal—if you are unhappy with the way your case turned out, talk to your lawyer about whether an appeal is an option.

MEDIATION AND SMALL-CLAIMS COURT

Not all disputes are worth the trouble and expense of a full-fledged trial, and some

> ▶ **THE NUMBER CRUNCH: SETTLEMENT OF CIVIL CASES**
>
> By some estimates, more than 90 percent of all civil cases are settled before trial.

disputes—like those between friends and neighbors—might be better solved if the parties could work things out informally and preserve their relationship. This section explains your options for avoiding trial altogether. This may seem a little strange after emphasizing the important role of the courts, but the fact is that the vast majority of disputes are resolved before they ever get to trial.

Resolving Your Dispute Out of Court

Q. What are my options if I want to resolve my civil case without proceeding to trial?

A. You have several options.

Negotiation

The lawyers in the case can meet and negotiate a settlement. If you don't have a lawyer, you should talk to the person with whom you have a dispute. Stay calm and reasonable. You may find that, if approached politely, your opponent will be willing to settle on a mutually acceptable basis. Make certain that the other person understands why you are unhappy and what you would consider a reasonable solution to the problem. Keep an open mind and listen to his or her side of the story. Making an effort to settle a dispute without a lawsuit is never a waste of time. In addition, many states require that a party first make a demand for payment or action before filing some types of lawsuits.

If you do reach a satisfactory compromise, ask your lawyer to get it in writing for both parties to sign—you will both want to establish what you are and are not agreeing to, and what (if any) issues still need to be resolved. Even if you and the other party are able to work out the main problem, it still may be necessary to appear before a judge if a lawsuit has been commenced. Your court appearance will be made easier if the agreement is in writing and can be submitted to the judge.

Mediation or Arbitration

If your attempts to negotiate a settlement are unsuccessful, you may want to try to resolve the dispute through mediation or arbitration.

In **mediation**, a trained mediator will help you and your opponent resolve your disagreement by identifying, defining, and discussing the things about which you disagree, in an effort to help you reach a mutual agreement. This is an informal, cooperative problem-solving process, and does not necessarily require you to know the law or to hire a lawyer, although often the parties find it useful to do so.

Arbitration, on the other hand, is a more formal proceeding in which you and your opponent will be asked to present evidence and witnesses to an arbitrator, who will issue a decision, usually in writing, to resolve the dispute. Arbitration may be binding or nonbinding. If the parties agree to a binding arbitration, it means they must accept the arbitrator's decision as final; if they agree to a nonbinding arbitration, it means the parties retain the right to go to court.

Send a Demand Letter

If negotiation and mediation have failed but you are still keen to avoid a trial, the next step is to ask your lawyer to write a carefully-thought-out letter to the person with whom you have a disagreement. This is called a **demand letter,** and should include an accurate summary of the history of the problem and a date by which you would like a response or settlement. This type of "settle-or-else" letter has many advantages. It helps you organize the facts and your thoughts logically. Your lawyer may be able to express your thoughts in a way that the other person might not have heard when you dealt with him or her directly. A demand letter may be just the push needed to get the other person to settle. If the letter sets reasonable time limits, it will often help to encourage settlement.

Settlement During Trial

In the event that all of your attempts to settle before trial are unsuccessful, you may find yourself preparing for litigation. This does not mean that it is no longer possible to settle your matter. It is often the case that as parties prepare their evidence and marshal their resources for trial, they become more interested in settling. In many cases, the judge

---

▶ **COURT-FACILITATED SETTLEMENTS**

Courts actively encourage settlements, and will often require the parties in a civil case to confer in order to give them a chance to avoid a full trial.

▶ **APPEALS**

In many small-claims courts, there is no right to appeal if you lose. However, you may be able to start **de novo**—that is, new—litigation in a court of general jurisdiction.

---

will order the parties to participate in settlement conferences, mediation, or arbitration. A party may make an offer to settle before the trial begins, during the trial, or after the trial—right up until the moment that the jury returns with the verdict.

Small-Claims Court

Q. What is small-claims court?

A. All states have these special courts, most often known as **small-claims courts,** but sometimes called magistrate's courts, justice of the peace courts, or pro se courts. As suggested by their name, small-claims courts are available only to resolve disputes involving small claims for money. The jurisdictional limits of small-claims courts may range from a few hundred dollars in some states to thousands of dollars in others. The popular TV program *The People's Court* is an example of the comparatively informal, quick justice provided by small-claims courts.

Q. May I represent myself?

A. Yes, you may represent yourself in small-claims court and do not necessarily need a lawyer to accompany you. In fact, there are some states in which a lawyer is not permitted to represent a party in small-claims court.

> ## ▶ JURISDICTION
>
> When we say a court has **jurisdiction** to hear a case, we mean it has the legal power and authority to decide the kinds of issues raised in the case. Not every court has jurisdiction to hear every kind of case. One of the first questions to answer before filing a lawsuit is which court has jurisdiction to hear the case: Can your case be heard by a small-claims court, or does a state or federal court have jurisdiction over the case?

Q. What are the advantages of filing a lawsuit in small-claims court?

A. First, if you choose to act as your own lawyer, you may not need to pay lawyer's fees. Second, small-claims court procedures are designed to be simpler and involve less paperwork than those of other courts. Third, it may be possible to conduct your proceeding after normal working hours. And finally, the case is often resolved in less time.

Q. Can I have a jury trial in small-claims court?

A. No, there is no jury; a judge will decide your case.

Q. It sounds like it won't take much work to bring my case in small-claims court. Is that true?

A. Not necessarily. You should only represent yourself in a small-claims procedure if you are willing to invest some time and effort in your case. If you act as your own lawyer, you will need to do research, gather documents, and investigate factual matters to prepare and present your case. In some cases, the other side may be represented by a lawyer.

Remember that a small-claims court is, in many respects, like any other court. You will need to be prepared on the date of the hearing—know what arguments you are going to make; have your evidence ready, with copies for the judge and opposition; and bring any witnesses who are going to give testimony. And, like other courts, small-claims courts operate according to laws and rules. Even the most careful preparation and the best presentation in court will not help if you cannot prove legally that the other person owes you the money. You must be able to prove **legal liability** in your case—in other words, that someone else's wrongful acts caused you to suffer a loss for which money damages are appropriate.

> ## ▶ SOME SUGGESTIONS
>
> Before you decide whether you should take advantage of small-claims court, ask yourself some simple questions. Is your claim one that has only to do with money? If so, is the amount for which you are suing considered a small claim in your state? Are the time and effort you will have to invest learning your state's law and presenting your case worth what you are likely to collect?

REMEMBER THIS

- There are many ways to resolve your dispute without going to court. You can sometimes save time and money—and end up with a better outcome—by avoiding trial.

- If your attempts at negotiation and mediation do fail, do some research and see whether your case could be handled in small-claims court. Your case might be dispatched more quickly than it would be in a state court, and you may not need a lawyer.

CIVIL VERSUS CRIMINAL LAW

Q. How do civil and criminal law differ?

A. Civil matters are private matters, which typically involve the plaintiff suing the defendant for a money award, often in combination with other orders of the court, like an injunction to make a party stop a particular course of action.

A crime is considered a wrong against the public. Although a criminal defendant may have injured only one victim directly, any violation of criminal law harms society. Criminal cases are always initiated by the government. The defendant in criminal cases is usually a person and is very rarely a corporation. While victims of a crime may be consulted, they have no power to make a prosecutor bring charges or to prevent the prosecutor from dropping charges. A convicted defendant may be ordered to pay a fine, or may be sentenced to probation, community service, jail, prison, or even death.

Q. Do criminal defendants have more rights than civil defendants?

A. Yes. The Bill of Rights—the first ten amendments to the U.S. Constitution—together with state constitutional provisions, treat a criminal conviction (and the possibility of a prison term or death sentence) as more serious than a finding of civil liability. Accordingly, it is more difficult to convict someone of a crime than it is to obtain a civil judgment against a defendant.

In a civil suit, the question that a trial judge or jury will ask is whether a plaintiff has proven that it was more likely than not that the defendant was legally responsible for the plaintiff's injury or loss. This preponderance-of-the-evidence standard means that if the evidence favors the plaintiff· by even the slightest bit, the plaintiff is entitled to a verdict in his or her favor. In a criminal case, on the other hand, the standard is much higher: The prosecution must prove the defendant's guilt beyond a reasonable doubt. Even if it is more likely than not that a criminal defendant is guilty of the crime charged, the proper verdict is "not guilty" if there remains a reasonable doubt about his or her guilt.

The U.S. Constitution guarantees criminal defendants many other rights, including the right to a jury trial when there is the possibility of a conviction resulting in a prison term of six months or more; the right to have a lawyer appointed if the defendant cannot afford to hire one when there is a possibility of a loss of liberty; the right to confront one's accusers; and the right to a swift and public trial. State constitutions may guarantee other rights, including rights to a jury trial in lesser offenses.

The chart on the following page outlines the primary differences between civil and criminal trials.

	CRIMINAL TRIALS	CIVIL TRIALS
How the trial is commenced	The government brings charges through its prosecutors.	One or more private citizen or corporation brings a complaint against one or more other private citizens or corporations. (Note that sometimes the government can be a party in a civil trial.)
Parties involved	Government v. defendant	Plaintiff v. defendant
Burden of proof	Beyond a reasonable doubt	Preponderance of the evidence
Possible results	Jail time, fines, community . service	Paying or recovering damages, restoring the wronged party to the position he or she would have occupied were it not for the wrong committed by the defendant.

THE BASICS OF CRIMINAL LAW

Whether they're inspired by TV shows about detectives and prosecutors or articles about the latest "trial of the century," most of us have some preconceptions about the criminal justice system. But how accurate are these preconceptions? Are all crimes treated the same way? What about crimes committed by kids? This section provides an introduction to issues related to the criminal justice system.

Q. How does the criminal justice system work?

A. It is useful to think of the criminal justice system as being made up of three main components:

- Law enforcement: the police investigate the alleged crime and arrest the defendant;
- Adjudication: after arrest, the defendant is charged and brought into the court system to have his or her case heard; and
- Corrections: if a defendant is convicted, he or she may enter the corrections system—jail or prison.

Q. Are more serious crimes treated differently than less serious ones?

A. Yes. Each state has a body of criminal law that categorizes certain offenses as felonies and others as misdemeanors.

The federal government and most states classify a **felony** as a crime that carries a minimum sentence of more than one year. A **misdemeanor** is an offense punishable by a sentence of one year or less. Some states draw the line based on the place of possible confinement. If incarceration would be in the state prison, the offense is considered a felony. If the offense is punishable by a term in a county jail or a state facility other than a prison or reformatory, it is considered a misdemeanor.

Felonies are more serious crimes than misdemeanors. Robbery, kidnapping, sexual assault, and murder are examples of felonies. Public drunkenness, resisting arrest, and simple battery are misdemeanors. Depending on the degree of the offense, however, the same offense might be either a misdemeanor or a felony. Petty larceny (stealing an item worth less than the dollar amount specified in the relevant state legislation) is a misdemeanor. If a person steals an item or items worth more than that amount, the offense is grand theft, which is a felony. Similarly, driving under the influence of drugs or alcohol may be a misdemeanor if it is a person's first offense. After a certain number of convictions for that same offense, however, the state may prosecute the next violation as a felony.

Q. How does the criminal justice system deal with children who commit crimes?

A. Children are generally dealt with in the juvenile court systems. These systems vary by state, but generally hear cases involving persons between the ages of ten and eighteen. Not all states agree that the maximum age is eighteen; in New York and many other states the maximum age is sixteen. In some circumstances, even juveniles under the age limit may be transferred to adult court. If the prosecution charges an older juvenile with a particularly serious or violent offense, the prosecutor may request that an adult court try

▶ THE REQUIREMENTS OF A CRIME

Most crimes require both a criminal act (**actus reus**) and a criminal intent (**mens rea**). Even if you committed a criminal act (for example, injuring someone), you might not have had the required mental state, or wrongful purpose, for it to be considered a crime.

Both criminal act and criminal intent must be proved beyond a reasonable doubt if a person is to be convicted of a crime. If the facts in your case show that you did not have a criminal intent, then all the elements of the case have not been proved, and you may not be convicted of a crime.

However, in certain circumstances you can be convicted of a crime even if you did not specifically intend to commit it. For example, a person who kills another person commits a crime if his or her actions were reckless or sufficiently negligent, even if the killing was unintentional. Thus, if you accidentally kill a pedestrian while driving 100 miles per hour on a city street, you have committed a crime even though there was no conscious intent to injure that person or anyone else.

the case. In some states, juveniles fourteen or older who are charged with serious acts like murder, rape, or armed robbery must be dealt with in adult courts unless the judge transfers them to juvenile court.

▶ THE CHARACTERISTICS OF SOME SERIOUS CRIMES

Crimes are defined by law and are set forth in a state's criminal or penal code. They also may be listed in a state's vehicle or health-and-safety code. Crimes can be as serious as murder or as minor as jaywalking. There are many categories of crimes, including drug offenses, weapons offenses, child and spousal abuse, child endangerment, welfare fraud, and driving under the influence. The following list describes only a few of the most serious common crimes.

Crimes Against the Person

Homicide   A person is guilty of criminal homicide if he or she purposely, knowingly, recklessly, or negligently causes the death of another human being, without legal justification or excuse.

Sexual Assault   Sexual assault includes forced sexual conduct or penetration without the victim's consent or when the victim is underage. These types of crimes often are called rape, sexual assault, sexual conduct, or sexual battery, and may include special designations when the victim is a child.

Robbery   Robbery is the unlawful taking or attempted taking, by force or threat of force, of property that is in the immediate possession of another.

Crimes Against Property

Burglary   Burglary consists of a person entering into, or remaining in, a residence, building, or vehicle without consent, with the intent to commit a felony or a larceny therein.

Larceny (Theft)   Larceny or theft is the unlawful taking or attempted taking of property from the possession of another, without force and without deceit, with intent permanently to deprive the owner of the property.

Arson   Arson is the intentional or attempted damaging or destroying of property—one's own property, or the property of another without their consent—by means of fire or explosion, with or without the intent to defraud.

Q. Are juvenile trials run the same way as adult criminal trials?

A. No. The juvenile court system often is different from the adult criminal justice system. Because juveniles do not have the constitu-tional right to a jury trial unless they are tried as adults, judges hear most juvenile cases. Juveniles also do not have the right to a public trial or to bail. However, the fundamental elements of due process do apply in a juvenile proceeding, just as they do in the criminal trial of an adult. For example, a child charged in a juvenile proceeding has the right to receive notice of charges in advance of any adjudication of delinquency; to be represented by a lawyer, including one paid for by the state if the family cannot afford one; to confront and cross-examine witnesses; to pretrial release, unless the child is a danger to himself or others; and to assert the Fifth Amendment privilege against self-incrimination. Finally, the state is required to prove its charges beyond a reasonable doubt, just as in the trial of any adult on a criminal charge.

Under most state laws, juvenile offenders do not commit "crimes." They commit **delinquent acts,** which are acts that would constitute crimes if committed by an adult. The trial phase of a juvenile case is referred to as an **adjudication hearing.** This means that the judge hears the evidence and determines whether the child is delinquent. The court then may take whatever action it deems to be in the child's best interest. The purpose is to rehabilitate, not to punish.

The chart below provides a quick comparison of adult criminal court with juvenile court.

REMEMBER THIS

- In criminal cases, the government is always the prosecuting party. The prosecution must prove its case beyond a reasonable doubt.

- Defendants have rights guaranteed by the U.S. Constitution, which help to ensure that they receive a fair trial. State law and state constitutions may protect other rights.

	ADULT CRIMINAL COURT	JUVENILE COURT
Person Accused	Defendant	Juvenile
Act	Alleged crime	Alleged delinquent act
Name of Proceeding	Trial	Adjudication Hearing
Right to Jury	Yes—if facing a prison term of more than six months	No
Right to Public Trial	Yes	No
Right to Bail	Yes	No
Right to an Attorney	Yes	Yes
Possible Outcomes	Sentence based on punishment, rehabilitation, and deterrence of future crimes.	Adjudication based on the child's best interest and the desire to rehabilitate.

▶ **THE IMMIGRATION CONSEQUENCES OF CONVICTION**

Noncitizens should be aware that a criminal conviction can often have tremendous consequences relating to immigration. For instance, the government can deport a noncitizen convicted of a crime—even when the crime is classified as a misdemeanor or even if the defendant is not sent to prison. Moreover, if a noncitizen defendant pleads guilty to a criminal offense, a judge rarely is required to explain these immigration-related consequences at the time the defendant enters his or her guilty plea. For these reasons, it's very important that if you are a noncitizen facing criminal charges, you explain your immigration status to your lawyer so that he or she can properly advise you. Even if you are not residing in this country legally, you should tell your lawyer about your immigration status. This information is protected by attorney-client privilege, and your lawyer is required to protect it from third parties.

- In the case of serious crimes, juveniles may be tried as adults in some states.

THE POLICE AND YOUR RIGHTS

Imagine you are looking through a store window and are suddenly grabbed by a police officer and frisked for weapons. Can the police lawfully do this to you? Or do they have to arrest you first? What would happen if you were arrested? Do you have to answer any questions the police might ask you?

It's a good idea to know what to expect in case you ever have to deal with the police—whether you're a victim reporting a crime, a witness, or a suspect. This section provides you with information about your rights when dealing with police, your rights to a lawyer, and the process of being charged with a crime.

Investigation Techniques

Q. How do the police investigate crimes?

A. When the police receive a report of a crime, they send investigating officers to the scene as soon as they can. If the officers arrest a suspect, they will transport that person to the police station or to jail for booking. The investigating officer will write an arrest report, detailing when and why he or she went to the scene, along with any observations made at the scene, and why he or she arrested the suspect. The officer also will fill out a property report, detailing what items—for example, drugs or cash—the police found on the suspect during booking. The officer also will list any evidence found at the scene.

If the crime is complex or serious, the police then assign an investigating officer, usually a detective, to the case. That officer will make a return visit to the crime scene, look for more evidence, and interview any other witnesses. If the police have not arrested anyone, the detective will analyze the evidence and try to narrow down the list of suspects. The detective will then question suspects and sometimes obtain a confession.

Q. Do the police have the right to tap my telephone? What about other forms of electronic surveillance?

A. The police have the right to tap your telephone if they can demonstrate probable cause—that is, if they can show the court that intercepting your telephone conversations is necessary to help solve certain crimes (such as treason, terrorism, drug trafficking, wire fraud, or money laundering).

The law considers wiretapping to be very intrusive. Therefore, it is closely regulated by federal and state law. A court will permit wiretapping only for a limited period of time. Moreover, the authorities that listen to your telephone calls must make efforts to minimize the intrusion by limiting the number of intercepted calls to those involving the investigation. For example, a court might authorize the tapping of a bookie's telephone only during the hours when it is likely that bets will be placed. After the wiretap period has ended, the authorities must inventory the calls and reveal to the court the content of the conversations they intercepted.

Less intrusive forms of legally permissible electronic surveillance include the **pen register** and the **trap and trace.** A pen register device records every number dialed from your telephone. A trap and trace records every number dialed from an outside line to your telephone. These devices do not enable anyone to listen to your conversations; they simply list telephone numbers.

It is also possible for the police to tap a cellular telephone. In order to do so lawfully,

however, they need a warrant. Similarly, police generally need a warrant in order to search e-mail records.

You should assume that any conversation from a jail or visitor's phone is being tapped. If you are in jail, do not discuss any aspect of your case with anyone except your lawyer.

Q. May the police use information against me that is obtained from a confidential informant?

A. Likely, yes. **Confidential informants** are people who supply information to the police

---

▶ HOW TO REPORT A CRIME

Call the police and say that you wish to report a crime. The police will likely want to talk to you to determine what you know about the incident so they can decide whether to investigate further.

If you were in any way involved in the crime, you might be considered a suspect. If this is the case you should call a lawyer immediately, before you talk to the police, unless someone's life or safety is in danger. A lawyer will be permitted to accompany you to the police station and be present to protect your interests during police questioning. Many people believe that what they say to the police is not admissible unless written down, recorded on tape, or said to a prosecutor or judge. That is not true. To be on the safe side, you should assume that anything you say to anyone but your lawyer could be used against you at trial.

on the condition that their identities will not be disclosed. The law allows police to use such information if it is reliable. The police often use such information to obtain search warrants. For example, an informant might tell the police where someone has hidden evidence of a crime. The police would then provide this information and a supporting affidavit containing other information (such as the informant's prior reliability, how the informant obtained the information, and evidence obtained from other sources that confirms the informant's story) to a judge or **magistrate** (a type of court official). If the judge or magistrate determines there is probable cause to believe the evidence will be found at the location specified, the judge or magistrate will issue a search warrant. The prosecutor must not reveal the confidential informant's identity unless he or she is ordered to do so by the court. In addition, the prosecutor can ask the judge for a protective order sealing the warrant and the supporting affidavit in order to keep the identity of the informant secret.

Searches

Q. When can the police legally search my home or items in it?

A. You have greater privacy rights in your home than you do in your car or public places. (See Chapter 14, "Automobiles," for information on car searches.) Therefore, the police normally cannot search your home unless they have a warrant. The warrant must specify what the police are looking for and the specific areas of the house they are allowed to search. The police may search outside those specified areas in some circumstances—for example, to prevent the destruction of evidence or to ensure the safety of the police.

Q. What happens to the evidence the police recover if they search me without a warrant?

A. If the police do search without a warrant, the search is presumed invalid, so you have the right to challenge it in court. If the judge finds there was a valid exception to the warrant requirement, he or she may allow the evidence to be presented at trial. On the other hand, if there was no such exception, the **exclusionary rule**—which prevents illegally obtained evidence from being introduced at trial—may prevent the evidence from being used against you.

Warrant Exceptions

Q. May the police search me without a warrant?

A. That depends on whether you are under arrest. If the police have lawfully arrested you, they are permitted to search you. They also are allowed to search the area under your immediate control—also known as your **wingspan,** which simply means the area where you can reach. This may include, for example, the glove box of your car.

If you are not under arrest, the police generally are not permitted to search you. There are a number of important exceptions to this rule. For example, the police may search you if you give your consent for them to do so. Keep in mind that consenting to a search may limit your defense in later proceedings. Your consent, for example, will make it difficult to challenge the legality of the search at a pretrial suppression hearing. Many people feel they should consent in order to show the po-

▶ ADMISSIBLE AND INADMISSIBLE EVIDENCE

What does it mean to say that evidence is "admissible" or "inadmissible"? If evidence is **admissible,** it can be admitted into evidence and relied upon in court. If there is some problem with the evidence—for example, if it was obtained unlawfully, or is likely to be unreliable for some reason (see the discussion on hearsay earlier in this chapter)—then a judge can rule that it is **inadmissible.** This means that it cannot be relied upon in court when the case is being argued. For example, if the police seize drugs, but they seize them by means of an unlawful search, the drugs are likely inadmissible as evidence.

lice they have nothing to hide. But what you may consider insignificant, such as a piece of paper with a telephone number written on it, may be incriminating if it links you to a crime. For this reason, your consent to a search should not be given lightly. The police also can search you for weapons if a police officer reasonably feels that he or she is in danger.

Q. Do the police need a warrant to stop me on the street?

A. In all likelihood, no. The police are always free to ask you questions in a public place. Likewise, you are free to refuse to answer their questions and to leave. However, if police have observed unusual activity suggesting that a crime is occurring and that you are in-volved, then they can stop and briefly detain and question you. The Supreme Court has held, for example, that people in high-crime areas may be pursued and stopped merely for running away at the sight of police. Once you have been stopped by a police officer, you do not have the right to walk away. However, you also do not have to answer any questions they may ask you. During these types of brief detentions, police do not have to issue Miranda warnings (see the sidebar titled "The Miranda Rule" later in this chapter).

Q. Do the police have a right to frisk me?

A. That depends on the circumstances. On the one hand, the Supreme Court has ruled that an anonymous tip that a person is carrying a gun is not, without more evidence, sufficient to justify a police officer's frisking of that person (by patting the outside of his or her clothing). On the other hand, suppose the police reasonably suspect that you are engaging in criminal activity and that you may be armed and dangerous. Then they may stop and frisk you for weapons. The one and only lawful purpose of a frisk is to dispel suspicions of danger to the officer and to other persons—in other words, to ensure that a person is not armed and dangerous. For example, suppose that the police observe you walking back and forth in front of a store after dark. They observe you looking around nervously, as though you were "casing" the store prior to breaking in. The police are permitted, under these circumstances, to stop you and conduct a frisk for weapons if they believe you may be armed. If the officer who frisks you has good reason to believe that you committed a crime, or are hiding an illegal item—a gun or drugs, for example—he or she then may search you more extensively.

Custody and Arrest

Q. What procedures must the police follow while making an arrest?

A. The police do not have to tell you the crime for which they are arresting you, though they probably will. They are not permitted to use excessive force or brutality when arresting you. If you resist arrest or act violently, the police are allowed to use reasonable force to make the arrest or to keep you from injuring yourself. It may constitute a separate crime to resist arrest.

While the police are arresting you, they probably will read you your Miranda rights. However, they do not have to read you these rights if they do not intend to ask you questions.

Q. After arresting me, may the police make me provide fingerprints, a handwriting sample, or a voice sample?

A. Generally, the police are permitted to force you to supply these types of samples. They will take your fingerprints during the booking procedure at the police station. And because the law considers handwriting and voice samples to be evidence of physical characteristics, you may not claim that the police are forcing you to incriminate yourself by providing them. The police may use these samples as evidence against you in court if they help prove that you committed a crime. For example, your handwriting may be compared to the signature on a forged check or to the writing on a note handed to a teller during a bank robbery.

Q. What are my rights if the police put me in a lineup?

A. In a lineup, several people who look somewhat similar are lined up to be observed by victims or witnesses. The police then ask the victim or witness if they can identify anyone in the lineup as the person who committed the crime.

If formal charges have been filed against you and the police put you in a lineup, you have a right to have a lawyer present to protect your rights. A lineup is not supposed to be unfairly suggestive. For example, if a victim claims that her assailant was approximately six feet tall with a red beard, her lineup could not include five short, clean-shaven, dark-haired men and only one tall, bearded redhead.

Similarly, the police are not permitted to suggest to a victim that a certain person in the lineup is their main suspect—for example, they may not point to one person and ask, "Could that be the man who stole your purse?"

When you are in a lineup, the police have the right to ask you to speak if the witnesses feel they can identify you by your voice. The law permits the police to have you speak the words used during the crime. For example, they might ask you to say "Give me your money."

Additionally, the police are not permitted to make suggestions during photographic identifications, when a witness is asked to pick the suspected or accused criminal from a set of similar photographs. A suspect does not have the right to have a lawyer present during a photographic identification.

Q. After the police finish their investigation, how do they recommend that criminal charges be brought?

A. Criminal cases go through a screening process before a defendant faces charges in court. This is a two-step process that begins with the police inquiry. The investigating officer (or another officer superior to the arrest-

▶ WHERE POLICE ARE PERMITTED TO MAKE ARRESTS

Whether the police are allowed to arrest you in a particular place may depend on whether they have a warrant for your arrest. The police make most arrests without a warrant. For example, if you commit a misdemeanor in an officer's presence, that officer is permitted to arrest you without a warrant. Similarly, if the officer has **probable cause** (the minimum level of evidence needed to make a lawful arrest) to believe that you committed a felony, then the officer is allowed to arrest you without a warrant, even if he or she did not see you commit the crime. The law permits warrantless arrests in public places, such as a street or a restaurant.

But unless there are exigent circumstances, the police must have a warrant or your consent in order to arrest you in your home. There are two types of warrants: an **arrest warrant** and a **search warrant.** To arrest you in your own home, the police must have an arrest warrant. If they lack a warrant but have probable cause for a warrantless arrest, they are permitted to put your home under surveillance. They may then wait until you leave your home and arrest you in a public place. When the police arrest you without a warrant, the law entitles you to a prompt hearing to determine whether there was probable cause for the arrest.

If the police wish to arrest you in someone else's home where you are staying as an overnight guest, the same rules apply. However, if you are only a brief visitor to another person's home, the police can arrest you without a warrant.

ing officer) will review the arrest report. That officer will determine whether there is enough evidence to recommend filing charges against the arrested person. If the officer decides not to recommend filing charges, then the police will release the arrested person.

If the officer recommends that a charge be filed, a prosecutor will review the officer's recommendation. Based on the arrest report and any follow-up investigation, the prosecutor's office will decide whether to file charges and what criminal offenses to allege.

Q. How long may police hold suspects before charges must be filed?

A. If the police have probable cause to believe a person has committed a crime but the prosecutor has not yet brought formal charges, the police may detain the suspect in custody for a short period of time, generally twenty-four to forty-eight hours. **Probable cause** is defined as facts sufficient to support a reasonable belief that criminal activity is probably taking place, or knowledge of circumstances indicating a fair probability that evidence of crime will be found. It requires more than a mere hunch, but less than proof beyond a reasonable doubt.

After this short period of detention, the police must release the arrested person, or bring formal charges and present the suspect before a judge. If released, the person may be rearrested at a later date if the police obtain sufficient evidence.

Q. For legal purposes, when am I deemed to be "in custody"?

A. The most obvious example of being in custody, of course, is when the police say "You're under arrest." But you might be in custody even if the police do not say those magic words. Generally, the law considers you in custody when you have been arrested or otherwise deprived of your freedom of movement in a significant way. This may occur when an officer is holding you at gunpoint, or when several officers are surrounding you. It may also occur when you are in handcuffs or when the police have locked you in the backseat of a police car. There are no absolute rules for determining when a person is in custody—the test is whether a reasonable person in the circumstances would have felt free to leave the scene, and a court will consider all the circumstances.

Q. Does being in custody affect my rights?

A. Yes. Under the U.S. Constitution, once you are in custody, you have the right to an attorney and the right to remain silent.

Q. What is an interrogation?

A. An **interrogation** might be a period of explicit questioning, such as the police asking

---

▶ THE MIRANDA RULE

In 1966, the U.S. Supreme Court ruled in *Miranda v. Arizona* that when law enforcement officers question people in custody, the evidence collected in their interviews cannot be used against them unless they have been informed of their constitutional rights to counsel and to remain silent. When a person is taken into custody, before he or she is questioned, the police must issue some version of the Miranda warning. For example: "You have the right to remain silent. If you give up the right to remain silent, anything you say can and will be used against you in a court of law. You have the right to a lawyer. If you desire a lawyer and cannot afford one, a lawyer will be obtained for you before police questioning."

The Miranda rule was developed to protect the individual's Fifth Amendment right against self-incrimination. Many people feel obligated to respond to police questioning. The Miranda warning ensures that people in custody realize they do not have to talk to the police, and that they have the right to the presence of a lawyer.

If the Miranda warning is not given before questioning, or if police continue to question a suspect after he or she indicates a desire to consult with a lawyer before speaking, statements by the suspect generally are inadmissible. However, it may be difficult for your lawyer to prevent your statements from being used against you in all circumstances. For this reason, the best rule is to remain silent until you can consult with a lawyer. You have the right to a lawyer. Insist on it.

▶ CONFESSIONS

A lot of people believe that only written, signed confessions are admissible as evidence. This is not true. Oral and unsigned written confessions are also admissible.

If you make a confession without a lawyer present, the admissibility of that confession will depend on whether you gave up your right to a lawyer and your right to remain silent. If you voluntarily talked to the police after they read you your Miranda rights, you might have waived (given up) your right to counsel and your protection against self-incrimination, and the prosecution probably could use the confession against you in court. This is true even if the police lied to you or tricked you into talking. Once you talk to the police, you do so at your own risk.

However, if the police continued to question you after you told them you wanted a lawyer, your confession would likely be inadmissible, because your lawyer probably could persuade the judge to exclude the confession from evidence.

Remember that you are permitted to change your mind about wanting a lawyer. If you voluntarily begin to talk to the police, but then tell them that you want a lawyer present, the questioning must stop immediately. Or if you have talked to the police once, you may refuse to talk to them a second time until a lawyer arrives.

Miranda rights must be read only when an individual is in police custody and is under interrogation. So, if you made a confession when you were not in custody or when you were not being interrogated, then the confession may be admissible even if you did not have a lawyer when you made it. For example, if you attend a dinner party and tell another guest, who happens to be a police officer, that you hit another car on your way to the party and then left the scene, you cannot later claim that your confession (your admission that you left the scene of an accident) is inadmissible because you were not read your Miranda rights.

---

you, "Did you kill John Doe?" But interrogation might also be less obvious, such as comments made by the police that are intended to elicit incriminating information from you. It is legal for the police to lie to you about what they know or suspect, or about what other people have said about you. The police may try to trick you into talking. This is one reason why it is so important to have a lawyer present during your interrogation.

Lawyers and Criminal Law

Q. When do I have a right to a lawyer—before a police interrogation, during it, or both?

A. You have a constitutional **right to counsel**—the right to have a lawyer's advice—before and during police interrogation. If the police are asking you questions and you think they may suspect you of a crime, tell them that you do not want to answer questions and that you want a lawyer, regardless of whether you have been given Miranda warnings. Police frequently obtain damaging admissions before you are in custody, and prior to providing Miranda warnings. Do not answer any questions until your lawyer arrives. If the police place you in a lineup, the law entitles you to have a lawyer present if you have been formally charged. You also have the right to a lawyer at all of your court appearances.

Q. If the police arrest a friend or a relative, may I send a lawyer to the jail to offer help?

A. Yes, but the right to counsel is personal. This means that the person who is under arrest must tell the police that he or she wants a lawyer. In some states, if your friend waives the right to counsel and agrees to talk to the police, the police do not have to tell your friend that you are sending a lawyer. In other states, if your friend has not requested a lawyer, the police are even permitted to turn away the lawyer upon his or her arrival at the station without telling your friend. If a friend telephones you, the best thing you can do is to say that a lawyer is on the way to offer help. Your friend should tell the police that he or she does not want to answer questions until he or she has had the opportunity to talk to a lawyer.

Q. How do I find a lawyer?

A. If you have a family lawyer, call him or her immediately. If your family lawyer does not do criminal work, he or she may be able to recommend another lawyer who does. If you cannot afford a lawyer, tell the police you wish to have a lawyer appointed on your behalf. A defense attorney—whether private, a public defender, or assigned—will be appointed on your behalf.

Q. What should I look for in a lawyer? How do I know I can trust my lawyer?

A. See Chapter 1, page 6 for guidance about finding an attorney and developing the attorney-client relationship.

Q. May I represent myself without a lawyer?

A. Yes. You have a right to represent yourself before the trial, and the court may even allow you to act as a lawyer in your own defense at trial. The law refers to self-representation as **pro se** representation. If you request to proceed pro se, the judge must allow you to represent yourself if he or she determines that you are mentally and/or physically able to represent yourself, that you are making an informed and voluntary decision to give up your constitutional right to counsel, and that you are aware of the dangers and disadvantages of self-representation.

Q. What if I can't afford an attorney?

A. The U.S. Supreme Court and most state constitutions provide that even indigent people have the right to an attorney during criminal proceedings (some constitutions limit this right to cases involving crimes that could result in a prison term). Consequently, if you can't afford an attorney, but would like one to represent you during criminal proceedings, the court will appoint one. See Chapter 1, page 8 for a discussion about how these appointment systems work.

Q. Is it better to represent myself than to rely on a court-appointed defender?

A. No. It usually is not a good idea for untrained people to try to represent themselves in criminal cases. The opponent will be a skilled prosecutor who has conducted many trials. The rules of evidence at trial are complicated, and an untrained person may miss many opportunities to present his or her strongest case. The judge or jury will not necessarily be sympathetic toward you simply because you decided to go it alone.

Some defendants choose to represent themselves because they feel they can do a better job than a public defender or a lawyer whom the court has appointed to represent them free of charge. This simply is not true. First, any lawyer is sure to know more than you do about the legal system. Lawyers must complete a three- or four-year program in law school and pass a rigorous bar examination. Second, do not assume that the public defender is an inadequate lawyer who could not get a "real job" in a law firm. Many top law students choose public-interest work because they want to help people. Public defenders often have substantial experience defending people in criminal cases.

In addition, most people charged with a crime are too close emotionally to their own problems. Therefore, they cannot maintain the clear, coolheaded thinking that is necessary in court. Even lawyers charged with a crime usually hire other lawyers to represent them. Those lawyers are heeding the old adage, "A lawyer who represents himself has a fool for a client."

By representing yourself, you give up a very important constitutional right: the right to counsel. If you represent yourself and are convicted, you cannot claim that your incompetence as a lawyer denied you effective assistance of counsel.

For these reasons, self-representation is a risk that most criminal defendants should not take. Remember that you have the right to dismiss your lawyer for good cause (although if you do not have a good reason for wanting to dismiss your appointed counsel, the judge may refuse to replace him or her). If the court will allow it, you can change lawyers or reconsider representing yourself—though the court may require you to proceed immediately with the case, without extra time for you or your new lawyer to prepare.

Once you have experienced the complexities of the legal process, you probably will realize that you need a professional to protect your interests.

Criminal Charges

Q. How are criminal charges brought against someone?

A. There are three basic ways in which formal charges may be brought: by information, indictment, or citation. An **information** is a written document filed by a prosecutor alleging that the defendant committed a crime. The information may be based upon a criminal complaint, which is a petition to the prosecutor requesting that criminal charges be initiated.

An **indictment** is a formal charge imposed by a **grand jury,** which is a group of citizens convened by the court. Its function is to determine whether there is sufficient evidence to charge a person with a crime and to bring him or her to trial. The grand jury conducts its proceedings in secret and has broad investigative powers. The federal system and about half of the states use grand juries in felony cases. The majority of defendants are charged not by a grand jury, but through some other mechanism.

A **citation** is issued by a police officer,

most often for a misdemeanor or other minor criminal matter such as jaywalking, littering, or a minor traffic offense. The normal penalty is a fine, which may range from under $20 to several hundred dollars. In some municipalities, a citation for an offense could result in a short jail sentence. If the police cite you for such an offense, they will issue you a ticket. You usually will have the option of not contesting the citation by mailing in the ticket with the specified payment. Or, if you feel the police have ticketed you wrongly, you have the right to contest the citation at a hearing.

None of these mechanisms determines the guilt or innocence of defendants. Rather, each indicates that the issuing authority has determined there is sufficient evidence to bring a person to trial.

Q. What is the grand jury's role in charging individuals with crimes?

A. In about half the states, grand juries must be used to bring charges for felonies. In the other states, they may or may not be used to bring charges for felonies—prosecutors have discretion to use them or bring charges on their own.

Grand juries also have a second role in many states: investigating public corruption or undertaking such tasks as monitoring conditions in the jails.

Q. What's the difference between a grand jury and a trial jury?

A. The purpose of the grand jury is not to decide guilt or innocence—that's the role of the trial jury. Instead, the grand jury determines whether there is sufficient evidence to bring a person to trial.

In general, grand jurors answer this question: "Is there sufficient information to indicate that the suspect should be held accountable for a crime?" If people are indicted, they have the opportunity to defend themselves at the ensuing trial. The judge or the jury at the trial will determine whether a person is guilty of the charges brought by the grand jury.

Q. Why is it called a "grand" jury?

A. Because it's usually bigger than a trial jury. A grand jury is a body of citizens that varies in size depending on the jurisdiction, but usually includes more than twelve and as many as twenty-three jurors. (Trial juries, which usually consist of twelve persons or fewer, are sometimes called petit juries, because "petit" is the French word for "small").

Q. How does a grand jury work?

A. The jurors are summoned by the court to serve for a certain period of time, often many months, though they may be called into session only a few days a month. They may consider a number of cases during their term of service. They do not have to agree unanimously to issue an indictment, though state law often requires a vote of two-thirds or three-quarters of the jurors to indict. Typically, the prosecutor works very closely with the grand jury. Using the grand jury's broad investigative power to compel witnesses to appear and answer questions or submit documents, records, and other evidence, the prosecutor and jurors weigh the evidence and try to decide whether it is sufficient to issue an indictment against one or more persons.

Unlike trials, grand jury proceedings are secret. In many states, it is a crime to reveal information about a grand jury's proceedings. The public, the news media, and the person being investigated have no right to be present. The secrecy of the proceedings is intended to encourage witnesses to speak freely without fear of retaliation. It also protects the persons being investigated in the event that the evidence is deemed insufficient and an indictment isn't issued.

In most jurisdictions, people called to testify before a grand jury are not allowed to have their lawyers present. The lawyers for the persons under investigation also rarely play any role in grand jury proceedings, meaning that the grand jury makes its findings without hearing both sides of the case. Nor is a judge usually present during grand jury sessions, since normal rules of evidence don't apply in grand jury proceedings, making the role of the prosecutor all the more important.

Q. Once I'm charged with an offense, does that mean I'll definitely have to go to court?

A. Not necessarily. Police or prosecutors may suggest a **diversion program,** which is also known as **supervision.** The result of successful completion of a diversion program is that the charge is dismissed and no documentation of the incident is recorded on the charged person's criminal record. Diversion programs usually are run by the prosecutor's office. A guilty plea may be required as a condition of being placed on diversion in some states. Diversion ordinarily involves your participation in a service program designed to rehabilitate you. For example, some states allow a first-time drug offender to attend a program such as Cocaine Anonymous instead of being tried. In many jurisdictions, diversion is only available for some crimes, such as misdemeanors.

Q. What does it mean if I have been charged with "attempt"?

A. An **attempt** means that you had the intent to commit the crime, and you took some step toward committing the crime, but for some reason did not complete it. Suppose you went into a bank and demanded money from a teller at gunpoint. Then an alarm rang, so you ran out of the bank before you could get the money. The prosecutor probably would bring charges of attempted robbery. Conviction for an attempted crime usually carries a somewhat lesser sentence than for the crime itself, although in some states the sentence is identical.

Q. What is a conspiracy?

A. A **conspiracy** is an agreement between two or more people to commit a crime, followed by any activity aimed at carrying out the agreement. Conspiracy itself is a separate crime from the crime being planned by the conspirators. Therefore, the prosecutor can bring charges of conspiracy even if you did not complete the crime you intended to commit. Because conspiracy charges carry separate penalties, you can be convicted of both conspiracy and a crime that you or your fellow conspirators accomplished during the conspiracy (the **substantive** count). If you are convicted of both the crime and the conspiracy to commit the crime, then you will receive a sentence that takes into account both convictions.

Q. What is complicity or accomplice liability?

A. **Complicity,** also known as aiding and abetting, is the act of being an **accomplice.** An accomplice is someone who helps in, or in some states merely encourages, the commission of a crime. Courts sometimes refer to such a person as an **aider** or an **abettor.** This person did not commit the crime, but his or her actions helped enable someone else to do so. Examples of complicity include supplying weapons or supplies, acting as a lookout, or driving a getaway car. Another example would be bringing a victim to the scene of a crime, or signaling the victim's approach to people who intended to commit a crime. The doctrine of accomplice liability dictates that anyone who helps in the commission of a crime is as guilty as the person who committed the crime itself, and could be punished as severely as they would be if convicted of that crime.

REMEMBER THIS

- The police have some rights to search you or your home even if you're not under arrest and they do not have a warrant. Remember: If you consent to a search, you may limit the range of your defense in later proceedings. If the police search you or your home unlawfully, then anything they find may be inadmissible at trial.

- If you are being arrested, the police must tell you of your Miranda rights if they intend to ask you questions.

- If the police are asking you questions and you think they may suspect you of a crime, you should refuse to answer questions until you see a lawyer, even if you have not yet been read your Miranda rights. You have the right to a lawyer. Insist on it.

CRIMINAL COURT PROCEDURES

Going to court can be intimidating, whether you're a suspect, a witness, or a victim. But one day you may be forced to become involved with the court system. In this section you'll learn how the system works, and what to expect—just in case.

Initial Criminal Court Proceedings

Q. When will a defendant first appear in court?

A. The first step is an initial appearance (often referred to as a **first appearance**) before a judge or a magistrate. The police may not hold a defendant for more than a reasonable period of time without an initial or first appearance. In some jurisdictions, this may be twenty-four or forty-eight hours; in others, it may be seventy-two hours. Sometimes defendants will be released before the first appearance, but must appear when ordered or risk having a judge issue a bench warrant for their arrest.

The purpose of the first appearance is to ensure that the defendant is informed of the charges and made aware of his or her rights. It is also an opportunity for the defendant to end the proceedings quickly with a guilty plea if he or she so desires. If the defendant was arrested without a warrant, as is common, this is the time at which the judge will determine whether there was probable cause for the arrest.

For misdemeanors and felonies, a first appearance involves the following steps:

Misdemeanors

- The charge(s) are read to the defendant and the penalties for conviction are explained.
- The judge or magistrate advises the defendant of his or her right to trial and right to trial by jury, if applicable.
- The right to counsel is explained, and the judge or magistrate appoints a lawyer if the defendant requests one and is found

to be **indigent** (too poor to afford a private lawyer).

- The defendant enters a plea.
  - If the defendant enters a not guilty plea, a trial date will be set.
  - If the defendant pleads guilty, either a date will be set for sentencing or the magistrate or judge will impose probation, fines, or other sentences immediately.
  - In some jurisdictions, the judge or magistrate may allow a defendant to plead **nolo contendere,** or "no contest." In many jurisdictions, a plea of no contest is equivalent to a guilty plea, except that the defendant does not directly admit guilt. (See the discussion on nolo contendere pleas later in this section.)
- If the defendant has pled not guilty, the judge or magistrate sets the amount of the defendant's bail. (See the discussion on bail later in this chapter).

Felonies

- The process is similar to that of first appearances for misdemeanors. However, felony first appearances involve the additional step of a **preliminary hearing,** which is a safeguard warranted by the more serious nature of the charges.
- First, the charge or charges are read to the defendant, and the penalties for conviction are explained.
- The defendant is advised of his or her right to a preliminary hearing and is informed about the purpose of that proceeding. The defendant is also advised of his or her right to trial, and right to trial by jury in trial court.
- The right to counsel is explained, and the judge or magistrate appoints a lawyer if

the defendant requests one and is found to be indigent.

- In most jurisdictions, the defendant does not enter a plea.
- The matter is set for a preliminary hearing. This is a hearing to establish if a crime has been committed and if there is probable cause to believe that the defendant committed the offense(s) alleged in the complaint.
- The judge or magistrate sets the amount of the defendant's bail.

Q. What is involved in a preliminary hearing?

A. The preliminary hearing differs from a first appearance in several regards.

At a preliminary hearing, the government must demonstrate to a judge or magistrate that there is sufficient evidence, or **probable cause,** to believe that the suspect committed the crime with which he or she is charged. Defendants usually must be present at these hearings, although they do not commonly offer evidence in their defense. Victims seldom appear at preliminary hearings, and often the hearing will feature just a single witness—the police officer who investigated the crime or who arrested the defendant. The proceeding has a function similar to that of a grand jury: to safeguard against unfettered government action.

If the court finds that there is no probable cause, the matter is dismissed. (This is the equivalent of a grand jury declining to press charges.) If this happens, the defendant is released. However, if the court finds that there is probable cause (as is usually the case), the matter is transferred to trial court. The matter is then said to be **bound over** to the other court for trial. In light of evidence that comes to light in the preliminary hearing, bail may be continued or reset at a different amount.

Note that in the federal system, the government can prosecute for felonies only by obtaining an indictment voted upon by a grand jury. If you are indicted by a grand jury, you have no right to a preliminary hearing because the grand jury has already determined that there is probable cause to believe you committed the offense with which you are charged.

Q. Am I likely to be released before my trial?

A. You are not guaranteed the right to be released before trial. The judge will consider whether you are likely to flee or whether, if released, you might pose a danger to the community. Factors that may work in your favor include strong family ties in the area, long-time local residence, and current local employment.

Release on recognizance (or **own recognizance** or **personal recognizance**), often referred to as **ROR, OR,** or **PR,** is common for most offenses. This does not involve posting bail money, but you will have to make a binding promise to return to court on a date specified by the judge. Some types of release do not involve posting money bail, but the defendant will be liable for money if he or she later fails to appear. This type of financial condition is usually referred to as an **unsecured bond.**

If the court grants you ROR status or releases you on bail, you must reappear in court as agreed. If you do not appear, the judge could revoke your bail or ROR status. Failure to appear also may be considered a separate criminal act, and the judge could issue a bench warrant for your arrest.

If the judge decides that financial bail is appropriate, he or she must establish the amount you must post in order to be released. Your bail may not be excessive, meaning that you may not be required to pay an unreasonably high amount. Some states have bail schedules that set forth different types of charges and the bail applicable to each. In addition, the judge may condition your release upon a hearing that demonstrates the source of your bail payment is legitimate.

Q. Is there a difference between a plea of guilty and a plea of nolo contendere?

A. Yes. The vast majority of criminal cases eventually result in pleas of guilty or nolo contendere. A guilty plea is a specific admission of guilt, while a plea of nolo contendere is a plea of "no contest." In a few jurisdictions, a defendant may elect to **stand mute** instead of making a plea. When the judge asks

---

▶ **BAIL**

Bail is money or property that you provide to ensure that you will appear in court for trial. Bail is not a fine. It is not supposed to be used as punishment. The purpose of bail is simply to ensure that you will appear for all trial and pretrial hearings for which you must be present. If you fail to appear, you forfeit the bail. If you do not have the money or property to post bail, a relative or friend can post bail on your behalf (or you can go to a bail bondsman, described below). After the trial ends, the court will refund the bail money, usually keeping a percentage to cover administrative costs.

▶ THE ROLE OF A BAIL BONDSMAN

Many defendants cannot raise the entire amount of their bail. In some states, defendants may arrange for their release through a bail bondsman, who guarantees to pay the bail amount to the court if the defendant fails to appear for trial.

There are inherent problems with commercial bail bonding. First, the defendant will pay a nonrefundable premium to the bondsman, usually 10 percent of the bail amount set. Second, the defendant or a party acting on behalf of the defendant must put down collateral for the entire bond. Third, should the defendant abscond, a bail bondsman is likely to hire a bounty hunter who has powers exceeding those of police officers in terms of crossing jurisdictional borders and the use of force.

for a plea, the defense lawyer states, "My client stands mute." The court will then enter a plea of not guilty. By standing mute, the accused avoids admitting to the correctness of the proceedings against him or her until that point, and preserves his or her right to attack the validity of the proceedings on appeal.

Q. Why plead nolo contendere?

A. In some states, the practical effect of a nolo contendere plea is to avoid automatic civil liability. As an example, suppose that a nursing home operator is accused of abusing patients. If the operator pleads guilty, anyone who later sues him for civil damages will not have to prove that the abuse occurred—they can simply refer to the guilty plea as proof of wrongdoing. However, if the operator pleads nolo contendere, then the civil court will have to decide whether the alleged acts actually took place.

Q. Must the judge accept my plea?

A. A plea of not guilty must be accepted. A judge cannot accept a guilty plea unless he or she is sure that you understand the rights you are giving up, and that you are doing so of

your own will—that is, free from coercion and threats. In many states, the judge also must determine that there is a factual basis for your plea—in other words, that you actually are guilty of the offense. If you assert that you are innocent, but want to make a guilty plea for the sake of expediency, you are entitled to do so as long as the judge finds a factual basis for the plea, and finds that you are competent to enter a guilty plea.

Q. What are plea bargains?

A. Plea bargains are legal transactions in which a defendant pleads guilty to a lesser charge or pleads guilty to the original charge in exchange for some other form of leniency, such as a lower sentence or dismissal of more serious charges in a multiple-count case. The rationale is based on the notion of judicial economy—plea bargains avoid the time and expense of a trial, freeing up the courts to hear other cases. The benefit to defendants is that the process is completed sooner than it would be if they went to trial. Furthermore, defendants are afforded a sense of certainty; they know what the outcome of their case will be, rather than taking their chances at trial.

Generally, plea bargain offers are more generous in the early stages of prosecution. This provides an incentive to the defendant to bring the case to an early conclusion. Early disposition of a case is generally desirable for prosecutors and judges, because it eliminates the need for additional court appearances that are required if a case goes to trial.

In most cases, the defense is better off waiting to investigate the case thoroughly and then considering a later offer or possible dismissal of the charges. However, keep in mind that if you do not accept a plea bargain offer when the prosecution first makes it, the prosecutor may reduce or withdraw the offer.

Q. Does every defendant get offered a plea bargain?

A. No. You do not have the right to have the prosecutor negotiate a plea with you or your lawyer.

Q. Does the judge have to accept my plea bargain?

A. Not necessarily. In most jurisdictions, the court has no obligation to adhere to the bargain the prosecution offers, but in many cases the judge will accept the plea if a legal basis for it is established in court and the judge feels the bargain is fair. Before accepting your guilty plea, the judge will explain the maximum time to which you may be sentenced and the maximum fine, if any, that may be imposed. That time may exceed the sentencing recommendation of the prosecution, or the judge could impose a shorter term in the interests of justice. If you do not accept at that point, your guilty or nolo contendere plea will not be entered and you will go to trial.

The plea bargaining process is not without its critics. Some victims' rights groups feel it is immoral for criminals to serve less time through plea bargaining than they would if convicted of the crimes committed. In response to citizen pressure, some states such as California have passed laws severely restricting or even prohibiting plea bargaining in the case of certain serious or violent crimes.

Q. Can the charges against me be dropped?

A. Yes. This can occur for several reasons. For example, charges may be dropped if there is insufficient evidence, which means the police either could not find enough evidence to link you to a crime or found evidence pointing to your innocence. Witness problems also prompt prosecutors to drop charges—for example, if those who observed a crime fail to appear in court, are reluctant to testify, or testify inconsistently. Sometimes cases are dropped **in the interests of justice**, a broad rationale indicating that the prosecutor does not feel the case is significant enough to pursue. This might happen, for example, in a case involving only minor property damage.

Evidence in Criminal Cases

Q. How may I recognize and preserve evidence to help me at my trial?

A. Physical evidence—such as a gun or piece of clothing—can be very important in helping a judge or jury piece together what actually happened. Judges and jurors were not present when the alleged crime took place. Physical evidence can provide a way to show that your version of the facts is correct.

You should preserve any items that might be useful as evidence, whether you think the evidence will help or harm your case. It is against the law to destroy evidence. In any event, let your lawyer determine whether the evidence is harmful. For example, you might believe that the prosecution will use a gun bearing your fingerprints as evidence against you in a shooting. But if your lawyer can show that the gun was too big or the trigger too difficult for someone of your size to pull, and thus that you couldn't have fired it, then the evidence could help your case. In this example, the only logical explanation for your fingerprints being on the gun would be that you picked up the gun after the shooting. This explanation could cause the jury to have reasonable doubt about your guilt.

Q. What kind of evidence may the prosecution use against me at trial?

A. The prosecution may use almost any type of admissible evidence that will help establish your guilt. This includes physical evidence, such as a murder weapon or items stolen during a burglary. Testimonial evidence, which involves **testimony** (oral statements) from one or more persons on the witness stand, is likely to be used as well. For example, the owner of a stolen car might testify that nobody had permission to take the car on the day the crime occurred.

The prosecution also may introduce circumstantial evidence of a crime. For example, if a defendant hurriedly packed and moved out of state within hours after a crime took place, the prosecutor might introduce this fact in order to suggest the defendant's consciousness of guilt. Circumstantial evidence is best explained by saying what it is *not*: it is not direct evidence, meaning that it is not the testimony of a witness who saw or heard something directly. Rather, **circumstantial evidence** is indirect evidence: it is proof of one or more facts from which another fact can be established. For example, suppose X has been murdered, and Z is a suspect. Z's fingerprints are found on a book in X's bedroom. A judge or jury may infer that Z was in the bedroom, because the fingerprints are

---

▶ **OVERLOOKED EVIDENCE**

Some evidence is far less obvious than a gun. At a crime scene, tiny items such as rug fibers, hair, cigarette ashes, matches, and even DNA samples may become important evidence in your defense. Therefore, if you are at the scene of a crime before the police arrive, you should leave everything undisturbed. Do not vacuum, move items, or touch anything. The police will secure the area and record everything to maintain what the law calls "crime scene integrity." Once evidence gets misplaced or damaged, a crucial link to winning your case may be lost. In addition, the judge or the jury might view tampering with the evidence as an indication of your guilt.

The nature of the offense will determine the types of evidence to preserve. For instance, if the prosecution charges you with an economic crime such as fraud, you must preserve any important documents relating to the transactions in which the alleged fraud took place.

circumstantial evidence of Z's presence. Circumstantial evidence is usually not as effective as direct evidence, because it sometimes may lead people to draw the wrong conclusions. However, circumstantial evidence is generally admissible unless the connection between the fact and the inference is too weak to be of help in deciding the case. In a trial, juries must consider both direct and circumstantial evidence. The law permits juries to give equal weight to both, but it is for the jury to decide how much weight to give to any evidence. Many convictions for various crimes have rested largely on circumstantial evidence.

Q. Can a witness testify about anything so long as it is true?

A. No. Testimony must be relevant to the crime and must not be based on hearsay. If a lawyer asks a witness to testify about statements that someone else made outside the courtroom, the opposing lawyer may object to the admissibility of the testimony because it is **hearsay.** The problem with hearsay is that the person who made the statement is not a witness at the trial and is thus unavailable for cross-examination. For more information on hearsay, see the discussion on page 35 in the section titled "Trials."

Defenses Against Criminal Charges

Q. If I am charged with a crime, what are my possible defenses?

A. To defend against criminal charges, the defense may assert a variety of affirmative defenses, including that the defendant was insane at the time of the crime; that the defendant was improperly induced by the government to commit the crime (**entrapment**); or that natural forces outside of the defendant's control forced him or her to commit the crime in order to prevent greater injury (**necessity**).

A defendant may also provide evidence showing that the state has failed to prove the elements of the crime charged. This is not strictly a defense, but would possibly be sufficient to ensure a not guilty verdict. A defendant also may present evidence of an **alibi**—that is, evidence that he or she was not at the scene of the crime when it was committed.

Q. What is an affirmative defense?

A. In arguing an **affirmative defense,** a defendant concedes that he or she committed the crime, but argues that the crime is excusable because his or her actions were justified. For example, a person accused of a violent crime will not be found guilty if he establishes that he was justified in using the force involved; this is generally referred to as **self-defense,** though the defense may also be applied to situations involving defense of another person or defense of property. Another defense might be that the defendant was forced by another person to commit the crime, and had no alternative but to perform the acts in question.

Q. How does a defendant's mental health affect the legal process?

A. Under our system, it is unconstitutional to make anyone stand trial if they are mentally **incompetent.** This means that defendants must be able to comprehend the nature of the charges against them, and to assist properly in their own defenses (such as by explaining to a lawyer what happened and which witnesses may be able to substantiate their accounts). When a defense lawyer has reason to question a client's competency, he or she will ask the judge to order a psychiatric evaluation. A defendant who is deemed incompetent may be committed to a psychiatric facility for treatment, where he or she will stay until he or she is competent to stand trial. In some states, the psychiatric patient must be released after a certain period.

Q. Is incompetence the same as insanity?

A. No. Being incompetent to stand trial differs from being insane at the time of the offense. **Insanity** is a defense to certain crimes that require proof of intent. For example, it could be argued that one who is insane cannot commit first-degree murder because his or her mind is incapable of premeditating and deliberating (planning the crime).

A few states have abolished the insanity defense but allow psychiatric evidence at trial on the issue of intent. For example, evidence might be introduced to show that a defendant in a drug case was delusional and believed he was a doctor dispensing medication, and thus could not have formed the intent to sell an illegal substance.

Most states require formal notice of plans to raise the insanity defense. In cases where the insanity defense is to be raised, the defendant enters a plea of not guilty and proceeds to trial. If convicted, the individual may be found guilty, not guilty by reason of insanity, or, in a few states, guilty but mentally ill. Defendants found not guilty by reason of insanity are placed in mental health facilities until their mental condition improves to the point where they are no longer a threat to themselves or the community.

Criminal Pretrial Procedures

Q. Does discovery take place in criminal cases like it does in civil cases?

A. Not quite. Discovery is a process that allows the parties (the state and a criminal defendant in criminal cases, and the plaintiff and defendant in civil cases) to learn the strengths and weaknesses of each other's cases—for example, by obtaining the names and statements of witnesses the other side intends to call at trial. Because the defendant in a criminal case has certain constitutional safeguards (such as the right against self-incrimination), discovery in criminal cases is far more limited than in the civil context.

Q. What must be turned over for discovery during a criminal trial?

A. It is common for discovery rules or laws to require both parties to provide, in advance of trial, lists of witnesses and physical evidence that may be introduced at the trial. The state usually must hand over any statements made by the defendant that it intends to introduce at trial. Typically it must also reveal the criminal records of defendants and witnesses, as well as any benefits offered or provided to witnesses, such as reduced charges granted in exchange for testimony. Defendants are entitled to receive the same kinds of discovery material as are made available to the state. Defendants often must reveal to the prosecution in advance of trial their intention to rely on certain defenses, such as insanity. The prosecution is required as a matter of federal constitutional law to hand over to the defense all evidence favorable to the defendant that concerns either factual guilt or sentencing issues.

Q. Other than simply turning over documents and evidence, what are other forms of discovery?

A. Interrogatories are written questions about the facts and background of the case, which the opposing party must answer in writing. **Depositions** involve the same types of questions, but are oral examinations conducted in a conference room without a judge present. These common civil discovery procedures are rare in criminal cases, although some states such as Florida do permit the taking of depositions in criminal cases. In addition, a rule of federal criminal procedure permits the taking of a witness's deposition where the prosecution or defense can show that it is necessary to preserve his or her testimony because the witness's testimony is material and he or she will be unavailable for trial.

In a civil case, the parties must participate in depositions if requested by the opposing side; in a criminal case, because of the guarantees of the Fifth Amendment, it would be unconstitutional to force the accused to answer questions about the case (unless he or she elects to testify at trial). Criminal defendants must be present at depositions in their cases (or waive that right) because of the Sixth Amendment right to be present and to confront witnesses.

Trial

Q. What happens at trial?

A. First, the jury is selected—unless the defendant elects, and the prosecution agrees, to have a trial by judge, commonly referred to as a **bench trial.** Once the jury has been **impaneled** (seated for the duration of the trial), the proceedings begin. See pages 75–78 for a detailed discussion of jury selection and jury duty.

Opening statements then follow. The prosecutor addresses the jury first, explaining the nature of the case and what he or she intends to prove. Then the defense lawyer may offer an opening statement, or may reserve the opening statement until after the prosecution has finished its case.

Next, the prosecution presents its case in chief, which usually involves direct testimony by witnesses and the introduction of any physical evidence against the defendant, such as a gun or other implements of the alleged crime. Defense lawyers may cross-examine the prosecution witnesses by asking questions designed to raise doubt about the government's case. After all prosecution witnesses have testified, the process repeats itself in reverse: the defense presents its case in chief, calling any witnesses it may have, and the prosecution cross-examines them.

Because the prosecution bears the burden of proving the defendant's guilt beyond a reasonable doubt, the defense is not required

---

▸ YOUR RIGHT TO A JURY

In criminal cases, the right to a jury trial under the federal Constitution extends to defendants facing prison sentences of six months or more. In addition, Congress has provided for the jury trial option in some instances where the federal Constitution does not require one. State constitutions also may guarantee broader rights to a jury trial.

to offer any witnesses, nor are defendants required to testify unless they so choose upon the advice of their lawyers.

When the defense has rested, the prosecutor will give a closing argument, summing up the evidence presented against the defendant. The defense lawyers then will make their own closing argument. The prosecutor has one last chance for a rebuttal argument, addressing the points made by the defense in closing. (Note that the order of the closing arguments may vary in some states.) When the closing arguments have concluded, the judge instructs the jury on the law to apply in deciding the case.

Sentencing

Q. If a judge or a jury convicts me, how and when will the court sentence me?

A. In felony cases, sentencing is a separate procedure from the trial, and usually is held several weeks or even months after conviction. After the verdict is read, the court will order a presentencing report from the probation department, which contains, among other things, the offender's criminal record and a sentence recommendation.

In misdemeanor cases, on the other hand, sentencing usually immediately follows a finding of guilt and presentencing investigations are not conducted.

In most states the judge has some discretion in choosing your sentence. For misdemeanors, the judge usually chooses among a fine, probation, a suspended sentence, or a jail term (or a combination of these). For felonies, the choice is often between imprisonment and probation, depending on the crime.

For state offenses, the criminal code often suggests the minimum and maximum sentences for each specific crime. Often these are designated as a range, such as three to five years. For federal offenses, there are similar sentencing guidelines.

Repeat-offender laws have been enacted in some states to deter and punish people who commit crimes repeatedly. Under repeat-offender legislation, people who commit crimes within a certain time period after their release from prison, and are convicted of those crimes, must be sentenced by judges to the maximum sentences provided by statute. Offenders must then serve 100 percent of their sentences.

Q. Is the judge the only person who may decide the sentence?

A. In most states and in federal courts, the judge alone determines sentencing. The exception in some states is those cases in which the defendant may receive the death penalty, in which case the jury, not the judge, will determine whether the death penalty should be imposed. In death penalty cases, the penalty phase becomes a mini-trial of its own, with witnesses commonly testifying about the defendant's character and family upbringing, in an effort to show why he or she should be sentenced in a certain way.

Q. What determines the sentence I will receive?

A. The primary factors are the sentencing range provided in the penal code and your prior convictions, if any. The judge also may consider any aggravating or mitigating factors. **Aggravating factors,** such as the violent nature of a crime or a high degree of sophistication in planning it, warrant a tougher sentence. **Mitigating factors** are factors that may warrant a more lenient sentence; they may include a good family history, a stable employment record, or any benefits you have bestowed on the community, such as by performing volunteer work.

In addition, before imposing your sentence, the judge must allow you to make a statement. You should discuss this with your lawyer in advance. Sometimes a plea for mercy or a promise to improve your behavior will be effective at this point, but this will depend upon your individual circumstances and case.

Q. Are there any alternatives to jail or prison sentences?

A. Yes. For crimes not covered by mandatory sentences of incarceration, judges may impose what are called **alternative sentences.** Some alternative sentences involve the offender making some sort of payment; others involve the offender being supervised; and others involve enrollment in a residential program or attendance in a day program.

One such option is monetary. The judge may order you to pay a fine as punishment, or to make **restitution** (repayment to a victim who lost money because of your crime). Another possibility is **probation.** When you are on probation, the court releases you into the community. During probation, you must obey the conditions set forth by the court, which may include periodic drug testing, completing a GED, job training, abstinence from alcohol and drugs, and staying away from the victim. If you violate these conditions, the court can revoke your probation and resentence you.

These types of alternative sentences frequently are combined. For example, a person on probation also may be required, as a term of release, to make restitution to the victim.

A less restrictive sentence involves **community service.** The court could require you to spend a certain number of hours (usually hundreds or thousands) doing service work at a community center.

If the court requires you to remain in custody, you may be eligible for a residential program, such as a halfway house or a "boot camp." In a halfway house, you may be allowed to leave during the day to work at a job or go to school, but you must return to the building every evening. There are also day-reporting programs, which work in the opposite way from halfway houses: with these programs, you are required to attend certain events during the day, but can return home at night.

▶ THE RIGHTS OF PRISONERS

The law entitles prisoners to fair treatment as human beings. This means that jailers may not subject prisoners to brutality and that prisoners are entitled to food, water, medical attention, and access to the legal system. Such access includes typewriters and a library in which to perform legal research.

If your state laws provide for a right to **parole** (early release from prison), you can apply for parole when you become eligible. If the parole board denies your request for parole, you must be told the reason for the denial, and you must be given an opportunity to be heard. Parole is not available in the federal system.

In a boot camp, you are housed at a facility and may not leave at all. Your experience will be similar to what you might experience at a boot camp in the military—rising early in the morning, and performing demanding physical labor during the day. You also will be allowed to attend educational or job-training classes and may receive counseling. Boot camp programs are notoriously difficult to complete. However, failure to complete such a program successfully usually results in the participant's immediate incarceration.

Appeals of Criminal Cases

Q. May I appeal my conviction?

A. A convicted person has the right to appeal a conviction at least once. Appeal is not a right under the federal Constitution, but all jurisdictions permit those who are convicted to make one appeal. Also, the federal Constitution has been interpreted by the U.S. Supreme Court to guarantee counsel for all indigent persons during the appeals process.

On appeal, the defendant can raise claims that mistakes were made in applying and interpreting the law during the trial. For example, the defendant might claim that the judge erroneously admitted hearsay testimony, gave improper jury instructions, should not have permitted the prosecution to use evidence obtained in violation of the defendant's constitutional rights, or permitted the prosecution to make improper closing arguments. There are very few grounds for appeal if the defendant pleaded guilty. If the appellate court agrees that there were significant errors during the trial, the defendant will be granted a new trial.

There is one ground for reversal that bars retrial and leads to the defendant being freed:

if the court finds that, at the trial, the government failed to prove all of the elements of the offense beyond a reasonable doubt. For more information on the appellate process, see the earlier discussion in this chapter on pages 37–39.

Q. What if the law changes after a court convicts me?

A. If a court convicted you for something that is no longer a crime, you might be able to have your conviction overturned. This also might be possible if a trial court denied you a right that the U.S. Supreme Court later rules is a constitutional guarantee. Your rights will depend on whether the new rule or law is retroactive—that is, applied to past court decisions. This is generally a complex legal notion, and you should consider working with your attorney in deciding whether to appeal on the basis of a change in the law.

Q. Will the same lawyer who represented me at trial also handle my appeal?

A. Because trial and appellate (appeals) work are two different types of legal practice, the lawyer who represented you at the trial will not file or handle your appeal automatically. Trials require the skills of a lawyer who has experience in the courtroom and working before juries. Appeals involve a large amount of writing and legal research, as well as the ability to argue legal doctrines before a judge. It is recommended that you obtain a lawyer for your appeal.

If you want to appeal your conviction, be sure to inform your lawyer specifically and clearly of that fact—the U.S. Supreme Court has determined that a lawyer's failure to file a notice of appeal does not necessarily constitute ineffective assistance of counsel so long as the defendant did not convey clearly his wishes on the subject. In many states, the public defender (or another assigned counsel) generally will handle the appeal for those unable to pay.

Q. Are there any other options if I think my conviction was wrongful?

A. Yes. You can consider filing a habeas corpus petition. Literally, **habeas corpus** means "you may have the body." A habeas corpus proceeding challenges a conviction on the grounds that you are being held in prison in violation of your constitutional rights. Habeas corpus is not an appeal; it is a separate civil proceeding used after a direct appeal has been unsuccessful, and it is a federal civil proceeding initiated in federal district court. A common challenge under habeas corpus is that defendants received "ineffective assistance of counsel" at trial, meaning that their lawyers did not do a competent job of defending them. Such a claim is difficult to prove and will require the defendant-appellant to find a different lawyer to argue the incompetence of the previous lawyer. Legal arguments in a habeas corpus case generally are made through written motions, although an evidentiary hearing may be held as needed. Many jurisdictions strictly require that habeas corpus petitions be filed within a certain amount of time after a decision is rendered on final appeal.

REMEMBER THIS

- Trial procedure may be different depending on whether you have been charged with a felony or a misdemeanor.
- You may be eligible for ROR release, bail, or other conditions that ensure appearance and protect the community from

▶ EXPERT WITNESSES

Expert witnesses are specialists in certain fields—such as narcotics, psychology, medicine, or engineering—who are called to testify at a trial. Their testimony is another form of evidence that the judge or the jury may consider. In cases where laypeople are unlikely to understand the evidence without help, experts typically offer an opinion about what they think the evidence means. For example, in a case involving drugs, a narcotics expert might testify that the quantity of drugs seized and the way the drugs are packaged indicates the existence of a commercial drug operation. Or a fingerprint expert might compare the prints lifted from a crime scene to a fingerprint sample taken from the defendant, and then provide a professional opinion about whether the prints match.

The U.S. Supreme Court has ruled that in federal cases, the trial judge must act as a "gatekeeper" and rule upon the admissibility of expert testimony before it is offered. The judge will determine if the expert can testify by weighing the qualifications of the expert and the opinion he or she is offering, considering such factors as the reliability of the principles and methods used by the expert to arrive at his or her opinion.

danger. Money bail typically is a last resort. Talk to your lawyer, and investigate all your options before you approach a bail bondsman.

- If you are a victim of a crime or you witness a crime being committed, do not interfere with the crime scene. You could disturb valuable evidence.

- If you are a defendant and you are convicted at trial, you have the right to an appeal.

WITNESSES

Q. Who may serve as a witness?

A. During a criminal trial, the prosecution and the defense may both present witnesses. Witnesses might be victims or defendants who are testifying voluntarily on their own behalf, or people who are compelled to testify through the use of a subpoena. A witness might also be someone testifying as an impartial eyewitness to a crime, or someone with information about the crime.

Q. What should I do if I receive a subpoena?

A. A **subpoena** or **summons** is a legal document compelling you to appear or to produce certain evidence before a court or a grand jury. As soon as you receive a subpoena, you should take certain steps to protect your interests. First, be sure to preserve all related documents so that you will not risk being charged with obstruction of justice. Find a lawyer and speak only to him or her about the subpoena. Do not confide in friends or contact others who may be in the same situation, since they may be cooperating with the authorities and could end up testifying in court against you.

If you receive a subpoena ordering you to appear in court or before a grand jury at a certain date and time, you must obey or risk being held in contempt of court and receiving a fine or a jail sentence.

The subpoena may compel you to produce an item you possess, instead of or in addition to your testimony. This type of subpoena, known as a **subpoena duces tecum (SDT)**, compels you to produce certain evidence, usually in the form of documents. Before you obey this type of subpoena, call a lawyer. Depending on the content of the documents, you might be able to fight the subpoena on the grounds that it constitutes forced self-incrimination. Or, based upon the items listed in the subpoena, your lawyer may be able to offer your cooperation to the authorities in an effort to show that no crime has been committed or that, if a crime was committed, you were not part of it.

In some cases, your lawyer may be able to negotiate a deal in which you are granted immunity in return for producing the documents listed in the subpoena. The Supreme Court has determined that, if a government subpoena seeks discovery of potentially incriminating documents, and if you respond to that subpoena in exchange for being granted immunity, then the government cannot later use against you the fact that you produced those documents.

Do not deal with the authorities yourself. Your lawyer will need to ensure that your cooperation will not be used against you at a later date.

Q. May the court force me to testify?

A. If you are a defendant, no. The Fifth Amendment of the U.S. Constitution gives you the right to not incriminate yourself.

If you are a witness to or the victim of a crime, you have to testify, even if you don't want to get involved. You may refuse to answer a question on the witness stand if you feel the answers might incriminate you—unless the district attorney or prosecutor has granted you immunity in exchange for your testimony, in which case you must answer. A witness should rely on the advice of his or her lawyer regarding whether to refuse to answer questions. If you find yourself in this situation, your lawyer should be a person who has no role in the proceedings other than to advise you.

Sometimes a victim gets cold feet and changes his or her mind about testifying. This is especially true if the victim knows the defendant or is afraid of being retaliated against for testifying. If you are the victim and no longer want to go forward with testifying, you should make your wishes known to the prosecutor. However, even if you reported the crime and later decide you want the charges dropped, the prosecutor might not agree. The prosecutor often considers a victim's wishes, but technically the injured person is only a witness. Therefore, it is up to the district attorney or prosecutor to decide whether to proceed with the case and whether to subpoena a witness to testify.

Q. What do I do if I'm called to be a witness at a trial?

A. The most important thing is to be honest. When you are on the witness stand, the law requires you to tell the truth. Testifying can be tiring and frustrating. Try to remain relaxed and keep a pleasant attitude. The worst thing you can do is to appear angry, lose your temper, or argue with the lawyer who is asking the questions. If the judge and the jury disapprove of your behavior or attitude, they might not believe your testimony. If you are called as

witness, keep in mind the following key pieces of advice:

- Answer the questions as completely as possible, but stick to the point. Do not add details that are not necessary to answer the question.
- If you do not understand the question, politely ask the lawyer to rephrase it. Do not answer any questions if you are unsure of the answer. If you do not know the answer, your answer should be "I don't know."
- Always give verbal answers. A nod of the head cannot be recorded by the court reporter.

▶ **TYPES OF IMMUNITY**

If you refuse to testify by asserting your Fifth Amendment right against self-incrimination, the prosecutor can compel you to testify by providing you with immunity. There are two types of immunity that can be provided to a witness: use immunity and transactional immunity.

The different types of immunity provide different protections. If you are granted **use immunity,** the prosecutor is not permitted to use what you say, or evidence derived from what you say, to help prosecute you later. **Transactional immunity** provides far greater protection. If you are granted transactional immunity, the prosecution may never prosecute you for the crime at issue, even based on evidence independent of your testimony.

▶ WITNESS ASSISTANCE

Most district attorney's or prosecutor's offices have witness assistance departments that provide a number of services to simplify the process for prosecution witnesses. Many will give you directions to court and even arrange transportation if necessary. If you must travel a significant distance to testify, these departments may also provide you with a per diem (daily allowance) for food and lodging. Witness assistance coordinators can also help you with other necessary arrangements (such as child care) so that you can testify.

If testifying puts you in danger, witness protection programs are available. The police will escort you between your home and court if necessary. If you are a confidential informant and you fear for your life, steps may also be taken to hide your identity.

The defense generally does not have the same level of resources as the government. Thus, it may not be able to pay you a daily allowance. Despite this, if you have been subpoenaed, you must appear.

- If you hear a lawyer object after a question is asked, do not answer the question. Wait until the judge rules on the objection. The judge will tell you whether you may answer the question.

Q. Should I take the stand in my own defense?

A. You should listen to your lawyer's advice, but the final decision regarding whether to testify is yours. Many defendants do not testify. The judge will instruct the jury not to hold it against you if you do not testify, because the Fifth Amendment gives you the right not to incriminate yourself.

Many defendants feel that they should testify because they are innocent and have nothing to hide. But a defendant should bear in mind that he or she will be subject to tough cross-examination from the prosecutor. For instance, if you take the stand, the prosecutor may ask you whether you have any prior felony convictions. You must answer truthfully. If you do not take the stand, no one will reveal such information to the jury.

REMEMBER THIS

- If you hear an objection when testifying, immediately stop speaking. Before continuing with your testimony, wait for the judge to give you further instructions.

- If you are served with a subpoena, contact your lawyer. Speak only with your lawyer about it.

JURIES

Q. What is the purpose of a jury?

A. The right to trial by a jury of one's peers is a cornerstone of the individual freedoms guaranteed by the U.S. Constitution's Bill of Rights. A jury stands between the power of the government and the rights of the accused. The government cannot take away someone's right to life, liberty, or property until it has convinced the twelve citizens of the jury that the defendant is guilty beyond a reasonable doubt.

Q. Does the U.S. Constitution guarantee me a right to a jury trial in every case?

A. No, you do not have the right to a jury trial in every case. In civil cases, the Seventh Amendment guarantees the right to a jury trial in "suits at common law." As a general rule, **suits at common law** are civil suits in which money is sought as compensation for an asserted injury or loss—for example, breach of contract or personal injury actions. The Seventh Amendment's right to a jury trial does not apply if the plaintiff is seeking an **equitable** (i.e., nonmonetary) remedy for his or her injury or loss—for example, an order to the defendant to cease certain conduct or turn over certain property.

However, Congress has provided for the jury trial option in some instances where the federal Constitution does not require it. Additionally, the U.S. Supreme Court has ruled that a defendant who is facing incarceration lasting six months or longer is entitled to a trial by jury. In both criminal and civil cases, state constitutions may also guarantee broader rights to a jury trial.

Q. What is the difference between a legal and equitable claim?

A. Whether a claim is legal or equitable can generally be determined by the remedy the plaintiff is seeking. As noted above, a request for money damages is, historically, a **legal** claim, while a request that the court order a party to take or stop some action is an **equitable** claim. The question can be more complicated in cases where there are a number of different claims, some legal, some equitable, and some with both legal and equitable characteristics.

Q. Will I automatically get a jury trial if I'm constitutionally entitled to one?

A. No. Typically, you must make a written demand for a jury trial. For tactical reasons, some parties may prefer to have their case decided by a judge alone.

Q. How does a bench trial, where a judge conducts the trial without a jury, differ from a jury trial?

A. In a jury trial, the fact-finding function belongs to the jury, and the judge provides the jury with instructions on how to apply the law to those facts. In a **bench trial,** on the other hand, the judge must determine the facts and then apply the law to those facts.

Q. Should I exercise my right to a jury trial, or waive it in favor of a bench trial (a trial before a judge)?

A. This is a decision that you and your lawyer must make. Your chances might be better with a jury, because the prosecutor will have to convince every single juror that you are guilty. On the other hand, you should bear in mind that juries are unpredictable. In some rare cases, you might stand a better chance of acquittal with a judge. Listen to your lawyer's advice, but remember that in most jurisdictions, you cannot waive trial by jury without the consent of the prosecutor.

Q. How are potential jurors selected?

A. Jurors must be representative of the community in which the trial is being conducted.

Courts usually obtain the names of prospective jurors from a regularly maintained list or group of lists, such as lists of registered voters or licensed drivers. When a case is set for trial by jury, the clerk of court uses this list to provide the court with a randomly selected pool of potential jurors representing a fair cross section of the community. The jurors who will actually hear the case are then chosen by a process in which the members of the jury panel are questioned. This process is known as **voir dire.**

Q. How are the jury members selected for my particular case?

A. Potential jurors are questioned in open court by the judge or the parties' lawyers, depending on local statutes and court rules. The goal is to discover any potential bias or prejudice relating to the parties or to issues in the case. If a juror concedes such a bias or prejudice, or if evidence suggests that he or she may have such a bias or prejudice, the lawyer may ask the court to **strike the juror for cause** and remove him or her from the panel of potential jurors in that case.

In addition to challenges for cause, each lawyer can make **peremptory challenges.** These challenges permit a lawyer to excuse a potential juror without stating a cause. Based on the type of lawsuit being tried, each side is limited to a certain number of peremptory challenges. Moreover, peremptory challenges cannot be used to remove potential jurors on the basis of race or gender.

Q. How many jurors sit on a jury?

A. That depends on where the case is being heard. A federal criminal trial jury usually has twelve members. In some states, there may be fewer than twelve jurors in criminal misde-meanor cases. In more serious felony cases, in which the punishment may be more than a year of imprisonment in a penitentiary, twelve jurors are often required.

Q. What are jury deliberations?

A. After closing arguments, the judge will **charge** the jury—that is, give them instructions about how to apply the law to the evidence they have observed at trial. The jury then retires to a private room for **deliberations,** which are discussions among the jurors as they review the evidence and attempt to reach a unanimous verdict. Deliberations are carried out in complete secrecy, to ensure fairness to the person on trial. If the jurors have questions, they may send a note to the judge, who usually will respond in writing to clear up any confusion based on legal issues.

Q. Must all jury verdicts be unanimous?

A. In the federal system, jury decisions must be unanimous. If the jury cannot reach a unanimous decision, a mistrial is declared. (A jury that is irrevocably divided is called a **hung jury.**) In the case of a hung jury, the case may be retried later or dismissed.

In the state court system, requirements regarding unanimity among jurors vary from state to state. In more than a third of the states, agreement of only three-fourths or five-sixths of the jurors is needed to render a verdict in civil cases.

Q. Will the court protect jurors against danger of threats or violence?

A. The law entitles jurors to such protection. Very occasionally, the court **sequesters** the jury for the duration of the trial—that is, houses it in a hotel to isolate it from outside influences. Even if a jury is not sequestered for the entire trial, it is not uncommon for the jury to be sequestered during its deliberations. Police officers or court officials escort the jury to and from court. After the trial, the police will continue as best they can to ensure the safety of discharged jurors, at least for a time. On rare occasions the court can even empanel an anonymous jury.

Q. If I am called for jury duty and I have a job, will I lose my paycheck for the time I spend performing jury service?

A. That depends. Some states require that employers continue to pay employees their full salary, or a percentage of it, during jury service. Some employers do this voluntarily. All states provide jurors with a daily fee for service ranging from $10 to $40.

Q. If I am impaneled as a juror, what do I need to know?

A. Although it may not feel like an honor, realize that you are serving your country and exercising one of the vital rights of American citizenship. Remember that juries need to be representative of the community from which they are selected, and that service by everyone assists in achieving that goal.

You should also be aware that the judge will likely impose certain restrictions on you, such as:

- not allowing you to read newspaper articles or watch any news stories relating to your case;
- not permitting you to talk to other jurors about the trial before deliberations; and
- not allowing you to talk about the case to any lawyers you may know.

Jury service is becoming less burdensome than it used to be, due to an increase in the amount that jurors are paid; continuation by many employers of jurors' regular salaries for some period; and adoption in some jurisdictions of much shorter terms of jury service, a concept known in many states as **one day— one trial.** Many jurisdictions also provide that a juror will not be selected again for a specified number of years after serving.

Q. What if I am selected as an alternate juror?

A. At the beginning of the trial, the judge may order that more jurors be seated than are required for the verdict. These extra jurors are known as **alternate jurors,** and they are selected to guard against the possibility that some of the jurors will become ill or otherwise be unable to complete the trial. An alternate attends the trial along with the regular jurors, but does not participate in reaching a verdict unless one of the regular jurors is unable to continue.

No matter what procedures are used, it is important for alternate jurors to always pay attention to testimony, because they may be required to participate in the verdict should another juror be unable to complete his or her service.

REMEMBER THIS

- Deliberations are carried out in complete secrecy. This is necessary to ensure a fair trial.
- Serving as a juror is an important civic responsibility.
- If you serve on a jury, don't talk to any of your fellow jurors about the case during the trial.

VICTIM'S RIGHTS

Q. How does the criminal justice system protect victims?

A. Victims are a critical component of the criminal justice process. They have a right to be treated with fairness and respect for their dignity and privacy. Yet, historically, victims' rights were almost nonexistent. Today, many states have passed constitutional amendments protecting victims' rights, and numerous federal and state laws protect victims' rights to notice and participation in the criminal justice system. These laws are often collectively known as the Crime Victims' Bill of Rights; they may also protect certain rights of witnesses.

Q. Who is protected by these laws?

A. While laws differ in their definitions of who is a victim for purposes of triggering victims' rights, the laws generally protect victims of violent crimes, domestic violence, and sexual abuse. Some also cover victims of identity theft or telemarketing fraud, and sometimes certain witnesses to crimes. In addition to providing protection, the laws may require victim and witness cooperation in the apprehension and prosecution of the offender. The laws differ in terms of the procedures set forth for securing victims' rights. Some require the provision of notices and information automatically, but many require victims to activate their rights by calling, writing, or otherwise notifying the appropriate authorities.

Q. What kind of protections and rights are victims afforded?

A. One of the most basic rights available to victims is the right to notice of proceedings. This may include a general overview of the criminal justice process, as well as specific notice of dates, times, and places at which court hearings relating to the victim's case are taking place. For example, most laws provide notice of the time and date of trial and sentencing. Most also require that victims be given notice of parole hearings or early release, such as release on parole. An emerging technology called **automated victim notification** can help victims stay informed about their cases automatically. These systems have different names in different states, but they generally allow a victim to call a computerized toll-free phone number and provide a defendant's name, case number, or other identifying information to receive computerized updates on the status of the case and the next court date or prison release date. Some of these systems also allow victims to register their numbers so they can be notified automatically of any change in court date or in the status of the defendant.

Another critical right of victims is the right to participate in the criminal justice process. Most often, the victim is the key eyewitness, and therefore the victim's testimony is critical. Many laws require that victims be provided with a waiting area separate from the defendant, so that victims are not harassed or intimidated while attending court proceedings. Many victims' rights laws also provide that victims be taken into consideration when setting bond. Special bond conditions may be entered to prevent the alleged offender from contacting the victim while the case is pending. Victims also have the right to provide input during sentencing through a victim impact statement. Special conditions also may be attached to sentences to prevent offenders from contacting victims upon their release.

Crime victims suffer personal and financial losses as a result of crime, and many laws require notice of available services and assistance to enable victims to obtain the emotional and financial support needed for their recovery. For example, free or low-cost counseling may be available to crime victims. Also, government-run crime victims' compensation programs often help pay out-of-pocket costs, like medical bills or employment losses that have occurred as a result of crime. Restitution is mandatory for many crimes, and offenders can be ordered to pay for the damages they caused the victim.

Q. If I have been a crime victim, where can I get help?

A. Police or prosecutors should be able to provide information about your rights as a crime victim or witness. Many of these agencies have specialized crime victim advocates who can help secure the necessary information to help you participate in your case. Some states have developed ombudsman programs that oversee complaints; others have a designated statewide office that handles victims' rights information and complaints of violations of victims' rights. Government services are free of charge. Private agencies also exist in many jurisdictions and may provide free or low-cost services such as advocacy or counseling for crime victims.

REMEMBER THIS

- Crime victims have rights, such as the right to notification and financial recovery.

- If you have been a crime victim, local agencies and government offices may be able to assist you free of charge in protecting your rights.

Family Law

Tim and Sophie are young, in love, and recently married. They just bought a house and are talking about having kids. Looks like this marriage business could be fun. But who owns the house? What happens to the house if the marriage ends? Whose decision is it for them to have children? And what happens to their children if they separate or divorce?

It is difficult to give simple answers to many of the legal questions that a person may have about marriage, parenthood, separation, or divorce, because the laws vary from state to state. In addition, because so many of the issues before a court allow for judicial discretion, judges applying identical laws may decide cases with similar facts in different ways.

This chapter describes some of the laws and court rulings common to most states. If you have questions or simply want to be sure you understand how the law applies in your own state or to a specific situation, you may wish to speak to a family lawyer in your state. Many lawyers handle family law either exclusively or as a significant portion of their general practice. Lawyers specializing in family law also may refer to themselves as **domestic relations** or **matrimonial law** specialists.

MARRIAGE

This section explores the legal implications of marriage. Weddings often focus on family, ceremony, and celebration, so it's easy to forget that the government also has an interest in your marriage. State legislatures have passed many laws regulating marriage and divorce. Some of these laws can also affect couples who live together without being married.

Requirements for Getting Married

Q. *Legally, what is marriage?*

A. Marriage is a private bond between two people, but it is also an important social and legal institution. Most states define marriage as a civil contract between a man and a woman to become husband and wife.

The moment a man and a woman marry, their relationship acquires a legal status. Married couples have financial and personal duties to each other during marriage and after separation or divorce. State laws determine the extent of these duties. As the U.S. Supreme Court said about marriage in 1888: "The relation once formed, the law steps in and holds the parties to various obligations and liabilities."

Society recognizes marriage as an expression of several broad ideas. Among other things, marriage represents

- a way for two people to express commitment, strengthen intimate bonds, and provide mutual emotional support;
- a (comparatively) stable structure within which to raise children; and
- a financial partnership in which spouses may choose from a variety of roles. Both spouses may work inside or outside the home to support the family, or the husband may support the wife, or the wife may support the husband.

As our society becomes more complex, there is no short answer to the question "What is marriage?". Definitions of and opinions about the proper functions of marriage continue to change. For example, the womens' and gay rights movements have resulted in more equal treatment of men and women and the creation of new legal relationships, including domestic partnerships and civil unions for same-sex couples. Thus, the traditional concept of marriage remains, but it continues to evolve.

Q. What are the legal requirements for getting married?

A. The requirements are simple, although they vary from state to state. In general, there are three main requirements:

1. A man and a woman wishing to marry must obtain a license in the state in which they wish to be married, usually from a county clerk, a city clerk, or a clerk of court. Usually they must pay a small fee for the license.

2. Parties who wish to marry must have the capacity to do so. This means that neither can be married to someone else, the parties must be of a certain age, and both must understand that they are being married and what it means to be married. If, because of drunkenness, mental illness, or some other problem, one of the parties lacks capacity, the marriage may not be valid.

3. A few states require the man and the woman to have blood tests for venereal disease before the license is issued, although most states do not. In states that require a blood test, some will not issue a license if one or both of the parties have venereal disease, while others will allow the marriage if the couple knows the disease is present. In a few states, a couple must show proof of immunity from or vaccination for certain diseases, or proof that they have completed a general physical examination.

Q. Are there any other factors that may prevent a couple from getting married?

A. Yes. Close blood relatives generally cannot marry, although first cousins are allowed to marry in some states. Of those states that allow first cousins to marry, a few require that one of the cousins be unable to conceive children.

Further, some states require a waiting period, generally three days, between the time the license is issued and the time of the marriage ceremony.

Q. How old do I have to be to get married?

A. You can marry at eighteen without parental consent. Most states also allow persons age sixteen and seventeen to marry with the consent of their parents or a judge.

Q. When does a couple become married?

A. Most states consider a couple to be married when the ceremony ends and the officiant says, "I now pronounce you husband and wife." Failure to have sexual relations—otherwise known as lack of consummation—does not affect the validity of the marriage. In all states, the proper official must record the marriage license, which is considered proof that the marriage happened.

Q. Is a particular type of marriage ceremony required?

A. No. The law is quite flexible with regards to the particularities of a marriage ceremony.

> ### ► PERSONS WHO MAY CONDUCT MARRIAGE CEREMONIES
>
> Civil ceremonies are usually conducted by judges. In some states, county clerks or other government officials may conduct civil ceremonies. Religious ceremonies are normally conducted by religious officials, such as ministers, priests, or rabbis. Native American ceremonies may be presided over by a tribal chief or other designated official. Contrary to popular legend, no state authorizes ship captains to perform marriages.

A ceremony may be religious or civil. The person or persons conducting the ceremony should indicate that the man and woman agree to be married. A religious ceremony should be conducted according to the customs of the applicable religion—or, in the case of a Native American group, the applicable tribe. Most states also require one or two witnesses to sign the marriage certificate.

Q. Are marriages that take place in other countries recognized by the U.S.?

A. Generally, yes. If a marriage was performed and was recognized as valid in the country in which it was performed, it will be recognized in the United States. However, in some cases marriages may not be recognized if such recognition would be contrary to United States public policy. For example, even with parental consent, the marriage of an adult to a person below the minimum age at which marriage is allowed in the United States—for example, the marriage of an adult to an eight-year-old—might not be recognized if the couple moved to the United States while one of the parties was still a child. However, if the parties were both adults, there might be a different result—for example, if the marriage happened twenty years ago and the eight-year-old is now twenty-eight. Similar restrictions could apply for parties in multiple marriages (such as polygamists), even if such marriages are valid under the laws of the parties' home country.

Q. Does a woman's last name change automatically when she gets married?

A. No. A woman's name changes only if she wants it to change. In the past, a woman would often change her last name to her husband's name when she married. Today, however, society recognizes a woman's right to take her husband's name, keep her original name, or use both names. The general rule is that if a woman uses a chosen name consistently and honestly, then it will be recognized as her true name. The same law may apply to men who take their wives' names upon marriage. For details about how to change your name, see the sidebar entitled "What's in a Name?" on page 109.

Invalid Marriages

Q. What happens if a couple got married, but didn't actually meet all of the requirements for a valid marriage?

A. The marriage may be considered invalid. A marriage may be invalid if it involves close relatives, underage persons, or people incapable of entering into the marriage contract because of mental incompetence, or if a prior marriage exists and a divorce has not been completed. Sometimes people discover that their marriage is invalid only when filing for divorce.

In some states, the **putative spouse doctrine** offers some protection to the innocent party if the parties went through a ceremonial marriage. A putative (meaning "supposed") spouse may be entitled to the same benefits and rights as a legal spouse for as long as she or he reasonably believed the marriage to be valid. In states that do not accept the putative spouse doctrine, people who mistakenly believe they are married have the same status as unmarried couples who live together.

After a long union that both parties honestly believed was a valid marriage, a court may refuse to declare the marriage invalid and require a divorce to end the marriage.

Q. What if one person tricks the other into thinking there has been a valid marriage?

A. Sometimes the law treats an invalid marriage as valid if one person tricked the other into thinking that the couple had a valid marriage. If so, a court might not allow the deceiving partner to declare the marriage invalid. In legal terms, the court **estops** (prevents) the deceiver from denying that the marriage exists. In addition, a court may find that the doctrine of **laches** (meaning "long delay") prevents even the innocent party, who originally did not know about the invalid marriage, from having the marriage declared invalid. This may occur if, after learning that the marriage was not valid, the innocent party took no action for a significant period of time.

Duties of Marriage

Q. Does either spouse have a duty to work outside the home?

A. No. During a marriage, a court will not involve itself in private family decisions about who works and who does not; such decisions are left to the husband and wife. A husband or wife cannot, as a matter of law, force his or her spouse to work.

Q. If a couple separates or divorces, can a court require them to work outside the home?

A. No, not directly. If a couple separates or divorces, a court cannot directly order one or both of them to work. The court can, however, declare that one or both parties owe a duty of financial support to the other party (**alimony,** also called maintenance or spousal support) or to the children (**child support**). If so, the court will set an amount that must be paid. If there are no actual earnings from which to pay support, the court might base its amount on the earning capacity or ability of one or both of the parties. Payment of alimony and child support will be discussed later in this chapter.

Q. Are there legal remedies if a husband or wife refuses to have sexual relations with his or her spouse?

A. A court will not order a person to have sexual relations with his or her spouse. A spouse who forces sexual relations with a partner can be charged with rape under state criminal law. In some states, the refusal to have sexual relations with a spouse is specific grounds for divorce or annulment of the marriage. In other states, refusal to have sexual relations may be grounds for divorce because it constitutes an irreconcilable difference or a form of mental cruelty.

Q. May husbands and wives sue each other?

A. Yes. Husbands and wives can, of course, sue each other for divorce. They can also sue each other in connection with financial deals in which one may have cheated the other. The vast majority of states also allow one spouse to sue the other for deliberate personal injuries, such as those suffered in a beating. In addition, some states allow husbands and wives to sue each other in connection with an auto accident in which the driver-spouse accidentally injures the passenger-spouse. Other states will not allow such suits, for fear that the person suing would, in effect, be trying to collect money from an insurance company rather than from his or her spouse.

▶ **LOSS OF CONSORTIUM**

Loss of consortium refers to the loss of companionship and sexual relationship with one's spouse. The concept also can apply more broadly to the loss of companionship and affection from other family members, such as a child or parent. In personal injury actions, plaintiffs may seek damages from the defendant for loss of consortium, in addition to payment for other losses such as medical expenses, lost wages, and physical pain and suffering. For example, if a man is injured in an auto accident caused by a negligent driver and is unable to have sexual relations with his wife because of the accident, both the husband and the wife may seek damages for that loss.

Q. Can spouses testify against each other in court?

A. Yes. Husbands and wives routinely testify against each other in divorce cases. There is an old rule that husbands and wives cannot testify about communications made between them during the marriage. Although the rule may be applied in some circumstances, it generally does not apply if the husband and wife are involved in a lawsuit against each other.

Living Together Outside of Marriage

Q. Can two people live together without being married?

A. Of course. This is an increasingly common situation. Generally, two unrelated people can legally live together anywhere they want. A few states still have laws prohibiting **fornication**—sexual relations between a man and woman who are not married—but such laws are virtually never enforced.

Q. Are common-law marriages allowed?

A. In most states, no. In times past, particularly in the frontier days, it was common for states to consider a woman and man married if they lived together for a certain length of time, had sexual intercourse, and held themselves out as husband and wife, even if they never went through a marriage ceremony. Today, a few states recognize common-law marriages. In those states, in order for a common-law marriage to be legal, the partners must clearly represent themselves to others as husband and wife; merely living together is not sufficient to constitute a marriage.

In states that recognize common-law marriage, the partners have the same rights and duties as they would if a ceremonial marriage had taken place.

Q. If I move to another state, will my common-law marriage be recognized?

A. If a common-law marriage begins in a state that recognizes the validity of common-law marriages, then most other states will accept it as valid.

Q. Is there such thing as a common-law divorce?

A. No. A legal common-law marriage can end only with a formal divorce.

Q. May two unmarried people who are living together enter into agreements about sharing expenses or acquiring property?

A. Yes. People may want to agree about who will pay what, and about how they will share property they might acquire. From a legal standpoint, it is best to make the agreements specific and in writing. An oral agreement might be enforceable, but its existence may be difficult to prove if the parties have different views about the terms to which they agreed. In order for an agreement to be enforceable, each party should provide some benefit to the other party, such as agreeing to pay a certain portion of expenses. If an agreement appears to create a gift from one party to the other, with the other party providing nothing in return, then it might not be enforceable.

Q. Will a court enforce an agreement in which one unmarried partner agrees to keep house, and the other agrees to provide financial support?

A. The answer to this question varies from state to state. To begin with, such agreements are rarely formalized in writing, so their exis-

tence is often difficult to prove in court. Second, to the extent that one person is promising financial support to the other, that promise is usually contingent on a continuation of the relationship. For example, if one partner tells the other, "I'll take care of you," the statement may be too vague to be enforceable; if it means anything, it probably means something along the lines of "I'll support you financially as long as we are living together." So if the couple breaks up, a court probably would not find an enforceable promise for continued support.

There is a potential third problem: If a court thinks an agreement amounts to providing financial support in exchange for sexual relations, the court will not enforce it. Such an agreement is considered akin to a contract for prostitution.

Courts are more inclined to enforce agreements that provide for tangible behaviors or results, such as the payment of expenses or rights to property. A promise to provide housekeeping services or emotional support for a partner may be sincere, but is ultimately much more amorphous than a promise to pay half the phone bill or share the proceeds of a condominium sale.

Same-Sex Marriages

Q. Can a same-sex couple marry?

A. As of late 2007, the state of Massachusetts was the only state to formally recognize same-sex marriage (although resolution of this issue is currently pending in several other states). If two members of the same sex were to go through a marriage ceremony, most states would not consider the marriage to be valid—and, if the parties were to split up, they could not seek a legal divorce. Vermont allows same-sex couples to form **civil unions,** which provide same-sex couples with the same benefits and protections as heterosexual couples who enter into marriages. Other states and cities recognize domestic partnerships in lieu of same-sex marriages.

Q. What is a domestic partnership?

A. Some states and cities have passed laws providing for **domestic partnerships,** which can exist between homosexual persons and, in some cases, between heterosexual persons who are living together without being married. To become domestic partners, a couple must register their relationship at a government office and declare themselves to be in a "committed" relationship. Domestic partnerships provide some—but not all—of the legal benefits of marriage. Such benefits include the right to coverage on a family health insurance policy, the right to family leave to care for a sick partner (to the same extent a person would be able to use such leave to care for a sick spouse), the right to bereavement leave, visiting rights at hospitals and jails, and rent control benefits (to the same extent a spouse would be entitled to such benefits). As with benefits afforded to spouses, benefits afforded to domestic partners are generally available only to one partner. Thus, a person may have only one domestic partner at a time, and a domestic partnership must be dissolved before a person may legally enter into a new domestic partnership with someone else. If you are interested in finding out whether your state or city sanctions domestic partnerships, contact your local gay-and-lesbian rights organization.

Q. If a same-sex marriage, civil union, or domestic partnership is valid in one state, must another state recognize it?

A. No. The Defense of Marriage Act (DOMA) denies federal recognition of gay marriage. This means that each state can decide whether to recognize gay marriages from another state. The implication of DOMA is that if a same-sex couple is married in Massachusetts, they must stay there in order for their marriage to be legally recognized. This is not the case with heterosexual marriages. Under the Full Faith and Credit Clause of the U.S. Constitution, states generally must recognize heterosexual marriages from other states.

Q. Can a state restrict a same-sex relationship in other ways?

A. Some states have tried to restrict same-sex relationships, but outside of refusing to recognize same-sex marriages, these efforts are likely unconstitutional. Some states still have laws against **sodomy,** which, among other things, is prohibited sexual relations between people of the same sex. However, such laws have rarely been enforced in the case of private, consensual conduct between adults. In the 2003 case *Lawrence and Garner v. Texas,* the U.S. Supreme Court invalidated a Texas law that criminalized oral and anal sex by consenting gay couples. This effectively rendered unconstitutional state sodomy laws as they applied to private, consensual intimacy.

REMEMBER THIS

- State law dictates the requirements for getting married, including the length of the waiting period, if any, between issuance of the marriage license and the marriage ceremony.

- Marriage ceremonies can be religious or civil, or performed according to the customs of a Native American tribe.

- A few states allow common-law marriages, which are marriages that occur without a formal ceremony or marriage license.

- Domestic partnerships, civil unions, and same-sex marriages that are permitted in one state will not necessarily be recognized by another.

MONEY MATTERS DURING MARRIAGE

During marriage, which spouse owns the house, bank accounts, and cars? What if one spouse dies or the marriage ends? The answers to these questions will depend on many factors, including who has title to the property, whether it is separate property or marital property, and whether there is a premarital agreement or will that covers the property. This section addresses each of these issues.

Premarital Agreements

Q. What is a premarital agreement?

A. A **premarital agreement**, also known as an **antenuptial agreement** or **prenuptial agreement**, is a contract entered into by a man and a woman before they marry. The agreement usually describes what each party's rights will be if they divorce or if one of them dies. The agreement may also address how the couple intend to arrange their finances during their marriage, even if they never divorce. Premarital agreements most commonly deal with issues of property and spousal support—who is entitled to what property and how much support, if any, will be paid in the event of divorce.

Q. Why do couples enter into premarital agreements?

A. A person might enter into a premarital agreement for many reasons, but usually it is to protect money or assets. People use premarital agreements to clarify their expectations and rights for the future, and to avoid uncertainties about how a divorce court might divide property and decide spousal support if the marriage fails. For people marrying a second or third time, there might be a desire to ensure that a majority of assets or personal belongings are passed on to children or grandchildren from prior marriages rather than to a current spouse.

Q. What does a spouse give up by signing a premarital agreement?

A. In signing a premarital agreement, a spouse agrees to have his or her property rights and support obligations determined by the agreement rather than by the usual rules of law that a court would apply in the event of divorce or death. In terms of establishing rights and obligations, a premarital agreement can be more or less permissive than state law.

In most states, courts divide property as the court considers fair, and the result can be unpredictable: the split could be fifty-fifty, or something else. If one spouse dies, courts normally follow the instructions of that person's will, but in most states the surviving spouse is entitled to between one-third and one-half of the estate, regardless of what is set forth in the will. However, if the husband and wife have a valid premarital agreement, that agreement will supersede the usual laws for dividing property and income upon divorce or death. In many cases, the less-wealthy spouse will receive less under the premarital agreement than he or she would have received under the usual laws that govern divorce or wills.

Q. Why would a spouse sign a premarital agreement if he or she would receive less under the agreement than under other laws?

A. That answer depends on the individual. Some people liken a prenuptial agreement to a custom-made suit, tailored to fit the circumstances of the particular couple, while a marriage without such an agreement is like an "off-the-rack" garment, designed by the state to fit the "generic" couple. Some people may want to avoid uncertainty about what a court might decide if their marriage ends in divorce. Others may simply subscribe to the philosophy "love conquers all," meaning that the less-wealthy person wishes to marry the other party regardless of the financial details. For others, the premarital agreement may provide ample security, even if it is not as generous as a judge might be. Still others may not like the agreement, but they may be willing to take their chances and hope the arrangements work out for the best.

Q. What are the requirements for a valid premarital agreement?

A. In general, a premarital agreement must be in writing and signed by both parties. In most states, the parties must fully and clearly disclose to each other in writing their income and assets. This way the parties will know more about what they might be giving up. In some states, it may be possible to waive full disclosure of income and assets, but the waiver must be made knowingly, and it is still best if each party has a general idea of the other's net worth. If an agreement will grant the couple rights and responsibilities different than what would be the case in the absence of an agreement, it's important to state what those rights would have been. This will make it clear that both parties understood what they were giving up (and receiving) by entering into the agreement.

In addition, a person may not enter into a premarital agreement as the result of fraud or duress. An agreement is likely to be invalid on the basis of fraud if one person (par-ticularly the wealthier one) deliberately misstates his or her financial condition. For example, if a man hides assets from his future wife so that she will agree to a low level of support in case of divorce, a court may declare the agreement invalid. Similarly, if one person exerts excessive emotional pressure on the other to sign the agreement, a court might declare the agreement to be invalid because of duress.

Q. When should a couple enter into a premarital agreement?

A. Most states do not specify a time period within which a premarital agreement must be signed. Generally, however, it is better to negotiate and sign the agreement well before the wedding. This shows that each person has thoroughly considered the agreement and is signing it voluntarily. If the wealthier person shows the agreement to the prospective spouse only one day before the wedding, a court may later deem that agreement invalid.

Q. Must the parties to a premarital agreement be represented by lawyers?

A. No, but it is a good idea. Lawyers can help make sure that the agreement is drafted properly and that both parties are making informed decisions. The lawyer for the wealthier party usually prepares the initial draft of the agreement. The less-wealthy party should then have a lawyer review the agreement, even if the lawyer reviews it only briefly and at minimal cost. Although a lawyer's input is not necessary for a valid agreement, an agreement is more likely to be enforceable if each person's interests are represented and significant back-and-forth negotiations have taken place. In some jurisdictions, it may be necessary in the prenuptial agreement to have the involved attorneys waive certain rights.

Q. Do premarital agreements need to provide for a certain amount of support?

A. No. The law does not require that a specific amount of support be paid in the event of divorce or separation.

Some states will enforce an agreement to provide no spousal support, so long as lack of support does not leave the less-wealthy party so poor that she or he is eligible for welfare. Many courts will apply broader notions of fairness and require an amount of support that enables a higher than subsistence level standard of living.

Some lawyers think it is a good idea for premarital agreements to contain an **escalator clause,** otherwise known as a **phase-in provision.** This type of provision increases the amount of assets or support provided to the less-wealthy spouse based on the length of the marriage, or based on an increase in the wealthier party's assets or income after the agreement is made. However, some states may invalidate escalator clauses on the grounds that they encourage divorce. This may be the case, for example, if the wealthier spouse has an incentive to file for divorce earlier than he or she would have in the absence of an escalator clause, in order to avoid paying stepped-up levels of support.

Q. May premarital agreements decide future issues of custody and child support?

A. No. A court may consider parts of a premarital agreement regarding child custody or support, but is not bound by them. Broadly speaking, parties cannot bargain away the rights of their children, particularly before the children are even born. Child support and custody issues will be discussed in more detail later in this chapter.

Q. What happens if one spouse dies and there is no prenuptial agreement in place?

A. If the spouse left a will, his or her property should be distributed according to its provisions. If the will makes no provision for the surviving spouse, a court may not invalidate the will, but will nevertheless permit the surviving spouse to obtain a portion of the property. If there is no will, the property will be distributed according to the laws of the state. See chapter 18, "Estate Planning," for more information about what happens to an estate when a spouse dies.

Ownership of Property

Q. Which spouse owns what property?

A. Most property that is acquired during marriage with money earned by either party during the marriage is considered **marital** or **community property.** If one or both spouses buys a house or establishes a business during the marriage, that property will usually be considered marital property, particularly if the house or business is purchased with the husband's and wife's earnings obtained during marriage.

Separate property is property that each spouse owned before the marriage. In most states, separate property also includes inheritances and gifts (except perhaps gifts between spouses) acquired during marriage. During the marriage (and afterward), each spouse usually keeps control of his or her separate property, and may sell it or use it to buy other property or to borrow money. Income earned from separate property, such as interest, dividends, or rent, is generally considered separate property. Note that in some states, these profits may become marital property.

Q. Can separate property become marital property?

A. Yes, if it is mixed or commingled with marital property. For example, if a wife owned an apartment building before the marriage and she deposited rent checks into a joint checking account, then the rent probably would be considered marital property. The building is likely to remain the wife's separate property as long as she kept it in her own name. However, if the wife changed the title of the building to include the names of both herself and her husband, then the building would likely be considered marital property. In addition, if one spouse performed a great deal of work on the other spouse's separate property, that property may be deemed "converted" into marital property, or the spouse who contributed the work may have the right to some form of repayment for the work performed. If a husband or wife decides to use nonmarital funds for a common purpose, such as purchasing a home in joint tenancy, those funds will normally become marital property. The courts of most, but not all, states will view the nonmarital property as a gift to the marriage.

The main way to keep nonmarital property separate is to keep it in one's own name and not mix it with marital property. This issue is particularly important if the marriage ends and property must be divided.

Q. What is the community property system?

A. Eight states—Arizona, California, Idaho, Louisiana, Nevada, New Mexico, Texas, and Washington (plus Puerto Rico) have adopted a different concept of property rights during a marriage. Though the specifics of the law vary from state to state, these states generally consider any property acquired during a marriage, except by gift or inheritance, to be community property. This is true even if one spouse supplies all of the income during a marriage. In this type of system, each spouse owns half the community property, and each may transfer his or her interest without the other's signature. But there is no right of survivorship, which means that when one spouse dies, half of the couple's property—including, if they own one, half of the couple's house— must go through probate.

The law of Wisconsin also has certain community property features. In addition, Alaska changed its law in 1998 to allow married seniors to select community property as an alternative form of ownership. Under this law, a couple may voluntarily decide to enter into a written community property agreement or community property trust. If they don't choose to do so, their property will not be held as community property.

Debts and Taxes

Q. Is one spouse responsible for debts incurred by the other?

A. That depends on the nature and timing of the debt, as well as the state in which the couple lives. If both husband and wife have cosigned for the debt, both will be responsible for it. For instance, assume the husband and wife apply together for a charge card. If both sign the application form, both will be responsible for paying off the entire balance to the credit card company or store, even if only one of them made the purchases and the other disapproved.

▶ THREE FORMS OF CO-OWNERSHIP

There are three common forms of ownership available to couples living in non-community property states and some community property states. (For more information on the various forms of ownership, see Chapter 7, "Buying and Selling a Home," and Chapter 8, "Home Ownership.")

Joint Tenancy

This is a form of ownership that exists when two or more people own property that includes a right of survivorship. Each person has the right to possess the property. If one partner dies, the survivor becomes the sole owner.

Tenancy by the Entirety

Allowed in less than half the states, this is a type of co-ownership of property by a husband and wife. Like joint tenancy, it includes a right of survivorship.

Tenancy in Common

This is a form of co-ownership that gives each person control over his or her share of the property. Moreover, the shares need not be equal. A tenancy in common does not provide a right of survivorship; when one owner dies, his or her share passes to that person's heirs, either by will or in accordance with state law.

Q. Can one spouse be held liable for the debts of the other even if he or she doesn't cosign for the debt?

A. Again, the answer to this question depends on the nature of the debt and where the couple lives. Some states have family-expense statutes that make a husband or wife liable for expenses incurred for the benefit of the family, even if the other spouse did not sign for or approve of the expense in advance. Still other states impose this family-expense obligation even if it is not formally imposed by law. Thus, if a wife charges groceries at a local store or takes the couple's child to a doctor for care, the husband could be liable for the applicable expenses, because the expenses were incurred for the benefit of the family.

In community property states, a husband or wife is generally responsible for the debts of the other, even in the absence of a cosignature.

Q. Is one spouse responsible for debts brought into the marriage by the other spouse?

A. Not in most states. In states that do not recognize community property, such debts belong to the spouse who incurred them. But in community property states, a spouse may, under special circumstances, become liable for the other spouse's premarital debts.

Q. Can my marital status impact my credit rights?

A. No. The law forbids denying credit on the basis of marital status. See Chapter 7, "Consumer Credit," for more information on this topic.

Q. Which spouse is responsible for paying taxes?

A. If the names and signatures of both spouses appear on a state or federal personal income tax return, both parties are liable for all of the taxes associated with that return. If a couple files jointly, the Internal Revenue Service generally holds each one responsible for the entire debt, though an innocent spouse who is not aware of income concealed by the other spouse may not be responsible for unpaid taxes on the hidden income. A spouse whose tax status is "married filing separately" is not responsible for the other's tax debt.

Q. May one spouse make a tax-free gift to the other spouse?

A. A person may give his or her spouse any amount of money without paying federal gift taxes, so long as the spouse is a U.S. resident and the gift is an outright gift—that is, made without any restrictions or obligation of repayment. But the same is not true with respect to gifts made to other family members. Gifts to children or other relatives may be taxable if they exceed a certain amount per year.

Doing Business Together

Q. May husbands and wives go into business together?

A. Certainly. Wives and husbands can be business partners. They can set up a corporation and act as owners and employees of the corporation; they can form a partnership; or one spouse can own the business and employ the other. Wages and benefits can be paid, just as they are for any other employee. If wages and benefits are paid to a spouse or a child, the amount usually should not be unreasonable or exceed fair market value. If artificially high payments are made, the business could get into trouble with the Internal Revenue Service.

Q. Is a husband or wife liable for the other's business debts?

A. Usually, no. As long as a spouse does not cosign for the other's business debts, he or she normally will not be liable for them. However, a spouse will be responsible if he or she cosigned for the debt or if the couple resides in a community property state. It is common for institutions that lend money to small businesses to seek personal guarantees of payment from the owner of the business, and not just from the business itself. In the event the debt is not paid, lenders prefer to have as many pockets as possible to reach into. If the business owner owns a home, the lender may want to use the home as collateral for the business loan. In these cases, the business owner's spouse may be asked to sign a paper allowing use of the home as collateral. This means that the home could be lost if the business cannot pay its debts.

Q. May a couple file jointly for bankruptcy?

A. Yes. Bankruptcy provides relief for people who have more debts than they can pay. See Chapter 11, "Consumer Bankruptcy," for more information.

REMEMBER THIS

- Although state law varies, there are several ways to increase the likelihood that a premarital agreement will be enforced:
  - Each party should fully disclose his or her assets and income before the agreement is signed.

○ The parties should understand what the agreement means. It may be helpful for each party to be represented by a lawyer, though representation is not always required.

○ The agreement should provide for a reasonable amount of assets or income for the less-wealthy spouse, though the amount need not be as high as a divorce court would order.

- If a person entering a marriage has property that he or she wishes to retain in the event of divorce, that person should keep the property in his or her own name, in a separate account, and should not mix it with assets or income earned during the marriage.

- Wives and husbands can own real estate together in different ways, including joint tenancy, tenancy in common, and, in some states, tenancy by the entirety. The different forms of title affect rights to the property upon the death of one of the parties, and also affect the rights of creditors to obtain the property in connection with a debt owed by one of the parties.

- If both husband and wife sign a joint tax return, both are generally liable for any unpaid taxes. However, if one spouse hides income and does not pay taxes on it, the other spouse may be able to avoid liability for the unpaid tax on the grounds that he or she is an "innocent spouse."

CHILDREN

This section begins by examining the decision to have children, and goes on to discuss the rights and responsibilities of parents and children, along with issues relating to adoption and paternity.

The Decision to Have Children

Q. Who makes the decision to become a parent?

A. In the 1973 case *Roe v. Wade,* the Supreme Court held that the decision to have a child is very personal and is protected by the right to privacy under the U.S. Constitution. This means that individuals who wish to have a child cannot be barred from doing so (unless perhaps they are incarcerated). Individuals who do not wish to have a child have a legal right to obtain and use contraceptives.

Q. What if one spouse wants children and the other does not?

A. If one person in a marriage wants a child and the other does not, the spouses' disagreement could be the basis for a divorce. (Divorce options will be discussed later in this chapter.)

Beyond divorce, remedies are limited. The courts cannot force a woman to become pregnant, nor compel a man to make his wife pregnant. Similarly, a court cannot force a pregnant woman to terminate her pregnancy, nor can the law require a wife to obtain her husband's permission for an abortion.

Abortion

Q. What is the current status of abortion law?

A. As of early 2008, women have the constitutional right to an abortion. Some regulation and restriction of abortion is permitted, provided there is no "undue burden" on a female's right to privacy. For further information on abortion rights and restrictions, see the discussion in Chapter 4, "Health-Care Law."

Childbirth

Q. Are there any rules prohibiting parents from giving birth to their children at home?

A. No. Generally, at-home births are an option for parents. However, the mother should obtain good prenatal care, and should ensure that her health-care provider believes the delivery will not pose significant risks to her or her child. Some states allow nurse-midwives to practice only at hospitals or under the direct supervision of a physician. Other states allow nurse-midwives to deliver children at the parents' home or at a birthing center. If you are considering this option, you should consult with your health-care provider in order to ensure that your birthing option is both legal and, more importantly, safe.

Q. If the delivery takes place at a hospital, may the father or a sibling be present?

A. Most hospitals permit the father of a child to be present at the child's birth. Hospitals often prefer that the father and mother undergo some prenatal training before the delivery. Couples should check with their hospitals about other rules, and about whether siblings are allowed in the delivery room.

Rights and Responsibilities of Parents

Q. What are the rights of parents?

A. Parents have the right to direct the care, control, and upbringing of their children for as long as the children are minors. This gives parents the power to make various decisions on behalf of their children, including where to live, what school to attend, what religion to follow, and what medical treatment to obtain. Only in life-threatening or extreme situations will the courts step in to overrule the parents' decisions. For example, if a child might die without medical care that his or her parents refuse to provide, a judge may make the child a ward of the state and order that the care be provided. Parents have been prosecuted for withholding medical treatment from seriously ill children, even when they acted in accordance with their religious beliefs.

There may be certain medical procedures that the law allows "mature minors" to elect for themselves, even if their parents do not consent. For example, parents have no absolute veto power over a minor's decision to use contraceptives or to obtain an abortion. In addition, some states allow children of a certain age to seek mental health treatment or treatment for venereal disease without notifying their parents.

Parents also have the legal authority to control their children's behavior and social lives. Parents may discipline or punish their children appropriately. They may not, however, use cruel methods or excessive force, as this would constitute child abuse.

Q. Can parental rights be terminated?

A. Yes. A parent's rights can be terminated if a parent is unfit or has abused or abandoned a child. For more information on terminating parental rights, see the discussion on abuse and neglect laws.

Q. What is the definition of "unfit parent"?

A. Parental unfitness is determined by state law. Generally, an **unfit parent** is one who has failed to have regular contact with a child or to contribute to his or her support. A parent is also unfit if he or she has been abusive or has otherwise failed to provide adequate care for the child.

Q. What are the legal rights of children?

A. Children have a unique legal status. The law defines children as unmarried persons under the age of majority—usually eighteen—who have not left home to support themselves. The law protects children from abuse and neglect. It also entitles them to the protection of the state. Children may be removed from their home if removal is necessary to ensure them a safe, supportive environment. This removal may be temporary or permanent.

Children have a right to be supported by their parents. At minimum, this means that parents must provide food, shelter, clothing, medical care, and education.

The law allows children to sue, though in most instances an adult legal representative must initiate the lawsuit. This representative is often referred to as a **guardian ad litem** or **next friend.**

Q. What are the rights of children who are accused of committing crimes?

A. Children accused of committing crimes are subject to the juvenile courts of the state in which the crime was committed, rather than the regular criminal justice system. Juvenile courts provide children with only some of the due process safeguards that adults receive. In return, juvenile courts have more freedom to deal with juveniles in an effort to rehabilitate them. See Chapter 2, "How the Legal System Works," for a discussion of juvenile courts.

▶ **MONEY EARNED OR INHERITED BY CHILDREN**

Generally, parents do not have unlimited control over their child's money. If a child receives money from earnings, an inheritance, or a personal injury case, that money must be used for the child's benefit. If a child has substantial funds, some states will appoint a guardian under court supervision. Usually the guardians of a child's money will be his or her parents, unless the court appoints someone else to do the job. The parents are legally required to manage the money properly and to use it for their child's needs.

Q. How long do parents' legal obligations to their children continue?

A. Parents are legally responsible for their children until they reach the age of majority (usually eighteen), marry, or leave home to support themselves. In some states, divorced parents may be obliged to pay for a child's college or trade school education. In addition, a parent's duty to support a disabled child might continue for the child's entire life.

Q. Are parents financially responsible for their children's actions?

A. On this point, the law varies from state to state. In some states, parents have no financial responsibilities for damages resulting from their child's actions. In others, parents are financially responsible for damage caused by their children, but the state may place limits on the amount of liability. If damages exceed the applicable state limit, the child could be sued personally; if the child has assets, those assets could be seized to satisfy the judgment. In some states, the law provides that if parents know or should have known their child has a proclivity toward violent or malicious behavior, the parents may be required to take reasonable steps to control the child or give warning to persons whom the child might harm.

Generally, if a child has an auto accident while driving a parent's car, the parent's auto insurance policy will cover any losses to the same extent it would if the parent had been driving the car (although parents usually have to pay higher insurance premiums to cover young drivers).

▶ THE DUTIES OF ADULT CHILDREN TO THEIR PARENTS

In most states, adult children have no responsibilities toward their parents and their parents have no duties toward them. In some states, however, children must support parents who would otherwise be on welfare. In some cases, children may also be required to contribute to the support of parents in a state hospital or mental institution. In such circumstances, a child's ability to pay—not the actual cost of the care—usually determines how much he or she must contribute. Some courts will allow children to avoid paying support if they can show that the parents did not care for them when they were underage.

Adoption

Q. How does one adopt a child?

A. Adoption laws vary. For a minor child who is not related to the adoptive parent or parents, there are generally two types of adoptions: agency adoptions and private or independent adoptions.

Q. What is an agency adoption?

A. As the name implies, in an **agency adoption** the parents work through a state-licensed agency. The agency often supervises the care of biological mothers who are willing to have their children adopted by others, and it assists in the placement of children after birth. Some agencies have long waiting lists of would-be parents. Some agencies specialize in placing children who are born in foreign countries.

Q. What is a private adoption?

A. **Private adoptions** bypass the use of agencies, and may bypass long waiting lists as well. The process begins when people wishing to adopt contact a lawyer who specializes in adoptions. The lawyer may work with physicians who are aware of women willing to give up children for adoption. Sometimes would-be parents will place ads in newspapers seeking women who are willing to place their babies for adoption.

In most states, adoptive parents are allowed to pay a biological mother's medical expenses and certain other costs during the pregnancy. But adoptive parents are not allowed to pay the biological mother specifically to give up the child. The law treats this as a black-market adoption—in other words, as the buying and selling of children—and it is a crime in every state.

Q. Do I need a lawyer when I am adopting?

A. No, but it may be a good idea. Assuming there are no complications with the adoption, you can likely do the required paperwork on your own or with the help of an adoption agency. However, if the adoption is complicated—for example, if you are adopting from another country—then having a lawyer may help tremendously.

Q. Is court approval necessary for an adoption?

A. Yes. Court approval is needed for both agency and private adoptions. Many states also require that the adoptive parents be screened and approved by a social service agency.

Q. Can a biological mother revoke her consent to adoption?

A. Yes, but there are limits on her right to revoke consent. In most states, a biological mother who initially consents to a child's adoption before birth may revoke that consent after birth. In other words, the mother's consent is usually not final until a certain period of time after the birth takes place. In most states, that time period is relatively short, such as two to eight days. If a biological mother consents to adoption within a specified period of time after the child's birth, the law makes it extremely difficult for her to revoke her consent. Generally, following an after-birth consent, a biological mother may revoke her consent only if she can show that there was fraud or duress. Fraud could be found if the adoption agency or lawyer lied to the biological mother about the consequences of what she was doing. Duress might exist if a person at the adoption agency threatened the biological mother with humiliation if she did not sign. A biological mother's change of heart is not normally sufficient grounds for revoking an after-birth adoption consent.

Q. Is the biological father's consent necessary?

A. Generally, yes—if the biological father's identity is known, and if he does not abandon his parental rights. The biological father should be notified of the birth and pending adoption so that he may consent or object. If the father's identity is not known, the adoption may proceed without his consent. If a biological father is not notified, he may later contest the adoption if he acts within a certain period of time after the child's birth or adoption (normally one to six months).

Q. If biological parents give up a child for adoption, what rights and obligations do they retain?

A. In general, they lose all rights and have no obligations. They have no right of contact with the child, and cannot obtain information about the child. And they have no obligation to support the child.

▶ **RELATED ADOPTION**

A **related adoption** is one in which a child's relatives, such as grandparents or an aunt and uncle, formally adopt a child as their own. This might occur if the child's biological parents are deceased or are otherwise unable to care for the child.

Q. What is the legal status of an adopted child?

A. An adopted child has exactly the same rights as a biological child. Similarly, adoptive parents have the same obligations to the child as they would to a biological child.

Q. What is a stepparent adoption?

A. A **stepparent adoption** is one in which a child's biological parent marries someone who wishes to adopt the biological parent's child, and is able to do so because the other biological parent consents or because consent is unnecessary—for example, if the other parent has died or has had parental rights terminated. If the other biological parent does not consent to the adoption of the child, the child cannot be adopted by the stepparent unless a court first finds that the biological parent is unfit. If the biological parent is found unfit, his or her parental rights are terminated, and the child can then be adopted. For more information on terminating parental rights, see the section on abuse and neglect laws later in this chapter.

Q. What happens if a stepparent adopts the child of his or her spouse, and they later divorce?

A. A divorce does not affect the legality of the adoption. The stepparent continues to have all the rights and responsibilities of a biological parent, including a right to seek custody or visitation and a duty to support the child.

Q. Can a single person adopt a child?

A. Yes. Many states allow single persons to adopt, although some agencies strongly prefer to place a child with a married couple. Other agencies—particularly those dealing with

---

▶ OPEN ADOPTION

An **open adoption** is one in which the adoptive parents agree to let the biological parent or parents have some continued contact with the child. Such contact might include periodic visits or an exchange of pictures and other information between the adoptive family and the biological parent or parents. The nature of the contact is often specified in the adoption agreement. Open adoptions are a relatively new phenomenon, and in many states the law is still developing.

---

children who might be hard to place—might be more willing to place a child with a single person. Single-parent adoptions are usually possible in the case of private adoptions.

Q. Can lesbian or gay couples adopt a child?

A. Yes, in some states including New York and California, gay and lesbian couples are able to adopt a child.

Q. Who has access to adoption records?

A. In most states, court adoption records are sealed and can only be opened by court order, although a few states allow all adopted children access to their adoption records. Procedures and standards for opening records vary by state. Increasingly, states require that certain nonidentifying information, such as the medical history of the biological family, be made available to the adoptive parents at the time of adoption. Some states also have registries in which parties to the adoption can agree to a later exchange of information, including names and addresses.

Paternity

Q. In cases involving traditional conception, how is paternity determined?

A. Most contested paternity issues are decided these days by DNA testing, which is the testing of a person's genetic material. Throughout most of the twentieth century, blood tests could prove that a man was *not* the father of a child, but could not affirmatively prove that he *was* the father. However, modern DNA tests are nearly 100 percent accurate in proving or disproving paternity.

Q. May an unmarried woman legally force the father of her baby to support the child?

A. Yes. Both parents, married or not, have a duty to support their child. If the father admits paternity, the father often will be asked to sign an **affidavit** (a legal statement) to that effect. Then, if necessary, it will be easier to force the father to help support his child. If he does not admit to being the father, the mother may file a paternity suit against him. If the suit succeeds, the court will require the father to provide support.

▶ **INTERNATIONAL ADOPTION**

When adopting a child from a foreign country, you enter into a private legal matter with a foreign court. Therefore, you must comply with the rules of that foreign court. United States law and the protections of U.S. courts do not apply to an individual undertaking a foreign adoption.

Adoptive parents must comply with U.S. immigration law and applicable state law when returning to the United States with an adopted child. As of January 2008, in most cases a U.S. court will recognize a foreign adoption decree. However, the legality of such an adoption can be challenged if an adoption decree was not entered. If this is the case, you can ask a state court to let you "readopt" the child. This will protect you and the child, as well as further safeguard the legal status of the adoption.

If you are interested in adopting a child from a foreign country, you should always use a licensed and reputable adoption agency or attorney. As the number of adoptions from overseas has increased, so has the number of fraudulent adoption services. To avoid being victimized, contact your state's department of children and family services or a local bar association. Because this is a rapidly changing area of the law, ensuring that you have the best advocates working on your behalf can prevent lost time, money, and possible heartache.

Often the court will also require the father to pay a portion of the mother's pregnancy and childbirth expenses.

Q. If paternity is established, how much will the father have to pay in support?

A. Unwed parents must support their children to the same extent as married or divorced parents. Child support guidelines, which have been enacted in all states, set forth the amount of required support. A more detailed discussion of child support obligations appears later in this chapter.

Q. What happens if a father refuses to pay support?

A. If a father refuses to support his child, a court may garnish his wages, seize his property or bank accounts, revoke his driver's license or professional license, and perhaps even send him to jail.

Q. Can a father be required to visit with his child?

A. Generally, neither parent can be required to visit with a child.

Q. What are a husband's legal options if his wife bears a child that is not his?

A. If a woman is married, the law presumes that her husband is the father of her child, and the husband must support the child unless he can prove in court that he is not the father. Some states will not allow a husband to disprove the paternity of a child born during the marriage. If a state does allow a husband to disprove paternity, the law may establish a certain time period after birth (such as two years) within which the husband must do so.

Q. May the father of a child whose mother is married to another person file suit to establish paternity of the child?

A. The law varies from state to state. Some states allow a man to file suit to prove paternity of a child born to a woman who is married to someone else. The man who filed suit might then be able to obtain visitation—or, in unusual circumstances, obtain custody. Other states prohibit such suits and automatically presume that the woman's husband is the father.

Q. Do medically assisted pregnancies affect parental rights?

A. As medical science advances, there are a variety of ways in which individuals can become parents through medical assistance, including artificial insemination and in vitro fertilization. These types of medical procedures have legal implications that vary by state. Generally, however, if both husband and wife consent to artificial insemination or in vitro fertilization, the rights and duties of the husband, the wife, and the child will be the same as if the child had been naturally conceived.

Q. What are some types of medically assisted pregnancies?

A. There are many types of medically assisted pregnancies, including those that involve a donor egg, a donor sperm, or another woman carrying a couple's child. When a woman agrees to bear a child for someone else, a process known as **surrogate motherhood,** she may or may not receive payment for her services. Surrogate pregnancies usually occur when a woman cannot conceive or carry a child to term. In most cases, through artificial insemination, the husband or significant other's sperm fertilizes an egg belonging to either the woman or the surrogate mother. The husband or significant other is thus the biological father of the child. The surrogate mother agrees to give up all parental rights at birth, and the wife or significant other of the biological father legally adopts the child. Some states permit surrogate parenting arrangements; others prohibit them. If you are considering this option, it is important that you consult with an attorney experienced in this area who can discuss these issues with you and draft any relevant documents or agreements.

Abuse and Neglect Laws

Q. What is child neglect?

A. **Child neglect** or **child endangerment** occurs when parents or legal guardians willfully fail to supply a child with basic necessities, including food, shelter, clothes, medical treatment, and supervision.

Q. What persons and what types of actions are covered by child abuse laws?

A. It is a crime for adults to abuse children in their care. The term "adult" refers to parents, foster parents, legal guardians, other adults in the home, family members, and babysitters. In disciplining children, supervising adults may not impose unreasonable physical punishment. For example, adults may not beat children so severely that they require medical treatment. Child abuse laws prohibit not only physical abuse (such as beatings or starvation), but also other types of cruelty, such as subjecting a child to extreme humiliation.

Moreover, a person may be guilty of child abuse that he or she did not personally com-

> ### ▶ TAKING CHILDREN AWAY FROM THEIR PARENTS
>
> Even if a criminal case is not brought, the state may remove children from the custody of their parents if there is reason to believe the parents are physically, sexually, or emotionally abusing one or more of the children. The state may also remove the children if the parents are unable or unwilling to provide adequate care, supervision, or support.

mit if that person had legal responsibility for the child and failed to protect the child from an abuser.

Q. How does one report a suspected case of child abuse?

A. Many states sponsor toll-free numbers that people can call to report instances of child abuse. Calls can also be made to the state or county department that handles human services or children's issues. If an emergency exists, call the police.

Q. If welfare officials or the court take children away from their parents, is the removal temporary or permanent?

A. The goal is usually to reunite the family after correcting the problems that led to the removal. However, this is not always possible. Among the factors a court will consider are the severity and frequency of the parents' deficiency or bad conduct, the efforts of the parents to correct the situation, and the amount of time that correcting the situation would

> ▶ **THE DUTY TO REPORT NEGLECT AND ABUSE**
>
> Laws require a wide range of people who have contact with children to report suspected child abuse or neglect. Such people include doctors, nurses, teachers, social workers, and child care providers. A person who is required to report suspected neglect or abuse may face civil or criminal penalties for failure to do so. In addition, states often encourage the reporting of suspected abuse by others, such as neighbors and family members, through special hotlines. In most states, persons who make reports of abuse are shielded from defamation suits by the accused parents if the reports are made in good faith. Most states keep central lists of suspected child abuse cases. This helps identify parents who, for example, take their children to different hospitals in order to conceal evidence that they have repeatedly abused them.

take. For example, if the parents make little or no effort to improve the child's care or if the abuse is unusually severe, then the state may ask a court to terminate all parental rights. If this happens, the legal bonds between parents and children may be completely and permanently severed, and another family may adopt the child.

REMEMBER THIS

- As of early 2008, women still have a right under the U.S. Constitution to terminate a pregnancy. States may require a waiting period for an abortion, and may require the consent of a parent or a judge before a minor can obtain an abortion.

- In some states, parents can be held financially liable for the "willful or malicious" acts of their children.

- In order for a child to be adopted, his or her natural parent(s) must be deceased, give consent, be found unfit, or be unable to be located. Generally, a person challenging an adoption that has already taken

place must file a legal action very soon after the adoption, or his or her rights to challenge the adoption will be lost.

- Married and unmarried parents owe a duty of support to their children.

- It is an offense for parents and guardians to willfully fail to meet a child's basic needs.

DOMESTIC VIOLENCE

Q. What kinds of actions constitute domestic violence?

A. Domestic violence statutes in most states apply not only to physical attacks, but also to other types of conduct, including emotional and verbal abuse and intimidation. Examples of conduct that could be considered domestic violence include creating a disturbance at a spouse's place of work, making harassing telephone calls, stalking, and threatening a spouse or family member (even if the threat is not carried out). Domestic violence isn't necessarily about violence—more often than not, it is about power and control.

Q. What are the legal remedies for domestic violence?

A. There are several remedies. Domestic violence may constitute a criminal act (either the crime of domestic violence itself, or the crimes of battery and assault). In most jurisdictions, a successful criminal prosecution can result in probation, a fine, or even jail time. Courts can also issue a protective order, ordering the alleged abuser to stop abusing or harassing someone. In addition, the order will often require the abuser to stay away from the abused person, the person's home, or the person's place of work. If the abuser continues to abuse the person protected by the order, the abuser can be charged with a criminal violation of the order in addition to being charged with other criminal offenses.

Q. Who can be protected by an order of protection?

A. An order of protection can cover anyone being victimized by a domestic abuser. Most state domestic violence laws have expanded to include many types of relationships, including marriages, parent-child relationships, relationships between dating couples, same-sex couples, siblings, in-laws, and numerous other types of intimate associations.

Q. If I seek a protective order, will I have to face my abuser in court?

A. Probably not. In cases involving protective orders, most states provide for immediate **ex parte** hearings—that is, hearings held without notice to the other party. This means that you may be able to obtain an order with-

out facing your abuser. Afterwards, the court will likely hold a full hearing which the abuser may attend. Most courtrooms are staffed with sheriffs and deputies, but if you think your safety will be threatened during a court hearing, talk to a court official or your attorney before the hearing.

Q. Do protective orders actually work?

A. Sometimes. Studies have shown that issuing a protective order or arresting a person who commits an act of domestic violence does reduce future incidents of domestic violence. When perpetrators of domestic violence see that the police and the court system treat domestic violence seriously, many may be deterred from future violence. But orders of protection are not guarantees of protection or safety. Some individuals will not change their behavior regardless of whether a court order has been issued—and a court order might even add to their rage. The legal system cannot offer perfect protection, although it can reduce violence overall.

Q. Where does one turn for help in cases of domestic violence?

A. In a crisis situation, calling 911 or the police is a good start. Many people complain that the police do not take accusations of domestic violence seriously. But while it is true that responses may vary, police generally treat domestic violence situations seriously, and police officers nowadays receive increased levels of training about how to handle these types of cases. An increasing number of hospitals, crisis intervention programs, and social service agencies have developed programs to help victims of domestic violence. Your local state's attorney or district attorney may also be able to help. Agencies offering help in cases of domestic violence might be found in the yellow pages under such headings as "domestic violence intervention," "human services organizations," or "crisis intervention."

REMEMBER THIS

- Domestic violence isn't necessarily about violence—more often than not it is about power and control.

- An order of protection can cover virtually anyone being victimized by a domestic abuser.

- Although orders of protection aren't perfect, they can help reduce violence.

- If you think your safety is in immediate danger, call 911 without hesitation.

SEPARATION, ANNULMENT, AND DIVORCE

Sometimes marriages do not succeed. In some cases, despite the best efforts of husband and wife, and perhaps despite the help of counselors and clergy, there is nothing to do but end the relationship. This often means that assets have to be divided and custody arrangements made. Sometimes people can work it out between themselves; sometimes people just can't agree, and the law must step in to help them. In these cases, just as the state was involved in creating the marriage, it also becomes involved in dissolving it.

Q. I think my marriage is over. What are my legal options?

A. Deciding that a marriage is over is difficult for any couple. However, even when you've decided to end your marriage, your decision-making responsibilities do not end. You must choose between several different legal options, including separation, annulment, and divorce. Each of these topics is discussed below. Depending on your situation, major differences may exist between the three options, including differences relating to property division, insurance rights, and tax implications. It is likely best for you and your spouse to consult an attorney to discuss which option is best.

Separation and Separate Maintenance

Q. What is a legal separation?

A. Legal separation allows a husband and wife to live separately, and to formalize their arrangement by a court order or written agreement. The order or agreement will specify what support, if any, one spouse will pay to the other. If the husband and wife have minor children, the agreement or court order will set forth arrangements regarding custody or visitation. Generally, a legal separation does not legally end a marriage.

A legal separation is not the same as a divorce. A separation recognizes the possibility that the couple might reunite. Its terms can be modified by the parties or the court if the couple divorces. Most important, people who are legally separated may not remarry. They must wait until a divorce is final before marrying again. When a husband and wife legally separate, they no longer accumulate community or marital property. Any property acquired after the legal separation will be considered each partner's separate or nonmarital property.

Q. Does a person have to be legally separated before obtaining a divorce?

A. No. In most states, a couple can proceed straight to a divorce without first seeking a legal separation. While waiting for the divorce, the couple might live separately (without a formal agreement); or, in some states, they could even live together pending the final divorce. A few states do require a period of separation before a divorce can be granted.

Q. Is there an advantage to a legal separation?

A. That depends on the needs of the parties. A legal separation offers structure for the parties while they are waiting for (or considering) a divorce. If one spouse is paying support for the other spouse or for the children, the spouse receiving the support may wish to put the terms in writing. Similarly, one or both parties may want a fixed schedule establishing who will be with the children at what times. If these terms are part of a written agreement or court order, the parties know what to count on, and one party can seek enforcement in the courts if the other party does not comply. In addition, if one or both parties wish to obtain a religious divorce or annulment, a legal separation may provide a useful transition while the parties await action by the religious tribunal. After the religious annulment or divorce is granted, the legal divorce may proceed. Depending on the wishes of the parties and tenets of the religion, the legal divorce could precede the religious divorce or annulment.

Most medical plans permit a legally separated spouse to continue to be covered in a family plan without additional cost. The parties may also file joint income tax returns if they so desire.

Q. Are there any tax advantages to a legal separation?

A. Potentially, yes, depending on the support obligations of the parties. These potential tax advantages are similar to those enjoyed by divorced couples. See page 115 for a further discussion of this topic.

Q. Are there psychological advantages to a legal separation?

A. For some people, yes. Some couples want to separate, but are unsure whether they want to go through a divorce. In these cases, separation can serve as a sort of trial period—relieving immediate pressures while the husband and wife sort out what they want to do with their lives. A formal legal separation

---

▶ SEPARATION AGREEMENTS

If the terms of a separation agreement differ from what one of the parties would like them to be after the divorce, then that party should be careful about agreeing to those terms. If the parties agree to the terms of a separation agreement but cannot agree to the terms of a divorce, and if the court thinks the terms of the separation agreement have worked out reasonably well for both parties, then the court may simply order the continuation of the terms of the separation agreement in the final judgment of divorce.

may provide some structure, security, and financial advantages during the period of separation.

Annulment

Q. What is an annulment?

A. An **annulment** is a court ruling that a marriage was never valid. The most common ground for annulment is fraud or misrepresentation. For example, one person may not have disclosed to the other a prior divorce, a criminal record, an infectious disease, or an inability to engage in sex or have children. Annulment may also be granted in cases involving bigamy, incest, or marriage to an underage person.

Q. How common are annulments?

A. Annulments are uncommon because divorces are easy to obtain, and because the bases for annulment are narrower than the bases for divorce. However, one party may prefer an annulment in order to avoid some obligations that a court might impose in a divorce. Also, in a few states, spousal support that terminated because of the recipient's second marriage may be reinstated if the second marriage is annulled.

Divorce

Q. What is a divorce?

A. A **divorce** or **dissolution of marriage** is a decree by a court that a valid marriage no longer exists. It leaves both parties free to remarry. The court will award custody, divide property, and order spousal and child support.

Q. Are most divorces contested?

A. No. Although divorces may be emotionally contentious, close to 95 percent of di-

---

> ▶ **DIVORCE WITHOUT LAWYERS**
>
> Most states permit do-it-yourself divorces, sometimes referred to as **summary divorces.** The ease or difficulty of obtaining a do-it-yourself divorce depends on local laws and rules as well as the complexities of the issues involved in the divorce. In a contested case, the complexities of property division, taxes, or custody may make it advisable for both parties to seek expert legal and financial advice.

---

vorces do not involve a contested trial. Usually the parties negotiate and settle property division, spousal support, and child custody issues between themselves, often with the help of a lawyer. Sometimes parties reach an agreement by mediation, in which a trained mediator helps them identify and accommodate common interests. The parties then present their agreement to a judge. Approval is virtually automatic if the agreement is fair.

If parties are unable to agree about property, support, or child custody, they may ask the court to decide one or more of those matters. One spouse may sue the other for divorce, alleging certain faults or offenses by the defendant. But this has become far less common than it once was. Most divorces now are no-fault divorces.

Q. It's no one's fault that our marriage is ending. Can we still get a divorce?

A. Yes. Your situation calls for a no-fault divorce. A **no-fault divorce** is one in which neither person blames the other for the breakdown of the marriage. There are no accusations, and no need to prove guilt or cause. Common bases for no-fault divorces include **irreconcilable differences** and **irretrievable marriage breakdown.** As those terms imply, the marriage is considered over, but the court and the relevant legal documents make no effort to assign blame. Another common basis for no-fault divorce is the parties living separately for a certain period of time, such as for six months or a year, with the intent that the separation be permanent.

Q. Why does the law provide for no-fault divorces?

A. No-fault divorce is considered a relatively nonabrasive and practical way to end a marriage. The laws of no-fault divorce recognize that human relationships are complex, and that it is difficult to trace the breakdown of a marriage solely to the actions of one person. However, some critics of no-fault divorces

fear that an economically dependent spouse may not be adequately protected if the other spouse can easily obtain a divorce.

All states offer some form of no-fault divorce, but many states also retain fault-based grounds as an alternative way of obtaining a divorce. Some spouses want the emotional release of proving fault on the part of their mates. However, courts are not very good forums for dealing with personal issues, and usually the accuser ends up less satisfied than he or she expected.

Q. What are the grounds for obtaining a divorce based on fault?

A. Permissible grounds for **fault-based divorce** vary somewhat from state to state. Many states permit divorce in cases involving adultery, physical cruelty, mental cruelty, attempted murder, desertion, habitual drunkenness, use of addictive drugs, insanity, impotence, or infection of one's spouse with venereal disease.

▶ WHAT'S IN A NAME?

When a woman divorces, she may either resume her maiden name or keep her married name. As more and more men change their names when they get married, this option is increasingly available to both genders. If you decide to change your legal name because of a marriage, divorce, or for other reasons, you should notify government agencies and private companies that have records of your name. This includes the Internal Revenue Service, the Social Security Administration, the Passport Agency (within the U.S. State Department), the post office, state tax agencies, the driver's license bureau, the voter registration bureau, professional licensing agencies, professional societies, unions, mortgage companies, banks, charge card companies, utility companies, magazines, newspapers, dentists, and schools and colleges that you attended or that your children attend. It can be useful, though generally it is not necessary, for a divorce decree to state that a party will resume his or her unmarried name.

Q. What's the difference between a fault-based and a no-fault divorce?

A. It depends on the state. In a few states, fault may be taken into consideration when the court divides property and sets levels of spousal support, even if the divorce is granted on no-fault grounds. In other states, fault is not supposed to be considered in these situations. In some states, fault will be considered only if it directly causes waste or dissipation of marital assets. In some states, a spouse who commits adultery may not be able to receive spousal support. In cases involving child custody, fault is not supposed to be considered unless that fault harmed the child. For example, a discreet extramarital affair would not normally be taken into account by a court when making custody decisions. But an affair or series of affairs that repeatedly placed the child in stressful situations would likely be something the court would consider.

Property

Q. In divorce cases, how often do judges decide who gets what?

A. Judges rule on major contested issues in only a relatively small number of cases. Instead, the parties—often with help from lawyers—usually reach an agreement between themselves that they present to a judge for approval. If the agreement is fair, approval is usually granted after a short hearing.

Q. How do judges decide disputed property issues?

A. Laws vary by state. As a starting point, many states allow parties to keep their **nonmarital** or **separate property.** Nonmarital property includes property that a spouse brought into the marriage and kept in his or her own name during the marriage. It also includes inheritances received and kept separate during the marriage. It also may include

---

▶ **CHECKLIST: WHAT TO REMEMBER WHEN GOING THROUGH A DIVORCE**

- **Options.** Make sure you have assessed all of your options. Is this a marriage that can be saved through counseling? Does annulment or a separation make more sense?

- **Come to an agreement.** If at all possible, you and your spouse should work with an attorney or mediator to come to an agreement regarding the divorce and any support or financial issues.

- **Court order.** Regardless of whether you and your spouse can reach an agreement, you will need to obtain a court order officially recognizing the end of the marriage. Comply with the order regarding any property settlements, support obligations, and custody arrangements.

- **Name.** If either party is changing their name, be sure to notify all necessary government agencies and private companies.

> ▶ **SETTLEMENTS AND THE LAW**
>
> The settlement reached by the parties may be influenced by the rules of law that a judge would use in court to decide the case. If it is predictable that a matter would be decided in a certain way by a judge, it is seldom worth taking the issue to trial. In many cases, the cost of pursuing a disputed property issue at trial will exceed the possible monetary gain of a victory in court.

gifts to just one spouse during the marriage. Some states permit division of separate as well as marital property when parties divorce, but the origin of the property is considered when deciding who receives it. After allocating separate property, the court divides marital or community property.

Q. What property will the judge divide?

A. Judges usually divide marital or community property. **Marital** or **community property** is defined somewhat differently by different states, but it generally includes property and income acquired during the marriage. Wages earned during the marriage usually would be considered marital property, as would a home or furniture purchased during the marriage with marital earnings or assets.

Q. What if the property obtained during the marriage is in the name of one party only?

A. Such property will usually be considered marital property if it was paid for with marital funds, such as wages. For example, if a wife buys a car during the marriage and pays for it with her wages, the car is marital property, even though it is in her name only. A pension is also usually considered marital property, even though it may have been earned during the marriage by the labor of only one spouse. If a pension was completely earned before the marriage, it probably would be considered nonmarital or separate property. Marital or community property can be divided by the court between the parties. If real property is held in the name of only one spouse, there may be legal presumptions affecting who has the burden of proof regarding ownership of the property.

Q. How should a husband or wife keep nonmarital property separate, and thus less likely to be lost in a divorce?

A. See page 92 for further discussion about maintaining the integrity of separate property. It is important to note that property distribution laws are very complicated, and can vary widely between states; understanding them usually requires a lawyer's help.

Q. How do courts divide marital or community property?

A. Again, the answer varies from state to state. A few states, such as California, take a rather simple approach: they believe that property should be divided equally. In these states, the net value of all marital property and debt will be divided fifty-fifty, unless the husband and wife have a premarital agreement stating otherwise. However, most states apply a concept known as equitable distribution.

Q. What is equitable distribution?

A. **Equitable distribution** is the division of marital property by a court in a way that it deems valid, just, and equitable. States applying principles of equitable distribution view marriage as a shared enterprise in which both spouses usually contribute significantly to the acquisition and preservation of property. The division of property may be fifty-fifty, sixty-forty, seventy-thirty, or whatever the court deems appropriate. In some cases, one spouse may even receive all of the property, with nothing awarded to the other, though such situations are very unusual. The percentage to which each party is entitled may vary from one type of asset to another.

In cases involving equitable distribution, courts consider a variety of factors and need not weigh the factors equally. This gives more discretion to the judge and allows more consideration of the financial situation of both spouses after the divorce. However, it also makes the resolution of property issues less predictable. There are several factors courts consider when applying principles of equitable distribution:

Nonmarital Property

If one spouse has significantly more non-marital property than the other, the court may award more marital property to the less-wealthy spouse.

Earning Power

If one spouse has more earning power than the other, the court may award more marital property to the spouse with less earning power.

Who Earned the Property

When awarding property, often courts will favor the party who worked hard to acquire or maintain the property.

Services as a Homemaker

Courts recognize that keeping a home and raising children is hard work, and that homemaking services often enable the spouse working outside the home to earn more money. Thus, provision of homemaking services is a factor that weighs in favor of the homemaker. Applying a related concept, some courts also consider whether one spouse's earning capacity was impaired because he or she worked as a homemaker. If this was the case, the court might treat the homemaker-spouse more favorably.

Waste and Dissipation

If one spouse wasted money during the marriage, it could count against him or her when it comes time to divide property. This factor is sometimes known as **economic fault,** and may be considered even by courts that do not consider other kinds of fault. Examples of economic fault include excessive spending and the diversion of money due to an addiction.

Fault

Some states will take into consideration the issue of noneconomic fault, as in the case of spousal abuse or marital infidelity, but most states do not consider it relevant to property division.

Duration of Marriage

A longer marriage may weigh in favor of a larger property award to the spouse with less wealth or earning power.

Age and Health of the Parties

If one spouse is in poor health or is significantly older than the other, the court may award a larger percentage of property to the sicker or older spouse.

Q. What if the parties have more debt than assets?

A. In that situation, the court (or the parties by agreement) will divide whatever property

▶ WHO GETS THE HOUSE?

The decision of who gets the house depends on the facts of each case. If the parties have minor children and can afford to keep their house, the law usually favors awarding the house to the spouse who will have custody of the children most of the time. If the parties cannot afford to keep the house, it may be sold and the proceeds divided (or perhaps given to one party). In some cases, there is a middle-ground approach: The spouse who has primary custody of the children will have a right to live in the house for a certain number of years. At the end of that time, that spouse will buy out the other spouse's interest or sell the house and divide the proceeds.

the parties have, and will then allocate to each party the responsibility for paying off particular debts.

Alimony/Maintenance

Q. What is alimony?

A. **Alimony,** also known as **maintenance** or **spousal support,** is money paid from one spouse to another for day-to-day support. Sometimes alimony can also be used to repay debts.

Q. When do courts award alimony?

A. A court will order alimony on the basis of one spouse's need and the other spouse's ability to pay. Although most alimony payments are made from men to women, it is possible that a woman could be required to pay support to her economically dependent husband. Alimony is awarded less often now than it was in the past, because today there are more two-income couples and fewer marriages in which one person is financially dependent on the other.

Q. Does alimony continue indefinitely?

A. That depends on the purpose behind the alimony award and the positions of the parties. There are different types of support, including rehabilitative, permanent, and reimbursement support.

Q. What is rehabilitative support?

A. A common type of spousal support is **rehabilitative support.** Its purpose is to enable education or job training, so that a spouse who was financially dependent or disadvantaged during marriage can become self-supporting. Rehabilitative support is designed to help make up for opportunities lost by a spouse who left a job or did not pursue a career in order to help the other spouse's career or to assume family duties. It may also be awarded to a spouse who worked outside the home during the marriage, but sacrificed his or her career development because of family priorities. Rehabilitative support is usually awarded only for a limited time.

Q. What is permanent support?

A. Courts award **permanent spousal support** to provide money for a spouse who cannot become economically independent or maintain a lifestyle that the court considers appropriate given the resources of the parties. A common reason for ordering permanent maintenance is that the recipient, because of advanced age or chronic illness, will never be able to maintain a reasonable standard of living without it. Some courts will order that permanent support be paid to a spouse who, although working, will never have earning power approaching that of the more prosperous spouse. When deciding the amount of permanent support, courts often use the same criteria as for dividing property.

Although this type of support is called permanent support, the level of support can change or cease if the ability of the payer or the needs of the recipient change significantly. For example, support generally ceases if the recipient remarries or begins to live with someone else.

Q. If one spouse supports the other through graduate or professional school, does the supporting spouse have a right to be compensated for increasing the earning capacity of the other spouse?

A. Some courts offer compensation for parties who helped to put a spouse through school. The supporting spouse may have expected that both parties would benefit from

the educated spouse's enhanced earning capacity, but the marriage ended before any material benefits were earned. In some states, a spouse's professional license or other manifestation of enhanced earnings may be treated as a valuable asset if acquired during the marriage.

The supporting spouse may not need rehabilitation if he or she has worked during the entire marriage, and if there is no significant property to be distributed because marital resources were devoted to funding the other spouse's educational effort. In these types of cases, courts may award compensation to the supporting spouse, usually in the form of periodic payments. The amount paid may be based upon the contributions of the supporting spouse to the educational expenses and general support of the spouse who leaves the marriage with an advanced degree. In some states, support also may be based upon a portion of the increased earnings of the educated spouse. The courts may reduce or terminate such payments if the expected increased earnings do not occur, but the payments do not cease upon remarriage of the recipient. This type of payment is often called **reimbursement alimony** or **alimony in gross.**

Q. Are there tax consequences to making or receiving alimony or support payments?

A. Yes, potentially. If one spouse is paying support for the other, the payer can deduct that money from his or her income for tax purposes. The payment will then be considered taxable income to the recipient. If the payer is in a higher tax bracket than the recipient, this will reduce the couple's combined tax liability. In any case, it will reduce the payer's taxes and raise the recipient's.

> ▶ **HEALTH INSURANCE AFTER DIVORCE**

Passed in the 1980s, a federal law known as COBRA requires most employer-sponsored group health plans to offer divorced spouses of covered workers continued coverage at group rates for eighteen months. The divorced spouse must pay for the coverage, and the person seeking coverage must request coverage soon after the divorce is final.

Q. What if a couple is separated but not yet formally divorced, and one spouse is making support payments to the other? Are there tax consequences to this arrangement?

A. Yes, if the parties are legally separated by written agreement or court order. The deduction is not available for those who have an informal separation.

Q. Why would a spouse agree to receive support if the arrangement increases his or her taxes and provides a tax advantage to the other spouse?

A. Because the tax advantage to the payer is what encourages the payment of support in the first place, and it may ultimately motivate the payer to provide a greater amount of support. This makes the arrangement worth the recipient's while, despite his or her increased tax bill. Some couples and their lawyers may calculate a tentative amount of support that would be paid if the payer enjoyed no tax benefit. Then they calculate the potential tax benefit involved if the payer takes a deduction and the recipient counts the support as income. They then increase the level of support to whatever amount allows both parties to share equally in the value of the tax savings. This arrangement benefits both parties: the increased support usually exceeds the added taxes the recipient will pay, and because of the tax savings, the payer will have fewer out-of-pocket expenses for that year.

Custody

Q. What is child custody?

A. Child **custody** is the right and duty to care for a minor child on a day-to-day basis

and to make major decisions about the child. In sole custody arrangements, one parent takes care of the child most of the time and makes major decisions about the child. In joint custody arrangements, both parents share in making major decisions, and both parents also might spend substantial amounts of time with the child. Different states may use different terms (e.g., **timeshare, possession,** or **conservatorship**) to refer to custody. Some states refer to time spent with children as **physical custody** and to decision-making authority as **legal custody.** A court need not award physical custody and legal custody the same way. In other words, a court might award physical custody to one parent (with the other receiving visitation rights) but decide that decision-making authority (i.e., legal custody) is to be shared jointly by both parents. A more extensive description of these custody issues is provided below.

Q. How do courts decide custody?

A. If the parents cannot agree on a custody arrangement for their child, the court decides custody according to the **best interest of the child.** Determining the best interest of the child involves consideration of many factors, which may include the health and sex of the child, the primary caregiver prior to the divorce, parenting skills and willingness to care for the child, the emotional ties between child and parent, willingness to facilitate visitation by the other parent, and each parent's moral fitness.

Q. Do mothers automatically receive custody?

A. No. Under the laws of almost all states, mothers and fathers have equal rights to custody. Courts are not supposed to assume that a child is automatically better off with the mother or the father. Of course, judges, like the rest of us, are products of their background and personal experience. Some judges may have a deep-seated belief that mothers can take care of children better than fathers and that fathers have little experience in parenting. Conversely, some judges may believe that fathers are automatically better at raising boys—particularly older boys. Judges with such biases may apply these views when they decide custody cases, although they are supposed to base decisions on the facts of each case and not on automatic presumptions. As a group, judges are fair and unbiased in their decisions, and the level of bias is lower than it was in years past. Bias on the part of individual judges can be avoided if the parents are able to decide between themselves what the custody or parenting arrangements should be.

In a contested custody case, both the father and mother have an equal burden of proving to the court that obtaining custody is in the best interest of their child. A small number of states have laws providing that, if everything else is equal, the mother may be preferred; but even in those states, many fathers have succeeded in obtaining custody.

▶ INTERNATIONAL CHILD CUSTODY

When confronted with an international child custody dispute, courts in the United States treat foreign nations as sister states. This means that courts must recognize and enforce foreign-issued child custody orders that were created in a manner consistent with the procedures used by a state court. Thus, if a foreign custody order was issued before an order in the U.S., and if it meets the jurisdictional standards set forth in the Uniform Child Custody Jurisdiction and Enforcement Act (UCCJEA), then the foreign order and its contents will be recognized and enforced. In some cases, when a foreign order conflicts with an order granted in the United States, the foreign order may take priority.

An international custody order will *not* be enforced if it resulted from a foreign proceeding that violates basic principles of human rights or is contrary to the general public policy of the state. While the law varies on what constitutes a violation of human rights, in general, courts will first address whether the foreign order was issued with the same type of procedural safeguards afforded in the United States, including notice requirements and the right to legal representation.

Although it may seem odd for American courts to honor a foreign order above one granted in the United States, treating foreign countries as sister states promotes predictability and creates goodwill between U.S. states and foreign countries. This in turn increases the likelihood that a prior order issued in the United States will be honored by a foreign court. This approach also increases family stability for a child caught in an international custody dispute.

Q. What is the most important factor that courts consider when deciding custody?

A. The deciding factors will vary with the facts of each case. If one parent has a serious problem with alcoholism or mental illness, has abused the child, or has committed domestic violence, that could be the deciding factor. The court will next consider evidence relating to the child's needs and each parent's ability to meet those needs, and will award custody accordingly. Regardless of which parent has primary custody, children are usually best served when the child has continuous, meaningful contact with both parents.

Q. May a child decide where he or she wants to live?

A. The wishes of a child can be an important consideration. The weight a court ascribes to the child's wishes will depend on the child's age and maturity, and on the quality of his or her reasons for wanting to live with one parent or the other. A court is more likely to honor the preferences of an older child, although the court will want to assess the quality of his or her reasons. If a child wants to be with a parent only because that parent offers more freedom and less discipline, then a judge is not likely to honor the preference. Similarly, a child whose reasons are vague or whose answers seem coached may not have his or her preferences honored.

On the other hand, if a child expresses a good reason related to his or her own best interest—such as genuinely feeling closer to one parent—then the court will probably honor the child's preference. Although most states treat a child's wishes as only one factor among many to be considered, a few states allow a child of twelve or fourteen the "absolute right" to choose the parent with whom he or she will live, as long as the parent is fit.

Q. Will my child have to testify during the custody hearing?

A. This will depend on the facts of your case and on the age and maturity level of your child. Judges may talk to the child in the judge's chambers rather than in open court. In some jurisdictions, but not all, the mother and father's lawyers have a right to be present during the judge's interview of the child, although a judge may ask the lawyers to waive that right. In some cases, the judge may appoint a mental health professional, such as a psychiatrist, psychologist, or social worker, to talk to the child and report to the court.

Q. If a parent has a sexual relationship outside of marriage, how does that affect a court's custody decision?

A. In most states, affairs or nonmarital sexual relations are not a factor in custody decisions, unless it can be shown that the relationship has harmed the child. For example, a discreet affair that took place during the parents' marriage might not be considered significant by the court. Similarly, if a divorced parent lives with a person to whom he or she is not married, the live-in relationship may not by itself factor significantly into the court's custody decision, though the quality of the relationship between the child and the live-in partner may be considered.

If the parent's nonmarital sexual relationship or relationships have placed the child in embarrassing situations or caused significant, provable stress to the child, then those relationship(s) would be a negative factor considered by the court when awarding custody. In a few states, courts are inclined to assume that a parent's nonmarital sexual relationship is harmful to the child. With changes in technology, virtual sexual conduct and online relationships have begun to play a role in marital problems, and in turn, in custody decisions. These will be treated like traditional nonmarital relations in that they will only be considered a factor if they harmed the child.

Q. If a parent is homosexual, what impact does that have on custody decisions?

A. The impact varies dramatically from state to state. Courts in a few states seem willing to assume harmful impact to a child from a parent's homosexual relationship. Courts in other states treat homosexual and heterosexual relationships equally, and will not consider the relationship to be a significant factor unless specific harm to the child is shown.

Q. If one parent is trying to undermine the child's relationship with the other parent, how does that affect custody?

A. Most states favor an ongoing, healthy relationship between the child and both parents. If one parent is trying to undermine the child's relationship with the other parent, that effort will be viewed negatively by the court. If other factors are close to equal, a court may grant custody to the parent who is more likely to encourage an open and positive relationship with the other parent, unless that other parent has been abusive or otherwise harmed the child.

Q. If one parent is religious and the other is not, may the court favor the more religious parent?

A. Normally, no. Under the First Amendment to the U.S. Constitution, both parents have a right to practice (or not practice) religion as they see fit. A judge cannot make value judgments about whether a child is better off with or without religious training or about which religion is better. If a child has been brought up with particular religious beliefs, and religious activities are important to the child, a court might favor promoting continuity in the child's life, but the court should not favor religion per se. In some cases, a parent's unusual or nonmainstream religious activities may become an issue, especially if specific harm to the child is shown.

Q. Can custody decisions be changed?

A. Yes. A court can change child custody arrangements to meet the changing needs of the child and to respond to changes in the parents' lives. Because courts favor stability for the child and do not want to encourage contentious litigation, a parent seeking to change a custody arrangement must show that the conditions have changed substantially, and usually unpredictably, since the last custody order. The parent must also show that changing the custody arrangement would be better for the child. Sometimes the parent must show that not changing custody would be harmful to the child.

Q. What legal remedies are available if a parent abducts a child?

A. Abduction of a child by a parent is a crime under state laws and, under certain circumstances, may also be a federal offense. Local police, state police, and in some cases the FBI can help in locating missing children. Parents who abduct their children can also be forced to pay the expenses incurred by the other parent in trying to find and return the child. To recover such expenses, a parent would probably need the help of a private lawyer.

If a parent with custody fears that the

▶ INTERNATIONAL CHILD ABDUCTION

Globalization has changed family relations as much as it has changed political and economic relations. Because of increased family mobilization, tourism, and international marriages, international child abductions have become more frequent. The abduction of a child to a foreign country by a parent or stranger is considered not to be in the best interests of the child.

The United States is a party to the Hague Convention on the Civil Aspects of International Child Abduction. By signing this treaty, the United States has entered into agreement with over fifty foreign countries to respect and enforce properly issued custody orders, as well as to facilitate the return of any child who may have been abducted to one of these countries. A custodial parent whose child was abducted to a country participating in the treaty should file a petition for the return of the child in cooperation with the United States Department of State.

Unfortunately, fewer options exist for a parent if the child is taken to a country that has not signed the Hague Treaty. Because a foreign court not bound by the treaty does not have to honor an American custody order, securing the child's return to the United States becomes more difficult. Thus, a parent who fears that a child may be abducted to a non-Hague Convention country should become familiar with and utilize American laws to prevent abduction.

The United States has numerous federal and state laws designed to protect a child from abduction. Together, these laws provide for clear and stable custody orders, deter abduction, and provide for criminal penalties in cases of abduction.

A parent who fears that a child has been abducted to a foreign country should immediately contact the Office of Children's Affairs in the Department of Consular Affairs, which is part of the United States Department of State, and should also contact an attorney familiar with international family law.

---

other parent will abduct the child, he or she should immediately consult a lawyer.

Visitation

Q. If a parent does not receive custody, how much access or visitation is he or she likely to receive?

A. Visitation schedules vary with the desires of the parents and the inclinations of a judge. A standard visitation schedule might allow access to the child every other weekend (Friday evening through Sunday); one weeknight per week (i.e., for dinner); during the child's winter and spring breaks in alternating years; on alternate major holidays; and for several weeks in the summer. If parents live far apart and regular weekend visitation is not feasible, it is common to allocate more summer vacation and school holidays to the noncustodial parent. For parents who do not like the terms "visitation" or "custody," it is possible to draft a custody and visitation order that avoids those terms and simply describes the times at which the child will be with each parent. Instead of "visitation" and "custody," some states use terms such as **parenting time** or **access to the child.**

Q. Under what circumstances may a court deny the noncustodial parent visitation?

A. A noncustodial parent is entitled to visitation unless there is harm to the child. For example, if the noncustodial parent has molested the child, is likely to kidnap the child, has a long history of domestic violence, or is likely to use illegal drugs while caring for the child, a court will probably deny or restrict visitation. Visitation might be allowed only under supervision, such as at a social service agency or in the company of a responsible relative. A parent should not deny the other parent visitation without advance approval from the court unless a true emergency exists, such as a noncustodial parent coming to pick up the child while drunk.

Q. Does failing to pay child support obligations impact a parent's visitation rights?

A. Generally, no. State laws traditionally state that failure to pay child support will not adversely affect rights to visitation. However, as discussed later in this chapter, such failure could result in fines or jail time, which would impact visitation.

Joint Custody

Q. What is joint custody?

A. Joint custody—sometimes referred to as **shared custody** or **shared parenting**—has two components: joint legal custody and joint physical custody. A joint custody order can incorporate one or both of these components.

Q. What is joint legal custody?

A. **Joint legal custody** is an arrangement in which parents share in major decisions affecting the child, or in which each parent makes such decisions when the child is in his or her care. The custody order may describe the issues on which the parents must share decisions. The most common issues are school, health care, and religious training. Other issues on which the parents may make joint decisions include extracurricular activities, summer camp, the appropriate age for dating or driving, and methods of discipline. Many joint custody orders specify procedures parents should follow in the event they cannot agree on an issue. The most common procedure is for the parents to consult a mediator.

Q. What is joint physical custody?

A. **Joint physical custody** is an arrangement in which the child spends time with both parents. The amount of time spent with each parent is flexible. The length of time spent with one parent could be relatively modest, such as every other weekend, or the amount of time could be equally divided between the parents. Parents who opt for equal time-sharing have come up with many alternatives: from alternate two-day periods; to alternate months; to alternate four- and six-month periods. If the child is attending school and spends a substantial amount of time with both parents, it usually is best if the parents live relatively close to each other. Some parents even keep the child in a single home while they rotate staying in the home with the child.

Q. Are courts required to order joint custody if a parent asks for it?

A. No. In most states, joint custody is an option. Courts may order joint custody or sole custody according to what the judge thinks is in the best interest of the child. In eleven states, legislatures have declared a general preference for joint custody. That usually means the courts are supposed to order joint custody if a parent asks for it, unless there is a good reason for not doing so. The most common reason for not ordering joint custody is the parents' inability to cooperate. In these cases, courts are concerned that a child will be caught in the middle of a tug-of-war. Parents who do not cooperate also will have difficulty with sole custody and visitation arrangements, but the frequency of conflicts in those situations may be less. If a parent opposes joint custody because he or she (without good reason) is trying to undermine the child's relationship with the other parent, then the court may weigh this behavior negatively in granting custody to the other parent.

Moving the Child Out of State

Q. May the custodial parent move out of state with the child?

A. The law on this varies from state to state. Some states routinely allow the custodial parent to move out of state with the child if there is a good-faith reason for the move. However, many states examine requests to move on a case-by-case basis and decide the issue after considering several factors. Some states also impose notice requirements obligating the parent who wants to move with the child to notify the other parent a certain number of days (usually thirty, sixty, or ninety days) before the proposed move, so that the noncusto-

dial parent has an opportunity to challenge the move.

Q. What are good-faith reasons for a move?

A. The most common good-faith reasons for a move are obtaining significantly better employment in another state, following a new spouse to a job in another state, and a desire to live near family members.

Q. What factors will a court consider when deciding whether to allow a move?

A. The court considers several factors when deciding whether to allow an out-of-state move:

1. The quality of the custodial parent's reason for the move. A good-faith reason and a likelihood that the move will enhance the quality of life for the child and custodial parent will help the custodial parent's case. A bad-faith reason, such as a desire to undermine the child's relationship with the noncustodial parent, makes it more likely that a court will deny permission for the move.

2. The quality of the noncustodial parent's reasons for opposing the move. A parent who has been very active in the child's life, sees the child often, and wants to preserve the relationship makes a stronger case for denying permission to move. A parent who has not seen the child very much, or who often misses visitation, has a weaker case.

3. The quality of the relationship between the child and both parents.

4. The degree to which visitation can be restructured to preserve or foster a good relationship between the child and the

nonmoving parent, including the issue of whether substitute visitation is still possible.

Child Support

Q. How do courts set child support?

A. Under federal law, all states have guidelines for determining child support. These guidelines consist of formulas that take into account the income of the parties, the number of children, and perhaps some other factors. The formulas are based on studies of how much families ordinarily spend to raise children, and aim to approximate the proportion of parental income that would have been spent on child support if the family had not been divided by divorce. Courts plug numbers into the applicable formulas to determine the amount of support that should be paid.

Q. When working with guideline formulas, how are the parents' incomes determined?

A. Courts use different methods in different states. Some take into account the parents' net income, while others look at gross income. **Gross income** is the parents' income from all (or almost all) sources, including wages, investments, and other sources. **Net income** is equal to gross income minus taxes, health insurance costs, and perhaps union dues. For self-employed persons, the determination may be complex. In determining net income, courts will allow deductions for reasonable business expenses. But courts may disallow deductions for unusually high business expenses or for depreciation that reduces income artificially without hurting the parent's cash flow. Thus, certain expenses that are deductible for tax purposes may not be de-

---

▶ **PERCENTAGE OF NONCUSTODIAL PARENT'S INCOME DEVOTED TO CHILD SUPPORT**

In cases where only the noncustodial parent's income is taken into account, New York and Illinois courts use the following guidelines for determining child support:

Number of children	Percentage of net income devoted to child support	
	Illinois	New York
1	20%	17%
2	28%	25%
3	32%	29%
4	40%	31%
5	45%	35% for five or fewer children
		50% for six or more children

ductible from income for the purpose of setting child support.

Q. How much child support should a noncustodial parent expect to pay?

A. That question is difficult to answer precisely because guidelines vary among states, and because courts may depart from the guidelines. However, a few examples are provided below.

Q. What is an example of a typical guideline that is based only on the income of the noncustodial parent?

A. See page 122 for a chart comparing the guidelines in effect in Illinois and New York in the year 2008.

Q. What's an example of a support formula based on the incomes of both parents?

A. Support guidelines based on the incomes of both parents often are referred to as **income shares models.** Under these guidelines, the court first adds the income of both parents. Then the court consults a long table—or a computer program—that assesses the total obligation of support as a percentage of the combined incomes and the number of children. Generally, the percentage drops as the combined incomes rise, on the assumption that financially well-off parents spend a smaller portion of their incomes on their children than parents who are less well off. The court then multiplies the combined incomes by the percent figure and obtains a dollar amount. The responsibility to pay that amount of support is then divided between the parents in proportion to each of their incomes.

Assume a father and mother have two children and a combined annual gross income of $60,000: $40,000 earned by the father and $20,000 earned by the mother. Let's say the schedules set the guideline amount for support at $13,092 per year ($1,091 per month). Since the father earns two-thirds of the parties' combined income, he would pay two-thirds of the children's support ($8,728 a year) and the mother would pay one-third ($4,364). If one parent had primary custody of the children, the other probably would make a cash payment to that parent. The parent with primary custody probably would not make a cash payment as such, but would be presumed to be spending that amount on the children.

Q. Why might the court award more support than the guidelines specify?

A. The parties can argue that because of special circumstances, a court should order more or less support than is specified by the applicable guideline. Some common reasons for awarding support above the base guideline amount include high child care expenses, high medical or dental expenses for the child that are not covered by insurance, and voluntary unemployment or underemployment of the parent who is supposed to pay support. Expenses for summer camps and private schools also might be a basis for setting higher support levels, particularly if private schools or summer camps were part of the family's lifestyle during the marriage.

Q. Why might the court award less support than is specified in the guidelines?

A. Again, the answer to this question varies from state to state. But common reasons for setting support below the guideline amounts include support obligations from earlier marriages and large debts related to family expenses. If the support guidelines are based on the income of only the noncustodial parent, and if the custodial parent has an unusually high income, then the noncustodial parent can argue that the custodial parent's high income is a reason for setting support below the guideline amount. Also, if there is no maximum income level (cap) to which the guidelines may be applied, then the high income of the noncustodial parent may be a basis for setting a lower level of support.

Q. Is child support paid while the child is with the noncustodial parent for summer vacation or long breaks?

A. In most cases, yes. Courts figure that many major expenses for the benefit of the child—such as rent, mortgage, utilities,

---

▶ COLLEGE EXPENSES

The obligation of divorced parents to pay for a child's college or trade school education (and related expenses) depends on the state and on any agreements between the parents. Courts in some states will require parents to pay for a child's college expenses, assuming the parents can afford it and the child is a good enough student to benefit from college. Courts in other states terminate child support at eighteen. Regardless of the state's law on compulsory payment of college expenses, the mother and father can agree as part of their divorce settlement to pay for these costs. Courts usually will enforce those agreements.

---

clothes, and insurance—have to be paid whether the child is with the custodial parent or not. So usually a full support payment is due. On the other hand, the parties—with the court's approval—may agree on payments in different amounts during vacation periods when the child is with the noncustodial parent. The lower amount paid during these periods might reflect savings to the custodial parent for food expenses or child care.

Q. How is child support enforced if a parent does not pay?

A. The state and federal governments have a variety of techniques for enforcing payments of child support. The most common is **wage deduction,** by which the employer sends a portion of the parent's wages to a state agency that then sends the money to the parent who has custody of the child. A federal law requires that all child support orders must provide for an automatic wage deduction unless the parties have agreed otherwise or the court waives the automatic order. The state also can intercept the nonpaying parent's federal and state tax refunds. Liens can be placed on property, such as real estate and automobiles. A parent who has not paid support can be held in contempt of court, which may result in a fine or a jail term. In addition, a parent who has not paid support can lose his or her driver's license or professional license. Government lawyers may help with collection of child support, though their efficiency varies from state to state.

Child support enforcement is a matter of increasing federal concern. It is a federal crime to willfully fail to pay child support to a child who resides in another state if the past-due amount has been unpaid for over one year or exceeds $5,000. Punishments under federal law can include fines and imprisonment.

A parent may not reduce child support payments without a court order: the unpaid amounts will accumulate as a debt, even if a court later decides that there was a good reason for the reduction.

Grandparents and Stepparents

Q. What are grandparents' rights to visitation?

A. Although all states once had statutes allowing grandparents to seek visitation, the U.S. Supreme Court issued a ruling in 2000 that will make it more difficult for grandparents to obtain court-ordered visits with their grandchildren. In the case of *Troxel v. Granville,* the Court found that fit parents should be given more deference in decisions about persons with whom the child will associate. The Court left open the possibility that some grandparents could obtain court-ordered visitation if, for example, the grandparents can show that they had a particularly strong relationship with their grandchildren, that it would harm the child not to continue the relationship, and that it is in the child's best interest to continue visitation. In these cases, the burden of proof is on the grandparents.

Q. May courts award grandparents custody of their grandchildren?

A. Yes. But usually this happens only if neither parent wants the children, or if the parents are unfit. Courts examine such factors as the grandparents' age, health, and ability to care for the children. Courts will not deny grandparents custody because of their age, as long as they are healthy.

Some custody disputes between grandparents and parents arise when the grandparents have been raising their grandchildren for a considerable time under an informal arrangement. The grandparents may have become the "psychological parents" of the grandchildren by the time the parent or parents seek to regain custody. In this circumstance, courts in many states will allow the grandparents to retain custody, even if the parents are fit.

Q. What are a stepparent's duties and rights?

A. The responsibilities of a stepparent depend on state law. A stepparent is not usually liable for a spouse's child from another marriage, unless the stepparent has adopted the child. Until then, the child's biological parents are liable for his or her support. However, some states make stepparents liable for the stepchild's support as long as the stepparent and the stepchild are living together.

A stepparent who does not adopt a spouse's child may not normally claim custody of the spouse's child if the marriage ends in divorce, although some states allow a stepparent to seek visitation. A stepchild does not share in the estate of a stepparent, unless the stepparent has provided for the stepchild in a will. However, unmarried stepchildren under eighteen may receive supplemental retirement benefits or survivor's benefits under Social Security.

MEDIATION AND COLLABORATIVE LAW

Q. What is mediation?

A. Mediation is a process in which the parties to a divorce (or some other dispute) try to resolve their disagreements outside of court with the help of a mediator, who facilitates their negotiation. The mediator cannot force a settlement, but tries to assist the parties in clarifying their interests and working out their own solution. In divorce actions, mediators are often involved in custody and visitation disputes. They can also handle property disputes, support disputes, and other issues. If the parties resolve their disagreements through mediation, the lawyers for both the parties should be involved in finalizing and approving the agreement.

Q. Is mediation mandatory in divorce actions?

A. That depends on local rules. Many courts require mediation of custody and visitation disputes. In these cases, the mother and father must talk with a court-appointed mediator to try to resolve the problem before putting their case before a judge. The mediator cannot force a resolution, but the parties can be told to try mediation before coming to court.

Q. What is the professional background of divorce mediators?

A. Most mediators are either lawyers or mental health professionals. Some court-related mediators have degrees in social work or psychology. Private mediators are often lawyers, although many are mental health professionals. Mediators who are mental health professionals are not serving as therapists, and mediators who are lawyers are not serving as lawyers. Instead, they are professionals who are trying to help people work out their differences. Mediators generally are not licensed or regulated by the state, although the ABA has adopted standards that apply to mediators, and many states do have some cer-

tification requirements for court-mandated mediation.

Q. What are the advantages of mediation?

A. Mediation often is cheaper and quicker than taking a case before a judge. A good mediator can help the parties build their problem-solving skills, and that can help them avoid later disputes. Most people who settle their cases through mediation leave the process feeling better than they would have felt if they had gone through a bitter court fight. Often mediation is confidential, mean-

---

▶ **COLLABORATIVE LAW**

Collaborative law is a relatively new discipline for people who wish to resolve their disputes without a contested court hearing. Collaborative law can be applied in divorces and in other types of disputes. Under principles of collaborative law, the parties hire lawyers with the understanding that the lawyers can be used only to help settle the dispute. The parties and their lawyers work together as a team to reach a settlement that they all think is fair, or at least a settlement they can live with. The parties agree that in the event their case does not settle, they will have to hire new lawyers to handle a trial. Collaborative law is usually a (comparatively) peaceful and inexpensive way to resolve a dispute. If a settlement is not reached, however, there will be added costs in hiring new lawyers and putting on a trial.

ing that conversations that take place in mediation cannot be used against the participants if the mediation does not result in a complete agreement. This allows parties to speak freely with less fear that what they say might later be used against them.

Q. What are the disadvantages of mediation?

A. Mediation can be a problem if one or both parties are withholding information. For example, if the purpose of mediation is to settle financial issues and one party is hiding assets or income, the other party might be better off with a lawyer who can vigorously investigate the matter. Mediators are usually good at exploring the parties' needs, goals, and possible solutions, but mediators do not have the legal resources of a lawyer to look for hidden information.

Another problem with mediation can arise if one party is very passive and likely to be bulldozed by the other. In that situation, the mediated agreement might be lopsided in favor of the stronger party. A good mediator, however, will see to it that a weaker party's needs are expressed and protected. Mediators should refuse to proceed with mediation if it looks as though one side will take improper advantage of the other.

Some professionals think that mediation is not appropriate if the case involves domestic violence. One concern is that mediation will provide a forum in which the abuser can harm the victim again. Another concern is that victims of physical abuse are not able to adequately express and protect their own interests. However, other professionals believe that disputes in families with a history of domestic violence can still be mediated, particularly if the abused party is not significantly intimidated by the other party.

A final potential drawback to mediation is that if mediation does not succeed, the parties may have wasted time and money on the process and still face the expenses of a trial.

REMEMBER THIS

- All states provide no-fault grounds for divorce, such as irreconcilable differences or irretrievable breakdown. Most states also have fault-based grounds for divorce, such as adultery, physical cruelty, mental cruelty, abandonment, or addiction to drugs or alcohol. The degree to which fault is a factor in dividing property or setting support for a spouse varies from state to state.

- Upon divorce, in most states, wives and husbands are entitled to keep their own nonmarital or separate property. Such property can include money or investments earned before marriage and inheritances received before or after the marriage—assuming the property was kept in the wife's or the husband's own name and was not mixed with marital property.

- Unless there is a valid prenuptial agreement, the court has the power to divide marital or community property—which generally is property acquired during the marriage—between the husband and the wife. Marital or community property includes wages and pensions earned during the marriage, even if only one partner earned them.

- A court can award alimony (also referred to as "maintenance") to the spouse with fewer financial means. The alimony can be temporary or permanent, depending on the facts of the case and the law of the state.

- Child custody (also referred to as "parenting time") is supposed to be decided according to the best interest of the child. In almost all states, judges may not give an automatic preference to one parent or the other based on the parent's gender. Important factors in deciding custody include which parent has been the primary caretaker of the child, the quality of the relationship between the child and each parent, and the child's preferences. Joint custody is a common option for parents, although it may not necessarily entail a fixed schedule of time that the child spends with each parent.

- Child support is set with reference to state guidelines. Courts generally set child support according to guidelines adopted by the state unless there is a good reason for doing otherwise. There are a variety of methods for enforcing child support orders, the most common of which is automatic deduction from wages.

- People can seek to resolve their family law disputes through mediation. A mediator cannot impose a settlement on the parties, but the mediator can work with the parties to focus on genuine needs and to resolve a dispute without the cost and stress of litigation.

Health-Care Law

LoAnne is a single mother at her first day of work on a new part-time job. The benefits paperwork lists three health plans from which LoAnne can choose. She skims through the policy books for each plan, but they all look the same to her; the only difference she notices is the price. LoAnne does not want to spend the rest of her day wading through pages of boring legal and medical jargon. She figures that all health plans are similar, and that it doesn't really matter which one she chooses. She enrolls in the least expensive health plan, makes sure that her daughter will be covered, and gives the forms to her supervisor. Six months later, LoAnne is laid off from the job. Will she still have health insurance? For how long? How much will it cost her? Will her daughter still be covered? Does she have any options if she does not find another job? If she doesn't have insurance and there is an emergency, can she get treatment?

In the past, many of us accepted medical treatment without question. Now, enlightened consumers of health care are taking a more active role in assessing their treatment and their options. This has led to patients becoming informed about their health, and taking an active part in decisions about their health care. It has become even more important to be informed about health-care options as the law struggles to keep up with technological and scientific advances.

Each section of this chapter is self-contained; however, before drawing conclusions or inferences from any particular question, read the entire section in which the question is found. This will help you to keep the answers in context, and will make you aware of any qualifications to the information provided.

PATIENTS' RIGHTS

This section explores issues relating to patients' rights, including confidentiality, emergency care, and informed consent.

Confidentiality and Privacy

Q. What information is included in my medical records?

A. Your medical file contains personal information, including, but not limited to

- your name, address, and phone number;
- your age, sex, and marital status;
- the names and ages of your children;
- your occupation and Social Security number;

- results of lab tests and physical examinations;
- whether you have a living will, health-care power of attorney, or health-care proxy; and
- your family medical history, including risk factors (such as smoking, obesity, or high blood pressure), allergies, immunizations, and any medications prescribed.

Q. Who has access to my medical information?

A. Any time you enter a hospital or other medical facility, you automatically agree to let anyone directly involved with your care see your medical record. This includes secretaries, nurses, interns, residents, doctors, nutritionists, pharmacists, and technicians. This probably doesn't come as a surprise—it makes sense for these people to have access to your records. But there are dozens of other people and organizations that may also be able to access your medical information:

- *Insurance companies* require you to release your records before they will issue a policy or make payment under an existing policy. Medical information gathered by one insurance company may be shared with others through the Medical Information Bureau.
- *Government agencies* may request your medical records to verify claims made through Medicare, Medicaid, Social Security Disability, and workers' compensation.
- The *Medical Information Bureau* (MIB) is a central database of medical information. Approximately 15 million Americans and Canadians are on file in the MIB's computers. Insurance firms use the services of the MIB primarily to obtain infor-

mation about life insurance and individual health insurance policy applicants. A decision about whether to insure you is not supposed to be based solely on an MIB report.

- *Employers* usually obtain medical information about their employees by asking employees to authorize disclosure of medical records. When employers pay medical insurance, they may require insurance companies to provide them with copies of employees' medical records.
- *Other disclosures* of medical information occur when medical institutions such as hospitals or individual physicians are evaluated for quality of service. This evaluation is required for most hospitals to receive their licenses. Your identity generally is not disclosed when medical practices are evaluated. Occasionally, your medical information is used for health research and is sometimes disclosed to public health agencies like the Centers for Disease Control. However, specific names usually are not included with the disclosed information.

▶ BE CAREFUL WHAT YOU REVEAL ONLINE

A tremendous amount of health-related information is available on the Internet. Many newsgroups and chat rooms are available for individuals to share information on specific diseases and health conditions. Websites dispense a wide variety of information. Remember that there is no guarantee that information you disclose in any of these forums is confidential.

Q. What does it mean for medical information to be confidential?

A. **Confidentiality** means that a doctor should not reveal your personal information to anyone except people that are caring for you. Confidentiality involves an expectation that what you tell your doctor will be repeated only to those involved in your treatment. It is your decision whether other uses may be made of your personal information. It should be up to you whether your information is released to pharmaceutical companies, other patients, or anyone else not involved in your care. Your doctor's duty to honor your confidentiality is rooted in the Hippocratic oath.

Most information in your health record did not originate during the doctor-patient relationship. Laws regulating health informational privacy protect against unauthorized disclosure of all personally identifiable information, even if it was not disclosed in the context of a doctor-patient relationship.

Q. What is doctor-patient privilege?

A. **Doctor-patient privilege** is an obligation that prevents a doctor from disclosing a patient's personal information during a legal proceeding without the patient's consent. Not every state grants patients this right, and the privilege is not absolute—it may be overridden by a court order.

Q. How does the law protect my privacy and confidentiality?

A. The most significant law relating to medical privacy and confidentiality is the Standards for Privacy of Individually Identifiable Health Information, also known as the **privacy rule.** Developed by the Department of Health and Human Services (HHS), and issued as part of the Health Insurance Portability and Accountability Act of 1996 (HIPAA), the rule gives you some control over how your personal health information is used and disclosed.

Q. Who must comply with the privacy rule?

A. The rule applies to most health plans, doctors, hospitals, clinics, pharmacies, and nursing homes.

Q. How will I know if my health-care providers follow the privacy rule?

A. When you go to a doctor, a dentist, or a hospital, you probably will be presented with a form in the waiting room, and asked to sign it before treatment. This form discloses the ways in which the provider may use (and must protect) information about you. For covered health-care providers with direct treatment relationships with individuals, the HIPAA privacy rule requires them to provide patients with this type of notice no later than the date of their first delivery of service (i.e., the date of the patient's first visit). Health-care providers must also make a good-faith effort to obtain a patient's written acknowledgment of receipt of the notice. There will also be a posted notice on the premises, in a prominent location where patients are likely to see it, that includes the same information that is distributed directly to the individual.

Q. How does the privacy rule protect my medical privacy?

A. Under the rule, you have significant rights to help you understand and control how your health information is used, including the following:

- **Access to Medical Records:** The rule gives you the right to see and obtain copies of your medical records and request corrections if you identify errors and mistakes. (Note that you may be charged for the cost of copying and sending the records.)

- **Notice of Privacy Practices:** Doctors, hospitals, and health plans must provide you with a notice containing information on how they may use your personal medical information.

- **Limits on Use of Personal Medical Information:** The rule sets limits on how doctors, hospitals, health plans, and other organizations may use individually identifiable health information. The rule does not restrict the ability of doctors, nurses, and other providers to share the information needed to treat you. However, your personal health information may not be used for purposes not related to health care.
  - In addition, you must sign a specific authorization before a covered entity can release your medical information to a life insurer, a bank, a marketing firm, or another outside business for purposes not related to your health care.

- **Prohibition on Marketing:** The rule sets limits on the use of your information for marketing purposes. Doctors, hospitals, health plans, and pharmacies must obtain your specific authorization before disclosing your health information for marketing purposes. However, the rule does allow communication with patients about treatment options and other health-related information, including disease management programs.

- **Confidential Communications:** Under the privacy rule, you can request that your doctor or health plan take reasonable steps to ensure that their communications with you are confidential. For example, you could ask a doctor to call your office rather than home, and the doctor's office should comply with your request if it can be reasonably accommodated.

- **Stronger State Laws:** The federal privacy standards do not affect state laws that provide additional privacy protections for patients, like those covering mental health, HIV infection, and AIDS information. When a state law requires a certain disclosure—such as reporting an infectious disease outbreak to the public health authorities—federal privacy regulations do not outrank state law.

Q. What must hospitals, doctors, and health plans do in order to comply with the privacy rule?

A. The privacy rule requires hospitals, doctors, health plans, pharmacies, clinics, and nursing homes to establish policies and procedures to ensure the confidentiality of protected health information about their patients. This includes having written privacy procedures in place, and educating employees about those procedures.

Q. Can doctors ever give my personal medical information to others without my permission?

A. In theory, you have the right to dictate which people can and cannot see your medical information. In the real world, doctors, nurses, and other health-care workers have considerable discretion in releasing your personal information. Doctors may, for example, release your personal information in the following circumstances:

- **When you are unconscious.** If you are unconscious or unable to make decisions regarding your care, the doctor has the right to provide your family members with all the information necessary to make an informed decision on your behalf. Otherwise, doctors should use only very general terms, such as "stable," when describing your condition.
- **If you have a health-care agent.** Many people have anticipated that at some point in the future they might not be able to make decisions, and have written and signed a living will, a **health-care advance directive,** a durable power of attorney for health care, or a health-care proxy. Through any of these devices, you can appoint a **health-care agent** to make decisions for you. If you have such a document, then that person alone is entitled to information regarding your medical condition. See Chapter 16, "The Rights of Older Americans," for more information on your options in this area.
- **If your case involves vital statistics.** Just as the law requires some information to be kept under wraps, it also requires doctors, nurses, and other health professionals to release information in certain circumstances. For instance, most states have laws requiring doctors to file birth and death certificates. Doctors are also usually required to report injuries caused by guns or sharp instruments, such as knives.
- **When there is abuse or danger to others.** There is a duty to protect that is spelled out by law in many states. For instance, when child abuse is suspected, doctors, nurses, and other health professionals must report the abuse. The same is true for situations in which a doctor or

therapist decides that the patient is a danger to others.

- **When you have a communicable disease.** Many states require doctors to report cases of communicable diseases, including smallpox, tuberculosis, pneumonia, measles, chicken pox, mumps, syphilis, gonorrhea, AIDS, and HIV. AIDS and HIV present a special challenge to patient privacy and confidentiality. Some states use unique identifiers in their records rather than names.

- **In HIV or AIDS cases.** In general, confidentiality is needed so that people will be comfortable being tested for AIDS or HIV. But that need for confidentiality must be balanced with the desire to protect others from contracting the disease. While doctors in all states are required to report AIDS cases to state public health departments, states differ in how this information is used.

- **In legal proceedings.** Any time you make your health or physical condition the focus of a lawsuit, as in a suit for workers' compensation, a suit over injuries from a car accident or medical malpractice, and in some child custody cases, your doctor can be brought into court to testify about your medical condition—even if privilege exists between the doctor and the patient. Of course, if your medical condition is not really an issue during the proceeding, privacy rights do prevail.

- **When communicating with other doctors.** A doctor is allowed to discuss a patient with health-care professionals who are not involved in the patient's care, but only if the patient consents or the doctor doesn't reveal the patient's identity. In other circumstances, you have a right to maintain your privacy. For example, imagine that a doctor shows up to examine you—and is trailed by a group of medical students. You have the right to refuse to let the medical students watch your examination.

Q. Do I have a right to know what's in my child's medical record?

A. To a certain extent, you control what goes into your child's medical record, particularly when your child is very young. For example, if you do not tell your child's pediatrician that your child received medical treatment from an ophthalmologist or a chiropractor, the pediatrician will not be aware of that treatment.

The situation is very different for older children, who might be able to keep information from you. What happens when your child becomes a teenager? Do you still get to see your child's medical information?

The federal privacy rule generally gives parents the right to access information about their minor child. However, the federal rules do not overrule state laws, so in most cases the states have the final say.

The law differs from state to state. The rules often hinge on what the state defines as the age of majority for health-care purposes—in a few states, it's fourteen; in others, it's eighteen—and the age of majority may vary in a state depending on the circumstances. Many states have particular statutes dealing with minors' records and treatment for sexually transmitted diseases or for abortions.

Q. What can I do if I believe my privacy rights have been violated?

A. If you think your private information has been disclosed, you may file a formal complaint regarding the privacy practices of a covered health plan or provider. Such a complaint must be filed within 180 days of when you knew the act occurred. You can complain directly to the covered provider or health plan, or to the Office for Civil Rights (OCR), which is charged with investigating complaints and enforcing the privacy regulation. Information about filing complaints should be included in each covered entity's notice of privacy practices.

Q. What happens to my doctor if he or she releases my information without my consent?

A. Almost half of the states can take disciplinary action against a doctor if it is discovered that the doctor released confidential information without the patient's consent. This may include revoking the doctor's medical license, though reprimand is the more likely remedy.

Emergency Care

Q. What is an emergency medical condition?

A. An **emergency medical condition** is a condition involving symptoms so severe that any delay in medical treatment could reasonably be expected to seriously harm you. In the

---

▶ HOW TO PROTECT YOUR MEDICAL INFORMATION

- Tell your doctor that you are concerned about who has access to your medical information. Ask her what steps are generally taken to keep that information confidential. Don't let your concerns be brushed aside.

- Take your time and read every form you are asked to sign at the doctor's office or the hospital. If you want insurance to pay your claim, you will have to sign the release form allowing the doctor to send your information to the insurance company. On the other hand, you can also specify that the doctor may only release the specific information necessary to pay the claim—and no more.

- For particularly private medical issues, pay for the visit, medication, or therapy yourself so that the information will not be sent to the insurance company for reimbursement. This may seem unfair after you've already had to pay insurance premiums, but it is the best way to keep the information out of your insurance company's database.

- Ask your doctor for the clinic or hospital's policy on discussions about patients among the medical staff. Notice whether the staff discusses the personal information of patients while at the nurses' station, in the elevator, or in the cafeteria.

- If you believe medical staff members are not treating your medical information confidentially, discuss your concerns with your doctor. If you feel your doctor is violating your confidentiality or privacy, report the situation to a managing partner in the clinic or to the chief of staff—after all, even doctors have bosses. You can also report the problem to your state's medical licensing board and the local medical professional association. Both numbers can be found in your phone book.

case of a pregnant woman, it also includes cases in which any serious harm could come to the unborn child. In fact, any woman in labor is considered to have an emergency medical condition.

Q. I'm not insured. If there's an emergency and I have to go to the hospital, do they have to treat me?

A. At one time, some hospitals engaged in "patient dumping"—refusing to treat patients who were uninsured or poor, or otherwise considered undesirable. These patients were either turned away or transferred to other hospitals. The result was that patients did not receive immediate treatment. At its worst, it meant that some patients died because of the delay.

To deal with this problem, Congress enacted an "antidumping" law. The Emergency Medical Treatment and Active Labor Act (EMTALA) requires hospitals to:

- give you an appropriate examination when you visit the emergency room;
- decide whether an emergency medical condition exists; and
- stabilize you.

A health-care facility is required to report another health-care facility if it suspects that the other facility is violating EMTALA. If a facility is found to violate EMTALA, it could be fined or even lose its right to participate in the Medicare and Medicaid programs. In addition, hospitals' own policies may limit dumping. Many not-for-profit hospitals are required to provide some level of charity care beyond the level mandated by EMTALA.

There are exceptions to the antidumping law. For example, if a person is being brought to an emergency room by ambulance, the hospital may divert the ambulance to another facility if it is full or cannot handle the problem. In some instances, an unstable patient will need to be transferred to receive specialized treatment at another hospital. To authorize this, the doctor must certify that the benefits of the treatment at the other hospital will outweigh the risks of the transfer.

EMTALA requires that the hospital provide treatment to stabilize patients, but it does not require the hospital to provide treatment after stabilization.

Q. Which hospitals must comply with EMTALA?

A. EMTALA applies only to hospitals that have emergency rooms and that receive federal Medicare funds. This does not mean that you, as a patient, need to be on Medicare. It means that the hospital must participate in the Medicare program. Nearly every hospital in the country with an emergency room participates in the Medicare program, which ensures that most patients will receive the care needed. Hospitals that do not participate in Medicare are not subject to EMTALA, but may be subject to similar state laws.

Q. What is an "appropriate medical examination" under EMTALA?

A. Unfortunately, there is no clear standard in the law as to what constitutes an appropriate medical examination. In general, the hospital must give you a medical screening within the hospital's capabilities, although this standard has yet to be tested in most courts.

Usually, the court will look at whether you received treatment that was somehow different from treatment received by other patients. For example, suppose you walk into an emergency room with abdominal pains and no health insurance. After waiting four hours to see a doctor, you're given a five-minute examination, told it's probably the flu, and sent home.

To prove that you were not given an appropriate medical examination, you would have to show that other patients with abdominal pain—and health insurance—were given a more thorough examination. You do not have to prove that you were treated differently because of your race, sex, political beliefs, religion, or some other improper motive. It doesn't matter why the examination was inappropriate. It only matters that it was not appropriate.

Q. When is a patient stabilized?

A. A patient is considered **stabilized** when it is unlikely that the patient's condition will worsen significantly during, or because of, transfer to another facility or location. A pregnant woman is not considered stabilized until she delivers the placenta.

▶ WHY PATIENTS LOSE EMTALA CASES

Hospitals win most cases brought under EMTALA. The patient usually loses because he or she was unable to provide enough evidence that the medical examination provided was not appropriate. In other cases, patients have lost because they could not prove they ever actually went to the emergency room, or because they could not prove that their transfer was improper, even if the paperwork regarding the transfer was filled out incorrectly.

Q. Is it ever a good idea for a hospital to transfer a patient?

A. A hospital may transfer a patient if:

- the patient requests the transfer in writing; or
- the doctor certifies that the benefits of transferring the patient outweigh the risks.

There are times when transferring a patient is simply the best possible course of treatment—for example, if the problem is unique or if another facility would handle the problem better.

Q. How should a patient be transferred?

A. When a hospital transfers a patient:

- the transport, such as an ambulance, must have adequate equipment and personnel;
- the hospital to which the patient is being transferred must agree to accept the patient; and
- the first hospital must give all the patient's medical records to the second hospital.

Q. Do I have a say in whether I get transferred?

A. As the patient, you may refuse to agree to a transfer, or you may request the transfer yourself.

Q. Can I sue the hospital for malpractice if there is a problem with my emergency care?

A. Yes. In an EMTALA claim, you must prove that the hospital is required to comply with EMTALA, that you went to the hospital seeking treatment, and that the hospital either did not properly screen you or that the hospital sent you away before stabilizing your condition. Unlike with other medical malpractice claims, the majority of courts hold that EMTALA creates a private right of action against the hospital only. Therefore, money damages are usually not obtainable from individual doctors.

EMTALA claims are different from medical malpractice claims against doctors, but most lawsuits contain both types of claims.

In addition to money payable to you, the hospital may also be fined as much as $50,000, payable to the government.

Informed Consent

Q. What is informed consent?

A. In a nutshell, a requirement of **informed consent** means that a doctor cannot treat you until he or she explains the procedure to you and you agree to the treatment. Informed consent protects your freedom to make decisions about your body. It allows you—rather than your doctor—to decide whether to undergo a particular treatment, despite your doctor's expertise and medical training. With informed consent, the patient makes the decision about treatment—and is the one who has to live with the decision, whatever the outcome.

Q. I trust my doctor to make the best decision for me in medical matters that I don't understand. Why do we need informed consent?

A. The principle of informed consent evolved so that patients could better share in decisions about their treatment. Of course, a patient also has the right to waive the right to

full disclosure. After all, there are some health-care consumers who simply do not want to know the risks associated with a medical procedure, and believe that ignorance is bliss.

Q. My doctor told me about a medical procedure in very technical language that I didn't understand. I consented, but I didn't really know what I was getting myself into. Does this count as informed consent?

A. You are properly informed when the doctor explains to you all the facts necessary to make a knowledgeable decision regarding your medical care. This information should be given to you when you are calm, sober, and preferably not medicated. There are times, of course, when you will have to make a fast, nerve-racking decision about treatment for yourself or a family member. When time is of the essence, the doctor should give you as much information as possible so that you can make a sound decision, but this will no doubt be less in-depth information than the doctor would provide in other, non-life-threatening situations.

In order for you to provide informed consent, you must actually understand the information the doctor gives you. If your alternatives are couched in medical jargon that you do not understand, you cannot legally consent to the treatment because, in effect, you have no idea what your doctor is talking about. To be informed, you need to be given the information in terms you can understand. Of course, if you don't understand the information the doctor gives you, then you need to tell the doctor so that he or she can try again—doctors can't read your mind, and you can't expect them to divine whether you've understood the information or not.

Q. In order for me to provide informed consent, what exactly must my doctor tell me?

A. In order to make an informed choice about treatment, a patient needs to know the following:

- The details of the proposed treatment or procedure, explained in terms the patient can understand. Even the brightest among us can get lost when wading through medical jargon.
- The benefits, risks, and side effects of the treatment.
- The risks of not treating the ailment.
- Any available alternative treatments, along with the risks those alternative treatments entail.
- The rate of success for the treatment, and how the doctor defines "success."
- Information on whether the procedure is experimental.
- A description of the recuperation period, including a time frame and possible complications.
- Conflicts of interest. Patients need to know if a doctor has something to gain financially by referring the patients to

particular facilities or by recommending specific treatments.

This does not mean that the doctor has to warn you about every conceivable ache, pain, or minor side effect that may occur as a result of your treatment. But it does mean that the doctor has to tell you about any facts that might cause a reasonable person to decide against the treatment. For example, a reasonable person might decide not to have surgery after finding out it carries a 50 percent risk of paralysis. The doctor needs to tell the patient about this risk in order for his or her consent to be "informed."

In most states, a jury will consider four questions to determine whether a patient's consent was informed:

1. Did the patient understand enough of the information to give an effective consent?

> ▶ **WHAT SHOULD I ASK MY DOCTOR?**
>
> There are several questions you can ask your doctor in order to make sure your consent is informed:
>
> - What is the problem?
> - How serious is it?
> - How accurate are the test results?
> - When does treatment have to begin in order to be most effective?
> - Can you describe the treatment?
> - What are the risks involved?
> - What are the odds it will be successful?
> - What if it is not successful?
> - What are the side effects?
> - If I choose not to treat the problem, what risks are involved?
> - What alternative treatments are available?
> - Will medical students or residents be involved with my treatment?
> - Will students or residents be practicing any procedures on me that are unrelated to my care?
> - How many times have you performed the procedure?
> - What is your success rate?
> - What other facilities or practitioners perform this procedure?

2. Was the patient given the same information as other patients in the same situation?
3. If the patient had been given sufficient information, would he or she have consented to the treatment?
4. Was the patient warned about the complication that later arose?

A patient cannot bring a lawsuit if he or she was not injured, even if he or she did not give an informed consent. However, the patient may still file a complaint with the state licensing agency against the doctor for professional misconduct, regardless of whether an injury resulted. The doctor may then face some form of discipline from that agency.

Q. My doctor gave me some information and then asked me to sign a consent form. Is this the way consent is usually given?

A. Many doctors will ask you to sign a consent form, simply to provide evidence of the fact that you consented in the medical record; this is for the doctor's and your own protection. However, informed consent does not necessarily mean written consent. The whole purpose of informed consent is to give you enough information to enable you to share in decisions regarding your health care. Whether you need to sign an informed-consent form is a less important question than whether you actually want to agree to the treatment.

You are not required by law to sign any kind of consent form for most procedures. But keep in mind that, if you refuse to sign such a form, a doctor can refuse to treat you. Some states have laws that require the execution of specific informed-consent forms for some procedures, including HIV testing and sterilization.

Q. Do I have to agree to everything that appears on a consent form?

A. No. You have the option to cross out any clauses in a consent form if you don't agree with or consent to them. To cross out a clause, just put an "X" through it and write your initials nearby. The doctor must then explain any risks involved with the restrictions you have placed on your treatment. The doctor may require that the restrictions be noted in your medical record. If the restrictions are so strict as to make the procedure unsound, the doctor can choose not to proceed with the treatment.

Q. When is informed consent unnecessary?

A. There are times when it is simply not possible for a doctor to explain a medical treatment or procedure to you. There are also times when it is not necessary for a doctor to provide you with such information. For example, doctors are not required to obtain informed consent from you in an emergency

---

> ▶ **CATCHALL CONSENTS**
>
> Written informed-consent forms vary from doctor to doctor and from hospital to hospital. Some are so vague that they seem to cover every imaginable situation that might arise. In cases involving forms this vague, many courts have concluded that the patient did not consent at all.

---

situation if you are unable to give or withhold consent.

Q. Can I withdraw my consent if I change my mind?

A. You can withdraw your consent at any time, but this may affect your treatment. Obviously, it is best to change your mind before the doctor begins a surgical procedure. Once you withdraw your consent, the doctor has to discuss with you the effects of not proceeding with the treatment, but the ultimate decision is generally up to you.

Q. What if a patient can't speak English?

A. Informed consent is the right of all patients, including those who are physically disabled or tourists and immigrants who do not speak English. The law requires that doctors and facilities take steps to ensure that these people are fully informed as to their treatment options before the treatment begins. For example, deaf people have the right to have someone communicate with them using sign language. If a person does not speak English, an interpreter usually will be used to ensure that the patient understands the illness or injury and the treatment options.

Q. Can I choose to refuse treatment?

A. After being informed of your diagnosis, as well as your treatment options and the risks involved, you can choose not to undergo treatment. You can refuse any treatment, including life-sustaining treatment, as long as you are an adult, unless perhaps you are mentally incompetent under state laws and have lost your ability to make informed decisions. Although you have the right to refuse treatment, the public health department has the right to isolate you if you have a contagious disease and are a danger to others.

REMEMBER THIS

- The federal privacy rule protects the privacy of your medical records. Additional protections are provided by the confidentiality of the doctor-patient relationship.

- Emergency room doctors are required to examine you, determine whether there is an emergency, and then—if there is an emergency—either stabilize you or transfer you to another hospital.

- An appropriate medical examination is one that a doctor would give to any patient with your symptoms, vital signs, and complaints, regardless of your race, gender, religion, insurance status, or income level.

- Informed consent requires that your doctor must explain the treatment or procedure to you, along with all of the risks and alternatives. You must then agree to be treated before the doctor may proceed.

- For most procedures, consent does not require a written form. If you are given a form, you are not required to sign it, although if you refuse to do so, the doctor can choose not to treat you.

HEALTH-CARE OPTIONS

This section explains patients' options regarding payment for medical care, and explores current issues relating to managed care.

Health Insurance and Managed-Care Organizations

Q. What is a health insurance policy?

A. A traditional **health insurance policy** is like insurance for your house or your car— you pay a premium, and the insurance company promises to pay your health-care services. Generally, in addition to the premium, you are also responsible for payment of deductibles and co-payments (a percentage of actual charges or a fixed amount per visit), which are predetermined in the policy. You are free to choose your health-care provider, which then applies to the insurance company for reimbursement.

Q. Are there alternatives to traditional health insurance?

A. Yes. As part of an effort to control health-care costs, entities called **managed-care organizations** (**MCOs**) have developed new forms of health insurance and health service plans. The result has been lower premiums, generally achieved through a reduction in the patient's choice of health-care providers, a reduction in the type and amount of benefits available, stricter controls on the type and the amount of care given by providers, and/or negotiated reduction of compensation to health-care providers. There are several types of managed-care organizations.

Q. What is a preferred provider plan?

A. A **preferred provider plan** is a fairly flexible type of MCO, which gives you the opportunity to choose a health-care provider from a list of providers who are members of the sponsoring insurer's preferred provider organization (PPO). If you choose to see a health-care provider who is not a member of the PPO, then you will receive a reduced level of reimbursement.

Q. What are health maintenance organizations (HMOs)?

A. Private health service plans that promise to provide care, not merely pay for it, are often referred to as **health maintenance organizations (HMOs)**. Some are **closed-panel plans** that operate out of a central facility in which all the health-care providers are employed by the HMO. When you visit such a facility, you may see the doctor on duty, or your assigned physician.

Other HMOs are more loosely affiliated models, sometimes called **individual practice associations,** in which the participating health-care providers operate from their own offices.

Q. What about employer-sponsored plans?

A. Many large private employers provide health coverage by sponsoring self-funded, self-administered employee welfare benefit plans. These plans may look very much like preferred provider plans or HMOs, but they are administered for the employer by an insurance company.

Q. Are health insurers and MCOs governed by state or federal law?

A. Each state makes its own laws regarding the level of care that health insurers and MCOs must provide. Federal law limits the restrictions on preexisting conditions that insurers and MCOs may include in their policies.

Many state laws are similar to one another. More than half the states require health plans to pay for visits to the emergency room. In addition, almost every state now requires that new mothers be allowed to stay in the hospital for at least forty-eight hours after giving birth.

However, if an employer-sponsored health plan is exempt under the Employee Retirement Income Security Act of 1974 (ERISA), as discussed in the sidebar "Do You Have Access to External Review?" on page 145, then state and federal laws do not apply to the mandated coverage.

Q. What can I do if I have a dispute with my health insurance company or plan?

A. If a health insurance company or plan denies your claim or refuses to provide a benefit or service, you have several options:

- **Seek internal review.** Health insurance companies and plans are required to establish rules and procedures for handling complaints and grievances internally. Utilizing these procedures is an important first step in seeking resolution of a dispute. You can initiate an internal review with a phone call to a complaints hotline. You may need to follow up with a complaints form or a written complaint. Check your policy to see how long a review is likely to take—it could take anywhere from one business day to thirty days. If your dispute concerns the medical necessity of services to be provided, and if waiting for a standard review would seriously jeopardize your health, you may be eligible for an expedited review, and the plan will evaluate your dispute sooner.

- **Seek external review.** External review allows your case to be reviewed by a third party who is independent of the health-care plan. Most states have external-review procedures, which can be pursued once internal review has been exhausted. Your health-care plan or insurance company may automatically refer your dispute to external review if your internal review is unsuccessful; or you may need to request external review in writing within a certain time period after internal review. Most states will not review all disputes, only those involving **medical necessity.** This means that there must be a dispute between you and your health plan over whether a particular procedure, treatment, or pharmaceutical is essential for

your health and recovery. External review procedures differ from state to state, but are usually free or available for a small fee. Further, some plans might be exempt from review. See Sidebar "Do You Have Access to External Review?" on page 145.

- **Complain to the accrediting organization.** Most HMOs are accredited by nongovernmental groups such as the National Committee for Quality Assurance, the American Accreditation HealthCare Commission/URAC, or the Joint Commission on Accreditation of Health Care Organizations. HMOs rely on their accreditation by these organizations for marketing themselves to employers and unions. For this reason, making a well-documented complaint to the relevant organization and sending a copy to your HMO might achieve results.
- **Make a complaint about your doctor—and seek a second opinion.** If you think your doctor is withholding treatment, talk to your doctor about it. You might want to

---

▶ KEEP GOOD RECORDS FROM THE BEGINNING

When having a dispute with your health-care provider, keep a good paper trail to help with any reviews or complaints. This includes:

- Assembling a file containing all the paperwork you already have, such as bills or physician information. If you are denied care, ask for a record of the denial in writing.
- Keeping a log of every telephone call you make to the plan or insurance company. Record the date and the name of the person you talk to, and take notes about your conversation.
- Making copies of every document you send to the health plan or insurance company for your file, and recording the date on which you send any correspondence.
- If you send correspondence to any other parties—government agencies or accrediting organizations, for example—then send a copy to your health-care plan.

seek a second opinion about whether treatment is necessary. And if you believe your doctor is withholding treatment for his or her own pecuniary gain, you can file a complaint with your state's medical board.

- **Appeal to the state insurance department.** This is a good option if you are covered by an HMO. Since all plans have to be licensed by a state's insurance department, these departments truly do have the last word. They are especially useful if you feel there has been discrimination, unfair denial, or ambiguity with respect to the rules, disclosures, or booklets. HMOs are likely to respond out of concern that their license might be revoked or suspended.

Q. Can I sue my managed-care organization for malpractice?

A. A federal appeals court has ruled that MCOs and their medical directors can be sued for medical malpractice when they make a decision about the treatment of a patient that causes the patient harm. This applies to individual decisions, not to overall corporate policies. This means that consumers can sue an MCO for injuries resulting from the company's refusal to authorize medically necessary treatment.

Q. Are there any limits to my ability to bring a malpractice suit against my managed care organization?

A. Yes. ERISA bars people from bringing a claim against health plans that are offered by employers. Few people manage to bring malpractice cases against health plans. If you purchase your health plan on your own or through some other type of organization, rather than an employer, ERISA does not apply.

> ### ▶ DO YOU HAVE ACCESS TO EXTERNAL REVIEW?
>
> Some health plans do not provide access to external review. Under the Employee Retirement Income Security Act of 1974 (ERISA), some kinds of self-insured, employer-paid plans are exempted from the state's external review procedures. As a practical matter, this means that people who have disputes with their plans are limited to the internal grievance procedures and cannot sue in court for such things as breach of contract, breach of the implied covenant of good faith and fair dealing (bad faith), infliction of emotional distress, and fraud. As noted earlier, it also means that the plan may not have to comply with mandated coverage laws.
>
> Consult your employer's human resources department to determine if your plan is self-insured. If it is, then you probably cannot take advantage of your state's external review process.

Several states now have statutes that remove ERISA protection and explicitly allow individuals to bring suits against health plans. Courts increasingly are interpreting ERISA to allow such suits as well.

Q. Can I sue my health plan to recover the cost of my treatment?

A. ERISA does not bar claims for economic loss based on the denial of benefits. In other words, you can sue your health plan to try to recover the cost of your medical bills. Any amount you are awarded will be limited to the amount of the medical services that are disputed, and to your lawyer's fees. For example, if you have a bill for $2,900, that amount and the cost of your lawyer's fees is all you are allowed to recover from your health plan. To win coverage for medical bills, you will have to show that you complied with your health plan contract. Thus, if you go to the emergency room for a migraine at a time when your doctor is holding office hours, even though this is clearly not allowed under your policy, you may not be able to get coverage for the resulting medical bills.

Q. What happens if I lose my job? Does my employer stop paying for my health plan straight away?

A. A federal law called **COBRA,** short for **Consolidated Omnibus Budget Reconciliation Act,** gives employees some protection. It applies to almost all businesses that employ more than twenty people, and covers full-time and part-time employees. If you lose your job, or if your hours are reduced, COBRA allows you to purchase health coverage from your former employer, at the same price the employer paid, for up to eighteen months.

COBRA also kicks in during specific crises and transition times, such as divorce or death. In these types of situations, COBRA covers the employee's spouse and dependents for up to three years. COBRA also ensures coverage of a child who loses dependent child status—for example, by turning nineteen—for up to three years.

Continuing your coverage under COBRA can be expensive because you're still paying your contribution, plus the contribution your employer made, plus up to 2 percent for administrative costs. But often the cost is much lower than the cost of buying individual coverage.

Medicare and Medicaid

Q. What is Medicare?

A. Medicare is a federal insurance program. It pays medical bills using money from trust funds that have been funded over the years by tax dollars and employer contributions. It primarily serves people over the age of sixty-five, regardless of their income. It also serves younger disabled people and dialysis patients. Patients pay part of their medical costs through deductibles. Small monthly premiums are also required for nonhospital coverage. Medicare works in basically the same way everywhere in the United States, and is run by the Centers for Medicare & Medicaid Services (CMS), an agency of the federal government.

You can find detailed information on Medicare in Chapter 16, "The Rights of Older Americans."

Q. What is Medicaid?

A. Medicaid is a medical-assistance program that serves low-income people of every age. Unlike Medicare, which offers the same benefits to all enrollees regardless of income, Medicaid is managed by individual states. Thus, benefits and eligibility vary from state to state. Medical bills are paid from federal, state, and local tax funds.

Q. Who is eligible for Medicaid?

A. States have some discretion in determining which groups their Medicaid programs will cover and the financial criteria for Medicaid eligibility. Groups granted mandatory eligibility for Medicaid include

- Low-income families with children.
- Most Supplemental Security Income (SSI) recipients.
- Infants born to Medicaid-eligible pregnant women. Medicaid eligibility contin-

ues throughout the first year of life so long as the infant remains in the mother's household and she remains eligible, or would be eligible if she were still pregnant.

- Children under age six and pregnant women whose family income is at or below 133 percent of the federal poverty level.

States also have the option to provide Medicaid coverage for other "categorically needy" groups. These optional groups share characteristics of the mandatory groups, but the eligibility criteria are defined somewhat more liberally. The optional groups that states may cover as categorically needy (and for which they will receive federal matching funds) under the Medicaid program include

- some low income children;
- certain aged, blind, or disabled adults who have incomes above those requiring mandatory coverage;
- institutionalized individuals with income and resources below specified limits;
- people who would be eligible if institutionalized but are receiving care under home- and community-based services waivers;
- recipients of state supplementary payments; and
- low-income, uninsured women, screened and diagnosed through the Centers for Disease Control and Prevention's National Breast and Cervical Cancer Early Detection Program, who are determined to be in need of treatment for breast or cervical cancer.

Q. If I qualify for Medicaid, what sorts of services do I get?

A. Medicaid covers a broad spectrum of services. Certain benefits are mandated by federal law. They include

- inpatient and outpatient hospital services;
- doctors' and nurse practitioners' services;
- inpatient nursing-home care;
- home health-care services; and
- laboratory and X-ray charges.

You also may be entitled to services from podiatrists, optometrists, and chiropractors; mental health services; personal care in your home; dental care; physical therapy and other rehabilitation; prescription medications; eyeglasses; transportation services; and more. In all cases, you may receive these services only from a Medicaid-participating provider.

Q. What will Medicaid cost me?

A. Unlike Medicare, Medicaid does not require you to pay premiums or deductibles. Providers may not charge you additional fees beyond the Medicaid reimbursement amount. However, states are permitted to impose a nominal deductible charge or other form of cost sharing for certain categories of services and prescription drugs. If you are receiving Medicaid, a participating provider may not deny you services because of your inability to pay the charge.

Q. How do I apply for Medicaid?

A. You should contact the state or local agency that handles the Medicaid program.

▶ MEDIGAP

Medigap is a supplemental insurance policy that many people buy to cover some of the costs not covered by Medicare. Chapter 16, "The Rights of Older Americans," discusses Medigap in detail.

Its name will vary from place to place. It may be called Social Services, Public Aid, Public Welfare, Human Services, or something similar. Chapter 16, "The Rights of Older Americans," contains more detailed information on how to apply for Medicaid.

State Children's Health Insurance Program

Q. What is the State Children's Health Insurance Program? Does my state have this program?

A. The State Children's Health Insurance Program (SCHIP) is designed primarily to help children in working families with incomes too high to qualify for Medicaid but too low to afford private family coverage. All states and the District of Columbia offer health coverage through SCHIP and Medicaid.

Q. Are my kids eligible for SCHIP?

A. Each state can set its own income eligibility level. This level is adjusted every year, and varies depending on the size of the family. Contact your local human services department for information on eligibility and applying for SCHIP.

Q. What benefits can I receive under SCHIP?

A. Although benefits vary, children are generally eligible for

- regular checkups;
- immunizations;
- eyeglasses;
- doctor visits;
- prescription drug coverage; and
- hospital care.

Q. How much do I have to pay?

A. Health insurance provided to children through these programs is free or low-cost. Costs will vary depending on the state and your family's income, but any charges will be minimal. In some states, you may need to pay a premium or co-payment.

REMEMBER THIS

- Managed care is a way of keeping health-care costs lower, and thus more accessible.
- If your health plan is provided by your employer, ERISA may prevent you from having access to external-review procedures in your state.
- Be sure to read your health plan closely so that you know exactly what coverage you have for medical care.
- Medicare is an insurance program that primarily insures those over the age of sixty-five.
- Medicaid is a medical-assistance program that serves low-income earners of every age.
- Even if you're working, your child may be eligible for the State Children's Health Insurance Program.

REGULATING HEALTH-CARE PROFESSIONALS

Adequate regulation of the medical profession is crucial, because care that falls short of a high standard can sometimes result in injury or death. This section explores the licensing of health-care professionals and medical malpractice, as well as the legal and ethical issues arising from experimental research on humans.

Licensing of Health-Care Professionals and Hospitals

Q. Who licenses health-care professionals and facilities?

A. Each state government sets its own requirements for how doctors, nurses, hospitals, and other health-care professionals and facilities are licensed. The state does this to protect your health and safety.

Q. Does one medical license allow a doctor to practice all types of medicine?

A. Yes. Once a doctor is licensed to practice medicine, that doctor is licensed to practice any type of medicine. In theory, a dermatologist can deliver a baby, an obstetrician can perform liposuction, and a plastic surgeon can perform brain surgery. In reality, however, hospital regulations, fear of malpractice claims, and the threat of disciplinary actions discourage doctors from providing medical care outside their fields of expertise. Many hospitals insist that a doctor be certified in a particular specialty. Specialty boards certify physicians who have met certain published standards. Numerous specialty boards are recognized by the American Board of Medical Specialties (ABMS) and the American Medical Association (AMA). To become board certified, doctors must undergo specialized training, receive assessments from their supervisors, and complete written exams. In order to retain certification, specialists must periodically go through an additional process

involving continuing education in the specialty, review of credentials, and further examination.

Q. Who needs a license?

A. The answer to this question varies by state. In general, states will license chiropractors, dentists, doctors, surgeons, physical therapists, nurses, optometrists, psychologists, physician's assistants, respiratory therapists, pharmacists, and clinical social workers. Some states may also decide to license hearing-aid dispensers, eyeglass and contact lens dispensers, clinical laboratory technologists, and midwives. Many states also require homeopaths and naturopaths to be licensed.

Q. Why do doctors need a license?

A. State legislators believe that by requiring doctors to be licensed, they can help ensure that you will receive quality medical care. Requiring a license is a way of ensuring that doctors graduated from medical schools that taught them what they need to know in order

---

▶ **HOW TO FIND OUT IF A DOCTOR IS LICENSED**

To find out if your doctor is licensed, call the licensing board in your state. Licensing boards are usually listed in the phone book under your state's name and the heading "medical examination" or "licensing board." In addition to helping you confirm that your doctor is licensed, many states provide instructions on the Internet about how to lodge complaints against your doctor.

▶ THE MINIMUM REQUIREMENTS FOR OBTAINING A MEDICAL LICENSE

For a health professional to be licensed, he or she must usually

- graduate from an approved program, such as a medical or nursing school;
- pass a standardized licensing examination; and
- undergo a review of his or her personal history.

---

to treat you. License requirements can also prevent you from being treated by a person with a criminal history or a character defect. They also ensure that if a doctor does not care for you in medically acceptable ways, he or she may be disciplined by license revocation or suspension. A state may use its licensing standards as a way to promote public policy.

Q. What should I do if I find out my doctor is not licensed?

A. First of all, double-check the information—you don't want to make a false report. If you're certain that your doctor is not licensed, report him or her to your state's medical board. You should also report the doctor to the attorney general's office in your state, as he or she may be operating fraudulently. If the doctor is in fact practicing without a license, he or she may be subject to criminal prosecution. Depending on the situation, you may have a civil action against the person for battery, and you may be able to bring a lawsuit against him or her for monetary damages.

Q. When can a license be revoked?

A. It is difficult to get a health professional's license revoked. A professional license is considered property under the Constitution, so before it can be taken away, the person must be informed of the reason for the revocation and provided with a fair hearing. The most common ground for suspending a license is unprofessional conduct.

Q. Can I file a complaint with licensing authorities about a health-care professional?

A. Each state has several boards in charge of licensing, investigating complaints about, and disciplining doctors and other health-care professionals. To find out how to contact the appropriate board, look in the phone book or online. The board will tell you how to obtain a complaint form to begin the grievance process. Usually this form will be a release that you must sign allowing the board to look

---

▶ A WARNING ABOUT COMPLAINTS

Most customers who file complaints with the state licensing board find the complaint process frustrating. Customers are generally kept in the dark about what is happening. They do not have the right in most cases to attend hearings or see investigational documents, while the doctor sees everything the patient has filed.

at your medical records. You are not required to sign the form, but without looking at your records, the board may not be able to investigate your complaint fully. Some states require that your complaint form be notarized, which requires your name to appear on the form.

Q. Once I file the complaint form, what happens?

A. Usually, the board will examine the complaint form and decide whether the complaint should be investigated. In some situations, the board will not have the authority to investigate.

Q. How is my complaint investigated?

A. The medical board will notify your doctor of the complaint and ask him or her to respond. When the board receives your doctor's response, it will decide whether to continue the investigation. If an investigation is needed, the board will look at your medical records (and others as deemed necessary) and interview witnesses.

Q. How long does the investigation take?

A. Anywhere from a few weeks to several years, depending on the complexity of the complaint and the difficulty of the investigation. You can check on the status of your complaint by contacting the medical board.

Q. What happens after the investigation?

A. If the board finds that the complaint is unwarranted, it will dismiss the complaint. If it finds the complaint is justified, it may request that the complaint be investigated further. In some cases the complaint will be dismissed, but the board will notify the doctor that certain methods or actions must be changed in the future. It may order your doctor to undertake more training or to stop performing particular treatments. It may require that the doctor enter into treatment for substance or alcohol abuse. If the board finds that the doctor should be disciplined, there will be an administrative hearing, at which time the doctor may be disciplined in some way, including having his or her license revoked or suspended.

▶ **TYPES OF COMPLAINTS INVESTIGATED**

Types of complaints that a medical board will investigate include those relating to

- substandard medical care;
- illegal sale of drugs;
- professional misconduct;
- criminal convictions;
- sexual misconduct;
- neglect or abandonment of a patient;
- alcohol or substance abuse;
- mental or emotional illness that impairs the doctor's judgment;
- discrimination;
- billing for services not provided;
- false advertising;
- fraud;
- failure to provide medical records;
- overcharging for medical records; and
- failure to supervise staff.

Q. Do I have to give my name when I complain?

A. Some medical boards will not investigate a complaint that is anonymous, since it can be nearly impossible to investigate a complaint without access to the complaining patient's medical records. On the other hand, medical boards often will keep your name confidential if you so request. In other words, your doctor will not find out directly from investigators that it was you who complained, even though the medical board knows your name and sees your medical records. However, the doctor may be able to infer your identity when your records are sought.

Q. What happens to my complaint after it is dismissed, or after the doctor is disciplined?

A. These documents typically become part of the doctor's file kept by the medical board. In some states, the doctor's file is available to the public, because it is considered a public record.

Q. Can I appeal if my complaint is dismissed?

A. No. There is no appeal process through the medical board. In some cases, dismissal of a complaint indicates only that an investigation would not have provided sufficient proof to warrant disciplining the doctor.

Q. If the board does not take action, do I have other options?

A. Yes. The dismissal of your complaint by a medical board does not affect your right to bring a legal action against your doctor, such as for medical malpractice, unless the statute of limitations has run out.

Q. What constitutes the "unauthorized practice of medicine"?

A. The **unauthorized practice of medicine** occurs when an unlicensed person performs an action that is covered by the legal definition of "practicing medicine." This does not include simply offering general advice (as, for example, in a magazine article written for the general public), or offering informal advice (say, to a coworker about how to treat a cold). It does include presenting oneself as a licensed doctor when he or she has no such license. Each state has laws that forbid anyone but licensed doctors from practicing medicine.

Q. Do medical institutions need to be licensed?

A. Just as doctors must be licensed and meet certain standards, so must hospitals, nursing homes, and most other types of health-care facilities. However, unlike doctors, health-care facilities (including hospitals and nursing homes) are regulated by a combination of state and federal laws, including Medicaid and Medicare. These regulations dictate the type of care that may be provided and how the professional staff may be selected and trained, and provide standards for the maintenance and sanitation of the buildings and equipment. In addition, health-care facilities may choose to meet the standards of private accreditation organizations to boost their public image or increase their competitive edge.

Medical Malpractice

Q. What is medical malpractice?

A. **Medical malpractice** is negligence committed by a professional health-care provider— a doctor, nurse, dentist, technician, hospital, or nursing facility—whose performance of duties departs from a standard of practice of those with similar training and experience and results in harm to a patient. Most medical malpractice actions are filed against doctors who have failed to use reasonable care to treat a patient. Though million-dollar verdicts make headlines, in fact big jury awards are few and far between.

The goal of a medical malpractice lawsuit is to reimburse you if a doctor has injured you. Malpractice lawsuits are time consuming and costly for doctors, even if the doctor is insured or wins the case. The fear of malpractice is meant to keep doctors from making medical mistakes and from acting carelessly. In this way, the law can control the quality of health care. Malpractice puts the responsibility on doctors to act in a way that will not result in an injury to you. If doctors are forced to pay for the costs of their medical mistakes, they will be more careful to make sure that mistakes do not happen in the first place.

Medical malpractice is discussed further in Chapter 6, "Personal Injury."

Q. How would a jury decide if my doctor committed malpractice?

A. A jury will compare your doctor's conduct with how other doctors would have acted if faced with the same or similar circumstances. The doctor is not compared to a person in the general population. Instead, the doctor is compared to other doctors with the same type of medical training and skills.

Q. So if my treatment has a bad outcome, can I sue for malpractice?

A. If your doctor provides you with medical care and something bad happens, it does not automatically constitute malpractice. As long as your doctor uses reasonable care and skill in treating you, your doctor did not commit

> ▶ **PROVING MALPRACTICE**

To win your medical malpractice case, you will need to prove that

1. there was a doctor-patient relationship;
2. the medical care the doctor provided did not meet the standard of care that other doctors in the same or a similar situation would have provided;
3. you suffered an injury; and
4. your injury was the result of your doctor's failure to provide appropriate medical care.

malpractice. Five doctors could examine and diagnose the same person and offer five different opinions about what medical care is needed. But this does not mean that four of the doctors are wrong or incompetent; it just means that there may be many acceptable ways to treat a patient. The key is that all the doctors must act according to acceptable medical standards, and treat you as any reasonable doctor would treat you.

If your doctor is negligent but you are not injured as a result of his or her negligence, there is no malpractice. For there to be malpractice, the doctor has to be reckless or negligent, and that recklessness or negligence has to cause you an injury.

Research on Humans

Q. Why do we allow medical research on humans? Aren't there risks to the human subjects?

A. The advances in medicine that today we take for granted—dialysis, organ transplantation, the artificial heart, and prescription drug therapies to name just a few—are only available because, before these treatments were commonplace, there were patients willing to try them. Without experimentation and research on humans, medical technology could not improve.

At the same time, it's essential that the rights of human subjects to confidentiality and privacy be observed, that their informed consent be obtained before experimentation begins, and that research protocols be reviewed carefully for scientific merit. Unfortunately, there have been cases in the past where experimentation was forced on patients who were either unable to say no or did not know they were being used as research subjects.

It is also very important that financial arrangements be fully disclosed. Most medical institutions and clinics fail to tell you if they are getting paid for recruiting you into a study. This amount can be substantial—for example, a clinic might receive over $1,000 for recruiting a single participant.

Q. How is medical research regulated?

A. The National Research Act protects people who take part in medical research and experiments. The Act does not prevent doctors from experimenting on you. Rather, it establishes standards for research on humans that must be met if the researchers are to receive federal funds for their programs. These standards require the following:

- That you give informed consent to take part in experimental treatment. This means that the doctors must tell you about the procedure and the risks, side ef-

fects, and benefits associated with it. They must also tell you about any alternative procedures available to you.

- That you volunteer to take part in the research. Your doctor cannot force you or pressure you into being part of an experiment.

Q. Who enforces these standards?

A. The National Research Act requires that **institutional review boards (IRBs)** be established for all research funded by the U.S. Department of Health and Human Services or carried out on products regulated by the Food and Drug Administration. Since the federal government is a major source of research funds, IRBs have been set up at virtually all medical schools, universities, and hospitals where research on humans is conducted.

The IRB reviews proposed research plans or experiments and either approves or denies them. It ensures that each plan provides subjects with adequate opportunity to provide informed consent, and that it does not expose subjects to unreasonable risks. After the research is approved, the IRB provides continuing oversight to ensure that protections remain in force.

Q. How does an IRB make its decision?

A. It is the job of the IRB to assess both the dangers and merits of proposed research. In order to approve a research program, the IRB must find that seven conditions have been met:

1. The risk to subjects must be minimized as much as possible.
2. The risk to subjects must be reasonable compared to the benefits.
3. The selection of the subjects must be unbiased.

4. Each potential subject must be given adequate information to determine whether he or she wishes to participate.
5. The informed consent must be documented.
6. The data must be adequately monitored.
7. The subjects' privacy must be protected, and their personal data must be kept confidential.

Q. What does "informed consent" mean in this context?

A. While each state may require something a little different, the basic concept of informed consent remains the same for research as it does for medical treatment: You must be given sufficient opportunity to decide whether to be part of the research. When the research is explained to you, the researchers must use language that you understand. If they do not, your consent is not informed because you do not have all the information necessary to make your decision.

Q. How do I give informed consent?

A. Your informed consent to be a research subject will most likely be in written form and include eight parts:

1. An explanation of the research, including how long you would be expected to participate, a description of the procedures to be performed, and an explanation of which of the procedures are experimental.
2. A description of any risks or discomfort you might be expected to experience.
3. A description of any possible benefits to you or to others that may come out of the research. It is important to remember that any benefit of an experimental procedure or drug is highly speculative. The reason the researcher is conducting the experiment is that the researcher does not know if the procedure or drug is beneficial, and he or she wants to find out. You should be highly suspicious if a researcher characterizes additional medical exams as a benefit of the research. Keep in mind that getting "free" medicine is not necessarily a benefit.
4. An explanation of any other procedures or treatments that are available to you for your particular medical condition.
5. A description of how your privacy will be protected.
6. If the research involves more than minimal risk to you, a description of any medical treatments that are available if you are injured. In this case, the researcher should tell you whether you would be entitled to financial compensation for your injury. The researcher is not required to actually pay you—only to tell you whether compensation will be available in the event of injury.
7. The names of persons to contact for answers about the research or your rights as a research subject.
8. A statement that your participation is voluntary and that you can withdraw as a research subject at any time.

Q. What about research on children and the elderly?

A. The goal is to allow researchers to study children and the elderly while at the same time protecting them from abuse and mistreatment. Neither a child nor an elderly person suffering from a mental illness such as Alzheimer's disease has the legal capacity to consent to being part of a research study.

Researchers must get consent from the parents or guardians of the people they wish

▶ **PROBLEMS WITH INFORMED CONSENT**

Many persons battling illness wish to get into clinical trial programs, in the hope of benefiting from drugs or procedures not generally available. This predisposes many of them to trust their hopes and not their fears, and so they fail to give careful consideration to whether they really want to accept the risk of the experimental treatment.

What does this mean to you if you're contemplating entering a research program? You are your own best defense—make sure you investigate any possible research study as carefully as you can. Contact an experienced health research lawyer to get some advice, and make sure you understand how the information and results will be handled and whether they will be communicated to you. Ask questions until you are sure you fully understand the consent form and your concerns have been addressed.

to study in order to proceed with the research. When the research is on children, the researcher must also get assent from the children who participate.

Q. What if I think my rights were violated during a clinical test?

A. First, you should consider contacting the person or organization in charge of the testing (the appropriate contact information should be included on the written consent form). If the person or organization is unresponsive or

if you are uncomfortable with that option, contact the IRB, the U.S. Department of Health and Human Services, or the Food and Drug Administration.

Q. What about research on fetuses?

A. One of the biggest controversies in human research is the use of fetuses (either still in the uterus or aborted) and embryos. Research is allowed on fetuses within the uterus as long as the risk is minimized and the mother gives her consent. An additional ethical standard holds that the research must be of therapeutic benefit to the fetus.

Federal regulations and many state laws severely limit the research that may be conducted on aborted fetuses. In general, research on aborted fetuses is allowed only when needed to develop important biomedical knowledge that cannot be obtained in any other possible way. In addition, the mother must consent to the research.

Q. Is research allowed on embryos?

A. Couples who undergo fertility treatments and do not want the resulting embryos will sometimes donate the embryos for research. Current federal law prohibits research on embryos, as well as the creation of embryos for the sole purpose of research. This type of research offers some valuable potential, but also tends to generate religious, political, and legal controversy.

REMEMBER THIS

- Every state requires that doctors, nurses, hospitals, and laboratories be licensed.

- A license ensures that your doctor, nurse, hospital, or laboratory meets the minimum standards for providing medical care.

- Just because your doctor made a mistake or you had a bad result from medical treatment does not mean that your doctor committed malpractice.

- Subjects of human research must be volunteers.

- In order to serve as a research subject, you must be informed of the type of research being conducted, and you must agree to be a part of it.

- You have the right to withdraw from the research at any time.

SPECIFIC ISSUES IN HEALTH CARE

This section explores a number of specific health-care issues, including issues relating to assisted reproductive technologies, abortion, organ donation, and euthanasia.

Assisted Reproductive Technologies

Q. What are assisted reproductive technologies?

A. A person with a medical condition that impairs his or her ability to have a baby can use **assisted reproductive technologies** in order to conceive children. This term refers to in vitro fertilization, gamete intrafallopian transfer (GIFT), and other technologies aimed at facilitating reproduction.

Q. When does the law come into play?

A. When the use of assisted reproductive technology involves the parents' own gametes (egg and sperm), the couple must make decisions regarding the creation, storage, use, and disposition of their embryos, and must sign legal documents detailing those decisions. However, the process will be relatively free from legal complications relating to the identity of the parents or the baby.

In determining whether someone is a parent for legal purposes, courts generally ask whether that person intended to help create a child, and whether there is a genetic connection to the child. Courts consistently have held that a party should not be forced to be a genetic parent against his or her will. Agreements between parties to accept or relinquish parenting responsibilities are appropriately regulated by legislatures, which have taken a range of approaches—from banning such agreements to providing a legal framework for both the parties and judges to use in setting appropriate expectations for the arrangements.

Q. Does my insurance cover infertility treatments?

A. Few insurance plans directly cover treatment for infertility, although some policies are starting to cover in vitro fertilization (IVF) as its cost decreases and its success rates increase. Policies may also cover treatment for illnesses (such as endometriosis) that contribute to infertility. Some policies will cover infertility treatment if the couple has been trying to conceive for a year or more. Some individuals are fighting to get more coverage for infertility treatment, and some states now mandate that insurance companies include infertility treatment in their plans.

Q. Who owns the embryos produced through in vitro fertilization?

A. Not all courts are comfortable classifying embryos as "property." Nevertheless, it is

▶ FERTILITY TECHNIQUES

Two of the most common types of fertility treatment are in vitro fertilization and artificial insemination.

In vitro fertilization (IVF): The woman usually is given medication to make her body produce more eggs during ovulation. The woman's egg is then removed from her body and placed with a man's sperm into a dish containing a culture medium. If the sperm fertilizes the egg, an embryo results. An embryo or several embryos are then placed into the woman's uterus or frozen for later use. If the embryo attaches to the woman's uterus, pregnancy results. Transferring multiple embryos can result in multiple births.

Artificial insemination (often referred to as **intrauterine insemination,** or **IUI,** in the medical lexicon): Using a very thin catheter, sperm is placed in the woman's cervix or uterine cavity at the time mature eggs are released. The hope is that the sperm will fertilize at least one of the woman's eggs. Artificial insemination is a technology that is decades old, and still is used today.

However, things become much more difficult if the fight is between you and your spouse.

Q. What happens to the eggs, sperm, or embryos you don't use?

A. Whether you succeed in having all the babies you desire or decide to stop fertility treatments, there sometimes will be embryos or sperm left over. You can keep this genetic material frozen for possible future use by you, donate it to another person or couple for their use in creating a child, donate it for research, or have it destroyed. Regardless of your decision, the clinic should ask you—before you start treatments—what you want to do with your genetic material. This is an important step. You must have your decision in writing. Avoid relying on the clinic's informed-consent documents regarding how you want your tissue treated; instead, you should create a separate document.

A problem arises when a couple divorces and cannot agree on what to do with its leftover embryos. This kind of dispute raises complex emotional, legal, and ethical issues. If there is no agreement, the court will have to balance the interests of the people fighting for control.

Q. My first wife and I divorced, and I received control of the embryos in the settlement. My second wife and I want to use the embryos to have children. Can my ex-wife stop us?

A. Yes. Even when a husband and wife sign a clear agreement giving one partner control of the embryos, courts are reluctant to enforce the agreement because it forces one person to become a legal parent against his or her will. Therefore, as a matter of public policy, a court most likely would allow your ex-wife to step in

likely that you will have at least some property rights in your embryos if a third party (such as the fertility clinic) tries to interfere. In such cases, courts tend to provide parents with some form of property rights in their embryos, such as the rights to possess, use, or donate.

and prevent you from using the embryos with your second wife, because your first wife would be the child's or children's genetic mother.

Q. What is surrogacy?

A. In **traditional surrogacy**, a woman (the surrogate) undergoes intrauterine insemination with sperm from the man who wants to be the legal father. Thus, the baby has genetic material from both the father and the surrogate. If the baby is born in a state that does not have laws setting forth the rights of the intended parents, then the father's wife may have to adopt it through stepparent adoption proceedings. Because the surrogate has both a genetic and a gestational connection to the baby, like a traditional birth mother, her parental rights are protected under law.

In a **gestational carrier surrogacy**, an embryo is transferred to the woman who agrees to gestate the baby. This woman is known as the **gestational carrier**. The baby has no genetic material from the carrier. Here is where it gets confusing: The gametes (i.e., the egg and sperm used to conceive the baby) can come from either of the intended parents (or both), or from an egg donor or a sperm donor, or both. In gestational carrier arrangements, courts consistently have held that the intended parents are the legal parents of the child.

Q. Is surrogacy legal?

A. Whether a surrogacy agreement will stand up in court depends on the state in which you live. Both legislatures and courts are suspicious of any contract that involves the payment of fees in exchange for a baby. Some states will uphold the arrangement if there is a contract clearly outlining the responsibilities of the parties. Some states require the intended father's wife to adopt the baby as though she were the baby's stepparent. Some states refuse to recognize any type of contract that transfers parenthood from a surrogate to the couple who contracted with her; others won't recognize contracts where the surrogate is paid.

Q. Can children be "conceived" after a parent dies?

A. Through the use of assisted reproductive technology, children can be born months—

▶ DONOR SPERM AND PATERNITY RIGHTS

When artificial insemination is performed using anonymously donated sperm, the woman's husband is considered the legal father as long as

- he consented to the procedure in writing; and

- a doctor or other medical professional supervised the insemination.

On the other hand, if no doctor is involved, a donor may be granted paternity rights. State laws vary in the extent to which they clarify—or in some cases even address—issues relating to artificial insemination.

even years—after one or both of the parents die. If a couple freezes its embryos, the wife can have the embryos transferred after her husband's death. If both parents die, the person who "inherits" the embryos could have them transferred to a carrier, thus creating a child whose parents are deceased.

Q. Can children conceived after the death of a parent receive Social Security benefits?

A. Under the Social Security Act, survivors' benefits are disbursed in order to support children who were dependent on the wage earner at the time of his or her death. However, because they did not yet exist, children conceived after a parent's death could not possibly meet this requirement. Despite this fact, the Social Security Act is broadly interpreted by the courts so as to grant benefits to qualified applicants whenever possible. Some commentators predict that as Social Security funds begin to dwindle, courts will become more conservative in deciding who qualifies for these benefits. For now, however, these children usually receive benefits.

Q. Do inheritance laws apply to children conceived after the death of a parent?

A. State inheritance laws generally require a child to be born within 300 days of the person's death—in practical terms, this means conceived before the parent died—in order for the child to inherit from his or her parent's estate. This is because at the time these laws were written, the technology did not exist for a child to be conceived after one parent died. These laws permit the state to distribute the estate among the heirs without wondering who might come along down the road. It also protects the courts from having to investigate suspicious claims from people claiming to be heirs conceived after the parent died.

The state has to balance those concerns with the goal of keeping children off public assistance when they could be taken care of by the deceased parent's estate. It also does not want to punish children for the way in which they were conceived.

If you have stored gametes or embryos, then you (and the co-progenitor, if an embryo is stored) should have a specific provision in your will stating your intention regarding the disposition of your gametes or embryos, and whether you intend for them to be considered your child under your estate.

▶ CARRIER AGREEMENTS

Though such agreements continue to evolve, surrogacy agreements most commonly stipulate

- that the intended parents want to be included in prenatal doctor visits;
- that the intended parents will be present in the delivery room;
- that the carrier will refrain from behaviors that are harmful to the fetus; and
- that the parties will share medical information with each other.

Abortion

Q. Are there any limits on the right to an abortion?

A. The Supreme Court has imposed some limits on the right to an abortion. For example, there is no absolute right to have an abortion at any time, in any place. Furthermore, a state can pass laws regulating abortion as long as certain boundaries are not crossed. The state cannot completely override a woman's right to terminate a pregnancy, but the state does have an interest in protecting the health of pregnant women and the potentiality of human life. A man's right to prevent an abortion—or to force his partner to have an abortion—is not protected, because the pregnancy is not deemed to implicate a man's "bodily integrity."

Until the end of the first trimester, only the pregnant woman and her doctor can decide whether a pregnancy should be terminated.

After the first trimester, the state can pass laws regulating abortion as long as the laws are reasonably related to the pregnant mother's health. Once the fetus becomes **viable,** meaning that it can live outside the womb, the state can regulate—and even outlaw—abortion unless it is necessary to save the mother's life. There is no definite point, however, when a fetus becomes viable.

The legal standard for abortion is largely the same today as it was in 1973, with one major difference. Today, a court will examine state law to see if it places an undue burden on a woman's right to have an abortion. If it does not place an undue burden on her access to an abortion, then the law is upheld. Again, after a fetus becomes viable, the state can pass laws making it more difficult for a woman to obtain an abortion.

Q. Can minors have abortions without their parents' consent?

A. The rights of parents to raise their children as they see fit collides with a woman's right to privacy and abortion when she is under the age of eighteen. In cases involving women under the age of eighteen who seek abortions, the Supreme Court has said that limits on abortion are permitted so long as a judicial bypass option is available.

Q. What is a judicial bypass option?

A. All parental-consent laws are required to be very limited in their range, and they must include what is called a **judicial bypass option.** A judicial bypass option allows a woman under the age of eighteen to go to court for a judicial hearing. This option allows minor women to request that a judge waive parental-

---

▶ WAITING PERIODS

Some states require a waiting period, usually twenty-four hours, before a woman can obtain an abortion. During such waiting periods, the woman must make two visits to the clinic where the abortion will be performed. At the first visit, the woman will talk to the doctor or other medical professional about her choice to terminate the pregnancy. The doctor may be required to give specific information to the woman, the effect of which may be to discourage her from having the abortion. The woman then has to wait twenty-four hours before having the abortion, in order to think about whether she wants to terminate her pregnancy. Laws requiring this type of waiting period have been upheld as constitutional.

consent requirements, particularly when the minor is mature or when the judge finds that an abortion would be in the best interests of the minor.

This can be a traumatic experience for young women; after all, courtrooms are intimidating even to adults. To make things even more difficult, hearings are generally held during school hours, and the woman must discuss her most personal concerns with the judge, who is usually a total stranger.

REMEMBER THIS

- You have the right to control how your gametes or embryos are used.

- Before beginning infertility treatments, make sure you have a written agreement with the clinic as to how your eggs, sperm, or embryos will be dealt with once you end your treatments.

- States can pass laws regarding abortion as long as the laws do not place an undue burden on a woman's right to have an abortion.

- Husbands do not have the right to stop their wives from having abortions.

Organ Donation

Q. Who can be an organ donor?

A. Almost anyone may be an organ donor, depending on his or her medical condition and the circumstances surrounding his or her death. Organ donors must be at least eighteen years old (with a few exceptions), and there is no maximum age.

Q. What can be donated?

A. You can donate your entire body for anatomical study, or you can donate specific

▶ **ORGAN DONATION**

Organ donation is known in legal circles as an anatomical gift. For legal purposes, anatomical gifts may include organs, tissue, and even bones. For the purposes of this chapter, we will use the word "organ" as a general term referring to any part of the anatomy that can be donated.

organs and tissues. The most-needed organs are kidneys, hearts, livers, lungs, and pancreases. Sought-after types of tissue donation include eyes, skin, heart valves, bone, and bone marrow. You can also donate bone marrow or a kidney while you are still alive.

Q. Can I sell an organ?

A. No. The National Organ Transplant Act (NOTA), a federal law, makes it illegal to buy or sell organs for profit. People who violate this law can be sentenced to prison, fined, or both. It is also illegal under the law of most states to sell organs for profit. However, if you donate your organs, you can legally be reimbursed for some of the costs involved. For example, if you donate one of your kidneys, you may most likely accept payment for your lost wages and medical expenses. Pennsylvania offers a few hundred dollars to the families of deceased organ donors to cover funeral expenses. The amount of these payments must be reasonable. Any outlandish amount would be considered profit, and would thus be illegal.

Q. May a living child or a mentally incompetent person be an organ donor?

A. Sometimes, but only if there is some benefit to the child or the incompetent person. Legally, a child or mentally incompetent person is not able to consent to being an organ donor. The fear is that people needing organs will prey upon vulnerable people. However, there are rare situations in which the guardians of children or incompetent persons may lawfully allow them to be organ donors.

Q. Why did the hospital ask me if I was an organ donor when I was admitted for a minor procedure?

A. Federal law requires hospitals that participate in Medicare to ask you, when admitted, whether you are an organ donor. If you say yes, the hospital is required to get a copy of your donor card, driver's license, or advance directive indicating that you wish to donate your organs. If you say no, the hospital is required to tell you about your options for deciding whether to become an organ donor.

If you are near death and the hospital has no record of your decision to be an organ donor, the hospital is required to ask your next of kin to donate your organs. The purpose of these laws is to find out and document your wishes, as well as to increase the number of organs available for transplantation. But don't worry: Your doctor will make every effort to save your life even if you are an organ donor.

Q. When is a person considered dead?

A. Sounds like a silly question, doesn't it? But medical technology is advancing at breakneck speed, and "death" is constantly being redefined. For legal purposes, you are generally considered dead either when your circulatory and respiratory functions stop for good, or when your entire brain, including the brain stem, irreversibly stops functioning. If you are an organ donor and you are brain-dead, circu-

> ▶ **DONATING YOUR ORGANS**
>
> Every state has some form of a law called the Uniform Anatomical Gift Act (UAGA). If you are at least eighteen years old and of sound mind, this law allows you to
>
> - donate all or part of your body at your death;
>
> - designate that you are donating your organs for transplantation into another person or for medical research; and
>
> - name a hospital, doctor, person, or educational institution as the donee (i.e., recipient) of your organs or body.

latory and respiratory functions will be kept going by artificial life support to preserve your organs until they can be harvested for transplantation.

Q. What is non-heart-beating donation?

A. Non-heart-beating donation (NHBD) comprises a very small number of all organ donations, but is expected to increase in the future. It occurs when a patient is not brain-dead, but is on a ventilator and is in a vegetative state or considered "hopeless," and the family consents to having the ventilator withdrawn. When the ventilator is removed, doctors wait for the patient's heart and breathing to stop, declare cardiac death either immediately or after a waiting period of a few minutes, and then harvest the organs in an operating room.

If, as sometimes happens, the potential NHBD patient does not stop breathing when the ventilator is removed and continues to have a heartbeat, doctors usually wait an hour before canceling the harvest. Since the decision to withdraw treatment already has been made, if the patient continues breathing, he or she is returned to the hospital room to die without treatment being resumed.

Q. How can I be sure that my organs will, or will not, be donated?

A. It is not a good idea to include your wishes regarding organ donation in your will. Doctors will need to remove your organs or tissue in accordance with very specific timelines and using very delicate procedures. By the time your will is read, the opportunity to donate your organs will have passed. Instead, include your wishes regarding organ donation in your health-care advance directive, and communicate your wishes to your family regarding this issue.

In most states, your doctor requires your family's consent to harvest your organs, regardless of your wishes or whether you filled out an organ donor card. Even if your will or advance directive states that you would like to donate your organs, it is customary for doctors to ask your family to agree to the donation. In some states, hospitals are required by law to abide by the deceased person's wishes regardless of the family's consent. In practice, though, hospitals and doctors are reluctant to go against the wishes of family members in order to avoid malpractice lawsuits.

Q. What happens if I don't make a decision about organ donation?

A. If you do not indicate whether you want your organs donated, then your family will decide when you die whether to donate all or part of your body. If possible, your doctor will usually seek a decision from your spouse. If you do not have a spouse, the doctor will turn to your adult son or daughter. If you do not have children, the doctor will seek a decision from your parent, adult sibling, grandparent, or guardian.

Q. What should I do if I change my mind about being, or not being, an organ donor?

A. You can change your decision at any time. To revoke your decision to be an organ donor, write a statement to that effect and place a copy with your driver's license and your health-care advance directive. You can also revoke your decision orally, but this will be less dependable than a written statement. In either case, tell your family and loved ones about your decision so that there is no confusion about your wishes.

Q. Who chooses the recipients of organs?

A. The United Network for Organ Sharing (UNOS) keeps a national computer list of patients waiting for transplants. This list is used

> ▶ **WITNESSES USUALLY ARE UNNECESSARY**
>
> At one time, the law required that an organ card be signed in the presence of two witnesses. Today, the law does not require you to have witnesses, unless you do not intend to put your wishes in writing. In that case, if you want to be an organ donor, make your wishes clear in front of at least two people.

to match your organs with patients who might receive them through a transplant. Information about you, such as your blood type, is entered into the computer-match program. Possible recipients are listed according to the length of time they have been on the waiting list, their age, and their degree of compatibility with the characteristics of the donor's organs. Organs are offered to local patients first. If there is no patient locally that is a good match for the organ, the organ will be offered on a regional or a national level.

Suicide

Q. Is it legal to commit suicide?

A. It is not against the law to commit, or attempt to commit, suicide. The rationale is that suicide is usually prompted by a mental illness, and that people should not be criminally punished for being mentally disabled.

Q. Is it against the law to help someone else commit suicide?

A. It is against the law in most states to aid or assist someone else in committing suicide. Physician-assisted suicide is legal in only one state: Oregon. In 1997, Oregon enacted the Death with Dignity Act. This law allows—but does not require—doctors to prescribe medication to competent, terminally ill patients, with the knowledge that a patient will use the medication to end his or her life. This law is highly controversial.

Q. Is there a constitutional right to physician-assisted suicide?

A. No. In 1997, the Supreme Court upheld a Washington state ban on physician-assisted suicide. The Court said that such a ban did not infringe on a fundamental liberty under the Due Process Clause. The Court held that

---

> ▶ **EUTHANASIA VERSUS ASSISTED SUICIDE**
>
> **Euthanasia** (Greek for "easy death") is the act of painlessly putting to death a person who suffers from an incurable and painful disease or injury. It is sometimes called **mercy killing.**
>
> **Suicide,** on the other hand, is the taking of one's own life.
>
> Physician-assisted suicide is different from euthanasia. In **physician-assisted suicide,** patients ask a doctor to prescribe a lethal substance, and patients then administer it to themselves. In euthanasia, the doctor administers the lethal substance to the patient.

---

the ban was rationally related to legitimate government interests, such as prohibiting intentional killing and preserving human life, protecting the medical profession's integrity and ethics, maintaining physicians' role as their patients' healers, and preventing harm to those people who are the most vulnerable, including the poor, the elderly, disabled people, and the terminally ill.

The Court's rulings leave states free to enact laws allowing physicians to assist patients who wish to end their lives. These rulings simply mean that the states are not required by the Constitution to do so.

REMEMBER THIS

- Your doctor or hospital will ask your next of kin for their permission to take your organs, even if you sign an organ donor card

▶ **LIFE-SUSTAINING TREATMENT**

Most discussions about suicide or physician-assisted suicide inevitably turn to the issue of **life-sustaining treatment.** This term refers to those treatments necessary to keep a patient alive—for example, dialysis or mechanical ventilation. The termination of such treatments is a controversial and difficult decision for any family and patient. Generally, a doctor may stop providing life-sustaining treatment if the patient, having the ability to make decisions and fully understanding the consequences, states that he or she no longer wants the treatment, and if it is justifiable to withdraw treatment, or if treatment no longer offers any benefit to the patient.

If a patient is no longer competent to make such a decision, then doctors and family members often find themselves in a difficult position. Health-care advance directives can play an important role in such a situation, ensuring that your wishes and desires are carried out. These options are discussed more thoroughly in Chapter 16, "The Rights of Older Americans."

or specify organ donation in your health-care advance directive. If your next of kin refuses, the hospital probably will not remove your organs.

- Do not put your wishes regarding organ donation exclusively in your will. A better plan is to include your wishes in a health-care advance directive, and to discuss your wishes with your family and doctor.

By the time your will is located, it will be too late to donate your organs.

- It is not illegal to commit suicide.

- It is illegal in every state but Oregon for a doctor to assist a patient in committing suicide.

- States are free to enact laws allowing or prohibiting physician-assisted suicide.

CHAPTER FIVE

Children with Special Needs: Special Education

Robin is a bright, cheerful five-year-old. She attends kindergarten, and every day comes home with lots of stories for her parents. Last week, her parents received a letter from Robin's teachers saying that she might need special education. Her parents were shocked; they had never noticed any problems with their daughter. What did this letter mean? Could the school simply move Robin to a different classroom? How much input would her parents have in addressing Robin's needs?

If you or your child has a disability, you understand the worry, confusion, and stress associated with getting necessary services and education. **Special education** is the legal term for instruction that is specially designed to meet the unique needs of a child with a disability, and that is provided at no cost to the child's parents or guardians. This type of instruction can take place in a variety of settings and include a number of services.

The term "special education" refers to an instructional technique, not to a place. Thus, it does not mean simply placing a child with a disability in a particular classroom or program. Instead, each disabled child must be provided with a special education service appropriate to that particular child.

Special education programs are governed by a combination of state and federal statutes and administrative regulations. In addition to providing disabled children with a substantive right to free and appropriate public education, these statutes and regulations specify the procedures to be used for developing an Individualized Education Program for each child. The laws also set forth the procedures to be used for appealing decisions.

INTRODUCTION TO SPECIAL EDUCATION

Q. My child has recently been diagnosed with a disability. What is the first thing I should do?

A. Stop and take a deep breath. Going forward, your best bet is to educate yourself as much as possible about the disability and your options. Talk to your child's doctors, and study the relevant state and local laws. Also consider discussing your legal options with an attorney who specializes in education or special education.

Q. What laws regulate special education and disability services in the school setting?

A. A variety of federal and state laws set minimum standards for special education. The most common federal and state laws are discussed below.

Federal Laws

Q. What federal laws control special education?

A. Several federal laws protect children with special needs. The **Individuals with Disabilities Education Act (IDEA)** seeks to ensure that a free and appropriate education is available to all disabled children. The act provides state and local educational agencies with funds and also imposes obligations. A free and appropriate education must include special education and related services that are tailored to meet the unique needs of a particular child and are reasonably calculated to enable the child to receive educational benefits. The U.S. Department of Education's Office of Special Education and Rehabilitation Services administers the IDEA.

In addition, **Section 504** of the **Rehabilitation Act of 1973** prohibits discrimination in a federally funded program or activity on the basis of disability. Because virtually all public schools receive some federal funds, Section 504 is an additional tool for assuring that disabled school-age children receive a free appropriate public education. However, Section 504 won't apply when relief is available under the IDEA. Established by the U.S. Department of Education, the regulations implementing Section 504 in preschools, elementary schools, and secondary schools prohibit discrimination and require schools to take affirmative steps to ensure that children with disabilities receive an appropriate education.

Section 504 eligibility does not depend on whether a child is labeled "disabled." Rather, its protections are available to children who can be regarded in a functional sense as "handicapped." Section 504 defines a person with a **disability** as one "with a physical or mental impairment that substantially limits one or more life activities," or one with a record of such an impairment, or one who is regarded as having such an impairment. Children with asthma, attention deficit disorder, and epilepsy are included within this definition. Section 504 is monitored by the U.S. Department of Education's Office for Civil Rights.

Finally, the **Americans with Disabilities Act (ADA)** prohibits discrimination against qualified disabled individuals by any public agency that receives federal funds, such as a public school. When a claim under the ADA is the same as one under the IDEA, the ADA claim is dismissed. The ADA is administered by the federal Equal Employment Opportunities Commission.

State Laws

Q. Do state special education laws differ from federal ones?

A. Usually not. State special education laws substantially mirror the federal IDEA. However, states are not prohibited from setting higher standards. Parents should make sure they are following the guidelines applicable in their state. Many state education departments offer helpful materials to guide parents through the special education maze.

ELIGIBILITY FOR SPECIAL EDUCATION SERVICES

Q. Are all children with learning disabilities eligible for special education services?

▶ **YOUR LOCAL EDUCATION AGENCY**

Local educational agency (LEA) is a legal term referring to your local public board of education or other authority that is charged with administering, controlling, and directing the public elementary and secondary schools in your city, district, township, or county.

A. No. A child may ineligible for special education services despite having a learning disability, either because the child does not fit into one of the special education eligibility categories, or because the child's learning problems are not severe enough to qualify him or her for special education. However, such a child may be eligible for special services and program modifications under Section 504.

Q. What disabilities are covered by the IDEA?

A. Only children with disabilities as defined by the IDEA are entitled to protection under it. Specific covered disabilities include

- mental retardation;
- hearing impairments (including deafness);
- speech or language impairments;
- visual impairments (including blindness);
- serious emotional disturbance;
- orthopedic impairments;
- autism;
- traumatic brain injury;
- other health impairments; and
- specific learning disabilities.

For children aged three to five, some additional types of disabilities are covered. At the

▶ **CHILDREN WITH SPECIFIC LEARNING DISABILITIES**

The term **children with specific learning disabilities** refers to children with a disorder affecting one or more of the basic psychological processes involved in understanding or using language, spoken or written, where the disorder manifests itself in the imperfect ability to listen, think, speak, read, write, spell, or perform mathematical calculations. Such disorders include

- perceptual disabilities;
- brain injury;
- dyslexia; and
- developmental aphasia.

The definition of "children with specific learning disabilities" does not include children who have learning problems that are primarily the result of visual, hearing, or motor disabilities, of mental retardation, of emotional disturbance, or of environmental, cultural, or economic disadvantage.

state's discretion, covered children in that age group may include those experiencing IEP delays (as defined by the state) in physical development, cognitive development, communication development, social or emotional development, and/or adaptive development, if those developmental delays necessitate special education and related services.

Q. If my child is eligible for special education services, what rights do my child and I have?

A. Under special education law, parents and children have the right to

- receive a free, appropriate public education for the child;
- have the child be educated in the least restrictive environment possible;
- be given prior written notice of the parent's and the child's educational rights;
- be notified before any action or refusal to act by the local education agency;
- provide consent before the child's initial evaluation and placement for special education;
- withdraw permission for the child's evaluation, program, or placement;
- request an independent education evaluation at the local education agency's expense, and obtain an outside evaluation at the parent's own expense;
- be included as equal partners with school personnel in developing the child's Individualized Education Program (IEP);
- see and obtain copies of the child's education records;
- file a written complaint if the parent believes the local education agency has violated the rights of the parent or child; and
- request a due process hearing to resolve disagreements with the school.

Of course, how these rights will play out for your child depends on a number of factors. No two special-needs children are the same; as a result, no two special education plans are the same.

REFERRALS

Q. How does a parent find out if a child is eligible for special education and related services?

A. The process of obtaining special education and related services for a child begins with the written request for a **referral.** Anyone, including a child's parents, may refer a child. If a local education agency receives a referral from a person other than the child's parents, that agency must send written notice of the referral to the parents.

Q. What must the request for referral include?

A. A request for referral, also known as a **referral letter,** must include

- the child's name, address, birth date, and other identifying information;
- a description of the child's disability and, if the child is enrolled in school, the problems the child is having in school;
- a request that the child be evaluated by an Individualized Education Program (IEP) team;
- the date of the referral; and
- an address and daytime telephone number where the parent(s) can be reached.

The letter should be addressed to the local education agency's director of special education (the child's principal can usually provide the necessary contact information). Parents should keep a copy of the letter. In addition, it may be helpful to send a copy to the child's teacher, so that the teacher knows a request has been made.

Q. How must the local education agency respond to the request for referral?

A. It must accept and act on all referrals for children from birth to age twenty-one, so long as they live in the LEA's jurisdiction and have not graduated from high school. However, services do not have to be provided until the child turns three years old.

Q. What if the local education agency does not think an evaluation is needed?

A. If the agency does not agree that the child may need special education and related services, it may refuse to evaluate the child. The parent would then have to use the hearing process to require the LEA to evaluate the child.

EVALUATIONS

Evaluations are a crucial part of the early stages of special education. An evaluation is what identifies a child as needing services, and begins the process of identifying the child's specific needs. This section outlines the legal requirements for evaluations, as well as what parents can do to help.

Introduction

Q. When must the evaluation of a child be conducted?

▶ NOTICES

This chapter refers to various types of notice that parents are entitled to receive, including notice required after a referral, before an IEP team meeting, and when the local education agency refuses to take a requested action. Generally, a notice must contain

- a full explanation of all procedural rights available to parents;
- a description of the proposed or refused action, including an explanation for the school's decision;
- a description of the other options considered, along with an explanation of why these options were rejected;
- a description of each evaluation procedure, test, report, or other factor relied on in making the decision in question; and
- if the local education agency is initiating a hearing, information regarding any free or low-cost legal and other relevant services.

The notice must be clear and written in the parent's native language, unless this is clearly not feasible.

A. When a local education agency receives a referral, it has sixty calendar days to evaluate the child and (if the child qualifies for special education) to write an Individualized Education Program and offer placement. The sixty-day period begins when the LEA receives a letter of referral.

Q. My child's school told me that it wants to conduct an evaluation. Can they do this even if I don't want them to?

A. If this is the child's first referral, the local education agency cannot begin any evaluations until it has the parent's written consent. The consent must be voluntary and the parent can revoke it in writing at any time. A child with exceptional educational needs must be reevaluated at least once every three years. The parents or the LEA may request a reevaluation sooner if the circumstances warrant.

Q. What happens if I refuse or revoke my consent to an evaluation?

A. The LEA may initiate a hearing to determine whether it will conduct an evaluation without your consent.

Q. Will I receive notice of the evaluation?

A. Yes. Notices must conform with the requirements outlined on page 172.

Q. Who performs the evaluation?

A. The evaluation is performed by a multidisciplinary team called the IEP team. The IEP team is a group of educators who, based on their evaluations, will determine whether your child has a disability and needs special education and related services. The local education agency appoints members to the IEP team based on information in the referral.

Q. Who is on the IEP team?

A. All members of the IEP team must be employees of the local education agency. At least two members must be skilled in assessing children and in implementing programming for children with handicapping conditions, and at least one of these members must be a teacher licensed to teach children with the handicapping condition the child is suspected of having. In addition:

- If a child is suspected of having a learning disability, the IEP team must include the child's regular education teacher, if there is one.
- If a child is suspected of needing occupational therapy, the IEP team must include an occupational therapist.
- If a child is suspected of needing physical therapy, the IEP team must include a physical therapist.
- The IEP team must include other individuals as needed to evaluate and determine the needs of the child.

Q. What are the responsibilities of the IEP team?

A. The IEP team must examine all relevant available data concerning the child. If the child is suspected of being—or is currently identified as being—learning disabled, at least one member of the IEP team other than the child's regular teacher must observe the child's performance in the regular classroom. The child's parents must be involved and consulted throughout the entire IEP team process.

If necessary, the IEP team must consult with people other than school board employees, including

- the child's parents or relatives;
- foster parents;
- professionals such as therapists, physicians, or social workers who work with the child;
- friends;

- caregivers; and
- advocates such as an attorney or support group advisor.

All tests and other evaluation materials and procedures used by the IEP team must meet applicable legal requirements.

Q. What happens during the evaluation?

A. The IEP team must consider all areas related to the child's suspected disability—including, where appropriate

- vision;
- hearing;
- motor abilities;
- academic abilities;
- capacity for self-help;
- mobility skills;
- career and vocational abilities and interests; and
- social and emotional status.

Tests must be specific and administered by trained personnel following the correct guidelines. Rather than simply providing an IQ number or measuring the child's impaired skills, the tests must accurately measure a child's aptitude or achievement and assess specific areas of educational need. A psychological assessment must be conducted by a credentialed and trained school psychologist prepared to assess cultural and ethnic factors appropriate to the child.

Q. English is not my family's first language. Will that be taken into consideration during the evaluation?

A. Yes. Tests must be administered in the child's native language or mode of communi-

> ▶ **EDUCATIONAL RECORDS**
>
> Parents have a right to see their child's education records during any evaluation, placement decision, or challenge to a proposed action by the school, as well as during any hearings or appeals. Parent are specifically entitled to a copy of their child's IEP.

cation. If this is not feasible, an interpreter must be used. The testing materials must be selected and administered so as not to be racially, culturally, or sexually discriminatory.

The First IEP Team Meeting: Evaluating the Child

Q. Who schedules the IEP team meeting?

A. The local education agency sets a date for the IEP team to meet and discuss the evaluations and findings. A reasonable time beforehand, the local education agency will notify the parent of the meeting. The notice must include the following information:

- date, time, and location of the meeting;
- a statement that the purpose of the meeting is to determine whether the child has exceptional educational needs;
- names and titles of members of the IEP team and any additional persons who may be attending;
- a statement that the parent may attend the meeting and may bring an advocate; and
- if the child is a member of a minority group, a statement that a member of that

minority group may attend the meeting and provide input into the decision-making process.

If the meeting time and date are not convenient for you, immediately contact the local education agency to arrange a more convenient time.

Q. Am I entitled to a copy of the IEP team members' reports?

A. Yes. The IEP team members must make their individual reports available at the meeting, so long as the parent requests this in writing within ten days of being sent notice of the evaluation.

Q. An IEP team meeting has been scheduled for my child. What should I do to prepare?

A. If possible, you should arrange to bring a lawyer or advocate to the meeting with you. Before the team meeting, you and the advocate should

- clarify what the child is being evaluated for;
- determine who will be at the meeting;
- review records and reports, especially the most recent IEP team report, all individual reports, the current IEP, and the previous IEP;
- review any reports from private therapists or physicians;
- determine the child's needs;
- if an advocate will be present, discuss your role and that of the advocate, and notify the school that an advocate will be attending;
- determine what the legal issues are and research those issues; and
- develop a strategy.

Q. Are IEP team members required to attend?

A. Each member of the IEP team must either attend the meeting or be represented by a person with knowledge of the child and of the absent member's evaluations and findings. More than half of the IEP team members must be present in person.

Q. What does the IEP team do at the meeting?

A. At the meeting, the IEP team discusses and compares the evaluations and findings of each of its members. Based upon the evaluations and findings, and using applicable legal criteria, the IEP team will determine whether the child has a handicapping condition. As discussed below, this meeting is important because it will form the basis for the subsequent IEP team report on this question, which will be submitted to the local education agency's special education director for approval.

Q. What happens at the end of the meeting?

A. The participants should clarify what has been decided and the actions for which each participant will have future responsibility. Any unanswered questions or concerns should be raised before the meeting is over.

If the child is found to have a handicapping condition, the IEP team will determine whether the child needs special education as a result of that condition. If the IEP team concludes that a child has exceptional educational needs, it must consider and make recommendations regarding the related services the child may need.

IEP Team Report

Q. What does the IEP team do after the meeting?

A. After the meeting, the team writes an IEP team report, which at a minimum must include the following:

- a list of the found handicapping conditions;
- the team's conclusion regarding whether the child needs special education because of a handicapping condition;
- the team's conclusions regarding the need for occupational or physical therapy;
- a statement outlining the reasons for each of the team's findings and conclusions; and
- recommendations regarding any related services the child may need.

If the IEP team finds that the child does not have exceptional educational needs, the report must include

- an identification of the child's non-exceptional educational needs;
- a referral to any programs, other than special education programs, offered by the local education agency from which the child may benefit; and
- information about any programs and services, other than those offered by the local education agency, from which the child may benefit.

Q. There is someone with the title "director of special education" at my child's school. What is his or her role during this process?

A. The **director of special education** is an employee of the local education agency who is charged with a variety of special education ad-

ministrative responsibilities, including approving IEP team reports. If the director approves a report, a copy is sent to the local education agency board and the child's parent.

Special rules apply if the director approves an IEP team report signed by only a minority of team members. In that case, if the director attended the meeting that resulted in the proposed IEP team reports, the director must send to the governing board and to the child's parents a copy of all the separately proposed reports, and he or she must also indicate in writing which of the reports were selected and why. If the director did not attend the meeting, he or she must set a date to meet with the IEP team and discuss the proposed reports.

Q. Can the director reject the proposed IEP team report?

A. Yes. If the director does not accept the IEP team report or reports, he or she must send

---

▶ **IF YOU DON'T ATTEND THE MEETING**

If the child's parent is unable to attend the most recent IEP team meeting, the director must send the approved IEP team report and any separately proposed reports to the parent. The director also must notify the parent that he or she may request a conference with the director to discuss any of the proposed IEP team reports, as well as the approved report, and that an advocate may accompany the parent to this conference.

the report or reports back to the IEP team along with a list of questions. The director must schedule a meeting for the IEP team to discuss the director's concerns, and he or she must notify the child's parents of this meeting.

Q. The IEP team found that my child doesn't qualify for special education. What should I do with my copy of the report?

A. Keep all reports, even if the IEP team finds that your child does not need special education. You still may be able to use the report to create a more appropriate regular education program for your child. Or, if you disagree with the results, you may request an independent evaluation during which the report may prove helpful.

Reevaluation

Q. If a child is receiving special education, how often is he or she reevaluated?

A. The law requires an IEP team to reevaluate such children at least once every three years. A reevaluation can occur more frequently if either a parent or the local education agency feels it is necessary.

Independent Educational Evaluation

Q. I disagree with the local education agency's evaluation. May I seek an independent educational evaluation?

A. Yes. Parents may obtain an independent educational evaluation if they disagree with the local education agency's evaluation. Par-

ents have the right to select the independent evaluator. Reasons for seeking such an evaluation might include

- There is no one on the local education agency staff qualified to perform the evaluation.
- There is reason to believe the local education agency relied on insufficient testing when it made recommendations at the IEP meeting.
- The local education agency results are inconsistent with other testing, so clarification is needed.

Q. Who pays for an independent educational evaluation?

A. The local education agency is required to pay for the independent educational evaluation, unless one of the following occurs:

- The parent refuses to give the local education agency a complete copy of the independent educational evaluation.
- It is found at a hearing that the local education agency's evaluation is appropriate.
- The independent educational evaluation does not meet the statutory requirements.

Q. What should I do before obtaining an independent evaluation?

A. Before seeking an independent evaluation, parents should first select an independent evaluator and then ask the local education agency whether it believes the evaluator meets statutory requirements. If the local education agency finds that the parents' proposed independent evaluator does not meet legal requirements, it must inform the parents of that finding. The LEA must also inform the parents whether the agency will request a hearing to challenge payment of that evaluator.

Q. Can anyone other than a parent order an independent educational evaluation?

A. Yes. A hearing officer or a reviewing officer also may order an independent educational evaluation.

Q. What happens with the results of the independent educational evaluation?

A. The results of the independent educational evaluation must be considered by the local education agency when making any decision regarding

- the child's IEP team evaluation;
- the IEP itself; or
- the educational placement or provision of a free appropriate education for the child.

The independent educational evaluation also may be presented as evidence at a due process hearing.

Notice of Identification

Q. My child is currently identified as having exceptional needs. Will the school have to contact me if this status changes?

A. Yes. Whenever a local education agency proposes to change—or refuses to change—the identification of a child as having exceptional educational needs, it is legally required to send written notice to the child's parents. A parent then may initiate a due process hearing to contest the decision.

REMEMBER THIS

- Special education involves a variety of laws and policies. Parents should educate

themselves by asking questions and talking to their doctors, attorneys, other advocates, and school officials.

- During evaluation, parental consent is required. Parents have the right to revoke their consent at any point.

- An IEP team meeting should include the child's parents, a teacher licensed to deal with the child's handicapping condition, a regular education teacher, any necessary therapists, and, if appropriate, the child or the parents' advocate.

- If a parent disagrees with an IEP team decision, he or she may ask for an independent evaluation.

INDIVIDUALIZED EDUCATION PROGRAMS

Introduction

Q. So what exactly is an IEP?

A. The **Individualized Education Program** (**IEP**) is a document describing the program of specially designed instruction and related services for a child who (1) is three years of age or older, (2) has not graduated from high school, and (3) is determined by an IEP team to have exceptional educational needs. A child cannot access special education and related services unless he or she has a current IEP. This document should be developed collaboratively with the child's parents and school professionals.

Q. How does an IEP differ from an IEP team meeting report?

A. The formal IEP is a plan for your child's special education. The IEP team meeting re-

▶ IEP BEFORE PLACEMENT

An IEP must be developed before making a placement decision about a child. A school system violates the IDEA if it writes an IEP to support a placement decision that has already been made.

port is a summary of the team's initial findings with regard to whether your child is even eligible for special education services in the first place.

The Second IEP Meeting: Developing a Plan

Q. Is the second IEP meeting similar to the IEP team meeting that took place during the evaluation phase?

A. Procedurally, similarities include the scheduling requirements (both meetings must take place at a date and time agreed upon by the local education agency and parent), notification requirements (before both meetings, parents must receive a detailed notice outlining the purpose of the meeting and the parents' rights), and the preparation involved before each meeting. For a more de-

▶ IEP MEETING DEADLINES

The IEP meeting must be held within thirty days after approval of the IEP team report indicating that the child has exceptional educational needs.

tailed look at these issues, consult the "Evaluations" section earlier in this chapter.

Q. Who must be included in the second IEP meeting?

A. The IDEA requires the following participants at the meeting:

- a representative of the local education agency, other than the child's teacher, who is qualified to provide or supervise the provision of special education;
- one or both of the child's parents;
- the child, if appropriate; and
- a member of the IEP team that evaluated the child, or a person who is knowledgeable about the child's evaluation and is familiar with the IEP team report.

In addition

- If the purpose of the IEP meeting is to consider transition services for a child, then the local education agency must invite the child and a representative of any agency likely to be responsible for providing or paying for transition services.
- If a child is enrolled in a private school and receives (or is eligible to receive) special education from the board, or if the local education agency is considering placing the child in a private school, then a representative of the private school must attend.
- Others may attend the meeting at the discretion of the child's parents or the board.

The local education agency should not complete an IEP without a full discussion of the child's need for special education and the services offered. However, local education agency personnel may suggest goals or meet with the parents before the IEP meeting—if

▶ WHO HAS AUTHORITY?

The local education agency representative must have authority to commit the LEA to provide the services included in the IEP. Otherwise, the IEP could be vetoed by school administrators or other school officials.

▶ PARENT PARTICIPATION PARENTS ARE PART OF THE TEAM

Parents are expected to be equal participants, along with school personnel, in developing, reviewing, and revising their child's IEP.

the earlier meeting does not prevent team members (including parents) from providing input, and if it results in an IEP.

Q. What happens at an IEP meeting?

A. The IEP meeting generally proceeds as follows:

1. Discussion and description of the child's current level of functioning, including academic and nonacademic functioning.
2. Development of annual goals and short-term objectives derived from the child's current functioning.
3. Discussion and description of special education and related services, including the placement recommendation and significant details of the placement—such as class size, integration, and mainstreaming opportunities—that comprise the child's appropriate educational program.

Q. What are my responsibilities at the IEP meeting?

A. Make sure you understand what is happening. If you don't understand any acronyms or jargon, don't hesitate to ask for an explanation. Don't be concerned that asking ques-

tions will make you seem uninformed; on the contrary, asking questions will demonstrate that you are concerned about developing the appropriate education program for your child.

You can also contribute to the IEP meeting by bringing a written summary of your child's needs as you see them. This summary might include a description of the following:

- **Strengths.** Is your child outgoing and open? Optimistic and articulate? Imaginative? Whatever your child's particular strengths, mention them in your summary.
- **Weaknesses or problem areas.** Does your child have poor self-concept? Get into fights or have academic deficits? Does he or she tend to be disorganized, take longer than average to complete assignments, or get discouraged easily?
- **Functioning levels.** Does your child have difficulty with reading, mathematics, or spelling? Does he or she respond to individual attention? Need verbal reinforcement for presented material?
- **What your child needs to learn.** For example, does your child need a more positive self-concept? Need to achieve academic proficiency at his or her grade level?

Develop age-appropriate social skills or self-help skills? Acquire job training? Does he or she need to be better organized? Learn to work at a more rapid pace?

Q. May I bring others to the IEP meeting?

A. Yes. You can bring anyone to assist you in asserting your position, including an advocate, friend, caseworker, or attorney.

Q. May I tape-record IEP meetings?

A. Yes. In addition, as a parent you have the right to:

- inspect and review LEA-made tape recordings;
- request that the tape recordings be amended if you believe they contain information that is inaccurate, misleading, or in violation of the privacy rights or other rights of your child; and
- challenge any tape recording you believe is inaccurate, misleading, or in violation of your child's privacy rights or other rights.

Q. Can I have a language or sign interpreter at the IEP meeting?

A. Yes. The local education agency must take necessary steps to ensure that the parent understands what is said at the IEP meeting. If you need a language or sign interpreter, the local education agency must provide one to you at no cost.

Q. I can't attend the meeting. What should I do?

A. If a parent is unable to attend, the local education agency must ensure the parent's participation by some other means, such as by individual or conference telephone call. If no parent can attend the meeting or participate by other means, the local education agency must maintain a record of its attempts to have the parent attend or participate in the meeting.

Contents of the IEP

Q. What must the IEP include?

A. The IEP must include

- a statement of the child's present levels of educational performance in the areas of need as identified by the IEP team;
- a statement of annual goals, including short-term instructional objectives;
- a statement of the extent to which the child will be able to participate in regular educational programs;
- a statement of the specific special education and related services, including assistive technology services or devices if appropriate, to be provided;
- the projected dates for the start of services and their anticipated duration;
- appropriate objective criteria and evaluation procedures and schedules for determining (at least annually) whether the short-term instructional objectives are being achieved;
- beginning no later than age sixteen, an annual statement of needed transition services—and, if the child does not need transition services, a statement to that effect and a statement regarding the basis upon which the determination was made; and
- if a child has a visual handicap, a statement indicating whether the child needs to be taught Braille.

> ▶ **WHAT'S NEEDED—NOT WHAT'S AVAILABLE**
>
> The IEP must contain a statement of all services needed by the child, not just those that are available within the school system.

The IEP also should include a statement explaining why the chosen educational environment is the least restrictive environment. The statement must address the nature and severity of the child's disability, the issues with the regular education environment that warrant removal of the child, and the potential harmful effects on the child, on others, and on the services provided.

Q. What should be included in the present level of performance statement?

A. The **present level of performance** is a clear, descriptive statement of how the child is performing in a specific area of need identified by the IEP team. It should include a description of the child's strengths, interests, and weaknesses. The present level should reflect the child's unique needs in any area of education affected by the disability, including academic areas, nonacademic areas, and perceptual functioning. The child's performance should be described in objective, measurable terms.

Q. What are annual goals?

A. **Annual goals** are those the child can accomplish in one year. They should be directly related to present level of functioning. For each goal, the statement of annual goals should specify

- the child's area of need;
- the direction of the child's behavior; and
- the child's level of potential attainment.

Q. What are short-term instructional objectives?

A. **Short-term instructional objectives** are the specific, sequential steps the child must take in order to move past the present level of functioning and achieve an annual goal. A statement of these objectives should include a description of the skills or behaviors to be performed and the conditions under which the child will be expected to perform them—including a description of any necessary materials, instructions, time limits, prompts, or assistive technology.

Q. How do annual goals and short-term objectives work together?

A. Annual goals and short-term objectives allow a parent to track the child's progress and help determine if the child's educational program is appropriate. They also help form and guide the child's specific instructional plans and define the needed special education and related services. The local education agency must provide those programs and services necessary to meet the goals and objectives set forth in the child's IEP.

Q. What do evaluation procedures entail?

A. **Evaluation procedures** are used by the teacher to determine whether the child has met his or her goals. There are three components to an evaluation:

- **criteria**—i.e., the level of performance deemed acceptable for the child;
- **procedures**—the method for determining whether a goal has been met; and

- **schedule**—the timeline within which the teacher will evaluate each objective.

Q. What should be included in the statement of special education and related services?

A. Included in the IEP is a **statement of special education and related services,** a list of all the special education and related services the child should receive. These services can be specified in terms of school classes (i.e., specific classes the child must take) or actual time (i.e., the amount of time to be spent on each service). The IEP should specify the amount, frequency, and duration of each service. This includes describing any special transportation needs, adaptive physical education requirements, modifications to the child's regular school schedule, assistance or supervision needed during lunch hour or recess, appropriate disciplinary approaches, and extended school year requirements. The related services should be specified in detail, not merely described in general terms. When describing the amount of time to be spent in the regular education environment, the IEP should specify a list of classes, or an amount of percentage of the child's actual time—it should not merely specify a range of services.

Q. Should my child's IEP outline his or her exact instructional plan?

A. Not exactly. The IEP is not intended to be a detailed instructional plan. Instead, by specifying its goals and objectives, the IEP gives general direction to those who will implement it, and serves as the basis for developing a detailed instructional plan.

However, the IEP must specify all special education and related services that are needed. It must detail the amount of services to be provided, so that the local education agency's commitment of resources will be clear to parents and other IEP team members. The amount of time to be committed to each service must be appropriate to that specific service, and must be stated in a manner that is clear to all involved in the IEP's development and implementation.

Q. Must my child be moved out of a regular classroom?

A. No. Some special education students are able to remain in regular classes with certain modifications, supplementary aids, or services. Such modifications may include the use of a tape recorder, oral testing, or special seating. Any such modifications must be written into the child's IEP. See pages 185–187 for a more detailed discussion of placements.

Q. Can the IEP dictate the size of my child's class?

A. Yes. As we have seen, special education is instruction specially designed to meet the

---

▶ **CHANGES: AMOUNT OF SERVICES VERSUS SCHEDULING OF SERVICES**

Changes in the amount of services listed in the IEP cannot be made without another IEP meeting first being held. However, as long as there is no change in the overall amount of services provided, some adjustments in scheduling may occur without another IEP meeting, provided that the child's parents are notified.

unique needs of a disabled child. One of those unique needs may be a limit on class size. While a local education agency may disagree about the need for a class size limit, it may not categorically refuse to add class size to an IEP as a matter of policy. Such a policy would prevent the IEP team from developing an individualized educational program based on the unique needs of each child and, in turn, would violate federal and state disability laws.

Q. My child responds better to a certain teacher. Can the IEP require that he or she be placed in that teacher's class?

A. No. The IEP cannot require particular teachers, classrooms, or placements. However, the local education agency must provide services in a setting that meets the child's IEP goals and objectives. If the local education agency's proposed classroom or teacher cannot meet the child's IEP goals, you should ask the local education agency to change the classroom or teacher.

Q. How long does the IEP last? I think my child may benefit from summer school.

A. The IEP typically lasts from the beginning to the end of one school year. If a child requires services for longer than a typical school year, a separate IEP may be needed for the extended school year. See page 193 for further discussion of an extended school year.

Approving, Reviewing, and Challenging the IEP

Q. Must I consent to an IEP before it can be implemented?

A. Yes. If you disagree with parts of the IEP, you may consent to those portions that you agree with so that services can begin. The parts not agreed to cannot be implemented, and your issues may need to be resolved at a due process hearing. You may consent to the IEP as written, yet disagree with the actual placement site or classroom.

Q. Do I have to sign the IEP?

A. It is not required, although some educational agencies will ask parents to sign. By signing the IEP, parents indicate that they were present at the IEP meeting, but not necessarily that they agree with the IEP. If a parent does not agree with the IEP, the parent should indicate on the form that he or she disagrees with it.

Q. I have changed my mind about a part of the IEP. Can I withdraw my consent?

A. A parent may withdraw consent to any or all portions of the Individualized Education Program at any time after consultation with a member of the IEP team. The withdrawal of consent must be in writing.

Q. How often must the local education agency review a child's IEP?

A. At least once a year. A parent also may request a review of his or her child's IEP. Educational agencies should grant any reasonable request for an IEP meeting.

Q. May a local education agency unilaterally change an IEP without the parents' consent?

A. No. Once an agreed-upon IEP has been developed, school personnel may not unilaterally change it. In order to revise an IEP or change a placement, a local education agency must follow applicable procedures for IEP meetings and teams. The local education agency must give parents prior written notice of any proposed change, and the parents may initiate a hearing if they disagree.

Q. What should I do if I disagree with the IEP or some parts of it?

A. If you disagree with the Individualized Education Program, you should first attempt to resolve the disagreement informally with your local education agency. You may request a due process hearing if you are unable to resolve the disagreement informally. See page 197 for an in-depth discussion of due process hearings.

REMEMBER THIS

- An IEP is the document that describes the specially designed instruction and related services prescribed for a special-needs student.

- Parents play an important role in the development of an IEP. A parent must consent to the IEP before it can be implemented.

- An IEP should detail the child's present performance levels, as well as annual goals and short-term instructional objectives.

- An IEP must be reviewed at least once a year.

PLACEMENT OFFERS

Developing the Placement Offer

Q. What happens after an IEP has been developed and approved?

> ▶ **ECONOMIC ISSUES ARE NOT IMPORTANT**
>
> A local education agency must provide educational services based on the educational needs of the child. Educational agencies cannot legally use economic issues to deny a child services he or she needs according to the IDEA.

A. The next step is for the local education agency to develop a placement offer that carries out the IEP. The **placement offer** does two things:

- specifies the delivery model to be used and the level at which each of the services will be provided to implement the child's IEP; and
- specifies the location where services will be provided in conformance with the first part of the placement offer.

Q. Does placement require parental consent?

A. Yes. If this is the child's first placement, the parent must give written consent. Once consent is given to the first placement, it stays in effect for all future placements. However, consent can be revoked at any time and, after revocation, the LEA cannot continue the placement. However, if the local education agency believes the child is best served in special education, the local education agency can request a due process hearing

Q. How are placements determined?

A. Placement must be based on the child's unique needs as described in the IEP, rather than on the programs currently available.

Q. What must the local education agency take into consideration when making a placement offer?

A. The local education agency must take the following into consideration:

- To the maximum extent appropriate, the child must be educated with children who do not have exceptional educational needs.
- Special classes that would remove a child from a regular educational environment may be prescribed only when the nature or severity of a child's handicapping condition is such that education in regular classes would be unsatisfactory, even with the use of supplementary aids and services.
- Alternative programs needed to implement the child's IEP must be available.
- Appropriate nonacademic and extracurricular services and activities must be provided.
- Unless the IEP requires a different arrangement, the child shall be educated in the school he or she would attend if he or she did not have exceptional educational needs.
- Special education and related services shall be provided as close as possible to the child's home.
- A child may be placed in a special education program at the child's home or at a hospital only if a physician's written statement indicates that the child is unable to attend school.
- Any potential harmful effect on the child or on the quality of needed services must be taken into account.

Q. What if there is no appropriate placement at our local school?

A. If the local education agency operates (or can immediately establish) an appropriate special education program as required by the IEP and the placement offer, the local education agency must place the child in that program. If an appropriate special education placement is not available, the local education agency must determine whether an appropriate placement is offered by a different local education agency or state agency. In some circumstances, a child may be placed in a program offered by a public agency in another state, or in a private school.

Q. May children with different disabilities be placed together for instruction?

A. Yes. However, the placement must meet the child's IEP goals and objectives. If it does not, the placement is not appropriate.

Implementing a Placement Offer

Q. Once the placement is selected, how soon will it be implemented?

A. Before implementing a placement offer, the local education agency must send a copy of the offer to the child's parents. It must do this each time the placement is developed or changed. Unless a time extension has been agreed to, the placement offer must be sent to the parents within ninety days of the date the board received the referral or initiated a reevaluation of the child.

The placement offer must be implemented as soon as possible after the IEP meeting. There can be no undue delay in providing services. However, the placement offer may not be implemented until a reasonable amount of time has elapsed since the parent received notice of the placement offer.

Refusal to Initiate or Change Placement

Q. What if the LEA refuses to initiate or change a placement offer?

A. If the LEA refuses to initiate or change a placement offer, it must send notice of its refusal to the parents.

Disagreement with a Placement Offer

Q. What should I do if I disagree with the placement offer?

A. In most cases, you should follow the same procedures you would follow if you disagreed with the IEP. See page 187 for a discussion of this subject.

Residential Placement

Q. What is a residential placement?

A. The term **residential placement** usually refers to programs in which children are cared for at a location outside of their family home. Such programs include medical and nonmedical care in addition to room and board.

Q. When is a child entitled to residential placement?

A. If placement in a public or private residential program is necessary to provide special education and related services to a disabled child, the program must be provided at no cost to the child's parents. Typically, residential placement is indicated when a child requires structure, intensity, and consistency of programming beyond what is offered by a day program.

REMEMBER THIS

- A local education agency must provide educational services based on the educational needs of the child. Educational agencies cannot deny a child needed services based on economic issues.

- Program placement must be based on a child's unique needs as described in the child's IEP, rather than on the programs currently available in the local education agency's jurisdiction.

- If parents disagree with a placement offer, they should first send a letter to the local education agency explaining why they feel it is inappropriate.

SPECIAL EDUCATION: SETTINGS, SERVICES, AND COSTS

Special education laws employ complex terms and are based on complex theories. These theories include the notion that each child should be afforded a free appropriate public education (FAPE), educated in the least restrictive environment (LRE), and provided with necessary related services. But what exactly constitutes a FAPE? What should parents do if they think their child is being denied one? What exactly is a least restrictive environment? And what constitutes a related service? This section addresses these issues and others surrounding the theories central to special education.

Free Appropriate Public Education

Q. What is a free appropriate public education?

A. A free appropriate public education is an education that includes special education and related services, as well as appropriate preschool, elementary, or secondary school education provided in conformity with the required IEP. A package of special education and related services is considered appropriate if

- the IEP was developed in accordance with statutory procedures;
- it is reasonably calculated to enable the child to receive educational benefits; and
- it is likely to bring educational progress to the child.

Q. Does a free appropriate public education include nonacademic and extracurricular activities?

A. Yes. Educational agencies must take steps to provide nonacademic and extracurricular services and activities in a manner that affords disabled children an equal opportunity to participate. Such services and activities include athletics, recreational activities, special-interest groups or clubs, lunch and recess, and student employment, including employment by the school and assistance in making outside employment available. In arranging for these services, the local education agency must ensure that children with disabilities participate with nondisabled children to the maximum extent appropriate.

Least Restrictive Environment

Q. My child has been identified as needing special education services. Does the least-restrictive-environment rule mean that he or she can't be moved out of the regular classroom?

A. Not necessarily. Both the Individuals with Disabilities Education Act and Section 504 guarantee children with disabilities the right to participate in regular classroom and extracurricular activities with nondisabled children to the maximum extent appropriate in view of their individual needs, and with the help of supplementary aids and services or modifications to the regular education curriculum if necessary. Depending on the child's individual needs as documented by the IEP, the child may need to receive educational programming in a special education classroom, at a special school, at a nonpublic school, or at a residential facility. Whether your child will remain in a regular classroom will depend on your child's abilities and what the IEP requires.

Q. When may the school move my child into a setting other than a regular education classroom?

A. Only when a child's education cannot be achieved satisfactorily in the regular education classroom with one or more supplemen-

---

▶ EDUCATION WITHOUT COSTS

A **free** education is an education provided at no cost to the child or the child's parents or guardians. All special education and related services must be provided at public expense. Parents cannot normally be required to use their child's Social Security benefits or health insurance to pay for or defray the cost of special education or related services.

▶ **CHECKLIST: IS YOUR CHILD BEING EDUCATED IN THE LEAST RESTRICTIVE ENVIRONMENT?**

Answering the following questions can help determine whether a local education agency is complying with the least-restrictive-environment mandate:

- What are the educational benefits available to the child in a regular classroom, supplemented with appropriate aids and services, as compared with the educational benefits of a special education classroom?

- What are the nonacademic benefits of the child's interaction with children who are not disabled?

- What effect will the disabled child have on the teacher and the other children in the classroom?

---

tary aids and services. These issues must be considered both before and during the development of the IEP. If the local education agency proposes to remove a child from a mainstream setting, it bears the burden of proving that such a move (whether total or partial) is justified.

A child with disabilities will be a stronger candidate for an integrated environment or full inclusion if the child's IEP goals and objectives relate, at least in part, to the curriculum in use in the desired placement.

Q. What are supplementary aids and services?

A. Supplementary aids and services might include

- special seating arrangements;
- test and curriculum modifications;
- instructional or health aides to accompany the child; and
- adaptive equipment.

Q. Does my child's regular education teacher have any responsibility for ensuring that my child is educated in the least restrictive environment?

A. Yes. Regular education staff have a duty to cooperate in providing a disabled child with integration, full inclusion, and mainstreaming opportunities. The local education agency is responsible for:

- giving a copy of the child's IEP to the child's regular education teachers or informing them of its contents; and
- ensuring that a special education teacher or other appropriate support person is available to consult with the regular education teacher.

Related Services

Q. What are related services?

A. **Related services** are any services necessary to help a child benefit from special education. Examples of related services include transportation and such development, corrective, and other supportive services as may be required to assist a child with disabilities in benefiting from special education—including the early identification and assessment of disabling conditions.

Q. My child needs a service that isn't specifically mentioned in this book. Does this mean it won't qualify as a related service?

A. No. The statutory list of related services is not exhaustive. If a child needs a particular service in order to benefit from special education, and if the service is a developmental, supportive, or corrective one, it is considered "related" and should thus be provided.

Q. When is a child eligible for related services?

A. Once a child qualifies for special education services, that child is eligible for any related service required to meet his or her educational needs. On the other hand, the

---

> ▶ **WHAT IS A SUPPORTIVE SERVICE?**
>
> **Supportive services** can include speech pathology and audiology, psychological services, physical and occupational therapy, recreation (including therapeutic recreation), social-work services, and medical and counseling services (including rehabilitation counseling). For medical services to be considered supportive services, they must be for diagnostic and evaluation purposes only.

---

local education agency does not have to provide a service to a child with a disability just because he or she will benefit from the service, even if the child requires that service. Rather, the service is considered "related"—and thus must be provided—only if it is necessary to help the child benefit from *educational instruction.*

Q. Does it matter if my child is in a regular classroom setting?

A. No. Any child who meets the eligibility requirements for special education is entitled to related services, even if he or she is placed full-time in a regular classroom. In fact, even children with disabilities who are not eligible for special education are still entitled to receive supportive services necessary for them to benefit from their school programs.

Q. How often should related services be offered?

A. The frequency of a related service and the amount of time needed for each session must be determined based on each individual child's needs as determined at the IEP team meeting. The service's frequency and length should be specified in the IEP.

Q. When does a specific service count as a related service?

A. The following is a list of common related services, including a discussion of when they constitute related services.

Transportation

Transportation is considered a related service when, due to a child's disability or the distance of the child's home from school, it is necessary in order for the child to attend a special education program. So long as the IEP team determines that the child needs transportation, the child is entitled to receive it, even if the child is mainstreamed in regular classes.

Transportation options may include, but are not limited to: walking, riding the regular school bus, using public transportation (with reimbursement), riding a special bus from a pick-up point, portal-to-portal transportation by bus, taking a taxi, or voluntary driving by a reimbursed parent.

A local education agency cannot deny transportation services on the basis of how far the child lives from the school, or based on the parents' ability to provide transportation.

Physical Therapy and Occupational Therapy

These types of therapy address a child's fine motor functioning (e.g., the child's ability to write and draw) and gross motor functioning (e.g., the child's ability to run, walk, throw, or jump). A child's motor functioning may affect his or her independent living skills.

Speech Therapy and Language Therapy

Any child eligible for special education may receive speech and language therapy if he or she needs it to benefit from special education. Speech therapy addresses articulation difficulties. Language therapy addresses difficulties with memory, verbal expression, and listening. In order to receive these therapies as a related service, a child does not have to meet the special education eligibility criteria for speech or language disorders.

Mental Health Services

Psychological services include counseling and psychotherapy. Counseling generally focuses on school and school-related issues, such as behavior in school, grades, and curriculum. Psychotherapy generally focuses on a child's emotional status and feelings toward others. Psychotherapy is available when a child's emotional status has a negative effect on educational performance.

These types of mental health services must be provided to any child who needs them in order to benefit from special education. To receive these services, it is not necessary for the child to be classified as "seriously emotionally disturbed."

Communication Services and Equipment-Related Services

These types of services are considered related services when the IEP team decides that the child would benefit from them—for example, if the IEP team determines that a child would benefit from a computerized communications device and instruction in using the device. When dealing with a non-oral child, the local education agency should contract with a non-oral communications specialist to assess the necessity of such services.

Vision Therapy

If a child needs vision therapy in order to benefit from special education, the child is entitled to receive it as a related service. Vision therapy may include remedial or developmental instruction provided directly or in consultation with an optometrist, ophthalmologist, or by another qualified licensed physician or surgeon.

Medical Services

Services provided by a licensed physician to determine the nature of a child's medically related needs are considered a related service if the medical disability has resulted in the child needing special education and other related services. Related services also include school health services provided by a qualified school nurse or other qualified person.

Instructional Aides

Provision of an instructional aide is a related service if the child needs an aide in order to benefit from his or her education. This can include situations in which the child needs an aide to assist him or her in a regular classroom. Any required qualifications should be written in the IEP, as should the frequency, amount, and type of services the aide will provide.

Assistive Technology

An **assistive technology device** is any item, piece of equipment, or product system, whether acquired commercially or off-the-shelf and modified or customized, that is used to increase, maintain, or improve the functional capabilities of a child with disabilities. As a related service, the provision of assistive devices includes evaluating the needs of the child, purchasing, modifying or repairing such devices, and providing the training necessary for the child and others to use them effectively. Federal law requires that educational agencies ensure that assistive technology devices or services be made available as part of the child's

- special education;
- related services; and
- supplemental aids and services used to place children in the least restrictive environment.

Assistive devices that the U.S. Department of Education's Office of Special Education Programs has found to be "related services" include

- computers (including assistance in using them);
- auditory training equipment;
- computerized communication systems;
- devices for loading and unloading children from a bus; and
- liberator communication devices.

Q. My child needs hearing aids. Does this count as an assistive technology?

A. No. Individual-prescribed devices (such as glasses and hearing aids) are generally considered personal items, and educational agencies do not have the responsibility to provide them. In determining whether assistive technology is a related service, consideration is given to

- the importance of language to education;
- the availability of alternative systems;
- the child's prognosis;
- the technology's ability to improve gross motor skills and safety;
- the normalcy of the device in the context of the child's life;
- the family's acceptance of the device; and
- whether a child's IEP appropriately considers the child's potential.

Q. My child needs a computerized communication system to complete homework assignments. Can we bring it home?

A. Likely, yes. A child probably can use an assistive device at home if the child needs it to receive a free appropriate public education—for example, if the child needs it to complete school homework or practice functional skills.

Q. My son's school says he needs some form of an assistive device. Am I going to have to pay for it?

A. No. Educational agencies cannot require parents to buy assistive devices. Parents can be required to use private insurance for assistive devices only in limited circumstances.

Extended School Years

Q. I really think my daughter could benefit from year-round special education instruction. Can this be considered a special education service?

A. Yes, if the IEP team determines that an extended school year is necessary. The Individuals with Disabilities Education Act does not directly address providing special education and related services beyond the traditional school year. However, because special education programs must be designed to meet the unique needs of the individual child, if extended-school-year programming is required in order for a child with disabilities to receive a free appropriate public education, educational agencies must provide special education and related services on an extended-year basis.

Q. How is a child determined to need an extended school year?

A. The IEP team determines whether a child needs such a program by looking at the

- degree of impairment;
- availability of other resources;
- amount of regression; and
- rate of progress.

If interruption of the child's educational programming for summer break may cause substantial regression, and if that regression—compounded by the child's limited ability to relearn the skills previously learned—would render it impossible or unlikely that the child will attain the level of self-sufficiency and independence that would otherwise be expected in view of the child's disabling condition, an extended school year should be provided.

Q. What must be offered during the extended school year?

A. The special education and related services offered during the extended year must be comparable in standards, scope, and quality to the program offered during the regular academic year. In addition, the extended-school-year services must be provided at no cost to parents.

REMEMBER THIS

- A free and appropriate public education includes nonacademic and extracurricular activities.
- All children with disabilities have the right to participate in regular classroom and extracurricular activities with nondisabled children to the maximum extent appropriate. Whether your child will remain in a regular classroom will depend on your child's abilities and what the IEP requires.

▶ GET IT IN WRITING

If the IEP team recommends extended-year services, the recommendation should be written into the Individualized Education Program.

- Educational agencies cannot require parents to buy assistive devices. Parents can be required to use private insurance for assistive devices only in limited circumstances.

- An extended school year can become part of an IEP if it is necessary to meet the child's individual needs.

TRANSITION SERVICES

Q. My child, who has a disability, is about to graduate from high school. Will the school help him prepare for life after graduation?

A. Likely, yes. Local education agencies must provide transition services that should help with this process.

Q. What are transition services?

A. Transition services are a coordinated set of activities for a child, designed as part of an outcome-oriented process, which promote movement from school to post-school activities. Such services include postsecondary education, vocational training, integrated employment (including supported employment), continuing and adult education, adult services, assistance with independent living, and community participation. The set of activities must be based on the individual child's needs, taking into account the child's preferences and interests. The activities also must include instruction, community experiences, the development of employment and other post-school adult living objectives, and, when appropriate, acquisition of daily living skills and functional vocational evaluation.

Q. Who is entitled to transition services?

A. The Individuals with Disabilities Education Act requires that IEPs for children sixteen and older contain a statement of needed transition services for the transition to post-school life.

DISCIPLINE

Q. May the school discipline my special education child?

A. Yes. Under the Individuals with Disabilities Education Act, special-needs students can be disciplined. However, certain safeguards exist to ensure that your child isn't disciplined for behaviors that are merely manifestations of his or her disability.

Q. How is a special-needs child disciplined?

A. You and the IEP team can work together to create a modified discipline plan that will outline specific disciplinary procedures for your child. If a child's disability impacts the child's behavior, then the child's IEP should include any special education and related services that are needed to address the behavior.

Q. May a child with disabilities be suspended from school?

A. Yes. However, a child with disabilities generally cannot be suspended for more than ten days. If a pattern of short-term suspensions would result in a significant change in placement, and if the behavior for which the child is being suspended is a manifestation of the child's disability or is due to an inappropriate IEP or placement, then the child may not be suspended except in a genuine emergency, such as a threat to the health or safety of the child or others.

For offenses involving drugs and weapons, your special education child may be temporarily removed from school and placed in an alternative school or educational setting for up to forty-five school days. In addition, schools can unilaterally remove children for forty-five days for inflicting serious bodily injury.

Q. Recently, my child has been suspended a lot. I think this might be a sign that something is wrong with the placement. Can anything be done?

A. Yes. If a pattern of disciplinary suspension emerges, the local education agency should review the child's IEP and placement offer. The local education agency should take steps to ensure that the child's educational program addresses his or her unique needs and provides for educational interventions to address inappropriate behaviors arising from disability.

Q. May a child with disabilities be expelled from school?

A. Not if the expulsion is for misconduct directly related to the child's disability, or if the IEP team determines the child was not appropriately placed at the time of the misconduct. Because expulsion is a significant change in placement, before expelling a child with disabilities, the local education agency must follow specified procedures.

Q. What must happen before expulsion proceedings can begin?

A. Before expulsion proceedings can begin for any child enrolled in a special education program, the law requires certain procedures to be followed, including

- notifying parents in writing of the local education agency's intention to seek expulsion or suspension for more than ten days;
- conducting an evaluation of the child's educational needs;
- convening an IEP team meeting to determine if the misconduct is directly related to the child's disability or the result of an inappropriate placement; and
- informing the parents of their right to request both impartial administrative review of any IEP team decisions and judicial review of the final administrative determination.

Q. What happens at an IEP team meeting convened in this context?

A. The IEP team must attempt to reach agreement as to whether the misconduct was disability-related, and whether the child was appropriately placed at the time of the misconduct. If the misconduct was related to the child's disability, or if the child was inappropriately placed, then the local education agency may not proceed with expulsion and the IEP team must consider additional services or other placement options rather than expulsion.

Q. The IEP team cannot reach an agreement on these issues. Does this mean my child can stay in school?

A. Not necessarily. The local education agency will have to make these decisions and give you the right to appeal through a due process hearing. Any such hearing and any further judicial appeal of the hearing decision must be completed before the expulsion procedures begin. While the hearing or court proceedings are pending, the child must be returned to his or her last school placement unless the child's parents have agreed to a change in placement or the local education agency has obtained a court order permitting such a change.

Q. If the IEP Team decides that the misconduct was not related to the disability and that the placement was appropriate, does this mean my child can be expelled?

A. Yes. At that point, your child will be treated the same as nondisabled children with respect to expulsion. If you disagree with the IEP team's decisions, you may request a due process hearing. The child's placement may not be changed before the conclusion of the hearing. However, be aware that the local education agency may seek a court order preventing continuation of the placement if the continuation would likely result in injury to your child or others.

Q. If disciplinary issues arise, may school officials simply label my child as having "behavioral problems"?

A. No. School officials who simply label children as having "behavioral problems" instead of referring them for evaluations may be violating their obligations under federal and state disability laws.

Q. My child has been expelled. Will special education services stop?

A. No. The U.S. Department of Education prohibits a local education agency from terminating services for a special education child, even if the child has been expelled.

REMEMBER THIS

- Special education students aged sixteen or older are eligible for transition services.
- Special education students can be disciplined, provided certain guidelines are observed.
- A child with disabilities cannot be suspended for more than ten days.
- In order for a special-needs student to be expelled, the IEP team must first determine that the misconduct was not related to his or her disability, and that placement was appropriate.

DISAGREEING WITH A LOCAL EDUCATION AGENCY'S ACTION

Introduction

Q. If I disagree with something the school is doing, or not doing, and I don't think my concerns have been addressed at the IEP meeting, what are my options?

A. Generally there are two formal avenues for parents who wish to object: due process hearings and compliance complaints. A **due process hearing** involves a disagreement over what a child's program should include, while a **compliance complaint** involves a failure by the local education agency to follow the rules or to do what has already been agreed upon in the IEP.

Q. I am not ready to make a formal complaint. Do I have any less formal options?

A. Yes, and you should consider exhausting all informal avenues first. Special education is enhanced by cooperative relationships between parents and school officials. For this reason, before resorting to more formal means of objecting (compliance complaints or due process hearings), parents should explore informal means of resolving problems. These include

- talking with the person with whom there is a dispute in order to try to resolve it. If this is not successful, consider going up the chain of command (for example, from the school principal to the director of special education);
- identifying key issues; and
- seeking a solution to the problem, giving consideration to reasonable compromises in the child's best interest.

Q. I am challenging a change in my child's placement. Where will he or she be placed during these proceedings?

A. Once a parent initiates a complaint, the child's placement status is protected during any hearing, appeals, or judicial proceedings: the child remains in his or her present placement unless the parents and the state or local education agency agree otherwise. If the complaint involves an initial admission to school, the child, with parental consent, must be placed in the public school program until all administrative and judicial proceedings are completed.

Due Process Hearings

Q. The local education agency appears to have violated special education laws. What can I do?

A. When the local education agency appears to have violated special education laws or procedures, a parent, individual, public agency, or organization can file a complaint with the local education agency (with a copy to the appropriate state agency) within two years after they knew or should have known that an IDEA violation occurred.

The complaint should include

1. the name of the child;
2. the address of the child's residence;
3. the name of the school the child is attending;
4. in the case of a homeless child, available contact information for the child and the name of the school the child is attending; and
5. a description of the nature of the problem(s), including facts relating to the problem(s) and a proposed resolution of the problem(s).

Q. Can I pursue a more formal avenue of objection right off the bat, or must I first try to negotiate with the school?

A. Before a parent or guardian may request a due process hearing, the local education agency must be provided an opportunity to resolve the matter by convening a **resolution session.** This is a meeting between the parents and the relevant members of the IEP team who have specific knowledge of the facts at issue.

The resolution session is not required if the parent and the local education agency agree in writing to waive the meeting. If the local education agency has not resolved the issue within thirty days, then the due process hearing may occur. If a resolution is reached at the resolution session, the parties execute a legally binding agreement.

Q. Who conducts the hearing?

A. The hearing must be conducted by an impartial hearing officer who is not an employee or board member of the local education agency, and who does not have any conflicts of interest.

The hearing officer is selected by the local education agency with the written consent of the parents. If the parents do not respond within seven days of receiving written notification of a proposed hearing officer, the officer is considered acceptable.

If the parties are unable to agree on a hearing officer, the local education agency will ask the state to provide a list of three potential officers. The parents and the local education agency then each choose one name to strike from the list. The remaining person is the hearing officer.

Q. How should a parent prepare for a due process hearing?

A. In preparing for the hearing, a parent should

- analyze the issues and determine what evidence will be needed;
- assemble documents, including local education agency correspondence, school records, and independent evaluations;
- select witnesses, and contact them to determine if they will be available to testify;

▶ **OBJECT IN WRITING**

Any objection to a hearing officer should be confirmed in writing.

▶ **INDEPENDENT EVALUATIONS**

The hearing officer may order an independent educational evaluation of the child. For more information on independent evaluations, see page 177.

- analyze the local education agency's position;
- define the issues;
- if possible, **stipulate** to certain facts (meaning concede that those facts are true);
- explore settlement possibilities, and ask the hearing officer to mediate if you think it will be beneficial.

Q. Where is the hearing held?

A. The hearing must be conducted at a time and place that is reasonably convenient for the parents and child.

Q. How is the hearing conducted?

A. A due process hearing is similar in nature to a trial or other court hearing. The hearing normally begins with opening statements by each party describing what the party intends to prove. Each side calls witnesses to testify from their personal knowledge about the relevant facts. Expert witnesses may also testify. Documents may be considered if they are relevant to the issues at hand, and each party may cross-examine the other's witnesses. The hearing then concludes with the parties' closing arguments and post-hearing briefs, or with written arguments.

Q. *What are my rights at the hearing?*

A. Each party has the right to

- be accompanied and advised by counsel and by individuals with special knowledge or training;
- prohibit the introduction of any evidence not disclosed at least five days before the hearing;
- receive a free copy from the other party of each document offered into evidence by that party;
- have access to any reports, records, or clinical evaluations on which a decision was based, or that could have a bearing on the accuracy of the decision;
- obtain a verbatim record of the hearing;
- present an independent educational evaluation; and
- obtain written findings and decisions.

Q. *After the hearing, when must a decision be made?*

A. Unless an extension is granted, a copy of the final decision must be mailed to the parties within forty-five days of the receipt of request for a hearing.

Q. *Is the hearing officer's decision final and binding?*

A. Not totally. It is final and binding unless appealed in writing to the appropriate state agency within forty-five days of the decision. The state agency must appoint an impartial and independent reviewing officer to hear the appeal. In conducting the review, the independent reviewing officer must

- examine the entire hearing record;
- ensure compliance with due process;
- conduct a hearing in accordance with federal law, if additional evidence is necessary;
- provide opportunity for oral or written argument; and
- make an independent decision, with written findings provided to the parties.

Q. *May the parties submit briefs before the review?*

A. Yes. Each party has the right to submit a brief in support of its case.

Q. *When will the review of the hearing decision be conducted? How long will the process take?*

A. The review must be conducted at a time and place reasonably convenient to the parent and child. Copies of the final decision must be mailed to the parties within thirty days of receipt of the request for review, unless the reviewing officer grants an extension. The decision is final unless appealed to a court in a timely fashion.

Q. *If I'm unhappy with the decision of either the hearing officer or the independent review, can I take the issue to court?*

A. Yes. You may bring a civil action in any state or federal court that has jurisdiction.

▶ **PUBLIC HEARINGS**

Parents have the right to have the child present at the hearing and to make the hearing public (i.e., open for members of the public to attend).

The court will then review the evidence, giving due weight to administrative findings.

Complaints

Q. Are there any avenues of complaint other than a due process hearing?

A. Yes. Parents and others who believe IDEA or Section 504 rights have been violated may complain to the regional office of the Office for Civil Rights of the U.S. Department of Education. The complaint must be in writing and signed by the complaining party.

An investigator will investigate the allegations and make a written determination of whether the local education agency was "out of compliance" with the law or with the child's Individualized Education Program. If the agency was out of compliance, it may be ordered back into compliance. The state agency must investigate the complaint and issue a decision within sixty days.

Q. What issues can be complained about?

A. Under the law, a parent may complain "with respect to any matter relating to the identification, evaluation, or educational placement of the child, or the provision of a free appropriate public education to such child." Section 504 regulations also provide for parental complaints.

Remedies

Q. If the school violates special education laws, what are the possible remedies?

A. Due process hearing officers and courts can order a school system to take a number of actions in order to correct violations of the IDEA and Section 504, including

- modifying an IEP;
- implementing an existing IEP that is not being carried out;
- providing a particular placement;
- providing a particular related service;
- reimbursing parents for expenses for independent assessments, witness fees, and private-school tuition; and
- awarding damages.

Q. Can parents recover attorney's fees in an IDEA case?

A. Yes. The local education agency must notify parents that they can be awarded reasonable attorney's fees in certain circumstances. Speak with your attorney to determine your chances of recovering attorney's fees and the steps you will need to take in order to do so.

Q. I had to pay for parts of my child's special education before things were settled with the school. Can I recover this money?

A. Possibly. Compensatory education is available in some circumstances, as is reimbursement for special education and related services paid for by parents. Courts have recognized that without compensatory education, children whose parents lack the resources to place them in private programs and seek reimbursement have no way to vindicate their IDEA rights.

A parent need not precisely replicate the placement the local education agency should have provided; instead, parents may receive reimbursement for the costs incurred in providing special education or related services, so long as these educational services meet the standard of "appropriateness" established by the Individuals with Disabilities Education Act.

REMEMBER THIS

- If you think the local education agency has violated a duty under the law or under your child's IEP, you have two formal complaint options: a due process hearing or compliance complaint.

- During any challenges, your child's placement will be protected unless the school is able to get a court order mandating otherwise.

- Due process hearings are similar in nature to trials, and are conducted by impartial hearing officers.

Personal Injury

John was driving to work. He was in moving traffic when he felt the urge to sneeze. He sneezed, involuntarily closed his eyes, and his car swerved into another lane. John panicked, accidentally pressed the accelerator instead of the brake, and caused a major pileup. Noreen was waiting for the bus with her brother when she witnessed the accident. John's car ran up onto the sidewalk, and Noreen's brother was killed instantly. Noreen has become a nervous wreck. She is in therapy, has nightmares and flashbacks, and has had to leave her job. When a local newspaper covered the accident, its cover story stated that John (who was not injured in the accident) was drunk when he caused the pileup, even though he hadn't had a sip of alcohol.

In this scenario, several people may have personal injury claims. Certainly the people injured in the accident might be able to bring a case against John, but Noreen also might be able to bring a case against him for the injuries she suffered as a result of witnessing her brother's death. She may also be able to bring a claim on behalf of her deceased brother. Furthermore, John himself might have a defamation case against the newspaper if its story about him was maliciously false.

This chapter outlines the various steps involved with mounting a personal injury case, and discusses the differences between negligence, strict liability, and intentional wrongdoing.

Personal injury law, often referred to as **tort law,** is designed to protect you if you or your property are injured or harmed because of someone else's act or failure to act. A personal injury or tort lawsuit is a civil cause of action—not a criminal one. **Tort** is the legal term for a wrong that enables someone to recover damages. In tort law, there are three primary types of wrongdoing: negligence, strict liability, and intentional torts.

In most tort suits, the remedy is the same: payment of money by the defendant to the plaintiff. However, sometimes the remedy is an injunction rather than monetary damages—for example, if your neighbor plays loud music, you can file a nuisance action seeking an injunction to stop him.

Every tort claim addresses two basic issues: liability and damages. In other words, was the defendant liable for the damages you sustained? And, if so, what is the nature and extent of your damages? If you can prove both liability and damages, our justice system may award you compensation for your loss. Even if liability is established, parties to lawsuits frequently dispute the proper amount of damages. Some types of damages, such as lost wages and medical bills, are easier to calculate. However, reasonable minds can disagree about other kinds of damages, such as a person's expected future earnings, or how to measure pain and suffering.

THE BASICS OF PERSONAL INJURY LAW

Q. How do I know if I have a personal injury case?

A. First, someone must have had a legally recognized duty to you. Second, they must have breached that duty. And third, you must have suffered a legally recognized injury to your person or property as a consequence of that person's breach of duty. Keep in mind that your injury need not always be physical. Suits may be based on a variety of nonphysical losses and harms to your reputation or mental condition. To prove the intentional tort of assault, for example, you need not show that a person's action caused you actual physical harm—only that it caused an expectation that some harm would come to you. (Assault is discussed in more detail on page 228.) You also may have a case if someone has publicly attacked your reputation (the tort of **defamation**), invaded your privacy, or negligently or intentionally subjected you to emotional distress.

Q. If I have suffered a personal injury and think I have a case, how do I find a personal injury lawyer?

A. Talk with lawyers you know, ask friends and colleagues you respect about lawyers they know or have used, or contact a local bar association for referrals to lawyers who handle personal injury cases. You can find the telephone number of the local bar association in your telephone directory. Most lawyers offer free consultations, so you can meet with as many as you like. Choose the lawyer about whom you feel most confident—and with whom you feel most comfortable. Chapter 1, "When and How to Use a Lawyer," provides additional guidance on finding the right lawyer for your case.

Keep in mind that the law of torts is evolving. Some areas of tort law are complex, and require a lawyer with specialized expertise. For example, if you believe that you have a medical malpractice, product liability, or toxic tort case—that is, a case for damages resulting from exposure to various harmful (toxic)

> ▶ **WHY A TORT? AND WHAT'S A TORTFEASOR?**
>
> "Tort" comes from the French word "tortus," which means "twisted." Legally, a tort is a wrong for which someone can recover damages. Battery, assault, negligence, and defamation are just a few examples of torts. A **tortfeasor** is the person who committed the tort. "Feasor" comes from Old French and means "doer" or "maker."

substances—use particular care in selecting counsel.

Q. Do I have to hire an attorney?

A. No. You can always represent yourself **pro se** (meaning without a lawyer). However, remember that tort law imposes many important time limits that can seriously impact your legal rights. Make sure you are fully aware of all such requirements. For more information on the pros and cons of representing yourself, please see Chapter 1.

Q. I have a consultation set up with an attorney. Should I bring anything with me?

A. Yes. You should bring any documents that relate to your claim. For example, police reports include details about the parties, witnesses, and conditions surrounding auto accidents, fires, assaults, and other incidents. Copies of medical reports from doctors and hospitals should describe your injuries and treatment. Information about the other party's insurance carrier, if any, is also extremely helpful, as are photographs of the ac-

cident, the property, the scene, or your injury. The more information you provide your lawyer, the easier it will be to evaluate your claim. If you don't have any documents at the time of your first meeting, don't worry. Your lawyer will be able to help you obtain them.

Q. What kind of legal fees should I expect to pay for a personal injury case?

A. Personal injury lawyers generally charge their clients on a **contingency fee** basis. This means that your lawyer is paid a percentage of any amount recovered. This percentage may be negotiable, and should be addressed at the time you hire the lawyer. With whatever lawyer you choose to represent you, insist on a written retainer or fee agreement clarifying all fees and charges. Remember that, whether you win or lose the case, you will likely have to pay the expenses of investigating and pursuing it—court filing fees, payments to investigators, payments to court reporters and medical experts, and the expense of securing medical records and reports. Other types of fee arrangements, such as hourly arrangements, may also be used. See Chapter 1, "When and How to Use a Lawyer," for more information on the various types of fee arrangements.

Q. What can I expect after the first consultation?

A. If a lawyer believes your claim is covered by insurance, or that your damages are otherwise recoverable, the lawyer will gather information about your claim. In order to arrive at a figure for damages, your lawyer will need to determine the extent of your injuries, including pain and suffering, disability and/or disfigurement, the cost of medical treatment, and lost wages. Your lawyer may provide your damages figure to the insurer of the person

> ▶ **BEING SUED? INFORM YOUR INSURERS**
>
> If you are looking for a lawyer to defend you in a tort case relating to your vehicle or home, you should inform your auto or homeowner's insurer that you are being sued. Under most policies, they have a duty to defend you. Let them know about the suit even if you think the case has no merit or is not included under your policy. If you need your own lawyer to defend you, you should expect to pay an hourly rate for these services.

who injured you, or directly to the potential defendant. If the insurer considers it a valid claim, and you can agree on a value for damages, then the case may be resolved before an actual trial.

Q. What happens when I file a lawsuit?

A. When you sue someone, you are the **plaintiff,** and the other side is the **defendant.** Lawyers for each side typically begin gathering facts through the exchange of documents, through written questions called **interrogatories,** or through questions and answers recorded by a court reporter in proceedings called **depositions.** This exchange of information is called **discovery.**

After discovery, many cases settle before trial. See Chapter 2, "How the Legal System Works," for more information on settlement and trial procedures.

Q. What does it mean to settle a case?

A. **Settling** a case means that you agree to accept compensation in return for giving up

any further rights to proceed against the person who allegedly caused you damages. You will usually be required to sign a legally binding release discharging the obligations of the other side. Before settling, be sure to consider your situation carefully. Generally you cannot recover anything further if you later determine that your damages were greater than you thought.

Q. Will the court or the judge play a role in the settlement?

A. There is a chance the court could play a role. Courts generally encourage settlements. They hold status conferences to help judges manage the timelines of their cases, and settlement discussions are often part of these conferences. In many court systems, the judge will hold a settlement conference between the parties to determine the chances of settling the case. In other jurisdictions, disputes may be referred to arbitration, mediation, or another form of alternative dispute resolution.

Q. Will I learn about every settlement offer that gets made? Can my attorney reject offers without telling me?

A. No. If you are a plaintiff, legal ethics requires your lawyer to tell you the terms of every settlement offer. It is you, not the lawyer, who has the ultimate power to accept or reject a settlement.

Q. What if more than one person has caused my injury?

A. You must bring an action against each entity—whether a person or an organization—that caused your injury. The negligence of two drivers, for example, may have produced a collision in which you were injured. According to

▶ **SHOULD YOU SETTLE YOUR CASE?**

When deciding whether to settle your case, consider these important factors:

- the severity and permanence of the injury;
- the age of the victim (younger people generally have more future medical expenses);
- the duration of needed treatment and the size of medical bills;
- the amount of pain and suffering; and
- the value of lost wages, including the loss of future economic opportunities.

traditional legal principles, each driver could be held 100 percent liable to you. In a more recent legal trend, however, many jurisdictions have abolished this tradition, known as **joint and several liability,** and each defendant now is responsible only for the proportion of the harm that he or she caused. This is the rule of **comparative negligence,** which exists in most states, and is discussed more fully on page 210 and in Chapter 14, "Automobiles."

Q. What will I get if I win the trial?

A. If you win, a judge or jury may award you monetary damages for your injuries. Damages may include compensation for expenses such as medical bills and lost wages, as well as compensation for future wage losses. The judge or jury also may compensate you for medical expenses and for pain and suffering.

In addition, you may receive damages for any physical disfigurement or disability that resulted from your injury. All damages must be proved, meaning that you must show the judge or jury that there actually exists cause to award you such compensation.

In some states, the judge may change the amount awarded by a jury if the award is deemed excessive or inadequate.

Q. Will I have to take any extra steps to get my money?

A. A damages award does not necessarily translate into hard cash, especially if the person who caused your injury does not carry insurance, has inadequate assets, or is underinsured. Thus, you may have to take further legal steps to actually collect. For example, if a losing defendant does not pay the judgment, you may have to start collection proceedings. If the defendant owns property, you may be able to attach a claim to the property, or even foreclose on it. Another option would be to garnish the defendant's wages. Your lawyer will be able to help you in this regard. Investigating the ability of a defendant to pay should be one of the first steps you and your lawyer take, certainly before suit is filed. Experienced lawyers may be able to find sources of coverage that are not immediately apparent.

Q. Will the government punish the person who caused my injury?

A. Typically, government punishment becomes an issue during criminal cases, not civil cases. Defendants in civil cases for personal injury do not receive jail terms or fines as punishment.

In some states, juries and courts may award punitive damages in civil cases that involve extreme circumstances. Such damages are intended to punish defendants who have behaved maliciously, intentionally, or recklessly, so that they and other potential defendants are deterred from engaging in similar conduct in the future. Unlike fines, which go to the government, punitive damages are sometimes paid to the plaintiff, although an increasing number of jurisdictions earmark some or all of these damages for appropriate public use. For example, a judge may order that punitive damages be paid to a local charity.

Sometimes the actions that result in a personal injury case may also result in criminal charges. However, the resulting criminal case will be independent of your civil case. For more information on the differences between criminal and civil actions, see Chapter 2, "How the Legal System Works."

Q. I think I have a personal injury claim. How long do I have to file it?

A. Both federal and state laws set time limits, called **statutes of limitations,** within which you must file certain types of lawsuits. Depending on the nature of your claim, you may have less than one year after the date of injury to file a claim. If you miss the statutory deadline for filing a case, you lose your right to sue. Limitations in some types of cases, such as medical malpractice cases, may be calculated differently. For this reason, it is important to talk with a lawyer as soon as you receive or discover an injury.

Q. What if a person dies before bringing a personal injury lawsuit?

A. This depends on whether a person dies as a result of the injuries or from unrelated causes. If a person injured in an accident subsequently dies because of those injuries, that person's heirs may bring a lawsuit. Every state

has some law permitting an action when someone causes the wrongful death of another. If a person with a claim dies from unrelated causes, the claim survives in many cases, and may be brought by the executor or the personal representative of the deceased person's estate or heirs, although the amount that can be recovered may change.

Q. Do I have any other options aside from a lawsuit?

A. You are permitted to negotiate with the other party or his or her insurance company without filing suit. However, you will greatly increase your chance of a positive outcome if you have an experienced lawyer to protect your rights and present your claim.

There are other ways of bringing a complaint against a wrongdoer. Consumer protection agencies exist in every state. State attorney generals' offices also offer information and accept complaints. Or you can contact state boards that regulate the conduct of various service industries such as lawyers, doctors, veterinarians, and even barbers. Check the government listings in your telephone directory for the numbers of these agencies.

REMEMBER THIS

- If another person caused you to suffer injury, you may be able to recover compensation from that person, either through a claim or, ultimately, through a lawsuit.

- Take your time when selecting a personal injury lawyer.

- When you meet with a lawyer for the first time, bring supporting documents with you. Such documents may include police reports, medical reports, insurance policies, and documentation of lost wages.

- Most personal injury lawyers will represent you on a contingency fee basis. Read the fee agreement carefully.

- Many cases settle before ever reaching trial. You have the ultimate authority to decide whether to accept a settlement.

- Personal injury lawsuits must be filed within a specified period of time, called a statute of limitations.

NEGLIGENCE

Sometimes injuries just happen. No one intended to cause them, but doctors' bills, lost wages, and emotional losses still need to be covered. Who should cover these expenses? Under the law of negligence, the person who caused the injuries can be held responsible, even if he or she never intended any harm. But how do you prove cause? What if more than one person is responsible? How much money can you recover? This section sheds some light on these issues.

Q. I was injured, but the person who caused my injuries didn't intend to hurt me and claims that it was an accident. Can I still recover for my damages?

A. Possibly, if you can make a case for negligence. The most common type of tort case is based on negligence. A **negligent** person is one who is at fault, and has acted unreasonably under the circumstances and caused harm to another. Much of tort law is designed to compensate those who have been harmed by socially unreasonable conduct. Unlike someone who commits an intentional tort, a negligent tortfeasor does not intend to cause

harm or bring about a certain result. The person simply does not use reasonable care.

For instance, let's say that Jill is driving her car down the road when her cell phone rings. She picks up the phone and inadvertently swerves into another lane, striking another car. Jill did not intend to strike the other car, but Jill was negligent because she breached her duty to act with reasonable care while operating her car.

Q. How do I prove a legal case of negligence?

A. Generally, to bring a successful negligence action, you must prove four things:

1. duty;
2. breach of duty;
3. causation; and
4. damages.

In the above example, Jill had a **duty** to drive her car safely. When she swerved into the other lane, she **breached** that duty. Her actions in not paying attention to the road **caused** the harm, and she caused **damages** to be suffered by the other driver. If a legal case filed by the other driver proved the existence of these four elements, Jill's negligence would be established and she would be liable—that is, legally responsible—and probably would be required to pay money to the other driver.

Q. Can principles of negligence apply to situations other than car accidents?

A. Yes. Negligence reaches far beyond claims stemming from car accidents. It is the basis for liability in most personal injury lawsuits, including slip-and-fall cases and acts of professional negligence, such as medical and legal malpractice.

Q. What does it mean to have a duty?

A. A **duty of care** is a legal duty to behave reasonably under the circumstances. **Reasonable care** is the level of care that would be exercised by a reasonable person—that is, a person with an ordinary degree of reason, prudence, care, and foresight—in a similar situation.

Q. So what does it mean to breach the duty of care?

A. When a person fails to take reasonable care, that person breaches the duty of care. To understand this concept better, forget all the legal jargon and go back to the car accident example. A driver has a duty to use reasonable care to avoid injuring anyone he or she meets on the road. If a driver fails to use reasonable care and you are hurt as a result, the driver has breached his or her duty and is likely responsible for those injuries.

Q. What is causation?

A. **Causation** simply means that the breach of duty caused the injury or damages.

Q. So what are damages?

A. **Damages** are the loss or harm resulting from an accident or injury. In the car accident example, the damages may include medical bills from any injuries, the cost of getting your car repaired, and possibly any loss of wages during your recovery time.

Q. Who determines whether a defendant has acted reasonably?

A. After your lawyer presents the evidence, a judge or a jury will decide what a reasonable person would have done in similar circumstances. For example, in a case involving a driver who ran a stop sign, the judge or jury would decide whether a reasonable person under similar circumstances would also have failed to stop at the stop sign. Remember, you must suffer damages in order to have a valid personal injury lawsuit. In other words, you could not sue another driver if he or she ran a red light but did not hit your car and cause you damages.

Q. If I am hurt because someone failed to act, might that person be found negligent and therefore be liable?

A. Yes. Negligence stems from careless or thoughtless conduct or a failure to act when a reasonable person would have acted.

Automobile Collisions

Q. Can negligence be the basis for an auto collision case?

A. In general, yes. Automobile collisions, the area in which many personal injury actions arise, provide a good example of how the concept of negligence works. Tort law with respect to auto accidents works differently depending upon the state in which you live. This is because some states are **fault** states and others are **no-fault** states. For more information on fault and no-fault laws, see Chapter 14, "Automobiles."

Q. I was in a car accident, but it was partly my fault and partly the other driver's fault. Will this make a difference with regard to what damages are ultimately awarded?

A. Yes. In the past, the rule was that if you could prove the other driver contributed in any way to the accident, he or she could be totally barred from recovering anything from you. Now, most states have rejected such harsh results, and instead look at the comparative fault of the drivers. If a jury finds that you were negligent and that your negligence was 25 percent responsible for the injury, and that the defendant was 75 percent at fault, the defendant would be responsible for only 75 percent of your damages. Thus, in a case involving $100,000 in damages, the defendant would only have to pay $75,000. In some states, a plaintiff may recover even if he or she was more negligent than the defendant—that is, negligent in the amount of 51 percent or more. (See the sidebar below titled "Comparative and Contributory Negligence.")

Q. A neighbor who rides with me to work was injured when I got into a car accident. Do I have to pay her medical bills?

A. In many states today, no-fault automobile insurance would protect you—and often passengers in your car—by compensating those injured up to a specified level, regardless of who was at fault in the accident.

A few states still have **automobile guest statutes,** although there is a strong trend away from them. These statutes make drivers liable for injuries to nonpaying or guest pas-

---

▶ COMPARATIVE AND CONTRIBUTORY NEGLIGENCE

Different states have different systems of negligence law. The traditional system was a system of **contributory negligence.** In a contributory negligence system, a plaintiff could not recover any damages if he or she contributed to his or her injuries. Although there were some common-law doctrines that lessened the impact of this doctrine, contributory negligence was viewed as harsh and all-or-nothing, since plaintiffs either recovered all of their damages or no damages at all.

To avoid the all-or-nothing outcomes of contributory negligence, the vast majority of states have switched to a system of **comparative negligence.** Under this type of system, a jury compares the actions of the parties and then allocates fault between them. A defendant is obligated to pay only the amount of damages caused by his or her own negligence. So if you're the plaintiff and the jury finds that your own negligence caused 20 percent of the damage, then the defendant would only be responsible for 80 percent of your damages. To put it another way, your recovery is reduced by your own percentage of negligence.

There are different types of comparative negligence. Under a **pure** form of comparative negligence, a plaintiff can recover no matter how negligent he or she was. In other words, if a plaintiff suffered $10,000 in damages and was 80 percent at fault, in a pure comparative negligence system, he or she still could recover $2,000 ($10,000 − $10,000(.80) = $2,000).

In a **modified** or **50-percent** system, a plaintiff must be either equal to or less than 50 percent at fault in order to recover. In some states, the plaintiff's negligence must be less than 50 percent in order to recover. In other states, the plaintiff's negligence may be less than or equal to 50 percent.

sengers only if the drivers were "grossly negligent" by failing to use even slight care in their driving. In jurisdictions that still have such laws, the parties often litigate over whether the passenger was a guest. A neighbor also may be able to recover from you under ordinary negligence principles if she can prove that she was not a guest passenger. This usually requires some showing that both of you agreed to share expenses or shared similar responsibilities for the commute.

Courts also have held a driver liable for harm caused by known defects, but not for injuries caused by defects in the vehicle about which the driver had no knowledge.

Q. I sustained an injury when the bus I ride to work was involved in an accident. Will I be able to recover from the bus company?

A. Most likely. **Common carriers**—bus lines, airlines, and railroads (even elevators and escalators in some states)—owe their passengers "the highest degree of care" and are viewed as having a special responsibility to their passengers. Common carriers must exercise great caution in protecting their riders, and do everything they can to keep them safe.

Whether you win your case will depend on the circumstances of the accident. A jury will have to consider the facts of your case to determine if the driver acted negligently. But as an employee of a common carrier, the driver is required to provide you with a high degree of care. (If the bus were hit by another car, the other driver also may be liable for your injuries.)

Q. My car sustained damage when it hit a pothole on a city street. Can I recover from the city?

A. Some cities have **pothole ordinances,** a form of immunity that releases them from any liability for pothole accidents, except where they had prior notice of the pothole. Whether you can recover will depend on your city's law controlling liability and its immunities against suits. For instance, some states have **governmental tort liability acts,** which sharply limit suits against governmental bodies.

Q. I was in a car accident during my pregnancy and my baby was born with disabilities as a result of injuries from the accident. Does my child have any legal recourse?

A. Many states will permit a lawsuit by a child for the consequences of prenatal injuries (i.e., injuries taking place before birth). In states with no-fault automobile insurance, your child's right to sue often is limited. Most courts also will allow a wrongful death action if the baby dies from the injuries after birth.

Q. Someone recently stole my car and then wrecked it, injuring passengers in another vehicle. Now those passengers are trying to sue me. Can they win? Am I responsible?

A. Probably not, since the thief did not have your permission to use the car, although a lot would depend upon the law in your state. Suppose you left your car unlocked with the keys in it, making it easy for the thief to steal. This could be negligence. Even then, most courts generally will not hold you liable if the thief later injures someone by negligent driving. That is because courts hold that you could not foresee that your actions ultimately would result in such injuries.

In a few cases, though, courts have looked at whether your actions caused an unreasonable risk of harm to someone else. If you left your car parked with the engine running, for example, you might be liable if the car thief then injures children playing nearby.

In a no-fault state, on the other hand, it might be difficult—if not impossible—for the passengers to sue you.

Q. I was hit by a car that was driven by a drunk driver who was going home after a night out. What can I do, in addition to suing the drunk driver?

A. You may be able to collect from your own uninsured motorist or underinsured motorist coverage for damages you suffered from the drunk driver. In other words, if the drunk driver does not have automobile liability insurance, your uninsured or underinsured coverage from your own policy may provide you some relief.

If you live in a state that has a **dramshop act,** you may be able to recover damages from the owner of the tavern where the drunk driver was served the liquor. Such acts usually come into play when intoxicated bar patrons later injure somebody while driving. Some of these laws also hold tavern owners liable when drunken customers injure others on or off the premises. But some courts say that a tavern owner will not be liable unless the sale of the liquor itself was illegal.

Q. My wife was injured when her car was hit by another car. The other car was being driven by some kids who had been drinking at the home of our neighbor. May we take any action against the neighbor, who supplied the liquor to the minors?

A. Possibly. Some courts have imposed liability against neighbors or parents for serving alcohol to minors. Parents can be liable for **negligent supervision** of their children. As a general rule, courts have said that social hosts are not responsible for the conduct of their guests, unless the hosts routinely allow guests to drink too much or take illegal drugs—and then put them into cars.

Q. I was injured when my automobile collided with a truck driven by a delivery person. My medical bills are substantial, and the driver doesn't have many assets. Can I recover damages from the driver's employer, or must I file against the driver?

A. You may be able to recover from both. Under a theory known as **vicarious liability,** you probably can recover from the delivery person's employer. Under the law, employers may be held liable to third parties for acts committed by employees within the scope of their jobs. Although the employer was not negligent, it becomes indirectly liable for the negligence of its employee. The question will be whether the employee was making a delivery when the accident occurred. If so, the employer is liable, since making deliveries clearly is part of the driver's job. But if, for example, the employee first stopped at a restaurant for drinks and dinner with friends, then the employer may be able to escape liability. **Respondeat superior** is a type of vicarious liability applied in this context. Literally, "respondeat superior" means "let the superior respond." In practice, applying this liability principle means that if you are injured by an employee during the course of his or her employment, you usually can sue the employer.

Q. Why does the law permit vicarious liability? Doesn't this make someone legally responsible for another person's actions?

A. Yes. Many may feel that this concept is unfair to employers, who have to insure against this type of liability. However, the concept is often justified because it helps secure fair compensation for victims, and gives companies every incentive to deter harmful conduct by maintaining high standards and having rigorous training programs and procedures to guard against these risks.

In the example involving a person who is hit by a delivery truck, the truck driver himself might also be a defendant (in addition to his employer). But because the delivery company presumably has far greater resources than the driver, the employer is the more attractive target of the suit, and may thus face the primary liability.

Q. Is a rental company vicariously liable when the drivers of rented vehicles get into collisions?

A. Sometimes. In some states, car rental companies are liable for property damage or personal injury caused by operators of leased vehicles. This encourages rental companies to make sure they rent to competent and careful drivers. In these states, car rental companies must purchase liability insurance, and pass the cost of that insurance on to the consumer.

In other states, the car rental company is not liable for the renter's negligence. The car renter is primarily liable for damages, and must carry appropriate insurance as a condition of renting the car.

Q. Are there other instances in which a party not directly involved in causing a personal injury might be liable?

A. Yes. Besides vicarious liability per se, there are many other cases in which someone besides the direct perpetrator of the injury *may* be liable to the victim. In these cases, the question is whether the negligence of the

third party may have been a fundamental cause of the injury.

Examples include mall owners who may be liable for attacks in the mall (under the theory of **premises liability**, discussed later in this chapter), and tavern owners and social hosts who may be liable for the drunken driving of those to whom they have served alcohol. Laws governing third-party responsibility vary by state and circumstance. If you think someone else may be liable for your injuries, or if you may be liable for injuries caused by someone else, you should speak with a lawyer experienced in personal injury cases.

Q. A car ran over my dog. Can I recover from the driver?

A. Possibly, yes. A dog is considered property, and you have suffered property damage. However, in order to recover, you will have to show that the driver was negligent.

Injuries at Your Home and on Your Property

Q. A furniture delivery person was injured when he tripped over an extension cord in my living room. Can he recover damages from me?

A. He could sue, though it is not certain that he would win. Until recently, your liability for personal injuries incurred by a person at your home hinged on why the injured person was there. If the person was doing work for you, the law held that you had a special duty to make your home reasonably safe. Increasingly, the law holds landowners or property owners to a general duty of care to prevent injury to anyone coming onto their property—not just people performing work—unless the injury is caused by a dangerous condition that was open and obvious. In other words, some courts today will apply a reasonable person standard of care with respect to landowners. For more information on the various types of responsibilities owed to different people in your home, see Chapter 8, "Home Ownership."

Injuries on Others' Property

Q. What if I get injured while at the home of my neighbor, who invited me there for a party?

A. As a social guest, you might be able to recover from your neighbor, depending on how your injuries happened. Homeowners must tell their guests about—or make safe—any dangerous conditions that the guests are unlikely to recognize. Suppose, for example, that your injury was caused when you tripped on a throw rug. You may be able to recover if you can prove that your neighbor knew other people had tripped over the same rug, and knew that you were unlikely to realize its danger. Your neighbor probably should have warned you about it, removed it during the party, or secured it to the floor with tape or tacks.

Q. I was walking on a public sidewalk next to a construction site when I tripped and fell on a brick from the site, spraining my ankle. May I recover damages from the construction company?

A. In some circumstances, you will be able to recover damages from the construction company, which has a duty to take reasonable steps to keep sidewalks near its construction sites free from debris. If the company fails to remove such obstructions and you trip and fall, the company may be liable for your injuries.

Construction companies also should warn pedestrians that they could be injured if they stray from the sidewalk. However, posting a sign may not be sufficient. If a company fails to place barriers or warning lamps by a building pit, for example, it may be responsible if anyone falls into the pit and gets injured.

Q. I fell on a broken piece of city sidewalk and injured my ankle. Do I have a case against the city?

A. In many states, **municipal immunity statutes** prohibit recovery in many kinds of cases against a city or a town. If your state has no such statute or ordinance, however, you may have a case. Municipalities have a duty to keep streets and sidewalks in good repair. You might have a successful case against the city if you can show that it failed to maintain the sidewalk properly, or knew of the dangerous condition and had the opportunity to fix it but failed to do so.

Q. My daughter and her friends went snowmobiling on a nearby farm. When one of the snowmobiles ran into a fence, one of the kids got hurt. Is the farmer liable?

A. If landowners know that others are using their land for snowmobiling, most states require them to warn snowmobilers about hidden dangerous conditions, or to remove those conditions. Was the fence visible? Did the farmer recently build it? A few states have laws specifically dealing with liability when someone uses property for recreational purposes without permission. In those states, the farmer probably would not be liable if he did not authorize the group to be on his land and had not acted recklessly. You might want to ask a lawyer about your state's law. For more

> ▶ **IF YOU GET INJURED IN A STORE . . .**
>
> Suppose you were shopping in a hardware store and you tripped on a spilled can of paint, injuring your foot. Can you recover damages from the store? It depends on the facts of the case. Storeowners must keep their premises reasonably safe for customers by inspecting and discovering any dangerous conditions. They also must keep all aisles clear and properly maintained. A judge or jury will look at whether the owner was aware that the paint can was in the aisle, and how long it had been there. But a judge or jury also might find that you discovered the spilled paint and proceeded to walk right through it. Then the judge or jury might deny your damages claim, or find that you're comparatively at fault, thus reducing your recovery.

information on the duties land owners owe to guests and trespassers, see Chapter 8 "Home Ownership."

Q. I was injured on a ski lift. May I recover against the ski resort?

A. Possibly. Some states have laws limiting the liability of resorts, on the theory that there are certain risks a person assumes when skiing. However, some states hold that ski lifts are common carriers, like buses, and thus have expanded duties of care. In one of these states, you might have an excellent case.

Q. My son got injured during basic training in the U.S. Army. May he recover damages from the federal government?

A. No. People in the armed services who get injured during the course of their duties are not permitted to recover from the government for their injuries. The **Federal Tort Claims Act (FTCA)** allows people to sue the United States for certain tortious acts committed by its employees. However, the U.S. Supreme Court has stated that there is a broad exception for those serving in the military.

Q. If I have been injured by an employee of the federal government, and I am not in the military, can I sue the federal government to recover?

A. Possibly, yes. The FTCA provides that the federal government can be sued in tort "in the same manner and to the same extent as a private individual under the circumstances." If you are injured by an employee of the federal government who is acting within the scope of his or her office, you may bring suit in a federal district court against the government for negligent acts. But before suing in federal district court, you must first file a claim with the appropriate administrative agency that allegedly caused the harm. If the agency fails to respond or rejects the claim within six months, you can then sue in federal court. The federal courts must follow the law of the state in which the tort allegedly occurred. The federal judge serves as the judge and jury (fact finder) in these cases. There are many exceptions under

> ▶ **AVOIDING LIABILITY IF YOU'RE A LANDLORD**
>
> In recent years, many states have imposed a **warranty of habitability,** which requires landlords to maintain residential property in habitable condition. If you're a landlord, failing to maintain a property could cause you to be sued on the grounds that you violated this warranty. But negligence claims are also possible. For example, if guests are injured when an apartment's back porch collapses during a party, the landlord probably would be held liable, especially if he or she had been warned that the porch was sagging or was infested with termites and had not repaired it. Of course, the landlord may be able to argue that the porch collapsed because there were too many people on it. Landlords also must maintain any common areas of a building—including stairs, corridors, and walkways—for the benefit of both tenants and guests.
>
> If you are a landlord, there are ways to reduce your chances of liability. Consider having your insurance company inspect the premises, and then promptly repair any safety problems the inspector uncovers. If you inspect the premises yourself, look for unsafe wiring, loose railings, poor lighting, or similar flaws. You might also write tenants a letter each year asking them to point out any hazards or needed repairs they may have noticed. After all, if a tenant who lives in the building every day fails to notice a hazard, it is hard to argue that the landlord should have known about it. However, that still may not protect the landlord in a suit brought by a visitor who is injured while visiting. For more information on landlord liability, see page 361 in Chapter 9, "Renting Residential Property."

the FTCA. If you have been injured by an employee of the federal government, you should consult a lawyer who is well versed in this area of the law.

Medical Malpractice

Q. What is medical malpractice?

A. **Medical malpractice** is negligence committed by a professional health-care provider—a doctor, nurse, dentist, technician, or hospital or nursing facility—whose performance of duties departs from the standard of those with similar training and experience, resulting in harm to a patient. Most medical malpractice actions are filed against doctors and hospitals.

The profession itself sets the standard for malpractice through its own custom and practice.

Q. What should I do if I think I have a medical malpractice claim?

A. Talk to a lawyer who specializes in this area. Tell the lawyer exactly what happened to you, from the first to the last time you had contact with your doctor. Gather all your medical records from your doctors and hospitals—they must provide you with copies if you ask for them, though they may charge you for copying costs. Your lawyer will review all this information, and may have it reviewed by a doctor.

Q. How does a jury determine if a health-care provider's actions were within the standards of good medical practice?

A. A jury will consider testimony by experts—usually other professionals—who will testify whether they believe your provider's actions conformed with standard medical practice or fell below the accepted standard of care. For more details about medical malpractice, consult Chapter 4, "Health-Care Law."

Q. I signed a consent form before my doctor performed surgery. What did it really mean?

A. It is standard practice in hospitals for patients to sign a form giving their consent, or approval, for surgery. In the form, the patient usually consents to the specific surgery as well as to any other procedures that might become necessary.

If you can prove that your physician misrepresented the facts or failed adequately to inform you of the risks and benefits before surgery, your consent may be deemed invalid. The only time the law excuses doctors from providing such information is in emergencies, or when it would be harmful to a patient. But even if your doctor should have secured your consent and did not, you still may not automatically recover damages. You may still have to prove that, even if adequately informed, a reasonable person would not have consented to the surgery.

Q. If the consent form is considered valid, will this prevent me from recovering damages in a malpractice action against my doctor?

A. No. You still may be able to recover damages. A consent form does not release a physician from liability if he or she did not perform the operation following established procedures, or if he or she was otherwise negligent.

Q. What if I'm just not satisfied with the results of my surgery? Do I have a malpractice case?

A. In general, there are no guarantees of favorable medical results. In order to prevail in a medical malpractice case, you must show that an injury or damages resulted from the doctor's deviation from the appropriate standard of care for your condition.

Q. I became pregnant even though my husband had a vasectomy. Can we recover damages?

A. Yes, you may be able to win such a case. A number of negligence cases have been brought against physicians who performed unsuccessful vasectomies or other sterilization procedures that later resulted in unwanted children. Courts increasingly allow suits to be filed by the parents of children born as a result of wrongful conception or wrongful pregnancy. Damages generally are limited to those associated with the pregnancy and birth, and do not extend to support of the child.

Q. I don't think it was necessary for me to have a cesarean section when I delivered my daughter. Is there anything I can do about it?

A. Yes. Although most malpractice cases involving cesarean sections are brought against doctors who did not perform them when they

---

▶ **UNDERSTANDING MEDICAL MALPRACTICE**

See Chapter 4, "Health-Care Law," for more information on medical malpractice, including informed consent and what you must prove in order to make a successful malpractice case.

> ▶ **AS TIME GOES BY**

Assuming that you have a valid claim, a malpractice suit may last anywhere from two to seven years. If the judgment or verdict is appealed for some reason, your case may last even longer. The time frame for your case will depend on how complicated your claim is, as well as on the number of cases that were scheduled for trial before yours. It's because of factors like these, and the uncertainties of litigation, that most malpractice cases settle before trial.

should have, with resulting injuries to the mother or child, it is possible for a woman to win damages against her doctors for unnecessarily delivering her child by cesarean section.

To win such a case, it would be necessary for an expert to state that, in performing the cesarean section, the delivering doctor deviated from the appropriate standard of care.

Q. My aunt discovered that a sponge left inside her body years ago during an operation was the source of stomach trouble. May she still sue?

A. Like other personal injury cases, medical malpractice lawsuits are subject to specific statutes of limitations (time limits). Until recently, your aunt's suit may have been thrown out of court. In many states, time limits on filing used to begin when the injury occurred—in this example, that would have meant the clock started running on the day of the operation. But to alleviate harsh and unfair outcomes, many states have altered their laws. Now, the clock for filing a case does not begin to "tick" until people discover that they have

> ▶ **SHOULD YOU STOP AND HELP SOMEONE IN AN EMERGENCY?**

Generally, you do not have a duty to help someone in an emergency. The law says that if you did not cause the problem, and if you and the victim have no special relationship, you need not try to rescue a person. (Though of course, you are always free to go voluntarily to the aid of someone in trouble.)

To encourage people to help, many states have passed so-called **Good Samaritan laws** that excuse doctors—and sometimes other helpers—from liability for negligence for coming to the aid of someone in an emergency. Some states' Good Samaritan laws will protect a rescuer from ordinary negligence, but still allow the rescuer to be sued for gross (extreme) negligence.

In some states, if you injure someone while driving, you must help that injured person, regardless of who was at fault. Some courts look at the circumstances of the rescue. They say that, if you know someone is in extreme danger that could be avoided with little inconvenience on your part, you must provide reasonable care to the victim. Moreover, if you do start to help someone and then abandon your rescue efforts, you may be liable if you leave a victim in worse condition than you found him or her.

suffered an injury, or should have discovered it. This means that the clock would start running on your aunt's case on the day that she discovered the sponge (or on the day she should have discovered it).

Q. I think I have a valid medical malpractice case. How much can I win?

A. Forget about those huge sums you read about in the newspaper. In the majority of malpractice cases, the doctor wins. Moreover, many states put a limit, known as a **damage cap,** on the amount of punitive damages that may be awarded, and on noneconomic damages awarded on such grounds as pain and suffering. Others states impose damage caps for medical malpractice cases generally.

The dollar amounts of these caps vary, though they are often in the hundreds of thousands of dollars. While that still may sound like a lot of money, remember that you will have to pay lawyer's fees, or perhaps a percentage of your award in a contingency arrangement. There is a good chance that you will get less than the amount of the cap. The doctor may appeal if you win, or the judge may reduce the amount of your award.

Q. What exactly does a damage cap limit?

A. In some states, damage caps limit only punitive damages; in others, damage caps limit both punitive damages and any money that compensates you for your injury alone. Caps may vary from state to state, so it is important to speak with a knowledgeable attorney to determine the realistic value of your claim.

Q. Can a jury circumvent the limitations imposed by a damage cap?

A. Sometimes a jury may find ways to award money to a plaintiff, but label the award in a way that allows the plaintiff to avoid the damage cap. For example, in a state that imposes a cap on punitive damages, the jury might award the plaintiff a large amount of money, but label the award as an award for medical bills, lost wages, and pain and suffering. Because juries can sometimes circumvent damage caps in this way, some states do not allow lawyers or judges to tell the jurors that damage caps exist. That way, the jurors will not be tempted to change their decisions about compensation. The point is to keep the legal process fair for both you and the doctor.

Some Special Situations

Q. What about malpractice actions against professionals such as lawyers? I recently hired a lawyer who seemed inexperienced, and I was unhappy with the outcome of my case.

A. Like doctors, lawyers must possess and apply their knowledge and skills to the same extent as other reasonably qualified professionals. Not only must they exercise reasonable care in handling your case, they also must possess a minimum degree of special knowledge and ability. This means that they will be liable to you if their skills do not meet accepted standards in their area of practice. If you bring a case against a lawyer, you also must prove that the case would likely have succeeded if your lawyer had not mishandled it. Suits for legal malpractice usually result only in money damages; you cannot recover for the emotional distress of hiring a negligent lawyer.

If you are unsure about the basis for a malpractice case, check with the state agency that regulates lawyers in your state. Your state bar association will be able to tell you the name of the applicable agency.

Q. My daughter plays on the local park's basketball team. The park district asked us to sign a form promising that we won't hold the district responsible for any injuries she incurs. Can the park district do this?

A. The form you describe is a **waiver of liability** that contractually releases the organization from any liability should an injury occur. If you are worried about the safety of the activity, you should check out the facility and the coach before you sign the form.

If your child won't be permitted to participate in the activity unless you sign a waiver, a court may hold that the waiver is not really voluntary, and thus is not valid. Furthermore, signing the waiver might not mean that you are giving up your right to sue entirely. If an injury results because of intentional or reckless behavior, you probably will be able to seek damages.

Q. There was a fire at the motel where I was staying, and there was no sprinkler system and no escape route posted in the room. Isn't the motel required to implement those safety precautions?

A. The motel management probably should have exercised reasonable care in maintaining the fire alarms and fire escapes, and they should have helped you escape. As with common carriers (see page 211), the law generally requires that innkeepers, who have a special relationship with their guests, have a heightened duty of care.

Q. Someone attacked my daughter on her college campus. May she hold the school responsible for this attack?

A. Your daughter may have a valid claim of negligence against the college. Based on the legal theory known as **premises liability,** some courts have found entities such as universities, motels, convenience stores, and shopping malls liable for attacks because they did not exercise reasonable care in preventing victims from being harmed. However, courts are divided on this issue, and plaintiffs bear a heavy burden of proof in showing that the crime was foreseeable. The most important factor is whether there have been similar

---

▶ LIABILITY AT SPORTING EVENTS

Suppose you attend a baseball game, and a player hits a ball into the stands and injures you. What can you do? Spectators at a baseball game know they may be injured by a flying foul ball. That is why courts generally say that spectators assume the risk of being hurt by a ball. The same usually holds true if a golf ball hits you while you are watching a golf match. The legal term for this doctrine is **assumption of the risk.** It means that you agreed to face a known danger. But if the ball park has installed a screen to protect spectators, and if the screen has a hole in it, then you probably could argue that the ball park was negligent not to have it repaired.

crimes in the same location. A court will also consider the security precautions taken by the college to prevent these types of crimes.

Q. I was attacked after withdrawing money from an automated teller machine (ATM). What can I do?

A. Under the theory of premises liability discussed above, customers have sued banks for failing to protect them from assault at ATMs. While there used to be no duty to provide security against such crimes, some courts today recognize such a duty.

A key question is whether the crime was a reasonably foreseeable danger. The business owner will argue that third-party criminal attacks are inherently unforeseeable, and that the act of the third party (i.e., the criminal) is an intervening, superseding act that breaks the chain of causation. In other words, they will argue that the true cause of the harm is the act of the third party.

You may be able to overcome these arguments if you can show that the bank knew or should have known about prior incidents of crime at or near the location. In such a case, a judge or jury would determine if there were similar past occurrences, and if the likelihood of the crime was foreseeable. If so, they may hold that the bank had a duty to protect people using the machine, and that the bank was liable.

Recently, the banking industry has been successful in limiting banks' liability if they comply with security and lighting requirements.

Q. We recently got a call from a hospital saying that my mother had died of a heart attack. In fact, she had not died or suffered a heart attack, and the hospital was sim-

ply mistaken. The hospital's false report devastated us. What can we do?

A. You may be able to recover from the hospital for the **negligent infliction of emotional distress.** That is, you may be able to sue the hospital for negligently causing you to endure emotional pain. Courts generally have maintained that a person must have physical injuries to recover in such cases, but courts in some states have allowed recovery when there are no physical injuries. Other successful emotional distress suits have involved bystanders. For example, a court allowed a mother who saw her child fatally hit by a car to recover money damages against the driver of the car.

Q. The store where I bought my wedding gown failed to deliver it in time for the ceremony. What can I do?

A. Although you no doubt suffered some distress as a result of the store's actions, it is unlikely that you have a personal injury case. Although the experience may have been traumatic for you, successful plaintiffs generally must show some physical manifestation of mental anguish. You may, however, have a case for breach of contract. For more information about what to do in this kind of situation, see Chapter 12, "Contracts and Consumer Law."

REMEMBER THIS

- Negligence is unreasonable conduct that injures another person. To be negligent, a person must have acted unreasonably, or below the general standard of care of a reasonable person. A judge or jury usually determines what is reasonable.

- Common carriers and innkeepers owe their passengers and guests a high degree of care.

- If you slip and fall in a store and injure yourself, you may have a claim against the storeowner. Storeowners must keep their premises reasonably safe for their customers.

- Spectators generally cannot sue for injuries suffered at a sporting event, because many courts will hold that spectators assume the risk of such injuries when they attend a game. For instance, a court would likely find that a spectator at a baseball game assumed the risk of being struck by a foul ball.

▶ **IF YOU GET INJURED AT WORK**

Workers' compensation laws cover most workers injured on the job. Under these laws, employers compensate you for your injuries, including payment for medical expenses, lost wages, and permanent or temporary disability, regardless of who was at fault. All you have to do is give notice to your employer and file a claim with the state's workers' compensation commission or board. (See Chapter 15, "Law and the Workplace," for more details.)

In the unlikely event that you are not covered by such a law, you may be able to recover from your employer on a negligence claim. To do so, you must show that your employer failed to exercise reasonable care in providing you with safe working conditions, or that your employer failed to warn you of unsafe conditions that you were unlikely to discover.

- Medical malpractice is a form of professional negligence. Physicians and other health-care providers can be liable if they do not adhere to the necessary standard of care.

- Medical malpractice actions, like other tort actions, are subject to statutes of limitations. States provide for an exception when a plaintiff does not or should not have reason to know about the injury immediately.

- If you are injured on the job, your remedy generally will be limited to a workers' compensation claim, rather than a personal injury tort action.

STRICT LIABILITY

This section covers issues related to strict liability. Strict liability applies to situations where the person who caused the injuries did not act negligently, and certainly didn't intend to harm anyone. Yet, because of the type of activity they engage in, the law holds certain individuals to a higher standard and will find them liable for damages resulting from their behavior. This section outlines when and how someone can be held strictly liable for their actions.

Q. Is there any other basis for liability besides negligence?

A. Courts hold some people or companies **strictly liable** for certain activities that harm others, even when they have not acted negligently or with wrongful intent.

For example, people or companies engaged in blasting, storing dangerous or toxic substances, or keeping dangerous animals can be strictly liable for harm caused to others. Strict liability standards also apply in other areas of personal injury, such as workplace accidents. The most prominent example of strict liability is in product liability cases—holding manufacturers liable for injuries their products cause.

Q. What is the rationale for strict liability?

A. The theory behind imposing strict liability is that inherently dangerous activities pose an undue risk of harm to members of the community. Thus, anyone who conducts such an activity does so at his or her own risk, and is liable when something goes wrong—even innocently—and someone is harmed. The law reasons that the people who pose such risks are in the best position to pay for any injury that results.

Q. We live near a site where a gasoline company stores its flammable liquids. Would we be able to recover damages if an accident were to occur?

A. Probably. Courts have found such storage to be an **inherently dangerous activity**. This means that the act is hazardous by its very nature, whether it is done well or poorly. Courts are likely to impose strict liability against the company for injuries resulting from this type of activity.

However, before imposing liability, courts might look at the location of the storage. If storage in the middle of a large city poses unusual and unacceptable risks, then courts might impose strict liability. The same holds true when a factory emits smoke, dust, or noxious gases in the middle of a town. On the other hand, a company may not be held strictly liable if it conducts such activities in a remote rural area and is not performing the activity in an unusual manner.

Q. What if one of my animals escapes from our fenced-in yard and goes onto our neighbor's property and destroys their deck furniture?

A. In most jurisdictions, keepers of all animals, including domesticated ones, are strictly liable for damages resulting from the trespass of their animals on another person's property. Courts make exceptions for the owners of domestic dogs and cats, saying they are not strictly liable for trespasses unless the owner is negligent, or unless strict liability is imposed by statute or ordinance for certain breeds of dogs with aggressive traits (e.g., pit bulls).

Q. Am I liable if my dog, normally a friendly and playful pet, turns on my neighbor and bites her?

A. It may depend on where you live. A number of jurisdictions have enacted dog-bite statutes, which hold owners strictly liable for injuries inflicted by their animals. If there is no such law in your town, you still can be found liable under a common-law negligence claim if you knew the animal was likely to cause that kind of injury, and if you failed to exercise due care in controlling the pet. On the other hand, if you did not know or have any reason to suspect that your dog had such a dangerous trait, then a court generally will not hold you liable. It is important that you contact your local animal control department to find out about any regulations in your area.

Q. Our neighbors have a vicious watchdog. We are scared to death that the dog will bite one of our children, who often wander into the neighbor's yard. What can we do?

A. The situation you describe is a common one, and is precisely the reason a number of municipalities regulate dog ownership through ordinances. A great deal would depend on the ordinance that applies where you live. Unless your neighbor posts adequate warnings, he or she may be strictly liable for injuries caused by a vicious watchdog. (And even if he or she does post warnings, they may not be sufficient if a child is injured, since children may not be able to read or fully comprehend the signs.) Even if the dog never bit anybody before, such liability is often imposed when a breed of dog is known to be vicious or have certain dangerous traits.

Product Liability

Q. What is product liability?

A. A **product liability** case is a tort case brought against the manufacturer or seller of a product by a user or bystander who has suffered injuries or damages as a result of a defect in that product.

Q. How does strict liability apply to product liability cases?

A. **Strict product liability** allows tort actions against a manufacturer that sells a de-

fective product, if the defective product causes injury to its buyers or users. The defect can be a defect in the product's design, manufacture, or labeling.

Strict liability holds designers and manufacturers strictly liable for injuries from defective products. If you are injured by a defective product, you do not have to establish that the manufacturer was negligent. Rather, you only need to show that the product was defective.

Q. I was opening a jar of pickles when it exploded, and I was injured by flying glass. Was somebody at fault?

A. Yes. Someone was at fault, since jars ordinarily do not explode. Courts often decide such cases by applying principles of strict liability, meaning that instead of having to prove that someone was negligent, a plaintiff would only have to prove that the jar exploded and that he or she was injured by it.

However, some courts continue to decide

▶ TOXIC TORT CASES

Toxic torts involve many plaintiffs suing multiple defendants for damages resulting from harmful exposure to various harmful (toxic) substances. Toxic tort cases can be difficult to prove, and they often involve a significant legal dispute over the cause of the plaintiffs' harm—for example, over whether damages were caused by long-term exposure to toxins, or by factors peculiar to the plaintiffs' individual environments (e.g., long-term proximity to a smoker, or proclivity toward a certain health condition).

Examples of toxic tort cases include asbestos litigation, breast implant litigation, lead exposure litigation, litigation involving radiation spills, litigation over longterm exposure to chemical solvents, and the classic Agent Orange litigation stemming from chemical exposure in Vietnam. These types of cases become class-action lawsuits because a number of people allegedly were injured by exposure to a certain toxin or pollutant. Many cases like these are settled for millions of dollars, but because there are so many plaintiffs, each person may ultimately receive only a small part of the settlement.

> ▶ **VISITING A ZOO**
>
> Zoos go to great extremes to protect visitors from risks, generally by restraining or confining their animals. For that reason, courts usually do not impose strict liability when a visitor to a zoo gets injured. Instead, the visitor must show that the zoo was somehow negligent in confining the animal.

such cases by applying negligence principles. If the manufacturer sealed the jar and it was handled carefully between the time it left the manufacturer's possession and the time of the explosion, some courts assume—or consider this circumstantial evidence—that the manufacturer was negligent.

Q. Our brand-new power mower backfired and injured me. From whom may I recover damages?

A. This is a typical product liability case. Not only can you sue the mower's manufacturer, but you can also sue the distributor and the retailer. You may also have a claim against the assembler of a specific part of the product. If the manufacturer hired a design consultant, a quality-control engineer, or a technical writer to help with the instructions, these individuals could also be liable.

Q. A disclaimer that came with the mower said the manufacturer did not offer any sort of warranty. Can I still recover?

A. While limited warranties are sometimes enforced by courts, this type of full disclaimer often is not. Courts find such warranties invalid because you, as the consumer, are not in

an equal bargaining position. Courts also tend to rule that such clauses are **unconscionable** (i.e., grossly unfair) and contrary to public policy. (See Chapter 12, "Contracts and Consumer Law," for a discussion about contracts of adhesion and unconscionability.) Most courts limit the effect of limited warranties to repairs. A limited warranty is not a waiver of liability for injuries.

Q. My grandson was playing with a toy. The toy came apart, and he put one of the pieces into his mouth and started choking. Do we have any redress against the toy manufacturer?

A. You have no redress if your grandson merely gagged and then spit out the part, suffering no injury. On the other hand, if he choked and stopped breathing, causing brain damage, then you probably have an action against the manufacturer. As in any strict liability action, several questions would need to be answered to determine the manufacturer's culpability. Did it have a duty to warn consumers about the danger of the toy falling apart? If so, what was the likelihood that the toy would break into small parts that could be dangerous to a small child? Was anyone supervising your grandson while he was playing?

Because toy manufacturers outside the United States can be difficult to sue, you also might want to consider suing other parties in the toy's chain of distribution—the toy store, for example, or perhaps a fast-food chain that distributed the toy as part of a promotion. Such retailers also can be liable for injuries.

Also consider contacting the federal **Consumer Product Safety Commission (CPSC)**. The CPSC closely monitors such products and defects. Like others that put products into commerce, toy manufacturers have a duty to consider any foreseeable misuse of their products.

Q. I suffered a severe allergic reaction to some cosmetics I used, and my reaction necessitated medical treatment. May I recover money from the manufacturer?

A. Perhaps. Some courts will not hold a manufacturer liable for failing to warn you of the risk of an adverse reaction, unless you can prove that an ingredient in the product would likely cause a number of people to have such a reaction. You also must prove that the manufacturer knew or should have known this, and that your reaction occurred because you were one of many people likely to have such a reaction, and not because you are hypersensitive. In addition, courts will determine whether you used the product according to the directions provided with it—i.e., that you are not guilty of **misuse,** which is a defense to strict liability claims. If the court does not find strict liability, you still might recover on a negligence claim.

Q. I got hepatitis from a blood transfusion. Is someone liable?

A. In many states, laws protect suppliers against strict liability when people who receive blood transfusions contract an illness from contaminated blood. However, you may recover if you can show negligence on the part of the supplier.

Q. My father's job exposed him to asbestos twenty years ago. Now he has lung disease. Is it too late to file a claim?

A. It may not be too late. Many people who suffered injuries from toxic substances, such as asbestos, did not know at the time of exposure that the compounds were harmful. As a result, some states have enacted laws allowing people to file lawsuits for a certain amount of time after lung impairment begins or cancer is developed, rather than from the date of exposure. A lawyer can tell you whether your father still has time within the statutes of limitations applicable in your state.

Q. I was injured because of a brake defect in a used car I bought. May I recover from the dealer?

A. Some courts may deem a used-car dealer negligent for failing to inspect or discover such defects. But generally, courts are split on whether dealers in used goods should be subject to strict liability.

REMEMBER THIS

- Even though negligence is the most common principle applied in tort law, strict liability applies in certain circumstances—including cases involving injuries that result from abnormally dangerous activities, wild or trespassing animals, or defective products.

- Some jurisdictions hold dog owners strictly liable for injuries caused by their dogs. Other jurisdictions hold the owners liable only if they knew of their dog's vicious tendencies.

- The three most common types of product liability actions involve manufacturing defects, design defects, and failure to warn.

▶ **WHAT YOU SHOULD DO IF YOU ARE INJURED BY A PRODUCT**

- Keep the evidence. For example, if a heating fixture ruptures and injures someone in your family, keep as many pieces of the equipment as you can find, and disturb the site as little as possible.
- For any defective product, make note of the manufacturer's name, the model, and the serial number.
- Keep any packaging or instructions.
- Keep any receipts showing when and where the product was purchased.
- Take pictures of the site and of the injury.
- Make a record of exactly when the incident occurred and under what circumstances.
- Be sure you have accurate names and addresses for all doctors and hospitals treating the injury.

- If you are injured by a product, keep the evidence. Keep all receipts showing when the product was purchased. Make detailed records of when the incident occurred and what happened.

INTENTIONAL WRONGS

Not all torts are caused by accidents or negligence. Sometimes people intend to harm—or, at the very least, scare—other people. This can occasionally result in serious injuries, damages, and even death. Although the criminal justice system often punishes these offenders, victims may still suffer monetary and emotional losses. The law of intentional torts allows those who have been injured to recover for their injuries and damages. This section outlines the law of intentional torts, explains what you must prove in order to mount a suc-

▶ **BREAST IMPLANT LITIGATION**

There have been thousands of lawsuits filed by women who have undergone breast implantation and now allege that the implants contributed to a wide array of health problems, ranging from cancer and autoimmune diseases to joint pains. The suits generally say that the manufacturers were negligent, and that they knew the product was defective.

Like asbestos cases, many states have provided special extended statutes of limitations for breast implant cases. For example, while a typical statute of limitations in an auto accident is one year, some states provide that in breast implant or asbestos cases, the filing period can be as long as twenty or twenty-five years.

cessful intentional-torts case, and provides some practical examples.

Q. What if someone intends to hurt me? Can I recover for my damages?

A. Yes—if you can prove that the person committed an intentional tort.

Q. What are intentional torts?

A. **Intentional torts** are those in which the wrongdoer intends to act in a certain way. For example, let's say Jack picks up a golf club, swings it at Jill, and hits her in the shoulder. Jack has committed the intentional torts of assault and battery. He intended to strike Jill, causing harm.

Q. But isn't hitting someone a crime?

A. It can be. Conduct that forms the basis for an intentional tort can lead to both criminal and civil proceedings. In the above example, Jack can be criminally charged by the state and sued by Jill in a tort action. The state's case is a criminal action, while Jill's is a civil tort action.

Q. What are some typical intentional torts?

A. There are intentional torts against people, and intentional torts against property. Some common intentional torts against people include assault, battery, defamation, false imprisonment, and intentional infliction of emotional distress.

Intentional torts against property include trespass to land, trespass to **chattel** (i.e., personal property), and **conversion** (i.e., converting someone else's property into your own).

Q. Is a civil lawsuit based on liability for an intentional tort different from a lawsuit based on negligence or strict liability?

A. You may claim the same types of damages, but you must prove different things. A person who is found liable for an intentional tort does more than just act carelessly. The person committing the intentional tort knows the consequences of his or her action. For example, if you pick up a realistic model of an AK-47 and point it at somebody out the window of your car, you should know that you are going to scare that person. Under the law of intentional torts, you may be liable for an assault (the tort of causing people to reasonably fear that some harm will come to them), as that person may have had a reasonable expectation that they could be harmed.

You need not intend to harm a person in order to be liable for an intentional tort; in fact, you may even be liable for an intentional tort in cases where you were attempting to help a person. In one case, for example, a defendant was found liable for an intentional tort when he proceeded to set the broken arm of a woman who had fallen, despite her protests. Unlike in a negligence action, a plaintiff alleging an intentional tort does not need to show actual damages in order to recover.

Q. I got in a fistfight with a man whose car accidentally bumped into mine while we sat at a red light. I received a black eye in the fight, and would love to get even with him. Can I recover if I sue him?

A. Normally, you can recover damages in a civil battery case against someone who hits you. However, a court might hold that two people who get into a fistfight are effectively agreeing to be hit by one another. For this reason, a battery case probably would fail, though a lot would depend on the facts of the case.

Q. What is the tort of battery?

A. **Battery** is a harmful or offensive touching of one person by another. Anyone who touches you or comes into contact with some part of you—even your clothing—without your consent may be liable to you for battery. The law does not require that you suffer any harm or damage. In fact, in order to bring a battery claim, you don't even have to know that a battery is occurring at the time it takes place.

The person committing the battery may have meant no hatred or ill will. In one case, for example, a plaintiff successfully recovered damages for an unwanted kiss. However, damages for such technical batteries are typically small.

Q. What is the tort of assault? How is it different from battery?

A. An **assault** is a reasonable apprehension (expectation) of some harm that may come to you. Unlike a battery, you must know that an assault is occurring at the time it takes place. A court will look at the reasonableness of your feelings. The court will consider whether the closeness of the physical threat subjectively should have upset, frightened, or humiliated you. Words alone usually are not enough to bring a successful case for assault.

Q. My neighbor fired his shotgun to scare an unwelcome solicitor. One of the pellets grazed a passerby. Will my neighbor be liable?

A. Under a legal doctrine known as **transferred intent,** your neighbor could be liable

for a battery to the passerby. This is true even though the passerby was an unexpected victim whom your neighbor did not intend to harm. The solicitor also is likely to win an assault case against your neighbor. The firing of the gun placed the solicitor in reasonable apprehension of a battery, which is the legal definition of an assault.

Q. A security guard in a store suspected me of shoplifting and detained me. I have heard about something called false imprisonment. Do I have an action for that?

A. If the security guard was acting in good faith, most courts will allow the guard to detain you briefly on the store premises to investigate. Nonetheless, you may be able to recover damages for false imprisonment. Suppose the security guard genuinely restrained you against your will, intending to confine you. Damages for such an action generally include compensation for loss of time and any inconvenience, physical discomfort, or injuries. If the guard acted maliciously, you also may be able to receive punitive damages.

Q. Someone broke into my house in the middle of the night and attacked me. I chased the culprit, and knocked him down while he was running away down the street. Will I be liable for his injuries?

A. If you reasonably believe that someone is breaking into your house and attacking you, you have the right to defend yourself, even if you injure the intruder. If you believe someone is about to inflict bodily harm, you may use non-deadly force to defend yourself. In situations in which you believe an intruder is about to inflict death or serious bodily harm, courts allow you to use deadly force. The question then becomes whether the force you used was reasonable under the circumstances.

In this particular case, if the culprit was already running away, courts may say that there was no longer danger to you or your property. Then, outrageous as it sounds, you might well be liable for the injuries you caused to the culprit.

Q. We got behind on our bills, and a bill collector has been stopping by our house and calling us day and night. The bill collector intimidates us, calls us names, and threatens to destroy our credit record. We are nervous wrecks. What may we do?

A. You may be able to make a case that the collector's conduct constitutes a tort: the **intentional infliction of mental distress.** Courts recently have begun to recognize such actions in cases of extreme and outrageous conduct that is intentionally inflicted. But in order for you to recover damages, you must show that you have suffered more than hurt feelings. Without aggravating (i.e., intensifying) circumstances, most courts have not allowed recovery if a collector has merely been profane, obscene, abusive, threatening, or insulting. Rather, the collector would need to have used outrageous and extreme high-pressure methods for an extended period of time.

You also might want to consider a case against the collector's employer. Just as employers are vicariously (i.e., indirectly) liable for the negligent acts of an employee, employers can also be liable for the intentional acts of an employee. A court would need to determine whether the collector's particular conduct fell within the scope of his or her job. (See Chapter 10, "Consumer Credit," for more information about debt collection and your rights.)

Q. What about someone hurting my reputation? Is that a tort?

A. Yes. The tort of **defamation** involves your reputation. If information about you is revealed to a third person and is understood by that person to weaken your reputation, or if that information keeps others from associating with you, you may have a defamation claim. Libel and slander are two types of defamation.

To recover for defamation, you have to prove that the information in question is both false and defamatory. (If something is false, but doesn't damage your reputation, then you don't have a claim.) The defendants can raise truth as a defense. In other words, if they can prove that the information about you was true, then slander or libel could not have taken place. Your consent to the publication of defamatory information about yourself is also a complete defense against libel and slander.

Defamation generally is easier to prove if you are a private person; courts treat public officials and figures differently from private citizens. Public figures must show that a speaker or publisher either knew the words were false or made the statement with reckless disregard for the truth. Private individuals must show only that the defendant was negligent in that he or she failed to act with reasonable care in the situation.

Q. What is the difference between slander and libel?

A. A defamation action for **slander** rests on an oral communication made to another party that is understood to lower your reputation or keep others from associating with you. **Libel** generally involves written or printed defamation that has the same effect. Today, however, radio and television broadcasts of defamatory material are nearly universally considered libel.

Q. My late grandfather, who owned a textile factory, was called "unfair to labor" in a recent book about the industry. Is that libelous?

A. While it can be libelous to write that someone is unfair to labor—or is a crook, a drunk, or an anarchist, for example—no defamation action can be brought on behalf of someone who is deceased. If your family still owns the factory and the same accusation made against your grandfather was made against a living family member or against your business, a defamation action could then be brought.

Q. I have a tax-return preparation business, and a neighbor recently told a potential client that I knew nothing about tax law. Is that slander?

A. If the statement was untrue, you might have a case. If someone disseminates false information that affects you in your business, trade, or profession, you can recover in a slander action even without showing actual harm to your reputation or other damages. You can do the same in three other situations: if someone says that you committed a crime, that you

have a loathsome disease, or, in the case of a female, that you are unchaste (i.e., impure).

Of course, you can also recover damages in other types of slander cases—but in those cases, you will have to show that actual damages occurred.

Q. Are there defenses to defamation?

A. There are several defenses that will defeat a defamation claim. As mentioned above, consent is one; truth is another. And certain persons and proceedings (such as a judge in his or her courtroom, witnesses testifying about a relevant issue in a case, and certain communications by legislators) are said to be privileged. They are protected from defamation claims.

Many states have so-called **retraction statutes,** which enable media defendants to retract, or take back, defamatory statements. Many retraction statutes merely limit a defendant's liability. Some statutes, for example, prevent a plaintiff from recovering punitive damages if the defendant properly retracts the statement.

REMEMBER THIS

- An intentional wrongdoer (tortfeasor) knows the consequences of his or her actions.

- The major types of intentional torts against people are assault, battery, false imprisonment, intentional infliction of emotional distress, and defamation.

- A major difference between assault and battery is that assault does not require actual contact, while battery requires a harmful or offensive touching. Conduct that constitutes assault or battery can also form the basis for a criminal action.

- False imprisonment is the intentional confinement of someone against his or her will. Shopkeepers often have a limited privilege to detain those whom they reasonably suspect of shoplifting.

- Intentional infliction of emotional distress requires that the wrongdoer engage in extreme and outrageous conduct. Such conduct must go beyond the pale of social decency.

CHAPTER SEVEN

Buying and Selling a Home

Jason had substantial investments, but while he was looking for a new home, he was laid off from his job. He was highly marketable and knew he would get another job, so he continued his search for a home. Jason eventually found a home he liked and entered into negotiations. He was embarrassed and upset to find that even though the value of his investments exceeded the purchase price of the home, he was unable to get a mortgage loan because he had insufficient income. Will he have to wait until he gets a new job before he can buy the home? Does he have any other options? Should he find a lawyer to help him through the process? What happens to the contract that was being negotiated? Can Jason get out of it?

Buying or selling a home is often not as easy as it may appear. The laws where you live, the economy, your financial situation, the prevailing real estate market, current mortgage rates, and tax considerations will all affect you. You'll need to work with a variety of people, including real estate agents, lawyers, lenders, home inspectors, surveyors, appraisers, and insurance agents.

Practices and laws affecting real estate change over time (to address new consumer issues), and over geographic regions (with laws and customs varying from city to city and state to state).

This chapter provides you with guidance, whether you're buying or selling a home for the first time or the tenth. You'll learn real estate terminology, become acquainted with the roles of different participants in the home-buying process, and learn about your financing and tax options. The section entitled "The Steps Involved with Buying and Selling a Home" tells you what you need to know about the contract that controls the transaction.

As you read this chapter, remember that becoming familiar with both the buying and selling side of the process is useful even if you are engaging in only one side of the transaction. If you understand the interests of both parties, you will be able to anticipate issues and be better prepared to negotiate.

INTRODUCTION TO BUYING AND SELLING A HOME

Imagine you've found the home of your dreams. It's in the right neighborhood, has the perfect kitchen, and it's at the right price. You contact the seller, put your own house on the market, and start packing for the big move.

But wait a minute. Are you sure you can afford to buy this dream home? Is it really as good a deal as it looks? Do you know what steps you have to take in order to buy a home, and how long the process will take?

This section helps you answer these questions.

Q. Why is the purchase or sale of a home more complicated than buying or selling other objects, such as an expensive car?

A. Items of personal property, such as cars and boats, have different characteristics from real estate. Personal property is usually movable and, in many cases, owned for a relatively short period of time. Moreover, possession of personal property is a strong indicator of ownership. But because real estate (also known as **real property** or simply **land**) cannot be moved, possession does not necessarily equal ownership. And even if a person owns real estate, he or she may not have possession of it—for example, if the real estate is being rented to someone else.

Because of the differences between real and personal property, the law treats them differently. For example:

- Unlike with personal property, agreements regarding the sale of real estate must be in writing to be enforceable.

- In the absence of consumer protection laws or special representations by the seller, real property is sold "as is."
- Foreclosing a mortgage on real property is usually more difficult than repossessing personal property.
- Real estate and personal property are taxed differently.

Q. What is a home?

A. A **home** is a dwelling, but it need not be a single-family dwelling built on an individual parcel of land. Town houses, condominiums, and cooperatives are also considered homes. Each of these types of homes has unique features, which are discussed later in this chapter.

Q. Why should I buy a home?

A. People buy homes for different reasons. Some want to own property because it might reduce their living costs. Others enjoy the income tax benefits of ownership. In certain parts of the country, finding rental property is difficult, so ownership may be the only option. And, most importantly for some, homeowners often have more control than renters over their personal living environments.

Many prospective home buyers think of a home solely, or at least primarily, as an investment. However, this view may be misguided. There is no reason to assume that home prices will always rise, so owning a home by no means guarantees that the homeowner will turn a profit. Home prices can fall, sometimes dramatically.

Still, although the decision to buy a home should not be viewed solely as an investment decision, it is wise to approach home ownership as carefully as you would any major investment. After all, a home is the largest purchase many people will ever make.

Q. I have been told that when I buy a home, I will get title to the property. What is title?

A. If you have **title** to a piece of real estate, it means that you own the property and have the right to use it. If you are the legal owner of record, you have title to the property and are the title owner. However, your interest in the property may be affected by **title exceptions,** or **clouds on title,** which are possible claims that other parties may have to your title.

Q. What are some examples of title exceptions?

A. There are several kinds of title exceptions. For example, a **lien** is a claim against a property, often representing an unpaid debt of the owner or an unpaid judgment entered against the owner by a court. The most common form of lien against real property is a **mortgage** or **deed of trust.** If the titleholder does not pay the lien or claim, the creditor may ultimately have the right to sell the property to satisfy the debt.

Other types of title exceptions include mineral rights, mechanic's liens, unpaid taxes, private and public utility easements, and road rights-of-way. **Covenants of record** (also known as **restrictions of record**), which generally take the form of a written document setting forth restrictions on the use of the property, are another important kind of title exception. For example, if a home is part of a subdivision or common-ownership association (i.e., if the home has been built in conjunction with other homes), there may be a written document placing limits on the homeowner's ability to rent, or placing restrictions on the business activities that may be conducted on the property. Covenants written long ago may contain restrictions that are unenforceable

▶ WHAT IS A DEED?

A **deed** is a written document that contains the names of the seller and the purchaser, other personal information, certain conveyance language, and a legal description of the property. There are different kinds of deeds, but they must all contain at least this basic information. A deed is generally effective between the parties upon delivery, but in most states it must be recorded in the public records to be effective against third parties.

today, such as prohibitions against selling your home to a member of certain racial, religious, or ethnic groups. Other types of covenants, however, continue to be enforceable, so be sure you understand them before you agree to them. In addition to title exceptions, govern-ment regulations, such as zoning or occupancy laws, also affect the use of real estate.

Q. How can I tell if there is a problem with title?

A. A search of the public records should always be conducted prior to the closing. By uncovering evidence of any claims that appear in the public record, a **title search** reveals who owns the property—and what title exceptions affect it. A lawyer, an abstract company, or a title insurance company usually conducts such a search. The results are usually compiled in either an **abstract of title** or a **title insurance commitment** to help the buyer determine who owns the property and if any title exceptions exist. Keep in mind, however, that there may be other claims of interest in the property that do not appear in the public record.

If possible, any unacceptable title exceptions should be corrected before closing. Typically, the seller is responsible for remedying title defects.

▶ WHOSE MARKET IS IT?

You may have heard the terms "buyer's market" or "seller's market," but what do these terms really mean?

A **buyer's market** occurs when home sales are slow. Some factors indicating a buyer's market may include: homes taking longer to sell, increased foreclosures and unemployment, reductions in home prices, and numerous "for sale" signs. In a buyer's market, buyers have many homes to choose from and may be able to demand special considerations from sellers.

A **seller's market** occurs when homes sell quickly, when there are relatively few homes on the market, and, generally, when the local economy is good. In a seller's market, sellers can demand high prices for their homes and often dictate the terms of the contract.

▶ DIFFERENT KINDS OF INTERESTS IN REAL ESTATE

Suppose that a farmer leases land owned by a school district. The district owns the land, but the farmer owns the crops he plants on the land. The district sells mineral rights in the land to another person. If the district ever decides to sell the property, the local church has the option to buy it.

As this example demonstrates, being an owner of real estate can have different meanings. For example, owning land mean could mean that you own some or all of the following:

- the land and everything under it, including minerals and water;
- anything of value on the land, such as crops or timber;
- the airspace over the land; or
- improvements on the land, such as a home, a building, a barn, or a fence.

Ownership of the above elements may be individual or shared, and may also be subject to the rights of other parties. In addition, though you may not be an owner, you may have a legally protected interest in property owned by someone else if you have the right to buy or possess the land or improvements under it—as may be the case, for example, with an option or lease.

REMEMBER THIS

- Buying a home is a major decision and one of the largest purchases many people will ever make.

- Title to property can have exceptions, meaning that others may have claims to the title. A search of the public records should be conducted before closing the sale of property to ensure that the seller has good title to the real estate.

MEETING THE PLAYERS

Buying or selling a home involves many steps, conversations, and forms. Having someone like a qualified real estate agent or lawyer in your corner can make a big difference. When you're buying a home, especially your first, you should ensure that your agent and lawyer are working in your best interests and have no conflicts of interest. This section introduces you to the various players involved in a real estate transaction, and points out some of the issues that you should keep in mind when buying or selling.

Q. Who is involved in a real estate transaction?

A. Although it is possible for a home to be bought and sold strictly between the buyer and seller, this rarely happens. Buyers and sellers usually want to work with a real estate agent, a lawyer, and a home inspector. To obtain financing, buyers will need to consult with a mortgage broker or lending institution. They may also meet with a financial planner or accountant about financing, and an insurance broker to obtain homeowner's insurance.

In order to avoid paying a commission, either party may choose not to use the services of a real estate agent. However, few sellers would forego the services of a lawyer. A knowledgeable person needs to prepare the required documents. In some parts of the country, it is customary to rely on a title insurance company to prepare these documents. However, it is important to understand that the title company does not represent either party to the transaction, and its personnel cannot engage in the unauthorized practice of law by giving legal advice to either party.

The Real Estate Agent

Q. What is the role of a real estate agent?

A. The role of a real estate agent will depend on which party the agent represents. If a seller signs a listing agreement with a particular agent, the agent is working for the seller, and is usually referred to as the **listing agent.** The listing agent helps determine the asking price, suggests how to market the home, adds the property to a local Multiple Listing Service (MLS), schedules advertising and open houses, shows the home to prospective buyers, and otherwise facilitates the sale. Since the amount paid to an agent can be high, it may be possible to hire an agent to handle only limited aspects of the sale in exchange for a reduced commission.

If a second agent is involved in the show-ing of a house to a potential buyer (often referred to as a **cooperating, selling,** or **showing agent**), questions may arise as to whom this agent represents. In the past, many buyers erroneously assumed that any agent showing them properties was in fact their agent, and would be working on their behalf. Today, many states treat buyer representation as a consumer protection issue. As a result, depending on the state, it may now be the case that if an agent shows a property to a buyer, that cooperating agent will be deemed the buyer's agent.

If a listing agent shows a property to a buyer, it is possible that one agent, referred to as a **dual agent,** will act as both the seller's and buyer's agent. In such a case, there is potential for a conflict of interest. Such an agreement must be disclosed and approved by both the buyer and the seller, usually in writing, before the parties can proceed.

The buyer's agent works with the buyer to find potential homes. The agent contacts listing agents, helps the buyer view the home, assists the buyer in preparing an offer, monitors the transaction, and sometimes helps the buyer obtain financing.

It is extremely important that the parties understand the role of each agent, and whom each agent represents.

Q. What is a listing agreement?

A. The **listing agreement** is a contract that, once signed, is binding between the seller and the listing agency or agent. Its provisions include the length of the listing period, the commission rate, the responsibilities of the firm, and who will pay for advertising and other associated costs of the sale. One important term to look for in a listing agreement is the date when the commission must be paid. As a seller, you want to owe a commission to your listing agent only if the closing has occurred. Many "standard" listing agreements provide that the agent is owed a commission if the agent has procured a ready, willing, and able buyer. Read the listing agreement carefully. Do not hesitate to discuss any changes you would like to see incorporated.

There are several types of listing agreements. The type commonly used in your area will be dictated by custom and will often be nonnegotiable, although some aspects of the agreement—such as when the commission is earned, who will be responsible for advertising expenses, and the length of the contract—should always be negotiable. Most real estate firms prefer to have the exclusive right to sell listings. This type of agreement provides that the seller will pay the listing agent a commission no matter who sells the property, even if another agent or the seller finds the buyer, as long as the property is sold during the specified period.

Other types of listing agreements include open listings and exclusive agency listings. An **open listing** allows anyone to sell the property, including the seller. Under an open listing, the commission is paid only to the person who finds the buyer. An **exclusive agency listing** gives one agent the exclusive right to sell the property. In the event of a sale, only the exclusive agent is owed a commission by the seller, and the agent does not have to share the commission with anyone else. However, the seller in an exclusive agency agreement retains the right to find a buyer without the assistance of an agent, in which case the agent is not entitled to a commission.

Before signing a listing agreement, let your friends and neighbors know you are selling. If any of them express interest in buying, exclude them in writing from the listing agreement so that if one of them buys the property, you will not be required to pay any commission to the agent.

Q. Why should I list my home with a real estate agent?

A. Experienced, reputable agents can provide invaluable assistance to sellers. They can suggest the listing price, estimate how long it may take to sell the property, offer suggestions about how best to show the home, and deter-

▶ YOUR MLS OPTIONS

Some Internet services will list your property on an MLS and, though they provide no further services, will often charge less commission than a real estate agent. For some examples of this type of service, consult the "World at Your Fingertips" section at the end of this book.

This type of service may seem like a good option if you are trying to save money. However, if you do list your property on an MLS using Internet services, you will have to fill out all the details—the size of each room, special features of the house, and so on—by yourself. This is a time-consuming process. More importantly, real estate agents are skilled at presenting this kind of information in the best possible way. If you are considering this option, make sure you understand the amount of time you will have to invest in making your sale.

mine whether buyers who inquire about the property are in a position, financially and otherwise, to buy the property.

One of the most important reasons to use an agent is to have the property information listed on a **Multiple Listing Service,** or **MLS.** The MLS allows detailed information about the home to be made available to hundreds of other agents and buyers, usually online. An MLS can cover a local or regional area. Make sure that you select a listing agent who is a member of the MLS on which you want the property to appear.

Q. How do I choose an agent?

A. As a seller, you should be comfortable and have confidence in the agent you select. The firm and agent should be responsive to you, communicating all expressed interest in the home and following up on the visits of potential buyers. You might want to know how many buyers have seen the home and why no offers have been made. Is the agent trying to discover why? Is the price too high? Does the decor detract from the home? Should you make some minor repairs?

A buyer needs to consider many of the same factors as a seller. As a buyer, you will also want to make sure that the agent has a good record of locating the types of homes you want. For example, an agent who customarily has clients seeking $500,000 homes may not spend much time working for a client seeking a $100,000 home, the sale of which will generate a smaller commission than a more expensive home.

Q. What fee will I pay on the sale or purchase of my home?

A. Typically, real estate firms charge a percentage (generally from 5 percent to 7 percent) of the sale price. Some Internet-based firms have marketed themselves as low-commission realtors, advertising commissions as low as 2 percent.

Other less-common forms of fee payments include the **flat-fee method,** in which a set fee is charged regardless of the home's price, and the net method. The **net method,** which is out of favor with most courts and is illegal in some states, allows the broker to retain any amount of the selling price that exceeds an agreed-upon sale price. Whatever fee arrangement you choose, make sure you are comfortable with it, and that it is spelled out in the listing agreement.

On the buyer's agent's side, the sales commission is typically shared by the seller's agent and the buyer's agent. But be aware that this scenario could create a conflict of interest for the buyer's agent. If the agent is being compensated by the seller only if the deal is closed, he or she might not represent the buyer's interests vigorously.

Q. As a buyer, what should I tell a real estate agent about my personal situation?

A. If you have hired a buyer's agent, you should feel free to discuss all aspects of the sale. If you are working with anyone else, you may want to withhold certain information that could be useful to the seller. Remember: unless you have hired a buyer's agent, the agents you are working with may be representing the seller, not you, and thus may be required to disclose all relevant information you give them to the seller.

Buying and Selling Without an Agent

Q. Are there advantages to selling my home without an agent?

A. Yes. The advantage of selling without an agent is that you will not have to pay a sales

▶ SOME ADVANCE WORK BEFORE YOU BUY

If you are a prospective buyer, postpone negotiating and making offers until you get a feel for various neighborhoods and the type of home (i.e., style, price range) you are seeking. Shopping open houses is an excellent way to accomplish this. Before you have a specific home in mind, you also may want to be preapproved by a lender for a mortgage. This topic will be discussed further later in this chapter.

commission, which, depending on the sale price, can be a very substantial sum. However, you also will have to assume all the responsibilities and associated costs of selling your home. These include advertising, spending time with potential buyers, making required disclosures, and negotiating.

There are various resources that can help guide you through the process, and experts generally recommend that you hire both an appraiser and a lawyer. An appraiser can help you establish a price for your home, and the lawyer can help you with the legal issues and necessary documents.

Q. Are there disadvantages to selling my home without an agent?

A. There are at least three distinct disadvantages:

1. You will lack the resources that real estate agents have to attract buyers.
2. You will have to find the time to show your home and talk to potential buyers. This could also raise some security issues.

3. You will be directly involved in negotiating the sales price and other contract provisions. You will also have to make all legally required disclosures. (Your lawyer can prepare you for what to do when you receive an offer.)

At first glance, selling without a broker may seem easy. However, a professional real estate agent may be skilled at avoiding "deal breakers"—the kind of petty disagreements that can break up negotiations—and can also help you find solutions for larger disagreements.

If you have decided to sell on your own, remember that settling on the terms and conditions of sale, including the price, is a give-and-take process. For example, the fact that you love your renovated kitchen will not influence a potential buyer who intends to remodel anyway.

Q. Are there advantages to buying a home from a seller who is not using a real estate agent?

A. The major advantage of buying a home that is **for sale by owner,** or **FSBO,** should be a lower purchase price, because the seller will not be paying a commission on the sale. However, the truth is that many FSBOs are initially priced as high as they would be if they were listed with a real estate firm. If you are interested in a FSBO, check the prices of comparable homes on the market, as well as recent sales in the area to see if you will have room to negotiate a lower price.

Buying Foreclosed Property

Q. What are foreclosed properties?

A. Most often, foreclosed properties—called **REOs** (for **real estate owned by the**

lender)—are owned by the lending institution or government agency that backed a mortgage. For one reason or another, the owner failed to make payments on the loan and the lender **foreclosed** on the property (i.e., took possession of it). This means that the lender has taken title to the property and has become the owner.

Q. What types of property can be foreclosed?

A. Mortgages on all types of properties, including single-family homes and condominiums, can be foreclosed.

Q. How can I find out about foreclosed properties?

A. Foreclosures are sold individually or through auctions. Some institutions advertise their foreclosed properties; others deal strictly through real estate agents. Local real estate agents usually keep a current list of local foreclosed homes. The "World at Your Fingertips" section also lists several websites that offer lists of foreclosed properties for a fee (see page 728).

The Federal National Mortgage Association, commonly known as **Fannie Mae,** is a federally chartered corporation that makes mortgage funding available to lenders. Information on Fannie Mae foreclosures, as well as foreclosures by other federally backed loans, can also be found on the Internet.

The Federal Housing Administration (FHA) usually sells its foreclosed properties through an auction announced in the classified sections of local newspapers. Potential buyers submit bids on the day of the auction, accompanied by a certified check for a percentage of the bid price. The highest bidder usually gets the home.

Q. Are there any special issues I should be aware of when buying a foreclosed property?

A. Yes. Buying a foreclosed property can be risky if you are not familiar with the procedures involved. This type of sale may not feature the same safeguards that are present in a traditional sale, such as a lender and a title insurance company. Therefore, if you plan to buy foreclosed properties, it is important to familiarize yourself with the process and consult a lawyer who specializes in this area.

An additional drawback to buying a foreclosed property may be the condition of the property. Sometimes, an owner who was unable to keep up with payments to the lender (thus causing the foreclosure) was also unable to maintain the home properly.

The Fair Housing Act

Q. Can a homeowner legally refuse to sell a home to a potential buyer?

A. Yes. However, there are limits. The Fair Housing Act (FHA) addresses issues relating to housing discrimination. Specifically, this law prohibits housing discrimination by real estate firms and homeowners. This means that homeowners may not refuse to lease or sell property based on race, religion, gender, color, or national origin. In some localities, special housing discrimination ordinances or laws also cover sexual orientation. This does not mean, however, that sellers must sell their home to anyone who makes an offer. On the contrary, sellers may legitimately prefer one buyer over another for economic or noneconomic reasons—for example, if a buyer makes a higher bid, or has already secured a mortgage loan commitment, or promises to preserve the character of the house. But a buyer could take legal action if the seller refuses to sell and the buyer believes that the true motivation was illegal discrimination.

A homeowner who violates the anti-discrimination laws faces serious financial penalties. The potential buyer could sue for actual monetary losses as well as lawyer's fees, court costs, and even punitive damages. If the economic viability of an offer is in question, perhaps the safest thing for the seller to do is tell the potential buyer that his or her offer might be accepted once the loan commitment is actually obtained, so long as no other offers are received in the interim.

Q. What if an agent refuses to show me a home? Is this discrimination?

A. The agent could be engaging in steering. **Steering** is the practice of showing potential buyers, for reasons of race, religion, gender, color, or national origin, homes located only in certain neighborhoods. The FHA prohibits firms and agents from steering buyers.

Q. How can I tell if illegal discrimination is occurring, and what can I do about it?

A. You may suspect discrimination if

- somebody tells you that a listed home is no longer for sale, but it remains on the market;
- an agent avoids showing you homes in areas you have requested; or
- a seller refuses a full-price bid.

The federal Department of Housing and Urban Development (HUD) investigates such complaints; for the address at which you can file a complaint, see the "World at Your Fingertips" section at the end of this book. You may also be able to contact a local civil-rights organization for further advice about whom to

> ▶ **ORAL PROMISES**
>
> Beware of making oral promises. Many kinds of contracts do not have to be in writing to be valid. For example, if a seller orally promises to update the electrical system in a home, the buyer might be able to insist that the system be updated even if the matter does not arise in later negotiations.

contact. Usually, you will have to consult a lawyer about possible legal action against the homeowner.

Working with a Lawyer

Q. When should I see a lawyer about buying or selling a home?

A. As a buyer, you probably do not need to consult a lawyer when you begin your search. However, you will want a lawyer when you are ready to make an offer, and certainly when finalizing the purchase contract. Legal advice will be more helpful—and may be less expensive in the long run—before rather than after signing a contract.

In addition to giving you advice and help in negotiations, your lawyer will ensure that your interests are protected. If something goes wrong, you do not want to discover too late that you have signed away important rights, failed to include critical protections, or failed to receive what you expected.

As a seller, you will probably want to consult a lawyer early in the process and before signing a listing agreement with a real estate agent. As in the case of a buyer, it is important to understand the terms of the offer before accepting it. In addition, a lawyer will be instrumental in helping the seller comply with the terms of an accepted offer and preparing for the closing.

Q. How do I choose a lawyer?

A. To choose a lawyer, you will want to consider the following:

- **Area of specialty.** While it may not be necessary to find a lawyer who only specializes in real estate, you will want a lawyer who is familiar with the real estate laws and practices in your area. It is a good idea to select a lawyer who has had some recent real estate experience.
- **Office location.** Your lawyer will need to review agreements and papers and appear at the closing. Costs can be minimized with a local lawyer. However, thanks to technology, location may be less of a factor than it was in the past.
- **References.** Friends and colleagues can be a good source of references.
- **Comfort level.** Real estate transactions can be very trying. You will want to hire a lawyer who can smooth the way and who will vigorously protect your interests, but not one who will create unnecessary obstacles to your purchase or sale of a home.

Although most real estate agents can provide lawyer referrals, you may feel more comfortable with a lawyer who is completely independent of the agent.

Chapter 1 provides more information about how to hire a lawyer.

Q. What will I pay for a lawyer's services?

A. Fees for real estate closings vary depending on where you live, the complexity of the transaction, and the time required to com-

---

> ▶ **DO YOU KNOW WHAT YOU'RE SIGNING?**

Do not sign something assuming that it's unimportant, or that it's not a contract. Keep in mind that a typed or handwritten **letter of agreement** or **letter of understanding** signed by the parties will be binding if it meets the legal requirements of a contract. Even though many real estate agents use form contracts, you should have a lawyer review anything that you sign, either before you sign it or within the lawyer-review contingency period. This is particularly true if your agent has supplemented a form contract with any additional language.

---

plete it. The various types of legal fees are discussed in detail in Chapter 1, "When and How to Use a Lawyer."

REMEMBER THIS

- If you're selling a home and decide to use a real estate agent, take your time in choosing an agent. Make sure the agent has the time and expertise to do the best job possible.
- If you're buying a home and are working with an agent, make sure the agent is a buyer's agent, and has a duty to you and not to the seller. Hire an agent who has experience working with buyers, and who will be sensitive to the issues faced by buyers.
- Sellers should consult a lawyer before signing a listing agreement. Buyers won't

necessarily need to contact a lawyer when they start looking for a home, but a lawyer should enter the process before they make an offer, and certainly before they sign a contract to purchase.

FINANCING A HOME PURCHASE

From filling out numerous forms to disclosing personal financial information to making some very serious decisions, financing a home is a stressful process. Applying for a mortgage can be full of unpleasant surprises. For that reason, it's a good idea to investigate your finance options before you go too far down the homebuying path. Do you know how much you'll be able to borrow, and how much home you'll be able to afford? What's the difference between being prequalified for a loan and preapproved? This section explores basics of financing a home purchase, and provides you with an overview of your financing options.

The Basics

Q. How much home can I afford?

A. Unless you are paying cash for a home, how much you can afford depends on how much you can borrow—which in turn, depends on your income, assets, expenses, and debts (including automobile or education loans and outstanding credit card balances). How much you can afford will also vary with prevailing interest rates on mortgages, the amount of cash (if any) needed for a down payment, and closing costs. Knowing what

you can afford will narrow your search so that you don't waste time looking at homes that you can't afford, or that are worth less than you're willing to spend.

Q. Should I prequalify for a loan?

A. If you are a buyer and you prequalify for a loan, you can be secure knowing that the lender will loan you the prequalified amount, as long as the information you supplied was accurate and the property appraises for at least the value of the purchase price. If you are unsure what price range is appropriate, or if you are a first-time purchaser, then prequalifying for a loan can help smooth the process. You will avoid the disappointment of being unable to buy a home you thought you could afford. To prequalify for a loan, buyers will need to go through most of the steps of applying for the actual loan.

A better approach is to be preapproved. In the preapproval process, the lender analyzes and underwrites the loan, subject to the buyer finding a home and the lender obtaining a satisfactory appraisal of it, and subject to the buyer being satisfied with the condition and value of the property. Preapproval entails the same steps as prequalification, but generally takes longer. In a seller's market, buyers who are preapproved have an advantage over buyers who are prequalified or have no evidence of financing.

Q. Is there a formula for determining what I can afford?

A. The amount a lender will agree to loan a buyer is directly tied to the buyer's income and expenses. Typically, a lender expects you to pay no more than 28 percent of your gross monthly income for housing, which includes the loan payment, the property tax, the home-

---

▶ CAN YOU AFFORD A HOME?

Consider the following questions to determine whether you can afford to purchase a home:

- How much money have you saved for a down payment?
- What is your current income?
- What are your current expenses, such as car payments?
- What is your credit rating?
- What are the current interest rates on mortgages?
- What are your priorities and lifestyle?

---

owner's insurance, any monthly dues or assessments, and estimated utility costs.

A lender looks for a solid history of income, employment, and credit. Therefore, the amount of your debt and ongoing expenses are relevant—including automobile payments, credit card debt, education loans, child support, alimony, and so on. As a general rule, your total indebtedness, including monthly housing expenses, should not exceed 36 percent of your gross monthly income.

Q. What forms of financing are available?

A. Today, a wide variety of financing mechanisms exist to finance a home purchase.

The most common form of financing is provided by a financial institution, such as a bank or savings and loan. The buyer agrees to pay interest on the money borrowed, and the lender retains a **lien** (that is, a mortgage) on the property. Some buyers may qualify for federally insured loans that permit smaller-than-normal down payments and lower interest rates than prevailing market rates. In order to increase the amount borrowed (or reduce the down payment), it may be possible to place two mortgages on the property at the time of purchase—one that the buyer intends to pay off in the short term (generally, a home equity loan), and a second that the buyer views as more long-term.

In some cases, buyers are able to obtain financing directly from the seller, which also can take a variety of forms. In one type of financing, the seller acts just like a conventional lender, while the buyer pays a certain amount at closing and also pays principal and interest on the balance. The seller then places a mortgage lien on the property. In another form of financing, a buyer is able to assume the seller's mortgage. In such a case, the buyer pays the difference between what is

---

▶ LIFESTYLE CHOICES

When you are calculating how much home you can afford, consider your lifestyle and priorities. If costly vacations, dining out, and entertainment are important, you may want to buy a less expensive home than the lender says you can afford. However, many people find that they are willing to give up some luxuries or even stretch their budget to afford a more expensive home.

owed on the existing mortgage and the purchase price, and takes over the seller's payments on the mortgage. (Note that this can occur only if provisions in the mortgage state specifically that the mortgage is assumable. Most mortgages include a **due-on-sale** clause that prohibits this assumption.) In the event that a buyer assumes the seller's mortgage, the seller should remember that he or she remains liable to pay the mortgage, unless the seller's lender specifically and in writing releases the seller from this obligation. One final form of seller financing is the land contract. This option is discussed in detail below.

Q. How much do I need for a down payment?

Today, it may be possible to buy a home with little or no down payment. For example, some people may qualify for special government-insured loans offered through the Federal Housing Administration or the Veterans Administration (VA) or by state governments. Some private lenders also offer loans that require little or no down payment.

A. Generally, unless you can qualify for a special loan or creatively structure the financing, you will need a down payment equal to 20 percent of the home's purchase price to avoid paying the extra cost of **private mortgage insurance (PMI)**. If a buyer makes a down payment equaling less than 20 of the home's purchase price, then banking regulations require the buyer to carry PMI. This insures the lender against nonpayment of the difference between the customary down payment and the down payment actually paid.

Q. Do I have to pay PMI for the life of the loan?

A. No. The federal Home Ownership and Equity Protection Act helps consumers understand when they no longer need to pay private mortgage insurance. Once you have built up at least 20 percent equity in the home—meaning that the money owed is less than 80 percent of the home's value—the lender is no longer considered to be at risk. At that point, you can ask that the insurance be canceled. Be aware that the insurer will need written support from a certified appraiser as to the value of your home. Additionally, the lender must cancel the insurance when the mortgage balance falls below 78 percent of the home's original purchase price. Federal law now requires the lender to tell you annually that you have the right to cancel if you meet certain criteria.

▶ DOWN PAYMENTS

The term **down payment** refers to the approximate difference between the purchase price of a home and the amount of money borrowed to finance the home—that is, the cash that the buyer contributes when making a purchase. The down payment usually includes, but is not limited to, earnest money and closing costs.

Applying for a Loan

Q. How do I apply for a loan?

A. Obtaining a loan requires a lot of paperwork and fortitude. Problems with subprime mortgage lending and the large number of foreclosures in recent years have forced lenders to take a much more critical look at their lending

▶ **THE LAND CONTRACT**

A **land contract,** also known as a **contract for deed,** is another instrument for buying property. A land contract combines the transfer of title with seller financing. The buyer generally gives the seller a down payment and agrees to make monthly payments for some period of time. Typically, the buyer takes possession of the property and has all the benefits and burdens of ownership, but legal title is not transferred until the entire purchase price is paid.

Be warned that in some states, the buyer's right to complete the purchase may be secondary to the rights of anyone who obtains a lien against the seller after the contract is signed. Such lien holders can include anyone who obtains a judgment against the seller, contractors who furnish labor or materials to improve the property, and lenders who obtain a mortgage on the property from the seller.

The terms of such an arrangement should be in writing and the contract (or a notice of the contract) should be recorded. In addition, a prudent buyer should require that evidence of title, such as a warranty deed, be placed with a third party (for example, a title company), which would hold the document until payment is completed. Once all payments have been made, the deed is delivered to the buyer and recorded. In some places, if the buyer fails to make all payments, the seller must foreclose in order to clear title and take possession of the property.

practices. When you apply for a loan, it's a good bet that you will be asked about all aspects of your financial history. Loan applications vary, but most require the following information:

- **Employment history, salary history, and proof of employment.** This may require you to obtain a letter from your employer and recent wage stubs. You may be asked for copies of your federal tax returns for recent years or copies of your W-2 statements. While there is no law that requires you to submit this information, the lender has the right to turn down your request for a loan if you refuse to supply pertinent information. If you are using other income to qualify for the loan, such as income from property, child support, or income from investments, you will need to provide proof of these as well.

- **Credit history.** This includes the account numbers of all current credit cards. You may be asked to submit year-end statements that reveal how much interest was paid on these cards during the preceding year.

- **Outstanding debts.** These include automobile loans, alimony, child support payments, and credit card debt.

- **Assets.** These include the value of any items you own, such as automobiles, rental property, stocks, bonds, cash, savings accounts, IRAs, retirement accounts, mutual funds, and so on.

- **Source of your down payment.** The lender will want to make sure that you are not borrowing money to make your down payment. (If you are borrowing money, this will be taken into consideration.) If you are receiving a gift from relatives for a down payment, the lender will expect proof that it is truly a gift and that the amount will be forthcoming.

Q. How long does it take to get a home loan application approved?

A. When you apply for the loan, ask the lender how long the approval process is expected to take. Normally the process can take anywhere from one day to three months, depending on a variety of factors. If you have included a mortgage-contingency clause in your purchase contract, then when you apply for a loan, be sure to inform your lender of the date the clause expires. Usually, your lender will try to meet the deadline or alert you that approval will take more time. You may then be able to obtain an extension from the seller based on the mortgage contingency.

Once your loan is approved, the lender will provide you with a loan commitment. You should read this carefully, as it may set forth conditions you must meet before closing, such as clearing certain credit issues or even selling your current home. A copy of this commitment can be provided to the seller as assurance that your financing is in place.

Q. Is there anything that I must know about the loans I am considering? Does the law require the lender to tell me any specific facts?

A. Yes. Federal law requires that the lender reveal all costs of the loan, including such items as appraisal fees, escrow fees, fees for the lender's lawyer, service charges, and, of course, the interest rate on the loan. The interest rate must be expressed in terms of an **annual percentage rate (APR)**. This is calculated by including the interest to be paid along with other fees, such as any points paid to originate the loan. **Points** are interest charges paid up front when a borrower closes a loan, or fees imposed by a lender to cover certain expenses associated with making the loan. Points are usually expressed as a percentage of the amount loaned—for example, one point is typically equal to 1 percent of the loan amount.

Under the federal Truth in Lending Act, all lenders are required to use the same methods for computing the cost of credit and disclosing credit terms. This requirement helps borrowers compare the costs and terms of home loans.

The federal Equal Credit Opportunity Act prohibits discrimination in any aspect of a home loan transaction on the basis of race, religion, age, color, national origin, receipt of public-assistance funds, sex, marital status, or the exercise of any right under the Consumer Credit Protection Act. If a lender rejects your application, you are entitled to be informed in writing of the reason for the rejection.

Lenders are also prohibited from doing anything that discourages you from obtaining credit, including taking an excessively long time to process your application, being unwilling to discuss available types of loans, or failing to provide information required to apply for a loan. If you suspect discrimination, you can file a complaint. When making a complaint, be sure to include your name and address along with the name and address of the problematic person or financial institution, a short description of the alleged violation, and the date of the alleged violation.

Q. I want to buy a home, but my credit history is poor. Is there anything I can do?

A. Yes. You have several options. These include paying your bills on time, curtailing your borrowing, and working with a credit-reporting agency to fix any mistakes in your credit report. Chapter 10, "Consumer Credit," provides more detail about improving your credit report and fixing mistakes.

Q. I want to buy another home, but I have not sold my current home yet. Is there a way to finance until I can sell?

A. Some lenders offer a **bridge loan** to allow buyers to close on another home while waiting to sell their present home. You can usually obtain a bridge loan if you have a contract to sell your present home and you need the loan only for a specific, relatively short period of time. If you don't have a buyer for your home, obtaining a bridge loan may be more difficult. A bridge loan usually carries a higher interest rate than a traditional home loan.

It may also be possible to use the equity on your current home to provide the additional funds for the new home. To accomplish this, you would need to obtain a home equity line of credit on the current home, which could then be drawn upon at the time of the second purchase. The line of credit would be paid off at the time of the sale of the current property. Home equity lines of credit are generally interest-only loans.

▶ **SHOPPING FOR LOANS**

There are several ways to shop for home loans. By far the easiest way is on the web, which is awash with interest rate information and mortgage brokers competing with each other to get you the best deal. Most websites devoted to mortgages also feature useful mortgage and home finance calculators. To find dozens of these websites, search for "mortgage" and the name of the state where you are planning to buy.

You can also call a mortgage broker for information, but remember: the rate you are quoted on the phone may not be the rate you are offered when you actually apply.

Interest Rates

Q. How should interest rates affect my choice of a home?

A. The interest you pay on your loan is part of the cost of owning a home. For example, a 1-percent increase in the interest rate on a $100,000 loan adds approximately $85 to your monthly loan payment over the life of a thirty-year loan. Obviously, the lower the interest rate, the more you can afford to borrow.

Q. How do lenders determine the mortgage rate?

A. Mortgage rates for home loans are determined by the overall market in interest rates. Home loan rates are very interest-sensitive; when rates are rising, they are among the first rates to go up; however, when rates are declining, they are usually the last to be lowered. This is because most home loans are made at a fixed rate for a fairly long term (fifteen to thirty years), during which time inter-

> ## ▶ HOME EQUITY LINES OF CREDIT
>
> A **home equity line of credit** is a loan secured by the equity in your home. (**Equity** equals the value of your home, minus the amount remaining on your mortgage loan.) It functions as a line of credit, which means that you are free to draw down money as you need it, up to the value of the loan.

est rates may increase substantially. Thus, lenders attempt to protect themselves from making too many long-term loans at low rates by taking a slow approach to reducing interest rates. These rates can and will rise very quickly, if other interest rates begin to escalate. Current mortgage rates are easy to find on the Internet.

Q. Does it pay to shop around for an interest rate?

A. Since lenders are competitive, it pays to compare several options. Interest rates and fees charged to originate a loan may also vary among financial institutions. It may be possible to obtain a lower interest rate if the lender charges the prospective buyer a fee to obtain the loan, either as a flat fee or a percentage of the loan. All lenders are required to disclose the annual percentage rate (APR) they are charging. This allows borrowers to compare apples to apples.

One lender might offer an 8-percent, thirty-year fixed-rate loan with a flat fee of $200. A second lender might offer a 7-percent, thirty-year fixed-rate loan with two points. (Recall that **points** are interest charges paid up front when a borrower closes a loan, or fees imposed by a lender to cover certain expenses). A third lender might offer the loan without points or other fees, but at a higher interest rate. This could be an advantage for a buyer who wants to make as high a down payment as possible. Another buyer might prefer to pay higher points in exchange for a lower interest rate, because the IRS allows points to be deducted against taxable income in the year the home is purchased. (However, the IRS does not allow a single-year deduction for points paid in connection with a refinancing—in that situation, the deduction must be spread out over the life of the loan.)

Different Types of Loans

Q. What type of loan should I choose?

A. This answer will vary depending on your individual circumstances. The questions in this section will shed light on the most common types of loans. When making a decision about financing your home, remember that what works for your friend or neighbor might not always be your ideal option.

Q. What is a fixed-rate loan?

A. With a **fixed-rate loan,** the interest rate cannot be increased during the term of the loan—typically fifteen, twenty, or thirty years. With a fixed-rate loan, buyers have the comfort of knowing that their monthly loan payments will not increase during the life of the loan. But although the interest rate does not change, the way in which each payment is divided between principal and interest (also known as **amortization**) will change over the course of the loan period. (The **amortization schedule** is a table that shows how much of each payment will be applied toward principal and how much toward interest over the life of the loan.) At the beginning of the loan period, most of each payment will be applied toward interest. As the loan progresses, more money will be applied to paying off the principal. This means that the amount of interest deductible for federal income tax purposes will decline over the life of the loan.

The major difference between a fifteen-year fixed-rate loan and a thirty-year fixed-rate loan is that the borrower will pay higher monthly payments on the shorter-term loan in order to borrow the same amount of money. On a shorter loan, however, the buyer pays far less total interest, because he or she is using the money for a shorter period of time.

Q. *What is an adjustable-rate loan?*

A. **Adjustable-rate loans** vary, but they all share one common factor: the lender can change some of the loan terms during the life of the loan. Adjustable mortgages are classified differently based on whether the lender may change the rate of interest, the amount of the monthly payment, or the length of time allowed for repayment.

The major categories of adjustable-rate loans include:

- **Adjustable-rate mortgages (ARMs).** These loans typically offer a lower-than-market interest rate in the first year or first few years of the loan. The future interest rate, usually adjusted annually, is tied to an index that may move up or down but is not under the control of the lender. This may be the one-year Treasury bill index, or some other index that reflects changes in interest rates.

Note that the rate is tied to the index, but is not the same as the index. The mortgage might specify, for example, that the future rate will be two points above the average Treasury bill rate. Typically, ARMs are adjusted once a year on the anniversary of the loan. Additionally, ARMs usually provide for a cap—that is, they specify the highest rate that can be charged—and some may also provide for a minimum rate (i.e., a floor).

- **Convertible ARMs.** These loans usually offer a conversion factor that allows the borrower to convert to a fixed-rate loan during a specified period of time. For example, a convertible ARM could allow the borrower to convert to a fixed-rate loan once a year during the first five years of the loan. The interest rate to be paid upon conversion might also be tied to an index.

- **Renegotiable-rate mortgages** (also known as **rollover mortgages**). These loans typically set the interest rate and monthly payments for several years, and then allow both the rate and the principal payments to be changed depending on general market conditions. If the new terms are unacceptable, the borrower can pay the loan in full or refinance at prevailing interest rates.

- **Graduated-payment mortgages (GPMs).** With this type of loan, typically sought by young buyers who expect their incomes to rise, the payments are low in the first couple of years, and gradually rise during the life of the loan.

- **Shared-appreciation mortgages.** These loans offer lower-than-market interest rates and low payments in exchange for a lender's share in the appreciation of the property. Usually, the lender will require

▶ WHAT DOES THE BORROWER NEED TO SIGN?

The borrower will have to sign many documents; however, two are essential. The first is a **promissory note,** in which the borrower agrees to repay the lender the money borrowed, plus interest. The borrower may be responsible for repaying the money even if he or she later sells the home to a buyer who assumes the mortgage. The second is a **mortgage,** or **deed of trust.** The mortgage gives the lender a lien (i.e., security interest) in the real estate. This means that the lender may foreclose and sell the property to recoup the amount due under the loan.

that its share of equity be turned over when the home is sold or on a specified date.

Q. What is a balloon loan?

A. With a **balloon loan,** the buyer is expected to pay off the balance of the loan completely within a fixed period of time—usually in three, five, or seven years—instead of making regular payments to completely pay off the loan. The interest rate can be fixed or variable, but in all cases the (usually substantial) unpaid balance is due at the time specified. Usually, the borrower must either refinance or sell the home to pay off the loan. Because most payments made at the beginning of the loan term go toward paying off interest rather than principal, the balance due at the time of the loan payoff will probably be nearly the same as the amount of the original loan.

To attract buyers, builders often offer balloon loans during periods of high interest rates, when home sales are sluggish. In most cases, the interest rate will be lower than prevailing institutional home loan rates. However, if interest rates are high when full payment is due, refinancing may not be possible. The balloon can burst, resulting in foreclosure or forced sale and loss of the home.

▶ SUBPRIME MORTGAGES

What exactly are subprime mortgages and why might they be especially risky?

Generally, a **subprime mortgage** is a type of mortgage made to a borrower with low or modest income or little credit history. (Note that a subprime mortgage is rarely called "subprime" by the lender, who will usually just refer to it as an adjustable-rate mortgage.) Many of these loans have low initial "tease" rates that, over the life of the loan, will reset at higher rates. The problem occurs most frequently when interest rates go up while the value of the home goes down. When this happens, most borrowers will be forced to make higher loan payments than originally anticipated. In many cases, these payments can become so high that the borrowers end up defaulting on their loans, and in some cases, having their homes foreclosed.

Q. *How do FHA and VA loans work?*

A. The Federal Housing Administration (FHA) and the Veterans Administration (VA) are loan guarantors. They offer loans made by the federal government or approved lending institutions. The fees associated with these loans vary and may be paid at the closing, or paid monthly over a period of time. While FHA loans are not available through all lenders, in some areas they are very popular and can make the difference in obtaining a loan for some potential buyers who do not qualify for conventional financing. The VA offers government-insured loans to qualified veterans, often with no money down.

Income qualifications, down payments, and the maximum allowable loans under these plans change periodically. For first-time home buyers, local and state governments may also offer loan assistance to prospective buyers who meet eligibility requirements. For more information about these loan programs, consult your local FHA and VA offices and your real estate agent.

Q. *What are jumbo loans?*

A. **Jumbo loans** are loans that exceed the amount allowed by Fannie Mae and Freddie Mac. Fannie Mae and Freddie Mac are not loan guarantors; rather, they purchase loans from lenders and resell them to other organizations, such as insurance companies and pension funds. Interest rates on jumbo loans are typically slightly higher than the rates on other types of loans, but this is not always the case.

Q. *Do I always have to pay the full monthly interest on my loan?*

A. The answer to this question depends on the type of loan. In a typical home loan, the borrower pays off the interest and principal in installments. This reduction of the principal is known as **amortization.** In a **negatively amortized** loan, the installment payments do not cover all the interest due each month. This unpaid interest is added to the owed principal, resulting in a debt that increases rather than decreases.

The problem with negative amortization arises if home values decrease. If this happens, the size of the debt could increase to the point where it would exceed the homeowner's equity in the home. Sadly, upon the sale of the home, the owner would not be able to repay what he or she owes. Of course, in a down market, this could also happen with a conventional mortgage.

Often, the risks of negatively amortized loans outweigh the benefits of lower payments. If you're considering a negatively amortized loan, it may be more prudent to postpone buying a home until you can afford to make higher payments.

Key Provisions of Loan Documents

Q. *What is an assumable mortgage?*

A. An **assumable mortgage** allows you to transfer your existing mortgage debt to the buyer of your home. The new owner would **assume** (i.e., take over) your mortgage loan and pay you the difference between the amount you still owe and the agreed-upon sale price. Most lenders include a **due-on-sale clause** in the mortgage, which prohibits a buyer from assuming the existing mortgage. However, some don't. In addition, some lenders will allow a mortgage to be assumed by charging a fee or adjusting the interest rate.

▶ KNOWING YOUR HOME LOAN

If you are considering applying for any type of adjustable-rate loan, make sure you understand

- exactly how the mortgage works, including the spread between the interest rate and the index to which it is tied;
- how often the loan can be adjusted;
- the maximum increase (or decrease) that is allowed annually, and over the life of the loan; and
- the risks of negative amortization.

If the interest rate is attractive, a buyer should explore the possibility of assuming the existing loan. But before agreeing to assume the seller's loan payments, a prospective home buyer should obtain a written statement from the original lender stating:

- the amount still owed;
- that there are currently no defaults under the loan;
- the rate of interest for the remainder of the loan;
- the length of the repayment period remaining; and
- whether the lender has the right to call in the loan (i.e., demand payment of the entire amount), change any of the existing terms, or prevent future assumption by another buyer.

▶ INSURING PAYMENT OF YOUR HOME LOAN IN THE EVENT OF DEATH OR DISABILITY

Several types of insurance policies will pay your home loan if you die or become disabled. This type of **mortgage insurance policy** establishes an annual premium cost for the life of your loan. Because your loan declines as you pay down the principal, the amount of insurance coverage decreases each year, although the cost stays the same. In most cases, a term life insurance policy that can be used to pay off the loan in the event of your death is preferable to a mortgage insurance policy. Term life insurance is less expensive, and offers better protection and more flexibility. For example, it may give your spouse or other beneficiary the option of keeping the money in the bank and continuing to make payments—especially if the interest rate is low—whereas mortgage insurance must be used to pay off the loan. All insurance products are relatively complicated; consider consulting a financial professional or a lawyer before you buy.

Because temporary or permanent disability can also threaten your ability to pay your home loan, you may also want to consider buying a disability policy or participating in disability insurance offered by your employer. Disability insurance can add to your peace of mind and that of your lender.

Before assumption, the lender may require the buyer to go through the lender's normal application process so that the lender is sure the buyer is creditworthy. The particular assumption agreement will vary depending upon your location.

Q. What is a due-on-sale clause?

A. A **due-on-sale clause** should more accurately be called a due-on-transfer clause. Most mortgages include such a clause, which requires the seller to pay off the entire mortgage loan when selling or transferring the property. Therefore, this clause would prohibit a buyer from assuming the seller's mortgage. In addition, a due-on-sale clause may be triggered if the seller leases or further mortgages the property. The rationale behind such a clause is that the lender is making the loan to a particular person and does not want to find out that, without its consent, a different person owns the property or is living there. However, in some cases federal and state laws preempt the terms of the mortgage and allow such transfers.

Q. What is a late-payment charge?

A. Most home loans provide for a **late-payment charge,** which means that the borrower must pay a fee if the lender receives the monthly mortgage payment late. These charges can be very expensive. Make sure you know when your loan payment is due, and if you are mailing your payment, allow enough time for it to arrive by the due date.

Q. What is a prepayment penalty?

A. Although the practice is illegal or restricted in some states, some home loans may provide for a **prepayment penalty.** This is a charge imposed if the borrower pays off the loan ahead of schedule. This penalty is usually equal to 1 or 2 percent of the loan. Some home loans provide for a prepayment penalty only during the first few years of the loan.

REMEMBER THIS

- Determine what you can afford before you start looking for a home.
- If possible, try to get preapproved for a loan before you immerse yourself in the business of buying. If you can't wait for preapproval, then being prequalified is better than nothing.
- Take some time to shop for a loan. Have an idea about the kind of loan you want, and compare interest rates and fees to find the best loan. The Internet is a useful tool for loan shopping.
- Ask your lawyer to talk you through the small print, so you have a good understanding of your obligations under the loan.

THE STEPS INVOLVED IN BUYING AND SELLING A HOME

The contract is at the heart of the home sale; it sets forth the nuts and bolts of transferring ownership from seller to buyer. Your lawyer can help you navigate the complex obligations and contingencies in the contract, so that when you arrive at the closing, you can be certain that all the details have been covered.

Selling: Setting a Price for the Property

Q. How do I establish the price of my home?

A. First of all, there is no "right" price. The value of your home is almost entirely dependent on what someone is willing to pay for it, and on how long you are willing to wait to find that person. To find the optimum price at which their home will sell, most sellers rely on comparisons with recently sold homes in the area. A real estate agent can help by providing a list of homes sold through the local Multiple Listing Service (MLS) during the past year or so. You can also locate this information yourself on the Internet.

Once you have some basic sales information, you will need to compare the features of the homes that have been sold to those of your own home. For example, if your home is a three-bedroom, two-bath ranch on a typical lot, your agent can point out sales prices of similar homes to determine a listing price. Try to limit your study to homes that are similar to yours.

To narrow the price range further, you'll want to look at amenities sought by buyers. Expect the selling price to be higher if your home has features such as an updated kitchen, wood-burning fireplace, or a large lot, and expect the price to be lower if your home does not have such sought-after amenities. Most buyers also want good schools, ample transportation, quiet neighborhoods, and little if any commercial activity. The presence or absence of these factors will affect the selling price of your home.

Perhaps equally important are your reasons for selling and how long you can wait. Typically, the most interest in a home is generated in the first few weeks after it is listed. If you want to sell your home fast, you'll want to price it so that it stands out among comparable homes on the market. If you are willing to wait, you can afford to price it above the competition. Sellers who try to hold out for the highest price, however, may find themselves reducing the price down the line. A house that has been on the market beyond the average marketing time generates little interest from buyers, even when the price is reduced dramatically. Rightly or wrongly, most buyers will assume that the home has problems that they want to avoid.

Disclosures

Q. What is the seller obligated to disclose to the buyer?

A. Disclosure is generally addressed by state law, and requirements vary. Because this is an

---

▶ APPRAISALS

If, despite all your efforts, you cannot find comparable homes in your area (or even if you can), consider consulting an appraiser. An **appraisal** is a professional's opinion of a home's fair market value. The appraisal should be close to the probable selling price. However, keep in mind that the appraiser is basing the value in part on completed sales. In a seller's market, a real estate agent may be in a better position to estimate value, since the agent will have information regarding contracts that have not yet closed.

In order to ensure that a home is worth at least as much as the purchase price, lenders usually order their own appraisals, often paid for by the borrower, before approving a loan. If you intend to sell your home on your own, without a real estate agent, an appraisal can provide valuable market information. But remember: in the end, a home is only worth what someone will actually pay for it.

area of law that is rapidly changing, it is important to review your state's requirements before selling.

Some states require sellers to fill out a long form that explicitly asks about the seller's knowledge of various significant or **material defects** that might be present in the home, such as leaks in the roof, or unsafe concentrations of radon gas. In other states, sellers are not required to fill out disclosure forms, but are required to disclose any defects in equipment that should be functioning at the time of sale, such as the furnace, central air-conditioning, or hot-water heater. In others, unless you ask specific questions about defects, the seller is not required to disclose them, even if the seller has specific knowledge that one or more substantial defects exist. As a result, any problem buyers discover after the closing is their problem. To protect yourself, you should hire an inspector to look at the property. When in doubt, ask specific questions of the seller and obtain answers in writing if possible. In certain homes, federal laws do require disclosure of lead-based paints that can create a health risk.

As a seller, you may want to disclose known material defects that seriously affect the home's value, even if your state does not mandate such disclosure. Responding honestly to the buyer's questions and either repairing material defects or disclosing them will help to avoid future legal problems. Many lawsuits that involve real estate transactions are based on the seller's misrepresentation or failure to disclose.

Q. What are the real estate agent's obligations with respect to disclosure?

A. The Code of Ethics of the National Association of Realtors governs member real estate firms and agents. This code calls for disclosure by a realtor of all known pertinent facts about the property. Members must also attempt to get all of the buyer's questions answered. For example, if the buyer has noticed water damage in the basement, a member agent should ask the seller about it and tell the buyer about the cause of the problem. Some states require the broker to make additional disclosures that might affect the value or desirability of the property.

Making an Offer: The Purchase Contract

Q. How do I begin negotiations to buy a home?

A. Negotiations are handled in various ways depending on locality. Typically, transactions begin with negotiations over price, although other items such as date of possession may also be negotiated. The real estate agent will provide a formal offer form, which will convey the terms of your offer in writing to the seller. Once signed by both parties, the offer becomes a contract.

The offer should cover all the contingencies: an inspection contingency, a mortgage contingency, and a lawyer-approval contingency. Remember: once both parties sign this document, it is legally binding.

The offer should specify that it expires if the seller has not accepted it by a specified date. This date may be as soon as twenty-four hours from the time of receipt by the seller or the seller's agent. Also, the offer to purchase is usually valid only if both the buyer and seller sign it within a certain time period. As a general rule, a deposit called **earnest money** accompanies the offer. (Earnest monies are discussed further on page 259.)

The written offer to purchase may be passed back and forth between the buyer and seller before both accept all of the terms. Remember, however, that both parties must initial any agreed-upon changes. Once you have agreed on terms, you will want to arrange for a home inspection and review the document with your lawyer. In most cases, you will not want to apply for a specific loan on the property until the home inspection and lawyer review are completed.

In some areas, the purchase contract will include all provisions of the transaction. In other areas, another document will be drawn up by the buyer or the seller that covers such items as conveyance of title and provision for insurance. In either case, you will want your lawyer to make sure, before you sign, that the final document covers all aspects of the sale.

Q. What happens to the earnest money?

A. The buyer customarily deposits the earnest money with a third party, such as the seller's real estate agent, the seller's or the buyer's lawyer, or the title company. In some cases, when there is no third party to hold the money, the parties can set up a joint account at a bank or financial institution—an account that cannot be accessed without the approval of both parties. If the offer is rejected, the buyer will get the money back.

In most states, earnest money is not the same thing as a down payment. However, if the sale goes through, then the earnest money will be applied to the down payment. Earnest money symbolizes the buyer's commitment to take the necessary steps to complete the purchase. Thus, if a prospective buyer does little or nothing to complete the sale, or if the sale cannot close for other reasons attributable to the buyer, then he or she risks losing the earnest money.

Q. What happens to the earnest money if the seller backs out?

A. Generally, if the seller defaults, the purchase contract allows the buyer to get back the earnest money and any interest earned on it, unless the buyer has in some way violated the contract. If the seller refuses to return the earnest money, the buyer may have to sue the seller for it.

Q. What is the purchase contract?

A. The **purchase contract** may be called a **sales contract,** a **real estate contract,** a **purchase agreement,** a **sales agreement,** or a **purchase-and-sale agreement.** Whatever its name, this document is a legal contract that will govern the entire transaction. Before signing such a contract, you will want to review it carefully and have your lawyer review it. Remember: once the purchase contract is signed, you are obligated to fulfill your part of the contract.

Q. What are the key provisions of the purchase contract?

A. The contract can have many provisions. But at a minimum, the contract should include or specify the following

- the date of the contract;
- the purchase price of the home;
- the amount of the down payment, who is holding it, and the escrow terms if the amount of the down payment is being held in escrow;
- all items of personal property to be included in the sale, such as wall-to-wall carpeting, window treatments, appliances, or lighting fixtures;

- any items to be excluded from the sale, such as an heirloom chandelier;
- the date the deed will be transferred (i.e., the closing date);
- the various contingency clauses, such as clauses for mortgage, inspection, and lawyer-approval contingencies;
- a provision that the seller will provide good title to the home, or what is sometimes called **marketable title** (see "How Does a Seller Provide 'Good Title'?" below)
- any restrictions or limitations that could affect title;
- a provision for paying utility bills, property taxes, and similar expenses through the closing date;
- a provision for the return of the buyer's earnest money deposit if the sale is not completed;
- a provision for taking possession of the home, including a firm date for transfer, and a provision detailing what happens if the seller remains in the home past the agreed-upon date (this issue is discussed more fully below);
- a provision for a walk-through inspection within a specified period before the date of closing, to allow the buyer to ensure that conditions are as they should be;
- a provision specifying who is responsible for maintaining insurance until the closing;
- the allocation of closing costs, and the apportionment of taxes, fuel oil costs, homeowner's association dues, common charges, and any other items prepaid by the seller that will benefit the buyer;
- any disclosures required by state or federal law; and
- the signatures of the parties.

Q. What does an inspection contingency provide?

A. An **inspection contingency** protects the buyer's right to inspect. Most often the contingency falls within one of two categories. The first gives the buyer the right to have the property inspected by a professional home inspector of the buyer's choice, and at the buyer's expense. If the inspector finds defects, the buyer has the right to cancel the contract within a specified time. This type of contingency raises some concerns, since inspectors will almost always find some problems. As a result, buyers may get a few extra days to decide whether they want to follow through with the purchase, though the inspection contingency should not be used primarily for that purpose.

The second type of inspection contin-

▶ HOW DOES A SELLER PROVIDE "GOOD TITLE"?

Generally, the seller fulfills the obligation to show that he or she possesses **good title** (i.e., marketable title) by providing an abstract of title, a certificate of title, or a title insurance policy. This indicates that the seller has the authority to sell the home. In some states, the seller is required to deliver good title, which the buyer is expected to verify, at his or her own expense, by securing an abstract of title, a certificate of title, or a title insurance policy. If the buyer encounters problems in establishing title, he or she can reject the title at or before closing.

gency also gives the buyer the right to have an inspection performed. The difference is that the seller may then either repair any uncovered problems, or agree to reduce the contract selling price by the cost of the repairs. If a seller opts to do nothing, he or she must inform the buyer. Unless the parties can come to terms based on the buyer's inspection report, the buyer can cancel the contract and seek return of any earnest money previously paid.

Other types of inspection contingencies exist, usually incorporating some or all components of the two forms described above. Some people prefer the simplest form of contingency, with the hope that simplicity generates fewer back-and-forth discussions between the parties. Others may prefer a more tailored version based on some specific concern the buyer has about the property being sold. Generally, if the seller wants to sell, the parties can make a deal, even if there is a serious problem. (Inspections are discussed further on pages 264–266.)

Q. What is a lawyer-approval contingency?

A. A **lawyer-approval contingency** (or **lawyer-review clause**) is a common type of provision in a purchase contract. It makes the purchase contract subject to review and approval by the buyer's and the seller's respective lawyers within a short period of time, usually five to ten days after acceptance of the offer. This contingency ensures that the contract need not bind the parties if their lawyers find an unsatisfactory provision. The lawyer-approval contingency usually provides that formal notice of disapproval must be communicated within a set time period. Without such a contingency in the contract, both the seller and the buyer are bound by the terms of the contract upon execution, and those terms may be unclear or may fail to capture the parties' intent. This contingency raises some of the same concerns as the inspector contingency, because in almost every circumstance, a lawyer will likely be able to find a problem with a purchase contract.

Q. What is a mortgage contingency clause?

A. A **mortgage contingency clause** provides critical protection to the buyer. Such a clause generally provides that the contract is contingent on the buyer obtaining approval for a loan with certain characteristics. This common provision allows the buyer a certain period of time to obtain a firm written commitment for financing based on the described terms. The contingency usually lasts for thirty to sixty days, depending on the average amount of time needed to obtain a loan commitment.

Although the buyer is required to act in good faith to obtain the described financing, which would include timely application for the loan, a mortgage contingency allows the buyer to terminate the contract without penalty if the buyer is unable to obtain the financing within the specified time period and on the stated terms. Because this type of clause favors the buyer, some real estate agents insist that the buyer be preapproved by a lender, which provides the seller with some degree of certainty.

The seller may refuse to agree to a mortgage-contingency clause. The absence of such a clause might mean that the buyer will be forced to finance his or her home purchase at an unfavorable interest rate. In the worst-case scenario, the buyer might be unable to obtain a mortgage and will therefore forfeit the earnest money. The buyer might even forfeit the full down payment, if the down payment is already being held in escrow pending closing. Because of this risk, buyers should be very cautious about signing a purchase contract that does not include a mortgage-contingency clause.

Q. May the seller refuse to accept lawyer-review, inspection contingency, and mortgage contingency clauses?

A. Sellers are not required to accept any of the buyer protections set forth in these types of contingencies. In fact, sellers should be wary of contingencies—after all, the property could be off the market during the period of review, with no assurance that the sale will actually go through. However, most sellers will accept these and similar contingency clauses, provided that all contingencies are limited to a certain time period, after which they expire.

With respect to an inspection contingency, sellers should make sure that these types of clauses expire relatively quickly—say, ten days from the signing. Similarly, with a mortgage-contingency clause, sellers should ensure that the proposed interest rate is reasonable, and should also allow a limited but reasonable time for the mortgage commitment.

Q. Should I allow the seller to remain in the home after closing?

A. The better practice is almost always for the buyer to obtain possession at closing. Generally the buyer will be paying the mortgage as of the date of closing, and will not want to pay for two residences. In addition, the buyer assumes the risk that the seller will either damage the property while moving out, or fail to move out as promised. The buyer could be faced with the expensive and time-consuming task of having to evict the seller.

Sometimes, however, a buyer may allow the seller to remain for a specified period of

---

▶ FINDING AN "OUT" FROM THE CONTRACT

Depending on its wording, a contingency may allow the buyer to get out of the contract even after it is signed. As a buyer, it is important to be sure that the lawyer-review language gives the lawyer the right to review *and* the right to disapprove the contract. It is also important that the lawyer act within the stated period. In some jurisdictions, if the lawyer wants to terminate the contract, the lawyer need not state specific reasons as long as he or she is acting in good faith.

As a seller, you can refuse such a contingency, forcing the buyer's lawyer to review and make changes to the offer before it is submitted. In addition, it is possible to limit the buyer's lawyer to certain legal matters contained in the contract—for example, the lawyer might be limited to reviewing issues relating to the state of title.

time. If you are a buyer and find yourself in this situation, do not rely on oral promises or a statement about the date on which the seller promises to vacate the premises. Make sure that your purchase contract—or a separate document, such as a lease or use-and-occupancy agreement—states how long the seller may occupy the home after closing, and that it specifies the rent to be paid. The document should also specify any penalties that will apply in the event the seller does not move, does not pay rent, or causes any damage prior to vacating the premises. Most contracts provide that a certain amount of the seller's proceeds will be held in **escrow** after closing to ensure that the seller vacates as promised. Finally, be sure to clarify whose homeowner's insurance will apply during this interim period.

Q. Who is responsible for maintaining insurance until the closing?

A. The Uniform Vendor-Purchaser Risk of Loss Act applies in some states, which means that the seller assumes the risk of loss until either the transfer of title or possession. In some states, common law requires the seller to assume this risk.

Q. Can a buyer sue a seller for backing out of the contract?

A. Depending on the terms of the contract, it is possible that if the seller violates the terms of the contract or refuses to close the sale, the buyer will be able to force the seller to complete the transaction, or recover the earnest money and cancel the contract. It is also possible for the buyer to sue for money damages. For example, if a buyer incurred costs in obtaining a mortgage, or if the buyer incurred costs for renting temporary housing

▶ **DELETE WITH CAUTION**

Some buyers make the mistake of deleting the mortgage contingency clause from their purchase contract if they have been preapproved for a loan. But keep in mind that, even if you've been preapproved, the loan is still subject to your purchase of the particular property, and the lender will still need to appraise the property and review the condition of title. It's a good idea to err on the side of caution and retain the clause; or, if you do take the clause out, to insert a clause saying that the purchase is subject to the lender obtaining a satisfactory appraisal.

because the closing did not occur, then that buyer might have a case for damages.

Q. What is title insurance?

A. A **title insurance policy** serves at least two purposes. First, it provides a search of the legal records relating to the property, and discloses who is authorized to sell the property and what title exceptions exist. And second, in the case of the owner's title insurance policy, it provides that the title insurance company will defend against (and pay losses involved in) any claim covered by the policy's terms, up to the amount of the policy, as long as the buyer or the buyer's heirs own an interest in the property.

Title insurance is available from title companies and, in some states, from lawyers' groups. Prices for title insurance vary across the country, and the extent of the protection provided is only as broad as the language of the policy itself. The buyer's lawyer can help gauge whether the policy is adequate.

Lenders usually require buyers to obtain title insurance that protects only the lender. This is known as a **lender's** or **mortgage title policy.** The buyer may have to pay for this additional title insurance, or negotiate with the seller to purchase such a policy. For more information on title insurance, see Chapter 8, "Home Ownership."

Q. What is a survey, and what is its purpose?

A. A **survey** is an accurate depiction of the property being conveyed. There are different types of surveys, each providing varying amounts of detail about the property. All surveys indicate the boundaries of the property and the location of any improvements (for example, buildings and fences). The survey is an essential element of the closing in that it highlights any differences between what the buyer thinks he or she is purchasing and what is legally being conveyed (as indicated on the survey). For example, a survey may reveal that the backyard boundary of a property actually lies at a different point than the buyer originally thought.

Home Inspections

Q. What is involved in a home inspection?

A. Professional home inspections vary, but generally the aim is to discover any problems with the home that might not be readily apparent to an untrained eye. In most inspections, the inspector checks to make sure there are no material defects or problems with such items as the electrical, plumbing, heating, or air-conditioning systems. The inspector also may check for termites; check the age of the roof and whether it might need replacement; inspect the condition of the basic home structure, including its foundation; check for evidence of basement seepage; and check for other problems. Some inspectors check for radon concentrations, lead paint, mold, or other environmental hazards, and may also test the well water and the functioning of the septic system.

Inspection fees vary, depending on such factors as the size and type of building inspected. As a general rule, buyers should anticipate a fee somewhere between $250 and $500.

Q. I am buying a home and my inspector just uncovered some major problems. What should I do?

A. You have several options. Although an inspection contingency may allow you to walk away from the purchase, you may not want to do this if the home has other desirable qualities. One alternative is to negotiate with the seller to lower the previously agreed-upon price. For example, if the seller was unaware that the furnace needs replacement or that rotting timber needs replacement, the seller may be amenable to reducing the purchase price by the estimated cost of repairs. However, if you choose this option, be aware that it may affect the amount of the mortgage that can be obtained from a mortgage lender. Many lenders will take such a repair credit into account in determining the amount of financing available to the buyer. For example, if the agreed-upon purchase price was $300,000 subject to a repair credit of $20,000, you may find that the lender will only lend you 80 percent of $280,000 (as opposed to 80 percent of $300,000), so you may have to seek extra funds in order to make the repairs.

Alternatively, the price could remain the same, with the seller repairing the problems at his or her expense. If you pursue this alternative, you assume the risk that the seller will not complete the job to your satisfaction. Whatever the decision, it should be written into the contract.

While some buyers use an inspection to extract further concessions from the seller, it is unlikely that a seller will agree to substantially reduce the cost of a home to reflect the cost of correcting minor problems, such as a repairing a porcelain chip or replacing peeling wallpaper or worn carpeting. In fact, a seller facing a long list of minor repairs may wish to end negotiations, unless the seller has no other prospective buyers.

Q. I am selling my home and the buyer's inspectors claim to have found a bunch of problems that I just don't believe exist. What can I do?

A. Your response as a seller to a negative inspection report will depend on the buyer. Sometimes, such a report will scare away the buyer. If you strongly disagree with the inspection, you may want to obtain your own written inspection, copies of which you can provide to prospective buyers.

You can also try to negotiate a resolution to the problems discovered by the inspector. For example, if the inspector discovers that your home has inadequate or outdated electrical wiring, you may offer to have the wiring updated or to reduce the price by an agreed-upon sum to cover the buyer's costs of updating the wiring.

As a seller, be aware that some buyers will

> ▶ **DON'T PANIC!**
>
> A professional inspector should not be an alarmist; the idea is to point out problems without exaggerating defects. It is a good idea for the buyer to accompany the inspector during the inspection; this way, the buyer is able to ask questions and to ascertain the cost of any necessary or advisable repairs. Furthermore, the inspector may suggest ways to better insulate the home, or offer tips about maintenance.

take any problems and turn them into major roadblocks, hoping to force an anxious seller to reduce the selling price. If you find yourself dealing with such a buyer, you may be better off to simply refuse further negotiations, let the offer expire, return the buyer's deposit, and place the home back on the market. Even if you believe that the buyer's complaints are without merit, it could be time-consuming and costly to insist on compliance with the contract if there is an inspection contingency.

Q. Should a seller get a home inspection?

A. If you are worried about possible problems in your home, you can have your home inspected before you put it up for sale. This will allow you to examine your home from a buyer's perspective, and allow you time to fix any problems or reduce your asking price. The problem with doing this, though, is that inspectors vary greatly. The inspector you hire may not raise the same issues as your buyer's inspector.

Most buyers will probably want to pay for

their own inspections. If you do share your presale inspection report with a buyer, be sure to provide the entire report; otherwise, a court might find that you intentionally withheld negative information.

Q. I am planning on buying a new home that is currently under construction, so there is really nothing yet to inspect. What can I do? Is there anything special I should know?

A. If you are contracting with a builder on a home that is not yet built or finished, you want to ensure that you will get what you expect. For example, keep in mind that model homes typically feature optional upgrades rather than standard features. Make sure that the builder provides you with a complete list of standard and optional features. If you are choosing options, make sure the purchase contract includes their specific costs.

You will want to know other facts as well, such as the type and extent of any landscaping to be provided by the builder, any known plans for the development of surrounding property, and the exact provisions of any builder warranty. If possible, you will want a warranty that is insured by an insurance company, rather than a warranty guaranteed only by the builder. Finally, the builder should provide you with evidence that there are no mechanic's liens or construction liens on your property. The seller's contractors, subcontractors, and material suppliers can file such liens in the event the builder does not pay them for their work.

The purchase contract should address certain issues unique to new construction. For example, specific dates for completion and occupancy should be included if the home is not yet built. Although it is difficult to negotiate, the buyer can try to provide for a penalty or for the right to cancel the contract if the builder does not honor these dates. In addition, the contract should specify the method of calculating and prorating real estate taxes. It is also very important to visit the building site frequently. When it comes to your house, you are the person most concerned with protecting your best interests. Errors, delays, and other construction issues are much more easily handled and corrected if caught early.

In addition, you may want to consider having the finished structure inspected. Remember: it is the quality of the construction, not its newness, that is important. An independent inspection can provide you with assurance that you're getting what you expect.

Buying in a Multi-Unit Building or Development

Q. What is the difference between a condominium and a co-op?

A. A **condominium** is a common-interest community in which individual units are separately owned, but in which unit owners also own an individual interest in the building's common areas, such as hallways, roofs, exteriors, and any land surrounding the building. With a **cooperative,** or **co-op,** buyers generally purchase shares of stock in a corporation that owns a building, and then enter into a lease to occupy a particular apartment. A condominium owner has title to his or her unit; a co-op owner receives stock in the corporation that owns the building (based on the proportional share of the building that the unit comprises), and receives the right to lease a particular apartment in the building.

For more information relating to these types of properties—from tax considerations to community associations and insurance—see the section titled "Shared Ownership: Condos and Condominiums" in Chapter 8, "Home Ownership."

Q. Are there differences between common-interest home ownership and single-family home ownership?

A. In **single-family home ownership**, decisions and expenses are the responsibility of the owner—subject to zoning restrictions established by local law, restrictions contained in the declaration of the original builder, and the rules of any homeowner's association. As a general rule, multi-unit ownership is subject to more extensive regulation than single-family ownership. For example, more statutes, rules, and regulations generally govern what you may and may not do with your condominium, co-op, or other multi-unit dwelling.

Before finalizing an offer to purchase, it is important for the buyer to review and understand all restrictions affecting the property. Buyers should ask to see the applicable by-laws, operating budgets, management agreements, and other regulating documents. Many states require disclosures to the purchasers of units in a common-interest community. Some states have a central agency that licenses and regulates the development and sale of common-interest community units.

Q. What criteria should I consider when buying a condominium or a co-op?

A. First, read all of the governing documents and review the minutes of recent meetings involving the owners and board of directors. You should also talk to other owners or shareholders. Ask them what they like best about where they live, and what their complaints are. Along with any considerations that would apply when purchasing a single-family home (such as the type of neighborhood in which the home is located), prospective common-interest buyers should consider the following:

- **Percentage of owner-occupants and renters.** A high percentage of renters could indicate poor sales and/or absentee landlords who are insufficiently interested in maintaining the building.
- **Monthly maintenance fees and special assessments** (and the history thereof). You will also want to ask whether the association or corporation is involved in any lawsuits brought by builders, neighbors, or former owners.
- **Financial condition of the association or corporation.** Obtain a copy of the most recent financial statements and budgets.
- **Quality of construction.** Hire an inspector and make certain that he or she checks the soundproofing, the condition of shared common areas (such as the roof and patios), and the electrical, heating, and plumbing systems.
- **Bylaws and/or covenants.** If these are too restrictive, you may have trouble obtaining a loan or selling your unit or share. Covenants will also dictate whether you can lease, and will govern other uses of the property—including, for example, whether pets are allowed.

Chapter 8, "Home Ownership," also provides detailed information about shared ownership.

The Closing

Q. What happens at the closing?

A. The real estate **closing** (sometimes called the **settlement**) is the final stage in the process of buying a home. The closing is a meeting at which the buyer and seller, usually accompanied by their respective lawyers and real estate agents, complete the sale. The meeting may take place at an attorney's office, at one of the agents' firms, at the title company, or at some other neutral location. At this meeting, the buyer usually signs the promissory note and mortgage and obtains the lender's proceeds. The buyer is then able to make all the required payments due to the seller. The seller produces all documents necessary for the transfer of good title, and delivers a deed that transfers the title.

Before the closing, the parties and their lawyers should review all documents. A closing statement or settlement sheet is prepared, fully listing the financial aspects of the closing. The Real Estate Settlement Procedures Act (RESPA) applies in any transaction in which a buyer is obtaining a federally insured mortgage from a financial institution. This requires use of a settlement sheet developed by HUD that sets forth all credits and payments made at closing. In other closings, another form of settlement sheet may be used.

Both buyers and sellers should expect to sign a lot of papers at the closing.

Buyers should expect to sign or provide the following:

- a promissory note in which the buyer promises to pay the loan and interest in full;

▶ **OBTAINING A MORTGAGE ON A CO-OP**

Since a mortgage, by definition, is a lien on real estate, the owner of shares in a corporation cannot obtain a mortgage unless the owner places a lien against the entire building. It is unlikely that any one owner in a co-op would be permitted to lien the entire building. Because of this, historically it was not easy to obtain a loan to buy a co-op, and for that reason prices for co-ops were usually much lower than prices for condominiums.

Now, however, the owner of a co-op may be able to obtain other forms of financing similar to a mortgage, provided that the cooperative's association permits it. This is because the federal government amended the law to allow the Federal National Mortgage Association (Fannie Mae) to buy co-op loans, making them much easier for prospective co-op buyers to obtain. Generally, as a condition to obtaining a loan on a co-op, the lender will hold the stock to the cooperative as collateral.

Today, it is only slightly more difficult to obtain a loan for a co-op than for a condominium. You may have to put down more money than if you were buying real estate, and the rates may be slightly higher. Prices of cooperative units, however, generally remain lower because of the extra restrictions placed on co-op owners.

- the mortgage document;
- a Truth in Lending form, which requires the lender to disclose in advance the approximate annual percentage rate of the loan over the loan's term;
- a typed loan application form;
- a payment letter specifying the amount of the buyer's first payment and when it is due;
- a survey form stating that the buyer has seen and understands the survey of the property, and that the survey fairly depicts the property;
- a private mortgage insurance application or disclosure, usually required on loans involving a down payment of less than 10 percent;
- a termite inspection or other inspection form, indicating that the buyer has seen a report of any inspections that were made;
- a homeowner's insurance policy (in the case of a single-family home);
- an affidavit from the buyer stating that the buyer has the legal right to mortgage the property, and that there are no liens or encumbrances (judgments, mortgages, or taxes owed) on the property;
- if the buyer has used more than one name, an affidavit stating that the various names used in the documents all refer to the same person; and
- an agreement to cooperate with the lender to correct any errors or omissions in the loan documents.

The seller can expect to sign or provide the following documents:

- the deed transferring title;
- a bill of sale transferring ownership of any personal property that may be included in the sale of the real estate;
- an affidavit of title in which the seller states that he or she has the legal right to sell the real estate, and that there are no liens or encumbrances (judgments, mortgages, or taxes owed) on the property;
- an affidavit as to mechanic's liens and possession, indicating that the seller has not had any work done on the property that would give rise to a mechanic's lien, and that there are no parties other than the seller entitled to possess the property;
- in the case of a new home, an occupancy certificate indicating that the home complies with the local housing code; and
- a 1099-S reporting certificate verifying the terms of the sale and the seller's tax identification numbers for IRS reporting purposes.

Both buyer and seller will have to sign:

- an affidavit specifying the purchase price, and indicating the source of the funds that will satisfy the purchase price. This affidavit assures the lender that the buyer has not received any undisclosed loans from the seller that could negatively affect the buyer's ability to repay the lender's loan;
- a RESPA form developed by the federal Department of Housing and Urban Development, and sometimes a separate closing statement; and
- transfer declarations, as required by state or local authorities.

Q. Financially speaking, what happens at the closing?

A. At the time of closing, the seller and the buyer will total up various credits in order to determine how much money the buyer must pay. The allocation of expenses will depend on the terms of the purchase contract, as well as the law and customs in the area where the property is located. Before the closing, the real estate agent or lawyer should advise the buyer about how much money will be needed at the time of closing. Typically, the buyer will be required to have a certified or cashier's check or wired funds in the amount required to meet the applicable expenses.

The seller will usually receive credits for such items as fuel on hand (such as oil in the home heating tank), unused insurance premiums (if insurance is being assigned), prepaid taxes, and public utility charges such as water and sewer fees. Such credits will also include any other items prepaid by the seller that will benefit the buyer.

The buyer will usually receive credits for such items as the earnest money deposited, and taxes or special assessments that the seller has not paid but which, when they become due, will include the period during which the seller owned the property. The settlement sheet will also specify who is responsible for the payment of various expenses. These will include the sales commissions and the costs of the title search, inspections, recording fees, transaction taxes, and the like. Keep in mind that this list of fees is by no means exhaustive; you should talk to your agent or attorney beforehand to make sure you are aware of any additional fees that are common in your area.

Closing Costs

Q. How much will I need for closing costs?

A. In addition to the down payment, the buyer will need to pay for closing costs. These costs will vary depending on local custom and the specific terms of the purchase agreement. If you are obtaining a loan, the law requires

---

▶ **THE WALK-THROUGH**

As a buyer, it may be wise to inspect the property just before closing to ensure that

- the property is in the same condition as it was when you signed the contract, except for ordinary wear and tear;
- all repairs that the seller agreed to make have been completed in a satisfactory and workmanlike manner;
- all personal property to be included in the sale is actually at the property; and
- the seller has vacated the property and caused no damage while moving out.

If any of the foregoing conditions are not satisfied, the buyer should quickly notify his or her lawyer or real estate agent. The problem needs to be addressed prior to closing. If something is missing, the buyer needs to determine whether the item will be returned before closing. If the condition of the property is not right, repairs should be made.

the lender to provide an estimate of these costs as part of the loan application process.

Closing costs usually include all or most of the following:

Appraisal fee

This is the fee paid for an appraisal of the property. It is required by the lender and is often paid for by the borrower. The Federal Housing Administration and the Veterans Administration establish the appraisal fees for mortgages that they guarantee.

Lawyer's fees

Generally, buyers and sellers pay the fees for their own lawyers. However, in some states, buyers are required to pay for the lender's lawyer. This fee may be a fixed fee, or it may be calculated as a certain percentage of the mortgage.

Survey fee

The contract should specify whether the seller is obligated to provide a survey. If the seller is not so obligated, the buyer may need to obtain and pay for a survey, both for his or her own use and to satisfy the lender. You may be able to avoid this fee if the lender agrees to accept a recent survey conducted for the seller, along with an affidavit by the seller stating that the property lines have not changed since the survey, and that there have been no additional improvements to the property since the survey was made. In addition, the title company may perform a visual inspection of the property to verify the seller's statements. Even then, a title insurance company may require a new survey unless the survey has been recertified recently.

Loan discount fee

This is the lender's charge to the buyer for obtaining the loan, sometimes referred to as

points or the **loan origination fee.** The buyer may have paid some of this fee in advance to secure the loan.

Inspection fees

These are charges for general inspections or those required by local laws. The buyer or the seller may be responsible for these fees, depending on the contract, local law, and custom.

Title fees

These fees cover the cost of the title search.

Title insurance

The contract needs to spell out who pays for title insurance. It could be divided between the seller and buyer, or the seller may pay for the buyer's policy and the buyer may pay for the lender's, or the buyer may pay for both policies.

Transfer taxes

Imposed by the state, county, or city where the property is located, these are taxes on the transfer of the deed and, in some cases, on the mortgage.

Recording fees

The costs of recording the deed in order to change ownership, and of recording the buyer's mortgage, are paid by the buyer. The cost of recording the release of the seller's mortgage by the seller's lender, and of recording the release of any other liens found in the record of title, are paid by the seller.

Q. Is the seller responsible for any additional closing costs?

A. The parties can negotiate who will pay the other closing costs. These obligations should be set forth in the contract. Generally, the seller is responsible for paying the real estate agent's commission, real estate taxes on the property up to the date of closing, and any liens that may be outstanding on the property, including any money due the current lender. On occasion, the seller may pay some of the costs of the buyer's loan, in order to induce the buyer to go through with the sale.

Ownership Options

Q. What form of home ownership is best for me?

A. If more than one person is buying the home, ownership may be declared in one of several ways. Generally, married couples or other co-owners with equal interests in the property prefer to hold title as **joint tenants with right of survivorship.** This form of ownership enables one person to own the entire property in the event of the other person's death. At the time of a subsequent sale, the surviving person will need to present a death certificate. Some states also permit married couples to own as **tenants by the entirety,** provided that the home is their principal residence. This form of ownership also provides a right of survivorship, and provides some additional protection to the parties against loss of the home to a creditor of one spouse.

Married or unrelated people may also own property with separate interests, either equally or unequally, as **tenants in common,** or they may hold title as a business entity (e.g., a limited liability company or partnership). Depending on where you live, other forms of ownership may be available, such as land trusts or community property. The option that is best for you will depend on a variety of factors, such as where you live, your estate tax situation, and the provisions you want to make for children, stepchildren, or other relatives.

The deed to your home must specify the type of ownership, so buyers should select a form of ownership before the closing. (Chapter 8, "Home Ownership," provides more detailed information on these and other ownership options.) Be sure to consult a lawyer about the various advantages and disadvantages of different types of ownership, so that you can make an informed decision about the form of ownership that is best for you.

REMEMBER THIS

- Once you sign a contract, you're committed to buying (or selling) a home. Consult with your lawyer before you sign. Don't rush into things, and be sure to include the necessary contingencies—so that you have some options, for example, if your financing falls through.

- If you're a buyer, it's a good idea to get a home inspection to make sure that the home you're about to buy has no substantial defects.

- You might find the closing intimidating—there are many papers to sign and much to understand—but your lawyer should help lead you through the process smoothly.

- Consider how you and your spouse want to hold title to the property. Your decision could affect your estate planning, and it may be important should you and your spouse divorce.

TAX CONSIDERATIONS

You can't afford to forget about taxes when buying or selling a home. After all, you may have to pay transfer taxes, real estate taxes, or a capital gains tax, depending on whether you are buying or selling. Talking to your lawyer about tax issues will prevent you from being shocked when the bill arrives, and may even result in a lower tax obligation.

Tax Considerations When Buying Your Home

Q. At my closing, I had to pay a transfer tax. What is a transfer tax?

A. A **transfer tax** is a tax paid for the privilege of transferring ownership of real property. Depending on local law, state or local transfer taxes may be assessed on the amount paid to purchase a home. If the home is financed, there may also be a documentary tax on the note or mortgage. The **documentary tax** often applies to the recording of the promissory note or mortgage by the county clerk, and is often in the form of stamps that must be purchased and affixed to the documents before they can be recorded. There may also be an **intangible tax** on the loan, another kind of fee for recording the mortgage. Generally the seller pays the cost of the transfer tax, but in most cases this is negotiable. The buyer generally pays the cost of the documentary tax on the note or mortgage, as well as the tax on the loan.

Q. What taxes will I have to pay once I own my home?

A. Most homeowners have to pay taxes on their real estate. **Real estate tax** is a yearly tax based on the assessed value of the property, usually paid to the local government. As a general rule, this tax is divided among the municipality (city and town), the county, the school districts (including the local school district and community colleges), and other governmental units. Currently, if you itemize deductions on your federal tax return, these taxes are deductible against taxable income.

Depending on your state's laws, the amount you pay in property tax also may be deductible on your state income tax return.

Q. What aspects of home ownership are deductible against federal income tax?

A. When you file your federal income tax return, both property tax and interest on loans of up to $1 million in principal are deductible against your taxable income. Federal law also permits you to borrow up to $100,000 through a home equity loan, and to deduct the interest, as long as the total debt on the home (including the first mortgage) does not exceed the fair market value of the home. Note, however, that you must itemize in order to claim these deductions; they are not available to taxpayers who claim a standard deduction. New buyers may deduct any loan fees or points paid to obtain a mortgage in the tax year in which the points were paid, but only if the points were paid by funds other than the borrowed mortgage funds. (A point is equal to 1 percent of the amount borrowed.) Loan fees or points paid to refinance a mortgage cannot be claimed in a single year; they must be spread out over the life of the loan.

Be aware that transfer taxes, lawyer's fees, recording charges, and other lender charges, such as charges for the appraisal and the credit report, are not deductible. See Chapter 8, "Home Ownership," for more information about possible federal tax breaks.

Q. How can I calculate the current real estate taxes on a home?

A. The seller should be willing to disclose the amount of property taxes paid on the home over the last few years. If not, you or your lawyer can obtain this information from the local tax collector's office. If a title commitment is issued in connection with the sale, the amount of taxes will also be disclosed in the commitment.

Q. How are real estate taxes determined?

A. The most common method of determining real estate taxes involves two steps. First, the taxing body determines the total value of all real estate within its borders (i.e., it conducts **assessments**). It then calculates the total value of the budgets (spending plans) for the various governmental units for which it collects taxes. The ratio of budgets to assessments creates a tax rate, which is then multiplied by the value of your own assessment.

Q. Does my purchase of a home affect the real estate taxes?

A. Depending on how your state assesses property, a purchase can affect the amount of property taxes to be paid. In some states, property tax increases occur only when a home changes ownership. The tax assessor reassesses the home using the price paid as its new value; in some cases this means that the property taxes will skyrocket. Other states reassess property every three or four years. If you are buying a home at the end of this type of three- or four-year cycle, you may see a large increase in property taxes at the start of the new cycle. While taxes may not be the deciding factor in your decision to buy, you will want to take them into account in determining your total monthly housing costs.

Q. Is there anything I can do if my home is assessed at a higher value than I paid for it?

A. You may be able to appeal the assessment, based on your purchase price. Once you have purchased the home at fair market value, you can appeal to the assessor's board or office. You must prove, however, that the sale was an "arm's-length transaction." In other words, you cannot purchase the home from a relative at below-market cost and then expect that your appeal will be successful. If the assessor grants your appeal and reduces the assessment, your future taxes would be lowered. See Chapter 8, "Home Ownership," for more information on this topic, and on how to lower your property taxes.

Tax Considerations When Selling Your Home

Q. Do I have to pay federal capital gains taxes on the sale of my home?

A. Only if you have lived there for less than two years, or if the profit on the sale is more than $250,000 (or $500,000 for a married couple.)

Q. How do I determine my profit?

A. You can calculate your profit by subtracting the adjusted cost basis of your home from its adjusted sales price. You can compute the adjusted sales price by subtracting certain items (such as the sales commission, lawyer's fees, and fix-up expenses) from the price of your home when you bought it.

To calculate the adjusted sales price, start with the selling price. Then subtract the cost of capital improvements made while you owned the home, and closing costs not deducted when you bought it. Note that you may not subtract the cost of any repairs you made to your home. You can only subtract the cost of improvements, and the IRS is very strict about what it considers improvements. For example, repairing a water heater

ASSESSED VALUE VERSUS APPRAISED VALUE

The **assessed value** of a home, determined by the tax assessor, is usually only one part of an equation that determines the total tax bill. The assessed value may or may not reflect the **market value**—that is, the price at which the home would be expected to sell. Be aware that not all states assess homes at their full market value.

The **appraised value,** on the other hand, is an estimate of the property's market value, usually made by a trained appraiser. A lender will normally require an appraisal to determine that the selling price does not exceed the property's market value or fall below the value of the lender's mortgage. It is common for a lender's appraisal to equal the purchase price specified in the contract.

is not considered an improvement, but adding a dishwasher is. You can check with your accountant or on the IRS's website to find out whether an expense will count as an improvement. Also, you may deduct the labor costs paid to a tradesperson (such as a carpenter), but not any costs for your own labor. The IRS requires home sellers to complete a form in the year of the sale that includes these calculations. You will also want to keep all receipts relating to any expenses you are deducting. Without such documentation, the IRS is not likely to allow your deductions.

Q. Now I have calculated my profits. What about calculating my tax bill?

A. First, remember that if you haven't made a profit, you don't have to worry about paying taxes. However, the IRS does not allow you to deduct any loss on a primary residence. As already noted, you also don't have to pay capital gains tax on the sale of any residence you have lived in for at least two of the last five years, unless the profit is more than $250,000 per person or $500,000 per married couple. One complication, however, is that in calculating your profit, you have to count not only the profit made on this house, but on any other houses you sheltered by rollover prior to 1997. On the other hand, if special circumstances required you to move before living in your house for two years, you still can exclude part of the profit—for instance, half the profit if you lived there for only one year—up to your $250,000 limit.

Most people don't have to pay any capital gains taxes on their home unless they have enjoyed a very substantial profit. This exclusion applies for as many times as you sell a primary residence that meets the two-year test. But note that this door does not swing both ways. If you lose money on the sale of your home, you cannot deduct the loss and pay less in taxes, or carry the loss forward. Additionally, some homes, such as investment properties and vacation homes, may be subject to capital gains taxes. If you think you may be subject to capital gains taxes, speak with your tax lawyer or accountant.

Win or lose, whenever you sell a home, you have to file Form 2119. This is a form that reports the sale date, the price, and how much profit (if any) is subject to immediate taxation. This one-page form details the calculations required to determine gain on sale, adjusted sales price, and taxable gain. If you die without selling the home, all capital gains taxes are erased. Your beneficiaries will inherit the property at a new, stepped-up basis, and they will not have to pay any capital gains tax on the previous sale of your home or homes.

Q. Will I owe state and local taxes on my profits?

A. Only if you live in a state or city that requires you to pay state or local taxes on the profits of a home; not all states and cities do. Talk to your real estate agent or lawyer about the rules in your area.

Q. My neighbor told me that there is a way to donate your home to charity, still live in it, and get a tax break. This sounds too good to be true. Is it?

A. In some circumstances, this is indeed possible. A homeowner interested in converting home equity into income may want to consider a **gift annuity**, in which he or she donates the home to a qualified charitable institution and is eligible for a tax deduction against taxable income in the year in which the donation is made. In return, the institution provides an annuity to the donor and grants the donor a life estate in the home. This means that the donor may remain in the home for his or her lifetime, and is responsible for all taxes and maintenance on the home. At the donor's death, the property becomes the possession of the charitable institution.

This arrangement offers several tax advantages, particularly for homeowners who do not have heirs or who want to reduce the size of their taxable estate. Again, you should consult a financial professional or tax lawyer for more information.

REMEMBER THIS

- Investigate the amount of property tax you can expect to pay on the home you're buying. It might not be the deciding factor in your decision to buy, but you will want to take it into account nonetheless.

- It's a good idea to save all receipts relating to home improvements. If you sell your home, they may come in useful for capital gains tax purposes.

▶ SAVE YOUR RECEIPTS

If you are making improvements to your home, save your receipts. Eventually your house might gain just enough value that you will want to prove your basis has increased, and therefore that the profit is not as great as it appears.

Home Ownership

After years of saving, Howard has finally moved into his suburban town house, and he couldn't be happier. He has just finished painting, and has even begun to build a dog-house for his furry friend. Suddenly, a letter shows up in his mailbox from the community association telling him to stop construction, and claiming that the doghouse is in violation of community regulations. Can the community association do this? Can Howard get them to change their minds? What are his options?

Howard's daughter is planning on going to college next year, and Howard thinks he will need some extra cash to pay the tuition bills. Can he use his home as collateral to get a loan? If he decides to do this, what steps are involved? If he defaults on the loan, is there a chance that he could lose his home?

This chapter offers an introduction to the law of home ownership, including discussions of rights and restrictions, insurance, and the financial side of owning a home. As you read, remember that the laws of each state are different; what follows are simply basic legal principles that provide a framework for understanding state laws.

PROPERTY RIGHTS AND RESTRICTIONS

You may own your home, but that doesn't give you license to do anything you want with your property. For example, you probably won't be able to turn your garage into an all-night roller disco—after all, your neighbors have rights, too, and there are probably zoning regulations restricting the use of your property. And when you say you own your home, think about exactly what that means. Do you own it outright, in fee simple? Do you own it as a joint tenant, or as a tenant in common?

This section helps you understand your property rights and how to safeguard them; it also explores the rights of others, including your neighbors and the government.

Your Property Rights

Q. Are my rights as a home owner limited?

A. Generally, what you do with your home is up to you. You have a right to maintain or neglect, preserve or remodel, keep, sell, give away, or enjoy your home as you see fit.

However, these rights are not absolute. They are limited by federal, state, and local laws, because the people who live around you also have rights. For example, under the federal Fair Housing Act, you may not discriminate when renting your property. Under local ordinances, your home must also conform to zoning and building codes. The zoning code may prevent you from adding a three-story addition to your home. Or if your garage is falling down and creating a hazard, your neighbors could call the building inspector, or even sue you themselves, to force you to repair or raze it.

So be mindful of such matters as zoning, building codes, easements, water rights, and local ordinances on noise, or you could find yourself in trouble.

Q. How do zoning codes affect my property rights?

A. To avoid urban mishmash, municipalities often restrict business and industry to particular designated areas. Other areas are designated as residential zones, which may include apartment buildings, or are zoned strictly for single-family homes. If your neighborhood is zoned residential, you won't have to worry about a pool hall or gas station going up next to your house. However, there will also be certain restrictions on what you can do with your property.

If you plan to build any sort of addition or new structure, check with your local building department about zoning restrictions on your property. If you are still unsure, consult a lawyer.

Q. Can zoning codes prohibit me from running a business in my home?

A. A typical residential zoning ordinance probably would not preclude you from operating a home-based business, if the business would not alter the character of the neighborhood. Thus, telephone sales, freelance writing, or mail-order distribution would all likely be permitted. But if the home-based business will require signs and will cause an increase in traffic, local zoning ordinances may prohibit it. As a result, you should check with the local department of building and zoning before you make an investment in the business. Also, be sure to ask about any licenses you might need.

Q. Is there a way to avoid zoning restrictions?

A. Most communities allow you to apply for a variance if you wish to make a minor change to your property that would violate zoning restrictions. For example, if you want to build a deck that will be close to the sidewalk, and will thereby violate zoning regulations, you could seek a variance; or you might seek one if you want to build a two-story extension in a one-story zone. Essentially, a **variance** is per-

mission from the governing body to deviate from the zoning laws.

If your plans call for a major change, you may apply for a **zoning change.** For example, if you live near the boundary of an area zoned commercial, and if you want to turn your nineteenth-century house into a doctor's office, you might be able to persuade the zoning authorities to slightly extend the boundaries of the commercial zone. For both variances and zoning changes, you would have to show that the change would not hurt property values, and convince your neighbors that it would not diminish their property rights.

Q. I know there is a restriction on my property, but I don't think it comes from the government. Is this possible?

A. Yes. It is possible that your property is subject to a covenant. **Covenants,** also called **CCRs** (for **covenants, conditions, and restrictions**), consist of private restrictions designed to maintain quality control over a neighborhood. Builders may draw up covenants affecting new subdivisions they are developing—and in modern developments, these restrictions can be significant and extensive. In an older subdivision, the covenants might be recorded on the plat. A **plat** is a plan or map of a piece of land that illustrates the location and boundaries of the land. Covenants typically restrict such factors as lot size, square footage, architectural design, fences, and unsightly activities such as auto repair.

Q. How do covenants affect my property rights?

A. Covenants generally "run with the land." This means that they bind all future owners of the property, unless all owners in the affected subdivision join in releasing the covenants, or unless they expire after a certain term. Covenants may restrict your use of your land even if municipal zoning laws do not. You should receive a copy of the covenants from your real estate agent or lawyer before you buy your home. Read them carefully to avoid being surprised later.

If you don't obtain a copy of the covenants from your agent or your lawyer, a copy should be available from the applicable homeowner association. In addition, covenants are usually recorded in the public records.

Q. What is an easement?

A. An **easement** allows someone else the right to use part of your property for a specific purpose. For example, a common type of easement allows a power company to run a power line over your backyard.

Commonly, neighbors may also have an easement on your property. They might have an easement to use your driveway to get to their house (i.e., a **positive easement**) or one that restricts you from blocking their view of the lake (i.e., a **negative easement**).

Q. How are easements created?

A. An easement or profit (the right to enter someone else's land and take something of value from the land, such as crops or minerals) may be created by a deed or other instrument of agreement, by a will, or by implication—for example, if a previous owner divided a single lot in half and the only access to the back lot is through the front one. Or, if a neighbor has been using your property in some way for a long time, such as by driving on your private road, he or she may be able to claim a prescriptive easement to continue doing so whether you give permission or not.

Courts are willing to grant **prescriptive** easements if a person has been engaging in the activity in question for a given period of years, and if the property owner has not physically stopped him or her from doing so, such as by erecting a locked gate. Oddly, one of the requirements for gaining a prescriptive easement is that the property owner must have objected—for example, by telling a person repeatedly over the years not to drive on the

> ▶ **CHECKING OUT EASEMENTS**
>
> Easements are recorded at the county courthouse, but they may be scattered among various plats, deed books, and mortgage books. The best way to find them is through a professional title search, which most likely occurred if you obtained title insurance or an opinion of title before buying your house. If you discover an easement, check its wording. When a document grants an easement to a particular person, the restriction may cease when he or she dies or sells the property. But if it's granted to someone and "his heirs and assigns," it's probably in effect no matter who owns the property. Until the easement expires, your legal obligation is to refrain from interfering with that right. Conversely, the person in whose favor the easement is created may not extend or broaden the permitted use. For example, if you have an easement for a walkway over a neighbor's property, you can walk across the property, but you can't drive vehicles over it.

road—but not physically prevented the behavior in question. In contrast, if an owner gives someone permission to do something, that person cannot claim it as a right.

Q. What about regulations on activities in my home?

A. The general rule is that activities that take place in the privacy of your home are your own business. There are three exceptions: when your activities are illegal; when the activities make it difficult for other people to enjoy their own homes; and when you are violating zoning codes, such as by running a prohibited business out of your home. Local noise ordinances may restrict the hours during which you can conduct loud activities. In addition, most activities that are illegal in public are also illegal in private—such as selling cocaine or serving alcohol to minors.

Safeguarding Property Rights: Title Insurance

Q. What is meant by the term "good title"?

A. If you have **good title** to your home, it means that you legally own your home and have the authority to sell it.

Traditionally, good title was determined by a study of the public record. Searching the public record can uncover the chain of ownership back to the very beginning of the property chain (which typically begins with a patent or grant from the government), as well as any encumbrances. This type of study is called an **abstract,** and some buyers, especially in rural areas, still rely on an abstract and a lawyer's opinion as to what the abstract demonstrates for evidence of title. However,

in modern practice, **title insurance** is the most common way to assure good title.

The chief problem with the abstract system is its lack of accountability. For example, what happens if the abstract company (or a lawyer issuing an opinion on the property) fails to uncover a flaw in the title, and it costs you (the new owner) a great deal of money? You could sue, but you'd have to prove that someone was negligent. With title insurance, the insurer agrees to pay covered claims whether anyone was negligent or not. Essentially, title insurance provides indemnity (i.e., protection against damages) for matters typically discovered by a thorough search of the public record. The result is similar to what an abstract and a lawyer's opinion would achieve, but backed by insurance. The title insurance company also assumes the obligation to defend covered actions challenging title to the property.

Q. How does title insurance work?

A. Title insurance protects you from liability for matters that occurred before the pol-

> ▶ **HISTORIC HOMES**
>
> What if you own a two-hundred-year-old house with historic value? If your home is listed on the National Register of Historic Places, no federally funded or federally licensed program may alter the building without a hearing before a federal agency. Also be aware that some communities have their own historic preservation ordinances that may affect what you can do to your property.

icy's effective date, but were discovered later. You only have to pay once to be covered as long as you own the property. However, note that many lenders will insist on a new lender policy before refinancing, to ensure that their new loans will have first priority. They want to know if you have taken out a second mortgage, obtained a home improvement loan, or been subject to a court judgment between the time of the mortgages. (For more information about title insurance, see Chapter 7, "Buying and Selling a Home.")

Q. What's the difference between an owner's title insurance policy and a mortgagee policy?

A. Owner's title insurance policies commonly cover losses or damages you suffer if it turns out that the property you think you purchased really belongs to someone else, if there is a defect or **encumbrance** on the title, if the title is unmarketable, if a notice of zoning violation or eminent-domain action (such as condemnation or taking) is recorded, or if there is no legal access to the land.

A **mortgagee title insurance policy** includes all of these protections and a few more. But it protects only the lender. Particularly important policy clauses for the lender are the ones that cover losses the lender would suffer if another creditor were first in line to be repaid by the buyer.

Owners' policies are usually more expensive. If the same insurer issues both, the concurrent mortgagee policy will probably cost far less—in part because the insurer doesn't have to search the records twice. The limit of the owner's policy is typically the market value of the house at the time of purchase, while the limit of the lender's mortgagee policy is typically the amount of the mortgage.

> ### ▶ REFINANCING
>
> If you are refinancing, your new title insurer will probably rely on the work of the individual or company who did a title search when you bought the home. If you provide the prior owner's policy as evidence of good title, the new insurer will simply bring it up to date by checking what you have done to affect the title, such as selling part of the property to your neighbor. Providing an existing title policy to the new insurer usually will save you some money. If a big problem surfaces that the original title insurer should have caught, the second insurer may go after the first to cover the claim. Likewise, if you have an abstract, the insurer may bring it up to date and base the policy on that. Contact a lawyer if you have questions about your title policy.

The premium is based on the amount of coverage and may vary greatly by state.

Q. What isn't covered by title insurance?

A. An owner's policy usually does not cover one or more of the following, which are often referred to as **standard exceptions:**

- claims of people who turn out to be living in the house, such as the prior owner's tenants or someone living there without your knowledge, if their presence is not a matter of public record;
- boundary-line disputes;

- easements or claims of easements not shown by public records;
- unrecorded **mechanic's liens** (claims against the property by unpaid home improvement contractors);
- taxes or special assessments left off the public record; and
- claims relating to mineral and/or water rights (especially in the western states).

In most states, you can get extended coverage for these standard exceptions by paying an additional premium and furnishing additional evidence to the title company. Other common exclusions from coverage include payments relating to

- zoning;
- environmental protection laws;
- matters arising after the effective date of the policy;
- subdivision regulations;
- building codes and the effect of any violation of these codes;
- problems the insured caused, or that the insured already knew about on the effective date of the policy; and
- problems not shown in the public records and not disclosed to the insurer.

Exclusions need to be removed by special endorsements, and probably will result in additional premiums. (In some states, exclusions for problems not shown in the public record cannot be removed.) Even in a policy without general exceptions, title insurers will still list certain special exceptions—matters of record, such as subdivision restrictions, or anything else they find that might turn into a claim, from this year's property taxes to the power company's easement across the property. Check your current policy to see what's

on the list, in case there's anything you should be concerned about.

Ownership Options

Q. How does the deed affect property ownership?

A. The ownership description on the deed has long-term significance—both to the duration of the title and to your ability to transfer your interest to someone else. Today, the most common form of ownership is **fee simple.**

Fee simple is the most complete form of ownership because, in theory, title in fee simple is valid forever. People who own property in fee simple may sell it, rent it, transfer it to their beneficiaries, and to some extent limit its future use. With some other forms of ownership, such as an estate for years, title reverts to the former owner at some specified time.

While it is still possible to transfer a life estate in property that ends upon the owner's death, this is rarely done because it severely restricts the new owner's ability to sell the property.

Q. Will both my name and my spouse's name appear on the deed?

A. In many cases, you can decide for yourself. However, the way in which your deed classifies ownership has critical long-term implications. It affects who can transfer interests, how much of the property is available to one owner's creditors, whether the property goes through probate when one co-owner dies, and whether the surviving owner faces a tax on any capital gain when it is time to sell.

It's important to think about what you want the deed to accomplish because, depending on state law, at least three ownership options may be available: sole ownership, joint tenancy with right of survivorship, and tenancy in common. In some states, married couples also may opt for owning the property as tenants by the entirety or as community property. (For more on these topics, see Chapter 17, "Estate Planning.")

Q. What is the most common form of joint co-ownership?

A. For couples, married or unmarried, the most common form of ownership in most states is **joint tenancy with right of survivorship.** In this type of ownership, each person owns an undivided interest in the real estate. At the death of one joint tenant, the interest of the decedent is automatically transferred to the surviving owner, who then becomes the sole owner of the property. When property is held in joint tenancy with right of survivorship, the beneficiaries of a deceased joint tenant have no claim to the property, even if the deceased mistakenly tried to leave the property to them in a will. Most couples choose this form of ownership to avoid having their home involved in probate after the first spouse dies.

Tenancy by the entirety operates similarly, but requires that the tenants be spouses. This form of ownership is not recognized by some states. Consult a lawyer to determine the form of ownership most advantageous to you.

Q. What is a tenancy in common?

A. Tenancy in common gives each owner separate legal title to an undivided interest in the property. This gives the owners the right to sell, mortgage, or give away their own undivided interests in the property. When one owner dies, the deceased owner's interest in the property does not go to the other owners. Instead, it transfers to the decedent's estate.

This might be an appropriate form of ownership for those who want their beneficiaries, rather than the other owners, to inherit their interest in the property.

Q. What is the difference between joint tenants with right of survivorship and tenants in common?

A. The two forms of ownership have many similarities: in both cases, two or more people who own a property are each considered the owner of an undivided interest in the whole property. That is, if there are two owners, each is presumed to own half of the property (unless specified otherwise in the deed), but not a specific half (e.g., the north half or the south half). If there is a court judgment against one owner, a creditor may wind up owning that person's interest in the house. In some states, an owner may sell his or her interest to someone else, whether the other owner approves or not. Such a sale ends a joint tenancy, so the new owner becomes a tenant in common with the remaining original owner(s).

The chief difference between joint tenants and tenants in common, therefore, is the right of survivorship. If one joint tenant dies, the property automatically belongs to the other owner or owners, avoiding probate. If three people own it and one dies, the two surviving owners each become owners of an undivided one-half interest. But if the owners are tenants in common, the other owners have no rights of survivorship—they would receive the deceased's interest in the property only if it was specified in his or her will or by inheritance. Additionally, in a joint tenancy, each owner has an undivided interest in the whole. However, in a tenancy in common, the owners can have equal or unequal shares of ownership.

Q. How does one stipulate a joint tenancy?

A. The deed must specify this arrangement. The usual language for this is as follows: "Mary Smith and Amy Smith, as joint tenants with right of survivorship and not as tenants in common." That way, if there is a question—say, from Mary Smith's children, who think they should inherit her half-interest in the property—then the intent of the owners will be absolutely clear.

If joint tenancy is not specified in the deed, then the law assumes the owners are tenants in common (except in some states, where their ownership constitutes tenancy by the entirety if they are married to each other, as explained below).

Q. What is tenancy by the entirety?

A. If the co-owners are married to each other, at least one other ownership option, **tenancy by the entirety**, may be available to them, depending on the law of the state where the property is located. As with a joint tenancy, this form of ownership bears a right of survivorship; if one spouse dies, the surviving spouse continues to own the whole property. It differs from joint tenancy primarily in that the parties must be married.

In most states that still recognize this form of ownership, a husband and wife who purchase property together are considered tenants by the entirety, unless the deed very specifically states otherwise. If not, a deed saying "to John Smith and Mary Smith, his wife," creates a tenancy by the entirety.

Q. What if one spouse wants to transfer a half-interest in the property to someone else during the marriage?

A. The ability to do so will depend on where the couple lives. In most states that recognize tenancy by the entirety, one spouse's interest may be transferred, whether by sale or gift, only if both spouses sign the deed. However, in some states, either spouse may transfer his or her interest—including the right to survivorship. Therefore, it is important to know what law applies in your state.

Q. Are there other forms of ownership?

A. Yes, there is one more common type: **community property.** There are eight community property states—Arizona, California, Idaho, Louisiana, Nevada, New Mexico, Texas, and Washington—plus Puerto Rico. A ninth state, Wisconsin, also has certain community property features in its law. A tenth state, Alaska, changed its law in 1998 to allow married seniors to select community property as an alternative form of ownership.

If you live in a community property state, the law may assume that a house you acquired during marriage (by the efforts of either spouse) is community property, unless you specifically state otherwise in the deed. In order to transfer the property to someone else, both husband and wife typically must sign over the deed. Chapter 3, "Family Law," provides more information on community property.

Q. Which form of ownership is best?

A. That depends on your circumstances. You or your spouse may want to be able to give half of your house to someone else. For example, if you are currently in a second marriage but have children from your first, you may want to avoid joint tenancy, because joint tenancy would not allow your children to inherit your interest if you died before your spouse. But if you don't want the house to be included in the estate after one of you dies, then joint tenancy might be a good idea. If you are married and have reason to expect that creditors will come after your house, you may want the protection offered by a tenancy by the entirety, if it is available in your state, because property owned in this way generally is not subject to a judgment against one spouse.

If you live in a community property state, be aware of two significant tax advantages that result from holding the house as community property rather than in joint tenancy. The first advantage has to do with capital gains tax. A **capital gain** is an increase in the value of an asset. In this context, it is the difference between a house's selling price and its **basis,** which was the cost of the house when you took title (plus allowable adjustments). If you hold the property as community property, then when the surviving spouse inherits the whole, the property receives a new tax basis (called a **stepped-up basis**) that reflects its current value. The practical effect of this is to minimize capital gains taxes if the survivor sells the property soon thereafter. (However, unless your profit on the sale is more than $250,000, this benefit may be irrelevant. Currently, federal tax law allows people to exclude from taxable income any capital gains realized from the sale of their primary residence, up to $250,000 per person or $500,000 per couple, as many times as they wish—provided that they've lived in the house for at least two of the five years prior to the sale.)

The other tax advantage to community property involves estate taxes. Subject to reductions in some cases for pre-death transfers, every American may give up to $2 million upon death without paying federal estate taxes; in 2009, the amount rises to $3.5 million. If you and your spouse do not live in a community property state and hold all your

property as joint tenants, none of the jointly held property will be part of your spouse's estate if he or she dies first. Since property can generally pass between husband and wife without tax consequences, the surviving spouse will then own all the jointly held property free of federal estate taxes. But if the value of your estate exceeds the exemption amount upon your death, it will be subject to federal estate taxes when you die. However, if you live in a community property state, your late spouse's one-half share of your community property, along with whatever property he or she owned separately, is considered his or her estate. As a result, it will not be taxed unless it exceeds the exemption amount. This means that some or all of it could be passed to your children, tax free. Because of your spouse's death, your estate might not grow beyond the exemption amount, and thus may not be subject to tax upon your death.

Q. Should a married couple ever hold title to their house in only one name?

A. In deciding whether to hold property in a single name, couples should consider not only estate-planning issues, but also potential liability for court judgments. For example, take the case of a house held solely in the husband's name. Let's say he loses a lawsuit over a car accident and his insurance won't cover the judgment. Because the property is solely his own, he might be forced to sell it to cover the judgment. (In some states, some protection may be offered through a **homestead exemption,** which allows people to retain a modest residence despite having to satisfy a court judgment.)

Some people may want a house to be held solely in their spouse's name precisely to

▶ CHANGING THE FORM OF OWNERSHIP

It is fairly simple to change the form of home ownership, but you must ensure that you are using the correct type of deed and the correct wording. Consult an experienced property lawyer who will consider all the aspects of your situation, including estate-planning and tax implications, and who will ensure that the paperwork and filings are done correctly. Though the actual process is fairly simple, using the wrong type of deed or the wrong wording can have serious consequences. In some juris-dictions, a straightforward change may have a minimal cost; but elsewhere, transfer fees, taxes, and recording fees can add up.

avoid this type of liability. For example, a doctor without malpractice insurance might want to deed the house to her husband, so that it can't be taken away if she gets sued. Before making a decision, consult a lawyer about all aspects of your situation, including tax and possible fraud implications. Some mortgage lenders may require one spouse to be removed from the title if that spouse will not be named on a home loan.

Q. How does the form of ownership affect property settlement in a divorce?

A. In most divorces, the parties divide the property themselves in out-of-court settlements, often with the help of lawyers and me-diators. The husband and wife decide what is fair and reasonable in a process of give-and-take. In contested divorces, it's up to the judge to decide who gets what.

Today, most family courts are more concerned with what's fair than with whose name is on a deed. They consider a wide range of factors, from the length of the marriage to the needs of each party.

Q. So who gets the house?

A. If there are minor children, usually the home goes to the custodial parent. If there are other assets to divide, the noncustodial parent may get a bigger share of the assets to make up for the loss of the home. If not, courts typically award possession of the house to the custodial parent until the children grow up. Then the house is sold, and the proceeds are divided between the parties. If neither party can afford to maintain the home, the court may order it sold and the equity split. Chapter 3, "Family Law," contains more information on the division of property in a divorce.

Handling Property Constraints

Q. What is a lien?

A. A **lien** is a claim to property for the satisfaction of a debt. If you refuse to pay the debt, whoever files the lien may ask a court to raise the money by foreclosing on your property and selling it, leaving you with the difference between the selling price and the amount of the lien. It's possible to lose a $200,000 house over a $5,000 lien.

There are several types of liens, any of which creates a "cloud" on your title. For example, a **mechanic's lien** or **construction lien** can occur if contractors or subcontractors who worked on your house (or suppliers who have delivered materials) have not been paid. They may file a lien at the local recording office against your property. If the lien is not removed, it can lead to foreclosure or inhibit your ability to sell your home. Liens often are filed in connection with divorce decrees. If two homeowners divorce, the court often will grant one of them the right to remain in the house. However, when that owner sells the house, the former spouse may be entitled to half the equity. The divorce decree would probably grant that spouse a lien on the property. If everything goes as it should, the former spouse will receive full payment of his or her respective share at the closing. Sometimes a lien created by a divorce decree is not registered, so if a purchaser is buying a house that may be subject to a divorce decree, a lawyer should examine all relevant documents to ascertain whether a lien exists. Title insurers should also be on notice to check the divorce decree.

Likewise, if you bought a home with your

▶ **REMOVING A LIEN**

If you discover a lien on your property, see a lawyer to determine the best course of action. If the lien is valid and for an affordable amount, the best course of action may be to pay the debt and clear the title. Have the payee sign a release-of-lien form, and file it at the county recording office to clear the recorded title. If the amount of the lien is major or you believe that it's not your debt, consult with your lawyer about what action to take.

---

spouse but later divorced, your own divorce decree might give your former spouse a lien on the home for half the proceeds. That lien can hinder your ability to sell the home if your former spouse refuses to release the lien. A divorce lawyer may try to build a release mechanism—such as an escrow containing the deed and release—into the divorce decree.

Q. Can a lien be filed for unpaid child support?

A. Many states impose a lien on the property of parents who fail to pay child support. That lien would have to be paid off before the property could be sold.

Q. What is adverse possession?

A. Although you have a right to keep trespassers off your land, under the law it's possible for someone who occupies your property for many years to actually become its owner. This entitlement is called **adverse possession.** It's very unlikely to occur in urban or suburban areas, where lots are plotted and homeowners know when someone else has been using their property continuously. But if you own an unvisited beach house or hunting cabin, you might not know that someone has been living there continually for years.

For a claim of adverse possession to succeed, the person occupying the property must show that his or her occupation of the property was **open and hostile,** which means that it took place without permission. As with prescriptive easements, granting the person permission to use the property precludes his or her claim to ownership by adverse possession. The occupation must also have been **continuous,** meaning without interruption, for a certain number of years—generally ten to twenty, but sometimes fewer, depending on the state. And in many states, the occupier must have paid local property taxes on the land.

If you suspect that someone has been living in your hunting cabin or other property, check the property tax records for that county to see whether anyone has made tax payments on it.

Q. How can I prevent someone from taking adverse possession of my property?

A. A bit of vigilance will prevent problems in this area. You should post "no trespassing" signs to warn people that your property is private. Erect gates at entry points and keep them locked. Ask trespassers to leave, and call the police if they refuse. If you suspect that someone will continue to use your property despite your efforts (e.g., for a road to obtain lake access), consider granting that person written permission to do so, especially if the use doesn't interfere with your own. This will bar a future claim of adverse possession, which requires that permission not have been granted. To make the arrangement clear, ask for a written acknowledgment—and, if reasonable, a fee or payment. It is best to check with an attorney to make sure the written acknowledgement includes the proper language.

Q. What is an encroachment?

A. An **encroachment** occurs when your neighbor's house, garage, swimming pool, or other permanent fixture stands partially on your property or overhangs it.

In the case of a neighbor's roof overhanging your property, or a fence standing two feet on your side of the line, your rights might be tied to the prominence of the encroachment and how long it's been in place. If it was open, visible, and permanent when you bought your home, you may have taken your property sub-ject to the encroachment. In that case, the neighbor may have an implied easement on your property to continue using it in that manner. If the encroachment is less obvious, you may only discover it when you have a survey conducted for some other purpose. In that case, you might have a better chance of removing the encroachment.

It's even possible to encroach on an easement—for example, by locating the apron of your swimming pool on the telephone company's easement across your property for underground cables. In that case, the company would have a right to dig up the concrete and charge you for it.

Q. What are my options for handling an encroachment?

A. First, you could demand that the neighbors remove the encroachment. If they refuse, you could file a quiet-title lawsuit or ejectment lawsuit and obtain a court order. In a **quiet-title lawsuit,** you ask a judge to declare your title to the property, and clear the property of any other interests or claims. You could seek similar orders in an **ejectment action,** which is a legal action you can bring to determine who has superior title to the property.

Of course, this isn't the best course of action if you wish to maintain neighborly relations, especially if the fixture in question is something relatively insignificant, like the cornice of your neighbor's house. Furthermore, if prior owners of the neighboring property have used that bit of your land for quite a few years, your current neighbor could ask a court to declare a prescriptive easement in order to maintain the status quo.

Second, you could sell the disputed strip of land to your neighbors. Perhaps you didn't know quite where the boundary line was anyway, so you might agree on a new one and file it with the county recording office. If you or your neighbor has a mortgage, you will need to obtain the consent of the lender before either of you can transfer any land.

Third, you could grant your neighbor written permission to use your land for the stated purpose. This approach could actually ward off a future claim for prescriptive easement or adverse possession, because in order to successfully mount these types of claims, your neighbor would have to demonstrate that his use was open and hostile (i.e., without permission). If you like your current neighbor but worry that you may not like his successors, you might grant permission to use the land for only as long as that neighbor owns the property. Your lawyer could draw up a document granting permission and file it for you.

When someone has encroached slightly onto your property, the primary question becomes, how offensive do you really perceive the encroachment to be? Typically, disputes over encroachments arise when there's discord among neighbors. If everyone is getting along fine, chances are you can live quite happily, even if your neighbor's fence protrudes slightly onto your land. However, remember that the encroachment will need to be disclosed when you put your house on the market. When you go to sell your property, you will want to ensure that the buyer agrees to the encroachment in the purchase contract, so it doesn't become a title issue at closing.

Government Rights to Property

Q. Can the government force me to sell my property?

A. Since ancient times, governments have had the right to obtain private property for governmental purposes, such as building roads and public buildings. This principle is called **eminent domain.** In the United States, it's limited by the Bill of Rights, which grants a right to due process of law and fair compensation when the government takes a person's property. Federal and state governments may delegate their condemnation power (condemnation is an order that certain land should be assigned for public use, usually with reasonable compensation) to municipalities, highway authorities, forest preserve districts, public utilities, and other agencies. A public purpose can include anything from building a new freeway ramp to declaring your soggy back acres a protected wetland.

Q. What should I do if the government wants to take my land?

A. If the government wants your land, chances are you'll hear about it informally ahead of time. If you object to the taking, the best approach may be to rally your neighbors in the hopes of influencing the authorities' plans. For example, your town might be persuaded to narrow a proposed road that would otherwise encroach upon your yard.

Your first official notice will be a letter indicating the government's interest in acquiring your property (or a portion of it) for a certain purpose. That's when informal negotiations should kick into high gear. With or without your consent, the government will then have your property appraised and make you an offer, called the **pro tanto award,** which you may accept or refuse. If you accept it, the government may ask you to sign a document waiving your right to sue for more money. Some governmental units offer a bonus to entice people into accepting the pro tanto award, because offering such a bonus is cheaper than going to court.

If you think the offer is too low, retain a

lawyer experienced in eminent-domain cases to negotiate for you and to prepare your case for possible trial. If the case does go to trial, it will be a battle of experts who testify to the value of your property. That value will ultimately be decided by the jury.

Q. Can the government ever seize my property without paying me?

A. If you've been convicted of a crime, the federal government can seize any property used in the crime, including your house. The property may then be sold and the proceeds used to further the government's crime-fighting efforts. So if you own a crack house, your arrest and conviction may lead not only to jail time but also to permanent loss of the house and your equity in it. Additionally, in some areas, dilapidated properties can be demolished without compensation to the owner (however, this usually only happens after notice and a court proceeding).

Q. Can the government seize my house and later claim to have done so because of suspected criminal activity?

A. For those of us who steer clear of crime, the good news is that federal law makes it unlikely that the government will seize our property. The Civil Asset Forfeiture Reform Act prohibits the government from confiscating property unless it can show "by a preponderance of the evidence" that the property is substantially connected to a crime. This is a much higher standard of proof than probable cause. If the government does seize property and the owner is able to prove that the seizure was incorrect, the government must pay the owner's legal fees. And if the confiscation causes substantial hardship to the owner, the government must release the property.

> ▶ **FEES FOR EMINENT-DOMAIN CASES**
>
> Sometimes when a government authority condemns land, it also pays the lawyer's fees for the property owner. In other cases, lawyers who specialize in eminent-domain cases work on a contingency basis. In these cases, the lawyer's fee may be a specified percentage of the difference between the initial offer and the ultimate settlement. You might want to set up a fee arrangement in which you pay a flat fee or an hourly rate for initial review, negotiation, and counteroffer, and then switch to a contingent-fee arrangement if the matter turns into a lawsuit.

As long as you're staying away from crime, one thing you almost certainly don't have to worry about is the government seizing your property and selling it. To be on the safe side, avoid the appearance of criminal activity in your house and vehicles. And if it's possible your property may be seized, retain a knowledgeable, assertive lawyer as fast as you can.

REMEMBER THIS

- In general, owning property means you can do with it what you wish. However, because other people also have rights, your property rights may be restricted by state and federal laws, zoning and noise ordinances, and restrictive covenants.

- Your title insurance policy pays you and your lender if there are problems with the title to your property.

- The way that ownership is characterized in your deed—e.g., as sole ownership, joint tenancy with right of survivorship, tenancy in common, and so on—will be significant in the event of divorce, sale of the property, liability, or death of an owner. Make sure your deed says what you intend it to say.

- Your property might be subject to adverse claims such as liens or encroachments. Depending on the significance of such claims, you may want to consult a lawyer.

- Government entities have a right to take your land for public purposes, but they have to pay a fair price. If you start talking early to the applicable agency, you may be able to influence the project so that it doesn't result in significant encroachment on your property. If not, a lawyer experienced in the law of eminent domain can help you negotiate a fair price.

PROPERTY INSURANCE AND OTHER PROTECTIONS

Any time someone gets hurt on your property because of your carelessness, you may be legally responsible. The same applies when you or your children damage someone else's property. One of the major functions of property insurance is to provide coverage for your liability. The other major function is to help you repair or replace your property when it's stolen, damaged, or destroyed. Theft, fire, tornado, or any other type of calamity: if it happens to you, you'll be glad to have a good homeowner's policy in place. But it's important to know what your policy won't cover. It's also important

to know how to protect your property from preventable perils, such as burglary.

This section discusses liability issues, including when you're responsible for damages and how to reduce the chance that someone will get hurt. Then it moves to protecting your home and health from a wide range of perils. It includes suggestions on reducing your risk, and on making sure you'll have enough money in the unfortunate event that you have to start over.

Floor Wax and Dog Attacks: Liability Issues

Q. Am I responsible if someone has an accident in my home or on my property?

A. The question of legal responsibility hinges on whether your **negligence** (that is, carelessness) caused or contributed to the accident or injury. Homeowners are **liable,** meaning legally responsible, only if a court finds them to be negligent in some way. Of course, many cases settle out of court before such a finding is made, if the homeowner or her or his insurer believes that a court would find the owner negligent.

Most homeowners carry insurance, and the insurance company generally handles any claims against the homeowner. It's only when the insurer believes the claim is unreasonable that the matter is likely to land in court. Even then, the insurer will likely provide the lawyer and pay any damages awarded (up to the limit of the policy), along with court costs.

Still, facing a lawsuit and going to court is no fun. Lawsuits involve months of depositions, motions, and counter motions before the trial even gets started. Even after a verdict is rendered, a party may appeal, and the battle could go on for years. As a homeowner, you are far better off preventing injuries on your property and protecting yourself with a comprehensive insurance policy in the event that accidents or injuries do occur. For more information on negligence cases and how courts evaluate them, see Chapter 6, "Personal Injury."

Q. Am I responsible for anyone who enters my property?

A. Historically, the law identified various categories of people who might be injured on your property—from invited guests to trespassers. The category of the injured party dictated the homeowner's duty of care. Today, although some jurisdictions still treat trespassers differently than "lawful" visitors, courts in most states hold property owners to the same standard with respect to everyone: a duty to employ reasonable care in maintaining your property and to warn people of hazards. This means, for example, that if you permit someone to pick berries on your property, you are obliged to warn the berry picker that the local gun club is holding target practice nearby.

Generally, courts hold homeowners responsible only if they are in some way negligent. The law does not expect the homeowner to guarantee that someone visiting his or her house will not get hurt. But the homeowner is expected to take reasonable care to protect people from known hazards.

Q. What happens if someone is injured on my property and we are both at fault?

A. While your best defense to any charge of negligence is that you exercised due care, several other defenses are also available. In some cases and in some states, a jury may decide that, although a homeowner was partially responsible for what happened, the person injured was also partially responsible. This is called **comparative** or **contributory negligence.** For example, if you forget to tell your houseguest that you recently dug a pit in your backyard for a septic system, and if the guest decides to get a breath of fresh air and wander around your backyard in total darkness, then a jury might find you both partly responsible for your guest's broken leg. In that case, the jury might reduce the amount of the damage award you would otherwise pay.

In other cases, the jury might decide to absolve you of any responsibility because of what the law calls **assumption of risk.** For example, let's say your neighbor offers to help you fix your car. He crawls underneath it, and then you accidentally roll your car over him. If he was to sue you, the court might rule that the neighbor knew of the risk of crawling under the car, and that you thus are not liable.

Q. Is there any difference between someone being injured in my pond and someone being injured in my pool?

A. Generally, courts do not hold homeowners liable for injuries stemming from natural hazards such as lakes and streams, even if a child is hurt, unless some other negligence is involved. However, homeowners are more likely to be held responsible if the hazard was created artificially, as in the case of a pool.

Q. Do particular standards apply if children are injured?

A. Even though an uninvited child wandering into your yard to inspect the swimming pool might well be a trespasser, the law of **attractive nuisance** says that you have a special duty to erect barriers to protect children. If there is access to a dangerous part of your property, such as a swimming pool, then a child may find it and get injured, and you may be held liable. That's why precautions such as fences, locked gates, and swimming pool covers—and good liability insurance—are so important.

Q. Am I responsible for damage caused by my children?

A. As a rule, parents are liable for injury and damage caused by their minor children (eighteen years of age and younger). Usually, damage caused by children thirteen or under will be covered by your homeowner's policy. In many homeowner's policies, damage and injury are not covered if the children are older than thirteen and intentionally cause the damage or injury.

Q. If I host a party in my house, am I liable for my guests' actions?

A. Some courts have ruled that a host is not responsible for the conduct of guests, unless your parties routinely turn into brawls. Likewise, if one of your guests is horsing around and hurts himself, you probably will not be liable. But if you allow a minor to consume alcohol and then send him or her out behind the wheel, you could be liable for a resulting accident. For more information on host liability, see Chapter 6, "Personal Injury."

Q. Am I liable for the actions of my pets?

A. The law typically holds people responsible for the actions of their pets. Most states have so-called dog-bite statutes, which hold owners legally liable for injuries inflicted by their animals. Chapter 6, "Personal Injury," provides additional information on pet owner liability.

▶ RECREATIONAL USE OF PROPERTY

If you allow a person to use your land for free to hunt, fish, ski, or engage in some other recreational activity, you probably will not be held liable if the person gets hurt. In the 1970s, virtually all states enacted **recreational-use statutes,** designed to encourage people to offer their land for recreational use without fear of liability. However, these statutes do not protect you if you charge a fee for use of the land, or if you're malicious in your failure to warn of hazards. For more information about such statutes in your area, contact a local lawyer.

Q. Can I be held liable if one of my trees falls on my neighbor's house?

A. Traditionally, property owners were not responsible for damage caused by falling tree limbs and other natural occurrences on their property. However, they were responsible for damage caused by artificial conditions—for example, if a high wind blew a loose board from a lumber pile through a neighbor's window. In both types of cases, today's courts apply an ordinary standard of care to measure negligence. This means that maintaining your property in good condition is an important protection against a negligence suit.

For example, if your trees have visible rot, you should cut them down or trim rotted limbs before they can fall on your neighbor's property. Trees should be maintained well enough that, short of a tornado or hurricane, the wind won't blow limbs from your yard into your neighbor's. For more information on trees, see the section on neighbors later in this chapter.

Q. I am planning on starting an excavation on my property. Should I be worried about how this may affect my neighbor's property?

A. If you excavate near the property line and cause your neighbors' land to sink, you may be liable whether their house is affected or not. Check with a civil or geological engineer if you think you have reason to be concerned. Your builder or contractor will know of one, or you can find one yourself.

Similarly, if changes you make to the contours of your land cause excess rainwater to pour onto your neighbor's property and cause damage, then you may be liable. If you are planning to change the contours of your land, ask a lawyer or your local building inspector about your state law.

Q. What other kinds of problems should I be concerned about?

A. Basically, if you're acting reasonably and responsibly, maintaining your property and carrying homeowner's insurance, you shouldn't fret about liability. However, if you're planning any changes to your property, you should investigate local laws to ensure that you will not violate them. Pay particular attention to the following potential problem areas:

- **Waterfront areas.** If you live along a river or stream, state and local laws designed to protect wildlife habitats may prohibit you from clearing brush or changing the lay of the land. Don't make these kinds of changes without checking with your department of conservation, natural re-

sources, or wildlife, usually located in the state capital.

- **Pollution.** You could be liable for the cost of cleaning up pollution stemming from underground oil tanks or old dump sites on your property, whether or not some other party caused the problem in the first place. Look into this before you buy a piece of property, because there won't be much you can do about it afterward. Ask the seller if any such problems exist, and have your lawyer include a clause in your purchase agreement that covers you in the event such problems arise. If the unique nature of the property is cause for special concern, you might even consider hiring an environmental consultant.

- **Wetlands.** Federal laws govern the draining and filling of wetlands. If parts of your property are boggy for even part of the year, avoid serious legal trouble by ascertaining your responsibilities before making changes. You might start with your state's department of environmental protection, probably located in the state capital. The federal Office of Wetlands, Oceans, and Watersheds in Washington, D.C., also might be able to help.

- **Utility lines.** As a rule, you are not liable for maintenance of utility lines crossing your property. To be safe, don't do anything to cause potential damage to utility lines, such as planting fast-growing trees under them.

Q. What should I do if someone is injured on my property?

A. First and foremost, do all you can to help. Express concern, ask what injuries might have been suffered, make the victim as comfortable as possible, call for medical assis-

▶ **CHECKLIST FOR MAINTAINING A SAFE HOME**

- Repair steps and railings
- Cover holes
- Fix uneven walkways
- Install adequate lighting
- Clear walkways of ice and snow as soon as possible
- Be sure children don't leave toys on steps and sidewalks
- Replace throw rugs that slip or bunch up
- Reroute extension cords that stretch across high-traffic areas
- Repair frayed electrical cords
- Keep poisons and other hazards beyond the reach of children, even if no children live in the home
- Warn guests about icy conditions and other hazards
- Restrain your pet
- Erect barriers to your swimming pool, such as an automatic pool cover or a tall fence with a good lock, and install an alarm on any door leading to the pool
- Keep weapons securely locked and out of sight, where children cannot see or gain access to them
- Remove nails from stored lumber and secure any lumber piles
- Don't leave ladders standing against the side of the house or the garage
- Don't let children stand nearby when you mow the lawn
- Don't let your guests drive under the influence of alcohol or drugs

tance, and so on. But don't say anything to suggest or admit guilt or negligence. While it's natural to empathize with the injured party and to want to soothe any pain and suffering, as well as assuage your own feelings of guilt, it's not a good idea to complicate the situation by making potentially incriminating statements. Rather, leave it up to the law to decide who was responsible.

Notify your insurer in writing (and speak to your lawyer) as soon as possible. Don't talk with the other party or his or her lawyer about liability until you've taken these steps. Later you may well offer to defray some of the injured party's medical bills, but do this only after you have had the chance to review the situation with a clearer head, and after obtaining the appropriate advice.

Note that there is one situation in which the law requires you to act. If someone has been hurt on your property or is in danger, you may have a legal duty to offer humanitarian aid, even though you had nothing at all to do with the injury. For example, in one case, a Minnesota cattle buyer became severely ill while inspecting a farmer's cattle. A court later ruled that the farmer had a duty not to send the man, who was helpless and fainting, out on the road alone on a cold winter night.

Liability Insurance

Q. Does my homeowner's insurance cover accidental injuries in my home?

A. Likely, yes. The **liability insurance** portion of your homeowner's policy is designed to cover unintentional injuries on the premises and unintentional damage to other people's property. In other words, injuries caused by your negligence are covered; injuries you inflict on purpose are not. Given your potential liability as a homeowner, you're asking for trouble if you don't carry adequate liability insurance. It takes only one person who is seriously injured by your negligence to generate a huge liability award and to deplete your financial nest egg—not to mention your psychological well-being.

Q. What kind of liability coverage is provided by a typical homeowner's policy?

A. A typical homeowner's policy includes $100,000 of liability insurance, which won't go far if someone is severely injured. In exchange for a slight increase in your premium, you can raise the amount of coverage to $300,000 or $500,000. Some companies offer coverage of $1 million or more. Typically, coverage includes harm caused by your

children and pets, except intentional harm if your child is over thirteen. (If your pet attacks people routinely, the insurer may cancel your policy or refuse to renew it.)

Most standard homeowner's policies do not cover

- losses suffered by employees and clients of your home-based business, including children enrolled in home-based day care,

---

▶ WORKERS' COMPENSATION

If you have a home-based business that necessitates people coming into your house, be sure to obtain a separate business rider for your homeowner's policy. Also, if you have a swimming pool or other type of special hazard on your property, check the policy provisions to make sure you're covered.

If you have domestic employees, even part-time help such as a nanny, you may be required to carry workers' compensation insurance, which costs a little more than $100 per year. Workers' compensation sets limits on awards. If you don't have it, you could have to pay far larger damages, and there may be civil and criminal penalties. Contractors working on your house should already have workers' compensation for their employees. You should ask to see proof of such coverage, and don't hire them if they don't produce sufficient verification or don't have adequate coverage.

if you take in more than three children and have no special endorsement;

- claims by one member of the household against another; or
- damages arising from any disease that you pass on to someone.

Q. Can I get more coverage in case there is a major accident?

A. Yes. An **umbrella liability policy,** also called a **personal excess liability policy,** is designed to protect you in case of a big judgment that would quickly exhaust your regular policy coverage. Such policies are relatively inexpensive because insurers typically bet that you'll never need them. Their coverage picks up where your home and auto policies leave off; thus, you will need to have certain levels of basic home and auto liability insurance before you can qualify for an umbrella policy.

You will also have to meet certain eligibility requirements, such as owning no more than four cars. If you've been convicted for driving under the influence of alcohol in the past three years, you're not likely to get approved for coverage.

Some umbrella policies pay the deductible amount that isn't covered by basic policies. Others impose a deductible, called a **retained limit,** in certain circumstances. For example, if your homeowner's policy doesn't cover slander or libel (and most don't without a special endorsement), an umbrella policy with a retained limit might require you to pay the first $250 of a judgment for slander. A policy without such a limit would pay the entire amount.

Your premium for the umbrella policy will be determined based on the number of houses, rental units, and vehicles you own. If

---

> ▶ **WHO NEEDS AN UMBRELLA POLICY?**
>
> People usually determine their need for umbrella liability coverage based not so much on how many hazards are on their property as on the amount of assets they have to protect. After all, the wealthier you are, the more you have to lose. Some people buy $5 million in coverage, and some even take out umbrellas on their umbrellas. Consult your insurance agent to help decide what type and amount of coverage is best for you.

---

you have one house and two cars, a typical premium will cost $150 to $225 for $1 million of coverage. For only about $100 to $150 more in premium costs, you can obtain about $2 million in coverage.

Homeowner's Insurance

Q. What kind of homeowner's insurance do I need?

A. Broadly speaking, a homeowner's policy is designed to pay for the repair or replacement of your house and belongings, plus extra living expenses, in the event of damage or loss—for example, if you and your family have to stay in a motel for several months. It also covers claims and legal judgments against you for injuries people suffer in your home or for damage that you cause. How much the insurer pays will depend, of course, on the limits of your policy, which in turn depends on how much you've paid in premiums. Although details of insurance policies vary among companies, the general types of coverage are fairly standard and include:

- **Basic policies.** Called **HO-1** or **HO-A policies,** these inexpensive policies pay the actual cash value of your home and its contents in case of loss due to specific causes, such as fire. This minimal type of policy usually satisfies lenders, because they are interested only in your ability to repay the mortgage, not in your ability to rebuild your house.
- **Broad policies.** Called **HO-2** or **HO-B policies,** these policies provide at least 80 percent of the replacement value (rather than the actual cash value) of your home in the event of damage due to specific causes, such as fire and theft. In most cases, you're better off with this type of policy (i.e., a policy that provides replacement value), because it usually costs more to replace a house than its market (i.e., cash) value might indicate. Note that the value of your home's replacement cost is estimated by the insurance agent. For an additional small fee, guaranteed replacement-cost coverage will protect you if your agent has underestimated the cost of replacing your home. Many financial professionals recommend these types of policies.
- **Inflation guard clauses.** These clauses increase the face value of a policy either according to the annual increase in local construction costs, or by a given percentage every three months. This type of rider can reduce the chances that you will be underinsured, but it doesn't guarantee replacement cost.
- **Comprehensive or all-risk policies.** These types of policies provide the best level of protection, because they cover any damages except those arising from specific exclusions, such as floods and earthquakes. However, even an all-risk policy may require separate riders for luxury items, jewelry, and art.

Q. What isn't covered by a homeowner's insurance policy?

A. Most policies specifically exclude damage caused by floods and earthquakes, and some policies will exclude or limit coverage for theft in high-crime areas. This doesn't mean that you can't purchase insurance for these threats; it simply means that you must pay for riders on your policy. Homeowner's policies also provide little if any coverage for home businesses. If you're operating a home business, check with your agent to see whether your business is adequately protected.

Q. Does homeowner's insurance cover natural disasters?

A. Not necessarily, because the differing nature of these perils is treated differently throughout the insurance industry. Consumers are often confused about what their homeowner's policies cover and what they don't. Typically, differing levels of coverage are available for the following types of disasters:

- **Floods.** Flooding can arise from many sources—rivers, lakes, oceans, and so on. In some states, sinkholes are a big issue. Homeowner's policies absolutely exclude damage from flooding, except in a narrow range of cases, such as a burst pipe or water tank. Generally you can't get an endorsement to cover flood damage; however, if your community is flood-prone, you can probably buy a special policy as part of the National Flood Insurance Program, which is administered by private insurers and backed by the federal government. Any insurance agent can sell flood policies. The cost depends on what measures your community has taken to reduce the risk of flood damage. Until your community meets the standards of the federal flood-control program, only limited coverage is available: up to $35,000 for a single-family house and $10,000 for its contents, for a cost of about $250 per year. However, once your community meets the applicable standards, you can obtain up to $185,000 for a single-family house and $60,000 for its contents. Premiums will depend on the structure of the house and how close it is to the water, but in a moderately flood-prone area, $60,000 of coverage on a house and its contents might cost about $150 per year.

- **Earthquakes.** The state of California requires insurance carriers to offer earthquake coverage to anyone in the state who carries a homeowner's policy. Usually such coverage takes the form of an endorsement to the regular policy, expanding the coverage for a fee. But if a California policyholder decides not to buy or renew the endorsement, the carrier isn't obligated to give him or her a second chance. Of course, given the risk, earthquake endorsements in that part of the country don't come cheap. The annual premium on a $100,000 house could be anywhere from $230 to $1,800, depending on the location of the house and the materials used in its construction. Coverage for brick houses, for example, would be priced at the high end of the spectrum. Deductibles on earthquake endorsements usually equal 10 percent of the total coverage for the structure and its contents,

figured separately. In other parts of the country you can more easily obtain earthquake endorsements, often for next to nothing—but most people don't bother, because they don't expect to need them.

- **Tornadoes and hurricanes.** Although standard homeowner's policies cover windstorms, you may need extra protection if you live in an area that is especially prone to hurricanes or tornadoes. In these areas, standard coverage may not be available; you may have to buy a special policy, such as the beach and windstorm insurance plans available in Atlantic and Gulf Coast states. As with flood insurance, any licensed agent or broker in those states can sell this type of insurance.

- **Volcanoes.** Volcanoes are specifically listed as a covered peril in standard homeowner's policies.

Q. How much does homeowner's insurance cost?

A. The cost of homeowner's insurance varies greatly depending on the amount of coverage and the age, location, and replacement cost of your home. It pays to shop around for the cheapest insurance premiums, but be sure that you are comparing similar, if not identical, coverage. Ask your insurance agent what discounts are available for taking safety precautions, and what other steps you can take to reduce costs, especially if you can afford a higher deductible.

Q. What should I do if I need to file a claim?

A. The claims process for theft or damage to your home or its contents is fairly basic, but it will go more smoothly if you have taken in-

▶ SHOPPING FOR INSURANCE

Whether you're buying your first policy or shopping for a better price or better coverage, begin by listing your possessions and estimating their value. Get your house appraised, either by an insurance representative or an independent appraiser, to figure out what it would cost to rebuild at current prices. Note valuables that might require special coverage. Then take the following steps:

- Talk with several different agents about your insurance needs. Ask them to quote premium costs with higher and lower deductibles. Compare costs and coverage. And check the reputation of the companies you're considering—perhaps by using a rating service, which can study companies' financial stability and ability to pay claims. Your insurance agent should have the latest ratings for the companies he or she works with, and should be able to help you interpret the ratings scales.

- Watch out for policies that limit recovery on personal possessions—for example, to "four times the actual cash value." This could mean that you would receive less than the amount you need to replace your old possessions.

- Avoid policies that limit reimbursements to what the insurance company would pay for a given item, because the company could probably buy that item wholesale.

- Keep your agent informed about additions to your house and major purchases that might affect the level of coverage you need.

- Periodically review your coverage to make sure you're adequately insured.

---

ventory of your possessions and their value ahead of time. In case of theft, first call the police. Then call your insurance agent or insurance company immediately. Ask whether you are covered for the situation, whether the claim exceeds your deductible, how long it will take to process the claim, and whether you will need estimates for repairs. Follow up your call with a written explanation of what happened. If you need to make temporary repairs to secure your home or protect it from the elements, keep track of expenses—but don't make permanent repairs until an adjuster has inspected the damage.

Don't do business with someone who comes to your door after a loss, claiming to be an adjuster. Scam artists may be eager to take advantage of your misfortune.

Q. What can you do if you have a problem with your insurance company?

A. If you're dissatisfied with the way your adjuster handles your claim, first talk to your agent. If that doesn't help, call the company's consumer affairs department. Then try the National Insurance Consumer Helpline, which might be able to suggest a course of action. Finally, you could call your state's insurance department to complain and ask for help.

▶ **TAKING INVENTORY**

Although you don't need a detailed inventory in order to buy insurance, and although you can eventually get a sizable check from the insurance company without one, the claims adjusting process will proceed much more smoothly if you keep clear, accurate records. The time-honored method is to keep a household inventory booklet (available from your insurance agent) indicating the purchase dates of furniture, equipment, and valuables and estimating replacement costs. It helps to attach bills of sale, canceled checks, or appraisal records. The more detail you can include, the better.

Another option is to use a computer software package designed to categorize records of personal possessions and make it easy to update them. Some programs can even print out records room by room, in case of partial damage to your house.

For a visual record, consider either photographs or a videotaped tour of your house, complete with commentary. Include the insides of closets and cabinets, and close-ups of computers, jewelry, and other valuables.

Be sure to keep a backup copy of your inventory in a safe place, away from your home. Send a copy to your lawyer, store it in a safe-deposit box, or leave it with a friend.

If these approaches do not bring a satisfactory settlement, consider hiring your own adjuster for an independent appraisal of your damage. You'll have to pay a fee of 10 to 15 percent of your final settlement. But check with your state insurance department to find out whether public adjusters have to be licensed in your state.

Another option may be arbitration with your insurance carrier. If both parties agree to arbitration, or if it is required by your contract with the insurance company, an independent arbitrator will hear the arguments and decide what compensation you're entitled to. For disputes involving a few thousand dollars or less, it's probably cheaper to present your own case in small-claims court.

Security Issues

Q. What should I do if there's an intruder in my house?

A. Everyone's afraid of encountering an intruder at night. If it happens, try to avoid a confrontation; your life is more important than your possessions. If possible, run away and call the police. If you can't get yourself and your family out of the house, try to lock yourselves in a room and call the police.

Q. May I shoot the intruder?

A. The law says that you can use reasonable force to defend yourself if you're being attacked or have a reasonable belief that you will be attacked. In other words, you don't

▶ HOME SECURITY CHECKLIST

How easy would it be for a crook to get into your home? Experts advise homeowners to examine their homes as a burglar might. Identify the easiest place through which to enter your home, and make it more secure. In addition, ask yourself the following questions:

- Are there exterior lights at the front and back of the house?
- Are there shrubs around your doors and windows that could be used for cover? (If so, trim them.) Do you have a privacy fence that could provide burglars with too much privacy?
- Do you have deadbolt locks on your doors? Do you keep them locked, even if you're out working in the yard?
- Are your doors solid, at least 1¼ inches thick, and do they fit snugly in the frame?
- Have you installed a specially designed lock for your sliding-glass door?
- Could a burglar slide a window open from the outside and climb into your home? (If you have double-hung windows, a removable nail pinning the upper and lower halves together is quite effective.)
- Should you consider grates for your street-level windows? (Be aware that they can trap you inside the house in case of fire.)
- Would an alarm sound if an intruder stepped inside your home?
- Is there a sticker on your window indicating that you have an alarm system? (This may be enough to scare off some would-be intruders, whether you actually have an alarm system or not. However, keep in mind that some alarm stickers might help experienced burglars who know how to disable the alarm systems of particular companies; you can counteract this danger by displaying the sticker of one company but using the system of another company.)
- Do you ever leave your house keys with your car keys when you valet park your car? Do you carry house keys on a key ring with a name-and-address tag? Do you hide a key in a secret place outside your home? (Be careful not to do this; burglars know where to look.)
- When you go on vacation, could strangers tell that you're gone? (Don't let mail and newspapers pile up outside, and make sure that your lawn stays mowed and your walks stay shoveled. Use automatic timers for lights and a radio, and leave your blinds open in their usual position.)

▶ DISASTER PREPARATION AND YOUR HOME

Since the events of 9/11 and Hurricane Katrina, federal, state, and local governments have spent a great deal of time and money on disaster preparation. However, in order to ensure that your family and loved ones are ready in the event of a disaster, you should also take some steps on your own.

The first step toward disaster-readiness is simply talking with your family and developing a plan. This plan should include a meeting place for all family members to congregate in the event of an emergency or evacuation. You may want to consider selecting two places: one close to home, and another out-of-state in case it becomes dangerous to stay near home. You should also designate an out-of-state contact person for family members to call. During an emergency, it may be easier to call someone long distance than to reach local numbers.

You should also prepare emergency kits in order to ensure that, if something happens, your family will have a stockpile of necessities. When assembling a kit, focus first on the basics: fresh water, food, clean air, and warmth. Consider including the following:

- water (plan to have at least a three-day supply, allotting one gallon of water per person for each day);
- food (stock three days worth of nonperishable items);
- flashlights and extra batteries;
- a first-aid kit;
- a whistle (to signal for help);
- dust masks;
- moist towelettes, garbage bags, and plastic ties (to be used for personal sanitation);
- basic tools, including a hammer, a wrench, and pliers;
- a can opener; and
- local maps.

You may also want to include

- prescription medication;
- pet food and water for your pet;
- important documents such as personal identification, insurance forms, and bank records;
- money;
- sleeping bags and blankets;

- a change of clothes for each family member; and
- books, games, and other activities for children.

Remember: during an emergency, ATMs and computers may not work, so you will want to make sure that you have some cash, traveler's checks, and change on hand. When putting together an emergency kit, consider including copies of insurance policies, identification, and bank account statements. All paper should be kept in a waterproof, portable container.

While planning for your family's emergency care, take a minute to consider your pet. What is best for you is usually what is best for your pet, so consider ahead of time how your pet will be evacuated should it become necessary. Maintain copies of all your pet's identification documents and recent vet records, and keep a recent photo of you and your pet together. When creating your emergency plan, remember that public shelters don't always accept animals. You may want to consider developing a buddy system with a neighbor or friend. This would ensure that in case you are unable to return home, someone else would know to check on your pet and make sure it is safe and healthy.

have to wait until the intruder is actually coming at you with a knife. The key word here is "reasonable"; the jury would have to decide whether a reasonable person would have thought that an attack was imminent—for example, that a toy gun was real, or that a hand reaching into a pocket was actually reaching for a weapon.

Depending on the circumstances, you may end up in court if you shoot an intruder or whack him over the head with an iron pipe. You would have to argue that you acted in self-defense or in defense of your property, and it would be up to the jury to decide whether to believe you.

Q. What is considered "reasonable force"?

A. States vary widely on what they consider reasonable force. In general, if you use force against an intruder, use no more than appears

necessary. That is, if a shout sends the burglar running, don't pull a gun and shoot him in the back. If a single blow stops a burglar in his tracks, don't beat him to a pulp. If the intruder isn't threatening bodily harm to someone in the house, you're on shaky ground if you use deadly force. Some courts have held that a homeowner who could retreat safely isn't justified in beating or killing the intruder.

Q. What about booby-trapping your home to keep burglars out?

A. People have gotten into serious legal trouble for this sort of thing. Even if you're fed up with repeated break-ins, you can't set up a gun rigged to shoot anyone who comes through the window. First, it's not up to you to impose a death sentence on someone who might try to break in. And second, the next person through the window might be a firefighter trying to save you.

▶ ENVIRONMENTAL HAZARDS

Sometimes a home can look fine, yet contain deadly environmental hazards. In some cases, you may find out about a problem accidentally, such as when a remodeling contractor finds asbestos around a furnace. Or you might learn about lead the hard way when your children are diagnosed with developmental problems. The best way to discover and correct these types of hazards may be to hire an expert to test your home.

If you intend to test for household toxins such as radon, asbestos, or lead, research consultants carefully. To avoid scams, research the nature of each home toxin, the services available for eliminating it, and the procedures and precautions involved. For names of licensed professionals in your area, consult state or local health departments or EPA regional offices, and ask potential consultants for references from previous clients. (See "Remodeling" on page 317 of this chapter for information on hiring contractors.)

Toxic waste can create additional problems for homeowners. Residential property can harbor toxic wastes that are potentially dangerous to the homeowner and neighbors. For example, a private home may have a leaky heating-oil tank buried under the backyard. The law may hold homeowners responsible for the cost of cleaning up toxic waste sites, even if they had nothing to do with creating the problem. Responsible parties—who may include the current homeowner, the owner of the property when the pollution was caused, and the person or company who caused the pollution (which may be another party altogether)—are jointly and severally liable for cleanup costs. Being **jointly and severally** liable means that any one of these people can be forced to pay the entire cleanup cost. Often that person is the current homeowner, who is probably the easiest to find. Then it's up to the homeowner to find the other liable parties and sue to recover their portions of the cleanup cost.

One final note if you are selling your home: federal rules require sellers to disclose information about lead-based paint, and many states require sellers to inform potential buyers when they know about other hazards in the house, like asbestos or radon. Then it's up to the parties to work out who's responsible for the costs of eliminating the hazards.

Q. Does the law prohibit me from killing wild animals on my property?

A. It depends on the animal. Many states allow the killing of gophers, rattlesnakes, and coyotes, but most states impose hefty fines for killing other wild animals without a permit. Your state department of fish and wildlife has jurisdiction over wild animals, and a call to the nearest office will probably get you some advice. In some cases, it's not difficult to deter an invading animal. For example, an eight-foot-high fence will stop most deer. Dried blood or a commercial mixture should repel rabbits. Storing trash so that it's not accessible to raccoons quickly forces these very smart (and often rabid) animals to find new territory.

However, some animals are difficult to deter. Many states assist farmers with cash payments to reduce the damage caused by certain wild animals, and some reimburse farmers and ranchers for wildlife damage. Note that in most cases, reimbursement programs (which are funded by hunting license fees) aren't open to farmers who bar hunters from their land.

REMEMBER THIS

- If someone is injured on your property because of your negligence, you're legally responsible. It pays to be careful, warn people of hazards, and carry plenty of liability insurance.

- Your homeowner's policy also covers property damage. This includes damage to your own property from a variety of perils, and accidental damage to your neighbor's property caused by your family, your animals, your trees, or your personal property. Make sure your policy limits are high enough to enable you to start over in the event of a calamity.

- Standard homeowner's policies typically exclude coverage for floods. But if you're in a flood-prone area, you can probably obtain a special government-issued flood policy.

- It's better to prevent harm than to collect insurance for it. Take steps to protect your property and your safety.

MANAGING NEIGHBORHOOD PROBLEMS

What your neighbors do with their homes may well affect you—whether because there's a high fence blocking your view, an overgrown yard bringing down your property values, or the din of a teenage rock

> ▶ **A STEP-BY-STEP GUIDE FOR RESOLVING NEIGHBOR PROBLEMS**
>
> - **Step 1:** Discuss the problem with your neighbor, who may not be aware that her late-night parties bother you, or that Fifi is digging up your flower bed.
>
> - **Step 2:** If things don't change, warn your neighbor. Obtain a copy of the applicable local ordinance (check your local library or city hall for the applicable municipal code, or contact your local council representative). Mail it with a warning letter alerting your neighbor of the violation. Be sure you keep a copy of the letter. Wait a reasonable amount of time to see if the problem is resolved.
>
> - **Step 3:** Suggest mediation. Try to work out the problem with an impartial mediator to resolve the dispute informally.
>
> - **Step 4:** Contact the authorities. If all else fails, call the police and/or file a civil lawsuit.

band practicing at full volume in the next-door garage. This section explores your options for coping with problem neighbors.

Handling Disputes

Q. What's the best way to handle a dispute with a neighbor?

A. Unless you intend to move, resolving a problem amicably is in your best interest. Neighborhood spats typically originate from minor disputes over boundary lines, fences, junky cars, noise, pets, or trees. If a problem cannot be solved amicably by you and your neighbor, different disputes call for different remedies.

If you are unable to resolve things informally, you'll want to know how the law (as well as municipal and subdivision regulations and private covenants) can be put to use in your best interest.

Q. How can I tell if my neighbor is violating a zoning ordinance?

A. City or county zoning regulations may limit the height of fences, the use of property for commercial purposes, or the level of noise allowed at night. In some cases, city officials notice a violation and issue a citation, but usually it's up to the neighbors to complain. If you suspect a zoning violation is causing the problem, check with your city hall or town council to see if there's a regulation on the books. Either the town hall or the local library should have copies of municipal ordinances.

Q. What can I do if my neighbor is violating a zoning ordinance?

A. Notifying the neighbors that they are violating an ordinance may take care of the problem. To file a complaint, you may have to

> **▶ SAMPLE WARNING LETTER**
>
> Dear Neighbor,
>
> Just as you enjoy playing your stereo, I enjoy a quiet environment in my home. However, it's impossible for me to do so when your stereo is played at such a loud volume.
>
> Please read the enclosed municipal noise ordinance. You will see that the law requires that you keep your stereo to a reasonable volume.
>
> I trust that we can resolve this matter amicably, so that I will not have to contact the authorities. Thank you for your anticipated cooperation.
>
> Sincerely,
>
> Your Neighbor

contact the city attorney or the controlling agency, such as the local zoning board. If the city takes up the cause, it will require less effort and expense on your part than filing a lawsuit. You won't receive money, but your neighbor will be ordered to comply with the zoning rules, pay a fine to the city, or both.

Q. What if my neighbor's actions don't violate any ordinances, but are still egregious. Is there anything else I can do?

A. You can consider bringing a nuisance suit. **Nuisance** is the legal term for an unreasonable action that interferes with your enjoyment of your property. Anything from noxious gases to annoying wind chimes may consti-

▶ HANDLING DISPUTES IN COMMON-INTEREST COMMUNITIES

A **common-interest community** is a type of real estate in which owners of a unit have an obligation to pay money to another person, usually an association, for maintenance, taxes, upkeep, and insurance of property other than the individually owned unit. Condominiums and cooperatives are both types of common-interest community.

If you are embroiled in a dispute and you live in a common-interest community, check the bylaws and regulations of your development to see whether a rule prohibits the activity in question. Your homeowners' association can be a powerful ally. After all, if a neighbor's actions are bothering you, they may be equally troublesome to the other residents. If your neighbor refuses to comply with your initial requests, consider asking other neighbors to get involved. They may be willing to sign a petition or joint letter to the homeowners' association, which would be more likely to draw the attention of the board than a complaint from an individual.

The association will investigate the complaint, ask for input from the offending neighbor, and then take a vote as to whether official action is warranted. If the board feels that your neighbor has violated its governing rules, it will likely begin by issuing a formal warning letter. In extreme cases of noncompliance, the homeowners' association may refer the matter to the city attorney or file its own lawsuit against the offending resident.

---

tute a nuisance. The law of nuisance involves a balancing test: weighing the social value of the activity against the social value of your use and enjoyment of your property. Accordingly, authorities that deal with nuisance complaints expect them to be reasonable. Thus, your distaste for your neighbor's cooking odors may not be enough to sustain a nuisance complaint.

Q. What can you do about a nuisance problem?

A. If your local ordinances classify nuisance as a crime (usually a misdemeanor), the offender might be given a citation to appear in court on a given date, or he or she might even be arrested, held until bond is posted, and ordered to appear in court. If convicted, the offender may be fined and/or jailed. If your local

ordinances classify nuisance as a civil violation, your neighbor could face civil charges in court, which could result in a fine.

Your role as the complaining neighbor is limited to testifying. Again, any money collected will be in the form of fines paid to the city, not to you.

The other option is to file a lawsuit yourself. You would bear the expense of bringing the case to trial, including filing fees and the costs of legal counsel. But if you won, you could collect monetary damages from your neighbor, or obtain a judgment requiring him or her to remedy the problem. To prevail against your neighbor in court you will have to show that

- the neighbor is doing something that seriously bothers you;

- the neighbor's actions have reduced your ability to use and enjoy your property;
- the neighbor is responsible for his or her actions; and
- the neighbor's conduct is unreasonable or unlawful (this is only required in certain states).

In addition, you will have to request a specific amount of money or an injunction. An **injunction** is a court order directing a person to do or refrain from doing something—in this case, an order directing your neighbor to take steps to adequately deal with the annoyance.

Q. *How can I handle disputes over boundary lines?*

A. Disputes over boundary lines are less common than other neighbor-related problems, in part because of modern surveying techniques. Boundary lines may be set forth in the property description in your deed. However, sometimes if the property description was created decades or even centuries ago, the description in the deed may be a bit difficult to trace on the ground.

If you and your neighbor are unsure where the boundaries of your property lie, you have a number of alternatives:

- Spend a few hundred dollars to hire a surveyor.
- File a quiet-title lawsuit asking a judge to determine the location of the boundary line. This is more expensive than hiring a surveyor, because you will have to pay filing fees, lawyer's fees, and possibly a surveyor if the court so requires.
- Agree with your neighbor that a certain imaginary line or physical object, such as a fence or tree, will serve as the boundary between your properties. Have a lawyer draw up quitclaim deeds for both parties

---

▶ **WATCH THOSE BOUNDARIES**

Before you erect a fence or other structure on your land, make sure that the land is indeed yours. If you innocently but mistakenly erect a fence on your neighbor's property, you may be liable for trespassing on your neighbor's land. Your neighbor could ask the court for an injunction to make you tear down the fence, and could seek to recover for any damage you may have caused to his or her property.

If your neighbors start building on land you believe is rightfully yours, notify them immediately. If you allow the construction to continue and wait to complain, you may be giving up your right to that land. After years of uncontested use, courts sometimes grant the party that has used the land a prescriptive easement allowing them to continue using it. Or your neighbor could obtain rights over your land, right up to the fence.

---

to sign, each granting ownership to the other neighbor of any land on the other's side of the line. Be sure to record the deed by filing it in the county records office. This may require the mortgage holder's approval.

Q. *What can I do about noise?*

A. Noise is one of the most common sources of neighborhood tension. Some municipal ordinances limit noise to a given number of decibels.

However, timing is critical. Many municipalities regulate noise levels during certain "quiet times" when most people sleep. Quiet times typically begin between 10:00 P.M. and midnight and last until 7:00 or 8:00 A.M. on weekdays; on weekends, they often extend to 9:00 or 10:00 A.M. But some noises may be considered unreasonable at any time—for example, if a person plays an electric guitar so loudly that it makes a neighbor's walls shake.

As with any nuisance, start by asking the neighbor to turn down the volume, and explain why. Keep a log of the noise—when it occurred, how loud it was, and how it affected your household. If the neighbor doesn't respond to a letter, consult with local authorities about local ordinances that might be helpful. Consider a lawsuit only as a last resort.

Q. My neighbor is letting his property fall apart. Is there anything I can do?

A. Blighted property decreases the value of surrounding homes and will often incur the wrath of neighbors. However, unless homeowners are governed by subdivision rules on exterior maintenance, they are generally free to choose how their property looks. The exception occurs when a place is so neglected that it becomes a neighborhood eyesore, such as a yard overgrown with weeds or filled with trash, or a safety hazard, such as a dangerous structure.

If deterioration is a result of the offenders' financial problems, perhaps you and other neighbors could pitch in for a "cleanup" day. If it's simply a matter of sloth, ask the offenders to clean up or repair what is broken. If they refuse your request to maintain a reasonable standard of cleanliness, you may be able to get the city to force them to clean up the property, provided the city has an ordinance declaring blighted property to be a nuisance. If so requested by a resident—or if a city official observes the nuisance—the city may issue repeated notices to the offenders. Under certain circumstances, the city can place a lien on the blighted property to cover the cost of cleanup or other repairs.

Q. Besides calling the police, what can I do if my neighbor is engaging in illegal activities?

A. If the problem is with tenants, first contact the property owner, who may or may not know that the tenants are doing something illegal. Some cities require such tenants to be evicted, or will fine landlords who allow the nuisance to continue. In some cases, state and federal laws allow the government to seize property that is being used for illegal financial gain. The threat of forfeiting the house to the government is likely to persuade the homeowner to evict undesirable tenants. Another approach is for you and your neighbors to pursue a private lawsuit against a neighborhood nuisance. Neighbors can be a powerful, unifying force in these situations. You can also consider contacting local law enforcement to report the criminal activity.

Pets

Q. What can I do if my neighbor's animals are creating a problem?

A. If you have a problem with a neighbor's pet, knowing your local laws can help you resolve it. Your town probably has one or more ordinances (indexed under "dogs" or "animal control") that can be enforced in court. Such laws often limit the number of animals per household, the length of time a dog may bark, or the frequency of barking allowed. Leash laws require that dogs not run at large, and pooper-scooper laws require owners to clean up after their pets. If polite requests to your neighbor don't work, call your local animal control service. Unless the animal control authorities consider your complaint unreasonable, they will probably call the offending animal's owner with a warning, followed by a citation and possible fine if the problem persists. If the neighbor continues to allow his or her animal to annoy you, he or she can be fined repeatedly if you continue to complain. If the problem persists, you may need to bring a civil lawsuit for nuisance in order to get a court order. If your neighbor disobeys the court order, he or she could be found in contempt of court and face jail time or a hefty fine.

For animal problems, call the police only as a last resort. Police are generally not very interested in problem dogs, and bringing the police into the equation also may sever any further relations with your neighbor.

Trees

Q. What's the law regarding trees?

A. Trees can cause as much contention between neighbors as yapping dogs, whether they block people's view, crack their foundations, or drop debris on their driveways. The general rule is that a tree whose trunk stands entirely on the land of one person belongs to that person; if the trunk stands partly on the land of two or more people, it usually belongs to all the property owners.

Someone who cuts down, removes, or harms a tree without permission owes the tree's owner money for compensation. If nec-

essary, a court can determine the amount of money owed.

Q. Is there any way I can be prevented from cutting down the trees on my own property?

A. In most cases, the answer is no. But trees are not strictly private property like, say, barbecue grills. In some instances, neither the tree owner nor the neighbor has unlimited control over the fate of a tree. In some jurisdictions, the municipality has ordinances limiting a tree owner's right to cut down the tree. Or there may be a restrictive covenant in the relevant deeds that bears homage to trees. In addition, it is now quite common for communities to have ordinances barring the cutting down of trees. Commonly, public or private regulations will proscribe the cutting down of trees that exceed a certain diameter.

Q. Can I trim the overhanging limbs of my neighbor's tree?

A. You may trim the branches of a neighbor's tree that hang over your property, with certain restrictions:

- you may trim up to the boundary line only;
- you need permission to enter the tree owner's property (unless the tree poses imminent and grave harm to you or your property);
- you may not cut down the entire tree; and
- your trimming may not destroy the tree.

It's always best to notify the tree owner before starting any trimming, pruning, or cutting. If the owner objects to the trimming, offer reassurance that the job will be done professionally and responsibly, respecting the mutual rights of both parties.

▶ THE FRUITS OF YOUR NEIGHBOR'S LABOR

Fruit-bearing trees that overhang a neighbor's property pose a tasty dilemma. When apples drop onto the neighbor's property, is the fruit considered manna from heaven? According to a long-standing common law doctrine, the answer is no.

What if your neighbor's fruit poses a problem for you? If rotting fruit habitually falls from a neighbor's tree into your yard, notify your neighbor, and ask him or her to clean up the fruit and to trim the tree to avoid such droppings in the future. If he or she ignores your request or refuses to comply, your neighbor may be liable for any damages the errant fruit causes to your grass or garden. (The same thing goes for the fruit of a neighboring tree that may cause physical injury to you, such as a coconut that falls and smacks you on the head.)

Q. Am I liable for the encroachment of my trees or shrubbery on a neighbor's property?

A. The law varies by state, but generally it depends on the extent of the damage. Tree roots are likely the most serious (and potentially costly) problem. You will save money in the long run by hiring a landscaper or "tree surgeon" to take whatever steps are necessary to prevent root damage to your neighbor's home or walls.

Views

Q. What are my rights regarding the view from my property?

A. Generally there is no absolute right to a view, air, or light, unless such a right is created by law or by a subdivision rule. Such provisions are relatively common in coastal areas or other scenic-view locations. If a view is important to you or to the value of the property you are thinking of buying, be sure to investigate your legal rights to protect that view before closing the deal.

Q. Can my neighbor legally block my view?

A. That depends in part on where you live. The best way to protect a view is to purchase an easement from your neighbor, guaranteeing that he or she will not build anything on the land described in the easement if it would obstruct your view. (See page 280 for further information on easements.) You may cringe at the thought of paying to maintain a view that is already there, but in the long run an easement is likely to be less costly than bringing a lawsuit.

Unless you live in a community that has a view ordinance, you are unlikely to get relief in the courts without entering into this type of arrangement. But even if your community has a view ordinance, the mayor won't necessarily jump in and order your neighbor to tear down an obstruction. If the city does not feel that your complaint has merit, you will have to initiate a lawsuit and wait until your day in court to request an order requiring your neighbor to restore your view. Depending upon any court backlogs, the wait could be months. And of course, your neighbor might appeal the decision, causing another lengthy delay. In the interests of time and sanity, it may be advisable to forego the legal wrangling and negotiate with your neighbor.

If your city does not have a view ordinance, you can still ask a court to have the offending fence or tree removed if you can show that, by erecting or planting it, your neighbor was deliberately and maliciously trying to block your view. This type of behavior would fall under the category of "spite fences," which are discussed in the next section.

Fences

Q. What constitutes a fence?

A. The word **fence** does not refer merely to a picket or stockade-type barrier. Fence ordinances generally cover anything that serves as an enclosure or partition, including trees or hedges. Many zoning regulations restrict the height of fences, whether they are made of cut timber or living trees.

Q. Who owns a boundary fence?

A. A fence that sits directly on the property line of two neighbors is known as a **boundary fence.** With a boundary fence, the legal rights and responsibilities of the parties depend on a number of factors, including who "uses" the fence. Generally, boundary fences are somewhat like trees that straddle a property line: they belong to both property owners, both are responsible for the upkeep of the fence, and neither may remove or alter it without the other's permission. Of course, the owners are free to agree otherwise. One may wish to "buy" the fence from the other and have it recorded in the deed for posterity. Or one

neighbor may be willing to give up his or her "share" of the fence if the other agrees to pay for the maintenance.

Q. What can I do about a "spite fence"?

A. A **spite fence** is a fence that is excessively high, has no reasonable use, and was clearly constructed to annoy you. For example, suppose you live atop a canyon, and enjoy a beautiful view of the landscape below. You've been feuding with your neighbors, who live further down the slope. The neighbors suddenly erect a twenty-foot-high stockade fence near the

> ▶ **MEDIATION**
>
> **Mediators** are trained to listen to both sides in a dispute, identify problems, and suggest compromises and equitable solutions. They provide an impartial and unbiased forum in which neighbors can talk. The key to mediation, unlike a lawsuit, is that it's not an adversarial process. No judge makes a decision for either party. The parties are more likely to comply with the agreement, since both have consented to it. Be sure not to confuse mediation with arbitration, which is a similarly important proceeding and may, under certain circumstances, be as binding as a court order. Chapter 1, "When and How to Use a Lawyer," and Chapter 2, "How the Legal System Works," provide information on how to find a dispute resolution service.

property line. Unless your neighbors can demonstrate a reasonable need for such a high fence, such as extra privacy concerns, you can sue them under the doctrine of private nuisance. The case may be difficult to win, however, because most fences or other structures have some arguable utility to the owner.

Depending on the law of your state, your remedies may include an **injunction** (court order) to have the fence removed (or at least lowered to a less offensive height) or **compensatory damages** (a financial payment to you). Factors the court will consider to determine compensation include the diminished value of your property and any annoyance caused by the erection and maintenance of the fence.

REMEMBER THIS

- If you have a dispute with a neighbor, start by trying to work it out informally, then move to putting your request in writing. Suggest mediation if needed, and bring in the authorities as a last resort.

- Your town or city may have zoning, noise, or other ordinances that address the problem. Referring to the ordinance may give you some leverage with your neighbor.

- Trees, hedges, and fences that follow the property line belong to the neighbors on both sides, and both neighbors should share maintenance responsibilities.

- You may trim branches from your neighbor's tree that hang over your property, but it's best to talk with the neighbor about it first. The fruit of the tree belongs to the owner of the tree, whether it's good to eat or rotting in your grass.

REMODELING

The urge to improve your home is about as irresistible as the urge to improve your spouse. But home improvement is better protected by law—not to mention more likely to succeed! The protections provided by the law are a good thing, given the number of things that could go wrong—from a contractor who takes your deposit, tears off your roof, and gets too busy with other jobs to make further progress, to a kitchen remodeler who brings in subcontractors to do the work, then takes your check and skips town without paying them.

This section explains your legal rights during the remodeling process, provides information about the contracts governing your project, and tells you what to do if something goes wrong.

Legal Protections

Q. Which federal laws are applicable to remodeling projects?

A. For one thing, Federal Trade Commission (FTC) rules address the problem of false advertising. It's illegal for a vendor to advertise any product or service for less than it really costs, or to engage in the old **bait-and-switch** tactic. This happens when you are baited by an ad for a product or service, then told it isn't available and persuaded to switch to another, more-expensive version. The law requires vendors to offer a rain check whenever demand for an advertised bargain exceeds supply, unless the limited supply is clearly stated in the ad.

The federal Truth in Lending Act protects consumers who obtain financing for their projects. Whether you finance your home improvement through a bank, a credit union, or the contractor, the lender must prominently state the **annual percentage rate** of interest and the loan costs you will be charged.

Note that even if the terms appear reasonable, it can be a bad idea to have the contractor secure financing for your project, and in some cases it may also be illegal. If you qualify for a loan from a bank, take it; if you don't qualify, then you should think carefully about whether you can really afford to remodel.

These laws help keep most contractors honest, but they can't keep all the bad apples off the streets. Even if you report violations to the FTC, it is not likely to prosecute a small contractor. Federal enforcement tends to concentrate on major violations or patterns.

Q. What protection do I have once I sign a contract?

A. Your best federal protection may be the cooling-off period (known as the **right of rescission**) mandated by the Truth in Lending Act. Specifically, the law gives you three business days to cancel any contract that was signed in your home (or any location other than the seller's place of business) that involves any financial claim to your home—for example, a contract giving a contractor the right to file a lien against your home to enforce payment. This law also applies to any contract that involves the borrower making four or more payments—for example, if a contractor finances a project by using your home as collateral for a second mortgage.

If circumstances entitle you to a cooling-off period, the contractor must give you two copies of the Notice of Right of Rescission at the time you sign the contract. It must be sep-

arate from the contract—not buried in fine print—and a copy must be given to each owner, because any one owner may cancel. The notice must identify the transaction, disclose the security interest, inform you of your right to rescind, tell you how to exercise that right, and provide the date on which the rescission period expires.

Q. What kind of state and local laws apply to contractors?

A. State laws often are modeled after federal laws, and state and local agencies are much more apt than federal agencies to pursue a small contractor who has violated the law. If you suspect that a contractor is breaking the law, get in touch with your state attorney general's office, the contractor licensing authority in your state, or the local department of consumer affairs.

For information about legal protections and enforcement options in your state, contact your state or local consumer protection agency or the consumer fraud division of the local prosecutor's office.

Q. What's the best way to guard against swindlers?

A. Despite all the statutes, if you have to rely on the law to get your money back from a shoddy contractor, you will have to wait a long time (and may not get anything in the end, as contractors like this are frequently judgment proof). The best idea is not to engage contractors in the first place without a careful check of their reputation ahead of time. Be wary of contractors who

- Claim to work for a government agency. Always investigate these types of claims for yourself.

- Engage in door-to-door sales or try to attract your business through telephone solicitations. Be especially wary if the sales pitch demands an immediate decision—e.g., if you're urged to take advantage of prices that won't be available tomorrow. Most reputable contractors don't engage in such tactics.
- Offer an unsolicited free inspection of your furnace or basement. Many rip-off artists use this ruse to gain access to a home, and then either fake a problem or damage a sound furnace and good pipes.
- Claim your house is dangerous and needs immediate repair—unless you already know these things to be true.
- Have a company name, address, telephone number, or other credentials that can't be verified. Fly-by-night operators often use a post office box and answering service when hunting for victims.
- Leave delivery and installation costs out of their estimates.
- Offer to give you a rebate or referral fee for referring any of your friends.
- Insist on starting work before you sign a contract.

Chapter 12, "Contracts," provides additional information on contractor scams about which you should remain alert.

Hiring a Contractor

Q. How do I find a reputable contractor?

A. After determining what you want and what you can afford, ask for recommendations from people who have had similar work done, and talk to building inspectors, bankers, and trade association representatives—people who should know firsthand the work and reputation of contractors in your community.

For a large job, interview and solicit bids from two or three contractors from your list—but in order to facilitate sound comparisons, make sure they are bidding on exactly the same job. The lowest bid is not necessarily the best, because a contractor with a reputation for excellent workmanship (and for standing behind the work) might charge more. Even if the job is small enough to warrant only one bid, take time to check out your contractor's reputation and credentials.

▶ **CHECKLIST: SPEAKING WITH A FORMER CLIENT OF A POTENTIAL CONTRACTOR**

- Ask exactly what work the contractor performed. How did this person find out about the contractor?
- Jot down any other names that are mentioned, along with addresses and telephone numbers.
- Was the client comfortable with the way things were left at the end of each day? At the end of the project?
- What does the former client wish they had done differently to make the job go even more smoothly?
- What did the client's spouse (or roommate, neighbors, or children) think about the work and the construction process?
- Would this person hire the contractor to do another job? If so, what type of job?

If you select a contractor based on references, make sure those references have had work done that's similar to yours—for a kitchen remodeling, look for referrals from former clients who have also had their kitchens done, and so on. And don't just ask for references—actually call them. Most people won't mind chatting with you about their job. Chances are any such references provided by the contractor will be happy clients, so try to obtain a more detailed referral than simply "He's a great guy!" or "No problems at all!"

Q. What kinds of certification should the contractor provide?

A. If you are satisfied with a contractor's reputation, check his or her credentials before signing the contract. Find out if the contractor is licensed and bonded. Although not all states require licensing for home contractors, those that do keep records of each contractor's name and address, compliance with insurance laws, and agreement to operate within the law. If the company is a corporation, the state will have a record of the individual who is responsible. While some states only require contractors to register their names and addresses, quite a few require them to have some experience and pass an exam.

A state license doesn't ensure that the contractor will do a good job, but it's an indication that he or she has made an effort to comply with the law. Check with the state contractors licensing board to see if the license is current. Some states will also tell you if there have been complaints against a given contractor, and whether they proved to be valid. Otherwise, you can obtain this information from the local office of the Better Business Bureau or the office of consumer affairs.

Q. Are bonds important?

A. Dealing with a contractor who's bonded provides you with important protections. Be aware that there are two kinds of bonds involved in construction. The phrase **fully insured and bonded** generally means that the contractor's insurance coverage protects against employee theft, vandalism, or negligence. Especially if you have valuables to consider, ask to see a certificate or letter certifying such a policy.

The other kind of bond is a **performance bond,** which is an insurance company's assurance that the contractor can finish the job as stated in the contract. If the contractor defaults, the insurance company will pay another contractor to complete the work. Contractors must take out a separate bond for each job, so bonds are usually limited to jobs of $25,000 or more, and contractors pass on the cost to the owner. It is an expensive proposition, but a contractor who has been approved by a bonding company is a very good risk. You're the one who decides whether to require (and pay for) a bond.

Be aware that in some areas it is so expensive and difficult for contractors to purchase a performance bond that it may be impossible to find a contractor who has one.

Q. What else should I ask about?

A. Ask your contractor the following:

- Whether he or she carries workers' compensation insurance, to cover injuries that workers might sustain on the job. Your homeowner's insurance probably doesn't cover workers' compensation, so if the contractor doesn't carry it, you could be responsible for some hefty bills. In addition, the contractor should carry a builder's risk policy to cover any damage caused during construction.

- Whether he or she belongs to a trade association. Many associations require a contractor to have been in business a certain length of time, to have passed a credit check, and to meet all state legal requirements. It wouldn't hurt to call the association to make sure the contractor's membership is current and to inquire about complaints.

- Whether the contractor offers a warranty on work and materials. If so, what is the time limit on the warranty? Make sure any warranty is included in the contract. (Even if there is no specific warranty, most jurisdictions recognize an implied warranty of good workmanship that provides you with some protection.) For an additional fee, some contractors offer an

extended warranty. Some states have statutory warranties in addition to the contractual ones.

- Whether or not any civil judgments or lawsuits are pending against the contractor. (This information can also be obtained by contacting the local clerk of court.) If someone sued the contractor over something like poor workmanship, consider it a warning. Likewise, you might want to check with the nearest federal bankruptcy court to see whether the contractor has recently filed for bankruptcy—a possible indication of financial instability.

Q. What should the contract include?

A. A home improvement contract should address several specific issues, outlined below. This list contains things you may not require in every contract. For example, if your home is a hundred feet away from the nearest neighbors, then a contract for your kitchen remodeling probably won't require an anti-noise provision.

- **Preamble.** A preamble is an introduction that states the parties' names, addresses, and phone numbers, and the date the contract is executed. It should specify whether the contractor's business is a sole proprietorship, a partnership, or a corporation. (If it is a partnership or a corporation, make sure the person who signs is an authorized representative.) The preamble should also state that the remodeler is an independent contractor, not your employee. Otherwise, you might be responsible if the builder injures someone. You should also add the contractor's Federal Employer Identification Number. The contract price should state the total dollar amount, including sales tax, to be paid by

---

▶ THE IMPORTANCE OF A WRITTEN CONTRACT

Don't allow any work to begin until there is a signed contract. (Some people might take a chance on very small jobs, but this is definitely a risk.) Oral agreements can be enforced in court, but it is difficult to prove who said what if you don't get it down on paper. If the contractor gives you a standard contract to sign, take it home and study it carefully. Strike out unreasonable clauses and have both parties initial the changes. If you are uncertain about the meaning of provisions, and/or if it is a large or expensive job, make sure your lawyer reviews the contract.

the homeowner for services agreed to in the contract.

- **Starting and completion dates.** No contractor is likely to begin until after your right to rescission has safely passed. Specify an end date, stating exceptions for contingencies such as weather and strikes. You may want to add a bonus-penalty clause if the date is critical. If it's important to you, specify a daily starting time. Consider interim completion dates for key phases of big jobs.

- **Scope of work.** Contractors may shy away from broad clauses—for example, a clause stating that the contractor will provide "all labor, materials, and services necessary to complete the project." But when listing the tasks to be completed and the materials to be used, be wary of being so specific that anything not mentioned in the contract will be considered an "extra" or a "change order," and thus billed separately.

- **Description of materials.** See that complete descriptions of agreed-to products are listed, including brand names and order numbers. Plans and specifications, bids, estimates, and all other documents relating to the project are part of the scope of work. Make sure that copies of these are attached to all copies of the contract before you sign it.

- **Permits, licenses, and zoning.** Specify that the contractor will obtain all necessary licenses and permits and satisfy all zoning regulations and building codes, and indemnify the homeowner in case the contractor fails to do so.

- **Cleanup policy.** Will the contractor clean up daily? After each subproject? Only at the end? Where is refuse to be placed?

- **Storage.** Specify where materials and equipment will be kept. You are probably liable for damage to materials and equipment from fire or accidents, so be sure to check your homeowner's policy and make sure these are covered.

- **Parking.** If parking is a problem, the contract should deal with arrangements for the contractor's and subcontractors' vehicles.

- **Noise.** Some noise is inevitable during a remodeling project, but place limits on time and volume, according to local laws and neighborhood needs. You may wish to set specific times when work may begin and when it must end each day.

- **Theft.** Building materials are often stolen. The contract can make either the contractor or the owner responsible for any theft.

- **Damage.** What if a retaining wall collapses when the workers are digging the swimming pool? You'll want the contract to state that the contractor is responsible for damage to your property. If the contractor or a subcontractor will be doing any blasting to remove something from your property, the contract should state that the contractor is also responsible for damage to your neighbor's property.

- **Change orders.** Very few jobs go exactly as planned, which requires that the contract allow for simple and easy amendments. The contract should provide that change orders can be written up, signed by both parties, and attached to the contract as plans change or delays occur. See the sample below for specific wording of this contract clause.

- **Warranties.** The contract should assure that the materials are new, and that you will receive all warranties from manufacturers for appliances and other materials used on the job.

- **Progress payments.** Contractors don't expect to be paid entirely in advance, but they also don't expect to wait until the work is complete. It is customary to pay one-third upon signing a contract, to allow the contractor to buy supplies and get started. In smaller projects, two payments may suffice. In larger ones, plan to make payments after completion and approval of all major phases of the work. In all cases, make your final payment as large as possible, usually at least 10 percent, payable only after the entire job is completed.

- **Financing contingency.** If your ability to proceed with the project depends on securing outside financing, include a contingency clause stating that the contract is not binding if you are unable to secure the needed funds on acceptable terms.

- **Suppliers and subcontractors.** Ask for a list of subcontractors and suppliers and attach it to the contract with their addresses, telephone numbers, and Social Security numbers. Although you are not their boss, they probably have a right to place a lien on your home if the contractor does not pay them in full. It's only fair that you know who they are, should legal action become necessary. If you prefer, arrange to pay suppliers and subcontractors directly.

- **Lawyer's fees.** You should also consider including a provision in the contract stating that if the contractor breaches (violates) the terms of the contract, you are entitled to recover a reasonable lawyer's fee, in addition to damages. In many states, unless the contract contains such a provision, you will be unable to recover your legal fees from the contractor even if you win in court.

Troubleshooting the Project

Q. Who should obtain building permits, and when should they do it?

A. To find out whether building permits are needed, contact your local building department. Some municipalities require permits for just about anything; others require them only for major projects. The person who takes out the permit is considered liable for the work, so follow the usual custom of having the architect or the contractor obtain the permit. As a homeowner, you don't want to be responsible if the work isn't up to code, but you should know which permits are required and make sure they are obtained.

Q. What's the point of getting a permit, besides giving the town money?

A. First of all, the point is to abide by the law. Second, the inspector who checks your

---

▶ **CHANGE-ORDER CLAUSE**

The following wording can be used for a change-order clause in a contract:

Without invalidating this contract, the owner may order changes in the work, including additions, modifications, or deletions. Price and time will be adjusted accordingly. All such changes in the work shall be in writing, and signed by the contractor and owner and attached to this document.

house can assure you that you are paying for safe work. For example, altered fire-escape routes, often caused by a door or a doorway that was renovated without permit and inspection, can be dangerous; plumbing and electrical inspectors can ensure that the work is done according to code.

Also, if you have followed proper procedures, your house will be free of encumbrances when you want to sell it.

If you live in a condominium or a cooperative apartment, or in other common-interest property, your rights to renovate and remodel differ from those of single-family homeowners. Check your condominium declaration or your board to see if your renovation will be permitted.

Q. What should I watch out for when the job begins?

A. Be sure to keep a handle on the documents that can help you avoid problems later. In consultation with your contractor, draw up a schedule of what will be done when, and make sure it is followed. For example, if you don't have the wiring inspected before the drywall goes up, the inspector may require you to tear out the drywall.

Contractors report that their biggest problems with homeowners arise because owners request additional work along the way, and then object when they see the bill. The best way to avoid misunderstanding is with a specific written **change order,** as discussed on page 321.

Remember that if you want to make a change in what a subcontractor does, you should not ask the subcontractor directly to make the change. Your contract is with the contractor.

Q. What happens if someone is hurt on the job?

A. If you are dealing with an independent contractor, his or her insurance should cover expenses. But if you hired someone from down the street to paint your house, someone who doesn't maintain a separate business and who relied on you for tools and supervision, then that person is your employee, and any injuries he or she might suffer are your responsibility.

Q. What if someone is hurt after a job is completed because the work was done incorrectly?

A. If someone gets hurt later because a job was not performed correctly—for example, because the new basement steps were not nailed down properly—then your insurance company may pay the injured party, and then go after the responsible contractor.

Q. What can I do if the contractor violates the contract?

A. If you believe there has been a contract violation, first bring the matter to the attention of the contractor. To protect yourself, make a note of the conversation, summarizing your concerns and any agreements, and send it to the contractor. Keep a copy for yourself. Next, if the contractor doesn't remedy the problem within a reasonable time, ask your lawyer to write a letter.

If that doesn't work, check to see if your contract provides for **alternative dispute resolution (ADR)**—that is, mediation or arbitration. This would allow you and the contractor to call in a mutually acceptable third party to resolve the dispute without going to court. If your contract does not specify ADR, your initial letter and the lawyer's letter will provide a basis for a lawsuit, possibly in small-claims court, or for further action with a consumer protection agency.

Either way, your options are to push for **specific performance** (i.e., forcing the remodeler to do the work as agreed), or to have the remodeler pay any extra costs you incur by having someone else correct or complete the work.

Q. My contract mentions the possibility of a mechanic's lien if I don't pay. What does this mean?

A. A **mechanic's lien** is a claim created by law in order to secure payment for work performed or materials furnished in construction. A mechanic's lien is subordinate to any prior mortgage on your house, but the contractor may use it to enforce payment by threatening a foreclosure on your house. In some states, contractors and subcontractors must notify a homeowner if they intend to take out a lien. In others, you may only learn about the lien after it is filed at the local recording office. If you find out someone has filed a lien, call your lawyer immediately.

Q. How can I prevent a mechanic's lien from being filed?

A. It is possible to add a clause to the contract in which the contractor gives up his or her lien rights, but the contractor may not agree to such a clause, and in some states such a clause may not be valid. Moreover, even with a contractor's waiver, any subcontractor or supplier who is not paid by your contractor can file a lien against your home. Unless your job is covered by a performance bond, or your state has some sort of fund to protect homeowners from paying twice when

> ▶ **WHEN THE JOB IS DONE**
>
> Do not make final payment until:
> - all work is completed, inspected, and approved;
> - subcontractors are paid;
> - any liens are canceled; and
> - warranties are in the proper hands.

the contractor doesn't pay subcontractors or laborers, your chief protection against a lien is withholding final payment until all work has been properly completed to your satisfaction, and until your contractor supplies proof in writing that everyone who worked on your job has been paid. A release-of-lien form is useful because it provides places for all the subcontractors to sign. (This is one reason to have all subcontractors and suppliers named up front in your contract, so you can make sure everyone has signed off on the release-of-lien form.)

REMEMBER THIS

- The law protects homeowners from unscrupulous contractors. You have a right of rescission, which means you have three business days to cancel any contract signed in your home (or in any other location besides the contractor's place of business).
- Carefully check the reputation of contractors before they start repairing or remodeling your home.
- Make sure you have a complete written contract before work begins.

- Make sure all needed permits and inspections have been obtained.

- Don't make the final payment until you're sure the work is finished, all subcontractors have been paid, any liens are canceled, and you have any warranties in hand.

SHARED OWNERSHIP: CO-OPS AND CONDOMINIUMS

Common-interest communities, co-ops, condos, and clusters of town homes can all provide residents with some amazing benefits: living in a beautiful neighborhood without the yard work; access to tennis courts and swimming pools; and owning rather than renting. However, the thing that makes these types of property so enjoyable can also be one of their biggest drawbacks: strict restrictions on what owners can do with their property. The reason a spacious planned-unit development is such an attractive place to live is that community regulators prohibit certain behaviors—say, painting your house purple, or blasting a stereo from the window. But these restrictions also cause more tension and litigation than any other aspect of common-interest community living.

This section explains the various forms of common-interest communities, how they're governed, and the role played by their associations.

Q. What is a common-interest community?

A. **Common-interest communities** come in a variety of configurations, with a confusing array of names and forms of ownership. However, all share certain characteristics. They

are designed specifically for a certain type of community living by a single developer—or, in the case of existing buildings, by a single converter. They are created by a specific set of documents, usually drawn up by the developer and subject to change by the membership. And when the developer or converter departs, the community's affairs are governed by an association of all unit owners through its elected board.

The board has the authority to enforce restrictions and collect assessments to pay for maintenance and improvements. This is the essential characteristic of a common-interest community: the obligation to pay for the insurance, maintenance taxes, and upkeep of property other than one's individually owned portion of the community. It is a financial relationship, and most of the relevant laws in this area regulate that relationship.

Some communities are subject to covenants for architectural control. Others restrict the use of open space, but without the obligation to contribute money. Strictly speaking, these are not common-interest communities.

Q. What are the basic types of common-interest community?

A. Because state laws differ, the terminology can be confusing. But generally speaking, there are three distinct types of common-interest communities with three distinct types of ownership: the cooperative, the condominium, and the planned community or planned-unit development (PUD). You can't tell which is which by looking at the architectural form of the buildings. For example, in some states, "site condominiums" look just like single-family detached homes, but the land—not the home—is part of the condominium. However, the form of ownership has significant legal implications. Be sure you understand the type of ownership that is specified in your community's declaration.

Q. What's the difference between a cooperative and a condominium?

A. In a **cooperative,** the members are stockholders in a corporation that owns the entire building, including the residential units and all common elements such as corridors, elevators, and tennis courts. Stockholders don't actually own any real estate; the corporation owns it all, and stockholders lease their individual units from the corporation. Each stockholder pays a monthly maintenance charge, which is a proportionate share of the corporation's cash requirements for mortgage payments, operation, maintenance, repairs, taxes, and reserves. The corporation, governed by an elected board of directors, may veto a proposed transfer of stock with its lease, so it has considerable control over potential buyers.

Condominium ownership provides you exclusive title to your own unit, from the interior walls in, and ownership of an individual interest in the common elements of the condominium. With limitations, you are free to mortgage your unit or sell it. As in a cooperative, all unit owners must pay their share of the assessment for operation, maintenance, repairs, and reserves. The association is responsible for enforcing the rules and managing the common elements, but it doesn't actually own anything.

Q. How does a planned community work?

A. A **planned community** (or **planned-unit development**) is a hybrid subdivision combining certain aspects of cooperatives and condominiums. In these developments, each owner holds title to a unit—in many cases, a single-family, detached house. But all common areas, such as parks and playgrounds, belong to the incorporated homeowners' association, which all owners are required to join. The association is responsible for maintaining common areas and, in some cases, house exteriors. Homeowners pay a periodic assessment for common area expenses and reserves.

Some planned communities include condominiums or cooperatives. Others include commercial or even industrial areas, designed so people can live within walking distance of stores and work. Furthermore, several adjoining associations may belong to a **master association,** which charges an additional assessment for certain community-wide services. The master association may also be known as an **umbrella association,** a **master planned community,** or a **mixed-use association.**

Q. What kinds of restrictions can be imposed in common-interest communities?

A. The extent of restrictions varies. In a planned community of freestanding houses, rules may be limited to preserving the quality and cohesiveness of the development—for example, by requiring approval of any architectural or other exterior changes. Condominiums and cooperatives tend to have much more extensive rules and regulations, because generally people are living much closer together and often in the same building.

Mid-rise and high-rise condominiums rely on the concept of the airspace block. The title to a single-family house or town house often includes the land underneath it and the air above it, but if you own a high-rise apartment, there are other owners above and below. So you hold title, in effect, to a block of airspace—within four walls, a ceiling, and a floor.

Within that airspace block, you may alter or remove nonsupporting walls, replace the light fixtures, change the carpet however you wish, and make other changes that don't infringe on your neighbors' property rights. On the other hand, you are responsible for the maintenance and repair of paint, wallpaper, fixtures, and appliances, except for wires and pipes running through your walls that serve other units. Sometimes people accustomed to rental apartments are surprised to learn that their condominium building manager isn't responsible for fixing their hot-water heater or a blocked toilet.

Legal Rights and Restrictions

Q. What federal laws apply to common-interest communities?

A. Few federal laws directly affect the organization and operation of common-interest communities. However, under the Fair Housing Amendments Act, developments cannot discriminate against families with children, unless the development meets strict qualifications for senior-citizen developments. Otherwise, it is illegal to advertise a development as being "adults only," or to steer would-be buyers elsewhere because their children wouldn't be welcome.

The Fair Housing Amendments Act also prohibits discrimination against disabled persons. Developments must permit construction of facilities for disabled residents, although a disabled resident may be required to remove the construction upon leaving. Furthermore, all new multifamily buildings must provide access for the disabled in every unit on the ground floor, or provide access by elevator. Under HUD regulations, this includes wide doors, free passage for wheelchairs through units, bathroom walls strong enough for grab bars, and access to at least a representative portion of amenities.

The Federal Communications Commission requires that unit owners in common-interest communities be able to place certain forms of dish antennae (not exceeding one meter in diameter) on privately allocated spaces in common-interest communities without restriction.

Q. How do state laws apply to common-interest communities?

A. Most of the substantive law—and most of the confusion surrounding this topic—springs from an ever-changing patchwork of state statutes. The governance of cooperatives falls under state statutes governing corporations and nonprofit corporations. The same corporation statutes apply to associations governing planned communities.

In most states, condominiums don't have a corporation responsible for liabilities, taxes, and governance. That is why each state has a special set of laws detailing how condominiums must be organized and operated. These laws require each condominium to file a declaration and bylaws, with specific requirements regarding the rights and duties of the association. (In states where condominium associations are incorporated, the association must file articles of incorporation.) Planned communities require no specific statute, but some states include them in a law governing all common-interest communities.

Condominium statutes vary considerably by state, and many lack protections for consumers. While some states provide only the barest framework for creating a condominium, others are incredibly complex and detailed.

Q. What else governs a common-interest community?

A. In addition to federal and state laws, each individual community is governed by its own declaration and articles of incorporation, a set of bylaws, and various rules, regulations, and decisions promulgated by the association board.

A community association gains its authority from the legal documents that created it: the declaration, articles of incorporation, and bylaws. State statutes often back up that authority, whether in the statutes governing

---

▶ THE UNIFORM CONDOMINIUM ACT

In the hopes of bringing some uniformity to the law, the National Conference of Commissioners on Uniform State Laws has proposed model laws in this subject area. Fifteen states have adopted or adapted these laws, and numerous others are considering doing so. The Uniform Condominium Act (UCA) allows flexibility for developers while offering protection to consumers, such as requiring extensive disclosure before sale. It covers such matters as insurance, tort, and contract liability. The Uniform Common Interest Ownership Act (UCIOA) extends the same provisions to cooperatives and planned communities. So far, only a handful of states have adopted the UCIOA.

---

nonprofit corporations or the specific condominium or common-interest community act, or both. Broadly speaking, a community association may hold property, sue and be sued, receive gifts and bequests, make charitable contributions, make contracts, borrow or invest money, and assess unit owners for their share of the expense of maintaining and operating the community. Some state statutes grant even more far-reaching powers.

Q. Why are there so many documents?

A. By law, each common-interest community must file a set of master regulations, plus subsidiary documents called **articles,** plus a set of bylaws. For planned communities, the master regulations are called the **covenants, conditions, and restrictions (CCRs),** or the **declaration of covenants** or **master deed.** The same document for a condominium is called a declaration of condominium, a declaration, or a master deed.

A **condominium declaration** describes the land, building, and other improvements; the location of each unit; the percentage of each person's ownership; the common elements; and the intended use of each unit. Essentially, the declaration depicts the physical arrangement of the property, including a floor plan with tax-lot numbers for the various units. But under the laws of many states, it need not contain much operational detail.

Generally, declarations may only be amended by a supermajority vote of the unit owners, often two-thirds or three-quarters. Some amendments, such as those that change unit boundaries or assessment ratios, may require an even greater majority, sometimes unanimity. Most amendment provisions also require the consent of a certain number of the mortgage lenders.

The **articles of incorporation,** called **articles of association** in non-incorporated associations, are what legally establishes the association. They include the name, address, and purpose of the association, and specify the aggregate number of shares permitted; whether cumulative voting or other special voting or assessment rights are provided; and, in general, the power of the board to make, alter, and repeal reasonable bylaws.

Q. What do the bylaws regulate?

A. **Bylaws** dictate how the managing board will be elected and define its duties and powers. Bylaws cover such matters as whether the board will manage the property or engage a management firm; how disputes will be settled; how assessments and reserves are to be determined; what restrictions apply to the lease and sale of units; and to what extent board decisions bind unit owners. Basically, bylaws govern the internal operating standards of the community. In some older statutes, the bylaws may also include restrictions on use and insurance provisions.

Although bylaws in most corporations may be altered freely by the board or by a simple majority of the members, many condominium statutes require a two-thirds or even three-quarters majority in order to change them. States that have adopted the Uniform Condominium Act allow a bit more flexibility, to reduce the chance that a condominium will be unable to adapt to changing conditions.

The Board of Directors

Q. How is the board of directors established?

A. The board of directors or managers is elected by the membership to carry out day-to-day operations and oversee enforcement of the rules. A typical board has five to seven members who are elected on a rotating basis.

▶ CHALLENGING ASSOCIATION RULES

In the course of operating the association, boards periodically enact other rules and regulations regarding the details of community life, such as how parking spaces are allocated. These are subject to judicial review if a unit owner believes that the board overstepped its authority. In reviewing regulations, courts tend to consider four questions:

1 Is the rule consistent with the declaration and other superior documents?

2 Was the rule adopted in a good-faith effort to serve a purpose of the community?

3 Are the means adopted to serve the purpose reasonable?

4 Is the rule consistent with public policy?

If a court answers one of these questions with a "no," it might set aside the rule. In general, however, members are prevented from second-guessing board decisions by the **better judgment rule,** which states that if the decision was arrived at honestly and with no fraudulent intent, the board's decision will be upheld even if reasonable persons may disagree with it. This rule has also been called the "pure-heart-by-weak-mind" rule.

The board in turn elects officers, such as a chairman or president, a secretary, and a treasurer.

Q. What is the role of the board of directors?

A. Typically, the board has broad powers under state law. The board may raise or lower assessments and impose special assessments to cover specific repairs or improvements. It also may insist that unit owners obey the policies of the association.

Many associations grant the board of directors a right of first refusal to buy or lease a unit on behalf of the association. Generally, before agreeing to sell a unit, the owner must first offer to sell the unit to the board at a price that matches the good-faith price offered by an outside purchaser. Although this power is mostly used to keep out undesirable buyers, it can also be used to acquire a management office or superintendent's apartment. Some cooperatives require the right to approve any purchaser before a sale can be consummated.

Q. How does the board enforce the association's rules?

A. When a unit owner ignores the rules, the board may fine the owner. If the fines pile up and the owner refuses to pay, the board can exercise its right to enforce its lien against the owner's unit and, if necessary, foreclose on it. Some declarations permit the suspension of unit owner privileges—such as the right to use recreational facilities, or even the right to vote—while an assessment remains unpaid or another covenant remains in breach. Another approach is for the association to sue the violator, seeking an injunctive order to stop the practice in question. A violator who refuses to follow the court order could be found in contempt of court.

The uniform acts and many other statutes require that the unit owner who is alleged to have breached a covenant receive a notice and the right to a hearing before fines or other sanctions may be levied.

In theory, any unit owner may sign a complaint against another to initiate this process. In practice, though, most unit owners are hesitant to sign formal complaints against neighbors, even if they voice their concerns loudly to the board. If the community hires a management company—a standard practice in larger communities—then the company's routine maintenance inspections will include checking for violations of the rules. The employee who discovers the infraction will then serve as a complaining witness to the board, at which time it is likely that someone will be sent to speak with the alleged violator. Most board members try to be evenhanded in their enforcement, because they don't want to be criticized for punishing one violator and showing leniency towards another.

If the board decides to resort to the courts, it must do so promptly or risk losing the authority to enforce the rule. For example, if the rules say you cannot build a tool shed and you do it anyway, board members cannot ignore the shed for years and then one day sue to have you remove it.

Q. How does the board handle assessments?

A. One of the most onerous tasks of an association board is raising the monthly assessment that pays for maintenance and various services, from trash collection to snow removal. Some state statutes mandate certain levels of reserves to guard the community's financial stability and prepare for inevitable capital expenditures. Even without a mandate, a board is wise to build up a substantial reserve to avoid having to require a massive special assessment when the furnace needs to be replaced.

Some states require an association to get membership approval before raising assessments above a set limit, such as 15 or 20 percent. Many condominium declarations set similar dollar caps on increases in assessments without owner approval.

Q. What can the board do if I can't pay the assessment?

A. When unit owners are doing well, they may grouse about an assessment, but chances are they'll pay it. But what if a unit owner is in serious financial trouble, with several thousand dollars worth of assessments unpaid? If the owner goes bankrupt, creditors will line up for their share of what's left—and the community association will normally be somewhere far down the line. If the association can't obtain payment of the bankrupt owner's assessment, all the other property owners in the community will have to cover it.

One provision of the Uniform Common Interest Ownership Act, in effect in several states, gives community associations a super-priority lien, putting them first in line ahead of mortgage lenders for the bankrupt unit owner's share of the past six months' assessments.

Q. What can I do if the board isn't doing its job?

A. Most problems arise when a board neglects or abuses its duty to enforce the rules, or misuses the funds entrusted to it. If you suspect financial problems, you are entitled to review the association's financial documents, including its budget, financial report, bank loan documents, and record of reserves. Together with other concerned unit owners, you may hire an

independent accountant to conduct an audit, even if the board refuses to do so.

If you believe the board has become autocratic and tyrannical, review the minutes of the board meetings to see whether decisions were made in accordance with the association's bylaws, rules, and regulations. If not, some of the board's actions may be void.

When the board has seriously mismanaged its responsibilities, you have two basic options. The first and best option is to run for a position on the board yourself, and convince some suitably qualified neighbors to do the same. If the board has clearly exceeded its authority (or even undertaken activities with which a majority of the unit owners disagree), then the unit owners, by petition, may order a recall of some or all of the board members, by means of an election in which new board members can be elected. Another option, which should only be undertaken with great care, is to litigate the issue. Be aware, though, that the board has a right to assess unit owners to pay for its own defense, so you may have to pay for the legal representation of both sides—your own side and that of your opponent. Under the uniform acts, the loser will also have to pay the winner's fees. And remember that the business judgment rule, described earlier, will likely protect the decision of the board as long as it has been made in good faith. Arbitration or mediation may be a less costly approach. In fact, your bylaws might require it.

Handling Problems

Q. Can an owner obtain a variance from the association rules?

A. Under the rules of most community associations, you cannot make changes to the exterior of your home without the consent of the board. Normally, the board delegates the review of plans to an architectural control committee, which sets standards. As a homeowner requesting a variance, submit your plans to the committee and cross your fingers. Be aware, though, that many courts have denied covenant committees the authority to approve major violations of the restrictive covenants.

If the board denies your request, you will either have to change your plans or steel yourself for what may become a major battle.

Q. What can I do if my neighbor is creating a problem?

A. The first step is to check the association bylaws and regulations to see whether your neighbor is violating a rule. Then talk about it, first to the neighbor posing the problem and then to a member of the board, which will often act as an informal mediator.

If the neighbor is clearly violating the rules, the board may ask you to sign a formal complaint. This will begin a proceeding that could lead to fines against your neighbor, or even a court injunction to stop the behavior. If the problem isn't addressed in the bylaws and regulations and a polite request doesn't help, one option is to try alternative dispute resolution. Again, it is important to act promptly if a neighbor's behavior makes life unpleasant for you. If you've put up with the behavior for a long time, you may have trouble making your case.

Q. What can you do if the community has too many rental tenants?

A. Owner-occupants often object to renters, who are perceived as not caring about the property. Likewise, absentee owners generally want to keep up the rental value of a property, but don't want to pay for extras. And although restrictions apply to tenants as well as to owner-occupants, they are often more difficult to enforce.

If the board slaps a lien on a unit owner because of a rental tenant's behavior, the owner may terminate the tenant. If a majority of unit owners object to the number of renters, they may be able to band together and convince the board to change the bylaws to restrict leases.

Q. What can I do if I have a problem with the developer of a condominium?

A. In an increasing number of cases, condominium associations have sued their developers over shoddy construction, breach of contract, negligence, or fraud. These lawsuits are complex, time-consuming, and expensive. But the law expects a developer who cuts corners on construction or breaks promises to the unit owners to make up for the damage.

If yours is the only unit involved, it's up to you to hire a lawyer and try to settle the matter out of court, if possible. But if the problem involves common areas or common funds, the association may assess all unit owners to pay its legal fees in pursuing the developer. In some cases, the developer may agree to arbitration to save the time and expense of a lawsuit. But the important thing is to act quickly, because the longer you wait, the harder it is to find witnesses or collect a judgment. Many states allow only a limited amount of time, sometimes as little as one to three years, for bringing a lawsuit against a developer for breach of its warranties.

Association Insurance

Q. What kind of insurance does my association need to have?

A. This depends on the type of common-interest community. Condominium associations typically carry several insurance policies to cover damage to building exteriors and common elements, as well as liability for injuries on the premises.

- **Common-interest communities with attached dwellings or dwellings within a single building.** Most lenders and enabling statutes require a single policy of property insurance covering the entire building or attached-unit project. This policy should not name the unit owners as the insured party, but should name the association or a trustee as insured for the benefit of unit owners and their mortgage lenders.

  In such a community, you would only have to purchase property insurance on your unit's interior and contents. Your unit owner's insurance should also include a small amount, from $1,000 to $2,500, to cover uninsured losses to the overall community. This coverage may pick up your share of large deductibles in the community association insurance, or it may cover losses that are not covered by the association's insurance.

  In an attached-unit project, liability insurance should be maintained by the association to cover the entire project. Once again, this liability insurance should not name each unit owner individually, but should name the association as insured for the benefit of the unit owners. The association policy will cover your liability for association activities in common areas and within the community, and for association activities that occur outside of the community.

- **Common-interest communities with detached dwellings on their own lots.** Often, common insurance only covers common areas or areas that are the responsibility of the association. In these types of communities, the association insurance should cover the liability of the homeowners for the association's activities, as well as the property of the association.

Q. Does the association insurance protect the board members?

A. Associations usually carry errors-and-omissions liability policies on directors and officers, in case the board members are sued over their decisions. Many also carry an umbrella liability policy to cover catastrophic judgments.

Q. Who pays for the insurance?

A. As part of their regular assessment, unit owners pay the premiums on all association insurance.

Q. So how does my homeowner's insurance complement the association's? Do they overlap?

A. The issue of "dovetailing" between the association's policy and the unit owner's policy can be very complex, particularly in circumstances involving construction disputes or damage from the elements. Your insurance agent will need to review the condominium declaration carefully to ensure there is no gap in coverage between the policies. Your individual policy should cover your liability for injuries that occur outside the community, or that you cause on the premises that were not the responsibility of the association.

REMEMBER THIS

- Make sure you understand what type of common-interest community you live in, and which documents govern it.

- Before making changes to your unit, check the bylaws to make sure the changes are permitted.

- If a problem arises, take it to your association. If the association is the problem, work with your neighbors to elect new members.

- If you have a major problem with a developer or remodeler, see a lawyer promptly to assess your options.

THE FINANCIAL SIDE OF HOME OWNERSHIP

When you bought your home, you probably saved up for a down payment and obtained a mortgage that you'll be paying off for the next twenty years or so. But even though the business of actually buying a home may be over, you can't forget all about the dollars and cents. For the entire life of your mortgage, you'll want to keep an eye on your lender or mortgage service company to make sure you're not the victim of costly accounting errors. You'll also want to make sure that your family would have enough money to make mortgage payments if something happened to you. If interest rates are low, you may want to consider refinancing. If you run into financial problems, you'll want to know your legal rights and responsibilities, and what your lender can do to pro-

tect its interests. And when the day arrives when you finally have enough money, you'll want to know how to pay off your mortgage so you can own your home free and clear.

Understanding Your Mortgage

Q. Who owns the mortgage on my house?

A. Traditionally, banks and savings-and-loan institutions owned most residential mortgages. Today, it's much more common for the original lender to sell the mortgage to an investor, such as a mutual fund or an insurance company. This means that borrowers are usually dealing with a mortgage servicer, rather than the actual person or institution that owns the mortgage.

Q. What happens when my mortgage is transferred?

A. Most mortgages are sold soon after the loan is closed. This means that you'll probably deal with two or more mortgage servicing agents during the life of the mortgage. The mortgage servicer is responsible for collecting monthly payments and handling tasks relating to the escrow account, such as paying property taxes. The National Affordable Housing Act, which addresses the responsibilities of mortgage servicers, requires lenders to:

- Notify you at least fifteen days before the effective date of the transfer of your loan. (The servicer has up to thirty days after the transfer to notify you if you have defaulted on the loan, if the original servicer filed for bankruptcy, or if the servicer's functions are being taken over by a federal agency.)

- Include the following in the notice: the name and address of the new servicer; the date the current servicer will stop accepting mortgage payments; the date the new servicer will begin accepting payments; and a free or collect-call telephone number for both servicers, in case you have questions about the transfer.

- Adhere to the contracted terms of the mortgage. The new servicer may not change any terms, and this fact must be disclosed to the borrower. For example, if your former lender did not require that property taxes or homeowner's insurance be paid from an escrow account, the new servicer cannot demand that such an account be established.
- Provide a sixty-day grace period, during which a late fee cannot be charged if you mistakenly send your mortgage payment to your former servicer. Moreover, the new servicer cannot report late payments to a credit bureau.

Q. What can I do if I have a problem with a mortgage servicer?

A. Contact your servicer in writing. Include your account number and explain why you think there is a problem or error.

The servicer must acknowledge your inquiry in writing within twenty business days, and it has sixty business days to either correct your account or explain why it is accurate. While you're waiting, keep up with your mortgage payments, because not doing so could count as a default.

Q. I have heard that my mortgage lender went bankrupt. What should I do?

A. Recently, a number of lenders and mortgage servicers have become debtors in bankruptcy proceedings. Generally, they will continue to function as servicers for a period of time. Do not stop making payments merely

> ### ▶ IS YOUR ESCROW TOO BIG?
>
> The Real Estate Settlement Procedures Act limits the amount of money that can be held in an escrow account. The calculation is rather complex. Let's say the expenses paid by your escrow account add up to $3,600 per year, or $300 a month. The law requires that, at least once a year, the escrow account hold no more than twice the required monthly payment, or $600. The practical reason for this is that taxes are usually collected once or twice a year. Between collections, the account may have a sizable balance, but immediately after the collection it should have no more than $600.
>
> If you notice on your monthly statement that the amount in your escrow account is larger than twice your monthly payment, you have the right to question the lender. This happens more frequently than one might imagine, so take the time to figure out if your lender is adhering to escrow regulations. Otherwise, you're paying more in monthly payments than you should be.

because you are aware of such a bankruptcy. You will be notified when servicing rights have been transferred and to whom you should now send payments.

Q. What is an escrow account?

A. An **escrow account** is an account in which a lender sets aside part of your monthly mortgage payments to cover property tax, homeowner's insurance, and similar expenses.

Q. I have heard that the amount of my mortgage can impact how much value I have in my home. Is this true?

A. Sort of. What you are referring to is the concept of equity. **Equity** is the value of your unencumbered interest in your home. It's determined by subtracting the unpaid mortgage balance and any other home debts, such as a second mortgage or home equity loan, from the home's fair market value. For example, if your mortgage is $50,000 and your home is worth about $100,000, you would have $50,000 in equity, or 50 percent equity, in your home. If the value of your home has fallen, you may have less equity than when you bought the home.

Q. What can I do if falling home prices have eliminated my equity?

A. Homeowners can find themselves in this situation if they bought their homes when housing prices were soaring, and the home market later collapsed.

This is a difficult problem if you're trying to sell or refinance. If you sell, you may owe the lender more money than you receive from the sale, because the sale price is lower than the remaining mortgage. If you're trying to refinance, a lender will want to know that you have at least 20 percent equity in the home, but an appraisal may not bear this out. Don't accept the first appraisal. You may find that another appraiser will assign your home a higher value.

Unfortunately, if your equity has fallen below what you owe on your mortgage, there's little you can do. If you must sell, you'll have to take a loss on your home and perhaps pay the bank the remaining balance (in order to retain a good credit rating). If you're trying to refinance, you may be able to talk to your lender and renegotiate more favorable rates on your outstanding mortgage. The one exception is for homeowners who have FHA

▸ **CHECKLIST: WHAT TO DO WHEN YOU CAN'T PAY YOUR MORTGAGE**

Take the problem seriously. You could lose your home.

- Contact your lender as soon as possible. Call or write to explain your problem, and be sure to include your account number to speed the process.

- Ask if you can defer paying the principal for a few months, or if you can refinance the loan at a lower rate.

- If neither of the above options works, ask for time to sell the home yourself. If you're actively trying to sell your home, your lender may cooperate by reducing monthly payments.

- Contact the nearest housing counseling agency, which can offer advice and services to help you ward off foreclosure.

- Consider filing for bankruptcy, which in some states may ward off immediate foreclosure. But be sure to talk with a lawyer before beginning any bankruptcy proceeding.

and VA loans—they can apply for a special refinancing without an appraisal. (For more information, see the sidebar titled "Refinancing FHA and VA Loans" on page 340.)

Q. Is there anything I can do if I can't pay my mortgage?

A. The first thing to do if you're having trouble making your mortgage payments is to take the matter seriously. Many people refuse to face the fact that their home is on the line, and they delay doing anything until it's too late.

Lenders don't like to foreclose on property, because they may not retrieve the full amount of their loan. In most cases the homeowners would sell and repay the mortgage if they could, but they can't. Typically, the bank

---

▶ **WHAT TO DO IF YOUR HOME IS BEING FORECLOSED**

Foreclosures can happen quickly. Although traditional foreclosures involve court supervision, not all foreclosures require court orders. Depending on your state and the original terms of your loan, a foreclosure can be completed in as little as forty-five days or less. Still, if you are currently going through foreclosure, don't panic. Although this is a very stressful and serious situation, you do have options, and being proactive is in your best interest. In fact, if the foreclosure is still in its early stages, it is likely that your lender would prefer to work things out with you and not foreclose.

When you first receive notice of a foreclosure action, take some important steps. First, identify the parties involved. Today, most mortgages are sold and repackaged many times after the loan is first made. In some cases, the company that currently owns the loan won't actually be the one with the authority to renegotiate or modify it. This means that the company starting foreclosure proceedings isn't actually the party with which you will work. Although you may have originally worked with your local bank, your loan may now be owned by a larger company located in a different state. Knowing the parties should help prevent confusion and move the process along faster. It will also help protect against fraud. Once proceedings start, your name and address are public record, providing valuable information to individuals looking to prey on the vulnerable. Don't assume that any letter arriving in your mailbox is from a reputable or reliable source.

You should familiarize yourself with relevant state and federal laws and the policies of your specific lender. Because states vary greatly with regards to timing and notice requirements, knowing the specific laws governing your state and lender can save time and headaches.

If foreclosure is a realistic possibility for you, don't run from the problem—confront it head-on and get help. Help can come in various forms: credit and debt management advice from credit counselors, legal guidance from your attorneys, and sometimes even government action from state consumer protection agencies (if you think fraud or predatory lending has taken place).

ends up with a property that's not worth the outstanding amount on the mortgage. But a lender will recover all its money only if the homeowner has much more equity in the home than what's owed. There may be ways to work with the lender to reduce your monthly payments, or at least delay foreclosure until you can sell your house.

Q. What is foreclosure?

A. **Foreclosure** is a legal action in which a lender takes ownership of the property used to secure the loan because the owner failed to make mortgage payments. Foreclosure terminates the homeowner's ownership interest, as well as the interests of any junior lienholders. A foreclosure decree orders the sale of mortgaged real estate so the proceeds can satisfy the debt.

Q. If you have enough money, should you pay your mortgage down sooner than scheduled, or perhaps even pay it off completely?

A. That depends on your circumstances. It's usually considered a good idea to make extra payments on your principal when you can, because extra payments can reduce the term of the loan by several years and save you a bundle in interest.

But don't pay your mortgage off if it will leave you strapped for cash; you may need the financial cushion later. But if you can manage it without sacrificing other things you need, paying off your mortgage can be an excellent investment.

When you make the final payment, get a **certificate of satisfaction of mortgage** (sometimes called a **deed of reconveyance** or a **release of mortgage**). This document states that the loan has been paid in full. Have it signed by the lender, acknowledged (notarized), and entered in the public records.

This document is especially important if you've been paying a previous owner rather than a bank. In that case, ask your lawyer to draw up the certificate, then send it to the lender with a return envelope. If the previous owner balks, ask your lawyer to apply more pressure—it's extremely important to file this document.

If the bank offers to file the document for you, wait a few months and then check with the county register of deeds to make sure it's been done. If the lender was holding the abstract for your property, you should get it back. And if you were paying into an escrow account for tax and insurance bills, ask to see what's left and get a refund of any balance that remains in the account.

Refinancing and Home Loans

Q. When does it make sense to refinance your mortgage?

A. For some homeowners, the answer to this question is easy: if you have a double-digit interest rate on your mortgage when rates have dropped to below 8 percent, there's no question that you'll save money by refinancing. Even if you refinanced two years ago, refinancing again may make sense if interest rates have fallen a point or two.

> ▶ **FINANCES**

For more information on the various types of home loans available, and how they can impact what you owe, see Chapter 7, "Buying and Selling a Home."

Or you may need cash to pay college tuition. Borrowing the money against your home equity and deducting the interest is often cheaper than taking out an unsecured loan.

For other homeowners, the question is more difficult. You may want to take the following steps:

- Compare interest rates to figure out how much you would save on your monthly payments over the life of the mortgage. For example, on a $100,000 mortgage, an interest rate of 7 percent versus 8½ percent results in a savings of about $100 a month, or $1,200 a year on a thirty-year loan. To more precisely calculate the difference, you will want to get an amortization chart from a banker or real estate agent. Compare what you're currently paying each month in principal and interest with what you would be paying on the new loan.
- Include the costs of points, closing costs, title insurance, and other expenses for the new mortgage. Some lenders offer **no-fee mortgages** with rates maybe a quarter point higher, but with virtually no up-front fees, closing costs, or points. This makes sense if you expect to sell or refinance within a few years, but not if you'll be paying those higher rates year after year.
- Calculate the difference between your current payment's after-tax cost and your future payment's after-tax cost. Because the federal government gives you a tax break on mortgage interest (the amount of the break varies depending on your tax bracket), it's important to figure the tax break into your calculations, especially if you are (or expect to be) in the top tax bracket.

- Compare rates and charges between several lenders, including your current mortgage servicer.
- Consider switching from a thirty-year to a fifteen-year mortgage. You may be able to pay off your loan in half the time without increasing your monthly payment by much.

Note that the amount remaining on the loan must be less than your home is now worth. Mortgage lenders are bound by strict state and federal guidelines spelling out the

---

▶ **WHEN A BUYER ASSUMES YOUR LOAN . . . AND DEFAULTS**

Suppose that when you sell your house, you arrange for the buyer to assume your mortgage. Then the buyer runs into financial trouble and defaults on the mortgage. Are you liable for the loan?

That depends on when and how your mortgage originated. Some assumable mortgages dictate your responsibilities in case of an assumption. On most assumable conventional loans, you remain liable for the life of the loan. The same is true for older loans insured by the FHA. On these FHA-originated mortgages, you would share liability with the new owner for five years. If this happens to you, talk to your lawyer right away to figure out what to do. The law of such liability is very complicated, but all might not be lost.

percentage of current value they can lend. Generally speaking, you can refinance if your home is worth 10 percent more than the loan amount.

Q. Are there times when it doesn't make sense to refinance?

A. In almost all cases, you won't recover the closing costs for a few years. So if you plan to sell your home in the near future, it makes little sense to refinance.

Q. What's the difference between a home equity loan and a second mortgage?

A. They are similar in that the interest on both is tax deductible (up to $1 million of loans secured by the same property), and the home serves as collateral for both types of loans. They differ because a second mortgage usually consists of a fixed sum for a fixed period of time, while a home equity loan usually works as a line of credit on which you may draw over time. Typically, a home equity loan carries an adjustable interest rate, while a second mortgage carries a fixed rate, although this is not always the case.

Q. Which is better, a home equity loan or a second mortgage?

A. If you need a lump sum of cash, you're probably better off with a second mortgage because you will likely get a better interest rate. If you need money over a longer period of time, such as to pay college tuition or to pay for renovations planned over the next few years, it may be better to obtain a home equity loan. That way, you won't be paying interest on the money until you actually withdraw it.

▶ RENEGOTIATING YOUR MORTGAGE

Instead of refinancing, you may be able to get the savings you want by modifying your existing loan. Refinancing involves paying off the first loan and replacing it with a new one. But if your mortgage is fairly recent, you may be able to go back to the lender and renegotiate the terms to bring the existing loan in line with the market. This won't work if your original lender sold the loan to a mortgage service company.

Savings and loans and small-town banks, which often keep mortgage loans in their portfolios rather than selling them, are often willing to do this rather than lose your business. The new rate might be slightly higher than if you refinanced, but the costs could be significantly lower because there is likely to be less paperwork.

For recently originated loans, some lenders require only a one-page loan modification form and a modest one-time fee. Ask your lender if a loan modification is feasible for you.

Q. Do the same rules apply to refinancing as to obtaining an original mortgage?

A. When you refinance, you pay off the original mortgage and replace it with a new one. State and federal laws protect consumers in both obtaining a mortgage loan and refinancing, but you will want to go through the same steps as you would in obtaining a first mort-

▶ REFINANCING FHA AND VA LOANS

Homeowners who have an FHA or VA loan may be able to qualify for a special program called FHA Streamline Refinancing. This program does not require a home appraisal, employment verification, or qualifying ratios, as long as the mortgage is current. If you want to refinance an FHA or VA loan, call your local HUD office for information.

gage. (See Chapter 7, "Buying and Selling a Home," for advice on shopping for mortgage interest rates and mortgages.)

Q. Can I deduct the points I paid to refinance my mortgage on my federal tax return?

A. With one exception, points paid to refinance must be amortized over the life of the loan, while points paid to obtain an initial mortgage may be deducted the year the home was purchased. For example, if you paid two points to refinance a new thirty-year mortgage, you would be allowed to deduct one-thirtieth of the value of those points for each of the next thirty years. If you pay off the loan before it is due, however, you could deduct any remaining amount during the year the loan was paid in full.

An exception to this rule arises if you pay the points yourself and use part of the proceeds of the refinancing to pay for home improvements. Then you are allowed to deduct only a portion of the points in the year of the refinancing.

Tax Considerations

Q. What tax breaks are available to homeowners?

A. On your federal tax return, payments made for local property tax and mortgage in-

---

▶ CHECKLIST: STEPS TO TAKE BEFORE YOU REFINANCE

- Get a copy of your credit report before you apply, and correct any errors.
- Make sure you have at least 20 percent equity in your home; otherwise, you'll be expected to put down more money or be forced to pay private mortgage insurance (PMI). (PMI is more fully discussed in Chapter 7, "Buying and Selling a Home.")
- If you decide to use a mortgage broker, make sure you understand the fees charged, or the amount by which your interest rate will increase.
- Consider shortening the term of the loan, perhaps from thirty years to fifteen years; you'll pay more each month, but save a lot in interest payments over the life of the loan.
- Be prepared to wait. Refinancing can take three months or more because when mortgage interest rates decline, many homeowners jump at the chance to refinance.

terest (up to $1 million) are both deductible from your taxable income, as long as you itemize and do not take a standard deduction. (**Deductible** simply means that you don't have to pay federal taxes on that amount.) In the early years of a home loan, when most of your payment goes toward interest, deductibility might help you to shelter as much as a quarter to a third of your income from federal taxation. You can deduct mortgage interest on a vacation home, too, as long as it's not used principally as a rental property.

Federal tax law also allows you to deduct interest paid on up to $100,000 of a home equity loan, as long as the total debt on the home (including the first mortgage) does not exceed the fair market value of the home.

Depending on your state, you also may be eligible for a property tax deduction on your state income tax return.

Q. Is there any way to lower the property taxes on my house?

A. To lower property taxes, you need to lower the assessed value of your property, which is the basis for calculating your taxes. By providing evidence that the assessed value of your home or business property is too high, you should succeed in lowering the assessment and consequently your taxes. Chapter 7, "Buying and Selling a Home," outlines the various steps involved in obtaining an assessment and challenging an assessed value.

Q. How can I qualify for a tax deduction on a home office?

A. If you run a business from your home, your office expenses are probably deductible.

> ### ▶ FILING AN ASSESSMENT APPEAL
>
> Most municipalities allow a limited time for assessment appeals. Don't wait until you get your tax bill, when it is too late to appeal. In most states, the appeals procedures are relatively simple, and you may be able to represent yourself. If the case is complex or involves a large amount of money, you may want to consult a lawyer or real estate appraiser.

Depending on the size of your home and how much of it is designated as your office, the deduction can be significant enough to justify the extra effort needed to qualify. If your office meets the standards spelled out by the IRS, you can deduct the cost of repairs, furniture, computers and office equipment, extra telephone lines, and other business-related expenses. You can also deduct a proportional share of your home's depreciation (ordinary wear and tear), utility bills, and insurance. Although you can no longer deduct the entire cost of a desk or computer the first year, you may claim accelerated depreciation if you use the item more than 50 percent of the time for your job. This allows you to claim most of the deduction in the first two years.

Be aware, though, that you can deduct no more than your business actually generated. Also, remember that your deduction will lower the home's basis, which is the figure used to calculate capital gains.

REMEMBER THIS

- If you can't make your mortgage payments, contact your lender immediately to work something out. Don't just hope the problem will go away.

- Find out if refinancing your home or renegotiating your mortgage can save you money.

- If you think your property tax is too high, you might be able to find an error in the assessment or make your case before the assessment board.

- If you have a home office, you can deduct the expenses of running your business, including a portion of your home's depreciation.

CHAPTER NINE

Renting Residential Property

Venus was having problems with the heating in her apartment. She complained to her landlord, who promised to fix it, but three weeks later he still hadn't made repairs. Venus decided to stop paying rent until her landlord repaired the problem. Five weeks later, Venus went on vacation. When she returned, she found all of her possessions piled on the sidewalk outside her apartment, and the locks on her apartment had been changed. This was the first notice she'd had that she was facing eviction. Was Venus allowed to simply stop paying rent? What obligations did her landlord have to make the requested repairs? Could the landlord evict her like that?

   Renting an apartment—or any living space—is an important decision. As a tenant, you will probably spend more of your income on rent than on any other monthly expense. As a landlord, you will depend upon the tenant to pay the expenses of running the building, as well as to provide you with an income. You should make the decision to rent carefully. This chapter will help you to make a good decision that you won't regret.

This chapter also provides you with suggestions about how to handle problems that arise after you move in, and discusses your options—whether you're a landlord or a tenant—if those problems continue after you move out. The discussion in this chapter assumes that both the landlord and the tenant are private parties. If a government agency is involved, that will very likely bring an additional set of laws and rules into play.

> ### ▶ WHAT IS A LEASE?
>
> When the landlord has decided to rent to the tenant and the tenant has decided to rent from the landlord, they will enter into a lease. **Leases** (also known as **rental agreements**) are contracts, written or oral, in which the landlord grants to the tenant exclusive possession of the property in exchange for rent for a specified period of time.
>
> For more information on the basics of contract law as it relates to leases, see Chapter 12, "Contracts and Consumer Law."

RENTING BASICS

The landlord-tenant relationship is created when a landlord and tenant choose each other. The tenant has to want to rent from the landlord, and the landlord must accept the tenant's application to rent. How carefully the landlord and tenant make these decisions will likely affect the success of their relationship more than any other single factor.

This section explores the basics of the rental relationship, including leases and security deposits.

Leases

Q. What is a standard lease?

A. A **standard lease** is a lease that sets forth landlord-tenant rights and obligations using standard provisions that are common to most leases. Most standard lease forms are written by lawyers who work for landlords or the real estate industry, so the slant of a lease will often be in favor of the landlord. However, well-written and well-negotiated leases are preferable for both the landlord and the tenant, because they provide indisputable evidence of the terms of the agreement.

Q. Can a lease be oral?

A. In some situations, yes. However, the rights and options of both the landlord and tenant are better protected if everything is in writing.

Q. How long does a lease last?

A. The length of a lease is a matter that is negotiated between the tenant and landlord. Most leases fall into one of two categories: month-by-month or fixed-term. A **month-by-month lease** is one where rent is payable monthly, and the lease can be changed or terminated by either party after giving some specified amount of notice. Usually, notice must be given thirty days in advance. Occasionally, the landlord must give more notice to the tenant than the tenant must give to the landlord.

The advantage of a month-by-month lease for tenants is that they are free to simply give notice, move, and stop paying rent. For some tenants, this ease of mobility can be important. The disadvantage for tenants is that the landlord can raise the rent or otherwise change the rental conditions; for example, he or she might unexpectedly decide to disallow pets.

With a **fixed-term lease,** neither the landlord nor the tenant may terminate or modify the lease before the end of the term without the permission of the other. So long as a fixed-term lease is supplemented by an adequate security deposit, it will protect the landlord from a tenant's decision to move and stop paying rent, while also protecting the tenant from rent increases during the term of the lease.

▶ **LOCAL LAW IS IMPORTANT**

More than many other areas of law, landlord-tenant law is apt to be local in scope. Many laws and rules that affect the landlord-tenant relationship are unique to the community in which you live. Don't assume that you know what's in your community's laws. For specific answers to your questions, consult your local government, a tenants' union, a landlords' association, or a lawyer who practices in the landlord-tenant field.

Q. From the perspective of the landlord, what clauses in a lease are the most important?

A. The most important clause to landlords is the one that establishes the duty of the tenant to pay rent in full and on time. Typically this clause grants the landlord the right to charge a fee for late payments. Other important clauses grant the landlord the right to enforce the rules and regulations written into the lease.

Q. What are the most important lease clauses for tenants?

A. It's important that the lease state the duty of the landlord to maintain the physical condition of the premises. Also critical is the handling of the tenant's security deposit and the timing and mechanism for returning it to the tenant.

It is possible that the contract may contain clauses granting the tenant the right to terminate the lease if the landlord fails to make needed repairs, and to hire workers to correct defects in the premises and either charge the landlord for the cost or deduct it from the rent. However, these clauses are rare because landlords typically draft contracts weighted in their own favor. This is the reason that many courts have interpreted contracts as implying additional remedies for tenants.

▶ **SECURITY OF TENURE**

Security of tenure is a tenant's legal right to continue tenancy indefinitely, unless the tenant violates certain rules or regulations or the landlord has a compelling reason to reclaim possession of the premises.

Q. If either the tenant or the landlord doesn't like the lease, how should they go about changing it?

A. If one party can persuade the other to remove a particular provision, that provision should be blacked out in ink on all copies of the lease. Both the landlord and the tenant should then initial the marked-out sections.

Many preprinted forms contain large blank spaces for the landlord and tenant to write additional agreements, which will then become part of the lease. Both landlord and tenant should initial any inserted paragraphs. If the spaces are too small or there are no such spaces, the additional terms should be written on a separate sheet of paper and signed and dated by both the landlord and tenant. Remember: a lease doesn't have to look neat and clean. It just needs to clearly state the intent of the parties. Feel free to write all over it as you reach the agreed-upon terms.

Q. Does the law regulate the provisions in a lease?

A. Yes. Courts have restricted the enforceability of certain types of lease provisions. As a result, some of the most objectionable clauses in older leases are now illegal. For example, most state courts have struck down lease clauses requiring that a tenant accept an apartment "as is," and that the tenant pay the rent regardless of whether the landlord maintains the property. Today, if a landlord sues to evict for nonpayment of rent, tenants can defend themselves by arguing that the premises was not worth the full contract rent because of its deteriorated condition. This legal concept is called the **implied warranty of habitability** (for a further discussion of this topic, see page 354). It prevents the landlord from evading his or her responsibility to maintain the premises, even if the tenant signed a lease waiving the right to maintenance.

Many states and municipalities have enacted laws that prohibit other types of clauses as well. An example of a commonly prohibited type of clause is the **confession-of-judgment clause.** Such a clause would permit the landlord's lawyer to represent the tenant in court without any prior notice, service, or process. On the tenant's behalf, the lawyer could then waive a jury trial, confess judgment to the landlord's claims without offering any defense, waive all errors or omissions made by the landlord in making the complaint, and authorize an immediate eviction or wage deduction. In addition, many form leases include a waiver of jury trial—a clause that in many states is unenforceable.

▶ **NEGOTIATING THE LEASE**

A lease is not written in stone, even though it may seem that way. A residential lease is just a type of contract, subject to most of the same laws as all other contracts. Ultimately, the most important part of any contract is the agreement of the parties—i.e., the two parties negotiating terms that they can live by.

Lease Clauses to Consider

Q. Can tenants own pets?

A. With an oral lease, tenants probably have the right to own a pet unless the landlord specifies otherwise.

Written leases usually have a clause either

▶ MAY I COME IN?

Normally, a landlord has no right to enter a tenant's apartment unless the tenant gives consent. Under the general tenets of landlord-tenant law, the landlord has surrendered possession of the premises entirely to the tenant for the term of the lease.

But a written lease will almost always give the landlord the right to enter to show the premises to prospective buyers or tenants and to make necessary or agreed-upon repairs. A lease may require the landlord to give advance notice before entry (usually twenty-four or forty-eight hours), but some leases do not require any prior notice and restrict neither the time nor the frequency of entry.

State and local laws may also give landlords the right of access. Usually these ordinances require landlords to give reasonable advance notice, and to enter only at reasonable times and not so often as to be harassing.

Even if the landlord has the right to unlimited access, the police will normally ask a landlord to leave an apartment if the tenant so requests.

---

prohibiting pets on the premises or requiring tenants to get written permission from the landlord. A tenant who violates this clause can be evicted if the pet remains on the premises after the landlord asks for its removal.

Q. Is the lease canceled if the landlord sells the building or the tenant dies?

A. Most preprinted standard lease forms contain a paragraph dealing with heirs and successors. This paragraph typically provides that the lease does not expire upon the sale of the building or the death of the tenant. If the tenant dies during the term of the lease, the tenant's estate will continue to owe the rent until legally released; it will also have the right to occupy the premises. If there is no such provision in the written lease, or if the lease is oral, then the death of either party terminates the lease.

Most written leases also include a clause specifying that the lease does not expire on the sale of the building. Unless otherwise provided, an oral lease will also continue in effect under the new landlord without any changes.

Q. Does the tenant owe the landlord a late fee if the rent is not paid on the date specified in the lease?

A. Not unless a late fee is specified in the written lease. Some municipal ordinances restrict the amount of late fees that a landlord may charge. State courts have also ruled that such a fee may be charged as **liquidated damages** (i.e., a sum specified in advance), but cannot be so large as to constitute punishment.

Q. Is the landlord liable for the damages incurred by a tenant who was injured because of inadequate maintenance of the property?

A. Many leases contain clauses, called **exculpatory clauses,** in which the tenant automatically excuses the landlord from any liability for damages from any cause whatsoever. Only about half of the states prohibit such clauses in residential leases.

Courts in other states have interpreted exculpatory clauses narrowly, or have refused to enforce them because they are against public policy. If a tenant is injured, it will be up to a court to decide whether the injury resulted from some negligent act by the landlord.

Some courts have held that if the tenant's injury resulted from the landlord's violation of the housing code, the landlord is plainly negligent and liable. Other courts have required the tenant to prove negligence. That is, there must be evidence that the landlord knew or should have known of the defective condition before the tenant's injury. Furthermore, the landlord must have failed to make repairs within a reasonable time or in a careful manner.

Because the laws vary greatly, tenants who are injured on their rented property should consult a lawyer who has experience litigating these issues. Possible landlord liability for injuries is discussed at greater length in Chapter 6, "Personal Injury."

Q. If the landlord loses the building to the bank by foreclosure, is the tenant's lease still valid?

A. Most leases provide that the lease is subordinate to any mortgage. This means that if the landlord fails to make payments to the mortgage holder, and then loses the property, the bank can disregard the lease and evict the tenant. However, the bank must usually go to court first and get permission for the eviction.

Some leases do provide subordination or nondisturbance language, which explicitly provides that the lease remains in effect in the event of a foreclosure.

Q. If the property burns down, does the tenant still owe rent under the lease?

A. In most cases, no. But a few state laws still call for continued payment.

Q. If the local government condemns the property and decides to tear it down, is the tenant's lease still valid?

A. No. Most leases state that the landlord or the government may terminate the tenant's lease if the government condemns the property. The right of the government to condemn private property is called **eminent domain.** The government must compensate landlords for taking their property. The lease may provide that the tenants are not entitled to any of this money, but in some areas, the law may entitle them to a portion of the settlement.

If the building is condemned, the tenant will have to leave. However, the local government must still get the permission of the court to evict the tenant.

Q. Can the tenant, with the landlord's consent, operate a business out of the rented premises?

A. Maybe. It depends on the lease and on local law. Most leases provide that the tenant must use the premises solely for residential purposes, but the landlord may waive this requirement.

However, some businesses are illegal under zoning laws even if the landlord allows them. **Local zoning ordinances** govern how residential property may legally be used. In residential areas, some ordinances permit white-collar work, such as accounting, word processing, tutoring, and counseling, but for-

▶ WHOSE CHANDELIER IS IT?

Disputes often arise when tenants install fixtures, such as chandeliers or ceiling fans. A **fixture** is an object that is bolted or otherwise attached to the property.

Can a tenant install these kinds of fixtures? Under the general concept of landlord-tenant law, tenants may do anything they wish as long as they do not damage the property. But most leases do not allow a tenant to install such fixtures without the landlord's approval.

If tenants install fixtures, can they remove them when they move out? In the absence of a lease provision, fixtures belong to a landlord. Some leases permit removal of the fixtures if the wall or ceiling is restored to its original condition. Some states and cities have passed laws making it legal for tenants to remove fixtures that they purchased and installed. It might be easier for the tenant to avoid a potential problem by specifying in a separate attachment to the lease those items that will be attached, and inserting a clause entitling the tenant to remove them at the end of the lease.

---

bid commercial, retail, industrial, or manufacturing businesses.

Likewise, local zoning laws may prohibit people from living in a commercial, retail, industrial, or manufacturing building. Therefore, if the landlord rents manufacturing space to a residential tenant in violation of the zoning ordinance, the lease is unenforceable because it is for an illegal purpose.

Q. If the landlord provided laundry facilities in the building when the tenant signed the lease, but later discontinues this service, does this violate the lease?

A. Maybe. Most leases provide that the tenant's use of any facility in the building outside of the apartment is a license and not a lease. A **license** conveys permission to exercise a privilege in the use of certain property. Such licenses can generally be revoked by landlords and, unlike a lease, are not a guarantee of continued right to use.

But state statutes or municipal ordinances may define the term "premises" to include common areas of the property. In those jurisdictions, if a tenant agrees to rent certain premises, the landlord cannot discontinue services that were included on that premises when the tenant signed the lease. If the landlord discontinues such services, the tenant will probably be entitled to a reduction in rent.

Q. What can the tenant do if other tenants in the building make noise and interfere with the tenant's "right of quiet enjoyment" of the premises?

A. Traditionally, the **right of quiet enjoyment** referred to the ability of a tenant to live somewhere without being disturbed by another person's right (as granted by the landlord) to use the property. Today, the concept has been broadened to include the right to live somewhere without being disturbed by

---

▶ **CONDOS ARE SPECIAL**

A tenant who rents a condominium has obligations to the unit's owner, to the condo association, and of course to the other residents of the condo.

The condominium owner is the landlord. But the association sets the rules and regulations for the building and controls the common areas. Depending on local law, the association may have the right to seek eviction of a tenant who violates the rules. It may also have the right to seek the tenant's eviction if the owner fails to pay the regular association assessments.

All states and many municipalities have passed special condo laws, although in some cases they do not apply to buildings with only a few units. If you rent a condo, you should check the local law.

---

noise from other tenants. The reasoning is that if the landlord imposes upon his tenants the duty to be quiet, then those tenants have the right to force the landlord to enforce this duty so they will not be disturbed by the noise from other tenants.

Q. If there is a legal dispute between the landlord and the tenant, does the tenant have to pay the landlord's legal fees?

A. Most leases make the tenant responsible for the payment of all lawyer's fees incurred by the landlord in the enforcement of the lease provisions. But some state or local laws restrict that provision to situations in which

the landlord wins a lawsuit and the court awards fees.

Security Deposits

Q. What is a security deposit?

A. A **security deposit** is money set aside to protect the landlord in case the tenant damages the property or fails to pay rent. Usually, the tenant pays the security deposit before moving in. The landlord may ask for any amount, but some local laws restrict the deposit to the equivalent of one or two months' rent.

Q. What does a lease say about security deposits?

A. A preprinted standard lease form will probably contain a paragraph stating that the tenant has made the deposit to assure compliance with all terms of the lease. The lease will also set forth the conditions under which the landlord will return the deposit to the tenant. Most leases allow the landlord to keep all or part of the deposit if the tenant owes rent upon moving out or has caused property damage beyond normal wear and tear. Some of it may also be kept to pay for cleaning the property.

Q. Are deposits for cleaning, pets, parking, or garage door openers considered security deposits, and thus refundable?

A. Yes. If the tenant complies with all the terms of the lease agreement and leaves the premises in good condition, the tenant should get most (if not all) of his or her money back, whether the lease calls it a security deposit or by some other name. In some states, however, the landlord may charge the tenant a nonrefundable fee for anticipated damage. This is most common in the case of tenants who own pets.

Q. Must landlords hold security deposits in a separate bank account?

A. In some states, the law imposes a requirement on landlords to keep the security deposit in an account separate from their own money. This makes sense because, legally speaking, the money is not the landlord's. A security deposit belongs to the tenant until it is refunded or applied to cover unpaid rent or damage beyond normal wear and tear.

Q. Under what conditions does the landlord owe a refund of the security deposit?

A. The landlord will owe the tenant a refund if the rent was paid in full and there is no damage to the premises beyond normal wear and tear. The tenant should insist on accompanying the landlord during the final inspection, and should verify any items claimed by

the landlord to warrant deductions from the security deposit. If necessary, the tenant should dispute the charges.

Q. How does the tenant know what the landlord is deducting for?

A. Many states require the landlord to provide a tenant with an accounting that explains any deductions applied to the tenant's security deposit. Some states allow the tenant to automatically recover up to three times the security deposit if the landlord does not provide this accounting within one month of the tenant moving out. If your landlord is applying deductions to your security deposit and you don't know why, your first step should be to simply ask what the charges are for.

Q. What should the tenant do if the landlord does not refund the deposit or does not refund all of the deposit?

A. The tenant should first try to negotiate with the landlord, perhaps with the help of a mediator. If that fails, the tenant can take the landlord to small-claims court. Many states have a special small-claims court in which people can sue to collect relatively small amounts of money owed to them. The tenant, who will be the plaintiff in the lawsuit, is often required to appear without a lawyer. (In some states, the landlord may hire a lawyer.)

▶ INTEREST ON DEPOSITS

Some states have statutes requiring the landlord to pay interest on the security deposit. In these states, the landlord cannot avoid paying interest simply because a lease says the deposit does not earn interest.

If the landlord fails to pay interest on the security deposit, the law may provide for the tenant to recover damages from the landlord for that failure. The law may also provide that the landlord has to pay the lawyer's fees of the tenant who sues to collect the interest.

REMEMBER THIS

- A lease is a contract and, like all contracts, is negotiable. Both landlords and tenants have every right to propose changes in the draft lease, but the other party does not have to accept those changes.

- In addition to regulating the lease agreement, local and state law may have a lot to say about the rights and responsibilities of the landlord and tenant. The law may also render certain lease clauses illegal, even if both parties have agreed to them.

- The landlord has a right to ask for a security deposit, but the law may govern how much can be requested, whether the deposit gathers interest, and the terms under which the deposit must be returned.

THE TENANT

From the perspective of a tenant, what are the signs of a good landlord? What are your options if the landlord doesn't live up to all of his or her promises? Can you simply move out? This section addresses these and many other questions that many tenants have, and helps to explain the possible remedies should problems arise between you and your landlord.

Choosing a Landlord

Q. How can tenants choose a good landlord?

A. The first thing to do is check out the apartment. Look in every room and closet, open every door, drawer, and window, operate every appliance, and take your time. It is better to find problems now than after you move in. You should ask for any needed repairs or improvements as a condition of moving in. Good landlords will put their promises in writing.

The second thing to do is read the lease.

Most tenants never read a lease before signing it. There is no such thing as a "standard lease." You should ask for changes before you sign. Negotiating does not mean accepting whatever is offered. Simply because a lease includes a particular provision, it doesn't mean that the provision is legally enforceable. If it sounds ridiculous, it just may be.

The third thing to do is check out the landlord. This is not as hard as it may seem. Much of a landlord's history is part of the public record. Has the city cited the landlord for code violations? Have other tenants sued the landlord? Is the landlord known by tenants' unions, consumer services organiza-

---

▶ **THE MAILBOX TEST**

There is an easy way to judge how well a landlord maintains a building: look at the mailboxes and doorbells.

Are the tenants' names uniformly labeled—e.g., as though the landlord used a label maker? If so, you can surmise that the landlord at least cares about how the building appears.

Is the writing of the names all different, as if the tenants put up their own names? If so, the landlord is at best indifferent to the way the building looks.

Are the tenant's names written with a felt marker or etched into the metal? Are the mailboxes broken or unlocked? This suggests that nobody cares much about appearances. If you do, you should look elsewhere for an apartment.

tions, or other regulatory bodies? Prospective tenants can also learn a lot about a landlord by talking to other tenants in the building.

Q. Does the negotiation process give the prospective tenant some indications of whether the landlord will keep his or her promises?

A. There are winners and losers in the landlord derby. In first place are landlords who mean what they say and will back it up. They will agree to put promises in writing. They will also agree to make repairs and specify when they will make them. They are clearly landlords acting in good faith.

In second place are the landlords who make oral promises to get you to rent from them, but won't put the promises in writing. In last place are the landlords who will not make any promises. They have no word to trust. You should probably consider renting elsewhere.

If you are able to get the landlord to put a promise in writing, be certain to include an appropriate resolution in case one party breaks the promise.

Q. What information about a landlord is public record?

A. The Internet has made information more easily available than ever before. A skillful surfer may discover

- whether the landlord actually owns the building;
- whether the landlord has ever been taken to court by the city, other tenants, or workers the landlord has hired; and
- if there is a record of complaints against the landlord.

The regulatory consumer agencies in your area may maintain websites that record com-

---

> ▶ **GET IT FIXED BEFORE YOU MOVE IN!**
>
> If you see needed repairs when you inspect an apartment, make sure the repairs are satisfactorily completed before you sign a lease or hand over a security deposit. After you've signed the lease, the landlord no longer has any incentive to perform the repairs quickly.

---

plaints and evaluate customer satisfaction. Also, newspapers frequently carry stories about landlords and tenants; those articles can be discovered on the Web. Some websites list bad landlords. Check out these sites by typing "bad landlords" into your favorite browser.

Repairs and Property Maintenance

Q. Does the tenant have any obligation to the landlord regarding the maintenance of the premises?

A. Traditionally, the tenant has the duty not to commit **waste.** This means the tenant may not unreasonably and permanently damage the property.

Landlord-tenant laws have modified this concept. The tenant must comply with the sections of housing codes that require him or her to keep the premises clean, and to dispose of trash in a reasonable manner and in facilities that the landlord supplies. The tenant must not damage the property negligently or deliberately. When moving out, the tenant must return the property to the landlord in clean and repaired condition, except for reasonable wear and tear.

Some leases still place some of the burden of maintaining the apartment on the tenant. Some leases require the tenant to return the apartment to the landlord upon moving out in perfect condition, without any wear and tear. These lease clauses may be legal in some places, but even so, a landlord may not be able to enforce them.

Q. What is an express warranty of habitability?

A. An **express warranty of habitability** is a written provision in a lease stating that the landlord promises to make a specified repair or maintain the premises in a specified condition.

When the tenant signs a lease, he or she should make sure it lists all repairs that are needed, and that it contains a clause obligating the landlord to make future repairs when needed. Then, if the landlord fails to maintain the premises up to the express standard written into the lease, the landlord would be breaching the contract. The tenant could then sue the landlord for **specific performance** (a court order compelling the landlord to make the repairs) or for money damages for the breach.

Q. What if there is no express warranty of habitability? Does this mean that the landlord doesn't have to keep the building in good repair?

A. No. In this case, a court would likely say that the lease contains an **implied warranty of habitability.** The implied warranty of habitability is an unwritten promise that the landlord will maintain the apartment in the condition required by the housing code, and

will make the repairs necessary to keep the apartment in that condition. The courts have ruled that all landlords make this implied promise to their tenants. For this reason, lease clauses in which the tenant waives the right to maintenance have been declared illegal and unenforceable in almost all states.

If the landlord breaches the implied warranty of habitability, the tenant will probably have the right to withhold from the regular rent an amount that reasonably reflects the reduction in value of the apartment caused by the code violations. The landlord's breach will also give the tenant the right to sue the landlord for overpayment of rent if the tenant paid the full rent despite the presence of code violations. And the landlord's breach will give the tenant a defense if the landlord attempts to evict the tenant for failure to pay full rent.

Q. Does the implied warranty of habitability apply only to tenants living in slum buildings?

A. No. It applies to all tenants. The standard of required maintenance applies to all residential buildings, all landlords, and all tenants. Tenants at all income levels sometimes

---

▶ WILL THE LANDLORD HAVE TO FIX IT?

Remember the difference between repairs and improvements. On the one hand, a tenant is entitled to have things in good working order. On the other hand, a tenant may not be entitled to a new refrigerator if the old one is still working.

have problems with landlords providing inadequate maintenance.

Q. Can the tenant do anything if the landlord refuses to make repairs?

A. Yes. The tenant has a number of options, though not all are available in all states. (These options are discussed further later in this chapter.) For example, the tenant might

- take the landlord to court;
- repair the defect and deduct the cost from the rent;
- reduce the rent payment;
- terminate the lease; or
- complain to the municipal code enforcement agency.

If a tenant plans to take a landlord to court, there are likely three possible bases for legal argument:

1. A tenant might argue that the landlord violated the implied warranty of habitability (discussed above).
2. The tenant might argue that the landlord violated local ordinances. Many local landlord-tenant ordinances permit the tenant to seek a court order if the landlord fails to maintain the premises. The legal standard imposed on the landlord may be strict compliance with city codes. Local ordinances may also require the landlord to pay the tenant's lawyer's fees.
3. The tenant could go after the landlord under state consumer fraud statutes. A number of these statutes regulate the landlord-tenant relationship. Under these laws, it is fraud for a landlord to rent premises in defective condition. The reason this is considered fraudulent is that the city prohibits the landlord from renting substandard units, but the landlord does it anyway.

Repair-and-Deduct

Q. What is meant by "repair-and-deduct"?

A. **Repair-and-deduct** is a legal theory that permits the tenant to hire someone to make repairs, and then to deduct the cost of those repairs from the rent. State or local law may only cover repairs that are required to keep the premises habitable, such as the repair of a broken furnace or a leaking pipe.

Q. How does a tenant apply the theory of repair-and-deduct?

A. The tenant must serve written notice on the landlord. This notice must specifically enumerate the needed repairs, provide a reasonable amount of time for the landlord to comply, and state that if the landlord fails to do so, the tenant will hire someone to make the repairs and will deduct that cost from the rent.

Q. Are there any limitations on the use of repair-and-deduct?

A. Local laws may set a maximum dollar amount that the tenant can spend on re-

---

▶ **NOTICE**

When sending notice to your landlord of problems with the property or your intent to undertake repairs, send the notice with a return receipt so you have proof that your landlord received it.

pairs—for example, $500 or one month's rent.

However, in jurisdictions that have no explicit repair-and-deduct legislation (and thus rely solely on the implied warranty of habitability), the right to use repair-and-deduct is limited only by the reasonableness of the repairs. Under the right circumstances, for example, a tenant in these jurisdictions may even be able to buy a new furnace and deduct the cost from the rent.

Reduced Rent

Q. What is reduced rent?

A. In some states, when the premises do not comply with the standards of the local housing code, the tenant can pay the landlord a **reduced rent**—that is, an amount of rent lower than the full contract amount, which reflects the reduced value of the premises.

Q. How does a tenant go about paying reduced rent?

A. The tenant must serve written notice on the landlord. This notice must list specific repairs the tenant needs, provide a reasonable amount of time for the landlord to comply, and state that the tenant will pay a reduced rent unless the landlord makes the repairs within the time specified.

Q. May the tenant withhold all the rent?

A. A tenant might do that, especially to get the landlord's attention. But the landlord could reply with a notice to "pay up or get out." And if the premises remained habitable at least to some extent, some rent would continue to be owed. Bottom line: The tenant should pay some rent to the landlord as long as the tenant is still living there. (It would be up to a court to decide how much of a reduction is justified.)

▸ SHOULD YOU GO TO COURT?

If the state courts are responsive to municipalities' lawsuits for code enforcement, they will be responsive to tenants' lawsuits as well. In those cases, suing will be quite effective. On the other hand, if the courts in your region are not responsive to municipal code enforcement, then tenants may not do well in court. The ability to sue successfully, particularly under consumer fraud laws, often depends upon the sensitivity of the courts to tenants' rights.

Another potential obstacle is that the complexity of the court system often requires tenants to be represented by a lawyer. Poor tenants may have access to free or low-cost legal services, but most tenants are not eligible for such assistance.

For small problems that have not resulted in the loss of a large amount of money, it may be appropriate for a tenant or landlord to pursue a remedy in small-claims court. Chapter 2, "How the Legal System Works," provides more information on how small-claims courts work.

Withholding rent is very risky for a tenant. If the tenant fails to prove a breach of the implied warranty of habitability, the tenant might be evicted. For this reason, it is safer to pay the rent and sue for damages.

Q. *I want to pay a reduced rent because a plumbing problem has made over half of my apartment unusable. However, I'm afraid this could result in my eviction. Is there something I can do with the rent money to prove that I have it, but am refusing to pay it?*

A. Yes. You may want to put the withheld rent in an escrow account. This might be required by a local ordinance, or the court might order it for the duration of a trial. But whether required or not, it is a good idea to put the rent in escrow so the money will be readily available if needed.

Q. *If multiple tenants in my building have similar complaints, can we work together?*

A. Yes, you can possibly undertake a rent strike. A **rent strike** is a collective action, usually undertaken by tenants in the same building, in which the tenants withhold all or a portion of the rent. During a rent strike, it's best to place the rent money in escrow so that all the tenants know their neighbors are participating; this also protects the money and limits each individual tenant's liability.

Q. *How do the courts calculate rent reductions?*

A. The standards for rent reductions vary by state. Some courts base reductions on the fair market rental value of premises with code violations. Other courts use a **proportional use** standard, in which the reduction is deter-mined based on how much the defects reduce the use of the premises. For example, if a defect reduces the usability of the premises by 40 percent, then the rent may also be reduced by 40 percent.

Q. *If the tenant paid full rent but the premises were defective, can the tenant seek a rent reduction for rent already paid?*

A. Maybe, but the tenant would have to sue the landlord in order to collect. This concept is called **retroactive rent abatement.**

Both the implied warranty of habitability and local ordinances provide that the tenant has the right to recover damages from the landlord for failure to maintain the premises.

Lease Termination by the Tenant

Q. *If I move out before the expiration of the lease, is the lease terminated?*

A. No. The lease does not terminate just because you move out. The lease is a contract in which the tenant promises to pay the landlord for the right to possess the premises, whether the tenant actually lives there or not.

Q. *How can the tenant terminate the legal obligation of the lease?*

A. There are three ways for the tenant to terminate the rental obligation:

1. based on the legal misconduct by the landlord;
2. replacement by a new tenant (this may require the consent of the landlord); or
3. by agreement between the landlord and the tenant.

Failure to maintain the premises may constitute legal misconduct. Local laws may also provide for termination of the lease if the landlord violates other legal provisions, such as by abusing access to the premises or failing to disclose code violations cited by the municipality.

If another tenant replaces the existing tenant, the first tenant can avoid the rental obligation. The landlord cannot legally collect from the original tenant if the replacement tenant pays the full rent.

Obviously, the landlord and the tenant can also end the tenancy by mutual agreement. This simple approach is often overlooked, but should always be attempted first.

Q. How is one tenant replaced by another?

A. Under the common law, if there is no written lease, the tenant has the unrestricted right to transfer the leasehold to anyone else. A written lease will undoubtedly contain a provision giving the landlord the right of approval over prospective replacement tenants. An issue often arises over whether the landlord is acting reasonably in approving or disapproving the replacement tenant.

Q. What is the difference between reletting and subleasing?

A. In **reletting**, the landlord signs a completely new lease with a replacement tenant, and releases the original tenant from the obligation to pay rent.

In **subleasing** (or **subletting**), the first tenant rents to a new one (the **sublessor**). Although the sublessor now has the obligation to pay rent, the original tenant still remains responsible for the remainder of the lease term. Therefore, if the sublessor fails to pay,

---

▶ SUBLEASING

For many tenants, the commitment to a six- or twelve-month lease is inconvenient. For example, if you're a student, you might only need to live in an apartment for nine months; or perhaps your plans or your job might change, and you'll want to move earlier than you expected. When you have to leave your rented property and you don't want to break the lease, subleasing can be an appealing option.

It's a good idea to inform your landlord of a proposed sublet well in advance, and to seek the landlord's consent. Most of the time, there won't be a problem—after all, you'll be responsible for any damage your sublessor causes, as well as any rent they don't pay. In most states, landlords may not unreasonably deny consent to a proposed subtenant. If a landlord denies consent based on his or her personal taste, convenience, religious beliefs, sensibility, or desire to charge a higher rent, then the landlord may be deemed by some courts to have acted in bad faith, and the tenant might then assign the lease without the landlord's consent, or terminate the lease.

Rent-controlled apartments are the exception in some states. Generally, if a tenant of a rent-controlled apartment does not have an existing lease (and many tenants don't), then the tenant cannot sublet the apartment without the owner's written consent.

the landlord may sue the original tenant for the rent even though that tenant no longer uses the premises.

The original tenant may also be liable for damages if the new tenant breaches the lease or destroys the property.

Q. If a tenant moves out, does the landlord have to find a new tenant, or can the landlord simply continue to recover the rent owed by the original tenant?

A. In many places, the landlord is obligated to make a good-faith effort to find a new tenant promptly, so that the old tenant can discontinue paying rent. This is called the **duty to mitigate.** The first tenant can also help find a new tenant.

Q. Can a tenant remain in the premises after the expiration of the lease?

A. A tenant who stays after the expiration of a lease is called a **tenant at sufferance** or **holdover tenant.** The landlord can sue for eviction, or can choose to continue accepting rent, thus renewing the lease. The renewal will be on a month-to-month basis or for another year, depending on the terms of the lease and the provisions of the law. During the holding-over period, a lease provision or statute may give the landlord the right to charge up to double the original rent.

Since the landlord has the choice of eviction or renewal, the tenant who needs to stay past the expiration of the lease should try to negotiate an agreement with the landlord and get it in writing.

REMEMBER THIS

- The law imposes duties on both landlords and tenants, but ultimately it is the landlord's responsibility to maintain the property.

- A lease might give a tenant an explicit warranty about the condition of the property; if it doesn't, local law will impose an implied warranty.

- Tenants have many remedies for substandard housing, including complaining to housing authorities, suing the landlord, reducing the rent, doing the repairs and deducting the cost from the rent, and terminating the lease.

- If tenants want to leave rental property early, they will usually still owe rent, unless they have negotiated a settlement with the landlord or found a replacement tenant acceptable to the landlord.

THE LANDLORD

Renting real estate can be a very lucrative business for some landlords. However, renting can also quickly become a major headache: tenants who don't get along, building repairs, city inspectors, and, in the worst-case scenario, tenants who need to be evicted. How can a landlord find a good tenant? Can a landlord refuse to rent to someone? What options exist if a landlord wants to evict a tenant? This section outlines the rights and responsibilities of landlords, as well as the options for a landlord who wishes to terminate a lease.

Choosing a Tenant

Q. How can a landlord choose a good tenant?

A. Renting is a commercial relationship. You should approach selecting a tenant the same way you would approach selecting a building to buy. Ask yourself: Will I get the rent I want from the tenant without too many hassles?

Require the tenant to fill out a written application. You can purchase forms at stationery stores and real estate offices. Ask for current and former employers. Ask for current and former landlords. Go back five years, if possible. Make phone calls to verify this information.

Good tenants will appreciate that you check them out; they will want to know that you've checked out your other tenants and that they'll be good neighbors.

Q. How else can landlords evaluate prospective tenants?

A. They can hire companies that specialize in checking out prospective tenants. Landlords who only rent a few units may not possess all of the resources necessary to investigate prospects effectively. These companies charge a fee, but they truly earn that fee if they screen out undesirable tenants.

A check by a credit bureau will tell you about judgments against the tenant, bankruptcies, and slow payments to (or adverse information from) other creditors.

Q. Can I get into legal trouble by rejecting a prospective tenant?

A. Federal, state, and city laws prohibit discrimination. **Discrimination** means refusing to rent to people because of their race, national origin, sex, family status, handicaps, or disabilities. States and municipalities have often added additional categories. You should know the law in your city and state. The best way to avoid problems is to treat all prospective tenants the same.

Be careful not to refuse to show your rental property to members of certain races, genders, or national origins. This practice can

qualify as "steering" and is likely illegal. See page 243 in Chapter 7, "Buying and Selling a Home," for more information on this practice.

Q. In selecting tenants, is a landlord allowed to use any other criteria he or she wishes?

A. Yes. The landlord can use legal criteria to select tenants, such as their past history of tenancy, the amount of income they have available to pay rent, and their past criminal record. The landlord may also use personal criteria in selecting tenants—for example, by refusing to rent to people with purple hair or

---

▶ WHAT IS FAIR HOUSING?

Fair housing is a legal principle that prohibits landlords from refusing to rent property because a prospective tenant falls into one or more protected classes.

The federal Fair Housing Act forbids landlords from discriminating in choosing tenants because of their race, religion, ethnic origin, color, sex, physical or mental handicap, or family status. Landlords cannot refuse to rent to a family with children. It is also illegal under the Fair Housing Act for landlords to harass, intimidate, threaten, interfere with, or evict a tenant based on any of these same factors. Furthermore, the same law prohibits the landlord from attempting to evict a tenant for filing a complaint or lawsuit charging the landlord with discrimination.

nose rings. In some places, a landlord may even refuse to rent to certain people because of their occupation.

Repairs and Property Maintenance

Q. Does the landlord have the obligation to maintain the premises and to make repairs if defects occur?

A. Yes. Both court rulings and state and local laws impose on the landlord a duty to maintain rental property. If a government agency is enforcing a housing code, the agency can also go after the landlord for a defective condition, regardless of who actually caused it. (The landlord might have legal recourse against the tenant if the tenant damaged the property, but the landlord must still repair the property.)

For more information on the various warranties associated with rental properties and the consequences for violations, see the previous discussion on repairs and property maintenance in the section of this chapter titled "The Tenant."

Lease Termination by the Landlord

Q. At the end of a lease term, does the landlord need a reason to terminate the lease?

A. No. The landlord does not need a reason to terminate the lease, unless the lease requires written notice or provides for automatic renewal. However, the security of tenure or a retaliatory conduct law may govern the nonrenewal of the lease. Security of tenure is discussed in the sidebar on page 345, and retaliatory conduct is discussed on page 362.

Q. How does the landlord terminate the lease upon expiration of the term?

A. It depends on the type of lease. If there is an oral or written lease with month-to-month tenancy, the landlord ends it by serving written notice. The notice must give the tenant thirty days to vacate if rent is paid monthly, and seven days if it is paid weekly, although some states have different rules. Most cities or states require that this notice be delivered personally to the tenant, although some permit delivery by mail.

If there is a written lease with a specific duration or term, the lease automatically ends on the last day of the term. However, some municipal ordinances require a thirty-day written notice to the tenant before the end of the term.

Q. Can the landlord terminate the lease because the tenant is paying reduced rent?

A. It depends on the reason. If the tenant is paying reduced rent because of the landlord's breach of the implied warranty of habitability or violation of the housing code, then the landlord may not have the right to terminate the lease. A retaliatory conduct law may prohibit such a termination.

Q. I want to evict a tenant—what should I be aware of?

A. A landlord may not evict a tenant to retaliate for the tenant having exercised a right or remedy under the law. Protected rights include complaining to the government agency responsible for code enforcement, complaining to the landlord about code violations and the failure to make repairs, and organizing or joining a tenants' union.

Q. What type of conduct counts as retaliatory?

A. Landlord-tenant laws usually define four actions as retaliatory:

1. filing an eviction action or threatening to do so;
2. failing to renew a lease;
3. increasing the rent; and
4. decreasing services.

Q. How does the tenant prove that the landlord's conduct was retaliatory?

A. The tenant has to prove that the landlord knew about the tenant's protected conduct. The tenant also needs to prove that the defects complained of were code violations.

Sometimes, the law assumes that the conduct was retaliatory if the tenant engaged in a protected activity within a specified period of time, sometimes as long as twelve months, prior to the landlord's action. The landlord would then have the burden to prove some other valid motive for terminating the lease or increasing the rent.

Q. One of my tenants is causing some serious problems. Can I evict him?

A. Landlords can terminate a lease for cause in certain situations. For nonpayment of rent, the landlord can serve a written notice threatening to terminate the lease unless the tenant pays the past due rent within a certain number of days (depending upon the area, from three to ten days). If the rent is paid within the period specified by the notice, then the landlord must accept the rent and the tenant may stay.

For violation of the rules and regulations of the lease or damage to the premises, the landlord can serve a written notice terminat-ing the tenancy after a certain number of days (from ten to thirty days, depending upon the area). The most common violations include disturbing the neighboring tenants, possession of pets, and occupancy by persons not named on the lease. Some localities, but not all, provide that the tenant may remain if the violations end.

Q. What does all this emphasis on written notices mean to the landlord?

A. In every jurisdiction, the law imposes specific statutory obligations on the landlord regarding how to terminate the lease. If the landlord fails to give written notice where required, or if the notice is not properly written or not properly served on the tenant, then the landlord will not have the right to terminate. When the landlord goes to court, it is already too late to correct any deficiencies in the written notice.

Besides hiring a lawyer to advise during the entire procedure, the landlord can obtain standardized termination forms from stationery stores, the local apartment association, or the National Association of Realtors. Landlords should use these forms and fill in every blank space accurately to be sure that they follow the law.

Q. What can the landlord do if the tenant doesn't move out after the lease is terminated?

A. The landlord must take the tenant to eviction court. The landlord cannot simply decide to evict the tenant and carry out the eviction unilaterally. For an eviction to be legal, there must be a court order signed by a judge. Also, the sheriff or some other governmental agent must actually carry out the physical removal of the tenant from the apartment.

Q. Why would the landlord sue the tenant? Isn't it easier to ask the tenant to leave?

A. Of course, the landlord can ask the tenant to leave. But the landlord must sue the tenant if the tenant does not move after being asked. In that case, the landlord would be suing for **eviction,** which is legally known as **forcible entry and detainer** or **unlawful detainer.**

Q. What does the landlord need to do in order to evict a tenant?

A. If the tenant will not voluntarily leave the property, the landlord must take three steps in order to successfully evict.

1. **The landlord must serve the tenant a termination-of-tenancy notice.** This notice must be properly filled out and properly served upon the tenant. Each state has different, but quite specific, procedures that the landlord must follow. Al-

though the landlord may sue the tenant without a lawyer, a lawyer will probably protect the landlord from making the kind of legal errors that result in the court dismissing the lawsuit.

2. **The landlord must file a complaint with the local court, and have a summons served upon the tenant by a process server.** The landlord may have to pay a filing fee. Service of the summons must be proper. Once again, hiring a lawyer will help the landlord navigate the legal requirements.

3. **The landlord must win the trial.** Each state has different, but specific, trial rules. Trials for eviction often have different rules than other kinds of trials. For example, some states allow the tenant to file for a jury trial.

Q. How long does the eviction process take?

A. After the notice period expires, the landlord may file a lawsuit alleging forcible entry and unlawful detainer. The court will assign the case for trial as a **summary proceeding** (i.e., an expedited, quick process). The trial may be scheduled as soon as two weeks after the suit is filed. Assuming service was proper, the court will enter judgment after a default proceeding (if the tenant does not show up) or a trial (if the tenant does contest the suit).

In some states, the judge can order eviction immediately at the end of the trial. But the court customarily gives the tenant time to move out, usually one to four weeks. If the tenant remains after that period, the landlord must hire the sheriff or marshal to carry out a forcible eviction. This will take several weeks more. Further delays are possible if the tenant files a motion for more time, or objects to the court decision. Eviction may take still longer

▶ CHANGING THE LOCKS

Most people have heard stories about landlords changing the locks or shutting off the water or electricity in order to force out a tenant. This type of conduct is illegal.

In fact, some jurisdictions consider such action a criminal offense. If the tenant is not allowed back into an apartment, the landlord can be arrested, and can also be sued for monetary damages and lawyer's fees for an unlawful interruption of the occupancy.

if the tenant is being evicted during the winter months. Some municipalities prohibit eviction if the temperature falls below a certain level.

Q. What happens if the tenant does not show up in court?

A. If the tenant does not respond properly to the lawsuit or show up in court, the judge will issue a default judgment in favor of the landlord. This happens in most eviction suits.

Q. What kind of judgment may the court enter in an eviction case?

A. If the court rules in favor of the landlord, it may require the tenant simply to vacate the premises, or it may require the tenant to vacate and pay back rent, damages, court costs, and, in some cases, the landlord's lawyer's fees.

Q. Can the landlord take the tenant's possessions, or physically throw out the tenant after the court authorizes eviction?

A. No. The landlord must have the sheriff (or some other proper authority) carry out the physical eviction. Only the court can evict a tenant, and the purpose of the court proceedings is to prevent the landlord from undertaking "self-help" evictions. If the court issues a judgment for unpaid rent, the landlord must use normal debt-collection procedures, which may include wage garnishment and attachment of bank accounts.

Q. Is any of the tenant's property protected from seizure if the tenant owes money to the landlord?

A. Yes. All jurisdictions exempt some property from seizure by creditors, but they vary greatly in specifying which property is ex-

empt. States may exempt used cars of low value, household furnishings, clothing, tools or equipment used in the tenant's business, and most of the tenant's wages. Chapter 11, "Consumer Bankruptcy," provides more detailed information on this area of the law.

Q. Does the tenant owe rent after the termination of the lease and eviction?

A. The court may terminate the right of the tenant to occupy the premises. In many areas, however, the tenant can still be held liable for the payment of rent if the lease provides for it. But it is unusual for the landlord to sue the tenant a second time if the reason for the first lawsuit was nonpayment of rent. Debt collection against a tenant who was evicted for nonpayment of rent is often a waste of time, because the tenant who did not have the money to pay the rent usually does not have the money to pay a judgment.

REMEMBER THIS

• Landlords cannot discriminate against possible tenants on the basis of race, gender, national origin, or other protected classes.

• A landlord may not retaliate by terminating a tenancy if the tenant exercises any right or remedy under the law. Protected rights include complaining to the government agency responsible for code enforcement, complaining to the landlord about code violations and the failure to make repairs, and organizing or joining a tenants' union.

• Landlords can cancel a lease for such causes as nonpayment of rent and violation of rules, but if tenants do not move out willingly, landlords have to go to court to seek an eviction order. Tenants can defend against the eviction attempt in court.

THE RENTAL PROPERTY

The relationship between a tenant and landlord doesn't just involve those two parties; often the local government also has a say in the property's condition and upkeep. Housing codes play an important role in determining the maintenance required on a property, and can provide important remedies for dissatisfied tenants. This section explains the basics of municipal housing codes, outlines the enforcement process, and explains the process of terminating of a lease for municipal code violations.

Municipal Code Enforcement

Q. Can the municipal government force the landlord to maintain a property and make repairs?

A. Yes. If the municipality has a housing code, it will probably also have mechanisms for enforcing that code. The tenant can report the landlord to the municipal department responsible for enforcing the code. Municipalities often have employees to inspect properties for code violations.

Q. What is a housing code?

A. A **housing code** is a municipal ordinance (sometimes a state statute) that sets standards for the construction, rehabilitation, and maintenance of buildings. Housing codes govern new construction, energy conservation, fire regulations, fuel gas controls, private sewage disposal, mechanical equipment, plumbing, electrical, zoning, and general property maintenance.

Property owners must comply with these standards when constructing a new building, rehabbing or upgrading an old one, and making repairs. A standard provision in these codes prohibits a landlord from renting property that does not meet the code standards.

Q. What kind of standards do housing codes require landlords to meet?

A. Tenants should know what the local housing code requires, because they have the right to demand these required conditions of the landlord. Landlords should know the requirements because the municipality expects them to maintain these conditions in the property.

The following areas and issues are typically regulated heavily by local housing codes:

- The areas outside the apartment. This includes issues relating to garbage and refuse removal, stairs, porches, railings and handrails, windows and doors, screens, storm windows, walls and siding, roofs, chimneys, foundations, basements, signs, awnings, and other decorative features.
- The interior of the apartment, including walls, floors, and ceilings. Typically interiors must be kept free from holes, cracks, mold, water damage, lead-based paint, and insect infestation. Bathroom and kitchen floors must generally be waterproof.
- Light, ventilation, and space. Responsibilities typically include minimum lighting for halls and stairways, window or mechanical ventilation, and minimum adequate space for occupants.
- Plumbing facilities and fixtures. Landlords typically must provide running

water, adequate hot water, sufficient water flow, leak-free plumbing, and working fixtures.

- Mechanical systems, such as hot-water tanks, furnaces, air-conditioning systems, cooking equipment, and fireplaces.
- Electrical systems. Landlords typically must provide sufficient circuits and capacity, as well as working elevators (where applicable), fixtures, switches, and receptacles.
- Fire safety. Landlords may be required to supply smoke detectors, fire extinguishers, automatic sprinkler systems, adequate exits, and control over storage of flammable materials.
- Physical security. Landlords may be responsible for locks on windows and doors, peepholes, and shatterproof glass on windows.

Q. How does municipal code enforcement work?

A. Municipalities make two basic types of inspections: inspections upon complaint from residents, and inspections according to a preset plan.

A municipality's plan is simply a schedule of inspections. It may call for inspection of the common areas of every rental building every year, or inspections of all buildings with more than three stories every two years, or of every building in a certain neighborhood every three years, or any variation of that timetable. Some courts have restricted the right of the municipality to enter apartments in a building as part of a preset plan.

Some landlords have contested the right of municipal inspectors to enter their property; they call it trespassing. The municipality may have to go to court to get a warrant if the landlord refuses to let an inspector enter. The municipality does not need a warrant, how-

ever, if tenants invite the inspector onto the property.

If a local inspector finds any violations of the housing code, a citation can be issued against the landlord. Besides stating the violations, the citation may give the landlord a specified number of days to comply with the law.

If the landlord does not make the required repairs, the next stage of enforcement will probably be an administrative hearing. If the landlord fails to correct the violations after a hearing, the municipality can take the landlord to court.

Q. Is municipal code enforcement effective?

A. It certainly can be. If the landlord refuses to make repairs, the city can fine the landlord. If the landlord does not pay the fine, the city can place a lien on the property. The city can also foreclose on the lien. The city can appoint another person, called a **receiver,** to manage the building, collect the rents, and make repairs until the code violations are corrected. The city can even condemn the building and have it demolished at the landlord's expense.

If a municipality is committed to code enforcement, this is probably the most effective way to maintain the physical quality of housing in a community. If a municipality does not make code enforcement a priority, then compliance by landlords will to some degree be voluntary, and there is the risk that some landlords will only comply minimally.

Lease Termination for Code Violations

Q. Can the tenant terminate the lease if the landlord fails to maintain the premises?

A. Yes. Three different legal theories justify such an action. They are known as illegal lease, constructive eviction, and material noncompliance.

Q. What is an illegal lease?

A. If the landlord has been cited by the municipality for serious violations of the housing code, the tenant can argue the **illegal lease** concept—basically, that the lease is illegal because the code makes it against the law for the landlord to rent the premises in its present condition. This theory holds that the landlord should not benefit economically from an illegal act.

Q. What is constructive eviction?

A. Constructive eviction means that the property is in such poor condition that the tenant cannot reasonably be expected to live there. This would be the case, for example, if a property had no running water, no electricity, no heat, or a leaking roof in danger of collapse.

The tenant has to serve notice on the landlord of the conditions, but there is usually no minimum amount of time that the tenant is required to wait before vacating. The tenant must actually move out in order to argue constructive eviction. If constructive eviction applies, then the tenant will not be responsible for paying the rent.

Q. What is material noncompliance?

A. Material noncompliance means that the premises doesn't meet the minimum standards of the local or state housing code. To terminate the lease on these grounds, the tenant would have to serve written notice on the landlord, specify the conditions that represent material noncompliance, demand the correction of the conditions within a specified period of time, and inform the landlord of the date that the lease will terminate if the conditions are not corrected.

REMEMBER THIS

- Housing codes exist almost everywhere, and provide landlords with standards that they must meet.

- A tenant can terminate a lease for housing code violations based on three theories: illegal lease, constructive eviction, and material noncompliance.

Consumer Credit

A creditor denied credit to Will based on his bad credit history. In doing so, the creditor relied on negative information about Will from a credit report supplied by a major credit bureau. Will requests a copy of the credit report from the bureau. Much to his dismay, the report contains information about another individual with the same name as his. It also contains some information that's more than ten years old, and other information that's completely inaccurate. What can Will do to correct these mistakes? Can information remain on his report for that many years? What about the other person with Will's name—what happens if his debt collectors start to contact Will?

Credit can be valuable for many consumers, but it has many potential downsides. Some people overextend themselves by using credit to make purchases they can't afford. They consume rather than save, and become mired in staggering credit card debt with high interest rates.

This chapter explains credit and its costs, outlines the credit application process, explains the credit reporting process, and provides information about fair debt collection practices.

CREDIT BASICS

Imagine that you apply for a new credit card with a high limit. You have other cards with high balances, and you need some more credit to buy stuff that you want. You

---

▶ TYPES OF CREDIT

There are three basic forms of consumer credit:

- **Installment credit** (also known as **closed-end credit**). A consumer agrees to repay the amount owed in at least two equal installments over a set period of time. Automobile, personal, and furniture store loans are common examples of installment credit.

- **Charge account credit** (also known as **thirty-day credit**). Balances owed on charge accounts usually require payment in full within thirty days. Such arrangements are not considered to be installment credit, since the debt is not scheduled to be repaid in two or more installments. Travel and entertainment cards, such as those issued by American Express and Diners Club, operate this way, as do most charge accounts with local businesses.

- **Revolving credit** (also known as **open-end credit**). In this more flexible credit model, the consumer has the option of drawing on a preapproved open-end credit line and then paying off the entire outstanding balance, a specified minimum amount, or some amount in between. A consumer may use this type of credit, make a payment, and then use the credit again. Credit cards issued by Discover, MasterCard, Visa, and most major retail establishments are all examples of revolving credit.

In addition, some lease arrangements operate like consumer credit and may be subject to similar laws. These arrangements are discussed briefly later in this chapter. However, credit secured by real property—your home, for example—is discussed in Chapter 7, "Buying and Selling a Home," and in Chapter 8, "Home Ownership."

fill out the credit application, but a week later a rejection letter arrives saying that you do not qualify for the credit card. You ask yourself, is my credit really that bad? If I can't even get a credit card, how will I ever be able to get a loan to buy a new car or a home?

This section answers some important questions about credit—namely, what it is and how to get it.

Q. What exactly is credit?

A. **Credit** is essentially the sale of money for a specified price. Credit allows you to buy and use goods and services now—for example, a car or a washing machine—and pay for them later. Credit can also be used to pay for emergencies, such as a car repair or unexpected medical bill.

Q. Why does credit cost money?

A. To buy now and pay later, you must usually pay a finance charge, which consists of interest and other fees. This is because the supplier who waits for payment, or the lender who lent you the money, could have invested the money instead of lending it to you. The finance charge you pay compensates them for lost interest, as well as for the costs and risk involved in extending you credit.

Q. What is an APR?

A. **APR** stands for **annual percentage rate.** It refers to a way of expressing (in terms of a percentage) the amount of interest and certain other fees that you must pay in order to obtain credit. The APR relates your total finance charge to (1) the amount of credit you receive; and (2) the amount of time you have in which to repay it. When you buy credit, you buy a certain amount for a given number of months. The total dollar amount of your finance charge will depend on how many dollars worth of credit you obtain initially, and for how many months you use those dollars.

Q. I keep seeing references to the Truth in Lending Act. What is it?

A. The **Truth in Lending Act** (**TILA**) is a federal law that requires creditors, including banks, department stores, credit card issuers, and finance companies, to disclose the cost of credit in consumer transactions. TILA is part of a larger federal law known as the Consumer Credit Protection Act.

Under TILA, before you sign an installment contract, creditors must show you in writing the amount being financed, the monthly

---

▶ ## FEDERAL LAWS THAT AFFECT CONSUMER CREDIT

There are many federal laws that provide certain protections and rights to consumers. These include the Consumer Credit Protection Act of 1968 (CCPA), the Consumer Leasing Act (CLA), the Truth in Lending Act (TILA), the Fair Credit and Charge Card Disclosure Act, the Fair Credit Reporting Act (FCRA), the Equal Credit Opportunity Act, the Fair Credit Billing Act (FCBA), the Fair Debt Collection Practices Act (FDCPA), and the Identity Theft and Assumption Deterrence Act of 1998 (Identity Theft Act). These laws are discussed through this chapter. For additional information on such protections, contact your state or local consumer protection agency.

▶ CAREFULLY EVALUATE YOUR OPTIONS

It's critical to explore all of your financing options. Fortunately, the law allows you to obtain the information you need to shop comparatively. Use all of the available information, and consider your own needs carefully, to determine which loan or credit arrangement is best for you.

payment, the number of monthly payments, the dollar amount of the finance charge, and the APR. TILA also has rules about how open-end terms and conditions must be disclosed and explained to you.

TILA also regulates credit advertising. For example, if an automobile ad emphasizes a low monthly payment (i.e., by giving a dollar figure), then it must also provide you with other pertinent information, such as the APR.

Q. When shopping for credit, should I look only at APRs?

A. No. When buying on credit, it is not wise simply to compare APRs. Instead, you should decide how long you want to owe money to a creditor. If you want to minimize the amount of time during which you owe money, then you should choose the credit arrangement that offers the shortest time frame, even if the APR is higher. Or you may be able to negotiate better terms from one creditor if it shortens or lengthens the life of the loan.

REMEMBER THIS

- There are several forms of credit: noninstallment credit, installment or closed-end credit, and revolving or open-end credit. You should understand your credit arrangement, including finance charges, the monthly payments, the length of time

▶ POINTS TO CONSIDER WHEN USING INSTALLMENT CREDIT

When thinking about using credit, consider whether the interest is deductible on your federal income taxes. Almost all homeowners may deduct their entire mortgage interest for tax purposes. However, the interest that you pay on credit card debt and other debts is not deductible.

If you itemize deductions, you might consider financing major credit purchases through a home equity loan. This type of loan is discussed in the chapter on owning a home. However, remember that this type of loan puts your home at risk if you cannot repay. And if the items you are permitted to deduct for tax purposes are worth less than your standard income tax deduction, you will find that this approach will not help to reduce your tax bill.

You should also consider what will happen if you pay the loan off early. Make sure that you won't incur any unearned finance charges or prepayment penalties.

you must make such payments, interest charges, and whether interest charges are deductible.

- Not all credit costs the same. The Truth in Lending Act requires creditors to disclose the cost of credit to you, the consumer, before you sign the contract.

- You should look at several aspects of a credit arrangement beyond the annual percentage rate (APR)—for example, the length of the debt obligation. Remember that shopping for credit is like shopping for other products; compare and contrast your options to make the best deal.

CHOOSING A CREDIT CARD

This section examines terms that are typically offered to consumers by banks and other issuers of credit cards. It provides examples from actual solicitations, and explains how to determine whether a card offered to you is a good fit for your own credit needs.

Q. Who provides credit cards?

A. Many common credit cards such as Discover, MasterCard, and Visa are issued by various banks, savings and loans, and credit unions. Hence, if you do not like the terms on one card, you can always check with other issuers to see if their terms are preferable. Major retailers issue their own credit cards, and oil companies also offer their own cards, although many oil companies do not offer revolving credit.

Q. I am thinking about getting a credit card. Are there any protections for consumers?

A. First of all, it is illegal for card issuers to send you a credit card unless you have asked

for it, or unless it replaces a card you previously asked for. Under TILA, every solicitation for a credit card must contain a brief disclosure statement. More extensive disclosures are due before you use a credit card for which you have applied, and specific disclosures about finance and other charges and transactions are required with your periodic statement, which is usually monthly.

Q. How should I judge the APR listed in a solicitation?

A. Remember that the law requires credit grantors to quote the APR, which for credit cards usually includes the interest rate, but not other fees.

Q. Can I avoid paying a finance charge?

A. Most credit cards offer a grace period for repayments. The grace period is a period of time between the end of the billing cycle and the date on which you must pay the entire bill in order to avoid paying a finance charge. Typically such grace periods last between twenty and twenty-five days. The grace period is usually described on the disclosure statement in the following manner:

Grace period for repayment of the balance for purchases:

No finance charges are assessed on current purchases if the balance is paid in full each month within 25 days after billing.

Note that the grace period starts on the billing date. By the time you actually receive the bill, you may have only two weeks to make your payment. You must be careful to ensure that your payment is received by the due date. Be aware that the full balance must be paid each month to avoid interest, and that the grace period or interest-free period applies only to purchases. You usually do not get an interest-free period for cash advances, balance transfers, or convenience check transactions.

The credit grantor may adjust the grace period using the **retroactive** or **two-cycle balance method,** which is another method of assessing monthly charges on your bill. Under this system, if the opening balance on your bill was zero, and then you made credit purchases but did not pay your entire bill, your next monthly bill will include a finance charge for these purchases from the dates that they were posted.

Q. How do credit grantors calculate an account's balance?

A. As you can see from the examples below, finance charges may vary greatly depending on how the credit grantor calculates them. In the first example, the average daily balance of $300 determines the amount of finance charge owed. The average daily balance is the average of the $500 owed for half a month and the $100 ($500 minus $400) owed for the other half. You owe the $500 and the $100 each for half a month, because you paid the $400 in the middle of the month.

In the adjusted-balance method, which is used by relatively few creditors, you owe a finance charge only on the amount owed at the end of the period. Since you paid $400, and thus only owe $100, you pay a finance charge only on the $100.

In the previous-balance method, you owe a finance charge on the amount owed at the beginning of the pay period—the entire $500.

Q. Does the APR on a credit card always stay the same?

A. More and more credit card issuers set APRs that vary with some interest-rate index, such as the market rates on three-year U.S. Treasury bills or the prime rate charged by banks on short-term business loans. The **spread** is the percentage point added to the index to determine the rate you pay. An example of a disclosure on a variable-rate credit card offering is shown below:

Variable Rate Information
Your Annual Percentage Rate may vary quarterly. The rate will be the Prime Rate as published in The Wall Street Journal plus 9%.

	AVERAGE-DAILY-BALANCE METHOD	ADJUSTED-BALANCE METHOD	PREVIOUS-BALANCE METHOD
Monthly interest rate	1.5%	1.5%	1.5%
Previous balance	$500	$500	$500
Payment on 15th day	$400	$400	$400
Finance charge	$4.50	$1.50	$7.50
Calculation of finance charge	$300 × 1.5%	$100 × 1.5%	$500 × 1.5%

The rate will not go below 15.0% or exceed 19.9%.

The issuers of fixed-rate cards can also change the rate from time to time in accordance with the cardholder agreement and state and federal law.

Q. Is there a charge each year for the right to use a credit card?

A. Few (if any) credit cards issued by retailers have annual fees, but some credit cards issued by financial institutions do. If you usually pay your credit card accounts in full each month and do not expect to pay a finance charge, you should shop for a credit card with no annual fee or a fee that is low. However, if you often don't pay the balance in full each month, a low APR may be better for you than a low annual fee. A credit card solicitation must disclose any annual or other periodic fee, and certain other fees such as transaction fees, cash advance fees, and late fees.

Q. What other fees and charges should I look for on the disclosure statement?

A. In your disclosure statement, you will find a statement similar to the following (assuming these fees are part of the plan):

> **Transaction fee for cash advances, and fees for paying late or exceeding the credit limit**
> Transaction fee for cash advances: 2% of the amount of the advance ($1.00 minimum; $10.00 maximum).
> Late payment fee: $15.00, if the amount due is $2 or more.
> Over-the-limit fee: $15.00

Note that there may be other fees as well, such as replacement card fees, copy fees, wire

> ▶ **PAY AS MUCH AS YOU CAN AFFORD**
>
> If you cannot pay off the entire balance on your credit card, you should pay as much as you can afford. If you only pay the minimum amount shown on the bill every month, depending on the interest rate, it may take you more than ten years to pay off the debt—even if you never use the card again.

transfer fees, and insufficient-funds fees. Most credit card issuers set a limit on the amount of credit that they are willing to provide you at any one time. To encourage you not to exceed this limit, some banks may charge an over-the-limit fee. If you believe that you might be close to your credit limit from time to time, you might want to shop for a bank credit card that does not have an over-the-limit fee, or that has a very low one.

Q. What if I can't get a credit card from a financial institution—either because of a bad credit record or because I have not established a credit record?

A. You may want to consider applying for a secured credit card. Issued by a bank or other financial institution, a **secured credit card** is a credit card that is secured by a savings account. You need to shop carefully for the best terms. Your line of credit will typically be limited to 90 percent or 100 percent of your savings account. In shopping for a secured card, compare the rates paid on savings accounts, the APR charged, and the annual fees. The APR is important, since you may not be repaying your account in full each month. Also important are the late fees and any over-the-limit fees. These are sometimes quite high on secured credit cards.

Having a secured card is somewhat like using training wheels on a bicycle. Once you have shown you can handle a revolving-credit account, you should ask the institution that issued you the secured credit card to offer you the opportunity to switch to an unsecured card with more favorable terms. If the offer is not made, even after you have established a good credit record, apply for a regular credit card from another financial institution.

Protections for the Consumer

Q. How does the Truth in Lending Act affect me?

A. The federal Truth in Lending Act (TILA) helps you to choose credit wisely by requiring credit grantors to provide you with (and to highlight) important information before you make a decision. However, the law alone cannot protect you fully. You have to make it work by being an informed consumer.

TILA does not set interest rates or limit fees, nor does it tell you what rates are fair or unfair. In some states, laws exist to protect you from interest rates and fees that legislators have thought to be too high, but in most cases it is competition among lenders that serves to keep credit card rates in line. But in order for this competition to be effective, you must use the available information to select the credit card that fits you best.

Q. How can I limit the amount of interest and fees that I pay for credit?

A. Your shopping for credit plays a key role in limiting and minimizing the interest and fees

that you must pay. It does not matter whether you are looking for installment credit or revolving credit. And even though most states impose rate ceilings on various credit grantors or types of credit, shopping still saves you money.

In shopping for the best terms, check the *Wall Street Journal* and other newspapers that frequently publish credit card shopping guides covering all of the relevant terms discussed above. The Federal Reserve Board also gathers credit card rate terms for publication. Additionally, many online resources allow you to easily shop for a credit card and compare terms (see "The World at Your Fingertips" for information on these and other helpful websites).

Q. In shopping for a credit card, I found that one credit card issuer charges a higher rate than is allowed by state law. How can that be?

A. Many states impose rate ceilings on retail or bank credit cards. However, these limits do not always apply across the board. For example, under federal law, national banks may export their finance charge rates on credit cards. This means that a national bank may issue cards from an office in South Dakota—a state that has no rate ceiling on bank cards—so that the bank may then charge cardholders in Iowa (or some other state) any rate the agreement specifies. While most retailers selling to Iowa consumers may not charge rates on their credit cards higher than Iowa law permits, some major retailers have established credit card banks in other states, and will issue cards from those banks in order to charge higher rates. In those instances, they abide by the laws of the state in which the bank is located.

If you believe that the rate being charged does in fact violate state law, you should report the case to the state office of consumer protection (or similar office), your state's attorney general, or the federal authorities for national banks or federal credit unions. Competition and enforcement activities usually prevent such violations; but if there is a violation, you may be able to recover all of your finance charges plus a penalty, depending upon your state's law.

Q. What if a credit grantor fails to obey TILA?

A. You should inform the proper federal enforcement agency. To enforce your rights, you may bring a lawsuit for **actual damages** (i.e., any money loss that you suffer.) You may also sue for the greater of twice the finance charge or $100. However, the most you can recover, even if the finance charge is high, is $1,000. If you win the lawsuit, the law also entitles you to court costs and lawyer's fees.

Under some state laws, a violation of TILA is considered an unfair or deceptive act or practice (which may allow you to recover more than your actual damages), or a violation of other state laws.

Protections for Consumers Who Lease Products

Q. I am going to lease a car using credit. Does the law protect me?

A. Yes. The federal Consumer Leasing Act, which is part of the Truth in Lending Act, applies to any lease of consumer goods for more than four months in which the total contrac-

---

▶ CHECKLIST: WHAT TO LOOK FOR IN A CAR LEASE

- the **capitalized cost**—that is, the cost of the goods being leased (the capitalized cost is negotiable to the same extent that the price of goods is negotiable if you were buying them).

- the total amount of any initial payment you are required to pay.

- the number and amount of monthly payments.

- the total amount for fees, such as license fees and taxes.

- any penalty for default or late payments.

- the annual mileage allowance and the extra charges involved if you exceed the allowance.

- whether you can end the lease early, and the method of computing the charge if you do so.

- whether you may purchase the auto at the end of the lease, and for what price.

- any liability that you may have for the difference between the estimated value of the auto and its market value at the time you end the lease.

- any extra payment that you must make at the end of the lease.

tual obligation does not exceed $25,000. (It does not apply to leases of real estate.) This law requires the lessor (for example, the owner of the auto you lease) to disclose information before you sign the lease. You can report apparent violations of the Consumer Leasing Act to the same agencies that enforce TILA. The checklist on page 376 outlines the information that should be included in a lease.

REMEMBER THIS

- All credit cards are different. Selecting one is a decision that should be made carefully.

- Remember that federal law (e.g., the Truth in Lending Act) requires credit card companies to disclose the cost of credit to you. They must tell you the APR, how it's computed, any applicable fees, and a host of other financial information. However, bear in mind that TILA is primarily a disclosure statute. It does not set limits on the rates that credit card companies may charge.

- Some cards do not offer fixed APRs. Many cards have variable rates, usually tied to the prime rate.

- With credit cards, the interest-free period only applies to purchases. You lose your grace period, or interest-free period, if you do not pay in full at the end of the month. You usually pay interest from the date of the transaction for cash advances, balance transfers, and convenience check transactions.

- The federal Consumer Leasing Act applies to any lease of consumer goods for more than four months and under $25,000. This law requires lessors to disclose information to you, the lessee-consumer.

CREDIT RECORDS

A federal law, the Fair Credit Reporting Act, protects consumers from inaccurate information that could mar their consumer reports—for example, through identity theft, mix-ups, or flat-out mistakes. This section discusses consumer credit records, and the ways in which consumers can protect the accuracy of their credit information.

Establishing a Credit Record

Q. What is a credit bureau?

A. Credit bureaus (sometimes called **credit reporting agencies** or **consumer reporting agencies**) maintain computer files of your financial payment histories, public-record data, and personal identifying data. The federal Fair Credit Reporting Act (FCRA) governs their activities, as do the laws of many states. Credit bureaus do not make credit decisions. Instead, they provide data to credit grantors making credit decisions. The three nationwide consumer reporting agencies are Experian, Equifax, and TransUnion. You can find the credit bureaus in your area by going online or by looking under "credit reporting companies" in the yellow pages.

Q. If they don't actually make decisions about my credit record, then how exactly do credit bureaus work?

A. Credit grantors provide information on their customers' debts and payment histories to credit bureaus, usually on a monthly basis. The credit bureau then makes the data available to other credit grantors to whom the consumer has applied for credit. For this reason, a good credit record is very important for obtaining credit to purchase goods and services, to rent an apartment, or to buy a home. Insurance companies and potential employers may also examine credit reports when you apply for insurance or employment. The FCRA punishes people who obtain a credit report without authorization, as well as credit bureau employees who supply credit reports to unauthorized people.

Q. How can I get credit if I've never had it before?

A. First-time borrowers soon realize that in order to get credit they must have a credit history. Consumers have several ways to start building a good, solid credit history. For example:

- Open a checking or savings account. When credit grantors see such accounts, they can judge whether you have adequate money and know how to manage it.
- Apply for limited credit from a large, local department store. Once you obtain credit, use it. If you want to build a credit history, remember that some small local retailers, travel-and-entertainment card companies, credit unions, and gasoline card companies do not report your credit performance to a credit bureau.
- Obtain a secured credit card (discussed on page 374) or deposit money in a bank or savings and loan, and then borrow against it.
- Have someone cosign a loan with you. That person must have a favorable credit record and will face liability for the debt if you cannot pay. After you open a loan based on someone else's credit and pay it back, it will be easier for you to get credit on your own.
- Obtain a credit card with a low credit limit—for example, between $300 and

$500. Once you have demonstrated that you are able to manage that amount, the credit limit might be increased.
- Pay your rent and utility bills on time; some credit grantors will take this into account when making a decision.

Q. Should I get credit in my own name, even though I am married?

A. Yes. You should establish a credit history in your own name in case you get divorced or your spouse dies. This is also important if your spouse has a poor credit record and you do not want your credit records tarnished by your spouse's payment performance.

Q. My spouse recently passed away and I don't have any credit in my own name. Is there anything I can do?

A. Yes. Many divorced or widowed persons do not have credit histories separate from those of their former spouses. In these cases, credit grantors will look at the credit history of any accounts held jointly with a former spouse. In addition, even if the surviving spouse is not legally on the account, if he or she is listed as an authorized user, then a credit report may reflect his or her participation. Nonearning spouses can also obtain credit by using checks, receipts, or other records to show that they are worthy of credit. If their former spouses had poor credit records, nonearning spouses may show that the records do not reflect whether they themselves deserve credit by sending relevant evidence to credit grantors—for example, letters explaining that the nonearning spouse was not responsible for the poor repayment history, copies of contracts signed only by the former spouse, or other such evidence.

Checking Your Credit Record

Q. What does a credit report look like?

A. A basic credit report contains the following information:

- **Identification and employment data.** Your name, birth date, Social Security number, addresses (present and former), and employment history.
- **Public record information.** Events that are a matter of public record related to your creditworthiness, such as bankruptcies, foreclosures, or tax liens.
- **Payment history.** Your account record with different credit grantors, showing how much credit has been extended and how you have repaid it.
- **Inquiries.** Credit bureaus maintain a record of all credit grantors who have checked your credit record within the past six months.

Q. May I look at my credit record?

A. Yes. You have the right to know the content of credit files that contain information about you, and many consumer credit experts suggest that you examine these credit files at least once a year. A periodic checkup will enable you to find out what the credit bureaus will report to businesses that have a legitimate reason to check your credit record.

Q. When may I access my credit record? As often as I want?

A. The FCRA allows you to review your file at any time, and it is particularly important for you to do so if you plan to rent an apartment or apply for a home mortgage loan or other major loan or credit purchase. The FCRA requires each of the nationwide consumer reporting companies—Equifax, Experian, and TransUnion—to provide you with a free copy of your credit report, at your request, once per year. Otherwise, the credit bureau may charge you a reasonable fee for providing this service, unless your inquiry occurs after a creditor took adverse credit action against you or in certain other circumstances. A creditor may turn you down for credit or take other adverse credit action because of a report from a credit bureau. If this happens, the law requires that the credit grantor provide you with the bureau's name, address, and telephone number. You can request a copy of the credit bureau's report by telephone, mail, or in person. If a credit grantor has denied you credit within the past sixty days because

▶ UNDERSTANDING YOUR CREDIT REPORT

Contrary to popular belief, a credit bureau neither tracks your personal life nor explicitly evaluates credit applications. However, credit grantors do request a risk score summary that indicates the probability of bankruptcy or serious delinquency in the future. Credit bureaus are simply organizations that collect and transmit four principal types of information: identification and employment data, payment histories, credit-related inquiries, and public record information.

A good credit report is vital to your access to credit. Therefore, it is important for you to understand and find out what your credit report contains, how to improve your credit report, and how to deal with credit problems.

of data supplied by a credit bureau, the bureau cannot charge you for the information.

The FCRA also requires the credit bureau to tell you the names of the creditors who provided the data in your file, as well as the names of everyone who received a report on you in the last six months (or within the past two years for employment reports). The credit bureau must also help you interpret the data.

Q. How can I be sure that my credit record reflects only my own history, and not that of someone else with a similar name?

A. Because your credit record is critical to obtaining credit, it is very important to ensure that each item in your credit record actually reflects your own credit history, and not that of another person. Whenever you apply for credit, you should use the same name. Thus, if you are James R. Jones Jr., always add the "Jr." to your credit application. Do not sometimes identify yourself as "J. Randall Jones," and other times as "J. R. Jones." Finally, creditors will typically ask for your Social Security number on a credit application. The request is not to invade your privacy, but to ensure that your credit record does not get mixed up with that of another person with a name similar or identical to yours.

Maintaining a Good Credit Record

Q. What can I do if I believe the credit bureau has placed incorrect information in my file?

A. If you find that information in your credit report is inaccurate, incomplete, or outdated, you may challenge its accuracy or completeness by notifying the credit bureau. (For contact information, see the "World at Your Fingertips" section at the end of this book.)

Unless the credit bureau believes that your request is "frivolous or irrelevant," it must either verify the facts within thirty days or delete the information from its files. The "frivolous-or-irrelevant" provision is there in part to deter credit repair clinics from automatically challenging all negative information (whether or not a basis exists for such challenge), or from challenging the same negative information over and over again. If your complaint requires changes, the credit bureau will automatically notify the other nationwide bureaus and, if you request, notify any creditor that has checked your file in the past six months (two years for employment reports).

If reinvestigation of disputed information by a credit bureau does not resolve the matter to your satisfaction, you may file your version of the story in a maximum 100-word statement. The credit bureau must include your statement, or a clear and accurate summary of it, in all future credit reports containing the disputed item. You also may ask the bureau to mail copies of your statement to anyone who received a report containing the disputed item during the last six months (two years for employment reports).

Q. I had some credit problems a couple of years ago. How long does this information stay on my credit report?

A. Under the FCRA, consumer reporting agencies can report most negative information (such as late payments and accounts charged off) for seven years. Consumer reporting agencies can report records of bankruptcies for ten years (and up to twelve years for certain forms of bankruptcy). This negative information may continue to be used beyond these time limits when you apply for $150,000 or more in credit, a life insurance policy with a face amount of $150,000 or more, or a job paying at least $75,000 a year. The fact that negative information may remain on your credit report for such a long time underscores the importance of maintaining a good credit record. In many cases, however, the older information is less harmful to your credit score.

Credit and Divorce

Q. Can divorce impact my credit record?

A. Yes. Divorce can negatively affect people's credit for many reasons. People who are getting divorced should determine whether their various accounts are individual or joint accounts. If an account is an individual account, then only the individual on the account is responsible for the debts of that account. However, if the account is joint, both persons listed on the account are responsible. A joint account can prove costly when spouses or ex-spouses refuse to act responsibly or do not pay their bills. In **community property** states, both spouses may be responsible for all debts incurred during the marriage, even in the case of individual accounts.

Q. My spouse and I have some serious debt. When we divorce, can we split the debt?

A. Yes. Just as couples who are getting divorced usually negotiate a settlement in which they agree to divide their property, couples can also divide responsibility for debts. If the couple cannot agree on a settlement, the court will divide the assets and debts. For more information on divorce and debts, see Chapter 3, "Family Law."

REMEMBER THIS

- The Fair Credit Reporting Act (FCRA) provides a private right of action to con-

sumers, which allows them to ensure that their credit reports contain accurate information.

- Many creditors obtain information on consumers from major credit bureaus or credit reporting agencies. These credit bureaus have files containing your financial payment history, data from public records, and personal identification data.

- You are entitled to one free credit report every twelve months from each of the three nationwide consumer reporting agencies, as well as a free copy of your credit report whenever a creditor denies you credit based on a report generated by a credit bureau. In all other circumstances, the credit bureau is entitled to charge you a reasonable fee for providing a report.

- The FCRA imposes duties upon credit bureaus and reporting creditors to submit and maintain accurate information on consumers. If you dispute items on your credit report, the credit bureau must either verify the facts within a reasonable time or remove the information.

- Negative information does not stay on your credit report for life. Much information must be removed after seven years. However, records of bankruptcies can be reported for ten years (or in some cases up to twelve years).

APPLYING FOR CREDIT

The federal **Equal Credit Opportunity Act (ECOA)** prohibits discrimination against credit applicants on the basis of race, color, religion, national origin, sex, marital status, age, receipt of public assistance, or the fact that the applicant has in good faith exercised any right under the Consumer Credit Protection Act (which includes the ECOA, the Truth in Lending Act, and other federal consumer protection laws). This section explains how the law works, and outlines the steps involved with applying for credit.

The Credit Score

Q. How do creditors decide whether to issue credit?

A. Credit scoring systems are often used in making credit decisions. These systems weigh different factors deemed relevant to your creditworthiness. A credit scoring system at-tempts to determine how likely it is that you will pay your debts.

Not all credit scoring systems are alike. They attach different weights to different fac-tors. For this reason, each credit bureau may generate a different credit score for the same consumer. The following factors are generally used to calculate your credit score:

- **Payment history.** Have you paid your bills on time? (This factor typically com-prises 35 percent of your score.)
- **Amount of debt.** How much debt do you currently have? How much debt do you have as compared to your current credit limits? (30 percent)
- **Length of your credit history.** How long

▶ DETERMINING CREDITWORTHINESS

Credit grantors may use any of the following factors to decide whether to extend you credit:

- **Ability to repay:** This depends on the stability of your current job or income source, how much you earn, and the length of time you have worked or will receive your current income. Credit grantors may also consider your basic expenses, such as payments on rent, mortgage loans or other debts, utilities, college expenses, and taxes.

- **Credit history:** Your credit history reveals how much money you owe and whether you have large unused lines of open-end credit. Some important considerations are whether you have paid your bills on time, and whether you have filed for bankruptcy or had judgments issued against you.

- **Stability:** Credit grantors rate your stability based on how long you have lived at your current or former address, and by the length of time you have been with your current or former employer. Another consideration is whether you own your home or rent it.

- **Assets:** Assets such as a car or a home may be useful as collateral for a loan. Credit grantors also look at what else you may use for collateral, such as savings accounts or securities.

have your accounts been open? (15 percent)

- **Recent applications for credit.** Have you recently applied for several new accounts? If so, and if creditors denied your applications, such denials can negatively affect your credit score. (10 percent)

Under current law, if a consumer initiates an application for a consumer-purpose loan secured by one to four units of residential property, then creditors who use a consumer credit score as the basis for their decisions must disclose that credit score to the consumer. In such transactions, the consumer must receive a "Notice to the Home Loan Applicant" that spells out the lender's obligation to provide the credit score.

The Equal Credit Opportunity Act

Q. When I apply for credit, are there certain factors that credit grantors cannot consider?

A. Yes. The ECOA says that credit grantors may not use certain factors to discriminate against you in a credit deal. A credit grantor may not use age (provided that you are old enough to enter into a legally binding contract), race, color, national origin, sex, marital status, religion, receipt of public assistance, or the exercise of rights under the Consumer Credit Protection Act to

- discourage or prevent you from applying for credit;
- refuse you credit if you otherwise qualify;
- extend you credit on terms different from those granted to someone posing a similar risk (as determined by such factors as ability to repay, credit history, stability, and assets); or

- extend you less credit than you requested, if someone posing a similar risk would have received the same amount or more.

The ECOA does not, however, guarantee that you will receive credit. You must still meet the credit grantor's standards to qualify for the credit offered.

Q. When I apply for credit, may a credit grantor ask my age?

A. Yes, but if you are old enough to sign and be liable for a contract (usually eighteen, depending on state law), a grantor may not

- refuse to give you credit or decrease the amount of credit just because of your age;
- refuse to consider your retirement income in rating your credit application, if the creditor considers income in evaluating creditworthiness;
- cancel your credit account or require you to reapply just because you are a certain age or have retired; or
- refuse you credit or cancel your account because you cannot obtain life insurance (or similar insurance) due to your age.

The law does allow a credit grantor to consider certain age-related facts, including how long your income will continue or when you will reach retirement age.

Q. I am on public assistance. Can a credit grantor deny me credit because of this?

A. No, a credit grantor may not deny you credit for that reason alone. However, credit grantors may ask the age of your dependents, because you may lose federal benefits when they reach a certain age. A credit grantor may also consider whether you will continue to meet residency requirements for receiving benefits, and whether it will legally be able to access those benefits if you do not pay.

Q. Does my gender or marital status affect whether I am worthy of credit?

A. No. The law protects both men and women from discrimination based on gender and marital status. In general, a credit grantor may not deny you credit or take any adverse action because of your gender or because you are married, single, widowed, divorced, or separated. Specific prohibitions include

- A credit grantor usually cannot ask your gender when you apply for credit. One exception would occur if you applied for a loan to buy or build a home, or to repair, rehabilitate, or remodel a home. In those cases, asking your gender helps the federal government protect against housing discrimination, because it helps them to gather data about whether equally qualified females and males are able to obtain residential mortgage loans. You may refuse to answer this question.
- Normally, you do not have to use a gender title ("Mr.," "Miss," "Mrs.," or "Ms.") when applying for credit. Sometimes credit grantors may ask for your marital status, if that information relates to their right to obtain repayment. For example, a creditor would likely make such a request in a state with community property laws, or if the creditor will extend credit secured by collateral.
- A credit grantor cannot ask women if they use birth control or whether they plan to have children.
- You do not have to reveal child support or alimony payments to a credit grantor un-

less you wish the credit grantor to consider such payments as income.

Q. I am married and want to apply for credit. Do I have to include my spouse's name on the account?

A. No. Married people may open credit accounts that are not also in their spouses' names. People do not have to open joint accounts or take out loans with their spouses. Even if you have a joint account with your spouse, when a creditor sends information about your account to a credit bureau, it must report the information in each of your names, so you will not lose your separate identity for credit purposes. The credit bureau will maintain a separate file on you. Legally, a credit grantor may not

- refuse to open a separate credit account just because of your gender or marital status;
- require your spouse to cosign your account, unless you live in a community property state where spouses have liability for each other's debts; or
- ask about your spouse or ex-spouse when you apply for credit based on your own income. A credit grantor *may* seek this information if a community property state is involved, or if you rely in part on your income from alimony, child support, or maintenance payments from your ex-spouse for the purpose of obtaining credit.

Q. If my marital status changes, may a credit grantor force me to reapply for credit?

A. No. A credit grantor may not require you to reapply for credit just because you marry or divorce or because your spouse has died.

In addition, a credit grantor may not close

your account or change its terms unless a change in your creditworthiness occurs, such as a decrease in your income. For example, if you get a divorce, and you had previously used your spouse's income to obtain credit, a credit grantor may require that you reapply. However, the credit grantor must allow you to continue using the account while it considers your new application.

Denial of a Credit Application

Q. What happens if a credit grantor denies me credit?

A. Under the ECOA, a credit grantor must notify you whether it has approved or denied your credit application within thirty days after you have completed your application. If the credit grantor denies you credit, the creditor must provide you a written notice that lists the reasons for denying credit or tells you how to request such a list. The Fair Credit Reporting Act (FCRA) also requires that the creditor tell you if it used a credit report to deny you credit and, if so, the name and address of the credit bureau that provided the report. In these situations, the FCRA entitles you to ask for a free copy of your report. These rights also apply if a credit grantor takes any adverse action against you with regard to an existing line of credit, such as closing an account or reducing an open line of credit.

Q. A credit grantor took adverse actions against me and now won't tell me why. What are my options?

A. First, ask the credit grantor to supply a written explanation as required by law. If you think the credit grantor has illegally discriminated against you, tell the credit grantor why you think this and try to resolve the issue to your satisfaction. If the credit grantor contin-

ues the adverse action and has not given a satisfactory explanation, you may complain to the appropriate federal enforcement agency (the Federal Trade Commission or your local consumer protection agency may be able to refer you to the right federal agency). To make things right, you might have to sue or engage in mandatory arbitration.

Q. Do I have the option to sue if a credit grantor has discriminated against me?

A. Yes. Under the ECOA, you may sue for actual damages (the actual losses you suffered), plus punitive damages up to $10,000. The amount of punitive damages awarded depends on whether the credit grantor should have known it was violating the law, and on other factors like the number of violations committed by the creditor.

Credit Insurance

Q. What is credit insurance?

A. There are many different types of credit insurance. In the event of your death, **credit life insurance** will pay off the balance owed to your creditors. **Credit accident and health insurance** will make the monthly payments on covered debt for any period you cannot work as a result of an accident or illness. Occasionally, a creditor may offer you **credit unemployment insurance**, which would make payments on covered debt during a period of unemployment. Such policies may have a waiting period.

Q. Are there any legal requirements before a creditor offers credit insurance?

A. Yes. Generally, state laws impose certain requirements that creditors must observe when offering you credit insurance. For example

- The creditor should disclose to you in writing that your decision (i.e., whether to accept the insurance) typically will not factor into the creditor's decision whether to approve the extension of credit. However, if the creditor requires credit insurance, the creditor must include the premiums for the insurance in the APR it discloses to you under the federal Truth in Lending Act.
- The creditor must disclose in writing the cost of any credit insurance offered to you.
- You must give affirmative, written indication of your desire to obtain such insurance. Usually, this means that you must sign your name and check the "yes" box on a credit agreement.

Q. Do I have to have credit insurance?

A. No. If possible, you should decide ahead of time whether you want credit insurance. Once you are at the point of sale, the creditor may pressure you to accept it, just as a salesperson may pressure you to buy more options on a car. Tell the salesperson whether you want the insurance. Study the loan agreement or the retail installment sales contract to ensure that the creditor has adhered to your wishes. At the final closing of the loan or contract, check again. If you arranged a loan or other credit extension over the telephone or Internet, and if you specified "no credit insurance," then check the loan documents when you get the loan at the lender's office.

Q. Is credit insurance a good idea?

A. It depends. Whether you should buy credit insurance is a personal decision. If you think credit insurance makes sense, and especially if you are trying to protect your beneficiaries from having to pay off your mortgage, then you should investigate purchasing decreasing term life insurance. Though you may have to purchase a minimum amount, you would protect your family better, and get more for your money.

The cost per $100 of credit insurance is definitely higher than the cost per $100 of a decreasing term life insurance policy. However, if the credit life insurance covers, say, a $5,000 auto loan, then this comparison is not very meaningful, because most consumers cannot buy $5,000 decreasing term life policies. Depending on the insurer, a consumer typically must purchase a minimum of $50,000 or $100,000 in decreasing term life insurance.

As for insurance for credit cards, remember that such insurance makes only the minimum payment each month, even though you may have been paying a larger amount before the triggering disability or unemployment.

REMEMBER THIS

- The Equal Credit Opportunity Act prohibits discrimination against any credit applicant (or in any part of a credit transaction) based on race, color, religion, national origin, sex, marital status, age, receipt of public assistance, or the fact that the applicant has in good faith exercised any right under the Consumer Credit Protection Act.

- If you believe that a creditor discriminated against you based on one of the above-mentioned criteria, consider consulting with a lawyer.

- Under the Equal Credit Opportunity Act, a successful plaintiff who proves discrimination can recover actual and sometimes punitive damages.

- You should decide whether to purchase credit insurance based on an evaluation of your personal needs. If you have already purchased a term life insurance policy, you probably do not need credit insurance.

RESPONDING TO MISTAKES, POOR SERVICE, AND OTHER BILLING PROBLEMS

When it comes to assuring billing accuracy and high-quality customer service, paying with credit actually helps to assure you some level of safety and security. This section outlines how to correct billing mistakes, how to use your credit cards to deal with defective goods and services, and how to limit your liability should your credit cards be lost or stolen.

Correcting Billing Mistakes

Q. Will my credit rating suffer if my credit card bill contains an obvious error?

A. If you pay your bill despite the error, then no. If you don't pay your bill and don't bring the error to the creditor's attention, then yes. The Fair Credit Billing Act requires credit grantors to correct errors promptly once they are notified of an error.

Q. What exactly is a billing error?

A. A **billing error** means a charge

- for something that you didn't buy, or for a purchase made by someone not authorized to use your account;
- that is not properly identified on your monthly statement, or that is for an

amount different from the actual purchase price; or
- for something that you refused to accept on delivery because it was unsatisfactory, or that the supplier did not deliver according to your agreement.

Billing errors may also include:

- errors in arithmetic;
- failure to reflect a payment that you made, or another credit to your account;
- failure to mail the billing statement to your current address (if the credit grantor received notice of that address at least twenty days before the end of the billing period); and
- extensions of credit about which you request additional clarification.

> ## ▶ KEEP YOUR SALES RECEIPTS

When you buy an item on credit, it's a good idea to keep the receipt. For one thing, a receipt will enable you to return the item in case it is defective or damaged or the wrong size or color. Another reason to keep sales slips is to facilitate correction of billing errors. Creditors' monthly statements usually provide only the date and amount of a purchase, and the store and department from which you bought it. Therefore, you need to keep all sales slips, at least until you have checked them against your monthly billing statements. This also enables you to determine whether an unauthorized person is charging purchases to your account.

Q. What should I do if my bill seems wrong?

A. If you think your bill is incorrect, or if you simply want more details about it, take the following steps:

1. Technically, you should notify your creditor of the potential billing error in writing in order to preserve your legal rights. However, most creditors readily handle billing complaints over the telephone, and it is a lot faster and easier than writing a letter. If you call promptly after receiving a problematic bill, you will still have time to send a letter to protect your rights, if you need to. When you call, be prepared to provide your name, address, account number, and a description of the error. If you aren't satisfied with the results of your call, note the name of the person to whom you spoke and send a letter to the address your credit grantor supplies for this purpose, so that it receives the notice within sixty days after it mailed the bill containing the error. If you don't do this, you may lose your rights under the Fair Credit Billing Act. *The sixty-day period is very important.*

2. The letter should contain your name, address, and account number. State that you believe your bill contains an error, specify the error, explain why you believe it is wrong, and include the date and the suspected amount of the error.

Q. What happens after I notify the credit grantor about the possible billing error?

A. The law requires the credit grantor to acknowledge your letter within thirty days. (This does not apply if the credit grantor can fix the billing error in less time.) The credit grantor must correct your account within two billing periods. It should never take longer than ninety days from the time the credit grantor receives notice of your dispute. If the credit grantor does not correct the error, it must tell you why it believes the bill is not wrong.

If the credit grantor does not find an error, it must promptly send you a statement showing what you owe. The credit grantor may include any finance charges that accumulated and any minimum payments you missed while questioning the bill.

Q. Must I pay finance charges on the contested amount?

A. There are two possible outcomes. If the bill is not correct, you do not have to pay the finance charges on the amount in dispute. If you have already paid these amounts, the credit grantor should refund them. If the bill is correct, you must pay the amounts owed, including finance charges.

Q. While I am trying to solve a billing problem, may a credit grantor threaten my credit rating?

A. No. A creditor cannot threaten your credit rating because you fail to pay the disputed amount (or related finance or other charges) while you're trying to resolve a billing dispute. Once you have taken the steps described above by writing down your question and sending it to the credit grantor, the Fair Credit Billing Act prohibits your credit grantor from reporting the account as delinquent because of the disputed amount (or because of related finance or other charges) while the dispute is pending. Until the credit grantor answers your complaint, the Fair Credit Billing Act also forbids it from taking any action to collect the amount in dispute. You must, however, continue paying any undisputed amounts.

Q. What happens after the credit grantor has explained that my bill is correct?

A. The credit grantor may take action to collect if you do not pay, and may report you to the credit bureau as overdue for the amount in question.

Q. What if I still disagree with the credit grantor?

A. Notify the credit grantor in writing. The credit grantor must then report to the credit bureau that you have challenged the bill, and must give you written notice of the name and address of each person who has received information about your account after the dispute arose. When you settle the dispute, the creditor must report that outcome to each person who has received information about your account. If you are unable to settle the dispute to your satisfaction, you may want to consult a lawyer.

Q. What happens if the credit grantor does not follow all the rules within the proper time limits?

A. The law prohibits a creditor that does not follow the rules within the proper time limits from collecting the first $50 of the disputed amount. This is true even if it is money you truly owed. In addition, the creditor may be subject to remedies available for violations of the Truth in Lending Act.

Defective Goods and Services

Q. Can the law help me if I bought a product on credit that is defective or that is not delivered, or if the merchant has breached a contract with me?

A. Yes. If you use a credit card to purchase shoddy or damaged goods or poor-quality ser-vices, the Fair Credit Billing Act may help. If you have not already paid off the balance, it allows you to withhold payment still due for the disputed transaction once you notify the card issuer or merchant of your claim or defense, so long as you have made a real attempt to solve the problem with the merchant. You can demonstrate a real attempt by writing a letter or keeping notes from a phone call to the retailer's complaint department (i.e., a note, made by you on the date of the call, that includes the name of the person with whom you spoke).

You have this right even if you bought the goods or services with a non-retail credit card such as Visa, American Express, Discover, or MasterCard. Thus, if you purchase a tour or an air travel ticket using your general-purpose credit card, you could recover the cost from the card issuer if the tour or airline goes bankrupt. However, when you use your general-purpose credit card, the law limits your right to withhold payment to purchases totaling more than $50, and to purchases that took place in your home state or within one hundred miles of your home address. Card issuers will often shift this charge back to the merchant. These restrictions do not apply to store credit cards.

Q. If I refuse to pay for a defective good, should I be worried that the merchant will sue me?

A. It is possible the creditor might sue for payment. However, if the court finds the goods or services truly defective, you probably won't have to pay.

Q. What will happen to my credit report if I dispute a credit charge?

A. During the dispute period, the card issuer cannot report the amount as delinquent to a credit bureau.

Lost or Stolen Credit Cards

Q. Am I liable for the bills that may arise if I lose my credit card or someone steals it?

A. No. The Truth in Lending Act limits your liability for lost or stolen credit cards. You must notify the credit card company as soon as you notice the loss or theft of your card or cards. You do not have to pay any unauthorized charges made after you notify the company of the loss or theft of the card. Under TILA, the most you will have to pay for any unauthorized charges made before that time is $50 on each card.

Q. How may I prepare for the possibility of losing a credit card or having it stolen?

A. Keep a list of all your credit cards. This list should include your account numbers, and any information you'll need to notify the

---

▶ RESOLVING CREDIT DISPUTES

What if you believe that a credit grantor has treated you improperly? Resolving the problem involves a sequence of four possible steps—each one more aggressive than the last. (But don't worry—disputes can almost always be settled long before the third and fourth steps.)

1. Make sure you have accurate information about your rights and the credit grantor's obligations under the law.
2. If you are reasonably confident that your complaint is well founded, contact the creditor by phone or, if the matter is serious, by letter. Be sure to provide your name, address, and account number, and a statement of your concern. If your initial contact is by telephone, get the name of the person with whom you talked. To compete effectively, most credit grantors wish to keep good customers by settling complaints fairly and quickly. Nonetheless, create a "paper trail" by keeping a written record or log of all of your contacts with the creditor.
3. If you are not satisfied with the settlement offered by the creditor, the next step is to contact any state or federal agency that regulates your creditor. It is best to write to the appropriate agency and supply a copy of the written record that you have maintained. By sending your creditor a copy of the letter, you may focus attention on your complaint. While the regulatory agency may require some time to get to your problem, it will often be able to arrange a solution that will be satisfactory to you. To find these agencies, the FTC or your consumer protection office may be able to help. For the number of your consumer protection office, look online for local or state government listings.
4. If the regulatory agency fails to satisfy you, consult with a lawyer about pursuing the matter. Check to see if the lawyer will handle the case on a contingency-fee basis. Under this type of fee arrangement, you pay your lawyer only if you recover monies from the lawsuit.

card issuers in the event of theft or loss. Because you may lose credit cards when traveling, always take a copy of this list with you, and keep it separate from your credit cards. Also keep your Social Security number separate from your credit cards, because some issuers of credit cards use Social Security numbers to check the identity of card users. (The "Identity Theft" section of this chapter outlines additional steps you can take to protect yourself.)

REMEMBER THIS

- Creditors make mistakes. The Fair Credit Billing Act (FCBA) requires credit grantors to correct errors promptly. If you believe that a billing charge is incorrect, dispute the charge. Notify the credit grantor in writing. And if you have a meritorious dispute, don't delay. There are time limits built into the FCBA.

DEBT COLLECTION AND THE LAW

Many people in debt face the reality of having to answer calls from debt collectors. These can be stressful calls, especially for someone who is already concerned about his or her finances. This section discusses the legal issues surrounding debt collection.

Q. What can happen to me when I don't pay a debt?

A. As noted earlier, creditors will likely report your delinquencies to one or more credit bureaus, thus harming your credit record. In many states, they may seek a judgment and a court order to garnish your wages—in other words, the court may order your employer to pay some portion of your wages directly to the

creditor. Some income (such as Social Security income) is exempt from garnishment, and federal law sets a limit on what portion a creditor may take. Many state laws extend even greater protections. But if you have a good income, the probability is that some of it is subject to gar-

---

▶ HOW MUCH DEBT CAN YOU HANDLE?

Carrying too much debt poses numerous potential problems. If you have too much debt, you will have difficulty obtaining more credit or keeping existing lines of credit on your credit cards. Creditors may lower your credit limit, cancel your accounts, or not renew them. You may even face the possibility of bankruptcy, which is discussed in the next chapter. (Regardless of what others may tell you, bankruptcy has negative consequences. The fact that you filed for bankruptcy can stay on your credit record for up to ten years—sometimes more—and can handicap your access to various forms of credit for much of that time.)

As a rough guideline, one long-standing rule is that if your monthly payments on debts, excluding your home mortgage payment or rent, exceed 20 percent of your after-tax or take-home pay, then you have most likely reached your debt limit. Or, to put it another way, debt payments should consume no more than 30 percent of your pretax income. For information on how to work with your creditors if you are facing financial problems, see Chapter 11, "Consumer Bankruptcy."

nishment. Don't take garnishment lightly—it can even cost you your job. Your employer cannot fire you because of garnishment by one creditor, but may be able to fire you because of garnishment by multiple creditors.

Q. Will I know before a garnishment starts?

A. Yes. You will always have a chance to appear in court to defend yourself before the court approves a garnishment. If the court approves a garnishment, the creditor will then notify your employer to subtract a given amount from your paycheck each payday, and to pay that amount directly to the creditor until you repay the debt.

Q. Besides garnishment, how else can a creditor get at my assets?

A. For a car, truck, home appliance, or other durable good purchased on credit, your creditor probably has a lien on that item. This means that if you fail to pay as agreed, the creditor may recover (repossess) the item. Many state laws require that the creditor notify you in advance of its intent to repossess, so that you have one last chance to pay your outstanding debt on the item.

Remember, most agreements specify that when you default on your obligations under the loan, the entire debt—not just the monthly payment—becomes immediately due. Furthermore, recovery of the item by the creditor—for example, repossession of your car—does not necessarily end your obligation to the creditor. If your unpaid balance and your accumulated, unpaid finance charges, plus the creditor's costs of repossessing the item, exceed the net amount that the creditor obtains from the sale of the item, then you still may face liability to the creditor for the shortage. If the creditor thinks that you may be able to pay something toward the shortage,

the creditor can ask a court to assess a deficiency judgment for the shortage. Laws in a few states prevent some deficiency judgments.

If you are sued on a debt and believe you shouldn't have to pay, consult a lawyer. Failure to do so could lead to the court accepting the creditor's version of events.

Q. What is a debt collector?

A. Under the federal Fair Debt Collection Practices Act (FDCPA), a **debt collector** is someone, other than a creditor, who regularly collects debts on behalf of others. The FDCPA does not cover creditors, though some state laws do regulate debt collection by creditors. Thus, the FDCPA does not apply to a retailer who attempts to collect unpaid debts owed to it, but a law of the state where the delinquent consumer resides may apply.

Q. Does the law regulate how debt collectors can contact me?

A. Yes. Under the FDCPA, a debt collector may contact you by mail, in person, or by telephone or telegram during convenient hours. Unless you agree in writing (or a court specifically grants permission), a collector may not contact you at inconvenient or unusual times or places. Examples of poorly chosen times are before 8:00 A.M. or after 9:00 P.M. Also, a debt collector is not permitted to contact you at work if the collector knows or has reason to know that your employer forbids collectors from contacting employees at the workplace.

Also, debt collectors may not contact you if they know that a lawyer represents you.

Q. Can I stop a debt collector from contacting me?

A. Yes, by notifying the debt collector by mail not to contact you. After that, contact must stop. The law allows two exceptions to this general rule. First, the debt collector may tell you that it will no longer contact you, and that it will (or may) undertake some specific legal (or other) action. However, debt collectors may state this only if they actually plan to take such action. Second, debt collectors must stop contacting you if you notify them, by mail and within thirty days after they first contact you, that you dispute all or part of the debt, or if you request the name and address of the original creditor. However, debt collectors are permitted to resume collection activities if they send you proof of the debt, such as a copy of the bill, or the information you requested about the original creditor.

Q. What must a debt collector tell me about my debt?

A. Within five days of your first contact, a debt collector must send you a written notice stating

- the name of the creditor to whom you owe money;
- the amount of money you owe;
- that the debt collector will assume the debt is genuine, unless you challenge all or part of it within thirty days, and what to do if you believe you do not owe the money; and
- that if you ask for it, the debt collector will tell you the name and address of the original creditor, if different from the name and address of the current creditor.

Q. I am afraid the collector may start calling my friends and family and telling them about my financial problems. May they do that?

A. A debt collector may contact any person in order to locate you. However, in doing so, the collector usually may not talk to anyone

more than once, or refer to the debt when talking to that person. If debt collectors use the mail to contact you or another person, they may not send letters in envelopes identifying themselves as bill collectors. They may not send a postcard. Once collectors know that you have hired a lawyer, they may communicate only with your lawyer.

Q. Does the law restrict the actions of debt collectors in any other ways?

A. Yes. A debt collector may not harass, oppress, or abuse any person. For example, a debt collector may not

- use threats of violence to harm you, your property, or reputation;
- use obscene or profane language;
- repeatedly use the telephone to annoy you;
- make you accept collect calls or pay for telegrams; or
- publish a "shame list" or other roster of individuals who allegedly refuse to pay their debts (though the debt collector can report you to a credit bureau).

In addition, a debt collector may not use false statements when trying to collect a debt. For example, a debt collector may not

- misrepresent the amount of the debt;
- falsely imply that the debt collector is a lawyer; or
- threaten any action, such as seizing your property or seeking a garnishment, unless the action is lawful and the debt collector (or creditor) intends to take that action.

Q. A debt collector is harassing me and threatening me. What can I do?

A. If a creditor (for example, a retailer or bank) is making the collection effort, check with the consumer protection office of your state attorney general's office, and write that office a letter detailing your complaint (with a copy to the offending creditor). If the collection effort is from an independent debt collector, write to the nearest office of the Federal Trade Commission or its office in Washington, D.C. The FTC actively pursues violators, and may fine them heavily or even put them out of business.

In addition, if debt collectors violate the Fair Debt Collection Practices Act, you may sue them in state or federal court. However, you must do so within one year from the date on which they violated the law. You may recover money for the actual damage you suffered. In addition, the court may award you up to $1,000 for each violation. You may also recover court costs and your lawyer's fees.

Q. Where can I file a complaint about debt collection agencies?

A. You should file complaints about consumer credit reporting agencies or debt collection agencies with the Federal Trade Commission. The same goes for complaints about violations of the Truth in Lending Act and other federal laws involving credit issued by retail stores, department stores, and small loan and finance companies, and for credit-related complaints about oil companies, public utility companies, state credit unions, or travel-and-entertainment credit card companies. Depending on your state, you may also be able to file a complaint with the attorney general's office or the agency that oversees lenders and creditors.

REMEMBER THIS

- If you can only afford to make minimum payments on your credit card, you will likely face debt problems.

- Debt collectors may contact you at your home or at work by mail, in person, or by telephone after 8:00 A.M. or before 9:00 P.M. If a debt collector contacts you at other times, they violate the Fair Debt Collection Practices Act.

- You may notify a debt collector by mail to stop contacting you. You may also inform a debt collector to stop calling you at work.

- Debt collectors cannot harass, oppress or

▶ CREDIT REPAIR CLINICS: TOO GOOD TO BE TRUE?

Credit repair clinics can help you review and update your credit record and report. However, their fees can reach $1,000, whereas you can deal directly with a credit bureau on your own without paying such fees. If your credit report has an error, you may correct it yourself for free or at very little cost. If the information in your credit report is accurate, only time and better management of your debts will help. Be very suspicious and careful if a credit repair clinic promises that it can remove accurate records of bankruptcy and bad debts from your credit record, or if it promises to get you credit. Federal and some state laws regulate credit repair organizations, and federal law prevents a credit repair company from receiving any money from you before it has completed its services. If a credit program sounds too good to be true, it probably is.

▶ CREDIT COUNSELING

Credit counseling centers provide important help to some indebted individuals. These services include helping you set up a realistic budget so that you can better manage your debts, or contacting your creditors and arranging a repayment plan based on your budget. The National Foundation for Consumer Credit provides leadership for many nonprofit **consumer credit counseling services (CCCS)** throughout the U.S. CCCS offices get most of their fees from credit grantors, and typically charge consumers a small fee for setting up a budget plan. Hence, you may pay less to nonprofit offices than to for-profit centers, which must cover all their costs from charges to consumers who use the center's services. However, because of the source of their funding, nonprofit centers may favor arrangements that benefit creditors the most. For more information on credit counseling, see the following chapter, "Consumer Bankruptcy."

abuse you. They cannot repeatedly call you on the telephone to annoy you. The federal Fair Debt Collections Practices Act regulates the conduct of debt collectors. Read this law and become familiar with it if you are in debt.

IDENTITY THEFT

Identity theft occurs when one person steals another's personal information in order to commit fraud or theft. A common example is when someone uses another person's identity to open up a new credit card account. The thief then makes purchases and ruins the victim's credit by not paying the bills. A federal law provides that someone commits a crime when he or she "knowingly transfers or uses, without lawful authority, a means of identification of another person, with the intent to commit, or to aid or abet, any unlawful activity."

This section discusses how to limit identity theft, and what to do if you become a victim.

Q. What can I do to limit my chances of falling victim to identity theft?

A. There are steps you can take to minimize exposure to identity thieves

- Be careful to whom you reveal personally identifiable information. Do not give out this kind of information over the phone or online, unless you know with whom you are dealing.

- Do not use easily obtainable passwords for your bank and credit card accounts, such as your mother's maiden name or the name of your spouse.

- When you are writing checks to pay on your credit card accounts, don't put the complete account number on the check. The last four digits are sufficient, and that way your full account number will not be exposed.

- When your wallet is lost or missing, call the three national credit reporting organizations immediately to place a fraud alert (discussed below) on your name and Social Security number. (See page 231 of the "World at Your Fingertips" section for appropriate contact information.)

- If you do not receive a bill from a regular creditor, contact your creditor to make sure that it still has your current address. A thief may have changed your billing address.
- Many states have passed ID theft laws. Contact a local consumer protection agency or attorney general's office to learn more about applicable laws in your jurisdiction.

Q. *Files maintained by consumer reporting agencies contain a lot of sensitive personal information. How can I protect myself against identity theft relating to this information?*

A. The federal government has responded to the increasing risk of identity theft with new self-help options for consumers. Additional protections established by state law and offered by the marketplace are supplementing these federally created resources to give consumers a wide range of choices for guarding against identity theft.

In 2003, Congress amended the Fair

▶ CHECKLIST: PROTECTING YOUR CREDIT CARDS

- Sign new credit cards as soon as they arrive. Cut up and throw away expired credit cards. Destroy all unused preapproved credit applications.

- Keep a list of your credit card numbers, expiration dates, and the toll-free telephone number of each card issuer in a safe place, so that you can report missing or stolen credit cards and possible billing errors.

- Don't lay your credit card down on a counter or table. Hand it directly to the clerk or waiter. Take your card back promptly after the clerk is finished with it, and make sure that it is yours.

- Never leave your credit card or car rental agreement in the glove compartment of a car. Never leave your credit card in an unlocked desk drawer, grocery cart, or hotel room.

- Never sign a blank credit card receipt. Draw a line through any blank spaces above the total when you sign receipts.

- Open credit card bills promptly, and compare them with your receipts to check for unauthorized charges and billing errors.

- Never give your credit card or checking account number over the telephone, unless you have placed the call yourself. Never put your credit card number on a postcard or on the outside of an envelope.

Credit Reporting Act to enable consumers to add a **fraud alert** to any personal files maintained by a nationwide consumer reporting agency. These alerts include an **initial alert** and an **extended alert.** The initial alert lasts ninety days and the extended lasts seven years, and consumers may have to provide evidence that they have been a victim of identity theft. A third type of fraud alert is available to active duty military personnel. Fraud alerts are designed to protect consumers who fear that they may become victims of identity theft (for example, when a consumer's wallet is stolen) or when identity theft has actually occurred. When consumers place fraud alerts in their files, anyone who requests information from that file, including a credit score, also receives a notification about the alert. Creditors who receive this notification must take reasonable steps to verify the identity of the credit applicant before proceeding with the credit request. In other words, the fraud alert directs users of consumer report information to proceed with caution, and to ensure that they are dealing with the right consumer, rather than with an identity thief.

Q. I have been the victim of identity theft. Can I make sure that no information relating to the theft is connected to my credit report?

A. Yes. If you have already been a victim of identity theft, Congress allows you to block consumer reporting agencies from providing information that can be attributed to the theft. With this tool, you can limit the damage caused by identity theft.

State governments have supplemented these federal tools with an important self-help tool of their own: **credit freezes.** State credit freeze laws, effective in a majority of states,

enable consumers to prohibit consumer reporting agencies from providing information from their files to companies requesting credit reports. This is a more powerful anti-identity-theft weapon than the federal fraud alert. However, some consumers may find this option inconvenient, because it may interfere with or delay their ability to enter into a legitimate credit transaction.

If you know a particular item on your credit report (or on a bill that a creditor is trying to collect) is fraudulent—i.e., that someone else used your name to obtain credit—then you should file an **identity theft report.** The first step is to file a report with a law enforcement agency, under oath, explaining what happened. Get a copy of that report and send it to the creditor involved and to any credit bureau who reports the fraudulent debt in your name. The credit bureaus and the creditor must stop reporting that debt when they receive this report. If you are contacted by a debt collector about the fraudulent debt, send him or her a copy of the report. The debt collector must consult the creditor and, in most cases, must stop trying to collect. An identity theft report is a powerful tool.

Q. I have heard about credit monitoring. What is this? Is it different from a fraud alert?

A. Credit monitoring services are consumer tools that also help prevent identity theft. These services keep a close watch on a subscriber's credit report and alert the subscriber whenever a potential creditor has requested information from that report. This allows the subscriber to learn of possible credit transactions involving their file, and to stop unauthorized transactions before they occur. These services are usually offered in exchange for a monthly or annual fee, and some give subscribers access to their files and credit score.

REMEMBER THIS

- There are steps you can take to protect yourself from identity theft. For example, when you are writing checks to pay on your credit card accounts, don't write the complete account number on the check.

- If you think you have been the victim of identity theft, contact a credit reporting agency and ask to have a fraud alert placed on your file.

- If you have been a victim of identity theft, you should file a law enforcement report and provide a copy of that report to the national credit bureaus.

- Credit monitoring services can help you keep a close watch on your credit report, and will alert you whenever a potential creditor has requested information.

Consumer Bankruptcy

Jason's spending has been out of control for months. Most of his income is spent paying credit card bills, and he needs to borrow more just to pay rent. Jason's debts keep growing, and he is falling behind on some payments. Jason thinks he may have to declare bankruptcy, but he's worried that it will have implications if he wants to get a loan in the future.

Many Americans find themselves in serious debt. The creditors keep calling and the debt just keeps growing. For some individuals, bankruptcy law can provide relief and a fresh start. The purpose of this chapter is to provide you with information that will help you make informed choices, and to provide references to other sources of information about bankruptcy. See Chapter 3, "Family Law," for further topics regarding bankruptcy and marriage, and Chapter 10, "Consumer Credit," for further bankruptcy-related discussions.

INTRODUCTION TO BANKRUPTCY

Bankruptcy is one of several alternatives for consumers in financial distress. Some people can improve their situation by negotiating directly with creditors. Others can get help from a local financial counseling program, or from a consumer credit counseling service that has experience negotiating with creditors and formulating repayment plans. For others, bankruptcy may be the only realistic alternative. This section explores the topic of bankruptcy— what it is, how to file for it, and even how to avoid it through alternative means of debt relief.

Bankruptcy Defined

Q. What exactly is bankruptcy?

A. **Bankruptcy** is a legal process through which people and businesses can obtain a fresh financial start when they are in such financial difficulty that they cannot repay their debts. A fresh start is achieved by eliminating all or a portion of existing debts and/or by stretching out monthly payments under the protection and supervision of a court. The process is also designed to protect creditors, because general unsecured creditors share equally in whatever payments the debtor can afford to make.

During your bankruptcy case, creditors (with some limited exceptions) generally cannot try to collect their debts from you directly. And after the conclusion of the case, they cannot try to collect from you for any discharged debts. However, there is an enumerated list of debts that are not dischargeable (i.e., canceled) in bankruptcy—for example,

domestic support obligations, fraudulently incurred debts, DUI obligations, certain taxes, and student loans. These exceptions are discussed in detail later in this chapter.

Alternatives to Bankruptcy

Q. If I am having problems paying my bills, what is the first thing I should do?

A. A good first step is to assess your debt level as compared to your income level. Before you can make a plan as to your financial future, you need to determine what debts you owe and whether you can live within a strict budget. Many people can reduce their debt significantly simply by living within a self-imposed budget and not spending money on unnecessary items. They can learn to take charge of their lives and begin to reclaim their financial futures. For others, bankruptcy might be the only realistic option. But you can't make this decision until you carefully examine your income and debt.

Q. Right now, I cannot pay my debts. Besides bankruptcy, do I have any options?

A. Yes. You have several alternatives for handling debts that you cannot pay. Creditors might be willing to settle their claims for a smaller cash payment, or they might be willing to stretch out the term of your loan and reduce the size of the payments. This would allow you to pay off the debt by making smaller payments over a longer period of time, and the creditor would eventually receive the full economic benefit of its bargain.

You may also find that you are judgment proof and do not need to file for bankruptcy to protect your property and wages. **Judgment**

▶ THE LANGUAGE OF BANKRUPTCY

The Bankruptcy Code, and proceedings conducted in accordance with it, use a unique language. To help you understand this "foreign" language as you read this chapter, here are some frequently used terms relating to bankruptcy:

- **Automatic stay**—A legal requirement that, after a bankruptcy petition is filed, nearly all collection activities must stop.

- **Discharged debts**—Debts that the court has excused the debtor from paying.

- **Encumbered assets**—Assets pledged as collateral on a loan. The lender will commonly have a legal claim (also known as a **secured claim**) on encumbered assets until the loan is fully repaid. Some creditors may obtain a secured claim without the debtor's agreement, either because they have won a lawsuit and executed a lien against the debtor or because the law automatically provides a lien for certain claims (such as unpaid taxes or special service contracts that haven't been paid in full—e.g., construction liens, mechanics liens, etc.).

- **Exempt assets**—Enumerated assets that a debtor is allowed to keep, despite bankruptcy proceedings.

- **Liquidating**—Converting assets into cash to settle debts.

- **Secured debts**—Debts that creditors can collect on by seizing and selling certain assets of the debtor if payments are missed. Examples include a home mortgage or a car loan.

- **Unsecured debts**—Debts for which the creditor cannot seize your assets if you miss payments. Most consumer debts are unsecured. Examples include most credit card debt, doctors' bills, legal bills, and utility bills.

---

proof simply means that you have so little money and property that you couldn't pay a court judgment against you. If there's no point in creditors going after you in court, there may be less reason for you to declare bankruptcy.

Discuss this option with your credit counselor. However, remember that if you don't declare bankruptcy, creditors can continue their collection efforts and will be able to enforce court judgments against you if your financial situation improves.

Q. Is there anybody in particular I should contact about these options?

A. Yes. If you are behind on your payments, the collectors for each of your creditors may already be calling or writing you. You might be more successful if you phone each creditor, ask for the collection department, ask and note the name of the person you talk to, and explain your intent to repay the account and your need to stretch out the number of monthly payments and reduce the dollar amount of each payment. You might offer to come to the collection department office to discuss your situation. Ask each creditor to agree to a voluntary plan for the repayment of your debts.

When dealing with creditors, ask them to reduce late fees and interest. Get all agreements in writing before making payment. If you reach a settlement for a single payment, when the payment is made, be sure to indicate on the face and back of the check that the payment is "in full, final, and complete satisfaction" of your account, which you should identify by number. However, never give creditors information that would enable them to directly access your checking account, and make sure you maintain control over the payment.

▶ RECENT CHANGES IN BANKRUPTCY LAW

In April 2005, President Bush signed into law the Bankruptcy Abuse Prevention and Consumer Protection Act of 2005, the first major overhaul of bankruptcy legislation since 1978. The new law requires those who file for bankruptcy to consult with an "approved nonprofit budget and credit counseling agency" before filing. Other changes make it more difficult for people to file bankruptcy under Chapter 7, which means that more people will have to file under Chapter 13.

When filing for bankruptcy, make sure you hire a lawyer who is familiar with current federal bankruptcy laws.

Q. I owe many creditors. What should I do?

A. The problem of dealing with many creditors is that some of them might not want to give you more time to pay, unless they know what the other creditors are willing to do. Unless your debts are very large, it will be difficult for you to arrange for a meeting of your creditors and negotiate a reduction in your monthly payments or the amount of your debt. You can seek the help of a lawyer to negotiate an arrangement with your creditors. Some universities, local courts, military bases, credit unions, and housing authorities have credit counseling programs that may be able to help.

Your best bet may be to seek the help of a nonprofit consumer credit counseling service (CCCS). The repayment plans arranged through credit counseling centers enable you to make monthly payments that are then distributed by the program among creditors until all your debts are paid in full. Creditors usually prefer this kind of plan, since they will eventually get more of their money with this approach than they will under Chapter 7 bankruptcy. Also, any payments received by the creditor will not be recoverable from them as a preference payment. You should be aware that creditors provide most of the support for financial counseling services.

Under a repayment plan through a financial counseling service, you still might have to pay interest charges on your debts. However, many creditors will waive or reduce interest charges and delinquency fees.

Q. What does it mean to consolidate debt?

A. Occasionally, you may buy time by **consolidating** your debt. This means you take out a big loan to pay off your smaller debts.

> ▶ **A WORD OF WARNING**
>
> Be cautious when seeking a for-profit counseling service. If you choose a for-profit service, be sure you understand the fees. Investigate the service and its credentials carefully, and consider calling the local Better Business Bureau for information on the service.

Q. Should I consolidate my debt?

A. Whether consolidating your debts is a good idea depends on your desire to get out of debt, as well as several other factors. The primary danger of consolidation is that it is very easy to go out and borrow even more. In that case, you end up with even more total debt, and no additional income to meet the monthly payments. Indeed, if you have taken out a second mortgage on your home to get the consolidation loan, you might lose your home as well. You should also analyze the interest rate thoroughly. Make sure your consolidation loan's interest rate is lower than your credit cards' rate.

The Process of Filing for Bankruptcy

Q. What is the process of filing for bankruptcy?

A. Filing for bankruptcy is a very personal, very serious decision. The three primary causes of bankruptcy are divorce, loss of employment, and large medical expenses. Most people file when they have made a good-faith effort to repay their debts, but see no other way out. Such people and businesses may de-

clare bankruptcy by filing a petition with the U.S. Bankruptcy Court that asks the court to provide protection and relief under the Bankruptcy Code. In addition to that request, the debtor must provide information about his or her assets, liabilities, income, and expenditures. Complete disclosure, candor, and honesty are required. Often, debtors have a lawyer prepare and file the petition and other information for them, but some debtors represent themselves. After you have filed, under court supervision, either one of two results will follow. Either your nonexempt assets will be sold, or a three- to five-year repayment plan will be approved by the bankruptcy court. In both cases, the intent is to pay off as much of your debt as possible. Any unpaid debt will be discharged.

Q. Can anyone file for bankruptcy?

A. Yes, assuming they have completed the necessary steps beforehand. There are restrictions on filing for Chapter 7 bankruptcy, but these restrictions will not prevent you from being eligible for Chapter 13. Under the updated law, an individual debtor who earns more than the median income in his or her state may not be eligible to file a Chapter 7 case. (You can find more information about the differences between Chapter 7 and Chapter 13 bankruptcy later in this chapter.)

Federal law protects your right to file for bankruptcy. For example, you cannot contract away your right to file for bankruptcy. Also, you cannot be fired from your job solely because you filed for bankruptcy.

Q. Is there more than one type of bankruptcy?

A. Yes. There are several types, each set forth in a separate chapter of the federal Bankruptcy Code.

Proceedings under **Chapter 7** (also known as **straight bankruptcy**) involve surrendering your nonexempt assets and keeping your exempt assets (such as a limited amount of equity in your home, some jewelry, and an inexpensive car). A bankruptcy trustee is appointed in every Chapter 7 case to administer the nonexempt assets (if any), and distribute among the creditors either the assets or the proceeds from liquidating those assets. Some assets are exempt under Chapter 7, and cannot be sold to satisfy debts. The assets that are exempt depend on specific federal laws and on state laws that vary significantly from state to state.

Proceedings under **Chapter 13** (also known as **wage-earner bankruptcy**) require that you propose a plan for repaying all or a portion of your debt in installments from your income. Most plans are either three or five years, but some plans can be much shorter.

Chapter 11 generally covers businesses that are restructuring while continuing operations. While an individual may file for Chapter 11 bankruptcy, such proceedings are more expensive and complex, and consumer debtors normally use Chapter 7 or Chapter 13.

Under any chapter, once the bankruptcy case ends, you will likely be discharged from most of the debts you incurred before filing your bankruptcy petition (so-called **pre-petition debts**). This means the court has excused you from having to pay most debts. You then start over with a clean financial slate, except that the record of the bankruptcy can remain on your credit record for up to twelve years.

It should be noted, however, that in a Chapter 7 case, the discharge does not wipe out a secured creditor's lien, student loans, or support payments to children; these are still due and payable, along with certain other specifically non-discharged debts. In some cases, a discharge may be denied altogether.

Q. What are the advantages of filing for bankruptcy?

A. By far the most important advantage is that debtors can obtain a virtually fresh financial start.

Another big advantage is that collection efforts must stop. As soon as your petition is filed, an automatic stay takes effect and, by law, most collection activities must cease. If a creditor continues to try to collect the debt, the creditor may be cited for contempt of court or ordered to pay damages.

Q. What are the disadvantages of filing for bankruptcy?

A. Bankruptcy may be the best, or only, solution for extreme financial hardship. Although there is still a stigma associated with bankruptcy in some circles, that stigma has faded over the years as many people—including

---

▶ THE AUTOMATIC STAY AND YOUR CAR LOAN

As soon as you file for bankruptcy, an automatic stay takes effect, which means that most collection activities must cease. This stay applies even to the loan that you may have obtained to buy your car—meaning that in most cases, collection activities on your car loan should stop after filing. If you continue to make payments, the creditor will likely seek to have you reaffirm the car debt. If you miss payments, however, your creditor will probably petition to have the stay terminated in order to repossess the car. At the same time, you may seek to renegotiate the loan.

celebrities—have filed. However, bankruptcy should be used only as a last resort, since it has long-lasting consequences. The record of a Chapter 13 bankruptcy can remain on your credit record for up to twelve years, which is a long time in today's economic system. Moreover, once a bankruptcy petition is filed, there are strict time periods that must expire (two to eight years) before you can file another bankruptcy case and receive a discharge. If you have equity in your home or car, you may lose it, since that equity may be realized for the benefit of your creditors, depending on state laws.

In a Chapter 7 bankruptcy, you might also have to surrender some of your nonexempt personal property or your home to a bankruptcy trustee.

Q. When should I consider bankruptcy as an option?

A. Study the pros and cons carefully before resorting to bankruptcy as a means of solving your economic troubles. But do not wait until the last minute to get help—the day before a foreclosure or court date may be too late to get good advice or to take advantage of non-bankruptcy options. Get advice when you find you cannot pay your monthly expenses in full for more than three months, or if you face a sudden large debt, such as a medical bill, for which you cannot make payment arrangements.

Q. A bankruptcy filing could remain on my credit record for up to twelve years. How will that affect my future finances?

A. Twelve years is the outer limit for all types of bankruptcy. During that time, creditors may deny you credit or charge you significantly higher interest rates. So long as your credit record contains unfavorable information, you may have credit problems. This

> ▶ **IF YOU'RE SELF-EMPLOYED**
>
> Chapter 13 bankruptcy can be an effective tool for a self-employed individual; your business income and debts could be included in the payment plan and schedules.

means that you may have trouble renting an apartment, getting a loan to buy a car, or obtaining a mortgage for a house.

On the other hand, bankruptcy may improve your records. Because Chapter 7 provides for a discharge of debts no more than once every eight years, lenders know that a credit applicant who has just emerged from Chapter 7 cannot soon repeat the process.

Q. What are my chances of getting credit after declaring bankruptcy?

A. Your chances of getting credit after bankruptcy depend upon your willingness to work with lenders, and may require you to make payments at a higher rate of interest. Getting credit after bankruptcy certainly isn't impossible, but it may not be as easy as it was for you before bankruptcy.

Working with a Lawyer

Q. I think I need to file for bankruptcy. How should I find a lawyer to help?

A. There are a number of ways, but you should generally follow the recommendations for finding a good lawyer outlined in Chapter 1, "When and How to Use a Lawyer." In addition, consider the following options:

- Contact the American Board of Certification, which certifies lawyers specializing

---

▶ **DISCHARGE DATES**

The bankruptcy court enters a discharge order relatively early in a Chapter 7 case. In Chapter 13 cases, the borrower makes full or partial payment to creditors under a court-confirmed plan over a period of time (usually three to five years), and then receives a discharge. For both types of bankruptcy, debtors cannot obtain a discharge until they have taken an approved course in personal financial management.

---

in bankruptcy. Some states certify lawyers as bankruptcy specialists when they have significant experience in the field.

- Ask a lawyer you know to recommend a specialist. Suggestions from a friend, a relative, a neighbor, or an associate who has had a good experience with a particular lawyer also may help.
- Bar associations and groups for people with special needs, such as the elderly or persons with disabilities, often provide free referral services.
- Finding a bankruptcy lawyer online or by looking in the yellow pages of your telephone directory or advertisements in your local newspaper can be risky. Be sure to check the lawyer's references.

Q. I think I found a lawyer to represent me during my bankruptcy. How can I tell if he or she is good?

A. Be careful making your selection, and make sure that your lawyer has a good reputation and is familiar with current bankruptcy law and procedures. When you first talk with a prospective lawyer, does he or she seem to understand your problems and have solutions, or do you feel as though you're in a "factory" that merely processes paper? Also, how comfortable are you with this person? Remember, you will have to talk with your lawyer about some very personal mat-

ters—including your income and spending habits.

Q. How can I learn about fees?

A. You can, and should, discuss your lawyer's fees in advance. In addition, discuss whether your lawyer will charge additional fees if there are proceedings other than the filing of your case. The basic case will include preparing and filing the petitions, preparing and filing any additional schedules, and attending the creditors' meeting. In some states, it may also include preparing and filing a homestead deed. In a Chapter 7 bankruptcy, there may be reaffirmation agreements to negotiate and sign, objections to exemptions, or objections to the discharge of some or all of your debts. In a Chapter 13 case, there may be objections to your repayment plan or the way you value your assets. In either chapter, creditors may

---

▶ **DO IT YOURSELF?**

You are legally permitted to file your own bankruptcy petition. However, the more complicated your debt situation, the more risky it may be to represent yourself. For this reason, it is not advisable to hire a nonlawyer to help you file bankruptcy.

file motions for relief from the automatic stay, seeking court approval to repossess property or foreclose on real estate.

Under some Chapter 13 cases, you can pay the lawyer from the assets of your estate, which is administered by the court in the bankruptcy case. Generally, Chapter 13 is more expensive than Chapter 7, though it helps that the costs may be included in your repayment plan.

REMEMBER THIS

- Bankruptcy is a legal process through which people and businesses can obtain a fresh financial start. It is for people who are not in a financial position to repay their debts.

- You may try negotiating directly with creditors to obtain some financial relief. The creditors may reduce their interest rates or allow a longer payment plan.

- You may seek help from a local financial counseling program or a consumer credit counseling service. Such services may be able to help you consolidate (and reduce) your debt.

- Select a bankruptcy lawyer with care. Do not rely solely on advertisements. Contact your local bar association or refer to the American Board of Certification. Do not hire a nonlawyer to file your bankruptcy.

- During bankruptcy, creditors cannot call you to collect debts. Once a bankruptcy petition is filed, an automatic stay prohibits most collection activities.

- Use bankruptcy with caution; it might remain in your credit files for up to twelve years.

- Most consumer debts are unsecured, meaning that creditors will not be able to seize the relevant assets if you miss pay-

ments during bankruptcy. Some creditors are called secured creditors because they have the right to seize and sell the collateral—such as a car or your home—that secures your loan. Secured creditors have more protection in a bankruptcy than unsecured creditors.

STRAIGHT BANKRUPTCY: CHAPTER 7

This section discusses Chapter 7, or straight bankruptcy. It explains who can file Chapter 7 bankruptcy, and describes the procedures involved with filing—including an outline of the assets that a petitioner will be able to keep, and those that will have to be turned over.

Chapter 7 Defined

Q. What is Chapter 7 bankruptcy?

A. This type of bankruptcy is usually best suited to a person with a modest income, few assets, and comparatively high debts. Straight bankruptcy under Chapter 7 is available if less drastic remedies will not solve your financial problems. It allows you to discharge most of your debts. As noted in the previous section, Chapter 7 bankruptcy does not result in a discharge of all types of debt. If a debt is excepted from discharge, you are still legally responsible for it.

Q. What debts will not be eliminated if I file for Chapter 7?

A. Exceptions to Chapter 7 discharge include

- tax claims;
- alimony;
- child support (including past-due support);

- many property settlement obligations from a divorce or separation;
- most student loans;
- damages for "willful and malicious" acts such as assaulting another person; and
- fraudulent debts.

Q. I have decided to file for Chapter 7 bankruptcy. What will happen first?

A. Current bankruptcy law requires debtors to receive credit counseling within 180 days before filing for bankruptcy. Debtors must present to the bankruptcy court a certificate indicating that they have received such counseling. The counseling must be conducted by a nonprofit budget and credit counseling agency that is approved by the U.S. bankruptcy trustee or bankruptcy administrator.

Q. What is credit counseling?

A. **Credit counseling** can take place individually or in a group, in person, on the telephone, or over the Internet. Such counseling assists individuals by helping them create

---

▶ WHAT IS FRAUDULENT DEBT

If a person embarks on a credit card binge prior to a bankruptcy filing—purchasing more than $500 worth of luxury goods or services within ninety days before a filing, or more than $750 in cash advances within seventy days before a filing—then the court will presume that person to have committed fraud. Without a showing to rebut the presumption, such debts will not be discharged during a Chapter 7 bankruptcy.

---

budgets, learn to manage their money, and formulate plans for repaying their debt. In this context, the basic goal of credit counseling is to ensure that consumers have explored all of their options before filing for bankruptcy.

Q. After I complete credit counseling, what is the next step?

A. A Chapter 7 bankruptcy case begins when you file a petition with the U.S. Bankruptcy Court asking it to relieve you (or you and your spouse, if you are both filing) from your dischargeable debts. The bankruptcy court clerk or the Bankruptcy Noticing Center will notify your listed creditors that you have filed a bankruptcy petition, and creditors must immediately stop most collection efforts. A bankruptcy trustee will be appointed—usually a local bankruptcy lawyer approved by the Justice Department. As of the date you file your bankruptcy petition, your assets will be under the protection of the federal court.

Q. Will it cost me anything to file a Chapter 7 petition? What happens if I can't pay?

A. In order to file the necessary forms, debtors must pay a Chapter 7 statutory case-filing fee, an administrative fee, and a trustee surcharge fee. Individuals may pay the fees in installments within 120 days after the Chapter 7 case is filed; in certain circumstances, the court may also extend the length of this period to 180 days. Failure to pay the necessary fees could result in the dismissal of a bankruptcy petition, unless the court waives the fees.

Q. What forms am I expected to fill out?

A. Filing a petition for bankruptcy involves completing and filing a number of forms.

Many of these are referred to as **schedules**, which is just a fancy term for a written list or inventory. These forms include

- a list of creditors;
- a schedule of assets and liabilities;
- a schedule of current income and expenditures;
- a statement of your financial affairs;
- copies of all payment advances, or other evidence of payment received within sixty days before the date of the bankruptcy filing;
- a statement of your monthly net income, itemized to show how the amount is calculated;
- a statement disclosing any reasonably anticipated increase in your income or expenditures over the twelve-month period following the date of the bankruptcy filing; and
- a certificate from an approved nonprofit credit counseling agency.

If requested by a creditor or the trustee, you will also have to provide tax returns and a photo ID. If you are self-employed, a statement of your business affairs must also be included.

All of these forms will provide the bankruptcy court and parties in interest—that is, your creditors and the trustee—with a complete picture of what is called your **bankruptcy estate.**

Q. What should I list as my liabilities?

A. For purposes of a bankruptcy filing, your liabilities typically include

- your priority debts (such as taxes and past-due support payments);
- your debts to secured creditors (bills from auto and furniture dealers, home mortgages, and so on); and
- your debts to unsecured creditors (bills for department store credit cards, medical bills, and the like).

Be sure to list all of your creditors and their correct names and addresses. Remember, liabilities can also include any lawsuits in which you are a defendant or a potential defendant— for example, a claim against you arising out of a car accident. Even if you are current with your bills, if you omit some creditors from your filing or provide incorrect addresses, you might not be discharged from the applicable debts. It may be very helpful to access your credit report before filing to ensure that you have listed all of your outstanding debts.

Q. I just realized I forgot to list a creditor on my schedule of liabilities. What should I do?

A. Should you fail to list all of your creditors in your filing, the Federal Rules of Bankruptcy Procedure typically allow you to amend your petition. You will need to work with the judge and your attorney to make sure the petition is correctly amended.

Q. What should I include on my assets schedule?

A. When filing for bankruptcy, you should list all of your assets, which generally include

- all of your real property (for example, your home), including any that you own with your spouse or other persons;
- all of your personal property (such as household goods, cars, clothing, cash, retirement funds, bank accounts, accrued net wages, and tax refunds to which you may be entitled); and
- any lawsuits in which you are a plaintiff or a potential plaintiff (e.g., workers' compensation claims and/or personal injury claims).

In addition, you will need to designate which of your real or personal property you want to exempt from creditors.

Q. Do I have to include what I will earn after I file?

A. No. Your post-petition earnings from your job are not part of the Chapter 7 bankruptcy estate.

Q. Will I lose some of my assets if I file for Chapter 7?

A. More likely than not. Under Chapter 7, you will likely have to turn over many, if not all, of your nonexempt assets to the trustee. What happens depends upon the classification (i.e., value) of the asset and on state or federal law exemptions.

Q. What happens to my encumbered assets during a bankruptcy?

A. In bankruptcy, a claim is secured to the extent that it is backed up by collateral. Often the collateral is worth less than the amount of the debt it secures, such as a $1,200 car securing a loan balance of $3,000. On the other hand, sometimes a debt is secured by collateral having a value that exceeds the loan balance at the time of bankruptcy, such as a $65,000 home subject to a $30,000 mortgage. The lender is entitled to no more than it is actually owed. Thus, in the case of the $65,000 home secured by the $30,000 mortgage, the lender is entitled to no more than $30,000. The excess value of $35,000 is referred to as the **debtor's equity.**

If you cannot make the required payments on a secured claim (and also catch up on any back payments), then the creditor has a right to take back the collateral after having the automatic stay lifted (or after the discharge). However, you may be able to keep the encumbered item by redeeming it or reaffirming your debt (as explained on pages 413 and 414), or by continuing to make payments (allowed in some jurisdictions). Generally, the value of an asset is its retail value.

Q. What is the situation with unencumbered assets?

A. **Unencumbered assets** include: (1) assets on which there is no lien at all; and (2) the debtor's equity in assets that are collateral for over-secured claims. You may retain unencumbered assets to the extent that they are exempt; otherwise, they must be surrendered for distribution among those creditors holding unsecured claims, or the equivalent value must be paid to the trustee. However, if your unencumbered assets are worth less than a certain amount, or would be difficult to sell, then the trustee might abandon them if he or she decides it would not be cost effective to sell them and distribute the money to the creditors.

Q. What are exempt assets?

A. **Exempt assets** are those assets listed on your schedules that you may shield from your unsecured creditors.

Q. Can I convert any nonexempt assets into exempt assets without losing my bankruptcy discharge or my exemptions?

A. Yes, if you do it correctly. Pre-bankruptcy planning is an essential part of nearly every bankruptcy. A bankruptcy attorney's advice on this issue is valuable. In general, during the conversion process, you cannot use unsecured credit to increase your exempt assets, sell nonexempt assets for less than fair value, or mislead your creditors.

Q. So what assets are exempt?

A. Again, this depends on your specific state's law. However, the Bankruptcy Code provides a detailed list of exemptions available to debtors under federal law. In brief, these exemptions include

- $18,450 equity in your home or burial plot;
- $2,950 equity in one motor vehicle;
- $475 equity per item, up to $9,850 total equity, in household furnishings, household goods, apparel, appliances, etc.;
- $1,225 equity in jewelry;
- $975 equity in any property, plus up to $9,250 of any unused amount of the exemption for your home/burial plot;
- $1,850 equity in any implements, professional books, or tools of your trade;
- any unmatured life insurance contract you own, other than a credit life insurance contract;
- professionally prescribed health aids;
- your right to receive various benefits, including
  - benefits from Social Security, unemployment compensation, or local public assistance;
  - a veterans' benefit;
  - a disability, illness, or unemployment benefit;
  - alimony, support, or separate maintenance;
  - a payment under a stock bonus, pension, or similar plan or contract like a 401k; or
  - retirement funds in a tax-exempt fund or account; and
- your right to receive property that is traceable to
  - an award under a crime victim's reparation law;
  - a payment for the wrongful death of an individual of whom you were a dependent;
  - a payment under a life insurance contract that insured the life of an individual of whom you were a dependent on the date of such individual's death;
  - a payment, not to exceed $15,000, on account of personal bodily injury to you or to an individual of whom you are a dependent; or
  - a payment in compensation for the loss of future earnings of you or an individual of whom you are or were a dependent.

Every three years, the dollar amount of these exemptions is adjusted upward to reflect the annual increase in the cost of living.

Q. So if the value of my house is more than the exempt value, will I lose it? What exactly does the above list mean?

A. Let's use the example of your home to see how this works. As noted above, under the federal statute you can exempt from bankruptcy up to $18,450 of the equity in your home. A couple filing a joint Chapter 7 case may exempt twice this much (as outlined below)—a total of $36,900 worth of equity in their home. This is called their **homestead exemption.** If the home is worth $65,000 and has a $25,000 mortgage, then the couple has $40,000 worth of equity in their home. Since $36,900 is exempt by federal law, the couple's creditors can claim only $3,100 (the difference between the couple's equity of $40,000 and the $36,900 exemption). As a matter of practice, the couple would probably keep their home—perhaps at the cost of paying that $3,100 in nonexempt equity to the bankruptcy trustee—rather than have it sold for the benefit of their creditors.

Q. Do exemptions vary much between states?

A. Yes. Asset exemptions vary widely from state to state. For example, variations among the states are found with respect to a broad array of exempt assets such as cars, jewelry, household furnishings, and books.

Home exemptions also vary by state. For example, Florida has no dollar cap on homestead exemptions. It allows a homestead exemption that protects a debtor's home and property so long as the size of that property does not exceed half an acre (in a municipality) or 160 acres (anywhere else). In Georgia, by contrast, the homestead exemption is limited to $5,000.

Current federal bankruptcy law makes it harder to shield money, even in those states with high homestead exemptions. The law establishes that, regardless of state law, debtors may exempt no more than $125,000 of interest in a homestead that was purchased within forty months of a bankruptcy filing. Another limitation is that a person must live in a state for two years before claiming that particular state's favorable exemptions. However, you may still shelter more than $125,000 (if state law permits) if you bought your home (or a prior home) in the same state more than forty months before filing.

Q. How do exemptions work if you are married?

A. Spouses are permitted to file jointly for bankruptcy, but whether it is to their advantage to do so depends on many factors, such as how closely their finances are entwined and whether they live in a community or separate property state (see Chapter 8, "Home Ownership," for definitions of these terms). You should be wary of joint filing if divorce is a likely possibility.

In joint cases, each spouse must claim exemptions under the same law, with both relying either on state law or federal law. If they each want to claim exemptions under different law, they need to file separate cases. When married debtors elect to apply federal exemptions (and often when they elect to apply state exemptions), each spouse can claim the full exempt amount on his or her own behalf, in effect doubling the amount of exemptions to which a single person would be entitled.

In some cases, such as when one spouse has debts and the other is debt-free and has assets, it might be preferable for only the spouse with debts to file for bankruptcy. In about a third of states, creditors of only one spouse are barred (either completely or in large part) from reaching real and/or personal property owned by a debtor and non-debtor spouse as joint tenants or tenants by the entirety. Give your lawyer copies of your deeds, bank account statements, and car titles to find out whether your creditors can reach your assets.

Q. How do exemptions work if my creditor has a security interest in the property?

A. Exemptions do not ordinarily affect the rights of creditors to assets on which they have a secured claim. For example, a homestead exemption generally does not affect the right of a mortgage lender to foreclose on your home. Similarly, furniture bought on store credit may be subject to a purchase money security interest, and some credit card companies may attempt to create liens on items you purchase with their cards, in which case such creditors may have rights to your assets even in bankruptcy. Under some specific circumstances, the Bankruptcy Code may permit you to undo a lien or security interest and then assert exemption rights.

Chapter 7 in Action

Q. In a Chapter 7 filing, what property will I be required to turn over to the trustee?

A. The Bankruptcy Code requires that you give all nonexempt unencumbered assets to the trustee—that is, all the assets that aren't exempted by the law and aren't secured as collateral to a loan. Unless it would be too costly, the trustee will then liquidate (sell off) these nonexempt assets to pay your creditors.

Q. I have some items that probably won't be exempt, but it is really important to me not to lose them. Can I do anything?

A. Yes, you have a couple of options. If you are required to surrender some nonexempt property that you wish to keep—for example, a car—you may under certain circumstances arrange to **redeem** it (buy it back) for a price no greater than its current redemption value. **Redemption value** is the amount for which a retailer could sell the item, taking into consideration the item's age and condition. For example, if you owe $3,000 on your car, but its redemption value is only $1,200, you can recover the car by paying a lump sum of $1,200 to the creditor who has a lien on it at the time of redemption.

Q. Do I have to pay the redemption costs all at once?

A. Yes. The redemption price must be paid in full. Of course, it may be very hard to come up with $1,200, which must be paid from your personal assets, and not from property that has been set aside for distribution to creditors. Possible sources of funds would include your post-petition salary, proceeds from the voluntary sale of exempt assets, or loans from relatives or friends. Some companies specialize in making redemption loans on automobiles.

Q. Do I have any other options for hanging on to my property?

A. Yes. You may reaffirm a debt, if the applicable creditor allows it. By **reaffirming** a debt, you promise to pay the creditor (usually in full, but not always), and you may keep the property involved, so long as you keep your promise. But if you later default, the creditor can repossess the property and the remaining balance will not be discharged.

Q. If I decide to reaffirm, do I have any protections to prevent the creditor from going against the agreement and simply repossessing the property?

A. Yes. Bankruptcy law provides some protections for consumers considering reaffirma-

---

▶ **YOUR INTENTIONS**

Within fifteen days of filing, and usually as part of the papers you file, you must advise your secured creditors on a court form whether you intend to surrender or redeem any collateral, or reaffirm any debt. You can address the issue of reaffirmation at the creditor's meeting.

tion. Under the new law, creditors must provide extensive disclosures to debtors, including outlining the consequences of failing to pay and the debtor's right to cancel the reaffirmation.

If a debtor reaffirms a debt, the creditor must inform the debtor as to the amount of debt reaffirmed, the applicable interest rates, when payments will begin, and any filing requirements with the court. Additionally, reaffirmation of debts other than home mortgages must be approved by the debtor's lawyer or the court.

Q. Can I keep my property and just continue to make payments and not redeem or reaffirm?

A. Theoretically, no. Debtors are prohibited from retaining property without redeeming or reaffirming the debt by making installment payments. In other words, even if you are current on your car loan, you still must reaffirm or redeem that loan in order to keep the car.

Q. I have property that I want to protect from bankruptcy. Can't I just transfer title to a relative before I file?

A. Not if you are transferring the property simply to prevent it from being part of your bankruptcy estate. Bankruptcy trustees will look carefully at any attempts to hide assets or to avoid disclosing the true identity and value of your assets. You will be asked whether you have transferred property within two years prior to filing. If you have transferred property without receiving a reasonable amount in return, a trustee can cancel the transfer and recover the property for your bankruptcy estate and creditors. Moreover, if the trustee discovers that you made the transfer with the intention of defrauding any creditor, you may be

denied discharge, and may also face federal criminal charges for committing a fraudulent transfer.

Q. After I submit the required paperwork to the court, what happens next?

A. The bankruptcy court clerk will notify your creditors that you have filed a bankruptcy petition. Creditors must immediately stop most efforts to collect your debts. A trustee will then be appointed to determine the next steps.

Q. What will I have to do?

A. Procedures for filing bankruptcy vary greatly by state, but you may be required to take the following steps:

- In some states, you may have to file a homestead deed in the appropriate state court. A **homestead deed,** also called a **declaration of homestead,** is a document intended to protect your property from creditors. Generally, it describes the property and assigns an approximate value to it. The document may also have to be recorded in the appropriate office (such as a land record office) in the county in which you live. In some states, you may be required to take this step before you file for bankruptcy.

- You will be required to appear at a first meeting of creditors, where the trustee will examine you under oath about your petition, statement of financial affairs, and schedules. Creditors can also question you about your debts and assets, and will often attend this meeting to discuss reaffirmation, surrender of property, and related issues. Later, the trustee will determine whether to challenge any of your claimed exemptions or your right to a discharge.

- If you disagree with the trustee's decisions, you may protest to the court, which will make the final decision.

Q. So what exactly does the trustee do?

A. After determining your exemptions, the bankruptcy trustee will assemble, liquidate, and distribute the value of your nonexempt assets (if there are any). The trustee might **abandon**—that is, return to you—property that would bring no value to your unsecured creditors. This will include nonexempt assets with minimal resale value.

Q. How does the trustee decide which creditors get paid, and in what order?

A. The first creditors to be paid are secured creditors. The trustee will first distribute to secured creditors the value of their collateral, or the collateral itself if the collateral is worth no more than the debt. This means that the bank will get your house if you have no equity; it could keep it (which is unlikely) or sell it, but in neither case will your unsecured creditors benefit.

Next, the trustee will pay unsecured priority claims, such as most taxes and past-due support—for example, alimony and child support. If any funds are left, the trustee will distribute them to your general unsecured creditors, such as credit card companies, on a pro rata (proportionate) basis. In return, the court will discharge you from paying any remaining balance on your general unsecured debts.

The trustee will also pay the administrative claims, such as his or her commission fees (ranging between 3 and 25 percent, depending on the value the trustee recovers), and the fees of professionals, such as lawyers and accountants.

REMEMBER THIS

- Chapter 7 bankruptcy allows you to discharge most of your debts. In a Chapter 7 bankruptcy case, a trustee is appointed to investigate and supervise your case.

- When you file a Chapter 7 bankruptcy, you must file schedules and a statement of financial affairs. Information you must list on these forms includes your financial history, income, debts, and assets.

- If you are seeking to file for bankruptcy, you must file a certificate showing that you have received credit counseling and a budget plan from an approved nonprofit credit counseling service.

- Under either federal or state law, some of your assets may be exempt from creditors during bankruptcy. Exempt assets are beyond the reach of unsecured creditors and the bankruptcy trustee.

- You should consult with a bankruptcy attorney to maximize your exemptions by converting nonexempt to exempt assets.

- The Bankruptcy Code requires that you give all nonexempt, unencumbered assets to your trustee. If these assets have sufficient value to make a sale worthwhile, the trustee will liquidate them to pay creditors.

- Husbands and wives, depending on state law and the status of joint debt, may want to file jointly for bankruptcy.

- You may be able to reaffirm some debts—that is, promise to pay them—in order to keep certain assets, subject to the approval of the affected creditor.

- You cannot avoid the reach of creditors during bankruptcy simply by transferring title to property that you own. Improper transfers may cause you to lose your bankruptcy discharge, and may put you at risk for criminal prosecution.

- Bankruptcy does not discharge all debts. You are still liable for some tax claims, alimony, child support, fraudulent debts, student loans, and criminal obligations.

CHAPTER 13: WAGE-EARNER BANKRUPTCY

This section explores issues relating to Chapter 13 bankruptcy, which is also known as wage-earner or individual bankruptcy. It explains who can file and the procedures that must be followed, including the drafting of a payment plan.

Chapter 13 Defined

Q. What is Chapter 13 bankruptcy?

A. **Chapter 13 bankruptcy** allows individuals with regular incomes to pay a portion of their debts under a court-approved payment plan, and to keep both their exempt and nonexempt assets.

If you have a steady income, Chapter 13 allows you to pay all or a portion of your debts under the protection and supervision of the U.S. Bankruptcy Court. The law requires that your payments to creditors be no less than they would have been if you had filed a Chapter 7 case. Under Chapter 13, you will keep all your assets (both exempt and nonexempt) while the plan is in effect and after you have successfully completed it.

Q. Who is eligible for Chapter 13 bankruptcy?

A. Chapter 13 is available to almost everyone who has a regular income. The only other requirement is that you have less than $307,675 in unsecured debts (such as credit card debts) and less than $922,975 in secured debts (such as home mortgages and car loans). These figures are not doubled when husband and wife file a joint case, and are subject to periodic adjustments, currently every three years. Anyone with greater debts usually declares bankruptcy under Chapters 7 or 11 of the Bankruptcy Code.

Q. What are the main differences between Chapter 7 and 13?

A. The major difference is that in Chapter 7 you pay debts out of your nonexempt assets, while in Chapter 13 you pay debts out of your future income. As a result, a repayment plan under Chapter 13 normally allows you more time to pay your debts than does a Chapter 7 plan. It also involves you paying off more of those debts, and allows you to deal more easily with secured creditors (e.g., home mortgage lenders and companies providing financing for your purchase of a car or truck). The permitted repayment period is usually three years for people whose income is below your state's median income, and five years for those debtors whose disposable income is above the median in their state.

Not everyone is eligible for relief under Chapter 7. (Congress created a "means test" for Chapter 7 filers that is more fully explained on page 422 in the section titled "Chapter 7 or Chapter 13?") As a result, more people may file under Chapter 13 than under Chapter 7.

Typically, the amount that you repay under a Chapter 13 plan is equal to the total of your planned monthly payments over three to five years, assuming a good-faith effort to repay your debts. Thus, your payments represent either (1) full satisfaction of your debts; or (2) all of your disposable income for a three- to five-year period. **Disposable income** consists of whatever is left over from your total income after you have paid for taxes and reasonable and necessary living expenses. For some above-median-income debtors, allowable expenses are determined in large part by IRS regulations. It is important to consult with an attorney to determine what expenses are permitted. Under a Chapter 13 plan, debtors must also pay secured creditors the values of their liens over time, and cannot change the terms of their home mortgage loans. A debtor can, however, cure any delinquent payments on their mortgage loan over the life of the plan.

Chapter 13 in Action

Q. What is required in order to file a Chapter 13 bankruptcy?

A. As compared to Chapter 7, you need to provide more detailed information, including a statement of monthly net income itemized to show how the amount was calculated, copies of all payments received within sixty days before the filing of the petition, copies of federal tax returns, and a photo ID. As with Chapter 7, you will also have to file a certificate showing that you received credit counseling within 180 days before your bankruptcy filing.

You will also need to file a repayment plan within fifteen days of filing your petition. In your payment plan, you agree to pay a certain amount each month to your creditors. Your plan will indicate the amount of money you propose to pay each month, the total amount to

be paid, the percentage return you propose to pay to your creditors, and the expected length of the plan. You must make your first payment on this plan within thirty days after you file it.

Q. What does a Chapter 13 trustee do?

A. After you submit your plan to the court, a Chapter 13 trustee is appointed to handle your case. The trustee will verify the accuracy and reasonableness of your plan. The plan will then be distributed to your creditors, who will have the opportunity at a creditors' meeting to challenge your repayment proposal if they believe it doesn't meet the specific requirements of the Bankruptcy Code. You must attend the creditors' meeting, and answer questions under oath from your creditors and the trustee regarding your financial affairs and the proposed terms of the plan. The Chapter 13 trustee attends this meeting, but the judge does not.

The trustee will want to be sure that your plan provides enough money for you to live on, but will also challenge living expenses that seem unreasonably high. One issue will be whether you are making a good-faith and sincere effort to repay your debts, even if that effort means reducing your living standards, such as by eliminating entertainment expenses. Since the trustee's recommendation will carry considerable weight with the court, it pays to be honest and open with the information that you provide.

After the creditor's meeting, the bankruptcy judge will hold a confirmation hearing, and either confirm your plan or deny it. The confirmation hearing must be held twenty to forty-five days after the creditors' meeting. If the judge rejects the plan, you can propose another plan. If you are eligible to file Chapter 7, you could also convert your Chapter 13 bankruptcy into a Chapter 7 filing.

Remember that you must start making payments to the trustee, your landlord, and your secured creditors within thirty days of filing, regardless of whether the plan has been confirmed by a judge or not.

Q. Are there advantages to filing a Chapter 13 bankruptcy?

A. Yes, there are several positive features of a Chapter 13 plan. For one thing, under some circumstances, you can propose to repay a creditor at a lower interest rate than the rate stipulated in your original contract with that creditor (except in the case of a home mortgage). Moreover, your proposed repayment plan needn't provide that you pay back the entire amount you owe. Instead, you can reorganize your debts and submit a reasonable payback plan proposing that debts to secured creditors be paid back on your own schedule, without exorbitant interest. This flexibility can be a great advantage for Chapter 13 debtors.

But keep in mind that you still must put forth your best effort to repay your debts. A creditor might file an objection to a Chapter 13 plan if it will receive less under the plan than it would have under Chapter 7. Unsecured creditors are entitled to receive at least as much as they would have received under a Chapter 7 bankruptcy. This is called the **best interest of the creditors** rule.

Q. What happens to my secured collateral during a Chapter 13 bankruptcy?

A. Debtors are prohibited from the stripping down of security interests in motor vehicles acquired within 910 days of the petition filing, and of other secured debts incurred within one year of the bankruptcy. The term **stripping down** refers to the process, allowed under an older version of the bankruptcy laws, whereby debtors could propose a new value for property on which they owed money. Today, you must repay the full amount of the loans on such property.

Payment Plans

Q. How do I prepare my payment plan?

A. You have some flexibility in preparing a Chapter 13 bankruptcy plan. Your plan should take into account your income from all sources and your reasonable necessary expenses. It should also anticipate any known future changes in your income or expenses, such as retirement or a rent increase. What is left from your income after paying living expenses will be available for disbursement to your creditors. Note that some items, like child support payments and money used to pay certain debts, are excluded from your available income (and thus will not be disbursed to creditors).

Your plan must provide for payment in full of all priority claims—that is, certain taxes and family support obligations, including overdue child support and alimony. You can lose the protections of a Chapter 13 plan if you do not remain current with your family support obligations. Besides keeping up with such current obligations, you'll have to cure—that is, make up for—any payments you have missed in the past. You can arrange to pay such overdue debts over the life of your repayment plan.

Q. What happens after the plan is approved?

A. Once the court approves your payment plan, you must continue to make regular

▶ IF YOU'RE SELF-EMPLOYED

If you are self-employed and filing under Chapter 13, you will have to show your average monthly business expenses and income for the six months prior to the petition date. You will also need to include incidental income, such as part-time wages for babysitting, alimony and support income, and rental income.

monthly plan payments to the trustee. The trustee usually distributes payments among your creditors in accordance with your confirmed repayment plan. You will continue to pay for your ongoing utility and grocery bills and other everyday expenses. The court will grant you a Chapter 13 discharge after you complete the payments specified in your plan, usually in three to five years. If you are unable to complete the payments, you will not obtain a discharge of any of your debts unless you qualify for a **hardship discharge,** which requires proof of special circumstances beyond your control that made it im-

possible for you to make further plan payments (see page 420).

Q. My plan has been approved and I have started to make payments. Do I need to do anything else?

A. Yes. Chapter 13 imposes additional filing requirements on debtors during the lives of their repayment plans. Upon request from the judge or a party in interest (e.g., a trustee or creditor), debtors must submit annual financial statements showing the amount and sources of income and expenditures.

Q. What if I can't make the payments required under my plan?

A. You must do all you can to make the payments required under a Chapter 13 bankruptcy plan. If you don't make the required payments, the ramifications can be severe. If you fail to take the initiative in dealing with defaults under your Chapter 13 plan—for example, by seeking a change in the plan or a hardship discharge—a creditor or the trustee may seek to have your case either converted to Chapter 7, or dismissed outright. If the case is dismissed, the automatic stay that arose upon the filing of the Chapter 13 case is dissolved. This means that the collection calls will begin again, and your car

▶ CHAPTER 13 TRUSTEE

The role of Chapter 13 trustees varies among judicial districts. Some trustees work with debtors to help them learn to manage their finances, and may arrange for (or require) automatic payroll deductions to be credited directly to the trustee's account for disbursement to the various creditors. A small part of the monthly payments goes to the trustee for these services.

could be repossessed or your home fore-closed.

Q. If I defaulted on my payment plan and my creditors get the court to convert my case to Chapter 7, how will this impact me?

A. Conversion to Chapter 7 could be good or bad for you, depending on the circumstances. If you have little or no equity, Chapter 7 isn't much of a threat. You might even seek to have your Chapter 13 case converted to Chapter 7 on your own if you are having problems making the Chapter 13 plan payments.

However, if you have a lot of equity in your home or your car that you want to retain, then Chapter 7 could be something you'd prefer to avoid, since it would give your creditors a chance to recover nonexempt assets that you wish to protect. In that case, you'd have every reason to keep up with your Chapter 13 plan. Be aware, however, that conversion to Chapter 7 does not necessarily mean that you are eligible for a Chapter 7 discharge; conversion and eligibility for discharge are different matters entirely.

Q. I know I am going to miss a payment. What should I do?

A. You may want to consider a moratorium, modification, or discharge.

Sometimes, special circumstances can qualify a debtor for temporary relief from the requirements of a Chapter 13 plan. For example, if you have an accident that causes you to lose time from work temporarily, you may be able to arrange a **moratorium,** which means that you can miss a payment and catch up later.

Furthermore, if there is a major permanent reduction in your income—for example, from lost hours due to a chronic illness—the

trustee may support a **modification** in the plan if you meet certain legal requirements. Modification might entail stretching payments out over a longer period (not to exceed five years) and reducing the amount of each payment accordingly, or perhaps giving up some asset for which you had planned to make payments. If you complete performance of your modified plan, you are entitled to a full Chapter 13 discharge, provided you have satisfied the other requirements as well.

If there is no modification of your plan but you have defaulted on your plan payments as a result of circumstances for which you "should not justly be held accountable," and if your unsecured creditors have already received as much as they would have received under Chapter 7, you may qualify for a **hardship discharge** if you can show that a modification of the plan would be impractical. This is considered a Chapter 7—type discharge.

Q. I think a Chapter 13 discharge might be right for me. What debts will I be able to discharge?

A. Granted upon completion of a repayment plan, a Chapter 13 discharge covers more types of debt than a Chapter 7 discharge. However, it is important to note that the difference is much smaller than it was before the 2005 bankruptcy law was passed. Debts *not* discharged by Chapter 13 include

- taxes, where returns either were not filed or were fraudulent;
- debts left off the bankruptcy schedules;
- support obligations;
- student loans;
- debts for personal injuries caused by drunk driving;
- criminal fines;

▸ KEEP UP THOSE PAYMENTS

What happens to your home and home loan in Chapter 13? To avoid losing your home, you must make regular monthly payments to the Chapter 13 trustee, and make monthly future mortgage payments on your home as they become due after the filing. If you've skipped some mortgage payments before you filed your Chapter 13 bankruptcy, you can put the delinquent mortgage payments (with interest to account for your delay) under the Chapter 13 plan. In other words, you can spread them out. However, to ensure you keep your house, you must also make the future monthly payments on your home mortgage loan as they come due. If you don't, you may have to turn your home over to the lender.

- some restitution orders;
- debts for money obtained under false pretenses;
- debts for luxury goods bought on credit within ninety days of filing for bankruptcy;
- cash advances over $750 obtained within seventy days of filing; and
- funds obtained by embezzlement.

REMEMBER THIS

- Chapter 13 allows individuals with regular incomes to pay all or a portion of their debts under the protection and supervision of a court. Under Chapter 13, you file a bankruptcy petition and a proposed payment plan, which can extend from three to five years, with the U.S. Bankruptcy Court.
- The bankruptcy trustee will typically distribute your proposed payment plan to your creditors. Creditors will have a chance to challenge your proposals. Once the payment plan is approved by the court, you make monthly payments to the trustee, who then disburses the money among your creditors in accordance with the plan.
- If you cannot make payments under a Chapter 13 plan, you may be able to convert to a Chapter 7 plan or seek a dismissal of the Chapter 13 case.

CHAPTER 7 OR CHAPTER 13?

The differences between the two types of consumer bankruptcy can seem pretty confusing. Is one better than the other? Is there a choice to be made? This section compares the pluses and minuses of Chapter 7 and Chapter 13 bankruptcy, and will help you determine which one is a more feasible option for you.

Whose Choice?

Q. *Is the choice between Chapter 7 and Chapter 13 mine to make?*

A. When filing for bankruptcy, the choice between chapters is generally left to the debtor. Bear in mind, however, that the 2005 bankruptcy law may make you ineligible for Chapter 7 bankruptcy under the **means test** if you earn more than the median income in your state and have disposable income (income less living expenses) greater than $167 per month. If your disposable income is less than $100 per month, you still qualify for Chapter 7. If your monthly disposable income is between $100 and $167 per month, then a special calculation will be necessary.

Q. If I decide to file for Chapter 7 bankruptcy, can I be forced to change my filing to Chapter 13?

A. Yes. The trustee or any creditor can bring a motion in court to dismiss a Chapter 7 bankruptcy if the debtor's income is too high (that is, above the state median). In effect, this forces the debtor into Chapter 13 bankruptcy, if the debtor is able to file bankruptcy at all.

Under current law, a **means test** is used to determine whether a debtor's income is too high for a Chapter 7 case. The test is fairly complex and takes into account presumed income and a number of deductions. Under the means test, debtors must file a statement of their calculations with the court. If a debtor's disposable income is considered too high for Chapter 7 (greater than $167 per month), then creditors are notified within ten days of the filing of the petition, and can bring a motion to dismiss the bankruptcy petition. Median income varies by state.

If your income is under your state's median, your petition for bankruptcy still might be dismissed, although it is unlikely. Courts also have the option of dismissing a Chapter 7 bankruptcy on grounds of simple abuse, though the law does not clarify the precise meaning of this term.

Q. What if I decide that the trustee or creditor is right, and I want to change my Chapter 7 bankruptcy to a Chapter 13 bankruptcy. Can we all just agree to do it?

A. Yes. The law specifically provides for conversion of a bankruptcy case to Chapter 11 or 13, with the debtor's permission, as an alternative to dismissal.

Advantages of Each

Q. Are there advantages to a Chapter 13 bankruptcy as compared to a Chapter 7 bankruptcy?

A. Yes. Chapter 13 bankruptcy plans have several advantages over Chapter 7 plans. The main differences break down as follows:

- **Keeping your assets.** Perhaps the most important advantage is that Chapter 13 plans allow you to retain your assets, so long as you make the required payments.

- **Discharging debts.** Another distinction between Chapters 7 and 13 is that a few debts are dischargeable under Chapter 13 that are not dischargeable under Chapter 7 (such as property settlement debts and debts for willful property damage).

- **Cosigned loans.** Under Chapter 13, if you had people co-sign any of your consumer loans or other credit debts, and if the collateral for such loans is in your possession, then your creditors cannot collect from these cosigners until it is clear that the Chapter 13 plan will not pay the entire amount owed to the creditors. This is called a **co-debtor automatic stay.** In contrast, if you file Chapter 7, your creditors will have the right to demand payment from your cosigners immediately.

- **Reinstating your mortgage by curing delinquent mortgage payments on your home.** Chapter 13 permits you to make up your delinquent mortgage payments over the life of your plan, while you also continue to make your regular monthly payments.

- **Can be used more often.** Another advantage of Chapter 13 is that you can use it more often than Chapter 7. The law forbids you to receive a discharge under Chapter 7 more than once every eight years. However, Chapter 13 allows you to file repeatedly, and receive the benefits of the automatic stay, though each filing will appear on your credit record and will be reviewed by the trustee to prevent abuse. Remember that any Chapter 13 plans must be filed in good faith.

Q. So does that mean I can file for Chapter 13 as often as I want?

A. You can file, but under the new bankruptcy law, it may not be possible to complete the bankruptcy and be discharged from your debts. A Chapter 13 debtor will be denied discharge if he or she received a discharge in a case filed under Chapter 7, 11, or 12 during the previous four years, or in a Chapter 13 case filed during the previous two years. The advantage of being able to refile under Chapter 13 (even if debtors are not permitted discharge) is that debtors are given the temporary protection of the automatic stay. The benefits of having a period of time—up to five years—to deal with secured debt, a time in which unsecured creditors must suspend their collection efforts, may outweigh not being able to get a discharge at the end of that period.

Q. Are there advantages to filing under Chapter 7?

A. Yes, several.

1. There are many debtors for whom the advantages of Chapter 13 do not matter: debtors with no nonexempt assets they particularly wish to keep, no debts excepted from discharge under Chapter 13, no prior discharge within the last eight years, and no cosigners on their consumer debt loans.

2. You get to keep your post-petition earnings free and clear from discharged pre-bankruptcy debts.

3. Some debtors are not eligible for Chapter 13 bankruptcy, either because their income is not sufficiently regular to fund payments under a plan, or because the amount of their debt exceeds the statutory limits.

4. The discharge is normally within ninety days of filing, whereas in a Chapter 13 bankruptcy the discharge will occur only after all plan payments are made, which is normally three to five years after the filing.

REMEMBER THIS

- Most debtors can choose whether to file for bankruptcy under Chapter 7 or Chapter 13. However, the 2005 bankruptcy law means that some bankruptcies will be eligible for discharge only in Chapter 13.

SAVING YOUR HOME

Going through a bankruptcy can be a disruptive, painful, and often frightening process. Of all the difficult prospects people face during bankruptcy, the potential loss of one's home is likely among the most challenging. This section covers what you can do to preserve your home.

Q. I am going to declare bankruptcy. What are the chances I can keep my home?

A. You have a chance to keep your home—if you remember a few important things. Under either Chapter 7 or Chapter 13, you will be able to keep your home only if you continue to make the required ongoing monthly payments on your mortgage. If you've fallen behind, under Chapter 7 you must make arrangements acceptable to your mortgage lender to catch up on any delinquent payments, and it's up to the mortgage company to decide whether to work with you.

Under Chapter 13, you may be able to include any delinquent payments in your payment plan and pay them off over a specified period of time while maintaining ongoing monthly mortgage payments.

Another factor determining whether you'll keep your home is whether you own the property with your spouse. Let's say you have plenty of debt, but your spouse has little or none. Many states will completely block or significantly limit the ability of unsecured creditors to reach property that you own together with your non-filing spouse. (This is not true, however, in community property states.) Much may depend on how (i.e., in what form of joint ownership) you hold the home. Talk to a lawyer in your state about whether your can protect your home.

Q. I am going to proceed under Chapter 7. What will happen to my house?

A. There is a chance you may lose it. Even if you're willing to continue making the required monthly payments, you could still lose your home if you file for bankruptcy under Chapter 7.

With a Chapter 7 filing, if you have no equity in your home and you haven't made your payments, the creditor can foreclose on your home (i.e., take it from you) during or after bankruptcy, even if your unsecured debts are discharged. The Chapter 7 discharge does not release the lien. Of course, a lender can also foreclose on your home in these circumstances if you do not file for bankruptcy.

If you do have equity in your home, your unsecured creditors may also have an interest in your home, especially if it is worth more than the total of your mortgage debt and any applicable homestead exemption. In that case, the bankruptcy trustee may take possession of your home and sell it for the benefit of your unsecured creditors—in other words, it

---

▶ **HOMESTEAD EXEMPTIONS**

Homestead exemptions are discussed in more detail earlier in this chapter on page 412. This area of bankruptcy law varies greatly between states and can change quickly. Therefore, it is important to work with an experienced lawyer in your area to ensure you are doing everything you can to save your home.

▶ WHAT IF FORECLOSURE ISN'T ENOUGH?

A lender who recovers less from the sale of a house than the amount you owe will have an unsecured claim for the difference, which may be asserted and usually discharged in your bankruptcy case. In some states, a confirmation action in state court is required to verify the foreclosing mortgage company's entitlement to such a deficiency claim.

may become part of the assets collected for distribution by the trustee.

Q. Under what circumstances would the trustee take our home?

A. Whether the trustee will actually take your home will depend on two basic factors: how much equity you have in the home, and how much of the home's value is sheltered by exemption law from creditors.

Q. What if I file under Chapter 13. How can I keep my home then?

A. To preserve your home under a Chapter 13 plan, you ordinarily must agree to con- tinue your lender's lien on your home and to make the required ongoing monthly payments. You must also agree to pay any skipped payments (defaults) through your payment plan. Otherwise, you'll have to turn the property over to the lender.

It is possible that if housing values are greatly depressed, a lender might be willing to lower your monthly payments in order to gain some income and keep the house occupied. But don't count on it.

REMEMBER THIS

- Under either Chapter 7 or Chapter 13, you will not be able to keep your home if you don't make the required monthly payments on your mortgage after the filing.

- Whether the trustee will actually take your home will depend upon two basic factors: how much equity is in the home and how much of the home's value is sheltered by law from creditors.

- Often, there is a homestead exemption with a dollar amount that is shielded from creditors, but don't assume that you will be able to keep your home simply because you file for bankruptcy.

- With your home on the line, you're well advised to discuss your situation with a bankruptcy lawyer.

Contracts and Consumer Law

Brendan is buying a new 52-inch, flat-screen television. He has been saving for months now and can't wait to install it and watch the upcoming football season. Brendan has done all the research and knows exactly which brand to buy and from where. But what he hasn't researched is the sales contract he will have to sign, and the warranties the salesperson is suddenly offering him when he is ready to check out. Can he believe the salesperson's statement that "this is the best TV for the price?" Does the salesperson have the ability to change the warranty terms? What if Brendan disagrees with the delivery timetable set forth in the contract?

Contracts are a common part of our lives. Recognizing what constitutes a contract is key to understanding many legal questions. Very often a dispute centers not on whether someone has violated a contract, but on whether a contract existed in the first place. Other disputes center on whether a change in circumstances has made a contract unenforceable.

This chapter explains what contracts are and how they are created. It focuses on contracts common in daily life, such as leases and warranties, and highlights issues of interest to consumers. It also provides you with information about what you can do when things go wrong, whether the problem is breach of a contract term, or a company liquidating before sending you goods for which you've already paid. A final section outlines special consumer protections in such areas as advertising, door-to-door sales, telemarketing, and travel.

Keep in mind that these sections merely scratch the surface of contract law. This chapter will not deal in detail with the millions of contracts made every day between merchants and other businesses, or with contracts governing investment-related relationships.

AN INTRODUCTION TO CONTRACTS

This section provides an overview of the basics of contract law, including such topics as the parties to a contract, the issue of capacity, and contract formation.

Q. *What is a contract?*

A. Normally, a **contract** consists of legally enforceable, voluntary promises between competent parties to do (or not do) something. These are binding promises, which can be oral but are almost always more enforceable if written. Depending on the situation, a contract could obligate someone even if he or she wants to call the deal off before receiving anything from the other side. The details of the contract (who, how, what, how much, how many, when, and so on) are called its **provisions** or **terms.**

For a promise to qualify as enforceable, it must be supported by something of value that is bargained for between the participants or parties. This something, known as **consideration,** is most often money, but can also be some other bargained-for benefit or detriment. The final qualification for a contract is that the subject of the promise (including the consideration) may not be illegal.

Suppose a friend agrees to buy your car for $1,000. Your promise to sell and your friend's promise to buy are the promises required for contract formation. You benefit by getting the cash. Your friend benefits by getting the car. Because it is your own car (and thus yours to sell), the sale is legal, and you and your friend have a contract.

It is common for the word "contract" to be used as a verb meaning "to enter into a contract." We also speak of contractual relationships to refer to the whole of sometimes complex relationships, which may comprise one or many contracts.

Parties to a Contract

Q. *May anyone enter into a contract?*

A. No. To make an enforceable contact, parties must be able to understand what they're doing. This requires both maturity and mental capacity. Without both, one party could be at a disadvantage in the bargaining process.

Capacity

Q. What determines maturity to make a contract?

A. Maturity is defined by age—regardless of whether a person is in fact "mature." State laws permit people to make contracts if they have reached the age of majority (i.e., if they are no longer a minor), which is usually age eighteen.

Q. Does this mean that minors may not make contracts?

A. No. Minors may make contracts. But courts may choose not to enforce some of them. The law presumes that minors must be protected from their lack of maturity. So, for example, a Porsche salesman may not exploit a minor's naïveté by enforcing a signed sales contract whose real implications a young person is unlikely to have comprehended. Sometimes this results in minors receiving benefits (such as goods or services) and not having to pay for them, though they would have to return any goods still in their possession. This would apply even to minors who are **emancipated**—i.e., living entirely on their own—who get involved in contractual relationships, as well as to a minor who lives at home but is unsupervised for long enough to get into a contractual fix.

Q. What if my minor child enters into a sales contract for food that our family needs? Can we still get out of the contract?

A. Probably not. A court may require a minor or the minor's parents to pay the fair market value (not necessarily the contract price) for what courts call **necessaries**. The definition of a necessary depends entirely on the person and the situation—though it probably will always include food and probably will never include CDs, Nintendo cartridges, or Porsches. In some states, courts may require a minor to pay the fair value of goods or services purchased under a contract that minor has disavowed.

Q. Can lack of mental capacity invalidate a contract?

A. Probably, yes—but it would depend on the level of incapacity. While the age for legal ma-

---

▶ CAPACITY

We've discussed the fundamental requirements for competence to make a contract: maturity and mental capacity. Of course, it should go without saying that there's an even more fundamental requirement: that both parties be people.

In the case of a corporation or other legal entity that the law considers a "person," the requirement that the parties be people could be an issue. A problem in the formation or status of the entity could cause it to cease existing legally, thus making it impossible for that entity to enter into a contract. In that case, however, the individuals who signed the contract on behalf of the legally nonexistent entity could be personally liable for fulfilling the contract.

turity is easy to determine, the standards for determining mental capacity are remarkably complex and differ widely from one state to another. One common test is whether people have the capacity to understand what they were doing and to appreciate its effects when they made the deal. Another approach is evaluating whether people can control themselves, regardless of their level of understanding.

Q. May a person get out of a contract that was made while intoxicated?

A. At times. The courts don't like to let a voluntarily intoxicated person revoke a contract with innocent parties—but if that person was acting drunk when the contract was made, then the other party probably wasn't so innocent.

On the other hand, if the person didn't appear to be intoxicated when making the contract, then he or she probably will have to abide by it. In these types of cases, the key factor may be a person's medical history. Someone who can show a history of alcohol abuse or blackouts may be able to void the contract, regardless of his or her appearance when the contract was made. This is true especially if the other party knows about that person's medical history.

Authority and Agency

Q. May someone else enter into a contract on my behalf?

A. Yes, but only with your permission. The law refers to such an arrangement as **agency.** We couldn't do business without it. All sorts of people in our economy are agents, from the person who staffs the movie theater box office to the clerk who sells you clothes. They are **agents**—that is, someone with the authority to bind someone else (e.g., the movie theater

or the department store) by contract. (In these simple examples, the contracts provide that, in return for your money, the theater will show you a movie and the store will sell you the clothes you have chosen.)

The **principal** is the person or company for whom the agent acts. As long as agents do not exceed the authority granted them by their principals, the contracts they make bind their principals just as if the principals had made the contracts themselves. If something went wrong with the contract, you would sue the principal—not the agent—if you couldn't resolve the dispute in a friendly manner. An agent normally does not have any personal obligation.

While acting on behalf of principals, agents are required to put their own interests after those of the principal. Therefore, they may not personally profit beyond what the principal and the agent have agreed to in their agency contract. That means the agent cannot take advantage of any opportunity that, under the terms of the agency, is meant to be exploited by the principal.

Q. What happens when an agent exceeds the authority granted by a principal?

A. That depends on the circumstances. Suppose an agent exceeds her authority, but the person she's dealing with doesn't reasonably understand that she's exceeding it. If the principal knew (or reasonably should have known) that the agent has exceeded her authority in similar circumstances, but has done nothing about it, then the principal may be bound by the contract negotiated by the agent. On the other hand, if the principal is not aware that the agent exceeded her authority, then the contract will only be enforceable against the principal if it was reasonable for the other party to believe the agent was acting within her authority.

For example, suppose you visit a gas station and are waited on by a teenage boy wearing a service station uniform. While filling your tank, he also offers to sell you the whole service station in exchange for the car you are driving. It's not reasonable for you to assume that he has the power to make that contract, when common sense tells you he can only sell you his boss's gasoline for a fixed price. For this reason, the contract would not likely be enforceable.

By contrast, suppose an insurance agent sold you a policy for a larger amount than the insurance company had authorized. If the insurer never told you of the limit, then you would likely be acting reasonably to assume the policy amount had been authorized. As a result, you probably could collect on a claim for the full amount of the policy, even if that amount exceeded what the insurance company had authorized the agent to sell you.

Forming a Contract

Q. What steps must be taken in order to form a contract?

A. Generally, a contract is created when one party makes an offer and another party accepts that offer. For a contract to exist, the parties must assent to the transaction. **Assent** usually takes the form of offer and acceptance. Offer and acceptance are the fundamental parts of a contract, once capacity is established.

Q. What is an offer?

A. An **offer** is a communication by an offerer (the person making the offer) of a present intention to enter a contract that the offeree (the person to whom the offer is made) must receive.

Q. What makes an offer valid?

A. In a contract to buy and sell, in order for an offer to be valid, the answers to all of the following questions must be clear:

- Who is the offeree?
- What is the subject matter of the offer?
- How much of that subject matter does the offer involve (i.e., what quantity of goods or services are involved)?
- How much is to be paid (i.e., what is the price)?

Let's say you told your friend, "I'll sell you my mellow-yellow Mini Cooper for $1,000." Your friend is the offeree, and the car is the subject matter. Describing the car as a yellow Mini Cooper makes your friend reasonably sure that both of you are talking about the same car (and only one car). Finally, the price is $1,000. All of the necessary questions have been answered. Therefore, it's a perfectly good offer.

Q. Is an advertisement an offer?

A. No. Courts usually consider advertisements something short of an offer. They are an "expression of intent to sell," or an invitation to bargain.

Q. Does an offer stay open indefinitely?

A. Not unless the offeree has an option, which is a type of irrevocable offer for which the offeree bargains. Otherwise, an offer ends when

- the time to accept has expired—either after a "reasonable" amount of time or on the deadline stated in the offer;

- the offerer cancels the offer;
- the offeree rejects the offer; or
- the offeree dies or is incapacitated.

An offer is also closed, even if the offeree has an option, if

- a change in the law makes the contract illegal; or
- the subject matter of the contract is destroyed.

Q. What is an option?

A. An **option** is an agreement, usually unenforceable unless made for consideration, to keep an offer open for a certain period of time. For example, in return for a $50 deposit today, you might agree to give your friend until next Friday to accept your offer to sell her your car for $1,000. Now your friend has an option contract, and you may not sell the car to someone else—even for $1,200—without breaching that contract. An option puts a limit on your ability to revoke an offer.

Q. What constitutes acceptance of an offer?

A. **Acceptance** is the offeree's voluntary, communicated agreement or assent to the terms and conditions of the offer. **Assent** is some act or promise of agreement. A simple example of an assent might be your friend saying, "I agree to buy your yellow car for $1,000."

Generally, a valid acceptance requires that every agreed-upon term be the same as the terms of the offer. For sales and leases of goods, some flexibility is allowed if the intent to accept is clear—however, significant deviation will not suffice (i.e., an offer to sell 100 units cannot be accepted by an agreement to buy 25 or 200 units). You must communicate your acceptance by some reasonable means (by telephone, mail, or facsimile). On the other hand, a less-specific assent would also suffice, provided that it is crystal clear—for example, "It's a deal. I'll pick it up tomorrow." The standard is that the assent must be clear to a reasonable observer.

Q. Can silence signal acceptance?

A. In most cases, no. It isn't fair to allow someone to impose a contract on someone else. Yet there are circumstances in which failure to respond may have a contractual effect. Past dealings between the parties, for example, can create a situation in which silence constitutes acceptance. Suppose a fire-insurance company, according to past practice to which you have assented, sends you a renewal policy (essentially, a new contract for insurance) and bills you for the premium. If you kept the policy but later refused to pay the premium, you would be liable for the premium. This works to everyone's benefit: If your house burned down after the original insurance policy had expired, but before you had paid the renewal premium, then you obviously would want the policy still to be effective. And the insurer is protected from you deciding not to pay the premium until you know what claims you might have.

Q. Can an action qualify as acceptance?

A. Yes. Any conduct that would lead a reasonable observer to believe that the offeree had accepted the offer qualifies as an acceptance. Suppose you say, "John, I will pay you $50 to clean my house on Sunday at 9:00 A.M." If John shows up at 9:00 A.M. on Sunday and begins cleaning, he adequately shows acceptance (assuming you're home or would otherwise know that he showed up).

Q. When is acceptance effective?

A. A contract usually takes effect as soon as the offeree transmits or communicates the acceptance—unless the offerer has specified that the acceptance must be received before it is effective, or before an option expires. In these situations, there's no contract until the offerer receives the answer, and in the way specified. At times, the point at which the contract is effective is not easy to determine. However, this is not necessarily fatal to the contract.

Q. Is an "agreement to agree" a contract?

A. Generally not, because it suggests that important terms are still missing. Rarely will a court supply those terms itself.

Q. How much consideration, or payment, must there be for a contract to be valid?

A. There is no minimum amount; there's no absolute standard for determining whether a price is fair or reasonable. The courts presume that people will only make deals that they consider worthwhile. So if you want to sell your car to your friend for $1 instead of $1,000, you can. An exception may be found if the consideration provided is so out of line with what is received that it would "shock the conscience of the court." This idea of unconscionability will be discussed later in this chapter.

Q. Must both sides give consideration?

A. In general, yes. There's a crucial principle in contract law called **mutuality of obligation.** Both sides must be committed to giving up something. If either party reserves an unqualified right to bail out, then the other person's promise is not enforceable.

Q. Does consideration have to be money?

A. No. **Consideration** is anything that induces a party to enter a contract—a promise to act, a promise not to act, or a transfer of value—that the other party does not already have a preexisting duty to provide or perform. Consideration is a bargained-for benefit or advantage, or a bargained-for detriment or disadvantage. A benefit might be receiving $10 or first dibs on Super Bowl tickets. A disadvantage may involve promising not to do something, such as a promise not to sue someone. For these purposes, even quitting smoking, done with the reasonable expectation of some reward or benefit from someone else, is a detriment: Even though it's good for your health, it took effort that you otherwise would not have made.

Consideration cannot be merely illusory, or it is no promise at all.

Q. Must the consideration be a new obligation?

A. Yes, because someone already obligated to do something hasn't suffered any detriment. Suppose you agree to have a contractor paint your house this Thursday for $500. Before starting the job, however, his workers strike for higher wages. He tells you on Wednesday night that he settled the strike, but the job will now cost $650. You need the house painted before you leave town on Friday, and there's no time to hire another contractor, so you agree to the new price. But absent other circumstances, the new agreement is not enforceable. The contractor had already agreed to paint your house for $500. He should have figured any possible increased costs into the original price. You didn't get anything of benefit from the modified contract, since you had already received his promise to paint the house. Therefore, you only owe $500.

Q. Does that mean I can't renegotiate a contract?

A. No. It only means that no one can force you to renegotiate by taking advantage of an existing agreement. You could, of course, decide that the other party deserves more, or want to renegotiate so that you can use the other party on other jobs, or feel that the other party does the best job at any price. Considerations like these allow many sports stars to renegotiate their contracts.

Keep in mind that whenever you get involved in a deal, there is a risk that it might be less beneficial for you than you thought it would when you agreed to the contract terms. The other party doesn't have to guarantee you a profit, unless such a guarantee is part of your bargain.

Q. What if someone makes a promise to me without consideration, but I rely on it anyway?

A. Remember that a disadvantage to one party may constitute sufficient consideration for a contract. From that idea, the law has developed the concept of **promissory reliance**: that a contract may be formed if one party reasonably relies on the other's promise. In order to invoke the concept of promissory reliance, the relying party must do more than simply have his or her heart set on having the promise fulfilled. Rather, the party must do something he or she wouldn't have done in the absence of the promise, or fail to do something that he or she otherwise would have done. If one party's reliance on the other party's promise causes some loss, then the relying party may have an enforceable contract.

Suppose that rich Uncle Murray loves your kids. On previous occasions, he has asked you to buy them expensive presents and has reimbursed you for them. This past summer, Uncle Murray told you he would like you to build a swimming pool for the kids and send him the bill. You did so, but moody Uncle Murray changed his mind. Now he refuses to pay for the pool, and claims you can't enforce a promise to make a gift. The pool, however, is no longer considered a gift. You acted to your detriment in reasonable reliance on his promise, by paying for a pool you would not normally have built. Uncle Murray will have to pay, if you can prove that he induced you to build the pool—especially if this understanding was consistent with his behavior in previous gift-giving situations.

Q. Does a promise to make a gift constitute a contract?

A. Not if it is truly a promise to make a gift, without receiving anything in return. The reason is that a gift lacks the two-sided obligation discussed earlier. But if the person promising the gift is asking for anything in return, even by implication, then a contract may exist. Again, the key is whether any consideration was given.

Q. Can a joke be the basis for a contract?

A. It depends on whether a reasonable observer would understand that it was a joke, and on whether the acceptance was adequate. In our car example, you probably couldn't get out of the contract by saying, "How could you think I'd sell this for $1,000? It was a joke!" On the other hand, if someone sued you because you backed out on your promise to sell her the entire country of France for $15, then the joke

---

▶ **THE REASONABLE PERSON**

In any law book, the word "reasonable" will appear many times. Very often you'll see references to the "reasonable man" or the "reasonable person." Why is the law so preoccupied with this person?

The answer is that no contract can possibly predict the infinite number of disputes that might arise. Similarly, personal or property injury laws can't possibly foresee the countless ways humans and their property can harm other people or property. Since the law can't provide for every possibility, the standard of the "reasonable person" has evolved to furnish some uniform standards and to guide courts.

There are two principles that extend this fictional person's capacities into the realm of contracts. One is the concept of the reasonable observer, a reasonable person who sets the standard for whether an action or statement would reasonably suggest something—for example, an offer or acceptance of a contract, or repudiation of a contract. This person is not an eagle-eyed expert; instead, the reasonable person stands for common sense.

Closely related is the concept of "knew or should have known." If parties to a contract are considered to know, or be "on notice," of something—say, that their offer has been accepted—then it is not enough to ask whether they actually knew it. The law will not excuse parties from knowing something if they should have known it through the reasonable exercise of their senses and intelligence. Thus, it isn't enough to say, "I didn't know the car I sold you had no engine." That's something that someone selling a car should reasonably know.

---

would be on her, because no one could reasonably have thought you were serious.

Q. What is a condition?

A. People often use the word "condition" to refer to a term of a contract. More precisely, a **condition** is an event that must occur if the contract is to be performed. For example, in an auto sale contract, the sale might be made conditional by language such as: "The existence of this contract is conditional on our (the dealer's) ability to obtain financing for you on the terms specified in this order." Sim-

ilarly, the sale of real estate is often conditional on the buyer's obtaining specified financing or an acceptable home inspection report.

Neither party is required to agree to a condition that comes up during negotiations, and the one who wants the condition may have to pay extra for it. When a condition is put into negotiations, you must decide whether insisting on or agreeing to the condition is worthwhile to you, considering the risks and costs of not having the condition. In this respect, a condition is the same as any other term, such as price or quantity.

Drafting the Contract

Q. Do I need a lawyer to make a contract?

A. If you satisfy the maturity and mental-capacity requirements, then you don't need professional advice in order to make a contract. But it's a good idea to see a lawyer before you sign complex contracts, such as business deals, or contracts involving large amounts of money.

Q. Must contracts be in writing?

A. Technically, most types of contracts don't have to be written to be enforceable. For example, suppose you purchase an item in a store. You pay money in exchange for an item that the store warrants (by implication) will perform a certain function. Your receipt may be proof of the contract. In fact, with some important exceptions (discussed below), virtually any oral transaction could be enforceable—if you could prove that an agreement existed, and if you could prove what its terms were.

Courts will only enforce a contract that has been proven to exist. An oral contract can be very hard to prove—after all, you seldom have it on video. Usually an oral contract is deemed to exist if outside circumstances would have led a reasonable observer to conclude that it most likely existed—for example, in the case of payment for the delivery of goods. But even if an oral contract is shown to exist, there is always the problem of proving what its terms were. Even with written contracts, courts typically look only to unrefuted testimony to help them fill in the blanks regarding disputed contract terms, and are hesitant to add words or terms to any written document on the grounds that they were somehow implied.

Q. Are there any advantages to putting a contract in writing?

A. Yes. Although most states recognize and enforce oral contracts, the safest practice is to put any substantial agreement in writing. Get any promise from a salesperson or agent in writing, especially if there is already a written contract covering any part of the same deal—even if that contract is nothing more than an order form, a printed receipt, or a handwritten letter of agreement or understanding. Otherwise, the written contract may be regarded as a complete statement of the parties' understanding, and anything not included in that written contract could be deemed not to be part of the deal. Writing down the terms of a good-faith agreement is the best way to ensure that all parties know their rights and duties.

Q. Which contracts must be in writing?

A. Under state laws known as **statutes of frauds,** as modified by other state law or by the federal **ESIGN** Act (see the "E-Signature Bill Facilitates E-Commerce" sidebar, below), courts will enforce certain promises only if they are in writing or in other "record" form—for example, displayed on a computer screen and downloadable—and signed manually or electronically by the parties who are obligated to fulfill them. In most states, these types of promises include

- any promise to be responsible for someone else's debts—often called a **surety contract** or a **guaranty** (for example, an agreement by parents to guarantee payment of a bank loan made to their child);
- any promise that the parties cannot possibly fulfill within one year from when they made the promise;

- any promise involving the change of ownership of land or interests in land, such as a lease;
- any promise for the sale of goods worth more than $500 or the lease of goods worth more than $1,000;
- any promise to bequeath property (i.e., grant it to somebody after one's death); and
- any promise to sell stocks and bonds or to make a loan or other extension of credit.

Some states require written contracts for additional matters. These types of statutes prevent fraudulent claims in areas where it is uniquely difficult to prove that oral contracts have been made, or where important policies are at stake, such as the dependability of real estate ownership rights.

In the last few years, many states have allowed an increasing number of lawsuits containing claims based on unwritten contracts, even in situations that traditionally required a contract to be in writing. If you are facing a serious financial issue and fear that the statutes of frauds could prevent you from recovering, a lawyer may be able to help you.

Q. What are the rules regarding signatures?

A. A signature can be handwritten, but a stamped, photocopied, or engraved signature is often valid, as are signatures written by electronic pens. Even a simple mark or other indication of a name may be enough.

Furthermore, if there is sufficient evidence of trustworthiness, many states now permit e-mail from a specific account to be regarded as signed. Some states have set out specific requirements for e-mail signatures.

▶ E-SIGNATURE BILL FACILITATES E-COMMERCE

The Electronic Signatures in Global and National Commerce Act (ESIGN), a federal law, provides that online signatures have the same legal validity as pen-and-ink signatures for most—but not all—purposes. The law permits consumers to sign a mortgage or an insurance contract online, as well as perform other tasks, such as opening a brokerage account. A similar law enacted in some states is the Uniform Electronic Transactions Act.

These laws assure that a contract will not be denied legal status simply because the signature is electronic. However, the law does not give legal status to all electronic contracts. As a safeguard against fraud, most contracts and documents must be capable of being reproduced for later reference if they are to be enforceable.

Under these laws, no one is obligated to accept electronic signatures, and certain kinds of documents are typically exempted, including wills, codicils, and testamentary trusts; adoption papers; divorce papers or other documents relating to family matters; notices of foreclosures or evictions from one's primary residence; and cancellation of health or life insurance benefits.

What matters is whether the signature is authorized and intended to authenticate a writing—in other words, whether it is intended to indicate the signer's execution (completion and acceptance) of the writing. This means that you can authorize someone else to sign for you. This someone else, called an **agent** or **representative,** can even be a computer program or electronic agent. But the least risky and most persuasive evidence of assent is your own signature.

Q. Must contracts be notarized?

A. In general, no. **Notary publics** (or **notaries**), once important officials specially authorized to draw up contracts and transcribe official proceedings, now act mostly to administer oaths and to authenticate documents by attesting or certifying that a signature is genuine. Many commercial contracts, such as promissory notes or loan contracts, are routinely notarized to ensure they are authentic, even where this is not strictly required. Many technical documents required by law, such as certificates of incorporation, must be notarized if they are going to be recorded in a local or state filing office.

Assignment

Q. May I get someone else to perform my duties under a contract?

A. Yes, unless the contract prohibits such a transfer or the transfer might materially impair the other party's expectation. The law refers to a transfer of duties or responsibilities as a **delegation.** However, if someone contracts with you because of a special skill or talent that only you possess, then you may not be able to transfer your duty. Such cases are quite rare. Arguably, no car mechanics are so good at tuning an engine that they may not

delegate someone else to do it for them, unless they specifically promise to do it themselves. On the other hand, if you hire well-known entertainers to perform at your wedding, they may not send other entertainers as substitutes without your permission.

Q. Can I formalize this assumption of contract duties?

A. Yes, often with a surety contract or guaranty contract. A **surety contract** is an agreement in which one party, called the **surety,** accepts the responsibility for someone else's contractual obligations. For example, you might agree to pay back your son's bank loan if he does not. Usually, a surety is bound with the other person (the **principal**) on the same promise, often on the same document; under such an arrangement, the surety is sometimes called a **cosigner.**

A **guaranty contract** is similar, but the person who's vouching for the principal—called the **guarantor**—makes a separate promise, and is liable only if the principal breaches the contract and it is impossible to collect from him or her.

Q. May I give my rights under a contract to someone else?

A. Yes. A delegation or transfer of rights, called an **assignment,** is more flexible than a transfer of duties. For example, you may wish to transfer the right to receive money from a buyer for something you have sold. Generally, a contract right is yours to do with as you wish, as long as you didn't agree in the contract not to assign that right. You can sell it or give it away, though most states require you to put an assignment in writing, especially if it is a gift. If the assignment is the grant of a security interest, then in many cases a contractual or even a statutory restriction may be ignored.

Q. So can I assign my rights under any contract?

A. No, not necessarily. There are exceptions to the rule that assignments may be made freely. If an assignment would substantially increase the risk of the other contract party, or materially change that party's duty, then the contract may not be assignable, even if its terms contain no explicit agreement to the contrary.

For example, suppose you made a contract for fire insurance on your garage. Then a notorious convicted arsonist and insurance cheat contacted you, and asked you to sell him the garage and assign to him your rights under the garage's fire insurance policy. You would probably be in for a disappointment, even if the policy didn't prohibit assignment. Since the insurer made its decision to insure you based in part on your solid citizenship, insuring the arsonist would greatly increase its burden by imposing a risk that it never anticipated.

Limits to Forming a Contract

Q. May someone make a contract to do or sell something illegal?

A. No. For example, courts will not help someone collect an illegal gambling debt or payment for illegal drugs or prostitution. The law treats these contracts as if they never existed; they are unenforceable or void. This is the contract defense of **illegality.**

Similarly, even if they're not specifically outlawed, some contracts will not be enforced if a court determines that enforcement would violate public policy. An example would be a contract to become someone's slave, which may not be prohibited by statute but offends the law's view of the contracts permitted by our society.

> ▶ **MONEY ON THE LINE**
>
> What if it is illegal to gamble in your state, but you go online and gamble over the Internet using your credit card? Chances are you will still have to pay your losses. The website operator may be in violation of local law, and so may you. But your credit card agreement probably still requires you to pay your gambling debts. Until this area is regulated and controlled, you must assume that when you go online and put your money on the line, you may never see it again.

Q. What if the contract became illegal after the parties had already agreed to it? Is it enforceable?

A. Generally speaking, the Constitution forbids lawmakers from passing laws that would impair rights for which people bargain in contracts. Therefore, courts usually consider a contract in light of the applicable law when the contract was made—unless the change in the law involves a compelling public policy.

Obviously, a contract to sell someone a slave could not be enforced after slavery became illegal; neither could you enforce a contract to purchase a banned assault rifle that was made before the ban went into effect. This works both ways: A contract that was illegal when made usually will not be enforced, even though it would be legal if entered into today.

Q. Does the same hold true for a contract to do something immoral?

A. Courts will only enforce a moral code that the law (or public policy) already reflects, such as laws against prostitution or stealing. You may feel that X-rated movies or fur coats are immoral, but as long as they're legal, they can be the subjects of enforceable contracts.

Q. I was forced to sign a contract. Can it be enforced against me?

A. No. A contract that someone agrees to under duress is void. **Duress** is a threat or an act that overcomes someone's free will. The classic case of duress is a contract signed by someone "with a gun to his head." Because this kind of duress is very rare—and often very hard to prove—a duress defense is rarely successful.

Duress goes beyond persuasion or hard selling. It isn't duress when you say, "I would never pay that much for a Mini-Cooper if I had a choice." You do have a choice—to buy a Prius instead. But if you want that mellow-yellow Mini-Cooper, then you have to pay what the owner demands. In contrast, duress involves actual coercion, such as a threat of violence or imprisonment.

Q. Are there other kinds of duress besides physical threats?

A. Duress is a suspension of your free will. There may be duress in some circumstances in which there is no threat of physical violence—for example, if a person makes threats to bring a false lawsuit against you.

There is also economic duress. This was alluded to in the example on page 432, when the contractor demanded more money after his workers went on strike. This isn't the same as driving a hard bargain. Rather, the contractor had already made a deal. When the con-

---

▶ IS IT OR ISN'T IT A CONTRACT?

The principles discussed in this chapter will go a long way toward determining if people have formed a contract. You now know that a contract has to be made between willing, competent parties. Also, the contract must concern legal subject matter and must involve consideration.

But applying these principles isn't always easy. Sometimes special protections in the law complicate matters. If successfully invoked, only one of these may be needed to provide a complete defense against someone claiming you owe him or her money, or that you owe something else you supposedly promised. It would prompt a court to resolve the dispute as if there had never been a contract. Since the contract is **void,** neither party may enforce its terms in court against the other.

Other contracts are **voidable,** but not automatically void. What's the difference? A contract produced by fraud is not automatically void. People who are victimized by fraud have the option of asking a court to declare that contract void, or to **reform** (rewrite) it. On the other hand, if they went along with the contract for a substantial period of time, they could lose their right to get out of it. This is called **ratification,** and is based on the idea that they have, by their actions, made it clear that they are able to live with the terms. A checklist of contract defenses appears later in this chapter.

tractor threatened not to uphold his part of that deal, he left you with no practical choice but to agree. Courts have set aside contracts made under such economic duress.

Q. What should I do if someone forces me to sign a contract under duress?

A. Once you get out of danger, see a lawyer who can tell you how to protect yourself. The lawyer can help you determine whether you have assumed any obligation, and what legal rights you might have besides disavowing the contract. It's important to act quickly. Courts are especially skeptical of a claim of duress made long after the danger has passed.

Q. Are there other uses of unfair pressure, less severe than duress, that void a contract?

A. There is a contract defense called **undue influence,** which doesn't involve a threat. Rather, it's the unfair use of a relationship of trust to pressure someone into an unbalanced contract. Undue influence cases usually involve someone who starts out at a disadvantage, perhaps due to illness, age, or emotional vulnerability. The other person often has some duty to look out for the weaker one's interests.

An example would be a legal guardian who persuades his twelve-year-old charge to lend him $25,000 from his trust fund, free of interest. The loan contract would be unenforceable because of undue influence, regardless of whether the minor otherwise had the capacity to make a contract.

Q. What about fraud?

A. A court can cancel a contract because of **fraud** if one person knowingly made a **material misrepresentation** (i.e., an important untruth) with the intent to deceive, and if the other person reasonably relied on it to his or her disadvantage.

Consider our earlier example involving a car sale. You offered to sell your car to a friend. Suppose you knew it had a defective transmission, and you knew she wanted it for the purpose of driving. You told her it was working fine, and she relied on your statement. The contract you made may be set aside on the grounds of fraud.

Here, there is no reasonable argument that the statement was merely the seller's opinion, or exaggerated sales puffery that the buyer knew better than to believe literally. You didn't merely say it was a great car when really it was mediocre. Saying something is great is just the expression of an opinion, while fraud requires an outright lie—or, in many cases, a substantial failure to state a material fact about an important part of the contract. In this case, you told an outright lie, which caused your friend to pay you money for the car. If your friend took you to court, the contract would likely be canceled.

Q. If I enter into the contract under a mistaken impression, does that affect the contract's validity?

A. Probably not, if the other party didn't know about your mistake. This defense, **unilateral mistake,** is almost impossible to prove, even if the mistake is about the most important terms in the contract. If allowed liberally, this defense would lead to a lot of abuse. People could simply claim they made a mistake to get out of contracts they didn't like, even if they had no valid legal defense.

Q. Can a unilateral mistake ever count as a defense to a contract?

A. Courts have permitted a mistake defense most commonly if there has been an honest error in calculations, and if the other party knew or should have known of the mistake. The calculations must be material to the contract, and the overall effect must be to make the contract **unconscionable**—that is, unfairly burdensome.

Such mistakes may happen when a government agency puts public work out for bid. If a contractor mistakenly bids $5 million to construct a bridge and a road, when $5 million was actually the cost of building the bridge alone, and if the government *should* have known that the bid was far too low, then the contractor might be able to raise the mistake defense. But suppose that the government had no way to know that the bid was too low. Several months have now elapsed, and the government has materially relied on the mistaken figures (for example, by taking steps to move the process forward) before the mistake was discovered. It would then be unfair to the government to cancel the deal, and the defense would probably fail.

Of course, if you explicitly state your mistaken idea, then the other party has a duty to correct you. Then the issue is no longer one of mistake, but of fraud. In our car-sale example, suppose the car's heater worked—but not too well. If you (the seller) knew this, and if you hadn't discussed the issue of heaters with your friend, then you probably wouldn't have to tell her about it. But suppose your friend had told you, "The best thing about this car is that it's so hard to find one this old with a perfect heater." Then you would be obliged to tell your friend that the heater was faulty. If you didn't, many states would permit your friend to set aside the contract, or would allow your friend to collect damages for repairs required on the heater.

Having said this, the best defense is a good offense. Don't assume anything important or questionable. Ask the question now—before you sign.

Q. What if both sides make a mistake?

A. Then you don't have the mutual assent that is required to form a valid contract. To avoid injustice, the court will often set aside the contract, under the theory of **mutual mistake.**

The classic case of mutual mistake occurred when someone sold a supposedly infertile cow for $80. It turned out soon afterward that the cow was pregnant, which made her worth $800. The court ruled that since both parties thought they were dealing with a barren cow, the contract could be set aside.

Q. Does this mean that contracts always have a built-in guarantee against mistakes?

A. No. As you can imagine, this is a very tricky and unpredictable area. For example, a poor prediction is not a mistake, nor is a case in which both parties acknowledge they do not know the value of an item, and one of the parties is disappointed. Moreover, many people make purchases with the understanding that an object is worth more to one person than to the other. You wouldn't pay $80 for a cow if it were not worth at least $80.01 to you. That is, you figure you're somewhat better off with the cow than with the $80. (Economists call this amount the **marginal benefit.**) Similarly, the seller would not sell the cow if it were worth more than $79.99 to him or her. Both people have to be getting some benefit, or else they wouldn't agree to the sale.

Various courts draw the line between $80.01 and $800 at different places, if they are willing to draw it at all. Get competent legal advice about the law in your state if you are considering trying to void a contract because of a mistake.

Q. How long do I have to get out of a void or voidable contract?

A. The amount of time within which you must bring a lawsuit is governed by the **statute of limitations.** Deadlines vary, but usually you must bring the action within six years of the breach. The idea of this policy is that everyone is entitled, at some point, to close the book on a transaction. It encourages people to move on, and reduces uncertainty.

Changing Situations

Q. What if it becomes physically impossible to perform a contract?

A. Suppose you hire a contractor to paint your house on Thursday, and it burns down Wednesday night through no fault of your own. Unless there was an agreement allocating such risk to one party, the contract will be set aside because there's no way to perform it. You won't have to pay the painter, under the doctrine of **impossibility of performance.**

The same is true if the contract covers a specific kind of product, and it becomes unavailable because of an "act of God," such as an earthquake or a blizzard. Courts usually will not enforce such a contract.

For example, suppose you contract to deliver 100 barrels of a specific grade of oil from a specific Arabian oil field by a certain date. Then an earthquake devastates the oil field, making recovery of the oil impossible. You're probably off the hook under these circumstances.

This doctrine is also known as **impracticability of performance.** This term reflects the fact that performance need not be literally impossible in order to void the contract; instead, it may just be seriously impractical.

Q. What if changing circumstances make it much more costly to fulfill the contract, but it's still possible to do what the contract promised?

A. The courts probably would enforce the contract, on the grounds that the new circumstances were foreseeable, and that the possibility of increased costs was or could have been built into the contract. For instance, suppose that you contract to deliver 100 barrels of Arabian oil to a buyer, but fighting breaks out in the Persian Gulf, which interrupts shipping and greatly increases the cost of the oil. When a court considers these facts, it's likely to say that you should have foreseen the possibility of fighting, and built that risk into the price. The contract will likely stand.

Q. What if the contract can be performed, but to do so would be pointless?

A. Sometimes a change in conditions doesn't make performance impossible or impractical, but it does make performance meaningless. The legal term for this is **frustration of purpose.** One famous case involved a person who rented a London apartment to view the coronation processions for the king of England. Because of the king's illness, the coronation was postponed. The court excused the renter from paying for the room. Such cases, though, are rare. More typically, you take your chances when relying on another party's or outside force's action; many contracts include a term to that effect.

There are three criteria that must be satisfied in order for a contract to be set aside for frustration of purpose:

1. the frustration must be substantial—nearly total, and with almost no chance at improved benefit.
2. the change in circumstances must not have been reasonably foreseeable; and
3. the frustration must not have been your fault.

Q. May someone have a contract set aside simply because isn't fair?

A. It is possible, but not likely. Courts have the powerful weapon of unconscionability at their disposal. **Unconscionability** means that the bargaining process or the contract's provisions "shock the conscience of the court." For example, selling $10,000 worth of rumba lessons to a ninety-five-year-old widow living on Social Security would probably be held unconscionable. An unconscionable contract is a contract that is grossly unfair. Its terms suggest that one party took unfair advantage of the other during negotiations. The courts are reluctant to use this weapon, but consumers have a better chance with it than anyone else, especially in installment contracts.

Though courts sometimes will void contracts on grounds of unconscionability, it is uncommon for them to do so.

▶ **GETTING OUT OF A CONTRACT**

A contract may be set aside if competent parties have not made it voluntarily. It also may be set aside if there was grossly insufficient consideration. In addition, certain contracts must be in writing, or they are unenforceable. Here is a list of other contract defenses:

- Illegality
- Duress
- Undue influence
- Fraud
- Mistake
- Unconscionability
- Impossibility of performance
- Frustration of purpose

If you can prove any of these, the contract could be deemed void or voidable. In either case, it will be as if the contract never existed. If either party paid money, it would have to be returned.

REMEMBER THIS

- A contract requires an offer by one party and acceptance by the other. Without both, there is no deal.
- Each side must be surrendering something (such as an item, money, or the freedom to do nothing) in order for a contract to be valid.
- A promise may be a binding contract if the other party reasonably relies on it and sacrifices something of value (such as money or a good) in expectation that the pledge will be kept.
- You cannot be contractually bound to perform an illegal act.
- You should understand the distinction between fact and opinion. A seller commits fraud when he or she lies about a product, rendering a contract void. However, salesmanship allows a seller to opine about a product—for example, by saying that the product is the best he or she has ever seen.

- Contract claims come with time limits. Consumers have a limited time in which to sue after they realize the seller has not satisfied his or her end of the bargain.

WHEN THINGS GO WRONG

Now you know how contracts should work. But what happens when something goes wrong? A significant violation of a contract is known as a breach. This section outlines the remedies available for repairing a breach, and discusses how to obtain compensation for contractual losses. This section also explores your last resort when things go wrong: the different kinds of contract relief you can seek from a court.

Breach of Contract

Q. What is a breach of contract?

A. A breach of contract—also called a **default**—is one party's failure, without a legally valid excuse, to live up to any of his or her responsibilities under a contract. A breach occurs if a party

- fails to perform as promised;
- makes it impossible for the other party to perform; or
- repudiates the contract (i.e., announces an intent not to perform).

Q. What qualifies as a failure to perform?

A. One party must not have performed a material part of the contract by a reasonable (or stated) deadline. Suppose your friend promised to buy your car for $1,000, and to pay you "sometime early next week." It would be a material breach for your friend never to pay you, or to pay you in six months. If your friend paid you next Thursday, this probably would not constitute a breach if you did not explicitly make timely payment an essential part of the contract.

Q. How does one party breach a contract by rendering performance impossible?

A. Suppose you hire a cleaning service to clean your house on Sunday for $90. Early Sunday morning you go out for the day, neglecting to make arrangements to let the cleaning personnel into the house. You have breached the contract by making performance impossible. You would owe money on the contract, since the cleaning service was ready and able to clean your house, and since it presumably turned down requests to clean for other clients because of its contractual obligation to you.

Q. What if someone partially breaches a contract?

A. This happens when the breach does not go to the heart of the contract—for example, if someone fails to pay a bill by the specified date (as opposed to not paying the bill at all). It also may happen when the contract has several parts, each of which can be treated as a separate contract. If one of those parts is breached, you could sue for damages even though there isn't a total breach. An example of this would be a landowner hiring a contractor to perform a construction project within certain deadlines. Suppose these deadlines have already been missed, but overall the project is going well. As long as the delay (the breach) is not material, the owner can continue the contractual relationship but sue for whatever damages were suffered as a result of the delay. On the other hand, if the delay is material—i.e., so damaging to the project that it seriously undermines its value—then the breach strikes at the heart of the contract, and is considered total breach. The owner may terminate the contract and pursue remedies against the builder while hiring someone else to finish the job.

Q. What happens if one party announces that it will not live up to its end of the deal?

A. This may be considered repudiation, and may count as a breach. **Repudiation** is a clear statement made by one party, before performance is due, that the party cannot or will not perform a material part of its contract obligations. Suppose that on the day before your friend was to pick up the car that you promised to sell to her, you sent her a message saying that you decided to sell the car to someone else. This would be a repudiation. There can also be repudiation by means of an act, such as actually selling your car to another party.

One party refusing to perform because of an honest disagreement over the contract's terms does not count as repudiation.

Remedies for Breach of Contract

Q. What are the main types of remedies for a breach?

A. When someone commits a material breach, the other party is no longer obligated to keep its end of the bargain, and may proceed in several ways:

- The injured party may urge the breaching party to reconsider the breach.
- If the contract is with a merchant, then the injured party may get help from local, state, or federal consumer agencies.

▶ **SHOULD YOU BREACH A CONTRACT?**

Someday, someone may breach a contract with you. Or you may find yourself in a position where you have to breach a contract. Breaching a contract isn't always a bad thing, as long as you're ready to deal with the consequences. Sometimes the price you pay because of a breach is less damaging than performing a contract that turns out to be a big mistake.

Remember, though, that a contract is your pledge. If you want to be known for keeping your word, then you'll take your contract commitments seriously—even if you don't profit each time.

- The injured party may bring the breaching party to an agency for alternative dispute resolution.
- The injured party may sue the breaching party for damages or other remedies.

Q. What's the point of asking the breaching party to reconsider?

A. One advantage is that it's cheap. Often, the only cost is the price of a telephone call and a little pride. The breaching party may have breached the contract because of a misunderstanding. Or maybe you could renegotiate. That would almost certainly leave both of you better off than if you went to court. If you do hire a lawyer, the first thing the lawyer is likely to do is try to persuade the breaching party to perform.

Q. Should I keep records of my communications with a breaching party?

A. Yes. Once you see that you're in for a struggle, make a file. Keep copies of any letters you send, and transfer to this file all receipts, serial numbers, warranty cards, and the like.

Q. Assuming the breaching party does not budge, what else can I do?

A. If the dispute is between you and a merchant (someone who commonly sells goods of the kind you are purchasing), then you might want to contact the manufacturer of the product. If it involves a large chain of stores, contact the management of the chain. This goes for services, too.

If that doesn't help, contact a consumer protection agency, either in your city or state. The Federal Trade Commission (FTC) is unlikely to get involved in small disputes. However, if the FTC believes that what happened to you has happened to many other people nationwide, then it might be interested. The FTC's involvement carries a lot of weight. The same goes for your state attorney general or local consumer agency. Another resource is your local post office, where you can report any shady business practices that took place through the mail.

Q. If these methods don't work, what else can I do short of filing a lawsuit?

A. Other chapters in this book discuss many different types of alternative dispute resolution systems, such as mediation. Note that the contract itself may include a specific type of alternative dispute resolution that you must use. Sometimes, however, these agreements are not enforceable, and there is a burgeoning body of law refusing to enforce arbitration agreements in adhesion contracts.

Stopping Payment

Q. What if I want to cancel a contract or void a purchase that I made, but I already paid with a check?

A. First, you should call the seller and ask for the cancellation of your contract and the return of your check. If the seller won't cooperate, call your bank and stop payment on the check. Remember, you're still liable for the purchase price, and the seller may sue you—unless you have a legal excuse not to pay, such as breach by the seller. But if the seller's breach is small, a refusal to pay could put you in breach and make you liable for damages.

Also be aware that when you stop payment, you raise the stakes and lower the chance of a settlement. Merchants don't take kindly to this technique.

Q. Isn't stopping payment on a check a criminal act?

A. No. It's not the same as having insufficient funds, which may carry criminal penalties (see the sidebar, "Passing Bad Checks"). Stopping payment on a check is your legal right.

Q. How do I stop payment on a check?

A. Call your bank and provide the relevant information about the check. The bank will then send you a form to confirm your instructions in writing, which you must return within a certain number of days in order for the bank to honor your original request. Note that the bank may charge you for this service.

Don't try to avoid the fee by reducing your balance so the check won't clear. The bank may end up not paying other checks you've written, or it might even pay the check you don't want paid. More importantly, you will have gone from exercising a legal right (stopping payment) to committing a legal wrong (passing a bad check).

Q. Is there anything else that I should do after I place the order to stop payment?

A. You may inform the seller of your action, but you don't have to.

Q. What if the seller has already deposited the check in a bank account?

A. If the check has not cleared your account, then your bank may still put through the stop payment order. However, if your bank has already paid the check, then you'll have to try to void the contract and get your money back in other ways discussed in this chapter.

▶ **PASSING BAD CHECKS**

If you write a check for which you do not have sufficient funds, you may face criminal charges. Passing a bad check is a misdemeanor in many states, and can result in a fine and even a jail term. However, a single infraction rarely results in a criminal conviction, and will most likely result in a diversion program targeted at educating offenders so they don't repeat the same offense.

Q. I'm dissatisfied with goods or services that I've paid for with a credit or debit card. Can I use a stop payment order?

A. No. Stop payment orders only apply to checks. But under federal law, products you refuse to accept on delivery (or products that aren't delivered according to an agreement) are regarded as billing errors that the card issuer must investigate, and that the issuer may correct by granting you a credit. So long as the consumer has not accepted the goods, the appearance of a charge on the bill is considered a billing error. If the seller does not press the matter, the consumer will get a credit. If the seller protests, then the card issuer may or may not issue a credit, depending on the issuer's agreement and its customary practices with respect to merchants. See Chapter 10, "Consumer Credit," for more details.

Dealing with Failing or Failed Companies

Q. If I have a contract for services or goods with a company that goes out of business, what can I do?

A. You've just ordered and paid for an expensive item. The next day, you find out that the company has gone out of business. You're afraid that your money is gone.

If another firm bought the company, as in a corporate merger, then usually the new company must take responsibility for the contractual obligations of the old company.

If the company has ceased doing business, or is under the protection of bankruptcy laws, then your chances of recovering anything are small. If the company went through the bankruptcy process, then your contract could legally be disavowed, though any debt owed to you might not be. If the company is in bankruptcy, then the bankruptcy court may contact you, or you may need a lawyer's help to file your claim. If your claim isn't substantial, then it's usually not worth the trouble.

If you have an enforceable contract with a troubled company, another company may have to fulfill the remainder of your contract needs if the troubled company can't come through. Then you could try to bring a damages claim against the first company.

Q. My supplier went bankrupt, so I need to buy goods from another company. What can I do about the money the first company owes me under the contract?

A. If the company is in bankruptcy, you can file a claim against it through the bankruptcy court. You'll have to stand in line with the other creditors, and you may get only a small percentage of what is owed, if anything at all. If the business is a corporation that's dissolving under state law, you can file a claim against the corporation through the state agency (usually the secretary of state) for any losses you have accumulated. Whatever assets remain will be divided according to the number of claims filed and their amounts.

Q. If the financially troubled company is holding goods for me on layaway, can I still get my goods?

A. Most companies that go out of business will notify their customers they are closing— at the very least, they'll want customers to come in and finish their purchases because they need the cash. If a company has tried to contact you and you haven't responded, it may sell the goods you've placed on layaway, and you'll have no way to recover the merchandise—though the law still entitles you to any money you paid toward the purchase.

Q. If the merchandise is gone and I've paid money, how can I recover that money?

A. If the store is still open, it probably will pay you when you present your receipt for payments made toward the purchase price. If the store has closed, you might need to file a claim in the bankruptcy court or with the proper state agency, as described above.

Q. What can I do about merchandise that was under warranty? Who will cover it now that the seller has gone out of business?

A. If you've purchased a national brand of goods, there probably will be a service center or a licensed warranty center in your area. It may not be as convenient for you as the seller's store, but it should be able to handle your claim. You can also try contacting the manufacturer. Almost all manufacturers will stand behind their products regardless of where you purchased them. You may need to present an original receipt showing that the manufacturer's warranty still covers the product.

Lawsuits as Remedies

Q. What's the most common legal remedy for a contract breach?

A. The usual legal remedy is cancellation of the contract, followed by a suit for damages, usually **compensatory damages.** This is the amount of money it would take to put you in as good a position as if there had been no breach. The idea is to give you "the benefit of the bargain."

In some cases, you may not cancel, though you may recover damages for the breach. For example, if the seller has failed to deliver an item costing $10,000 and you buy it from another source for $12,000, your damages are $2,000. You may have to sue to obtain the difference. Because the legal fees may be a practical bar to such a lawsuit, you might want to consider bringing a small-claims action. (Chapters 1 and 2 can give you more information about procedures relating to small-claims courts.)

If the violation of a consumer protection law is established, the law may require the other side to pay your lawyer's fees, and you may be entitled to a minimum recovery without proof of actual damage. Also, if many people are involved, the state agency charged with consumer protection—such as the attorney general—may be persuaded to bring suit on behalf of all affected consumers.

Q. I think I can get compensatory damages, but I feel like the breaching party should have to pay more. What other kinds of damages might be awarded after a lawsuit?

A. There are several common types of damages:

- **Nominal damages:** Awarded when you win your case but have not proved much of a loss.
- **Liquidated damages:** An amount that is built into the contract. Although one or both parties have effectively breached the contract, this term will stand, as long as it fairly estimates the damages.
- **Consequential damages:** Losses caused by a defect in the product. These are discussed in more detail in the section on warranties. In formal contracts, the document typically excludes consequential damages. However, in informal contracts (including most retail cash purchases), they may be recoverable.
- **Punitive damages:** Available if the breaching party's behavior was offensive to the court. Punitive damages are virtu-

ally never recovered in a suit for breach of contract, but it may be possible to get punitive damages or some form of **statutory damages** (legal penalties) under a consumer fraud law or in a suit for fraud.

Q. Are there other remedies in a contract suit besides damages?

A. Yes. The most obvious remedy is a court order requiring the breaching party to perform as promised in the contract. This is known as **specific performance.** Courts are reluctant to award this, because they presume that the proper remedy for breach of a contract is the monetary equivalent of full performance, and because specific performance is awkward to enforce.

Q. What else can a court do?

A. A court may **rescind** (i.e., cancel) a contract that one party has breached. The court may then order the breaching party to pay the other side any expenses incurred; it could also order the return of goods sold. Or the court could **reform** the contract. This involves rewriting the contract according to what the court concludes the parties actually intended. These remedies are often used under the provisions of many states' consumer fraud laws.

REMEMBER THIS

- Stopping payment on a check without telling the seller decreases the chance for an out-of-court settlement.
- Keep copies of all correspondence. These documents will be important if you need to prove a breach.
- You will probably receive your goods if another company bought the company from which you made the purchase.
- You will have to wait in line behind creditors if the company is in bankruptcy.

- Compensatory damages are the usual remedy for breach.
- Punitive damages are rare in cases of breach.
- Specific performance is also an unusual remedy, and is generally ordered only in cases where the performer has a special talent.

SPECIAL TYPES OF CONTRACTS

Consumers generally do not ask to see sales contracts; often contracts are thrust upon them by sellers—especially at car dealerships, real estate agencies, or in an apartment manager's office. The contract terms generally appear on a form with numerous blanks on it, which can be filled in with the names of the parties, the financial terms, and so on. If you find yourself in this type of situation, you'll probably be expected to sign without asking any questions, and the other side probably won't be sympathetic if you ask for time to read the contract from start to finish.

This section will help you understand what you can do to protect yourself, and what to look for in various types of contracts.

Practical Contracts

Q. When I make a purchase and receive a sales contract, it has so much fine print. These look like standard forms—do I really need to read them?

A. Believe it or not, it pays to read form contracts. In most states, courts have held that people are bound by all the terms in a contract, even if they didn't read the contract before signing it (unless the other party engaged in fraud or unconscionable conduct). Don't trust the other party to tell you what a contract term means; even with good intentions, that party could be mistaken. Also, be suspicious if a salesperson urges you to disregard a term as unimportant. (Ask the salesperson, "If it's not important, is it okay to cross out the whole paragraph?") When a substantial amount of money is at stake, take the time to sit down with the form and underline any parts you don't understand. Then find out what they mean from someone you trust.

At the same time, you must be realistic about exercising your right to read a form contract. At the car rental counter at the airport, you probably don't have time to read the contract and get an explanation of each confusing term. And even if you did take the time, with whom would you negotiate? The sales clerk almost certainly doesn't have the authority to change the contract.

Similarly, when agreeing to the license terms of a commercially sold software program, no negotiation is possible. If you want the program, you have to agree. However, the contract forms and terms are usually available to examine while you are considering a transaction and before you are actually enter into a deal.

Q. What if taking the time to protect my legal rights results in my losing a great bargain?

A. Rarely will a truly great bargain not be there tomorrow. For all the great deals that work out fine, the one you will remember is the one that went sour—where the seller socked you with the fine print you didn't bother to read.

Q. If I understand a contract but don't like it, must I accept it?

A. No. You never have to accept a contract. Every part of a contract is open for negotiation, at least in theory. You can cross out parts you don't like. You can also add terms that the contract doesn't include, such as oral promises made by a salesperson. (However, make sure that any changes appear on all copies that will bear your signature; initial any pages that are altered but unsigned, and have the other party do the same.)

This doesn't mean that the other side must agree to your changes. But if you encounter a lot of resistance over what seem to be reasonable issues, take a hard look at the person with whom you are dealing—espe-cially if they resist your request to put oral promises in writing.

Q. What if I come across terms that I just can't figure out?

A. Until you understand every important term in a substantial contract, don't sign it. Legalese most often appears in contracts that include credit terms, such as when you buy something that requires installment payments. Chapter 10, "Consumer Credit," and Chapter 14, "Automobiles," explain many of these terms. If you still have questions, ask someone you trust (not a salesperson) to explain the terms to you. This could be someone experienced with the kind of contract you are considering, a state or local consumer agency, or a lawyer.

Q. Are there any laws that protect consumers against the use of confusing language?

A. Yes. Many states now require that some or most consumer contracts use plain English, and that potentially confusing sections or clauses be written in precise, standard terms that nearly anyone can understand. Federal and state truth-in-lending laws require providers of credit to furnish specific information about credit contracts in clearly understandable form. Finally, legal doctrines regulating contracts of adhesion may protect you.

Q. What are contracts of adhesion?

A. **Contracts of adhesion** are contracts that give you little or no power to change the preprinted terms, as is often the case with many of the form contracts discussed above, such as loan documents, insurance contracts, automobile leases, and "click box" contracts for software or other computer-

---

> ▶ **FILL IN THE BLANKS**

While some contracts may be standardized, there's no such thing as a standard contract. Many innocuous-looking forms are available in several different versions. One might be a "landlord's" contract, in which the preprinted terms favor the landlord, while a nearly identical one might be a "tenant's" contract. When entering into a "standard" contract, insist on crossing out or changing any term you don't like. If the other party refuses to accept changes that are important to you, don't sign the contract. Be sure all blanks are filled in, either with specific terms or with straight lines to indicate that nothing goes there. And insist on your own copy with the other party's original signature.

related merchandise. These are called contracts of adhesion because, if you want the deal, you have to "adhere," (i.e., stick) to the terms. They are standardized contracts and, for whatever reason, the other party simply refuses to negotiate.

Since no case-by-case negotiation takes place, contracts of adhesion are cost-efficient. But they can also be abusive. However, consumers do have some protections. Courts generally assume that contracts of adhesion have been drafted to provide maximum benefit to the lender, the lessor, or the insurance company. So when a dispute arises over terms or language, the courts usually interpret contracts in the way most favorable to the consumer.

This doesn't mean the consumer gets the benefit of the doubt regarding all terms of an adhesion contract; rather, courts will only apply this favorable interpretation to confusing or unclear clauses. To some extent, though, all contracts are interpreted to favor the party who didn't draft them—even when they're not contracts of adhesion.

Like the doctrines of unconscionability and fraud, a court's consumer-friendly approach to contracts of adhesion isn't something to depend on before signing a contract. It's simply something about which you and your lawyer should be aware in the event that a problem arises.

Q. My contract has an extra part called a rider. What is it? Will I be bound by it?

A. A **rider** is a sheet of paper (or several pages) reflecting an addition or amendment (i.e., change) to the main body of a contract. Often it's simpler to put changes in a rider, which supersedes any contradictory parts of

the main contract, than to try to incorporate the changes on the original form. If executed correctly, both sides are bound by the rider. Therefore, you should make sure you read all pages associated with the contract.

Q. What should I do about the fine print?

A. First, try to read it. If you sit down and examine the fine print sentence by sentence, you'll often find that you can understand a lot more than you expect, especially in states that have passed "plain-English" laws. You will at least, by expending the effort, identify which terms raise questions for you. The trick is not to be intimidated by the salesperson or the fine print.

Q. What can be so dangerous in fine print?

A. Very often the fine print contains terms that could greatly affect your rights. It may contain details about credit terms, your right to sue, and your right to a jury in a lawsuit.

Leases

Q. What is a lease?

A. A **lease** is a specific type of contract. It has all the elements of a contract explained earlier: It involves someone letting you use something for a specified time, and for a specified fee. There are two main kinds of leases. The first involves real estate, such as a lease for an apartment. The second includes all other kinds of property, such as leases for office equipment and vehicles.

Q. What should I look for in a lease for equipment or for a vehicle?

A. Usually on preprinted forms with very few blanks, these leases typically offer little room

▶ GET IT IN WRITING

When dealing with a written contract, a court will almost always treat the contract's terms as a complete and final representation of the agreement between the parties. The court usually will not even consider oral promises that are not included as part of the written contract. The main exception to this is when oral promises are used fraudulently to induce one party into signing a contract that he or she would otherwise have avoided. In all other cases, the general rule prohibiting evidence of oral promises protects both parties: they each know that, once they sign the contract, they have clearly and finally set the terms of their agreement.

If you're not completely satisfied with your agreement, don't be swayed if a salesperson orally promises you an extended warranty or a full refund. If it's not written into the contract, it may not be considered an enforceable part of your deal.

for bargaining. It is very important that you understand the terms and are sure you'll be able to meet them, especially if there's an option to buy. Make sure the lease states the price at which you'll be able to buy the item. It may specify the price as a dollar figure, or as a percentage of some amount that you should be able to figure out easily. Be sure that it's a price worth paying, at least from where you stand right now. Of course, if you have no intention of buying, then there's no problem—but you should be able to get a less-expensive deal by not including an option to buy in the contract.

Q. Are there laws designed to protect renters under residential leases?

A. Yes. Most states have laws that protect people who lease their homes. Chapter 9, "Renting Residential Property," discusses them fully.

Warranties

Q. What are warranties?

A. Warranties are obligations taken on by the provider or imposed on the provider by law. Some warranties deal with the quality of goods, while others deal with the ownership of goods.

Q. Does the law regulate warranties?

A. Yes. A federal law, the Magnuson-Moss Warranty Act, covers written warranties for consumer goods costing more than a few dollars. It does not require that merchants make written warranties. If they do make warranties, however, the law requires that they meet certain standards. The warranty must be available for you to read before you buy. It must be written in plain language and include

- the name and address of the company making the warranty;
- the product or parts covered;
- whether the warranty promises replacement, repair, or refund, and if there are any expenses (such as shipping or labor) you would have to pay in connection with any of the above;
- how long the warranty lasts;

- the damages that the warranty does not cover;
- the action you should take if something goes wrong;
- whether the company providing the warranty requires you to use any specific informal (i.e., out-of-court) methods to settle a dispute; and
- a brief description of your legal rights.

Many states have warranty laws that provide consumers who purchase new automobiles with greater protection than the Magnuson-Moss federal warranty law. These are commonly called **lemon laws.** Chapter 14, "Automobiles," contains more information about this topic.

Q. How can I get the best warranties?

A. Consider all warranty terms when you shop. The terms of a warranty are seldom negotiable—especially the warranty length, the types of problems the warranty covers, and what you must do to exercise your rights. But some elements, such as the price of an extended warranty, may be negotiable. Often the cost to the retailer is less than half the price the retailer asks the consumer to pay. This is an area where careful negotiations can result in substantial savings. Also remember that the dealer selling you the merchandise is not the only source of service contracts—you can always search online or elsewhere for a better deal.

Q. What is the difference between a full warranty and a limited warranty?

A. A **full** warranty is a promise that the product will be repaired or replaced free during the warranty period. If the warrantor (i.e., the company making the warranty) will repair the item, then it must be fixed within a reasonable time and it must be reasonably convenient for the consumer to get the item to and from the repair site. Many stores will offer a short full warranty of their own (thirty to ninety days), and some premium credit cards will double a warranty for up to a year for products purchased with that card. Repairs or replacement during the extended warranty period become the responsibility of the card issuer after the manufacturer's warranty expires.

Limited warranties are more common. They are less comprehensive, sometimes covering parts but not labor. Or the warranty may provide that the cost of repairs be split fifty-fifty for the first thirty days after purchase.

Q. What are express and implied warranties?

A. **Express warranties** are promises to back up the product, or promises about the product that the warrantor expresses either in writing or orally. Suppose your friend bought your car and you said, "I guarantee you'll get another 10,000 miles out of this transmission." That's an express warranty. It isn't an opinion about quality or value, such as "This car is the best yellow used car for sale in town." Rather, it's a specific statement of fact or a promise.

A warrantor does not state implied warranties—they're automatic in certain kinds of transactions. There are two main types of **implied warranties:** the implied warranty of merchantability and the implied warranty of fitness for a particular purpose.

Q. What is the implied warranty of merchantability?

A. When someone is in the business of selling or leasing a specific kind of product, the law requires that the product be adequate for the purpose for which it is purchased (or leased). This is the **implied warranty of merchantability.** This general rule of fairness means, for example, that a carton of milk in the supermarket dairy case will be drinkable milk, and not sour or otherwise unusable.

Let's look at a car-sale example. If the buyer's purpose is fairly ordinary—i.e., the buyer wants a car for general transportation—then the implied warranty of merchantability is what assures the buyer that the car will work. This warranty applies if the product does not work, even if great care was taken in its manufacture. For this reason, only a merchant makes the implied warranty of merchantability.

Q. What is the implied warranty of fitness for a particular purpose?

A. The **implied warranty of fitness for a particular purpose** means that any seller or lessor is presumed to guarantee that an item will be fit for the buyer's particular purpose, as long as the seller has reason to know that the buyer is relying on the seller to supply a suitable item. For example, if your friend tells you she needs a car that could tow a trailer full of granite up steep mountains in the snow, and if you sell her your car as a suitable vehicle for performing this task, then your friend has relied on your skill and judgment about the car. When you sell her the car knowing that she intends to use it for a specific purpose, you make an implied warranty that the car will in fact be able to accomplish that purpose.

Q. How long do warranties last?

A. It depends on the type of transaction and warranty involved, and on the applicable law. In most states, you have up to four years after the start of a transaction to enforce an implied warranty. A written warranty will disclose how long it lasts.

Q. Can a merchant eliminate a warranty?

A. Not after you've made the deal. But before you buy, unwritten express warranties and (in most states) implied warranties of merchantability or fitness may be excluded or disclaimed, if the contract or disclaimer is in writing and the relevant language is obvious. The word "merchantability" may have to appear in order for a disclaimer of an implied warranty to be valid, or a contract may have to state that the product is delivered "as is." In contrast, a less communicative written statement may disclaim the implied warranty of fitness for a particular purpose. In any event, a person may not disclaim an express warranty that's written into the contract.

▶ **WARRANTY SENSE**

The best-made products usually have the best warranties, because they're less likely to need them. Thus, the manufacturer can guarantee a long period with little risk.

Ultimately, don't be pressured by a salesperson into accepting a warranty. They're frequently a major source of profit on a transaction. Ask the salesperson: if the product is well made, then why should you be so concerned about insuring yourself against repair costs?

Q. Is disclaiming a warranty common?

A. In the case of written warranties, disclaimer is not allowed. If there are no such warranties, then disclaimer is common. With sales contracts for many consumer products, a warranty is stated and the contract states a specific remedy. This means that the buyer gets a warranty, and the seller or the lessor is also protected (because the consumer's remedy is limited to what is set forth in the contract). For example, the contract may provide that the seller will repair or replace the merchandise if necessary, but that the customer has no right to get money back.

Q. Does the law ever overrule the guarantees contained in a warranty?

A. Yes. **Lemon laws** provide a good example. Most states have these laws, which provide extra guarantees to people who have been unlucky enough to buy new cars (and in some cases other products) that are so bad that they fit the statutory definition of a "lemon." (Chapter 14, "Automobiles," has more information on these laws.)

Q. My warranty limitations exclude some forms of consequential damages. What are consequential damages?

A. Consequential damages are losses caused by a product's defect, including lost time and expense that result from the defect and repair costs. For example, if your new computer crashes and destroys weeks of work, the warrantor may give you a new computer, but almost certainly won't reimburse you for your lost time, work, or software—much less a lost job or client. However, you usually may recover damages in cases of personal injury that result from a product's defect.

Q. How can I protect my warranty rights?

A. First, keep your receipts through the warranty period. They provide proof of when the warranty starts and ends, and are more important than the warranty return card. (Often this card is simply a marketing device designed to provide manufacturers with more information about you.) Remember that any violation of the manufacturer's operating and

---

▶ READ WARRANTIES BEFORE YOU BUY

Don't wait until a product needs repair to find out what's covered in a written warranty. Compare the terms and conditions of the warranty before you buy, and look for the warranty that best meets your needs.

How long is the warranty, and when does it start and end? Will the warranty pay 100 percent of repair costs? Does it cover parts but not labor? What kinds of problems are covered? What do you have to do to enforce your rights? And when do you have to do it? Are regular inspections or maintenance required? Do you have to ship the product to the repair center? If so, who pays for shipping? What about a loaner? Who offers the warranty—the manufacturer or the retailer? How reliable is each?

service instructions probably will void the warranty.

If a problem arises, try the store where you got the item first. If you end up contacting the manufacturer, do so only as instructed in the warranty. Keep a list of all communications. It's a good idea to contact the manufacturer in writing, keeping copies of all correspondence, at the address specified in the warranty. That's especially true if you aren't getting quick responses. Your correspondence file will protect your warranty rights near the end of the coverage period.

SPECIAL CONSUMER PROTECTIONS

Advertising

Q. Store advertisements usually are not considered offers. Are there any exceptions to this rule?

A. Yes. Suppose a store advertises that it will give a free gift or special discount "to the first 100 customers." If so, the store has made an offer. You can accept it by successfully making the specified effort—that is, by being one of the first hundred customers to show up at the store.

Q. How exact must advertisements be?

A. They must be accurate regarding material aspects of the product or service listed in the offer. It's no crime to sell a dress that looks better on the fashion model in the ad than on a normal person. And if an advertisement pictures green spark plugs and you got gray ones instead, the ad did not materially mislead you. But if the ad stated that the plugs would last

for a long time, and they failed right away, then you probably were misled.

Q. What is false advertising?

A. False advertising is an unfair method of competition forbidden under federal law and state consumer fraud statutes. The advertiser's intent isn't important. What counts is the overall impression that an ad conveys.

False advertising misleads consumers about a product's place of origin (e.g., putting French labels on sweaters made in Arkansas), the product's nature or quality (e.g., promising first-quality socks but delivering irregulars or seconds), or a product's maker. With respect to services, false advertising occurs when the consumer is misled into thinking that a person has qualifications (such as being a master carpenter) that he or she actually does not have.

Q. What about contests and investment schemes?

A. The rule is this: Any contest or get-rich-quick scheme that requires you to part with your money is probably a losing proposition. Often these types of schemes are pyramid schemes. Someone may contact you and tell you about real people who made a bundle. And that part is actually true: some people did get a lot of money. But they likely did it illegally—by inducing people like you to pony up. The only way you could do the same is to con a large number of people into making the same mistake you did. The courts have held these types of scams—and any promotion that promises an unrealistic return—to be false advertising. Some cases might involve violations of securities laws. One good rule of thumb is that no legitimate speculative investment will ever promise or even strongly suggest a specific return.

If you are contacted by mail regarding what seems like a fraudulent scheme, contact the office of the U.S. Postal Service Inspector General. Otherwise, report such a pitch to your state or city consumer protection office or state attorney general and the Federal Trade Commission (FTC). Virtually all states now provide a mechanism for shutting down these scams and recovering victims' money, but the process may be long, and it may not always be successful.

Q. What is bait and switch?

A. The **bait** is an advertisement with the promise of an unbeatable deal. The **switch** occurs when you walk into the store and the salesperson tells you the advertised model isn't available, but a more expensive model is. This practice is illegal in most states if the advertised model was never available in reasonable quantities, or if the advertised model is falsely disparaged in order to discourage its sale. It is also illegal if the store never intended to sell the item, but advertised it just to get you into the store so that it could try to sell you a more expensive item.

You have a right to see the model that appeared in the ad. If the store is "fresh out of them," it may be guilty of false advertising. Don't let someone talk you into buying a model you can't afford. If insisting on your rights gets you nowhere, keep the ad, get the salesperson's name (and that of anyone else you spoke to), and report the matter to the state or local consumer protection office. This practice can also occur online and over the phone.

Telemarketing

Q. Should I ever buy a product or a service from a telemarketer?

A. The simple answer is: probably not. You know nothing about this person or the company he or she ostensibly represents. Request that he or she send you written information about the product or service, as well as a written contract with all terms and warranties. Do not trust yourself to understand—or the marketer to explain fully—the terms of the sale. If the marketer is legitimate, he or she can certainly send you the information in writing.

Q. I've had it with telemarketers and wish they'd stop calling. What can I do?

▶ BEWARE OF INTERNET SCAMS

Exercise the utmost care when participating in contests or the like over the Internet. It is difficult and often impossible to tell whom you are dealing with on the Web, and it's virtually impossible for a private citizen to get satisfaction after being swindled online—perhaps by someone who may not even be in this hemisphere. Common scams are those in which an e-mailer asks for assistance in recovering millions of dollars. All the consumer need do is provide the number of her bank account so the e-mailer can send the millions. Instead of filling up your bank account, the e-mailer will empty it out—before you are even aware of it. Don't fall for it.

▶ COMPLAIN, COMPLAIN, COMPLAIN

One of the best pieces of advice for consumers is to understand the importance of filing complaints with state attorneys general, other state consumer officials, or Better Business Bureau. The more people who complain about a particular problem, the more likely it is that a state will undertake an inquiry that could result in you getting some money back.

A. Many states have established do-not-call lists that compile the names and telephone numbers of residents who do not want to be contacted by telemarketers, who in turn must honor these requests. If you put yourself on your state's list, and telemarketers victimize you anyway, you may be able to get help from your state's authorities.

In addition, the federal Do-Not-Call Implementation Act authorizes the FTC to compile a list of people who do not wish to receive telemarketing calls. All you have to do is contact the FTC either online or by a toll-free number and tell the agency that you want to be added to the list. Placing your number on the registry will stop most telemarketing calls. However, you may still receive calls from political organizations, charities, people taking surveys by telephone, or companies with which you have an existing business relationship.

You can also contact the Direct Marketing Association, which represents the telemarketing industry, and request to be put on its do-not-call list.

Door-to-Door Sales

Q. Do any laws protect purchases made as a result of door-to-door sales?

A. Yes. Federal law requires a three-day cooling-off period for door-to-door sales. During that time, you can cancel purchases you make from someone who both solicits and closes the sale at your home.

You don't have to give any reason for changing your mind, and the three days don't start until you receive formal notice of your right to cancel. You can cancel almost any sale not made at a fixed place of business, such as sales made at your home, someone else's home, or a hotel. This cooling-off period applies to both credit and noncredit sales. It also forbids the company to charge you any cancellation fee.

The federal law applies to most cases, and many states have similar laws.

Q. What happens if I cancel my order during the cooling-off period?

A. State law usually will require the salesperson to refund your money, return any trade-in you made, and cancel and return the contract. The salesperson has ten business days to do this under federal law. If the salesperson waits longer than twenty days, you may be allowed to keep the goods for free.

Q. I feel confident about a door-to-door salesperson and plan to make a purchase. Is there anything specific I should look for in the contract?

A. Federal and state laws usually require such salespeople to provide you with the following details on your receipt:

- the seller's name and place of business;
- a description of the goods and services sold;
- the amount of money you paid, or the value of any goods delivered to you; and
- your rights during the cooling-off period.

Some of these laws also require that if the salesperson makes the sale in Spanish or another language, the seller must give you all the above details in that language.

Q. What about door-to-door home repair sales?

A. If someone shows up at your door and claims to have some leftover asphalt, shingles, or other material from a nearby job, and if that person offers you a sweet deal to fix your driveway, roof, or whatever else, tell that person to go somewhere else. Make your home repairs when you're ready, and only with contractors you know. (See Chapter 8, "Home Ownership," for more on home repairs.)

Buying by Mail

Q. If I buy something through the mail, how long does a mail-order company have to deliver goods that I ordered?

A. Under federal law, the goods must be in the mail within thirty days of your order. If they aren't, you must at least have received a letter informing you of the delay and when to expect delivery. The seller also must offer you a refund within one week if you don't want to wait any longer. An exception applies to goods that you understand not to be available until a certain time, such as magazines or flower seeds. Many states have laws that provide greater protections.

Q. May the company send substitute goods to me?

A. Yes, but you don't have to accept them. You can send them back and ask for a refund. However, if you keep the substitute goods,

---

▶ PROTECTING YOURSELF IN CATALOG PURCHASES

Shopping via catalogs, whether printed or online, has grown tremendously in the last few years. There are some drawbacks, including delays in receiving orders, uneven customer service, and inconvenience if repair or replacement is necessary. In addition, there is a possibility of fraud, since it's hard to assess the trustworthiness of a company without seeing a showroom or salespeople.

When ordering from a catalog, try to find established merchants that have been in business for at least a few years. Placing an order for an inexpensive item is a good way to check a company's performance before investing in more costly merchandise. Payment by credit card also is highly recommended—it usually makes it easier to resolve disputes.

then you have to pay the usual price for those goods, unless the company offers them for less. You can also try to negotiate. Since mail-order firms often depend on goodwill more than other companies do, a reputable company should be able to strike an acceptable deal with you.

Q. I received merchandise in the mail that I never ordered. What should I do?

A. Federal law requires the sender of an unordered item sent through the mail to mark the package "Free Sample." (The law permits charities to send you Easter Seals, Hanukkah candles, and the like, and to ask for a contribution.) Consumers who receive unordered merchandise in the mail should consider it a gift. They have no obligation to pay for the merchandise, and they may keep it. Sending you a bill for such merchandise may constitute mail fraud. After checking to make sure you or a family member didn't actually order the item, report such practices—or any harassment or threats aimed at forcing you to pay the bill—to the U.S. Postal Service and your state consumer protection bureau.

Time-Shares

Q. What are time-shares?

A. Time-shares are properties (usually residences at resorts) that are jointly owned by several people, with each person having the right to use the property during certain specified periods of time—say, for a week or so per year.

Q. What problems should I be aware of when buying a time-share?

▶ **ONLINE SHOPPING**

Much of what has been said in this chapter regarding mail and catalog sales applies to shopping for merchandise over the Internet—only more so. It is remarkably easy to find a slick website that has nothing real behind it. Do not assume, because it displays an authentic-looking trademark or accepts credit cards, that a merchant is what it seems to be. Avoid buying luxury goods over the Internet, except from established merchants you know from the "real world." Chances are that luxury goods from unknown merchants are counterfeits. See Chapter 13, "Computer Law," for more information on online shopping.

A. One problem is that expenses often offset the savings. If, like most people, you finance your time-share purchase over time, the interest costs alone may cancel out any profit you might have realized. Even if you pay cash, you lose the interest you could otherwise have earned on that money.

And unlike renters, who have the option of renting or not renting a property, time-share owners are generally locked in. In some cases, they may be able to exchange their property, but that involves a formal exchange program and costs money. They usually cannot sell the property except at a substantial loss.

Furthermore, your time-share contract will make you responsible for paying any increases in taxes, maintenance costs, or repair costs.

Q. Do time-shares ever break even?

A. Time-share sellers will often point out that, notwithstanding the problems already mentioned, time-shares allow you to enjoy "free" vacationing once they are paid off—so at some point you will break even. But the break-even point, which takes into account all of your costs, including interest, may not come for ten to twenty years.

Q. But if I don't like the time-share deal, can't I just sell it?

A. In theory, yes. However, practically speaking, many people who bought time-shares in the 1980s or 1990s are finding themselves with white elephants on their hands. You may have to unload the time-share for much less than you paid, if you can find a buyer at all. You may be stuck making an agreement with the sponsors in which they take back the time-share during the payment period and let you off the hook for the rest of the term. In this type of agreement, you get nothing back for what you've already paid (which might be several times what you would have paid in rent), but you will have no further obligations.

Pets

Q. What may I ask about a pet before I buy it?

A. You may ask anything. You have a right to know about the pet's health, family history or pedigree, training, and medical care.

Q. Do I have any protections when purchasing an animal?

A. Yes. Some states require pet stores to make detailed disclosures to buyers on such topics as the animal's health, age, and history (for example, immunization records and other health information). Some even have lemon laws that make it easier for buyers to get their money back if they have purchased a sick animal. If your state doesn't have such laws, then general warranty laws apply.

Q. What should I do if I am dissatisfied with my pet purchase?

A. Immediately notify the seller in writing, keeping a copy for yourself. Keep all contracts and papers—even the original advertisement, if there was one. If you have not received a replacement or refund within thirty days, consider filing a small-claims lawsuit.

Home and Appliance Repair and Improvements

Q. A handyman just ripped me off for some repairs that were done incorrectly. Are there laws that specifically protect consumers against shoddy workmanship and fraud in home repair contracts?

> ### ▶ CHECKLIST: WHAT SHOULD I DO BEFORE I PURCHASE A PET?
>
> Before you purchase a pet, you can and should ask any questions you feel are relevant—and get answers. These should include questions about
>
> - the pet's age;
> - the pet's current health;
> - the health history of the pet, including immunization and past illnesses;
> - any training the pet has had; and
> - the pet's family history and pedigree.

▶ DO PETS COME WITH GUARANTEES?

Suppose you buy a pet and it turns out to be sick or injured. Legally, what can you do? The answer may depend on whether you bought the pet from a pet shop or a private owner. It also may depend on whether you had a written contract, and what express and implied warranties exist under your state's laws. It also matters whether you bought this pet for a specific purpose, such as breeding it for competition. In general, it's best for you and the seller to sign a written agreement about your pet that will clarify most of a new owner's questions.

Another way of avoiding problems is to ask the seller for the name of the pet's veterinarian. Ask the vet for an opinion on the pet's health, which may alert you to potential problems before you complete the purchase.

A. Yes. Many states have registration requirements for companies offering home repair services, and may even set up guaranty funds to help you recover your money. They also may set up three-day cooling-off periods, letting you get out of a deal within three days without paying a penalty.

The Federal Trade Commission and federal truth-in-lending laws also police these types of cases.

Q. How may I protect myself?

A. Get several written estimates. Check into a contractor's track record with the Better Business Bureau and other customers before you sign a contract. Don't pay the full price in advance, and certainly not in cash. Don't sign a completion certificate or receipt until the contractor finishes the work to your satisfaction—including cleanup.

Q. Are there special things to look for in a home improvement contract?

A. Yes. Too often a contract of this type will read "work as per agreement." Instead, it should specify who will do the work, and in-clude a detailed description of the work, the materials to be used, and the dates of starting and completion. It also should contain all charges, including any finance charges if you are paying over a period of time. If the financing is to be provided by a third party, do not sign the repair contract before you sign the financing contract. In addition, the contract should include the hourly rate on which the total cost is to be based. Be sure any guarantee is in writing.

Be especially wary of any mortgage or security interest the contractor takes in your home, which means that you may lose your home if you don't meet the payments for the work. If the contractor takes a mortgage or security interest, federal law gives you three days to change your mind and cancel.

Consider having a lawyer look at the contract, especially if there's a security agreement. If problems do arise that threaten your rights to own your home, see a lawyer immediately.

Q. What about appliance repairs?

A. You can best protect your rights by getting a written estimate. At least make sure you get

---

▶ WHAT TO WATCH OUT FOR WITH HOME REPAIRS

Generally, as in any other contract, home repair contractors may not mislead you in any way to get the job. Be aware of these tricks:

- promising a lower price for allowing your home to be used as a model or to advertise the contractor's work;
- promising better-quality materials than the contractor will actually use (beware of bait and switch);
- providing "free gifts"—if these are offered, find out when you will receive them, or try to get a price reduction instead;
- not including delivery and installation costs in the price;
- starting work before you sign a contract, in order to intimidate you;
- claiming that your house is dangerous and needs repair;
- claiming that the contractor works for a government agency; or
- offering you a rebate or a referral fee if any of your friends agree to use the same contractor.

---

an oral estimate before work begins, and find out how the repair shop will figure the total charge, including parts and labor. Also, tell the repair shop to get your approval before beginning work. It will then be able to give you a better idea of how much the repair will cost.

Funeral Homes

Q. Do special rules apply to funeral home contracts?

A. Yes. When a loved one dies, bereaved survivors are in no mental state to negotiate a contract. Exploiting this vulnerability, some unsavory funeral homes used to charge exorbitant fees for burial services. To protect consumers, the Federal Trade Commission adopted the **Funeral Rule,** which requires mortuaries or funeral homes to quote you prices and other requested information over

the telephone. The intention is to prevent corrupt operators from requiring you to come to their showrooms, where they can take advantage of your weak emotional state.

Q. Does the Funeral Rule require anything else?

A. Yes. The general idea of the Funeral Rule is that the funeral home must inform you of your options every step of the way. If you visit a funeral home, it must give you a written list with all the prices and services offered—including the least expensive. You can keep this list. You have the right to choose any service offered, as long as it does not violate state law. The funeral home must give you a copy of applicable state law. The funeral home must reveal any fees charged for outside items, such as flowers, and may not charge a handling fee for purchases of caskets from third parties.

The home may not misstate state embalming requirements, and must give general information about embalming options. The Funeral Rule also entitles you to an itemized list of all charges.

Travel

Q. My hotel overbooked and now I don't have a room. Does this qualify as a breach of contract? What are my options?

A. It is a breach of contract if you paid in advance. Otherwise, the reservation is just a courtesy. Therefore, it is often worthwhile to pay for a hotel reservation by credit card when you make it. If you cancel within a couple of days before the reservation date, you probably will get a complete credit, depending on the credit card company's arrangement with the hotel. Also, many premium credit card companies guarantee their cardholders' hotel rooms if the rooms are reserved with that card. (Contact the credit card company if the hotel doesn't honor your reservation.)

If your room is unavailable even after you speak to the manager, you could have a contract claim. But it probably won't be worthwhile to pursue it legally because of the cost. Perhaps the best advice is to request firmly that the hotel arrange suitable alternative accommodations for you.

Q. What about an airline bumping me off my flight?

A. Generally, even if you have paid in advance, you do not have a contract to travel at a certain time. You only have a contract to travel to a certain city. However, if you check in on time and have a confirmed ticket, then you do have certain rights. Federal regulations require that if you get bumped against your wishes, the airline must give you a written statement describing your rights and explaining how the airline decides who gets on an oversold flight and who does not.

Travelers who don't get on the flight are often entitled to an on-the-spot payment as compensation. The amount depends on the price of their ticket and the length of the delay. There's no compensation if the airline can arrange to get you on another flight that is scheduled to arrive at your destination within one hour of your originally scheduled arrival time. However, if the substitute transportation is scheduled to arrive more than one hour but less than two hours after your original time of arrival, then the airline must pay you an amount equal to the one-way fare to your final destination, up to $200. You're entitled to up to $400 if your substitute transportation will not arrive within two hours (four hours for international flights).

If you're just delayed, not bumped, ask the airline staff what services it will provide. Ask about meals, telephone calls, and overnight accommodations.

You can complain to the U.S. Department of Transportation if you think an airline has abused you. But contact the airline first.

Q. How can I protect myself when paying for charter tours?

A. Your money often follows a twisting route to the tour operator. This leaves you vulnerable at the many different stops that exist in between. The best approach is to pay by credit card, which entitles you to the protections of the Fair Credit Billing Act. If you pay by check, the tour operator's brochure usually will specify the name of an escrow bank account in which all payments eventually go.

▶ **LAW EVOLVES TO MEET E-COMMERCE DEMANDS**

Many airline tickets and hotel rooms are bought online these days. Most consumer protection laws apply to these online merchants as well as to catalog and "brick-and-mortar" merchants. In addition, these laws are often supplemented in various states by laws aimed specifically at Web merchants. For more information on online shopping, see Chapter 13, "Computer Law."

Make out your check to that account. Also, if possible, put the destination, dates, and other details on the face of the check, which should guarantee that the payment goes where it should. That may help you get your money back if the tour is canceled, or if the tour operator or travel agent goes out of business. Your contract is with the tour operator.

U.S. Department of Transportation regulations require that, before your payment is accepted, you be shown and sign an operator/participant contract that describes your rights. Demand this contract if it is not offered to you.

Some operators carry bonds to reassure their customers, rather than using escrow accounts. If an operator doesn't have an escrow account, ask whether it is bonded and how you would be reimbursed in case of default.

Often, the travel agent will insist that the check be made out to the travel agency, because it is the policy of some agents to write a single check to the tour operator themselves. That's fine, but insist on a written guarantee from the tour operator and the agency, and make sure that the agency's check is made payable to the tour operator's escrow account. Reputable agents and operators should be willing to stand behind the tour.

You also can protect yourself by getting trip insurance. This guards you if you have to cancel the trip because of your illness or an illness in your immediate family. Various types of trip insurance, as well as message relaying and referrals to overseas legal and medical help, are also provided free by many premium credit cards.

REMEMBER THIS

- Form contracts are written on paper, not etched in stone. Do not be afraid to question terms you do not understand or do not like.

- If the seller won't budge on terms you do not understand or do not like, walk away.

- Beware of the salesperson who says, "It's just a standard contract."

- Take the time to read contracts, even when you feel rushed (such as when the pipes burst) or upset (like after a loved one dies).

- Protect yourself when you can by paying with a credit card and, in some cases, by purchasing insurance.

Computer Law

Heather doesn't have a lot of time to go shopping before the holidays, so she has decided to buy her gifts online. Point, click, and purchase. What could be easier? But is her credit card information safe? What are her options if the gifts never arrive? Can she shop online while she is at work? Will her employer find out?

Computers are everywhere, and they are changing the way we shop, work, and correspond. At the click of a mouse, we can purchase goods and have them delivered to our homes. Our home computers can connect us to our employers, in some cases eliminating the need to go to the office. Electronic mail enables us to communicate across long distances at less than the cost of a local phone call. And handheld devices have opened up even more possibilities.

But with this technology come potential dangers. Just how secure are those online purchases? Can my employer eavesdrop on my Internet and e-mail use at the office? Could I unwittingly enter into a contract online? What's to stop my kids from accessing sites I would rather they not visit?

This chapter examines how the law is responding, often slowly, to these issues, and provides helpful hints to protect computer users from potential harm. Remember, as technology rapidly develops and changes, so too do the associated laws. While this chapter gives you an overview of the legal issues related to computers and the Internet, you should try your best to keep up-to-date and current with important changes in this area.

> ▶ **WEBSITES AND E-MAILS**

Often this chapter directs you to seek out more information on the Internet, to send an e-mail, or to contact an agency or office. The appropriate contact information, websites, and e-mail addresses are available in the "World at Your Fingertips" section starting on page 722.

LAW ENFORCEMENT, COMPUTERS, AND YOUR FAMILY

The Internet has quickly become a valuable educational and research tool. At the click of a mouse, students can access information in seconds that it would have taken hours to find in a library just a generation ago. Young minds can let their imaginations soar as they visit websites covering virtually every subject.

But in the view of parents, caregivers, and lawmakers, this amazing technology also harbors great dangers. Many websites deal with subjects and contain images that are inappropriate for youngsters, such as pornography and violence.

This section covers what every parent should know about protecting their children on the Internet, as well as how laws affect you and your computer and how you can protect yourself.

Q. Does the law protect children who are online?

A. Congress has taken steps over the past decade to protect children by outlawing the transmission of obscene, indecent, or offensive messages to anyone under age eighteen. Lawmakers have also denied federal funding to libraries that fail to install blocking software.

While the law clearly allows parents and caregivers to restrict their children's Internet access, the First Amendment right of free speech puts some constraints on the ability of Congress and public libraries to similarly safeguard children.

Q. What can a parent do?

A. Concerned parents and caregivers should closely monitor the sites their children access and consider installing blocking software. Parents can refuse to give their children their own Internet accounts, thereby making it more difficult for them to disguise what sites and chat rooms they have visited.

However, remember that children can access the internet when outside the home. Children can get online at a friend's house or the library. In addition, most computers are preloaded with online software, and sex offenders can provide children with an online account to facilitate e-mail communication.

Parents should speak with their child about the dangers of communicating with strangers online, and should spend time with their child while he or she is on the computer. In addition, computers should be kept in a common area of the house, where a parent can monitor use.

Q. Are there stronger steps parents can take?

A. Most ISPs have parental permission restrictions you can set up, as do some browsers, such as Internet Explorer.

If more aggressive monitoring is in order, the FBI recommends that parents maintain access to their children's online accounts and randomly check their e-mail and any peer-to-peer sites they may have created, such as on MySpace. Be aware that some children host two such sites, one for their parents and one for their friends. In addition, parents should ask what safeguards are being used on computers at the public library and at friends' homes.

Parents have warned their children for generations to "Beware of strangers," and this warning should be expanded to include people that children encounter online. Parents should instruct their children never to meet with a person they have met online, or to post pictures of themselves on the Internet or in an online message to people they do not know in person. In addition, children should never disclose their name, address, or telephone number online. All it takes is a couple bits of this information for a stranger to locate your child.

Q. What signs of trouble should parents look for?

A. Parents should become suspicious if their child spends a lot of time online, particularly at night. While pedophiles are online all the time, many have day jobs that keep them from their computers until the evening and early-morning hours.

Parents also should be alarmed if they find pornographic pictures on their child's computer. The FBI says that pedophiles will often send graphic images as a way to broach the subject of sex with children. On your computer, you can run a search of the most common file formats used for pictures, such as ".jpg" and ".gif," and list them as thumbnails to see what's there. You can also look in your computer's history of visited sites (the **cache**) to find out the sites visited most recently.

Children may also exhibit certain behavior when they are engaging in inappropriate conversations online. For example, they will turn the computer off or quickly change websites when a parent enters the room. Parents should be suspicious if strange or unexpected gifts arrive in the mail, or if they notice a lot of hang-up phone calls.

Cyberbullying is also becoming more common, and parents should discuss this with their children. Teach your children not to respond to suggestive, obscene, belligerent, or harassing online messages, and teach them to report any bullying behavior to a trusted adult.

Q. What should a parent do if a child has received obscene photos or a sexual solicitation via e-mail?

A. The FBI advises parents to turn off the computer to preserve any evidence for law enforcement. Then call the police, the FBI, and the National Center for Missing and Exploited Children.

Q. My daughter surfs the Web a lot. I am worried about her privacy—are there any protections for her?

A. Federal law places restrictions on operators of websites and online services directed at children under thirteen. Under the Children's Online Privacy Protection Rule, issued by the Federal Trade Commission, these operators must post clear and comprehensive privacy policies on their websites describing what they plan to do with information provided by children.

These operators also must provide notice to parents and obtain parental consent before collecting personal information from children. In addition, the regulations require operators to provide parents access to their

---

▶ **COMPUTER-SAVVY BASICS**

- Online banking is pretty safe these days. Check your records for unauthorized transactions, and notify your bank quickly if there's anything amiss.

- You cannot stop spam, but you can contain it by doing the following:
  - Opt out of receiving commercial solicitations by using the "opt-out" functions contained in most privacy policies.
  - Limit the number of companies that know your e-mail address.
  - Read privacy agreements before buying items online.
  - Install software that screens out unwanted e-mail messages.
  - Create a separate e-mail account for your online purchases.

- Make sure your computer has up-to-date antivirus software.

- Do not open e-mails when you cannot identify the sender.

- Do not open attachments unless you know or have contacted the sender.

- Do not forward e-mails unless you know who sent you the message.

- The law is unclear as to whether people have an expectation of privacy with regard to their e-mails. It's probably safest to assume that you have no privacy rights, and act accordingly.

---

child's personal information, and to delete this information if the parents wish. The regulations also provide that operators may not require a child to provide personal information in order to participate on a site (beyond what is reasonably necessary to enable such participation).

Q. Regarding homework, how can a parent prevent children from plagiarizing?

A. Tell them that plagiarism is a form of stealing and, again, monitor the websites they visit.

Today's parents can remember being told in school that they should not simply copy what they read in the encyclopedia. Likewise, today's students must be told not to simply cut and paste what they read during their online research.

The advent of the Internet means that it has become much easier—and, correspondingly, more inviting—to plagiarize; children can simply cut and paste pages of information electronically. In addition, prewritten (and well-written) reports are available for sale—and even for free—online, making academic theft and cheating even more accessible to children. Parents should talk to their students about the possible repercussions of plagiarism. Your local school or library may be able to provide you with valuable information on how to talk to your children about these issues.

Q. I think my child may be gambling online. Don't those websites check to make sure the gambler is of age?

A. To access these sites, often the only thing a child needs is a credit or debit card. Therefore, parents and caregivers trying to prevent their children from accessing these sites should sharply restrict their access to these cards. Parents should also warn their children about the hazards of gambling, including the fact that the odds are always with the house (or, in this case, the website), and that they can lose their money, become addicted, and mess up their credit rating.

Q. Legally, are there any restrictions on when the police can search my e-mail?

A. This area of law has been changing a great deal in recent years. The Fourth Amendment creates a safeguard against unreasonable police searches and seizures that is based in large part on an individual's "reasonable expectation of privacy."

However, courts are undecided as to how much the Fourth Amendment applies to e-mail conversations. A major sticking point is whether people communicating by e-mail have a reasonable expectation of privacy, considering that these messages are collected and held by service providers. In at least one case, the U.S. court of appeals upheld a lower court order allowing the police to seize an individual's e-mail records in order to search for evidence of a crime.

Q. Is hacking illegal? My son is a whiz at computers, and I need to know how to guide him.

A. It is a federal crime to hack into, or illegally access, a computer system belonging to another person, company, or governmental agency. Agencies, companies, and individuals have turned to high-tech software to protect their computers against hackers. Nevertheless, computer-savvy individuals have in many cases been able to stay one step ahead of these programs, and have hacked into the websites and computers of numerous companies and agencies.

If by blind luck your son should stumble onto an unauthorized site, one option is simply to leave the site—perhaps by hitting the "back" button on your Web browser. Another is not to touch your computer, and to contact a lawyer to help safeguard your rights as you attempt to inform the appropriate people (the site's operators, law enforcement officials, etc.) of what has occurred.

▶ USING TECHNOLOGY TO FIGHT PLAGIARISM

From grade schools to colleges, schools today have become wise to the ways of plagiarism-friendly Internet sites, and have investigated and caught students who have bought reports rather than written their own. Some websites allow educators to detect plagiarism by comparing student submissions to billions of pages of Internet content.

REMEMBER THIS

- Responsibility for your children's online habits begins at home. Parents can monitor their children's Internet use in the home and install blocking software to prevent them from accessing pornographic, violent, racist, and gambling sites.

> ▶ **COPYRIGHT AND COMPUTERS**

Federal copyright laws apply to computers. You could be putting yourself at legal risk if you cut and paste words and pictures from an Internet site to include on your personal website or in a document you are producing, or if you copy software or illegally download music or software. Your safest bet before copying anything is to have the permission of the copyright holder (who may not always be the person who created the material you are copying). Or, under the **fair-use doctrine,** you may be able to copy protected material if you are using it as part of a criticism, a comment, a news report, or a valid educational or research tool. However, if you have any question about whether you have permission to copy, ask!

- Parents have significantly less control over their kids when the kids are outside the home.
- Several pieces of legislation designed to prevent children from accessing certain types of websites have been struck down by courts as violating the First Amendment.

ONLINE PURCHASES

More and more of us are buying products online, whether through the websites of established vendors who also have brick-and-mortar stores, from folks whose entire business is on the Internet, or through online auctions. E-shopping can be safe—if you follow some precautions and are aware of legal protections. This is a fluid, rapidly changing area of law. If you are a consumer encountering a problem with an online purchase—or a businessperson selling over the Internet—you should consult your lawyer to determine your rights and responsibilities under state and federal law.

This section covers common forms of online shopping, from auctions to airline tickets to personal finances.

Q. Is online shopping worth the risk?

A. Understand that the risks of buying online do not differ significantly in type from risks associated with buying from a brick-and-mortar store. But it may be more difficult to protect yourself if you buy online, and the level of risk may be somewhat higher than if you deal with an established local vendor. If you take reasonable precautions and act carefully, you can often achieve substantial savings by purchasing online.

Q. How do I shop safely online?

A. Common sense will prevent many potential problems in cyberspace. When shopping online, you lack many of the telltale signs of a company's reliability that you witness firsthand when shopping in person. Over the Internet, you cannot readily judge how well products are maintained, how well stocked or stable the company is, or how knowledgeable the salespeople are. Therefore, it might be best to shop online with companies you know and trust. Also, there are a number of seal-of-approval programs, such as the Better Business Bureau's, that allow you to assess an online company.

Q. What else can I do to protect myself when shopping online?

A. Before buying any electronics online, you should find a local brick-and-mortar store that sells the same item, and then go look at it. Check it out thoroughly to ensure that it has the features you want, and that it works as you expect. Be sure of the particular model that you want before buying it online. This will reduce the risks and problems you might encounter if you make the purchase and it proves unsatisfactory.

If you buy online, carefully check your order when it arrives. Verify that the item and model you received matches the one that you ordered in every respect. Check to verify that you received the manufacturer's U.S. warranty registration card, if you required one as part of your order.

You should also trust your instincts. If you do not feel comfortable buying an item over the Internet, or if you feel pressured to place your order immediately, maybe you should not complete the purchase.

Q. Is it safe to pay online by credit card?

A. A major concern of online shoppers is whether their credit card information is truly protected from thieves and computer hackers. Some credit card associations offer zero-liability policies. Under such policies, cardholders are not responsible for any amount of unauthorized purchases.

Another way to protect yourself is to make sure you use a recent version of a standard browser system, which will encrypt or scramble your information and thus increase the transaction's security. Most computers come with such a browser installed, or else you can upgrade for no charge. Software programs are also available.

> ▶ **USE THE WEB TO CHECK WEB MERCHANTS**
>
> You can reduce your exposure by doing some online investigation before you buy. Several website services provide information about vendors. These sites often include customer ratings and evaluations of the vendors, their policies, and their performances.

In addition, many online companies use Secure Sockets Layer (SSL) technology to **encrypt** (i.e., encode for security purposes) the credit card information you send over the Internet, and to provide you with assurance that your information will be protected en route to the company. These sites usually inform you that they are using this technology. For example, some sites use a padlock icon in the bottom right-hand corner to indicate an encrypted transmission. Or you can check whether the Web address on the page that asks for your credit card information begins with "https:" instead of "http:"—if so, then SSL technology is in place. Many websites will tell you when you are entering or leaving a secure page or site, and will prompt you to confirm that you want to do so. Of course, this doesn't protect your information once it has arrived with the company; it is up to you to ensure that you are purchasing from a company that employs comprehensive security policies.

Q. Is it safe to pay with a credit card?

A. Usually, yes. If you pay with a credit or debit card and a problem arises, then the federal Fair Credit Billing Act protects you. This law gives you the right to dispute charges and temporarily withhold payment while the charges are being investigated.

You can further protect yourself by keeping up-to-date records of your online transactions. Keep copies of your online communications with the company and your purchase order and confirmation number. Also, review your bank and credit card statements for billing errors or unauthorized purchases, which might have been made by someone who illegally accessed your information.

You can further limit your exposure by acquiring a low-limit credit card and using that card for your online purchases. The lower limit reduces potential exposure if the number is misappropriated.

Q. Are there other online payment methods?

A. Yes. Many websites accept payment by check. There is no need for you to write a real check; all you need to do is fill out your account details, and payment is automatically deducted from your checking account and will show up on your next bank statement. However, it is sometimes safer to pay by credit or debit card. Once the vendor negotiates your check or receives the wire transfer, the money is in the vendor's possession and it may take considerable effort to recover it if there is a problem.

The PayPal system used by eBay and other services works in a similar way. The payer and payee must both be registered with PayPal. If the payer wants to send money to the payee, the payer simply enters the payee's e-mail address and specifies the amount he wants to send. The transaction goes through the PayPal database, and money is electronically transferred from the payer's account to the payee's account. The payee receives an e-mail telling him that cash has been deposited in his bank account.

It is also possible to make some payments directly from your bank account if you use on-line banking. You simply need to give your bank the relevant information—the number of your utility account, the amount you wish to pay, and the date on which you would like to pay.

Be wary of any emails you receive asking you to confirm payment or shipping information. These emails may just be a ploy to try to get your credit card or other identification information. This practice is known as **phishing**. A common example of phishing involves you receiving an e-mail that appears to come from a reputable website (e.g., PayPal) asking you to click on a link in order to confirm your payment address. If you click through the link, you are taken to a website that appears credible, but if you enter your information, chances are good you are providing a criminal with the information needed to steal your identity. Other emails appear to come from banks, credit unions, eBay, and various social networking websites. Your email service's spam filter can help you avoid receiving phishing emails. However, if you do receive an email asking you to confirm or update any personal information, it is best to contact the company directly (not using the link in the email) to confirm the request. When in doubt, call the customer service number and speak to a real person. You can also find reports of phishing and other email-based schemes by searching online for them, or by visiting websites such as that of the Anti-Phishing Working Group.

Q. Can I use my debit card while shopping online? Will I be protected?

A. Yes. Some online companies use a debit card payment system, under which you set up an account with them, and authorize them to debit your account electronically after each

> ▶ **VALUABLE INFORMATION— ABOUT YOU**
>
> Be advised that online merchants will track your online buying habits. This information is valuable to marketing companies that might then send you unsolicited e-mails advertising products in which you have shown an interest or in which they believe you might have an interest. Be sure to check the privacy policies of all entities with whom you deal.

transaction. Debit cards can also be cards branded with credit card association marks that are processed using the credit card networks, or they might be cards from your bank that are processed through the ATM networks.

The federal Electronic Funds Transfer Act (EFTA) gives you many of the same protections for debit payments as you have for credit card payments. Within various time limits, you can point out mistakes on your statements, and the financial institution must investigate the mistakes, tell you the result of its investigation, and correct the problems after determining that errors have in fact occurred. Debit cards not issued by financial institutions may offer you fewer protections, though some, like Visa and MasterCard, protect you through zero-liability policies.

Q. I never signed anything; is the online company still under contract to send me my goods?

A. Yes, so long as it is clear through your correspondence that you have agreed to pay a specific price for a specific product. This clarity and specificity requirement prevents confusion and misunderstandings that can arise later, particularly in cyberspace, if the company fails to send you the items you ordered.

On the flip side, it is just as important to state clearly in your online correspondence with the company when you do not want to make a purchase. These messages should make it clear to the company that you do not wish to buy, that it should not send you the merchandise, and that you should not be charged anything.

Q. How do you "sign" a contract electronically?

A. These days, an increasing number of businesses are engaging in electronic commerce, allowing them to reach more consumers while cutting down on their paperwork and advertising costs. These transactions usually involve no face-to-face contact, no paper contract, no ink or "wet" or handwritten signature. And it might also mean confusion down the line about whether a contract has actually been made and what exactly has been agreed to. The general trend is to use technology to verify the identities of the parties, and to permit them to decide on acceptable electronic signing technologies. For more details about electronic signatures, see Chapter 12, "Contracts and Consumer Law."

Q. Are there any documents that can't be "signed" online?

A. Yes. The federal and state laws in this area may exempt certain documents, which means that electronic signatures may not be sufficient for wills, codicils, and testamentary trusts; adoptions, divorces, or other family-law matters; notices of foreclosures or evictions from one's primary residence; and cancellation of health or life insurance benefits.

Q. What can I do to make sure my order arrives?

A. You should take steps to protect your rights even before you place an order by

- Reviewing the company's return, refund, and shipping and handling policies. Look under the company's online contract agreement for "legal terms" or "disclaimers." If you cannot find the contract, ask the seller through an e-mail or telephone call to indicate where it is on the site or to provide it to you in writing.
- Printing and saving all company correspondence. You should print out and date a copy of the company's terms, conditions, warranties, item description, and confirming e-mails, and save them with the records of your purchase.

When your purchase arrives, examine the item carefully as soon as possible Contact the seller immediately if you discover a problem. Tell the seller in writing about any problems, ask for a repair or refund, and again keep a copy of your correspondence in case you have to take the company to court.

Q. What if my order never arrives?

A. Under federal regulations, companies that take orders over the Internet have up to thirty days to deliver the merchandise. Consumers who have not received their goods within thirty days may demand a refund. Companies that cannot make delivery within thirty days must tell the consumer, and inform the consumer of his or her right to cancel the order with a full refund.

Q. Are there special concerns when buying from foreign companies?

A. The online marketplace has made all stores appear local. But do not be lulled into assuming that the same rules apply both in the United States and abroad, even on the Internet.

Before ordering from a foreign company, the Federal Trade Commission advises that you ask the following questions:

- Are the prices posted in U.S. dollars or some other currency? If in another currency, the date of conversion to dollars may also be important.
- Does the company ship internationally?
- How long will delivery take?
- Will unexpected taxes or duties be added to the price?
- If a dispute arises, where will it be resolved?

The answer to the last question might be a deal breaker. Merchants, except in very rare cases, will want you to agree to have all disputes resolved in their local courts and under their local law as a condition of completing the sale. For example, if you are an Illinois resident upset that a French company has not sent you the wine you ordered, your only recourse might be to litigate the dispute in Paris rather than Chicago. Much as you might want to go to Paris, the expense of pursuing a case in a distant court is considerable, so think twice about ordering from an out-of-state or foreign company, especially for high-value goods.

Q. Are there any scams I should watch out for when buying online?

A. Internet and telephone vendors use a variety of techniques to try to take advantage of the unwary customer. You can protect yourself by taking these steps:

- **Understand gray-market goods.** Sometimes vendors will sell goods that were not manufactured or intended for sale in the United States. These products, sometimes called **gray-market goods,** have found their way to the United States through a circuitous route. Gray-market vendors will happily sell them to you at an often substantial discount. Many of these goods are made by well-known manufacturers, arrive in excellent condition, and work perfectly fine. On the other hand, gray-market goods may also arrive without a set of instructions in English. More important, they will almost definitely arrive without a U.S. warranty. The absence of a U.S. warranty means that if something fails, you have to pay to repair or replace it.

- **Beware of the "U.S. warranty" scam.** Some vendors, particularly in the consumer electronics area, anticipating that a customer will know enough to ask for a U.S. warranty, sell gray-market goods with a third-party warranty contract provided by a U.S.-based repair on warranty service. Since the third-party warranty comes from a U.S. firm, the vendor will "truthfully" tell you that the item has a U.S. warranty. These third-party warranties often do not match the breadth of coverage of the manufacturer's warranty. Unless you feel like gambling when you order, be clear that you want goods with the manufacturer's U.S. warranty, not gray-market goods.

- **Watch out for the shipping-charges scam.** Some discount vendors will quote you a very favorable price. While you are congratulating yourself on the great deal, the vendor will then recover some profit by adding an excessive amount for shipping and handling—say $60 or $75 when the true cost should be $20 or $30. Consider the cost of shipping a part of the ac-

quisition cost when comparing prices among vendors.

- **Turn down service contracts.** Often with consumer electronics items, you will have the opportunity to purchase a vendor or third-party extended-service contract to supplement the manufacturer's warranty. Distinguish these from extended warranties from the manufacturer. They are either a store arrangement or a third-party warranty package. Generally, the service contract or extended warranty costs 10 to 30 percent of the cost of the item, depending upon its scope and term and which vendor offers it. The primary purpose of these contracts appears to be creating an opportunity for the vendor to make a few extra dollars. These extended warranty packages often do not represent a good value, and you probably should forgo the "opportunity."

Q. Are there any other online scams I should watch out for?

A. Internet scams are so common that the Federal Trade Commission has a term for them: **dot cons.**

Among the most common scams are Internet sites that appeal to computer users' prurient interests by promising them they can visit adult Web pages for free simply by providing credit card information to confirm they are at least eighteen years old. But the next thing these computer users see is not what they expected; rather, they see unfamiliar charges on their credit card bills. To protect yourself from this and similar scams, the FTC advises that you share your credit card information only with companies you trust.

A typical scam known as the Nigerian scam promises riches if the e-mail addressee provides the name of his or her bank, account numbers, and other identifying information. This information is requested supposedly by a foreign government official, who promises the recipient a percentage of the millions of dollars he is trying to transfer out of his country. Once he receives that information, the con artist has all the personal data he needs to pass himself off as the e-mail recipient, and can easily draw funds from that person's account. To avoid being a victim, recipients of this type of e-mail should simply delete it. The old adage holds true: if it sounds too good to be true, it probably is.

Other scams to look out for involve e-mails that appear to come from banks or other institutes that you know and trust, asking you to confirm your credit card or bank account information. For more information on this practice, called phishing, see the discussion above on page 474. A similar scam, referred to as **vishing,** involves a computerized phone system that calls victims, notifying them that their credit or bank cards may have been used for fraudulent activity. The victims are then prompted to key in their account number and other identifying information, allowing the scammer access to their accounts.

Cyberspace Auctions

Q. If I am planning on bidding during a cyber-auction, how should I protect myself?

A. With online auctions, the rule "Let the buyer beware" applies. If yours was the highest bid, you will likely deal directly with the seller (not the auction house) to complete the deal.

Hence, it is essential for you to be knowledgeable about Web-based auctions. You should take special care to familiarize yourself not only with the rules and policies of the auction site itself, but with the legal terms (warranties, refund policy, etc.) of the seller's items on which you wish to bid. Also, if you are buying from an individual, some auction sites offer feedback pages where customers can discuss their experiences with a particu-

---

▶ COMPETITION MAY PROTECT PRIVACY

The best advice for finding an Internet service provider (ISP) that will protect your privacy is to examine ISP agreements carefully before signing up. Peruse the privacy policy to find out what information the seller is gathering from you, how the information will be used, and how you can stop it from being shared with marketers. If a provider's site does not have a privacy policy posted, you may not want to do business with that company. If the ISP does have a privacy policy, there will probably be a link to it from the company's home page, or it might be included with the legal terms.

Note also that privacy policies can change, and typically you agree to be bound by the privacy policy as is and as amended. If you don't like the privacy policy once it changes, find out how you can opt out. Shop around for possible deals on bundled services. Look for ISPs that provide anti-spam and child safety features for free.

lar seller. Before submitting a bid, check these reviews. Additionally, some sites offer insurance protection for your purchases.

Other precautions include verifying the seller's identity and asking about return policies. You should also find out what the seller charges for shipping and handling. Consider restricting your shopping to cyberspace auctioneers that provide fraud resolution, fraud protection, or similar services to ensure the privacy and integrity of online transactions.

Q. How should I pay if I win an online auction?

A. It is risky to pay by certified check or money order. If you pay by credit card, you can challenge the charge with the credit card company if the merchandise does not come or is not what you thought you had bought. You can also protect yourself by paying upon delivery.

Professional Services

Q. I have been searching online to find a new doctor, and I think I found a good one. Is there anything I should be aware of?

A. The truth is that often you cannot be sure that a professional's Web page contains the unvarnished truth. A Web page, like any advertisement, is subject to potential embellishment of the facts.

Common sense again plays a crucial part in your decision making. Just as you should not hire a doctor, a lawyer, or other professional without doing diligent research (i.e., inquiring about references or board certification), you should not retain professional services based solely on an Internet advertisement. Because of the Internet's global reach, you must also confirm that the professional is in fact licensed to practice in your state (assuming that a license is required).

Q. How can I tell if the professional I found online is reputable?

A. To assuage client and patient concerns, several professional organizations have begun establishing "seals of approval" for the websites of practitioners who adhere to standards of privacy and quality. For example, Hi-Ethics administers such a program for health-related websites.

Another safeguard may come through domain registration. For example, RegistryPro is developing a service by which **domain names** (i.e., the unique addresses of websites) are issued to accounting, medical, or legal professionals only after confirmation that they are currently licensed and are who they claim to be. While authenticated domain names do not guarantee that everything said on a professional's website is true, at least there will be assurances of identity and licensure status.

Airline Tickets

Q. Should I buy an airline ticket online?

A. Buying a ticket online could save you money. But be careful: Many of these great rates are nonrefundable, or involve other restrictions on changes to your travel plans or your ability to fly standby. Many airlines now offer to e-mail schedule updates, and allow you to check the status of your flights and check in online before leaving for the airport. Always print out your reservation details, and confirm the flight the day before you are scheduled to leave.

Q. Last time I bought an airline ticket from a travel website, I was stranded at the airport because my plane was overbooked. Are there steps I can take to prevent this from happening?

A. Read the policy statement of the airline or the agency that is operating the website. Often, airlines contract out their online reservations to an agency whose policies differ from the airline's. These statements cover the company's obligations in the event the flight is canceled or rescheduled.

Generally, the onus is on you to confirm your reservations. If possible, book seat assignments ahead of time, so that you are less likely to get bumped if the flight is oversold. Check online ratings of various airlines to see how frequently they suffer from late departures and oversold flights. You may also find that being a member of a frequent flyer club can help when dealing with an airline—not surprisingly, an airline is generally less likely to bump a loyal customer.

Q. If I get to the airport with my bags but there's no flight, what recourse do I have?

A. So long as you can show that you had booked a seat, the airline will treat you as if you had purchased a paper ticket (airlines vary on their policies regarding stranded ticketed passengers). An electronic ticket should provide proof of purchase. To be extra careful, you might want to arrive at the airport with a printout of a confirmation e-mail from the travel site (or a printout of your reservation from the website) as additional proof.

Stocks and Securities

Q. How do I protect myself from falling into a trading trap in which the website operators promise big returns?

A. Trading stocks online or off-line can be akin to gambling. Be careful of any site promising a sure thing. The Federal Trade Commission recommends that investors on the Internet check out the stock promoter with state and federal securities regulators, and talk to people who have invested through the website.

The U.S. Securities and Exchange Commission (SEC), which oversees publicly traded companies, also warns computer users of the dangers of investing online. In particular, the SEC says online investors should beware of "**pump-and-dump**" stock scams in which unsavory individuals tout a company on a website, in an online investment newsletter, or via e-mail with the sole purpose of creating high demand for the stock and pumping up its price. The perpetrators of the scam then sell their stock when the price is high, resulting in a quick and sharp fall in the stock price. The unwitting investors then usually lose their money.

Q. The investment newsletters and websites seem so thorough—what should I watch out for?

A. Some of those sleek online documents and sites, which often read like unbiased reviews, are actually paid for by companies to trumpet their stocks. Such publications are not illegal, so long as the newsletters disclose who paid for them and how much and how they paid. Nevertheless, the SEC warns that many newsletters fail to disclose this information. The SEC cautions that you should never make an investment based solely on something you read online, especially if the company isn't well known. A good rule of thumb is to think twice about investing in small companies that don't file regular SEC reports, unless you are willing to investigate the company thoroughly and check the validity of every statement.

Q. Commentators on investment bulletin boards sound so knowledgeable—should I heed their advice?

A. Not unless you know the commentators and trust their advice. The SEC says many messages on these Internet sites are not always trustworthy. Often these "unbiased observers" turn out to be company insiders, large shareholders, or paid promoters looking to create the illusion of widespread interest.

Online Pharmacies

Q. Are there any advantages to buying through an online pharmacy?

A. There may be advantages to using online pharmacies—such as saving money, trouble, and embarrassment—but remember that you always need a prescription to get drugs that aren't available over-the-counter. And as with any online purchase, you need to do your homework.

Q. How can consumers protect themselves when purchasing from online pharmacies?

A. The FDA website provides a number of good cautions, including:

- Before buying, check with the National Association of Boards of Pharmacy to determine whether a website is a licensed pharmacy in good standing. Purchasing a medication from an illegal website puts you at risk. You may receive a contaminated or counterfeit product, the wrong product, an incorrect dose, or no product at all.

- Taking an unsafe or inappropriate medication puts you at risk for dangerous drug interactions and other serious health consequences.

- Don't buy from sites that offer to prescribe a prescription drug for the first time without a physical exam, sell a prescription drug without a prescription, or sell drugs not approved by the FDA.

- Don't do business with sites that have no access to a registered pharmacist to answer questions.

- Avoid sites that do not identify the person or entity with whom you are dealing, or that do not provide a U.S. address and phone number to contact if there's a problem.

- Steer clear of sites that include undocumented case histories claiming amazing results.

- Consumers who suspect that a site is illegal can report it to the FDA.

REMEMBER THIS

- Use common sense when you're shopping online. If you are not familiar with the name and reputation of a company, find out more before you buy.

- On the Internet, use the safest way to pay: a credit card.

- Just because you can now purchase goods electronically does not mean you can forget the old adage "Get it in writing." Keep a copy on paper, or an electronic copy on your computer, so that you can retrieve it later.

- If you're booking travel online, print out your booking information and bring it with you to the airport.

- Take care with online trading—don't assume that online newsletters are giving impartial advice, and investigate companies thoroughly before investing.

COMPUTERS ON THE JOB

Warning: Your employer may monitor your work computer. So be careful what websites you visit, what e-mails you send and receive, what games you play, and how long you spend online. And if you think returning to the home page and deleting e-mails will cover your wayward computer use, you are sadly mistaken. Cookies and other memory caches enable employers to see your files even after you have "deleted" them.

This section covers all the ways in which employers may monitor what you do on your office computer.

Q. May employers really monitor my computer activity?

A. The overwhelming majority of legal commentators, as well as courts that have decided such cases, say yes. The office computer, they note, is no different than your work telephone, the use of which employers have traditionally and quite legally limited to work-related communications.

In fact, many employers now have written policies saying they can and will monitor office computers. Companies defend their examinations of employee e-mails and website visits as necessary to protect proprietary information from being downloaded and e-mailed, to discourage workplace harassment, to reduce waste, fraud, and abuse of company resources, and to ensure that office computers are being used for company business.

Q. Can a party other than my employer search my e-mail and monitor my Internet use on a work computer?

A. Yes. Companies are sometimes the targets of lawsuits, either from customers, clients, or former employees. During litigation, the parties can receive the court's permission to examine a wide range of documents and e-mail communications pertaining to the alleged wrongdoing. As part of this discovery process, lawyers for those suing can gain access to a company's computers, and to the sites visited and people contacted by employees. This information, though not actively sought by your employer, could nonetheless come to its attention during the discovery process. The company will need to gather relevant information to turn over to the other side in response to its request for records, and will likely review the records before disclosing them to find out what the other side's lawyers will see.

Q. May I use my work computer for personal e-mail and online shopping?

A. The official answer is, only if your employer lets you. Such overt permission is very rare. But informally, employers don't generally object—so long as the use is minimal, does not interfere with your job, and is perhaps subject to other restrictions (for example, very few—if any—companies want you visiting pornography sites on their computers).

All in all, it's best to be cautious. Before sending that e-mail or visiting that website, ask yourself if your company lets you make personal calls or shop on company time. Now ask yourself if you mind having your employer see the content of your e-mail or discover when and where you shop. Even if your employer allows these practices, it's best to use your work computer sparingly for personal business.

Q. What if I am working from home on my own computer?

A. The computer age, as never before, has enabled employees to work from home. Workers can now use their home computers and be fully networked into their employers' office computer systems.

Those working at home, however, should know that while the employees are connected to the company's computer network, the employer can access records of the websites that employees visit, just as if they were in the office. Breaching employment policies remains cause for disciplinary action, even if you are working from the comfort of your home office.

Q. I worked from home for years and my company put some programs on my home computer. Now that I am retiring, must I return all the software?

A. Yes. The software belongs to your employer, or is licensed from another company by your employer, who lets you install it or download it to your computer for the very limited purpose of doing the company's work. Once that employment ends, the law or perhaps an agreement with your employer may require you to return the software to the company.

The law is not settled, however, on the issue of whether companies can require ex-employees to surrender their home computers for the former employer's inspection. Employers, having lent their software to the employees, might want to ensure that no company-owned programs or proprietary information has been downloaded to the personal computer. Companies, especially those that have licensed their own software, are especially concerned with protecting their products and confidential data. A lot of companies provide in their employee nondisclosure agreements that they have the right to inspect any computer that you may use in order to ensure that confidentiality is maintained.

Q. Do these rules also apply to freelancers and contractors?

A. Yes, unless the contract between the company and freelancer states otherwise. Rarely will a company cede any equipment to someone who is not an employee.

In this highly computer-connected world, an increasing number of people are opening home consulting businesses in which they perform outside work for other companies. Their home computers become a smorgasbord of software programs from the companies they serve. These workers are called contractors for a reason: They are governed by a contract with each company.

The contract will generally spell out the terms under which a company allows a consultant to use its software and related equipment. This permitted use is often very limited so as not to blur any legal lines between a contractor, who relies predominantly on his or her own materials, and an employee, who has freer rein on the company's equipment.

Even in the absence of a written contract,

one hallmark of a freelance relationship is that you use your own equipment. Anything given to you by the company is for a limited purpose and must be returned. You will likely be required to sign nondisclosure agreements that allow the company to inspect your computers if there is reason to determine compliance with the company's policy.

REMEMBER THIS

- Be careful how you use your computer at the office. A good rule is to imagine that your employer is looking over your shoulder whenever you access websites or send or receive e-mail.

- Be aware that many employers have termination policies in place for employees who visit offensive websites.

- Exercise the same caution when you are working from home on the company's computer network that you would exercise if you were working in the office.

- Your company's software belongs to the company, even though it is on your personal computer. When the company wants it back, return it.

Automobiles

Kimberly just bought a new car, but now she is having problems making payments. Can the dealer take the car back if she defaults? Robert is making his payments on time, but his new car has been a disaster. He has had to take it to the shop three times in the last week and can't get to work on time. What are his remedies? Can he simply return the car?

What does he need to know when dealing with the repair shop? Mary has a totally different car issue: she has been stopped by the police. Mary doesn't think she has done anything wrong, but what does she need to know before she talks to an officer? Can the police search her? Can they search her car?

Every driver should have at least a basic knowledge of the implications of buying or leasing and operating a motor vehicle. This chapter covers everything about the law and automobiles—the initial contract, consumer protection, maintenance and inspection, traffic law, and insurance.

BUYING, RENTING, AND LEASING A CAR

If you are going to buy a new or used car, you are about to make a major purchase and part with some hard-earned dollars. Even if you're leasing instead of buying, you're still looking at spending thousands of dollars. With all this money on the line, you'd better pay attention to the legal implications.

This section highlights the laws that protect you when buying or leasing a car, and provides guidance regarding the confusing world of vehicle financing.

BUYING A NEW CAR

Q. When shopping for a new car, how much can I rely on ads? Do they have to disclose everything about the car? What information should an automobile advertisement include?

A. This is an area largely regulated by state laws. In some states, the ad must state the number of that particular type of vehicle that is available. Other required items may include price, dealer- and factory-installed options, and warranty terms. In addition, if the vehicle is "on sale," the ad should state the sale's end date. As with all advertisements, don't take any promise too seriously until you get it in writing in the sales contract.

Q. What if the advertisement omits details?

A. If the dealer knows important facts about the vehicle, but fails to reveal them, the law may consider that a deceptive act. You may be able to cancel the deal and even recover damages in court. Clearing up the missing facts later does not erase the dealer's deceitful act. (For more information, see "Lemon Laws" on page 495.)

Q. Must a car contract be in writing?

A. Yes, for all but very inexpensive cars, according to the Statute of Frauds of the Uniform Commercial Code (UCC). The UCC, which is in effect in some form in every state but Louisiana, regulates the sales of most goods and securities. This means that the UCC governs almost all auto transactions. The UCC requires that any sale of goods of at least $500 must be in writing and signed by the party against whom enforcement is sought. If the contract is challenged, the courts will not be permitted to enforce it unless it is in writing.

Q. Who signs the contract?

A. Besides you, either an authorized salesperson or supervisor or manager signs it.

Q. What should I know before I sign the contract?

A. Before you sign, make sure you understand and accept all the contract terms, because you'll probably have to abide by a contract you have signed, even if you have not read it. Read the contract carefully. Ask questions. Cross out blank spaces to avoid any additions after you sign. If the dealer makes an oral promise but doesn't put it in the contract, it's extremely unlikely you'll be able to enforce it. The contract you sign binds you, and escaping from the contract is both difficult and expensive—so don't sign until you are fully satisfied. You can find more information about contracts and your ability to negotiate preprinted contracts in Chapter 12, "Contracts and Consumer Law."

Q. May I cancel the contract even after I sign it?

A. Read your contract carefully *before you sign* to review the cancellation provisions and to make sure that you understand everything. If you cancel for no reason, you risk losing your deposit. The dealer also might sue to recover lost profits (for time spent with you and for time spent on the car) and other damages.

You may be able to cancel the contract in some circumstances—for example, if a party to the contract is a minor or if the dealer breached a warranty, in which case you might attempt to cancel the contract because of the breach. (See Chapter 12, "Contracts and Consumer Law," for further discussion of canceling a contract.)

▶ **TERMS THE CONTRACT SHOULD INCLUDE**

The sales contract should include

- a description of the car;
- the vehicle identification number (VIN) (located on the driver's side of the dashboard near the windshield);
- a statement of whether the car is new, used, or has had a previous life as a demonstration vehicle, rental car, or taxicab;
- terms consistent with any oral agreements;
- details on any trade-in you will supply, including mileage and the dollar amount credited;
- warranty terms (see "Warranties and the Uniform Commercial Code" on page 497 of this chapter);
- financing terms, including price, deposit, trade-in allowance, annual percentage rate of interest (APR), and length of term; and
- a cancellation provision that enables you to get your deposit back if you have negotiated with the seller to allow for this.

> ▶ **LOSING YOUR DEPOSIT**
>
> If you decide to cancel a contract, you could lose your deposit. Your state may allow you to get a refund of your deposit in limited circumstances—for example, if you cancel the contract before a dealer representative signed the contract. In some states, you may be able to get a refund if you cannot get financing to buy the car.

Q. If I wind up in court in a contract dispute, may I offer information in addition to the contract?

A. Generally, under the **parol evidence rule,** courts look at the actual contract rather than at any outside information. Courts generally assume that both parties read and understood the contract before signing it, and will not consider evidence of any terms that were discussed before the contract was signed that vary or contradict the contract. However, you may be able to present evidence of an oral agreement made after the written agreement.

Q. What if I want to add something after I sign the contract?

A. Ask the dealer to write a contract **addendum** (a supplement), or write it yourself. Both parties should sign it. Make sure that whoever signs for the seller has the legal power to do so. Mention the original contract in the addendum, state that everyone should consider the addendum an inseparable part of the original contract, and state that the addendum overrides any inconsistent terms in the contract.

Q. What if something happens to the car after the contract is signed, but before I have possession of it?

A. This will likely depend on whether one of the parties is a car dealer, and on whether your contract has any provisions for such circumstances. After you have signed the contract, you should be very clear about whether the vehicle is insured and when your insurance covers the car. Under the Uniform Commercial Code (UCC), if the seller is a merchant (for example, a car dealer), then the risk of loss passes to buyers when they receive the car. If the seller is not a merchant, as in a private sale of a used car, then the risk passes to the buyer on tender of delivery. **Tender of delivery** usually occurs when the seller actually tries to deliver the car, or makes the vehicle available for pickup. A sales contract that specifies when the risk of loss passes will override this default provision.

Q. What if I do not have enough cash to buy a new car, even after my trade-in?

> ▶ **FINANCING INFORMATION**
>
> Chapter 10, "Consumer Credit," provides more detail about issues related to financing and credit, including the information creditors must provide, the legal protections available to borrowers, and your remedies should something go wrong.

A. You probably need financing. Banks, credit unions, loan companies, and car dealers are all potential funding sources. Interest rates will vary. Shop around for the best deal by comparing the various credit terms and annual percentage rates (APRs). For more information on comparing terms and APRs, see Chapter 10, "Consumer Credit."

Q. What happens if I can't pay my finance payments?

A. You may lose your car if you finance the purchase and do not make the payments when they become due (**default**). The creditor may be permitted to repossess your car, which may also affect your credit score.

Q. So if I don't pay, can the secured creditor just come and take my car away?

A. Afraid so. The only limitation on automobile repossessions is that the repossessor must do it without breaching the peace. In many states, the creditor does not even have to sue you or tell you about the default before reclaiming the vehicle.

Q. What is a breach of the peace?

A. A **breach of the peace** generally is any act likely to produce disorder or violence, such as an unauthorized entry into your home.

Q. What happens after the repossession?

A. If this happens to you, the first thing to do is consult a lawyer in your state to advise you of your rights. As a general rule, the creditor can resell the car after giving you notice of the upcoming sale. However, before that happens, you may have the right of **redemption**—in other words, the right to buy back the car (or in legal terms, **redeem the collateral**).

Q. How does the sale after repossession take place?

A. The sale has to be **commercially reasonable,** and this term may have different meanings in different states. Some states may require the creditor to get a court's permission before holding a sale. In all cases, you should receive notice from the creditor of the time, place, and manner of the sale. If the sale is public, you have the right to participate by placing a bid on the car.

If the sale does not bring in enough money to pay off the car debt and related expenses, you can be held responsible for the remainder. If the sale brings in more money than the amount of the debt owed (and any related expenses), then the creditor selling the car should give you the extra money.

▶ THE RIGHT TO REPOSSESSION

When you buy a car on credit, you may have to give the creditor rights in your car that have priority over the rights of your other creditors. When you are loaned the money, you sign a security agreement, which gives the creditor a security interest in your car (the **collateral**). You are agreeing to give the creditor a lien on the car. If you don't pay, the creditor may try to get the car back and sell it to satisfy your debt.

Q. What else can the creditor do with the car?

A. The creditor may keep the car to satisfy the debt fully. The law refers to this as **strict foreclosure.** There is no duty to return excess money in a strict foreclosure. However, creditors seldom exercise the option of strict foreclosure, because they want to sell cars—not keep them.

Q. My car has been repossessed, but I just got a big check that I have been waiting on. Can I buy my car back from the creditor?

A. You might be able to. This is called **redemption.** As a general rule, you (the debtor) must pay the entire balance due, plus any repossession costs and other reasonable charges. Watch out for consumer credit contracts containing acceleration clauses that become effective when you default. These force you to pay the entire outstanding debt, not just the amount overdue. Redemption rarely takes place. Even though many states do not give you such a right, see if you can make a deal with the creditor to pay the overdue payment and other charges to get the car back.

▶ WHAT IS A USED VEHICLE?

Under federal law, a used vehicle is one that was driven farther than the distance necessary to deliver a new car to the dealer or to test-drive it.

Buying a Used Car

Q. Do I need a written contract if I buy a used car?

A. It is a good idea to put any car-buying agreement in writing. As a general rule, you should have a written contract if the price is more than $500. Depending on the law of your state and the amount of money at stake, the court might not be able to enforce a contract that is not in writing.

Q. Do I need to get anything else in writing?

A. You should have a **bill of sale.** Many states require you to present a bill of sale (and pay sales tax) to re-title and re-register a car. A bill of sale also may serve as a receipt. The bill of sale should contain

- the date of the sale;
- the year, make, and model of the car;
- the vehicle identification number (VIN);
- the odometer reading;

▶ SPECIAL RULES FOR USED CAR DEALERS

Under the Federal Trade Commission's **Used Car Rule,** used-car dealers are prohibited from misrepresenting the mechanical condition of a used car or any warranty terms. The rule defines **dealers** as those who sell six or more used cars in a twelve-month period. Dealers must also provide you with the terms of any written warranty they provide, and must post a Buyer's Guide on the side window of the car.

- the amount paid and the form of payment (cash, check, etc.); and
- the buyer's and seller's names, addresses, and phone numbers.

The seller should sign and date the bill of sale, and both parties should get a copy.

Q. How much information should the seller give to the buyer?

A. If possible, the seller should provide the buyer with the car's complete service records and other accurate information. No seller—whether a dealer or non-dealer—should lie about the car. If the buyer is disappointed because the car is not as described or does not perform as it was supposed to, then the buyer may have a breach of warranty action against the seller. If you are buying the car from a dealer, this information should all be included on the Buyer's Guide.

Q. Does the seller have to tell the buyer the car's mileage?

A. Yes. Federal law entitles the buyer of a used car to receive a mileage disclosure from the seller. On request, the seller must give a signed written statement to the buyer that provides the odometer reading at the time of transfer and certifies the odometer's accuracy. The written statement that must be completed and signed by the seller usually appears on the reverse side of the certification of title or ownership. Refusal to provide such a statement, or illegally tampering with the odometer, exposes the seller to stiff penalties.

Q. Are there other ways to find out about a car's history?

A. Yes. Websites such as AutoCheck and CARFAX make it easy to find services that will provide you with detailed repair information, odometer information, and histories for many used cars. The car's vehicle identification number (VIN) is the key to performing such searches.

▶ WHAT THE BUYER'S GUIDE MUST SAY

If you buy a used car from a dealer, you are entitled to receive a copy of the actual Buyer's Guide that was posted in your car. The Buyer's Guide contains the following information about the car:

- The warranty that is being offered:
  - If there is a warranty, the specific coverage must be outlined;
  - If the vehicle comes with implied warranties only, or is sold as is (meaning that no warranty is being offered), this must be made clear.
- A statement that you should request an inspection by an independent mechanic before you buy.
- A statement that you should get all promises in writing.
- A list of some of the major problems that may occur with any car.

> ▶ **INSPECT BEFORE YOU BUY**
>
> You should take the car to a mechanic for an inspection before you buy it. If the seller, whether a dealer or a private party, will not allow your mechanic to inspect it, do not buy the car unless it is such a good deal that you will not mind paying for car repairs later.

Q. I am selling my used car and thought I had a deal lined up, but now I am not so sure. Can I get out of a contract to sell?

A. The same contract laws that govern a new-car purchase also cover a used-car purchase. Whether you can get out of a contract to sell your car depends on the laws of your state, the terms of the contract, and how far along the contract process has progressed.

Q. May a court force me to sell my car to a buyer after I have decided I do not want to?

A. It depends on the circumstances. Courts try to "leave the parties as they find them," and usually will not force a buyer to make a purchase or a seller to sell an item. However, depending on the situation, a court might order the seller to go through with the contract.

Car Leasing and Renting

Q. What do I need to rent or to lease a car?

A. You must have a valid driver's license, and you may be required to show a good driving record. In several states, major car rental companies have electronic links to government computers, which they use to obtain driver records when someone wants to rent a car. They may refuse a rental contract if a person has had accidents or has too many violations on his or her record.

Some major rental and leasing companies require that customers have a major credit card and be at least eighteen years old; some consider only credit card holders age twenty-five or older. The company may waive the age requirement if you have an account number in your name through a motor club or other association, or if you have a rental account through your business. You must sign a contract when you rent or lease a car.

Q. What should a car rental contract include?

A. At an absolute minimum, it should list the base rate for the rental car, any extra fees, and the length of the rental period.

Q. Are there additional fees I could be charged?

A. Yes. The rental company might offer you the **collision damage waiver** (**CDW**) option. The rental company covers damage to your rented car if you accept the CDW. However, coverage does not include personal injuries or personal property damage. Before accepting this expensive option, make sure your own automobile, medical, and homeowner's insurance policies do not already protect you in an accident involving a rented car. If traveling on business, your company's insurance policy might cover you. Check with your credit card company to see if it offers any insurance benefits, and find out what they are.

Other additional fees might include drop-off fees, if you pick up and return the car in different locations. There may also be fuel charges, extra-mileage fees, and fees for renting equipment like child safety seats or ski racks.

Q. How does leasing differ from renting?

A. A lease is essentially a long-term rental. Leases usually have a one-year minimum. You may rent a car for shorter periods—e.g., a single day or week.

Q. What happens at the end of the lease? Will I have to pay for any damages?

A. This will depend on the type of lease you have entered. Generally, there are two types of leases: a closed-end lease and an open-end lease.

Q. What is a "closed-end" lease?

A. Under a **closed-end lease** contract, sometimes called a **walk-away lease,** the car's value when you return it does not matter unless you have put excessive mileage or extreme wear on the car. You simply return the car at the end of the term and walk away. Payments may be higher than under an open-end lease, because the **lessor** (the person or company leasing the car to you) takes the risk on the car's future worth.

Q. What is an "open-end" lease?

A. An **open-end lease** may involve lower lease payments. However, you gamble that the car will be worth a stated price, the **estimated residual value,** at the end of the lease. If the car's appraised value at the end equals or exceeds the specified residual value, you owe nothing. You may receive a refund of any excess value, if your contract provides for one. The downside: If the car is worth less than the estimated residual value at the end of the term, then you pay some or all of the difference, often called an **end-of-lease payment.** This amount can be substantial, and you still must return the car.

Q. How much does a lease cost?

A. The cost of a lease depends upon the specific terms of the lease. Up front, you probably will have to pay a security deposit and the first month's lease payment and possibly the last. You may have to pay an initial **capitalized cost reduction.** This is similar to a down payment when you buy a car. By paying a large amount up front, you could, in effect, reduce your monthly lease payments. But by doing this, you lose one of the advantages of leasing: lower up-front costs. Other expenses may include sales or use taxes and title and license fees, though the lessor may pay them. A lease may include insurance. If not, you must provide your own. You might have to pay for repairs and maintenance after any warranty period expires, unless the lessor agrees to pay under the lease. And at the end of the lease term, you may have to pay an excess mileage cost if you have a closed-end lease. Excessive wear and tear also may cost you.

Q. May I renew or extend my lease at the end of the term?

A. Yes, if your lease contained this option or you negotiated for it. Such an option may reduce your initial costs.

Q. I have leased a car, but now I have decided I would like to buy a different car. May I get out of my lease early?

A. You have signed a binding contract that obligates you to make payments for a stated term. However, your contract may contain an early termination clause. This might require that you make a minimum number of monthly payments before you may cancel, and may require you to pay an early termination charge, which can be substantial.

Q. The dealer I am working with is talking about a purchase option. What is this?

A. A **purchase option** allows you to buy the car when your lease term ends. The lessor must state the purchase price or the basis for setting this price in the initial lease.

REMEMBER THIS

- Contracts are extremely important. Be sure that you read and understand any contract before you sign on the dotted line. This goes for the contract that covers the purchase of the car, as well as any contract that deals with how you pay for the car or that deals with insurance for the car.

- If you default on your finance payments, your car may be repossessed. It's important to understand the differences between open-end and closed-end leases, as well as to understand the many provisions of car-leasing contracts, such as the terms on termination, option to renew, and purchase option. The time to negotiate is before you sign.

- If you are buying a used car, you should give the car a good going-over or pay for a professional inspection before you open your wallet. It may save you money or help you negotiate a contract if you detect problems that can be repaired before purchase.

CONSUMER PROTECTIONS

You have a right to know what you're buying, and unfair and deceptive practices laws exist in every state to protect consumers. If a seller makes misleading statements about a car and you buy the car because of those statements, you may have a case if something goes wrong.

This section covers all the ways in which you can protect yourself when you purchase a motor vehicle, including lemon laws, warranties, and recalls.

Unfair and Deceptive Acts and Practices

Q. The dealer told me the car I was buying was "a great little runabout." But it's had several breakdowns in the months since I bought it. Can I sue the seller for making a misleading statement?

A. Obviously, when a seller is trying to sell you a car, it is inevitable that he or she will attempt to make it sound as good as possible. Many general statements that sellers make are mere puffery or bluster, and you should take everything a seller says with a pinch of salt. For legal purposes, sales talk probably doesn't amount to misleading or deceptive conduct.

Q. So what counts as an unfair or deceptive act?

A. Each state's unfair or deceptive practices act provides different definitions. Generally, it is illegal for the dealer to fail to disclose any important facts about the car, or to attempt to make such facts difficult for the buyer to see.

Q. Must an unfair or deceptive act be intentional?

A. No. In most states, the seller does not even have to know about the deception. Rather, the court considers the effect that the seller's conduct might possibly have on the general public, or on the people to whom the seller advertised the product.

Q. What must I do in order to use an unfair and deceptive practices statute?

A. If you think that you are the victim of an unfair or deceptive act or practice, you should consult a lawyer who can advise you of your rights. There are time limits that apply, including with regards to the filing of a lawsuit, so you should not delay in seeking help.

Your state may require you to make a written demand for relief before you sue, and the law may allow the seller one last chance to make good.

▶ HOW TO SPOT UNFAIR OR DECEPTIVE BEHAVIOR

The most common violations to look for include

- hiding dangerous defects;
- not revealing that the dealer advertised the car at a lower price;
- odometer tampering;
- failing to reveal that the dealer is charging excessive preparation costs; and
- withholding facts about the car's previous use—for example, as a racing car.

If you do sue, many states require proof of injury. Loss of money or property is enough to prove this. You should also be able to show that the seller's actions actually caused the injury by showing that you bought the car because of the seller's unfair or deceptive act.

Q. What happens if I win?

A. Many states permit you to recover double or triple damages, as well as lawyer's fees. The purpose of these harsh penalties is to discourage sellers from committing unfair or deceptive acts in the future.

Lemon Laws

Q. What's a lemon?

A. Generally, a **lemon** is a car that continues to have a defect that substantially restricts its use, safety, or value, even after reasonable efforts at repair. There may be specific legal rules concerning how many repair attempts you must make over a period of time in order for a car to qualify as a lemon.

Q. What must I do to make lemon laws work for me?

A. First, you must notify the manufacturer and (in some states) the dealer about the defect. Keep a copy of every repair or service receipt. These receipts will prove that the required number of repair attempts has been made. This can be especially important if your car's defect had to be repaired at another garage or in another city because it was physically impossible to drive the car back to the seller's repair location.

Most states require that you go through an arbitration procedure before you can get a replacement or refund. Some states sponsor arbitration programs, which may be more objective than those run by manufacturers. Arbitration is usually free, and results often are binding only on the manufacturer; if you don't like the result, you can probably still take the manufacturer to court, depending on the applicable rules.

Some states require arbitration only if the manufacturer refuses to give you a satisfactory replacement or a refund. You also may have the option of bypassing arbitration and going directly to court.

If you successfully pursue a lemon law claim, you may get a refund of what you paid for the car, as well as reimbursement for things like taxes, registration fees, and finance charges. If you choose, you may get a replacement car. Be sure that it is of comparable value to the lemon it is replacing, and that it satisfies you completely.

Q. Do lemon laws cover used cars?

A. That depends on state law. A growing number of states apply lemon laws to used cars, and in some states lemon laws may apply to car sales by both dealers and private sellers. Sometimes a state's lemon laws are related to state law regarding safety inspection stickers. A used car might pass the safety inspection and still be a lemon. Some state laws define "lemon" for used cars the same way they do for new cars: by using a formula that takes into account repair attempts and/or time spent in the shop.

Q. What if a used car fails inspection right after I buy it?

A. Depending on the applicable state **safety inspection sticker law,** you may have certain legal rights if a used car fails inspection right after you buy it. These safety sticker laws usually protect you if two conditions are met. First, the car must fail inspection within a certain period after the date of sale. Second, the repair costs must exceed a stated percentage of the purchase price. If both of these conditions are met, then you may have the right to cancel the deal within a certain period. You must return the car to the place of

---

▶ OTHER LAWS THAT PROTECT CAR BUYERS

A number of statutes besides lemon laws protect car buyers, including

- The federal Anti-Tampering Odometer Law, which prohibits acts that falsify odometer mileage readings.

- The federal Automobile Information Disclosure Act, which requires manufacturers and importers of new cars to affix a sticker, called the Monroney label, on the windshield or side window of the car. The Monroney label lists the car's base price; the options installed by the manufacturer, along with their suggested retail prices; how much the manufacturer has charged for transportation; and the car's fuel economy (miles per gallon). Only the buyer is allowed to remove the Monroney label.

Every state has enacted laws against unfair and deceptive acts and practices, which are a strong source of protection for buyers of new or used cars.

sale, even if it requires towing. If the seller offers to make repairs, you can decide whether to accept the offer or get your money back. Again, all of these details may vary, depending on state law.

Q. May I drive the car while I decide whether it is a lemon?

A. Yes, you may drive the car (if it is drivable), but be aware that if the car does indeed turn out to be a lemon, the law usually allows the seller to deduct a certain amount from your refund based on the miles you have driven. This applies to both new and used cars.

Warranties and the Uniform Commercial Code

Q. What is a warranty?

A. A **warranty** is a guarantee of a product's quality and performance. A warranty may be written or oral. The Uniform Commercial Code (UCC) provides for three kinds of warranties by a car seller: an express warranty, an implied warranty of merchantability, and an implied warranty of fitness for a particular purpose. A seller may also sell a car "as is,"

▶ **AS-IS SALES OF USED CARS**

When buying a used car, be alert to whether the sale is "as is." All states provide for implied warranties for used cars bought from dealers, unless the warranty is disclaimed specifically, and in writing, by the words "sold as is" or "sold with all faults."

---

which means it is not covered by any warranties.

Q. Can I see the warranty before I buy the car?

A. Likely, yes. The Magnuson-Moss Warranty Act is a federal law that applies to all cars manufactured after 1975. If you are buying the car from a dealer and the warranty is in writing, then the law gives you the right to see the car's warranty before you buy. The warranty information is more detailed than the Buyer's Guide, and includes an explanation of how to obtain warranty service. Any written warranty must have a conspicuous label indicating whether the warranty is limited or full. In addition, if a written warranty is provided, then implied warranties may not be disclaimed. The law also creates remedies for breach of warranty, including the right to sue for breach of express warranties, implied warranties, or a service contract. If you win, you can recover your lawyer's fees and your court costs. However, be careful—this law does not apply to as-is sales, or to cars bought from private sellers.

Q. What kind of warranty will my car come with?

A. Below is a brief overview of the types of warranties that can apply to a car purchase. For more information on warranties, see Chapter 12, "Contracts and Consumer Law."

Q. What about the seller's personal opinion of the car?

A. An opinion or recommendation does not form an express warranty. Sales talk—for example, "This car runs like a dream"—will not create an express warranty. However, statements such as "This car needs no repairs," or "This car has a V-8 engine," will.

TYPE OF WARRANTY	HOW IS IT CREATED?	MUST IT BE IN WRITING?	WHAT IS COVERED? WHAT ARE SOME OF THE LIMITATIONS?
Express Warranty	Whenever a seller gives any description, makes any declaration of fact, or makes any promise on which the buyer relies when deciding to make the purchase.	Can be made orally, in writing, or through an advertisement.	An express warranty only extends to those factors outlined by the seller.
Implied Warranty of Merchantability	Applies automatically if the seller is a merchant, such as a car dealer. Most people agree that the implied warranty of merchantability is part of a new car purchase. All states impose implied warranties for used cars bought from dealers, unless the warranty is disclaimed specifically, and in writing, by words like "as is" or "with all faults."	Does not need to be written or expressly stated—it exists due to the status of the seller.	An implied warranty of merchantability is a representation that the car will do what it is supposed to do. This includes a **quality guaranty,** meaning that the car should possess the level of quality needed to pass without objection in the trade; and a **fitness guaranty,** meaning that the car should serve the buyer's ordinary purposes. An implied warranty of merchantability may have limited duration.

TYPE OF WARRANTY	HOW IS IT CREATED?	MUST IT BE IN WRITING?	WHAT IS COVERED? WHAT ARE SOME OF THE LIMITATIONS?
Implied Warranty of Fitness for a Particular Purpose	An implied warranty of fitness for a particular purpose is created when you tell the seller that you need the vehicle for a special purpose, such as towing a trailer, and the seller recommends a specific vehicle. You buy it, relying on the seller's skill or judgment.	No.	The seller is guaranteeing that the vehicle can do what you told the seller you needed it to do.
"As-Is" Warranty	The bill of sale must state that you are buying the car "as is." This type of sale can involve either a dealer or a non-dealer.	Yes.	If you bought a car as is, it means that you accepted it with all its faults. Any post-sale defects are your problem. The implied warranty of merchantability does not automatically arise in as-is purchases. Some states do not permit as-is sales for used cars.

Q. What is the difference between a limited warranty and a full warranty?

A. A **full warranty** provides for a refund or free replacement part, including installation, if the dealer cannot fix a car or a part after a reasonable number of attempts. A dealer must replace the car or the part within a reasonable time. A full warranty applies to anyone who owns the car during the warranty period.

A **limited warranty** is any kind of warranty that is not a full warranty, meaning that at least one of the above promises is missing. Most car dealers do not give full warranties on the entire car, but may do so on a specific part, such as the battery. Most used-car warranties are limited.

Q. What if the seller gives me express and implied warranties that are inconsistent?

A. According to the Uniform Commercial Code, the parties' "mutual intention" decides which warranty takes priority. If there is no way to decide this, the following rules determine priority:

1. Specific or technical language usually wins over descriptive language that is inconsistent and general.
2. Express warranties override inconsistent implied warranties of merchantability.
3. Implied warranties of fitness for a particular purpose survive other inconsistent warranties.

Q. What are my options if the seller will not honor the warranties?

A. If you discover the defect within a short period of time after the purchase (e.g., one or two weeks), then you may be able to **reject** the car. To do this, you must provide the seller with specific information about what is wrong. You need only show that the car does not conform to the contract; the defect need not be major. If you want to reject the car, you should behave as if you are no longer the owner and should not drive it, except to return it. You may hold the car for the seller to reclaim, or you may return it yourself.

Unfortunately, sometimes the law regards the mere act of driving the car off the dealer's lot as acceptance, as long as you had a chance to inspect the car—even if you do not discover the defect for some time. Acceptance may also occur if you take possession of the car despite knowing about its defects. Acceptance does not mean that the seller no longer has to honor its warranties, but rather that you'll have to try to enforce them through negotiation, threat of suit, or actually filing suit.

Q. My car has defects, but I have already accepted the car and driven it home. What can I do?

A. Once you have accepted the car, you must continue to make your payments; for the time being, at least, you are considered the car's owner and are responsible for its costs. You may not reject a car that you've already accepted, unless you accepted it on the assumption that the seller would repair the defect within a reasonable period.

However, you may be able to revoke your acceptance. You must give the seller notice of the defect, and show that it substantially impairs the value of the car to you. **Revocation** involves a higher standard than rejection. Generally, the defect will have to be major. After revoking acceptance, you must act as if you have rejected the car. Leave the car in your driveway until the seller reclaims it, or return it yourself.

Q. May I get my money back if I reject the car or revoke acceptance?

A. You should be able to. If your written demand for a refund is denied, you will probably have to sue the seller. The seller has the right to deduct from your refund a specified amount per mile driven. If your rejection is found to be wrongful, the seller may recover damages against you.

Q. May I simply use lemon laws and consumer protection statutes instead of warranties?

A. You may use any of these options. But note that there are differences among these laws, and that they may provide for different remedies. If you are in the position to take legal action against a seller, consult a lawyer about what options you have under federal and state law.

Recalls

Q. What is a recall?

A. A **recall** is a request by a manufacturer that consumers return a defective product. The manufacturer then repairs or replaces the product.

Q. For cars, what defects does the recall process include?

A. Generally, recalls concern defects that affect the car's safety, cause the car to fall below federal safety standards, and are common to a particular type of car or equipment. The defect can be in performance, construction, components, or materials found in the car or in related equipment, such as child safety seats.

Q. Who pays for the recall—the manufacturer or the owner?

A. If the first buyer bought the car less than eight years ago, then the manufacturer must remedy the defect for free.

Q. Once recalled, what does the manufacturer do?

A. The manufacturer has the option of repairing the defect, replacing the car, or refunding the purchase price. If the manufacturer chooses to repair the defect, it must do so within a reasonable time. If the manufac-

---

▶ WATCH OUT FOR SECRET WARRANTIES

A **secret warranty** develops when a manufacturer knows that many cars have the same problem, but tells dealers to charge customers to repair the problem unless the customer complains. A secret warranty is not really a warranty at all—it is more like a deceptive practice in that it represents a manufacturer's unpublicized policy about making repairs to problem cars. Unlike a recall (see the discussion above), the manufacturer is not required to notify owners of the problem. A secret warranty hides what the manufacturer knows about the defect, and allows the manufacturer to make money from unsuspecting consumers who do not complain.

If you suspect that a warranty should have covered your car repair or that the defect is widespread, complain to the dealer. The dealer may fix your car without charging you. Follow up with a complaint to the consumer protection division of your state attorney general's office. If government officials find that a secret warranty exists, the manufacturer may be required to notify owners, to pay for repairs, and to reimburse those owners who have already paid to fix the problem.

turer does not opt to repair the defect, then the manufacturer may choose to replace the vehicle or refund the purchase price. When refunding the purchase price, a manufacturer may deduct a certain amount for depreciation (loss in value).

REMEMBER THIS

- State protections against unfair and deceptive acts and practices may provide a remedy if you think that a car dealer has illegally crossed the line between bluster and misrepresentation.

- Lemon laws may offer you protection if your new car does not run despite repeated efforts at repair.

- Your car may be covered by express or implied warranties, depending on the circumstances surrounding the purchase and the applicable law. If you bought the car "as is" or "with all faults," then the usual implied warranties do not apply.

- If the seller will not honor your warranties, you can try to reject the car or revoke your acceptance.

- If a recall is issued on your vehicle, you should be able to get your car repaired or replaced within a reasonable time.

INSPECTIONS AND REPAIRS

States and vehicle owners both help to ensure that our roads are safe. One way states try to see that vehicles meet minimum safety standards is by imposing an inspection sticker requirement. As an owner, at some stage you will need to make repairs on your car. You will need to decide whether to take your car to a dealer or to a local mechanic, or make repairs yourself.

This section reveals how to protect yourself against fraudulent practices, incompetence, and overcharging. Many states have statutes specifically governing car repairs, or have included car repairs in their unfair and deceptive practices statutes.

Inspections

Q. I just received a notice that the state wants to inspect my car. What exactly does the state inspect?

A. Inspection standards vary by state. Most states check the car's lights, brakes, windshield wipers, and horn. Some states also inspect the tires, the windows, the body, and the seat belts. Many also test the emission levels, taking into account the automobile's make, model, and age.

Q. What if I am buying a car? Should I be worried about an inspection?

A. A new car should pass inspection easily. Someone other than the seller should inspect a used car. In many states, a used car sale is not final until the car passes inspection. In other states, failing inspection cancels the sale at the buyer's option. Contact your state department of motor vehicles for further information.

Q. Where do I get my car inspected?

A. States often authorize certain private repair shops and car dealers to make inspections. Some states have government-operated inspection stations.

Q. What will happen if my car does not pass the state's safety inspection?

A. The rules vary. You may get a "failed" sticker attached to your windshield. You may have a grace period that allows you to make repairs or to get your car off the road. If you fail to comply, you could face fines and other penalties.

Repairs

Q. Where should I take my car for repairs?

A. You can take your car to a dealer, which may be required under the terms of the warranty. Or you could take it to an independent garage or a franchise operation specializing in specific repairs. You could even try to repair it yourself. Each option has its advantages and disadvantages. If your car is under warranty, make sure that you understand its terms. Some warranties include language requiring that a dealer make repairs. If you take the car to another mechanic or try to make repairs yourself, you may invalidate the warranty.

In lieu of a manufacturer's warranties, you may have warranties from the shop that performed repairs on your car. If the repair shop makes an express warranty, you are protected as long as you abide by the terms of the warranty. Some state courts have held that the implied warranty of merchantability covers car repairs.

Q. Isn't it always best to take my car to a dealer?

A. Dealers may charge more. Yet a dealer may be more familiar with your car than other repair shops, and may have newer and better equipment with which to service it. Manufacturers want to ensure that dealerships run quality repair operations, so they invest in training mechanics.

> ► **MECHANIC QUALIFICATIONS**
>
> To help determine whether a mechanic is qualified, ask if he or she has been certified by the National Institute for Automotive Service Excellence (ASE). A certified mechanic has taken one or more written tests in areas such as engine repair and electrical systems. If a mechanic passes all of the tested areas, then the ASE will certify him or her as a General Automobile Mechanic.
>
> Of course, certification is not everything. Often you can discover the best mechanics from recommendations and word of mouth.

Q. Can I bring my car to a service station?

A. This is a good option for non-warranty work if the mechanics have adequate training and test equipment. Parts might cost more, but labor might be less expensive than dealer repairs. If you regularly use a particular service station, the mechanics might get to know your car and be able to spot potential problems early.

Q. What about highly advertised repair chains?

A. Specialty shops may repair one part of a car, such as brakes or mufflers. Some repair franchises advertise complete car care services. Sheer size and volume means lower costs than dealers and independent mechanics. If you know what repairs your car needs, franchise shops can be a good deal.

Q. Must I receive a cost estimate for the repairs before work actually begins?

A. Getting a cost estimate is always a good idea, and it may be required in some states. Some states may provide that the final cost of repairs cannot exceed a certain percentage or dollar value of the original estimate, unless the customer consents. Repair shops generally have the right to charge for making estimates, but you must receive advance notice.

Q. I am not happy with how much the repairs ended up costing. Can I simply not pay?

A. In most states, if you refuse to pay for completed repairs, the shop may keep your car. For example, if you have authorized extensive work, but decide that the car isn't worth that much after the shop completes the work, and you refuse to pay, then the shop obtains a mechanic's lien on your car. The car's actual value, and the actual cost of the repairs, does not matter. If you abandon your car in this manner, the mechanic may ultimately sell your car so that it can recover as much of the cost of repairs as possible. In states that require written estimates and repair authorization, the shop does not obtain a mechanic's lien if it does not comply with these requirements. Of course, if you do pay for the repairs, the repair shop must return your car.

Q. What protections does the law provide to stop repair shops from ripping me off?

A. Most protections are found in your state's unfair and deceptive practices statutes. The unfair and deceptive practices statutes usually require price estimates and repair orders. Many states give you the right to keep or ex-

---

▶ **REPAIR CONTRACT**

The repair contract, often called the **repair order,** is essential to a satisfactory repair job. The repair order describes the work to be done and, once signed, creates a contract authorizing the mechanic to make the described repairs.

The repair order should contain

- the make, model, and year of your car;
- the repair date;
- the car's mileage;
- an accurate description of the problem;
- a list of parts to be used and their cost;
- the amount of labor estimated to be needed (i.e., the time to be spent fixing your car);
- the rate to be charged, either per hour or as a flat rate; and
- your name, address, and telephone number.

amine replaced parts, and require repair shops to prepare a detailed invoice, which must state the labor and parts supplied, warranty work done, guarantees, and installation of any used or rebuilt parts. In some states, you may have the right to same-day repairs, unless you agree to a longer period or the delay is beyond the shop's control. Shoddy repair work must be corrected at no charge, especially in states where the implied warranty of merchantability has been extended to repair work. Finally, many states require repair shops to post price lists conspicuously. If you think a repair shop has intentionally cheated you, you should notify your state attorney general's office and call your lawyer to discuss your options.

Q. I took my car in to get the breaks repaired, but the mechanic made repairs I didn't authorize. What can I do?

A. First, you may wish to complain to your state attorney general's office, the local branch of the Better Business Bureau, or even to the local chamber of commerce. If you are still not satisfied, you may sue—for example, if the shop made unnecessary repairs or reinstalled the original part rather

---

▶ **UNCONDITIONAL GUARANTEES**

Beware of "unconditional" guarantees offered by many franchise repair shops. There are always some limitations on written guarantees. As with any contract or document, be sure to read the fine print. The warranty may include special procedures that you are required to follow in order to obtain the benefits of the warranty.

---

than a replacement. If the shop tried its best to correct a fault by fixing something that was broken, even though it was not the problem's ultimate cause, you may simply want to pay the shop and be done with it.

Service Contracts

Q. What is a service contract?

A. A **service contract** is a contract for car repair services and maintenance for a set period of time. Manufacturers, insurance companies, and car dealers offer service contracts.

▶ **SERVICE CONTRACTS VERSUS WARRANTIES**

Unlike a warranty, a service contract may not come from the manufacturer. Service contracts are optional and expensive, and the coverage often overlaps with warranty protection. A service contract often contains more limitations and exclusions than a warranty, may require you to pay a deductible fee, and might not cover all parts and labor or routine maintenance. If a service contract is available on a used car, the appropriate box must be checked on the Buyer's Guide. Finally, if you believe that your service contract has been breached, you may be able to sue and possibly recover lawyer's fees and court costs, as well as damages.

Like all contracts, you should read a service contract carefully and understand what it says before you sign.

Q. Should I purchase a service contract on my automobile right away?

A. If you buy one at all, you should consider waiting until your warranty period expires. After all, why pay for duplicate coverage? Be sure to look out for exclusions and exceptions in the service contract, and be sure to understand what the contract really covers.

REMEMBER THIS

- You may invalidate a warranty if you do not take the car to the dealer for repairs; however, if the warranty is not an issue, you might save money by taking the car to a trusted mechanic.

- Be sure to get a written repair order that contains all the key information pertaining to the repair. Get an estimate in advance.

- If you will not or cannot pay your mechanics, they have a right to hold your car until you pay, or sell it to recover their costs after a given time period.

- Remember that a warranty and a service contract are two different things.

- Read the fine print on any service contract, and be wary of exclusions.

YOUR AUTOMOBILE AND THE POLICE

No one likes to think about the prospect of being pulled over by the police. The law in this area changes all the time, so if you

have a serious legal issue, you should consult a lawyer without delay.

This section covers a few basics that may prove helpful if you and your car have an encounter with the police.

The Stop

Q. An officer is signaling me to pull over. What should I do?

A. Pull over to the side of the road as quickly and safely as possible. Remain in your vehicle until the officer directs you otherwise. Get ready to produce your license, registration, and proof of insurance. Sit quietly and keep your hands in view, so the officer does not think that you may be reaching for a weapon.

Q. The officer is at my window. Now what?

A. Stay composed and politely ask why you were stopped. If you have any doubt that you were stopped by a real police officer—if, for example, you were pulled over by an unmarked vehicle—politely ask to see the officer's photo identification, not just his or her badge.

The Search

Q. Suppose the officer wants to search my car?

A. Ask why the officer wants to conduct a search. If you have nothing to hide, you could save time and effort if you simply let the search proceed. If you don't want the search to proceed, you should state clearly that you do not consent. Denying a search is not an admission of guilt. Ask courteously whether the officer has a search warrant or if you are under arrest. If the officer replies that you are under arrest, ask for an explanation.

▶ PROBABLE CAUSE

In the context of vehicle searches, probable cause is a reasonable basis for an officer to believe that a vehicle contains incriminating evidence.

Usually, the officer is permitted to conduct the search only if

- you consent;
- the officer has **probable cause** to believe that the vehicle contains incriminating evidence; or
- the officer reasonably believes that he must search the vehicle for his or her own protection.

Q. What if the officer insists on searching my car?

A. Don't interfere. You can always challenge the legitimacy of the search later in court.

Q. Can the police legitimately search my vehicle without a warrant?

A. That depends on the circumstances. A key factor is whether you've been arrested. For example, the police usually would not have the right to search your automobile when you are stopped only for a minor traffic offense such as speeding. However, if the violation requires that you be taken into custody (for example, if you were driving under the influence or with a suspended license), then the search generally would be permitted.

Even when an arrest is not involved, the police have more latitude to search a vehicle than to search a home. The U.S. Supreme Court recognizes an automobile exception to the Fourth Amendment's protection against warrantless searches. The rationale for permitting warrantless searches of cars is that the mobility of automobiles would allow drivers to escape with incriminating evidence in the time it would take police to secure a search warrant. The Court has held that a person expects less privacy in an automobile than at home.

The chart on page 508 outlines common examples of warrantless vehicle searches that have been presented to the courts.

Q. May the police search my car without a warrant after they have impounded it?

A. The police do not need a warrant to undertake a routine inventory of an impounded vehicle. The reason is that such an inventory protects the driver's possessions against theft, and also protects the police against claims of lost or stolen property. Such an inventory also protects the holding facility from dangerous materials that may be in the impounded vehicle, and may aid in the identification of the arrested person.

Q. Suppose the officer sees a packet of marijuana on the backseat?

A. Again, the law is always changing. If the police can see evidence readily from a place in which they have a right to be, then the law generally does not consider it a search. Instead, this constitutes a plain-view seizure. As long as the officer has a legitimate reason to be standing by the car, and as long as the officer easily sees what he or she has probable cause to believe is evidence of a crime, then the officer can make the seizure. The officer probably could also conduct a warrantless search of the rest of the passenger compartment of the vehicle, and possibly the trunk (if probable cause exists to believe the trunk may contain evidence).

TYPE OF SEARCH	DETAILS	ALLOWED WITHOUT A WARRANT?
Contraband search	When the police search a vehicle that they have probable cause to believe contains contraband (meaning controlled or banned substances and weapons).	Yes—the Supreme Court has declared that police do not need to obtain a search warrant for a contraband search.
Passenger search	When the police search the passenger's belongings.	Yes—if the belongings could contain the object the police are searching for.
Drug checkpoints	When the police set up road checkpoints for the primary purpose of intercepting narcotics.	No—the Supreme Court has said that without some individual suspicion, such stops violate the Constitution.
Glove compartment search	When the police officer searches the glove compartment of your vehicle.	Maybe. Generally, the police may search the immediate area "under the driver's command," which includes the glove compartment. Some state constitutions offer greater protections.
Container search	When the police search a closed container in your car.	Yes—if you are under arrest, the police do not need a warrant to search any container in your car. If you are not under arrest, the police can search a container that might reasonably contain evidence of a crime for which the officer had probable cause to search the vehicle in the first place. This means, if the police are looking for a large shotgun, they can't search a small medicine container, but can search a large box.

Q. What about passengers? Do they have the same rights as a driver?

A. Yes. The Supreme Court has ruled that a passenger has the same rights as a driver. This means that if a search would have violated a driver's constitutional rights, then it will be considered a violation of the passenger's rights and likely won't be admitted during a criminal trial (see Chapter 2 for more information about the admissibility of illegally seized evidence).

Roadblocks

Q. What is a roadblock?

A. A roadblock is a tool used by law enforcement to enforce driving and other criminal laws. Roadblocks usually involve police officers limiting a driver's ability to travel on an otherwise open road. A driver must go through the block and submit to a search before continuing.

Q. What are the constitutional constraints on roadblocks?

A. The U.S. Supreme Court has ruled that a search or seizure (such as at a checkpoint on the road) is unreasonable under the Fourth Amendment unless there is individualized suspicion of wrongdoing—that is, unless the police have a particular reason to pull a particular driver over—but there are a limited number of exceptions. For example, the Court has upheld brief, suspicionless seizures at a fixed checkpoint designed to intercept illegal aliens, and at a sobriety checkpoint aimed at removing drunk drivers from the road. The Court has also suggested that a similar roadblock to verify driver's licenses and registrations would be permissible to serve a highway safety interest.

Q. So the police can pull me over in a roadblock and demand to check my license and registration?

A. Yes, under certain circumstances. The U.S. Supreme Court has said that such roadblocks do not constitute an unreasonable search as long as police stop all the cars passing through the roadblock or follow some neutral policy, such as stopping every fourth car. The police can't single out your car unless they have a suspicion that you don't have your driver's license, that your vehicle is unregistered, or that you or your car may be seized for violating the law.

Q. And is it legal to design a roadblock to catch drunk drivers?

A. Yes, provided the selection of vehicles to be stopped is not arbitrary and the inconvenience to drivers is minimized. Courts have upheld such roadblocks as constitutional. In some states, the prosecution must show that a roadblock is the least intrusive way to enforce drunk-driving laws. Some states require that the ranking police officer who supervised a roadblock testify at the offender's trial.

Q. What about a roadblock set up at an international border?

A. The Supreme Court has held that roadblocks at borders are permissible on the basis of immigration and national-security concerns.

Drunk Driving

Q. I have heard of DUIs, DWIs, and OUIs. How are they different?

A. Different states call the offense of drunk driving by different names. These include **driving under the influence** (**DUI**), **driving**

while intoxicated (DWI), and **operating under the influence (OUI)**.

The offense of OUI, for example, usually does not require that the vehicle be in motion. In most states, a person may be charged with OUI if he or she is in actual physical control. Actual physical control may be shown when the person is seated in the driver's seat, in possession of the ignition key, and capable of starting the motor.

Q. What does "drunk driving" mean?

A. The elements of the basic offense vary by state. However, the Uniform Vehicle Code requires proof that the person is under the influence of alcohol or drugs. Depending on the controlling law, "being under the influence" could refer to any substance that impairs your ability to drive.

Most states agree that a person is **under the influence** if he or she has a diminished ability, either physically or mentally, to exercise clear judgment and to operate a vehicle with safety. The person must be driving or in actual physical control of a vehicle. Some states' legislations require prosecutors to prove that the person was driving "on a public highway" or was drinking "intoxicating liquor."

Q. How does the prosecution prove that a person was drunk driving?

A. The prosecution relies heavily, sometimes solely, on the arresting officer's testimony about the defendant's operation of the vehicle and the defendant's behavior (such as appearance, speech, and an odor of alcohol). The prosecution also relies on the results of field sobriety tests and chemical tests (breath, blood, or urine). For example, the arresting officer might give evidence that "the car was weaving over the center line of the highway," or that "the driver had slurred speech, heavy odor of alcohol, glassy bloodshot eyes, and could not walk straight."

Q. What are field sobriety tests?

A. Every police department has its own preferred tests. Police may ask you to stand on one foot for a specified amount of time, or to walk in a straight line. Or they may ask you to touch your nose with your index finger with your eyes closed and head back, and have you stare at a flashlight or a pen so that the officer can see how your eyes respond.

If you do not perform these field sobriety tests satisfactorily, the police will ask you to submit to a scientific test that shows how much (if any) alcohol is in your body. Many states will offer you one of three choices: provide a blood sample, provide a urine sample, or take a Breathalyzer test. The Breathalyzer test involves blowing into a balloon attached to a machine that measures the percentage of alcohol in your breath.

Q. Do I have to take field sobriety tests if the police ask me to?

A. In most states, the police are not allowed to force you to take these tests. However, depending on the law in your state, they might use your refusal as evidence against you in court. Also, in many states, refusal to submit to such tests will result in automatic suspension or revocation of your driver's license.

Q. Suppose I fail the tests?

A. It's not like school; you can't promise to study harder next time. However, a skilled lawyer may argue that the police administered the tests improperly, or that the tests were inaccurate for some reason. In addition, a lawyer may present qualifying evidence—for instance, if a chronic knee injury prevents you from supporting your weight on one foot, then your lawyer might cite this as a reason for your failure of the field sobriety test.

Q. How does a breath-testing device work?

A. A person blows into a small machine, which estimates the percentage of alcohol in the person's blood. The law fixes a standard measure, over which a person is deemed to be intoxicated. This measure might be 0.10 (one-tenth of 1 percent blood-alcohol concentration) or 0.08, depending on the state. The law often entitles the defendant to two breath tests that must measure within 0.02 (or some other specified percentage) of each other.

Q. If my test result is under 0.08 or 0.10, will the charge against me be dismissed?

A. Not necessarily. Even if you have a blood-alcohol level less than the prohibited level of 0.08 or 0.10, you may still be considered impaired. The prosecutor may decide to proceed to trial, in which event the officer's testimony as to impairment will be given as evidence, in addition to the breath test results.

Q. If the breath-testing device hits 0.10, am I in serious trouble?

A. Probably, but a lawyer may be able to show that the machine's operator received inadequate training, that the operator's certification had lapsed, or that the operator did not maintain the machine well. Other factors may also affect the breath-testing device's reading, and may be established through an expert witness. Diabetics, for example, have high levels of ketone (a naturally occurring chemical) in their bodies, which could yield false results when they are tested. In most cases, however, the result of a breath test will be allowed into evidence.

Q. If I am asked to take a test, which one should I take? A blood test or a Breathalyzer test?

A. There is no hard-and-fast answer to that question. The law varies by state and is always subject to change. If you find yourself in this situation, you should consult a lawyer if you are allowed to call one.

Unless you are certain that you have had less than three or four drinks in the past hour, or less than five drinks in the past several hours, common wisdom holds that it is a good idea to refuse the tests. It generally is more difficult to convict a driver of drunk driving if no chemical tests are taken.

On the other hand, if you refuse, then your driver's license will probably be suspended automatically for a long period of time. In some states, for example, it will be suspended for six months if you refuse to take a test, but only three months if you take and fail the test (if you are a first offender). In other states, the suspension period might be the same, but you will have to do several days of jail time if you refuse to take the test.

Q. May I change my mind after declining to take a blood or breath test?

A. You have no right to change your mind once you have refused a blood test. Even if you subsequently have a change of heart and agree to a test, your license can still be suspended on the basis of your initial refusal. It is a good idea to call a lawyer while you are thinking over a decision, if the police allow you to do so. However, in most states you will have to decide whether to submit to the test fairly soon after being asked to do so.

Q. What kind of penalty am I likely to get for drunk driving?

A. Consult a lawyer in your state, because penalties vary widely and depend on several factors, such as whether you are a repeat offender. A number of states require minimum penalties for a first-time offender, which might involve enrollment in an alcohol treatment program and a license suspension of a month or several months. A second-time offender might suffer a two-year license suspension or revocation of license. Some states impound the license plates or vehicles of habitual drunk drivers, and others revoke the licenses of habitual offenders.

Jail terms for first offenders are more common than they used to be. Community service and enrollment in mandatory alcohol programs, as well as heavy fines, are regularly doled out by courts in various combinations as a result of changing public perceptions about drunk driving.

Q. Can a restaurant get in trouble if a patron was drinking at the restaurant, then leaves and gets into an accident?

A. Yes. In civil courts throughout the country, "dramshop" cases and "social host" cases are gaining wider acceptance, and are expanding defendants' potential liability for negligence. These cases hold taverns and restaurants legally responsible for providing alcohol to intoxicated persons if they have knowledge that the person is likely to drive, and if the driver goes on to have an accident.

Licensing, License Suspension, and Revocation

Q. What do I need to do to get a driver's license?

A. The exact requirements vary, but you will likely need to

- be a certain age (generally sixteen or seventeen);
- pass a behind-the-wheel driving test;
- pass a written test on the rules of the road;
- show proof of having taken a driver's-education class; and
- show identification (usually a Social Security card, birth certification, and/or other state identification).

Q. I am moving to a different state. Will I need to get a new driver's license?

A. Yes. If you are permanently moving to another state, you will need to get a driver's license with your new state's licensing authority (usually the Department of Motor Vehicles, or DMV). You may be required to take a written or driving test. Check with your new state's DMV for the exact requirements and time frame.

Q. Must I take another examination in order to renew my license?

A. Some states permit renewal by mail. Most require a vision test and, in some instances, a new photograph for renewal. A few require a written test. Prerequisites for license renewal could include a vision test, a written test, a thumbprint, a signature, and a photograph. Some states impose additional requirements if a driver has amassed a certain number of traffic convictions, or if the driver is of a certain age or has certain physical problems. Some states require a road test for "elderly" drivers (those over a specific age that is set by state law) prior to renewal.

Q. May a physical or mental affliction prevent me from driving legally?

A. Yes. A few states require doctors to report physical and mental disorders of patients that could affect driver safety.

Q. Suppose the police stop me and I've left my license at home?

A. Driving a motor vehicle on a public street or highway without a license is an offense in most states. Often, a person accused of driving without a license might be able to avoid conviction if he or she is able to produce a license in court that was valid at the time of the stop.

Q. What conduct could lead to license suspension?

A. Grounds for suspension vary by state. A local lawyer will be able to give you details about your state laws. Refusal to submit to a field sobriety or Breathalyzer test will probably result in suspension.

Q. What conduct could lead to license revocation?

A. Your license may be revoked for violating specific laws, such as those pertaining to habitual reckless driving, drunken driving, nonpayment of your motor vehicle excise tax, using a motor vehicle to commit a felony, or fleeing from or eluding the police.

Q. Am I entitled to notice and a hearing before the state revokes my license?

A. Barring an emergency, due process under the Fourteenth Amendment generally requires

▶ THE DIFFERENCE BETWEEN LICENSE SUSPENSION, CANCELLATION, AND REVOCATION

Suspension involves the temporary withdrawal of your privilege to drive. The state may restore your driving privileges after a designated time period and payment of a fee. You may also be required to remedy the cause of the suspension; for example, by purchasing auto insurance.

License cancellation involves voluntarily giving up your driving privilege without penalty. Cancellation allows you to reapply for a license immediately.

Revocation aims both to discipline the driver and protect the public. Revocation involuntarily ends your driving privilege. Revocation of your license applies for a minimum period set by law, until you become eligible to apply for a new license. The state may conduct a reinstatement hearing and you may have to retake a driver's license examination.

notice and a chance to be heard before the state terminates a person's license privileges. However, for certain serious offenses, the state may simply rely on the court conviction to revoke the person's license without the need for any hearing.

Q. What if the state charges me with an offense that requires a license suspension?

A. Unless another law says otherwise, no notice is necessary before a state may suspend your license under the mandatory provisions of a law. As a driver, you are presumed to know the law.

Q. If the state does notify me, what will the notice say?

A. The time, place, and purpose of the hearing should appear on the notice of the hearing to suspend or revoke your license.

▶ THE PERILS OF DRIVING WITH A SUSPENDED OR REVOKED LICENSE

If you are stopped while driving with a suspended or revoked license, you are likely to be arrested. At a minimum, the offense is usually a serious misdemeanor that carries with it a stiff fine and possibly some time in jail. Some states consider it a felony, in which case the offender could end up in state prison or performing a significant amount of community service, particularly if the suspensions or revocation was based upon a DUI.

Q. Does the law entitle me to a jury trial?

A. No. A suspension/revocation hearing is an administrative, not judicial, proceeding. However, you are entitled to confront and cross-examine witnesses. It is a good idea to have a lawyer represent you at the hearing.

Q. State A suspended/revoked my license, but I have a valid license in State B. Can I still drive in State A?

A. Consult your lawyer if you find yourself in this situation. Under the law of some states, a valid driver's license from another jurisdiction does not enable you to drive on the highways of a state that has cancelled, suspended, or revoked your license. However, other states have held that a license properly issued by a foreign state under the Driver's License Compact ends the suspension or revocation of a motorist's original license.

Seat Belt Laws

Q. My kids hate wearing seat belts. Must they wear them?

A. All fifty states and the District of Columbia require children to be restrained while riding in motor vehicles. State laws vary, however, regarding the ages of children that are subject to the child restraint law.

Q. Do I have to wear a seat belt?

A. It depends where you live and perhaps where you sit in the car; you may only be required to wear belts if you are in the front seat.

Q. May I still recover payment for my injuries if I am in an accident and am not wearing my seat belt?

A. Most states reject the so-called seat belt defense, and will not accept evidence that plaintiffs did not buckle up as proof that they were negligent in a way that contributed to the injuries. In some jurisdictions, however, evidence of the plaintiff's failure to use a seat belt may reduce the amount of damages awarded to the plaintiff.

Speeding and Other Offenses

Q. I got stuck in a speed trap. What can I do about it?

A. If the speed limit was clearly marked and you were exceeding it, you should grit your teeth and pay the fine. If you think you've been unfairly prosecuted, you might report the trap to your auto club or state authorities to spare other drivers the same expense.

Q. I was stopped for speeding by a radar gun. Do those things stand up in court?

A. Courts today regularly accept the ability of radar to measure speeds accurately. That doesn't mean that you can't try to prove the particular radar gun in your case was poorly maintained, or that its operator misread the results or was inadequately trained, but you may face an uphill fight.

Q. Aren't radar detector devices the best way to avoid speed traps and radar guns?

A. Radar detector devices alert the driver to radar and speed guns, allowing the driver to slow down before he or she is detected exceeding the speed limit. A few states have declared radar detectors illegal for all vehicles, but in general the laws single out "commercial" vehicles over ten thousand pounds (i.e., trucks). Of course, your best and safest bet to avoid a speeding ticket is to obey speed limits.

Q. What are the elements of a speeding charge?

A. Regardless of the circumstances, it is a violation to exceed a fixed maximum speed limit at any time. However, some states allow drivers to justify the speed at which they were driving by considering traffic and road conditions and visibility.

Q. Are there any excuses I can offer that might prevent a police officer from writing up a speeding ticket?

A. If you are taking a pregnant or sick person to the hospital, you might be spared a citation, and you might even get a police escort to the hospital. Sometimes a court emergency (be sure to display the court papers to the officer) or a broken speedometer (be prepared to give the officer a test ride) may succeed. However, this excuse should be true—the last thing you want is to get caught lying to a police officer.

Q. What kind of information is included on a traffic ticket?

A. The color, model, and registration of your vehicle, and the date, time, and place of the alleged offense are provided on the ticket. You will probably also find the specific violation with which you have been charged, the officer's name and badge number, the fine schedule, and a notice of your ability to have a hearing to contest the ticket. Each jurisdiction has its own form. If the officer includes incorrect information in the ticket, such mistakes may provide you with a defense.

Q. I was charged with reckless driving—what exactly is this? How is it different from a simple speeding ticket?

A. Increasingly, states are following the Uniform Vehicle Code, which defines **reckless**

driving as "willful or wanton disregard for the safety of persons or property." Essentially, the prosecution must show that the driver was indifferent to the probable harmful results of his or her driving, and that the driver should have realized that such driving posed a hazard.

REMEMBER THIS

- License renewal laws vary by state, and the requirements may be different depending on your age, driving record, and other factors. Contact your state department of motor vehicles to see what you have to do.

- Criminal and traffic laws affecting motorists vary from state to state, but a little common sense goes a long way. Using care and keeping a wary eye on the speedometer will help you avoid trouble.

- Drunk driving is very serious business, and you should consult a lawyer if you face charges on this score.

- Driving on a suspended or revoked license is likely to get you arrested.

ACCIDENTS AND INSURANCE

This section is a guide to the major issues concerning accidents and insurance. The possibility that you will have an accident is one reason why insurance is so important. As with every topic in this chapter, laws and insurance regulations vary from place to place, so you should consult a lawyer if you need to understand the legal repercussions of a serious matter.

Accidents

Q. If I am in an accident, do I have to worry about civil law? Criminal law? Both?

A. The annoying answer is, "It depends." In some accidents, especially fender benders, it's likely that no one will get a ticket or face any other criminal problem. If insurance handles any property damage and no lawsuit is filed, then you won't have to worry about civil law, either.

But let's say the accident is more serious and the police charge at least one of the drivers with an offense. That criminal charge could mean a fine or jail time for the offender. But in the same case, a personal injury lawsuit for negligent driving could be filed, and this civil lawsuit could lead to money damages being paid by one driver to the other (or others).

Chapter 6, "Personal Injury," discusses the civil law on automobile collisions (including personal injury lawsuits arising from auto collisions) in more detail.

Q. According to the law, how safely must I drive?

A. You have to use reasonable care under the circumstances. **Negligence**—the failure to exercise reasonable care—is the most common basis for liability. Ordinary negligence is not a crime.

However, if your driving is really bad, to the extent that it is willful or wanton, then you may be guilty of reckless driving, which is a crime.

Q. Do I need to exercise more care toward pedestrians and passengers than toward other drivers?

A. No. The same standard applies to pedestrians, passengers, and other drivers. Motorists must exercise reasonable care under the circumstances toward pedestrians. In practical terms, this means keeping a careful lookout for pedestrians, and maintaining control over your vehicle to avoid injuring them. You must also sound your horn to warn of your approach when you believe that a pedestrian is unaware of danger. In some states, you must stop if you see a pedestrian anywhere in a crosswalk. The law does not, however, expect you to anticipate a pedestrian darting out into the roadway.

You must also exercise reasonable care under the circumstances toward passengers, although this may change based on your passengers' relationship to you. You will not be liable if a passenger sustains injury through no fault of your own.

Q. To what standard of care will I be held if someone else is driving my car, and I am a passenger?

A. Some states will assume you still have "control" over the vehicle. Other states require the owner to take steps to stop the negligent driving as soon as the owner becomes aware of it. In other words, if you are the owner of a car, you may be liable for the way in which another person drives it.

Q. Am I legally responsible even if I am not in the car when an accident occurs?

A. Possibly. You still might be liable for property damage, injuries, and even death if you permit someone else to operate your defective vehicle, or if you allow an inexperienced, habitually intoxicated, or otherwise incompetent person to drive your car. The law calls this **negligent entrustment.**

Q. What if my child is driving my car and an accident occurs?

A. Some jurisdictions recognize the **family purpose doctrine,** under which the "head" of the family who maintains a car for general family use may be held liable for the negligent driving of a family member who was authorized to use the vehicle.

Q. Should I contact a lawyer after an accident? What should I tell the lawyer?

A. If you are filing a lawsuit against another driver, you will need to hire your own lawyer. If the other driver is suing you, your insurance company may provide a lawyer for you.

If you do file suit, you will need to supply information to your lawyer about

- your family status and employment situation;
- the accident, including witnesses' names and addresses;
- your injuries; and
- your out-of-pocket expenses, such as doctors' bills, ambulance and hospital costs, automobile repairs, rental car costs, and any lost income.

Chapter 1, "When and How to Use a Lawyer," provides more information about hiring a lawyer.

Q. What might happen if I believe an accident is at least partly my fault?

A. At the accident scene, do not take responsibility or say you are at fault. You may not be in the best position to determine how an accident happened. Defective equipment in your vehicle, a malfunctioning traffic signal, or another driver's intoxication are among the many possible causes of the accident. If you accept blame and apologize to the other driver, your statements may be used as evidence against you at trial. Leave it to the judge or the jury to decide who is at fault.

Q. If the accident is partly my fault, may I still receive payment for my injuries?

A. The answer depends on whether you live in a contributory negligence, comparative negligence, or no-fault jurisdiction. These legal standards set out varying rules for determining fault in a collision.

Q. I have heard that I live in a "no-fault" state. What does this mean?

A. Negligence law for auto collisions exists in no-fault states, but it is limited in its application. No-fault laws essentially provide (1) that you must purchase a minimum amount of no-fault insurance in order to drive; and (2) that if you are injured, you will be compensated by your own insurance carrier for your economic losses up to a specified level, regardless of who was at fault in the accident. In other words, the state law regarding negligence in auto collision cases is modified in most instances, though lawsuits alleging negligence might be filed in certain circumstances, such as in the case of economic

---

▶ WHAT YOU SHOULD DO IF YOU HAVE AN ACCIDENT

If you are involved in an accident, try to keep these things in mind:

- Get out of the way. Try to park on the shoulder of the road, and do not obstruct traffic. Use your car's flashers or flares to warn approaching motorists of the accident.
- If asked, give the other driver your name, address, vehicle registration certificate, and proof of insurance.
- Get the same information from the other driver.
- Identify yourself to any police officers who respond to the scene, and show your license and proof of insurance if asked. Also, get the names and badge numbers of the police officers.
- Write down the names and addresses of all passengers and possible witnesses.
- If you have a camera handy, photograph the damaged cars, skid marks, and the accident scene.
- Draw a diagram of the accident and make notes about the weather and the lighting and road conditions.
- Do not make any statements about who was at fault. Do not admit blame to other parties or witnesses.
- If you sustained any injuries, seek medical attention promptly.
- As soon as possible after the accident, notify your insurance company.
- Consult a lawyer if you intend to file suit.

losses beyond a certain level, injuries that included some specified serious conditions such as permanent disfigurement, and property damage to your vehicle.

Q. What does "leaving the scene of an accident" mean?

A. Generally, drivers of vehicles involved in an accident in which personal injury or property damage occurs must stop and identify themselves and their vehicles. Drivers must also notify police, and help any injured persons. Even if the driver has a reason for leaving the scene or doesn't own the vehicle, he or she can still be liable. If you think you might have committed this offense, consult a lawyer about your state's criminal law.

Q. What are the defenses to such a charge?

A. As a rule, it is a complete defense if no personal injury or property damage resulted from the accident, or if you had no knowledge that an accident had occurred. On the other hand, claiming that you left intending to drive directly to the police station to report the accident probably would not be a good defense.

Q. If I collide with a parked car, am I required to do anything?

A. The law requires you to try to find the owner. Alternatively, you are permitted to attach a written note to the parked car identifying yourself and your vehicle. You also should notify the police.

Q. Must I tell the police if I am in an accident?

A. Alert the police immediately if someone is hurt or killed. Generally, if the accident involves a death, personal injury, or property damage above a specific amount set by state law, then you must notify the police and file a written accident report immediately or within a short time. Often, states require you to file the report with the bureau of motor vehicles or a similar state authority. Some states do not require you to report an accident if no one is injured or if property damage is less than a certain dollar amount. Other jurisdictions require a report only if no police officer responded to the accident scene.

Failure to file a written report is a misdemeanor in most states. Some states may suspend your driver's license until you file the report. Remember: by completing an accident report, you are verifying that the report contains a recital of all important facts known to you. Providing false information in a written report is illegal.

Insurance

Q. What is auto insurance?

A. Auto insurance protects you against financial loss in the event of an accident. Coverage varies by policy, but typically protects you against property damage to your vehicle, liability for injuries you cause to other people and property, and medical expenses that you or your passengers may incur.

Q. Am I legally required to have insurance?

A. Probably. Almost all states require you to buy insurance, though the states vary in the minimum level of coverage set by law for liability insurance. Some states require you to show proof of financial responsibility if you choose not to purchase insurance.

Q. What are "compulsory insurance" statutes?

A. Compulsory insurance statutes mandate that drivers file proof of insurance as a condition of receiving their vehicle registration. Many states require drivers to purchase certain insurance options, such as **collision**, which pays you for damage to your car irrespective of who was at fault, and **comprehensive**, which pays you for damage to your car caused by theft, fire, and vandalism.

Q. Does the lender who made the loan to buy my car have a say in the amount of insurance I buy?

A. Possibly. Many states allow lenders to protect their collateral by requiring you to purchase insurance options such as collision and comprehensive.

Q. What happens if I don't have insurance?

A. You may be asked to show proof of insurance any time police stop you on the road, and you may be sent to court if you don't have it. Some states impose minimum fines, and you'll also have to pay court costs. The court will then mandate that you get the insurance you should have had in the first place. If you're a repeat offender, the fine will be higher and you may lose your car and have your license suspended.

But the worst consequence, by far, is that you'll have no coverage if you're in an accident and cause damages. You could lose everything you've worked for, including your house.

Q. May my insurance agent force me to pay my premium in a lump sum?

A. Check your particular state's law. Some states limit the amount an agent may demand before renewing your insurance to a certain percentage of the premium. If you have not

> ## ▶ WHAT IS A DEDUCTIBLE?
>
> A **deductible** is the amount that you agree to pay if and when you make a claim. The higher the deductible you choose, the lower your annual insurance premium. But if you select a high deductible, then you'll need more cash on hand if you have an accident.

paid your premium payments in the recent past, however, an insurance agent may legally ask you to pay your entire premium before renewing your policy.

Q. May my insurance agent charge me a service fee for issuing or renewing a policy?

A. Consult your state's law. Some states prohibit such fees.

Q. How are insurance rates determined?

A. A classification system based on objective criteria is used to determine the risk of an accident, and to set the varying rates that drivers pay. Criteria include your age, sex, marital status, and geographic location; the age, make, and model of the car; and the car's primary use. (Cars used for recreation are statistically less likely to be involved in an accident than vehicles used for commuting.) In some states, the insurance rates are set by the state's insurance commission, which regulates insurance companies.

If you have been involved in several accidents over a short period of time, you are a high risk, so insurance companies would add a surcharge to the basic premium you pay. On the other hand, insurance carriers might offer safety discounts if your vehicle is equipped with automatic safety belts, antilock brakes, or air bags. Insurance companies will offer other types of discounts as well, such as for being a senior citizen or a good student, joining a car pool, or insuring multiple vehicles with the same carrier.

Q. My teenage son's insurance premium is much higher than mine. Is it unconstitutional to discriminate based on age?

A. No. Research shows that persons under age twenty-one, especially males, have the highest rate of car accidents. This is the justification for the disparity in rates between adults and minors.

Q. Will my insurance premium automatically increase if I have an accident?

A. Not necessarily. If the insurance carrier has to dole out $300 to $500 or more in claims, you are likely to see a premium increase. If you have been accident-free for the previous three years, the surcharge (if any) might still be less than your costs to pay for the repairs out-of-pocket. If you are on your third accident and just getting warmed up, prepare yourself for a 20- to 50-percent premium hike.

Q. Do I have to buy uninsured motorist coverage?

A. It depends where you live. Some states now require drivers to purchase such coverage, which enables you to collect from your insurer if you are injured in an accident caused by an uninsured driver. The insurance carrier, in turn, receives **subrogation rights** against the uninsured wrongdoer; that is, the

carrier takes your place (and your rights) in any legal claims against the uninsured driver. Skyrocketing hospital costs, combined with a tight economy that causes many people to underinsure (or fail to insure) their vehicles, make this coverage a good idea.

Q. How do I collect on my uninsured motorist coverage?

A. Generally, you must prove that the other driver was at fault, and that he or she was without liability insurance to compensate you. An uninsured motorist may actually have no coverage, or the motorist may be de facto uninsured if he or she is underage, unlicensed, or otherwise ineligible for protection under the policy covering the vehicle that caused the accident—as, for example, when the driver at fault used the vehicle without the owner's permission. Practically speaking, if the insurance carrier of the driver at fault denies coverage, then you are dealing with an uninsured motorist.

Q. How does underinsured motorist coverage work?

A. **Underinsured motorist coverage,** which exists in a majority of states, will cover the shortfall if an injured person suffers more damage than can be covered by the driver's insurance. If, for example, the driver who injured you has only $50,000 in bodily injury coverage, but you have $70,000 in damages, you can look to your own insurer to cover the $20,000 shortfall after you have recovered damages from the other driver's carrier.

Q. Do underinsured motorist policies differ?

A. Yes. A minority of states that recognize this insurance option weigh the insured victim's damages against the driver-at-fault's liability coverage, compensating the injured person only if the driver-at-fault's liability coverage is less than the damages the victim suffered or was entitled to receive. Other states examine the injured person's uninsured motorist coverage and the driver-at-fault's liability insurance, with the insurance carrier paying out only when the driver-at-fault's liability insurance limit is less than the victim's underinsured motorist coverage. Most policies enable the insurer to deduct ("set off") the amount the victim receives from the driver-at-fault from the sum it pays to the victim carrying the underinsured motorist protection.

REMEMBER THIS

- In an accident, try to keep your head and to be civil and cooperative with the police and the other parties. When the police ask, be ready to provide identification and proof of insurance.

- Be careful not to admit fault or guilt, or even apologize to the other party—let the courts determine who is responsible for the accident.

- Try to gather as much information as you can about the scene of the accident, and ask for the contact details of any witnesses.

- When shopping for insurance, make sure you understand the requirements in your state.

- Even if your state does not require it, you may want to look into uninsured (or underinsured) motorist coverage, in the event that you are involved in an accident with a driver with little or no coverage.

CHAPTER FIFTEEN

Law and the Workplace

Michelle was excited when her dream job offered her an interview. But at the interview, things hit a sour note. The interviewer asked Michelle tons of questions she had never been asked before during an interview: When did she plan on having children? What did her husband do for a living? Would she be willing to submit to a lie detector test? Michelle really wants the job, but something felt wrong about the interview. Did the interviewer have the right to ask these questions? Can hiring be based on these criteria? What can Michelle do now?

The law affects just about every aspect of work. Federal and state laws regulate the hiring process, the terms and conditions of employment, and the circumstances under which employees can be terminated.

The law helps shape the relationship between employer and employee. The law does not address every issue that can arise on the job, but a basic understanding of what the law does require can help both the employer and the employee anticipate problems and avoid trouble.

This chapter helps both employees and employers understand how the law affects their rights and obligations at work. It explains the laws and suggests places to turn for further details. While this chapter discusses both federal and state laws, it does not go into detail of specific state laws. Instead, since no two states' laws are exactly alike, we refer only generally to state law and to how it can affect the work relationship.

INTRODUCTION TO LAW AND THE WORKPLACE

Q. What is the law of the workplace?

A. There is no single "law of the workplace." Today's workplace law consists of federal and state statutes and regulations, civil service rules, collective bargaining agreements, individual contracts, company personnel handbooks, and employer practices.

Q. Does it matter if a person works for the federal or a state government, rather than a private employer?

A. Yes. Generally, individual contracts, collective bargaining agreements, and federal and state laws regulate the relationship between private employees and employers (e.g., retail businesses or manufacturers). However, the government is a public employer, and is subject not only to labor contracts and laws but also to the restrictions imposed by federal and state constitutions. For example, the First Amendment restricts government interference with free speech and prohibits the government from disciplining one of its workers who speaks out on issues of public concern. The First Amendment, however, generally does not apply to a private employer, and thus does not prohibit a private employer from firing such an employee. In addition, most governmental employment is also regulated by civil-service rules.

Q. How does being in a union affect workplace law?

A. A union contract does not eliminate employee labor law protections and responsibilities. When employees select a union as their bargaining representative, the union negotiates a **collective-bargaining agreement** (contract) with the employer. This contract contains the terms and conditions of employment for those employees in the bargaining unit. The contract is legally binding on both the employer and the employees, providing a source of enforceable employment rights. Individual employees cannot usually negotiate separate deals with the employer, but collective bargaining agreements in some fields such as professional sports and entertainment

▶ INDEPENDENT CONTRACTS AND WORKPLACE LAW

Workplace law regulates the relationship between employers and employees. As a matter of law, independent contractors are not employees. Generally, if an employer controls, directs, and supervises you in performing your work, then you are considered an employee. Courts also would consider you an employee if you're paid on a salary or wage basis rather than a per-project basis, and if the employer furnishes the equipment you use in the performance of the work.

But if the employer merely specifies the result to be achieved, and if you use personal judgment and discretion in achieving it, then you may be considered an **independent contractor.**

For example, ABC Company hires Jill to construct a fence, and agrees to pay her $1,000. ABC does not supervise Jill's work; it does not tell her how to build the fence or what time to report to work. The company cares only about getting the fence built. Jill's income is based on the profits she makes on the job after subtracting the cost of buying the fencing materials. Her relationship with ABC ends when she finishes the job. Jill is an independent contractor, not the employee.

often permit union members to negotiate separately.

If there is no union contract, then the employee deals directly with the employer and negotiates his or her own terms of employment. Generally, that employee does not have the protections of a written contract.

FEDERAL LAWS REGULATING THE WORKPLACE

Throughout this chapter, we'll often refer to federal law. Many of these laws affect not just one aspect of employment, but the entire spectrum of rights and responsibilities within the workplace.

In this section we'll introduce some of the most frequently encountered laws that we'll discuss in more depth in subsequent sections of this chapter.

Q. What do I need to know about the federal laws that apply to my job?

A. It is important to know what federal law applies to your situation for many reasons. First, this helps you determine what type of employee is covered and what behavior is prohibited. Second, knowing which laws apply to you helps you determine which federal agency can help you. Lastly, this information helps you determine possible remedies and the correct course of action for you.

The chart on pages 526–531 gives you a quick overview of the common federal laws that apply in the workplace. Don't expect to remember every detail, but feel free to refer back to this chart as you read the chapter.

NAME OF THE ACT	GOAL OF THE ACT	EMPLOYERS/ EMPLOYEES COVERED BY THE ACT	AGENCY CHARGED WITH ENFORCE- MENT
Title VII of the Civil Rights Act ("Title VII")	Prohibits discrimination or harassment in employment based on race, color, ethnicity, religion, sex, and national origin.	Covers both public (government) and private employers that employ at least fifteen people. Also covers unions and employment agencies. Similar state or local laws prohibiting employment discrimination may cover additional employers.	The Equal Employment Opportunity Commission (EEOC).
42 U.S.C. Section 1981 ("Section 1981")	Prohibits employment discrimination based on race or ethnicity.	Covers all public and private employers, regardless of size.	There is no federal agency charged with enforcing this law. This statute is enforced solely by individual lawsuits.
The Age Discrimination in Employment Act (ADEA)	Prohibits employment discrimination based on age. For purposes of this statute, age is defined as forty years of age or older. Thus, even under the ADEA, an employer could legally refuse to hire you for being twenty-five years old.	Covers public and private employers employing at least twenty employees. Also covers unions and employment agencies.	The EEOC.

NAME OF THE ACT	GOAL OF THE ACT	EMPLOYERS/ EMPLOYEES COVERED BY THE ACT	AGENCY CHARGED WITH ENFORCE-MENT
The Americans with Disabilities Act (ADA)	Prohibits employment discrimination against persons with disabilities, both physical and mental. The ADA also provides that an employer must provide an employee with reasonable accommodations of a known disability.	Covers public and private employers employing at least fifteen employees. It also covers unions and employment agencies. State or local laws prohibiting disability discrimination may cover employers not covered under the ADA.	The EEOC.
The Rehabilitation Act ("Rehab Act")	Prohibits discrimination in employment against persons with disabilities, both physical and mental. It also requires covered employers to take affirmative action to employ people with disabilities.	Applies to employers who are contractors or subcontractors of the federal government who have contracts in excess of $2,500 and to employers who receive federal funds.	The Office of Federal Contract Compliance, in the Department of Labor.
The National Labor Relations Act (NLRA)	Deals with the role of unions as the bargaining representative of employees, and prohibits discrimination by employers or unions based on union activity or other protected concerted activity.	Covers only private employers that have an impact on interstate commerce. It specifically excludes public employers, railway and airline employers, and people who are employed as agricultural laborers.	The National Labor Relations Board (NLRB).

NAME OF THE ACT	GOAL OF THE ACT	EMPLOYERS/ EMPLOYEES COVERED BY THE ACT	AGENCY CHARGED WITH ENFORCE- MENT
		The NLRA also covers labor unions.	
The Fair Labor Standards Act (FLSA)	Establishes mini- mum wage and overtime standards for employees and regulates child labor.	Generally covers a private employer if at least two em- ployees are en- gaged in interstate commerce activi- ties and if the annual volume of business is at least $500,000. It also covers hospitals, educational institu- tions, and state and federal public em- ployers. Addition- ally, it covers individual employ- ees who engage in interstate com- merce activities, even if their em- ployer does not gross $500,000 a year. Remember that state laws regulating mini- mum wages, over- time, and child labor may cover employers not covered by federal law.	The Wage and Hour Division of the Department of Labor

NAME OF THE ACT	GOAL OF THE ACT	EMPLOYERS/ EMPLOYEES COVERED BY THE ACT	AGENCY CHARGED WITH ENFORCE- MENT
Executive Order 11246	Provides that an employer can't lawfully discrimi- nate based on race, color, religion, sex, or national origin. The nondiscrimina- tion requirement is essentially the same as that im- posed under Title VII. Furthermore, in some cases the Order requires that the employer de- velop and use an affirmative action plan.	Imposes obligations on employers with a federal contract or subcontract worth at least $10,000. The affirmative- action requirement kicks in when the contract is worth at least $50,000, and when the contrac- tor employs at least fifty employees	The Office of Fed- eral Contract Com- pliance, part of the Department of Labor.

Q. How is the Americans with Disabilities Act different from the Rehabilitation Act?

A. The main difference is the type of covered employers. Whereas the ADA covers employers who employ at least 15 employees, the Rehabilitation Act applies to employers who are contractors or subcontractors of the federal government, and to employers who receive federal funds.

Q. I work for a state government agency. Can I sue my employer for violating an employment law?

A. It depends on what law you are claiming the state has violated. If it is a state law (and if the law applies to state employers), then you can file suit. However, if it is a federal law, you may not be able to file a lawsuit. The Eleventh Amendment to the Constitution provides that state governments have immunity from federal lawsuits filed by individuals. The Supreme Court has held that Congress can abolish state immunity only under very specific circumstances. Both Title VII and the Family Medical Leave Act have been held to overcome state immunity; therefore, individual employees can sue state employers under these two federal statutes. However, under the ADA, the ADEA, and the FLSA, individual employees cannot sue state employers for violating these federal laws.

▶ **THE MEANING OF "DISABILITY"**

Both the ADA and the Rehabilitation Act protect individuals with disabilities. The definition of the term **disability** is the same for both laws. A qualified individual with a disability is one who

- has a physical or mental impairment that substantially limits a major life activity;
- has a record of having such a physical or mental impairment; or
- is regarded as having such an impairment.

This broad definition includes any physiologically based impairment or any mental or psychological impairment, but it does not include mere physical characteristics or cultural, economic, or environmental impairment. For example, a person with dyslexia may have a disability, but a person who is illiterate does not; a person who is a dwarf may have a disability, but a person who is short does not.

The impairment must cause a substantial limitation to a major life activity, including walking, seeing, hearing, or being able to care for oneself. Temporary conditions, such as a broken leg or a cold, would not be considered substantial limitations. Whether an impairment causes a substantial limitation is determined on a case-by-case basis. Thus, for some people, epilepsy will cause a substantial limitation, while for others it will not.

The second meaning of the term includes people who no longer have a disability but have a record of a disability, such as a person who successfully recovered from a disabling disease.

The third meaning includes people who have a condition that does not substantially limit a major life activity but are faced with an employer who believes it does. For example, this definition would include a worker who has asymptomatic HIV/AIDS and is not hired because the prospective employer mistakenly believes that the worker is unable to care for himself and therefore would cause disruption in the workplace.

This immunity doesn't mean that the states do not have to comply with these laws. If states fail to comply, then the federal government (through the EEOC with respect to the ADEA and the ADA, and the Department of Labor with respect to the FLSA) can initiate lawsuits against the state to enforce compliance. Finally, immunity does not apply to local government employers, which can be sued by their employees for violating any federal law.

Q. Some of those laws only cover employees that are engaged in interstate commerce. How is this determined?

A. The Wage and Hour Division of the Department of Labor has identified five cate-

▶ OTHER FEDERAL LAWS REGULATING EMPLOYMENT

In addition to the laws described in the chart on page 526, there are several other federal laws that also affect employment. Here is an introductory list of these laws, grouped according to subject matter; we'll discuss some of them in more detail later in this chapter.

Unions The Railway Labor Act regulates union activity in the workplace and prohibits employment discrimination based on union activity. It only covers airlines and railways.

Wages and hours. The Davis-Bacon Act, the Service Contract Act, and the Walsh-Healy Public Contracts Act require employers with certain types of federal government contracts to pay their employees a minimum wage as determined by the secretary of labor.

Equal pay. The Equal Pay Act requires employers to pay equal wages to male and female employees who are performing substantially equivalent work.

Workplace safety. The Occupational Safety and Health Act (OSH Act) requires employers to furnish a workplace free from hazards likely to cause death or serious injury and to comply with safety and health standards promulgated under the law.

Mine safety. The Mine Safety and Health Act requires mine operators to comply with safety and health standards promulgated under the law.

Pensions and welfare benefit plans. The Employee Retirement Income Security Act (ERISA) establishes eligibility and vesting rights for employees in company pension plans, and establishes administrative, fiduciary, funding, and termination requirements. This law also regulates, to a lesser degree, other types of employee benefit plans, such as medical insurance or legal services.

Immigrant workers. The Immigration Reform and Control Act (IRCA) prohibits employers from hiring illegal aliens, requires employers to verify the work eligibility status of applicants, and protects lawfully admitted aliens by prohibiting discrimination in employment based on citizenship.

Other Terms of Employment

The Uniformed Services Employment and Reemployment Rights Act (USERRA) requires employers to reinstate employees who have served in the armed forces to their former jobs upon completion of their military duty, and prohibits employment discrimination because of an employee's past, current, or future military obligations.

The Worker Adjustment and Retraining Notification Act (WARN Act) requires employers to give sixty days' advance notice of plant closings or mass layoffs to workers, unions, and state and local governments.

The Employee Polygraph Protection Act (EPPA) prohibits employers from requiring employees or applicants to submit to polygraph examinations.

The Family and Medical Leave Act (FMLA) requires employers to grant employees up to 12 weeks of unpaid leave during any 12 month period because of the birth or adoption of a child, because the employee has a serious health condition, or because the employee has to care for a parent, spouse, or child with a serious health condition.

The Jury System Improvements Act prohibits disciplining or discharging an employee because of federal jury duty.

The Drug-Free Workplace Act requires federal government contractors and grantees to establish a drug-free awareness program for their employees.

gories of employees that it considers engaged in interstate commerce. They include

- employees participating in the actual movement of commerce—for example, employees in the telephone, telegraph, television, transportation, banking, and insurance industries;
- employees doing work related to the instrumentalities of commerce—for example, employees who maintain and repair roads, bridges, or telephone lines; or employees who work at warehouses, airports, or bus stations;
- employees who regularly cross state lines in the performance of their duties—for example, traveling salespersons or service technicians;
- employees who produce or work on goods for commerce—for example, assembly workers in an auto plant, coal miners, shipping department employees, or clerical and administrative workers who do the support work necessary to produce goods for commerce; and
- employees who are employed in a closely related process or occupation essential to

producing goods for commerce—for example, employees who build tool and die machines used by auto plants.

REMEMBER THIS

- The law of the workplace consists of federal law, state law, contracts such as collective-bargaining agreements, employee manuals, and much more.
- Workplace laws apply only to employees. Independent contractors generally are not considered employees.
- Because they work for the government, public employees have certain constitutional rights that private employees lack and are usually afforded job security under a civil service system as outlined on page 526.

THE HIRING PROCESS

Several stages are involved in hiring employees: soliciting and reviewing applications, interviewing candidates, and selecting a candidate. As you will see in this section, the law affects each of these stages.

Q. Are there laws that specifically relate to hiring?

A. Yes. Antidiscrimination laws prohibit discrimination in employment—including during the hiring process—based on race, color, ethnicity, religion, national origin, sex, age, disability, and union affiliation. Some federal and state laws regulate the use of certain types of tests and screening devices in the hiring process. Also, a state's common law of torts may impose a duty on employers not to invade employees' privacy unnecessarily.

Q. Do government employers face the same restrictions as private employers?

A. Yes. In fact, they likely face even more restrictions, because the U.S. Constitution and civil-service laws come into play. Because of the constitutional guarantee of freedom of association, government employers cannot discriminate in hiring based on political affiliation (unless party affiliation is a necessary requirement for effective performance of the job—as would be the case, for example, with a governor's speechwriter). Civil-service laws generally provide that hiring decisions should be based on the "merit" of the appli-

---

▶ EMPLOYING DOMESTIC WORKERS

Thinking of getting some work done around the house? Are your workers going to be employees or independent contractors? (See the discussion on the differences between employees and independent contractors on page 525.)

If a domestic worker is your employee, then certain federal employment laws regulate that relationship. Examples of domestic workers who may be considered employees include in-home child care workers, cooks, housekeepers, and babysitters.

You must make quarterly Social Security payments to the IRS for every domestic employee at least eighteen years of age who earns more than $1,200 per calendar year. You must also pay federal unemployment taxes for every domestic employee who earns more than $1,000 per calendar quarter. Consult your accountant for rules regarding withholding taxes from an employee's pay.

The Fair Labor Standards Act (FLSA) covers baby-sitters if they work more than twenty hours per week. The FLSA applies to other domestic employees who earn more than $50 during a calendar quarter and work for one or more employers for more than eight hours in any workweek. Any employee who meets this definition must be paid the federal minimum wage and overtime for hours worked in excess of forty during any one workweek for a single employer.

If a domestic employee resides in your house, then the overtime provisions of the FLSA do not apply, but the minimum wage requirements do. Finally, you may want to consider buying workers' compensation insurance for your domestic employee.

cant, which is usually determined by administering competitive examinations.

Job Postings and Qualifications

Q. I need to hire an employee. What should I include in my job advertisement?

A. The main idea is to avoid discrimination while at the same time targeting qualified candidates. Ads should avoid words suggesting a preferred race, sex, religion, national origin, or age. For example, using "recent college grad," instead of "college degree required," could discourage older qualified applicants from applying. Using the term "salesman" instead of "salesperson" may suggest that only men should apply. Using the phrase "equal opportunity employer" in an ad indicates that the employer will judge all applicants based on their qualifications for the job, without regard to race, sex, religion, national origin, age, or disability.

Q. Can employers set basic job requirements and work standards?

A. Yes, as long as they do not discriminate based on a protected classification. Qualifications listed for a job should be necessary for the performance of the job. Even neutral job requirements can cause discrimination. For example, requiring a college degree for a job as a janitor could disproportionately screen out minority applicants vis-à-vis white applicants, since disproportionately fewer minority students attend college. The minority applicants would be screened out based not on their ability to do the job but based on a factor (college education) unrelated to being a janitor.

Other examples of job requirements that appear neutral but may actually discriminate include:

- refusing to hire single custodial parents may discriminate against women, since women are more likely to have physical custody of their children;
- requiring applicants to speak fluent English for a job that does not require communication skills may discriminate against applicants whose nation of origin is not the U.S.; and
- height and weight standards may discriminate based on sex and national origin.

Whenever seemingly neutral requirements have a discriminatory effect, the employer must be able to show that the requirements are related to job performance. Thus, requirements for job-related experience and specific job-related skills are usually valid.

Q. What about disabilities? Does the ADA affect an employer's ability to establish basic job requirements and work standards?

A. Job requirements and work standards that would screen out a person based on his or her disability must be job-related and consistent with business necessity. Under the ADA, in order to be job related, a requirement must be related to the essential functions of the job and not merely an incidental aspect of job performance. For example, a job description for a receptionist position states that typing skills are required; however, the employer has never required the receptionist to type. This requirement, therefore, is not an essential function, and requiring typing skills could have the effect of screening out a person who is a paraplegic.

▶ YOU NEED A LICENSE FOR THESE JOBS

State rules limit some jobs to people who have licenses. Depending on the state, these might include cosmetologists, barbers, electricians, heating/air-conditioning technicians, engineers, nurses, builders, lawyers, accountants, dental hygienists, and physicians. Employers must restrict hiring to individuals who are properly licensed. If you're considering such a career, contact your state licensing authorities to see what requirements apply.

Q. How can an employer identify the essential functions of a job?

A. The EEOC regulations list several factors that help determine whether a function is essential:

- The extent to which the position exists to perform that function. For example, to determine whether typing is an essential function of a receptionist position, it may be helpful to ask whether the position exists solely for that purpose (i.e., to facilitate typing of letters and documents).
- The number of other employees available to perform the function. For example, even if a receptionist's main duty is not typing, perhaps the employer has only one other secretarial employee, and the receptionist will be called upon to fill in for that other employee (including typing duties) when the other employee is sick or on vacation.

- The amount of time spent performing the function. For example, if the receptionist typically spends 75 percent of his or her time typing documents, then typing will likely be considered essential.
- The effect of not requiring the person in this job to be able to perform the function. For example, a firefighter may be called upon to carry a heavy person from a burning building only rarely, but failing to perform this function could cost a life.
- The work experience of employees who have previously performed the job.

Q. If a person with a disability cannot perform an essential function of the job, can the employer refuse to hire that person?

A. Not necessarily. The question is whether the inability to perform the essential function of the job is due to lack of qualifications or due to a disability. If the employer is hiring for secretarial positions and an applicant has no typing skills, then the employer could refuse to hire him or her even if the applicant is disabled. (For more on this point, see the "The Protected Class Under the ADA" sidebar.)

However, if the applicant does possess typing skills, then the question becomes whether, with a **reasonable accommodation,** he or she would be able to perform the essential function of the job. For example, an applicant for a secretarial position who is blind may be unable to use the word processor. However, if the applicant could use the word processor if provided with a Braille keyboard, and thus be able to perform the essential function of the job, then the employer could not refuse to hire the applicant because of his or her disability.

> ▶ **EXAMPLES OF REASONABLE ACCOMMODATIONS**
>
> The following are examples of actions an employer may be required to take to provide a reasonable accommodation:
>
> - making existing facilities readily accessible;
> - restructuring the job;
> - modifying work schedules or making a job part-time;
> - modifying equipment; and
> - providing readers or interpreters.
>
> Employers are not required to provide equipment or devices primarily for personal use, such as corrective glasses, hearing aids, or wheelchairs.

Q. How does an employer know if an applicant or employee needs a "reasonable accommodation" to be able to perform the essential functions of the job?

A. The applicant or employee should inform the employer of the need for an accommodation. The ADA does not require the employer to provide an accommodation if it is unaware of the need for one.

Also, the employer may ask for documentation of the need for an accommodation when the disability is not an obvious one.

Q. Is an employer's obligation to provide an accommodation unlimited?

A. No. The ADA only requires the employer to provide reasonable accommodations that do not cause undue hardship. The law specifically lists what factors should be considered in determining **undue hardship:**

- the nature and cost of the accommodation needed;
- the overall financial resources of the facility involved, including the number of persons employed at the facility, the effect on expenses and resources, and the impact on operation;
- the overall financial resources of the employer as a whole, including the overall size of the business; and

> ▶ **THE PROTECTED CLASS UNDER THE ADA**
>
> The ADA protects "qualified individuals with a disability" from discrimination in employment. An individual with a disability is **qualified** if he or she has "the requisite skill, experience, education and other job-related requirements" for the job. For example, in deciding whether someone with epilepsy is qualified to teach, you'd ask whether he or she held a teaching certificate or a college degree in education. If not, then the person is not qualified, and is not a member of the protected class under the ADA.

• the type of operation of the employer, including the composition, structure, and function of the workforce and the relationship of the facility in question to the employer as a whole.

Whether an accommodation causes an undue hardship is determined on a case-by-case basis.

Q. Is it ever appropriate to indicate a preference for applicants of a specific sex or age?

A. Rarely. Antidiscrimination laws require employers to consider applicants as individuals and not make decisions based on stereotypical assumptions. For example, if a factory job requires a worker to regularly lift 40-pound loads, an employer cannot express a preference for young male applicants based on the stereotypical notion that young men are stronger than older people or women. Some women and older people can lift heavy loads, just as some young men cannot. Instead, the employer's job ad should state that the job requires "regularly lifting 40-pound loads."

In some rare circumstances, however, it is an objective fact that people who are members of a protected class cannot perform the job in question. For example, a filmmaker may hire only men for male roles, or a kosher deli may hire only Jewish people as butchers. In both of these examples, sex and religion are

---

▶ BONA FIDE OCCUPATIONAL QUALIFICATIONS

An employer might be able to make a hiring decision based on sex, religion, or national origin if it can prove that the particular characteristic is a bona fide occupational qualification (BFOQ) for the job in question. The employer must prove that its hiring decision falls within the very narrow limits allowed by the BFOQ defense. The employer must show both that

• all persons of the excluded class would be unable to perform the requirements of the job; and

• the requirements directly relate to the essence of the employer's business.

The evidence that the employer presents must be objective and not based on stereotyped beliefs about persons in the protected class.

Years ago some airlines tried to defend their decision not to hire men as flight attendants on the basis that males were unable to provide reassurance to anxious passengers or give courteous, personalized service. The court held that even if this were true, the ability to reassure and give courteous service did not relate to the essence of the employer's business, which was the safe transport of passengers.

The BFOQ defense applies in very limited circumstances, such as for actors or fashion models.

bona fide occupational qualifications (**BFOQ**). Both Title VII and the ADEA allow employers to limit a job to applicants of a specific group when the employer can prove that a protected characteristic is a BFOQ for the job in question.

Q. Some employers find applicants through word of mouth or by talking to their current employees. Is anything wrong with this?

A. It depends. Using the old-boy network generally results in applications mainly from other old boys. If the workers are mainly non-minorities, then news about the job vacancy will likely be limited to their circle of acquaintances, who may be mostly non-minorities as well. This has the effect of closing out minority applicants. An employer can avoid problems by disseminating news of job openings as widely as possible to reach a broad pool of applicants. Placing ads in newspapers and magazines with a widespread circulation base online, and using employment agencies, can help in reaching a variety of qualified applicants.

Interviews

Q. What should I know before I conduct a job interview?

A. By their very nature, job interviews are subjective. Employers cannot help but form impressions in judging an applicant's ambition, motivation, creativity, dependability, and responsibility. Realizing the inherently subjective nature of the process, employers should try to make an interview as objective (fact-based) as possible. Concentrating on objective information helps to prevent decisions based on conscious or subconscious prejudice, and focuses the hiring process on

an applicant's qualifications and employment experience.

Employers should also try to make job interviews as uniform as possible. They should ask the same set of questions of all applicants for the same position. This allows for a better basis for comparison and can also prevent discrimination in the content of a job interview. For example, asking a female applicant "Do you type?" but not asking a male applicant the same question could indicate discriminatory stereotyping.

Q. Does the law prohibit any specific questions?

A. Yes. The ADA prohibits an employer from asking an applicant whether he or she has a disability, or from inquiring into the nature or severity of a disability (though the employer may ask questions about the applicant's ability

---

▶ **RELIGIOUS INSTITUTIONS CAN EXPRESS A PREFERENCE FOR EMPLOYEES OF A PARTICULAR RELIGION**

Title VII expressly allows religious corporations and sectarian educational institutions to hire applicants of a particular religion. For example, a Catholic grade school could decide on the basis of religion to hire a Catholic teacher rather than a Protestant one. However, this exemption applies only to religion; the school may not discriminate in hiring teachers based on race, ethnicity, color, sex, national origin, age, or disability.

to do the job). The National Labor Relations Act prohibits employers from questioning employees about union membership or activities. Furthermore, an employer should not ask questions that may imply discrimination. Moreover, some state laws expressly prohibit certain types of pre-employment questions, such as questions about marital status or number of dependents.

Q. What types of questions may imply discrimination?

A. Direct questions relating to an applicant's age, marital status, family background, or religious affiliation may indicate discrimination. Questions or comments based on stereotyped notions may also imply discrimination.

Interview questions should relate to the requirements of the job and the applicant's qualifications, work experience, and history. Even when the information sought is related to the job, the interviewer must be careful that the way the question is asked does not imply discrimination. For example, an employer trying to determine whether a female applicant is going to stay with the company for the next few years should not ask, "Do you plan to get married?" or "Do you plan to have children?" or "What kind of birth control do you use?" More direct, job-related questions will permit an employer to obtain the desired information without being discriminatory. For example:

- "We're looking for employees who will make a commitment to the company. Is there any reason you might not stay with us for the next few years?"
- "What are your career objectives?"
- "Where do you see yourself in five years?"

Similarly, suppose an employer is trying to determine a female job candidate's commit-

ment to living in a particular area of the country. It is better to ask, "Do you intend to stay in the area?" rather than "Is your husband's employer likely to transfer him?"

If attendance is the issue, questions such as "Does your husband expect you to be home to cook dinner?" or "What will you do if your children get sick?" are indirect and inefficient. It is more direct to ask, "How was your attendance record with your prior employer?"

Q. What is "need-to-know," and how does it apply to job interviews?

A. As an employer, you should try to only ask "need-to-know" questions during an interview. The key is whether there is an objective, job-related reason why an employer wants to ask a question. However, be aware that questions that do not violate antidiscrimination laws may still create problems. The tort law in some states protects people from unwarranted invasions of personal privacy. An employer that makes offensive inquiries into an applicant's personal life, unrelated to the requirements of the job, may be liable for invasion of privacy.

Sometimes employers clearly need to obtain sensitive information. For example, whether an applicant has ever been convicted of a crime may substantially affect the applicant's fitness for a specific job. And employers do need to condition their job offers on candidates' production of proper documentation of their citizenship or work authorization. (However, asking about national origin may be viewed as discriminatory.)

Q. What should I do if an interviewer asks questions that seem inappropriate or discriminatory?

A. The tactful applicant might avoid answering the discriminatory question directly, and

▶ CHECKLIST: HOW EMPLOYERS CAN HIRE WITHOUT DISCRIMINATION

- Employers and prospective employees both benefit when job openings are clearly defined. Ideally, employers should prepare a detailed job description for each position, specifying what the work is and the required qualifications.

- It helps to use a standard application form that avoids irrelevant questions. Avoid asking about age, height, weight, marital status, and education or arrest record unless these facts relate to the job.

- Using a checklist based on the job description, the employer should rate applicants during the interview in an organized, consistent manner that is predicated on their respective qualifications for the job. If both sides come to the interview with a clear idea of what the job involves, the interview is more likely to focus on the qualifications essential for doing the job.

in that way alert the interviewer to the fact that the question was inappropriate. For example, if an interviewer asks if you have children, you could respond, "Oh—you're wondering whether I'll be able to work long hours. I can assure you that I will. My current boss can confirm that."

If the interviewer continues to ask inappropriate or discriminatory questions, you should make a written record of all such questions as soon as the interview is over. If you don't get the job, you may need a record of the discriminatory questions in order to file a charge with the EEOC.

Selecting a Candidate

Q. May an employer use a lie detector to find out if a job applicant or employee is honest?

A. The Employee Polygraph Protection Act (EPPA) generally prohibits employers from requiring applicants or employees to take a polygraph test. This federal law covers all private employers with at least two employees engaged in interstate commerce activities and an annual volume of business of at least $500,000. It does not apply to public employers. The law provides an exception to the use of a polygraph in two situations:

- An employer can use a polygraph in connection with an ongoing investigation into theft involving economic loss or injury to the business. The employer may only make this request of employees who had access to the missing property or whom the employer reasonably suspects were involved. An employee is free to refuse to take the test, and the employer cannot take action against the employee based on the refusal.

- Employers that provide security services can administer a polygraph to certain applicants, as can employers engaged in the manufacture of controlled substances.

Most states also have state laws that either prohibit or regulate the use of polygraph tests in employment. A few states prohibit all tests and devices purporting to determine honesty.

Q. May an employer run a background check on an applicant?

A. Background checks may be necessary for certain jobs. These include jobs involving security or trade secrets. Moreover, background checks may be helpful if the employer should later face a negligent hiring suit, and they should be conducted for any employee who interacts with the public, has access to homes, or has responsibility for children, the elderly, or the infirm.

Checks should be made fairly and without bias. They should concern only issues relating to performance of the specific job. An employer that unnecessarily pries into private information or uses unreasonable methods to obtain background data could be sued for invasion of privacy.

Q. May an employer run a credit check on an applicant?

A. Yes. Credit checks can be very helpful when the information is necessary for a job-related purpose. This might include any situation in which an employee handles credit cards or has access to merchandise, which is common in both the retail service industry and the wholesale sector (i.e., for warehouse workers and shippers).

However, it's wise not to use credit checks indiscriminately. Court cases under Title VII have held that requiring good credit can have a discriminatory result, since nonwhites are more likely than whites to live below the poverty level. Even if a credit check is necessary, the Fair Credit Reporting Act (a federal law discussed in Chapter 10, "Consumer Credit") requires employers to notify applicants if they intend to obtain credit information from a consumer reporting agency, and to get written authorization from the applicant. If an employer decides not to hire applicants based in whole or in part on a credit report, the employer must inform the applicant, provide a copy of the report, and tell the applicant about his or her rights under the Fair Credit Reporting Act.

Q. May an employer require applicants to undergo a physical examination?

A. Generally speaking, no. The ADA prohibits employers from requiring pre-employment physical examinations. However, after making an offer, an employer may require the applicant successfully to undergo a physical exam before starting the job if:

- all employees in the same job category must be required to take a physical exam;
- information obtained from the exam is maintained in a separate medical file and kept confidential; and
- the employer does not use the information to discriminate against the employee because of a disability.

Q. I am applying for a job. Can I be forced to take a drug test?

A. It depends on where you live and the type of job for which you are applying. Federal law does not prohibit drug-screening tests for private jobs. However, several states have placed restrictions on them. For example, Iowa and Rhode Island require employers to have probable cause before they use drug tests. Other states, such as Minnesota and North Carolina, have established guidelines that must be followed in administering drug tests.

Moreover, the method used by an employer in administering a drug test (such as direct observation of urination) could be considered outrageous, and could render the employer liable under tort law for invasion of privacy or intentional infliction of emotional distress.

Q. Can applicants for government jobs be subject to random drug testing?

A. The Fourth Amendment of the U.S. Constitution prohibits the government from engaging in unreasonable searches and seizures. This restriction acts as a limit on a public employer's ability to use a drug test on its employees. Courts have generally been reluctant to allow public employers to engage in random drug tests. Instead, they usually require the employer to show some reasonable suspicion of drug use, or some compelling evidence that public safety would be jeopardized if the employee used drugs. For example, drug testing has been upheld for customs officers who are directly involved in drug enforcement, and for employees who are required to carry firearms.

Q. Once I have a job, can my employer test me for drugs?

A. As with applicants, it depends. Federal law does not prohibit drug testing of private employees. In addition, some employers are required to conduct random and post-accident drug testing of certain employees covered by the Department of Transportation Regulations (see the "Drug Testing Requirements for Certain Occupations" sidebar for more information). In certain states, there are restrictions and limitations on the use of drug tests for employers. Additionally, in a workplace where employees are represented by a union, an employer must bargain with the union before it can begin testing employees for drugs.

Q. May an employer use other types of tests (such as a skills test or an intelligence test) to screen applicants?

A. Yes, but such tests should be job related. A test may have an illegal discriminatory result, even if it seems fair. For example, a test of English-language skills might disqualify an

---

▶ DRUG TESTING REQUIREMENTS FOR CERTAIN OCCUPATIONS

U.S. Department of Transportation (DOT) regulations require drug testing of railroad workers and employees who operate commercial motor vehicles in interstate commerce. Testing occurs before employment, and then periodically or for reasonable cause. The U.S. Federal Aviation Administration has similar regulations covering airline flight personnel.

The Drug-Free Workplace Act, while not requiring drug testing, does require all federal contractors with contracts worth at least $25,000 or more to establish a drug-free awareness program and tell their employees about the program. Some states also impose drug-testing requirements for certain jobs, mainly in the transportation industry.

▶ ADMINISTRATION OF EMPLOYMENT TESTS UNDER THE ADA

Under the ADA, employers must be careful how they administer employment tests. This is to ensure that administration of such tests does not screen out applicants based on a disability. Tests should be administered in a way that accurately reflects the applicant's job-related skills, rather than reflecting an applicant's disability. For example, an applicant with dyslexia or with a visual disability might fail a written test because he or she could not properly see the material, and not because of a lack of knowledge. In such a circumstance, the employer may be required to provide a reader to help the applicant read the test materials. Similarly, oral tests may screen out applicants with a hearing disability. Usually, it is the responsibility of applicants to tell the employer that they need an alternative method for administering the test.

unusual number of persons for whom English is a second language. Unless the job in question requires English proficiency, the test may be unlawful.

Extensive federal regulations govern the use of employment tests.

Q. Are there laws that govern the hiring of workers under eighteen years of age?

A. Yes. The Fair Labor Standards Act (FLSA) regulates the employment of minors. With few exceptions (such as newspaper delivery), children under fourteen years of age may not be employed. Children under the age of sixteen may only work in nonhazardous jobs, and their hours of work are limited. During the school term, work hours are limited to a maximum of three hours a day and eighteen hours a week. Outside the school term, children under sixteen may work up to eight hours a day and forty hours a week. In either case, children under sixteen may work only from 7:00 A.M. to 7:00 P.M. (9:00 P.M. in the summer). Workers who are sixteen and seventeen years old are not limited in the number of hours they may work, but are prohibited from working in hazardous jobs.

Many states have their own rules for youth employment. An employer must follow these rules if they are more restrictive than federal law. For example, many states require minors to get work permits from school authorities.

Q. Are there laws that govern the hiring of alien workers?

A. Yes. The Immigration Reform and Control Act (IRCA) prohibits all employers from hiring unauthorized aliens. As part of the hiring process, employers must complete an eligibility form (Form I-9) for each new employee. This form ensures that the employer has verified the identity and legal eligibility of the applicant to be employed in this country. Employers who hire unauthorized aliens may be fined and imprisoned.

The employment-related provisions of the IRCA are aimed solely at steps an employer must take to ensure that it hires only people eligible to work in the U.S. These provisions do not affect the immigration status of the applicant.

▶ **HOW TO VERIFY THE IDENTITY AND EMPLOYMENT ELIGIBILITY OF AN APPLICANT**

The following documents are considered acceptable verification under IRCA: a U.S. passport; a birth certificate indicating that the applicant was born in the United States; a naturalization certificate; a valid foreign passport with an endorsement authorizing employment in the United States; a resident alien card with photograph and authorization for employment in the United States; or a Social Security card and a driver's license with photograph. So long as an applicant has documents that properly verify his or her identity and eligibility, an employer cannot require a particular or different document.

Q. Must an employer verify the employment status of current workers?

A. The IRCA applies only to employees hired after November 6, 1986. An employer doesn't have to verify the employment eligibility of any workers hired before that date. However, if the employer has reason to believe that a worker hired before November 6, 1986, is an unauthorized alien, then the employer would face penalties if it did not verify the worker's status and, if the employee was not authorized to work, fire that worker.

REMEMBER THIS

- Many federal antidiscrimination laws affect hiring. These laws protect you from discrimination on the basis of race, color, ethnicity, religion, national origin, sex, age, disability, and union activity or affiliation.
- State and local laws may provide you with extra protection; for example, some protect against discrimination based on marital status, sexual orientation, or arrest record.

- Employers can set job standards and requirements, but they can't lawfully discriminate against members of protected groups, even indirectly.
- Employers should make job openings known widely in the community. Interviews should include questions that focus closely on the requirements of the job; they should especially avoid any questions based on stereotypes.
- Certain federal laws regulate aspects of the hiring process; for example, employers usually can't give lie detector tests, are regulated in hiring children, and have to verify the eligibility of new hires to work in the U.S.

ON THE JOB

The law affects almost everything an employer or employee does while on the job. This section provides a rundown on the laws relating to unlawful discrimination, sexual harassment, job safety, and privacy, as well as unions and wages and hours.

Discrimination in the Workplace

Q. Besides hiring, what other aspects of the employment relationship are regulated by antidiscrimination laws?

A. Antidiscrimination laws regulate all aspects of work, including hiring, firing, promotions, job duties, wages, benefits, and reviews. Generally speaking, the laws do not require an employer to create specific policies or procedures or to provide specific benefits. Rather, the employer is allowed to establish its own policies so long as they are applied to all employees in a nondiscriminatory manner and so long as the policies do not have the effect of discriminating against a protected class.

Q. How do I know if an action is discriminatory in violation of the law?

A. First, remember that the law does not forbid all discriminatory actions. The law only prohibits discrimination when it is based on a person's **protected status** under federal law. Under federal law, the term "protected status" includes race, religion, national origin, sex, age, disability, or union activity.

Thus, if an employer makes a decision because of an employee's race, that employer has engaged in prohibited discrimination. Paying a worker lower wages than other employees because of that worker's gender violates Title VII. But paying a worker lower wages than other employees because that worker is performing different kinds of job duties does not. The question is whether the reason for the difference is based on the employee's protected status. Different treatment based on protected status is called **intentional discrimination** or **disparate treatment.**

Title VII adds an additional level of protection. It prohibits conduct that has the effect of discriminating against people in a protected class even if the employer's reason for the different treatment is not based on protected class. For example, an employer may decide to hire only applicants who do not have custody of preschool-age children. On its face, the reason for the employer's hiring decision does not relate to applicants' protected-class status. However, the effect of this policy may disproportionately screen out female applicants as compared with male applicants, because more women are custodial parents than men. Therefore, this policy could have a **discriminatory effect,** also called **disparate impact.** Title VII prohibits disparate impact discrimination, unless the employer can prove that the policy is required by business necessity and is significantly related to the job requirements.

The ADA also adds additional protection. The ADA defines discrimination not only in terms of disparate treatment and disparate impact, but also in terms of a refusal to provide reasonable accommodation to an otherwise qualified individual with a disability. (The previous section of this chapter, "The Hiring Process," discusses this topic in more detail.)

▶ DEFINING "SEX DISCRIMINATION"

As used in Title VII, the term "sex discrimination" refers to gender and does not include discrimination based on sexual orientation. Some states and some cities have enacted antidiscrimination laws that also prohibit discrimination based on sexual orientation.

Q. My employer just laid off most of the younger female employees at my company, claiming that they had the least seniority. Does this count as disparate impact?

A. Not necessarily, if the layoffs were in furtherance of a bona fide seniority system. Bona fide seniority systems are immune from attack under Title VII and the ADEA. A seniority system is bona fide so long as it was not established for the purpose of discriminating against a protected class, and is applied equally to all employees covered by the system.

A bona fide seniority system may have unfortunate, but legal, effects. For example, layoffs based on seniority may be legal during a downturn in business, even if all the most recent hires (and therefore all the employees laid off) are female.

Q. What should I do if I think I have been illegally discriminated against?

A. It is usually a good idea to bring your complaint directly to the attention of the employer, and attempt to resolve the problem informally. The employer may not be aware that people within the organization are discriminating, or the employer may be able to address your complaint and fix the problem.

However, if you want to pursue a legal remedy, you should get expert advice and act relatively quickly. Antidiscrimination laws specify strict time limits. You will have to en-

---

▶ **TIME LIMITS FOR FILING**

If you have been discriminated against and want to proceed under federal laws, you must file a charge with the EEOC within 180 days from the date of the discriminatory act.

In the absence of any coordination between the EEOC and a state agency, you must first file a charge with the state agency responsible for enforcing the state law. The state agency has at least sixty days to investigate your complaint. After sixty days, the EEOC can investigate your complaint, but your complaint must be filed with the EEOC within 300 days from the date the discrimination occurred or within thirty days after the state agency terminates its proceedings, whichever occurs first.

There is an exception to this time limit if the discrimination occurred in a state that has a state law prohibiting discrimination. In most instances, work-sharing agreements between the EEOC and the state agencies mean that you can file with the EEOC and it will be immediately cross-filed with the state agency, thus allowing virtually all persons making a complaint the opportunity to file during the 300-day filing period.

When the EEOC completes its investigation of the charge, it sends you a letter stating whether the EEOC found reasonable cause to believe the law was violated. This letter is called a right to sue letter. A lawsuit under either Title VII or the ADA must be filed within ninety days of receipt of the right to sue letter. You may file a lawsuit even if the EEOC has not found reasonable cause.

sure that you are filing your suit with the correct agency—which depending on your job and location, could be the EEOC, the NLRB, or a state agency.

Lastly, if you are fired or not hired for discriminatory reasons, you should look for another job. Do so even if it seems that you are entitled to the former job. If you do not actively seek other work, it may appear as though you are not seriously interested in employment. This can weaken your claim and may limit any award of back pay.

Q. Am I protected if I complain about discrimination to my employer or if I file a charge?

A. Various federal laws make it unlawful for an employer to retaliate against an employee because the employee has filed a charge or claim of discrimination, participated in any discrimination proceeding, or otherwise opposed discrimination. So you are protected if you file a charge, testify at a hearing, or assist the government in an investigation. This protection applies to current employees, former employees, and applicants.

However, in order for an employee to be covered by the anti-retaliation provisions in the federal laws, that employee must have a reasonable and good-faith belief that the complained-of conduct violates the law. Parallel anti-retaliation protections may also exist under state law.

Q. Do the antidiscrimination laws protect only women and minorities?

A. No. Antidiscrimination laws protect all workers from employment decisions based on protected status. Thus, if an employer pays a female worker better wages than a male worker performing the same job, that employer may

have discriminated against the male worker based on his sex in violation of Title VII.

Q. But aren't there times when an employer can use a protected status in favor of a minority employee or candidate? What about affirmative action?

A. Yes, such use of a protected status is okay if it occurs through an affirmative action plan. An **affirmative-action plan** (AAP) establishes guidelines for recruiting, hiring, and promoting women and minorities in order to eliminate the present effects of past employment discrimination. An employer analyzes its current employment practices and the makeup of its workforce for any indications that women and minorities are excluded or disadvantaged. If the employer identifies some problems, it then devises new or different policies and practices aimed at solving the problems. The employer also develops goals by which it can measure its progress in correcting the problems.

Q. If an employer gives preferential treatment to a woman or minority employee under an AAP, isn't this reverse discrimination in violation of Title VII?

A. Not necessarily. The U.S. Supreme Court has held that voluntary AAPs remedying discoverable past discrimination are lawful. Evidence of such past discrimination might include obvious racial or sex imbalances in traditionally segregated job categories.

The question involves balancing the employment interests of non-minority employees with the interest of minority employees in being free from the effects of unlawful discrimination.

Q. Are employers required to have affirmative-action plans?

A. Title VII, the ADEA, and the ADA do not require affirmative-action plans. Employers who contract with federal, state, and local governments, however, are often required to develop AAPs. In addition, some employers voluntarily adopt AAPs.

Q. What factors do the courts consider in deciding the validity of an AAP?

A. The law is still developing in this area, but the courts tend to follow four basic guidelines:

1. The AAP should be designed to eliminate obvious racial or sex-based imbalances in the workforce.
2. The plan cannot "unnecessarily trammel the interests" of non-minority workers. It should not automatically exclude non-minority employees from consideration. The minority employee favored by the AAP should be qualified for the job; employers should avoid favoring unqualified workers.
3. The AAP should not adopt strict quotas. It should strive toward realistic goals, taking into account turnover, layoffs, lateral transfers, new job openings, and retirements. These goals should also take into account the number of qualified minorities in the area workforce. Moreover, goals should be temporary—designed to achieve, not maintain, racial balance.
4. Courts are more likely to validate AAPs that focus on recruiting, hiring, and promotion practices, rather than plans that give special treatment in the event of a layoff. The courts are more willing to protect incumbent employees' interests in

their current jobs than any speculative expectations employees might have about a job they don't currently hold.

Q. Is an employer required to pay workers the same wage when they are performing substantially the same job?

A. No. The law prohibits differences in wages only when the reason for the difference is the race, color, religion, national origin, sex, age, or disability of the worker. An employer is allowed to pay workers different wages based on seniority, merit, piece rate, location, or another nondiscriminatory factor.

Q. Some benefits cost more to provide based on an employee's age. Must an employer provide all employees with exactly the same benefits, even if it has to pay more for some of the employees?

A. Generally speaking, the employer cannot discriminate in providing benefits based on age. However, the ADEA recognizes that age affects the cost of providing some benefits. For example, the cost of providing life insurance for a sixty-year-old employee may be more than the cost of buying the same insurance for a twenty-year-old employee. So long as the employer pays the same amount in premiums for both the sixty-year-old and the twenty-year-old, it will not violate the ADEA even though the effect of paying the same premium is that the former will have less coverage than the latter. However, where age does not affect the cost of the benefit, the employer cannot discriminate based on age. For example, an employer could not grant three weeks vacation to all employees under fifty, but only give two weeks vacation to all employees over fifty.

▶ EQUAL PAY ACT

The Equal Pay Act (EPA) and Title VII prohibit an employer from discriminating in wages on the basis of sex if the employees are performing substantially equivalent work. Both statutes are enforced by the EEOC, but there are some differences between the two.

The EPA applies to all employers covered by the FLSA (i.e., with at least two workers engaged in interstate commerce and a $500,000 annual volume of business), whereas Title VII covers employers with fifteen or more employees.

The EPA prohibits wage discrimination based only on sex, whereas Title VII prohibits wage discrimination based on race, color, religion, national origin, and sex.

An employee who brings a lawsuit under the EPA may be entitled to recover twice the amount of lost wages, whereas under Title VII the employee may recover lost wages, compensatory damages if there is intentional discrimination, and punitive damages if there is malice or recklessness.

Q. If an employer provides health insurance for its employees, must it offer coverage to employees with disabilities?

A. Yes. Under the ADA, an employer cannot deny employees with disabilities equal access to health insurance coverage.

Q. Must health insurance cover all medical expenses of employees with a disability?

A. Not necessarily. Many insurance policies have **preexisting-condition clauses** that disallow coverage for medical conditions predating a person's employment by his or her current employer. Such clauses are lawful so long as they are not used as a subterfuge to evade the purposes of the ADA. Many health insurance policies also limit coverage for certain procedures or treatments to a specific number per year. For example, some provide reimbursement for only twelve psychiatric treatment sessions per year. Such limitations

are generally allowed. It is not clear, however, whether an employer could offer a health insurance policy that puts a cap on the amount of reimbursement for a specific disease (for example, a $5,000 reimbursement limit for cancer) as opposed to a cap on the amount of reimbursement that is available for any type of medical condition (for example, a $1 million lifetime limit).

Discrimination Based on Gender

Q. Can an employer fire or otherwise discriminate against an employee because she is pregnant?

A. No. The Pregnancy Discrimination Act, an amendment to Title VII, specifically includes discrimination because of pregnancy, childbirth, and related medical conditions as a type of sex discrimination. Thus, an employer cannot base employment decisions on the fact that a worker is pregnant. Moreover, the employer must treat pregnancy in the

▶ PREEXISTING MEDICAL CONDITIONS

The Health Insurance Portability and Accountability Act of 1996 (HIPAA) limits preexisting-condition clauses in health insurance contracts. Individuals with a preexisting medical condition that was diagnosed, or for which treatment was received, within six months before enrolling in a new health insurance plan are not covered for that condition for the first twelve months. Thereafter, the condition is covered for as long as the employee keeps the insurance. A preexisting-condition clause can never be applied to pregnancy, newborns, or adopted children.

An employee's new health plan must give "credit for time served"—that is, the amount of time you were enrolled in your previous plan—and deduct it from the exclusion period. Thus, if you've had twelve or more months of continuous group coverage, you'll have no preexisting-condition waiting period. And if you had prior coverage for ten months, you can be subject to only a two-month exclusion period when you switch jobs. In order to make sure that coverage is "continuous," you cannot let it lapse for more than sixty-two days.

same way as it would treat any other non-work-related employee medical condition.

Q. Must an employer provide health insurance coverage for pregnancy?

A. The answer depends on whether the employer provides any health insurance coverage at all. Antidiscrimination laws do not require an employer to provide any benefits, including health insurance. However, if an employer does provide such benefits, they must be available to all employees without regard to sex, race, color, ethnicity, religion, national origin, age, or disability. Thus, if an employer provides health insurance, it must include coverage for pregnancy and pregnancy-related conditions.

Q. May an employer require a worker to take leave when she becomes pregnant?

A. No, so long as she can continue to perform her job.

Q. When an employee takes time off to give birth to a child, will she get her old job back?

A. Title VII does not require the employer to provide either paid or unpaid leaves of absence with rights of reinstatement for pregnancy. What Title VII does require is that the employer treat absences due to pregnancy the same as it treats absences due to any other medical condition. For example, if an employer's leave policy provides for time off when employees are unable to work due to medical conditions, then a worker unable to work due to pregnancy has the same right to time off as a worker unable to work due to a broken leg.

The duration of any leave time also depends on the employer's policy. Thus, if the employer provides two weeks of medical leave per year, a pregnant employee would be entitled to her job back so long as her leave did not exceed two weeks.

This basic principle of equal treatment applies to other decisions regarding the pregnant worker. If disabled workers are paid while on disability leave, then the pregnant employee must be paid. If an employer requires that all employees submit a doctor's certification regarding their inability to work, then the employer may also require the pregnant worker to submit such a certification.

Q. Is an employer required to give employees maternity or paternity leave?

A. If an employer is covered under the terms of the FMLA, it is required to give employees who meet the eligibility requirements up to twelve weeks of unpaid time off to care for a new born or newly adopted child.

If there is a medical reason for an extended leave after childbirth, then the employer must treat the leave in the same way as it would treat any other request for medical or disability leave.

Some states have laws requiring employers to grant parental leave.

▶ THE FAMILY AND MEDICAL LEAVE ACT

The Family and Medical Leave Act (FMLA) is a federal law requiring employers to grant up to twelve weeks of unpaid leave, with the right to reinstatement, to employees under certain conditions. The law applies to private employers who employ at least fifty employees, and to all public employers. Employees are eligible for leave if they have worked for their employer for at least a year, if they have performed at least 1,250 hours of service for their employer in the previous twelve months, and if there are at least fifty employees at the employees' work site or at least fifty employees within seventy-five miles of that worksite.

The law requires employers to grant employees up to twelve weeks of unpaid leave during any twelve-month period for any one of the following reasons:

- because of the birth of a child and in order to care for the child;
- because of adoption or foster care placement of a child and in order to care for the child;
- because of a serious health condition that makes the employee unable to perform his or her duties; or
- in order to care for a spouse, a child, or a parent with a serious medical condition.

If the employer provides health insurance coverage for its employees, it must continue that coverage during the leave of absence with no additional charge to the employee. At the end of the leave period, the employer is required to reinstate the employee to his or her previous position or to an equivalent position.

Employees can enforce their entitlement to the rights granted under the FMLA by filing a lawsuit. A few states have enacted leave laws that apply to smaller employers or that allow for more than twelve weeks of unpaid leave for childbirth or serious health conditions. At least one state, California, has enacted legislation providing for six weeks of *paid* leave for reasons relating to childbirth, adoption, or serious health conditions.

Q. Must the employer's health insurance pay for abortions?

A. No. The Pregnancy Discrimination Act expressly provides that employers do not have to pay health insurance benefits for abortions, "except where the life of the mother would be endangered if the fetus were carried to term, or except where medical complications have arisen from an abortion."

Q. May employers provide health-care coverage for dependents of married male workers, but not for dependents of married female workers?

A. No. Title VII prohibits all sex-based discrimination with respect to benefits. Employers don't have to offer health insurance at all to employees or their spouses, but if they do, then they can't discriminate. Thus, if the employer provides health insurance benefits to the spouses of male workers, then it must provide the same coverage to the spouses of female workers. Moreover, the extent of the coverage provided for dependents must be equal. For example, if all medical expenses of female workers' spouses are covered, then all medical expenses of male workers' spouses must be covered.

Q. May employers fire female workers who get married?

A. Title VII does not protect workers based on their marital status. However, if the employer fires only female workers who get married and not male workers, then the employer has violated Title VII by engaging in disparate-treatment sex discrimination—because it has applied an employment policy only to women.

Some states have laws that expressly prohibit employment discrimination based on marital status. In those states, firing married

workers would violate the law, even if the employer applied its policy to both sexes.

Q. Since statistics show that women generally live longer than men, can employers provide different retirement and pension plans for each sex?

A. No. The U.S. Supreme Court has held that pension plans cannot discriminate based on sex.

Other Protections for Workers

Q. Employees who are in the army reserve must attend training camp every year. Is the employer required to give them time off?

A. Yes. The Uniformed Services Employment and Reemployment Rights Act (USERRA) requires all employers to grant unpaid of leaves of absence so that employees in the military may perform their military obligations. Upon completion of their military duties, employees are entitled to their previous jobs, with the same seniority, status, pay, and vacation as they would have enjoyed if they had not been absent. The reemployment rights granted by this law apply to all types of military service—active or reserve armed forces and National Guard—whether the employee is drafted or enlisted.

Q. Can an employer lay off an employee because he or she has been called for jury duty?

A. No. The Jury System Improvements Act is a federal law that prohibits an employer from disciplining or discharging an employee because he or she has been called to serve on a federal jury. Additionally, most states prohibit employers from firing a worker who is called to perform jury service in state courts.

Q. Can an employer fire an employee for refusing to work on a certain day if his or her religion requires attendance at services?

A. Title VII requires employers to accommodate the religious beliefs of their employees unless the accommodation would cause an undue hardship for the business. If other employees are willing to work the shift, and the employer would not have to pay them more, then the employer may be required to accommodate the employee. However, if the accommodation would cost the employer additional money, or would cause a disruption in the business or violate the provisions of a collective-bargaining agreement, then accommodation would probably be considered unreasonable. There are many types of relatively cost-free accommodations that an employer may make, such as

- allowing employees to wear religiously significant garments, such as a yarmulke or a hijab;
- allowing an employee to leave work early in order to attend a religious service, where the employee could make up the missed work by coming in early or staying late on another day; and
- permitting an employee to take a short prayer break that does not disrupt other employees' work.

Sexual Harassment

Q. Is sexual harassment illegal?

A. Yes. The U.S. Supreme Court has held that Title VII's prohibition against sex discrimination includes sexual harassment as a

> ▶ **TIME TO VOTE**
>
> Approximately thirty states, including New York, Ohio, and Maryland, have state laws requiring employers to grant employees time off from work in order to vote in elections. The purpose of these laws is to ensure that employees can take time off from work to vote, if their work hours would not ordinarily allow them sufficient time to do so. Thus, if an employee's work shift were from 3:00 P.M. until 11:00 P.M., the employer would not have to give the employee time off to vote. But if the employee worked from 8:00 A.M. until 6:00 P.M., the employer may be required to grant time off. Most of these laws apply to all types of elections, whether federal, state, or local, although a few are limited to particular types of elections. Most of the laws do not allow the employer to deduct wages for the time off.

type of illegal sex discrimination. Moreover, some states have laws expressly prohibiting sexual harassment. Most others interpret their laws prohibiting sex discrimination to include sexual harassment.

Q. How is sexual harassment defined?

A. The EEOC defines **sexual harassment** as "unwelcome sexual advances, requests for sexual favors, and other verbal or physical conduct of a sexual nature . . . when . . . submission to or rejection of such conduct is used as the basis for employment decisions . . . or such conduct has the purpose or effect of . . . creating an intimidating, hostile or offensive working environment."

Thus, sexual harassment consists of two types of prohibited conduct:

- quid pro quo—where submission to harassment is used as the basis for employment decisions; and
- hostile environment—where harassment creates an offensive working environment.

Sexual harassment can occur when severe or pervasive harassing conduct, not necessarily sexual in nature, is targeted at a person because of his or her sex. In these kinds of cases, it can be more difficult to show that the harassing conduct is because of sex—that is, to show that the reason the victim is being singled out for the comments is because she is a woman. Often, whether behavior counts as sexual harassment depends on the circumstances. Courts will consider the nature, severity, and frequency of the conduct as well as the conditions under which it occurred.

An employee who is a victim of sexual harassment can file a claim with the EEOC. If the state in which the employee lives prohibits this type of harassment, then the worker should also contact the proper state agency.

Q. Does the gender of the harasser or the victim matter?

A. No. Both men and women can be victims of sexual harassment, and harassment because of sex (as distinguished from harassment because of sexual orientation) is illegal under federal law whether the harasser is the same sex or the opposite sex. Harassment on the basis of sexual orientation is not illegal

---

> ▶ **HARASSMENT THAT'S NOT SEXUAL**
>
> Title VII also forbids words and conduct that vilify and denigrate people based on their race, religion, or national origin. Severe and pervasive racial, religious, and ethnic slurs can create a hostile work environment. This concept— **discriminatory harassment**—is very similar to the concept of sexual harassment caused by a hostile work environment, and the employer's liability for this conduct is based on similar principles.
>
> The ADEA and the ADA also prohibit comments related to age or disability that create a hostile work environment.

---

under federal law, but is illegal under some state and local laws.

Q. What is quid pro quo harassment?

A. **Quid pro quo harassment** occurs when an employee must submit to unwelcome sexual advances in order to receive some job benefit. For example, a supervisor promises an employee a raise if she will go out on a date with him, or tells an employee he will be fired if he doesn't engage in intimate conduct with her.

Only people with supervisory authority can engage in quid pro quo harassment, since it requires the harasser to have the authority to grant or withhold job benefits.

Courts look to whether the harassment results in a tangible employment action—that is, whether there was a significant change in employment status, such as firing, failure to promote, or a change in wage rate.

Q. If an employee "voluntarily" has sex with a supervisor, does this mean that she or he has not been sexually harassed?

A. Not necessarily. In order to constitute harassment, sexual advances must be "unwelcome." If an employee by her conduct shows that sexual advances are unwelcome, it does not matter that she eventually "voluntarily" succumbs to the harassment. In deciding whether the sexual advances are unwelcome, the courts often will allow evidence concerning the employee's dress, behavior, and language, as indications of whether the employee welcomed the advances.

Moreover, sexual advances that initially may have been welcomed subsequently may become unwelcome. Thus, an employee who engages in a welcomed office romance with a supervisor, but later decides to end it, may become the victim of quid pro quo harassment if the supervisor demotes the employee because of the refusal to continue the romance.

Q. Is an employer liable for quid pro quo harassment engaged in by its supervisors?

A. In general, an employer is held to be strictly liable—meaning the employer is liable even if it did not know about the harassment—when a supervisor engages in quid pro quo harassment that results in a tangible adverse employment action.

Q. What is hostile-environment harassment?

A. Hostile-environment harassment occurs when an employee is regularly subjected to comments of a sexual nature, offensive sexual materials, unwelcome physical contact, or derogatory and insulting comments because of his or her protected status, and when the actions have unreasonably interfered with the employee's work environment. Generally speaking, a single isolated incident will not constitute hostile-environment harassment unless it involves extremely outrageous and egregious conduct. The courts look to see whether the conduct in question is both serious and frequent.

▶ WHAT CAN VICTIMS OF SEXUAL OR DISCRIMINATORY HARASSMENT DO?

Employees subjected to sexual or discriminatory harassment should immediately notify their supervisors. If the supervisor is the harasser, then the employer should go to the company's human resources department. If the employer has an established anti-harassment policy that outlines a specific complaint procedure, then employees must utilize this procedure.

Victims should keep a written record of the harassment, detailing the place, time, people involved, and any witnesses. Victims can also express their disapproval of the conduct to the perpetrator and tell him or her to stop. Victims should also keep a written record of how, when, and to whom they have reported any harassment, and the results of such reports.

Supervisors, managers, coworkers, and even customers can be responsible for creating a hostile environment.

Q. Is an employer liable for hostile-environment harassment?

A. It depends on who has created it. The employer is liable when supervisors or managers are responsible for the hostile environment, unless the employer can prove that it exercised reasonable care to prevent and promptly correct harassing behavior and that the employee unreasonably failed to take advantage of any preventive or corrective opportunities provided by the employer.

When coworkers and/or customers create the harassment, the employer is liable if it is negligent in addressing the problem. Thus, if the employer knew or reasonably should have known of the harassment, and failed to take prompt and effective remedial action, it may be liable.

Remedial action usually requires a prompt investigation and corrective action. The action taken by the employer should be in proportion to the severity of the offense.

▶ CHECKLIST: HOW EMPLOYERS CAN PREVENT SEXUAL AND DISCRIMINATORY HARASSMENT

Employers can take several measures to prevent sexual and discriminatory harassment in the workplace:

- Develop a written policy dealing with harassment, indicating that sexual harassment is against the law and also violates company policy. The employer can contact the EEOC for its guidelines on sexual harassment. These will help the employer formulate its policy.

- Develop an effective complaint procedure for workers subjected to harassment.

- Provide a mechanism for employees to bypass their supervisor if the supervisor participates in the harassment or fails to take proper action.

- Promptly and effectively respond to harassment complaints.

- Undertake a complete and confidential investigation of any allegations of harassment and impose appropriate disciplinary action.

- Prevent harassment before it occurs. Employers should circulate or post the company anti-harassment policy and the EEOC rules on sexual harassment, express strong disapproval of sexual harassment, and tell employees of their right to be free from harassment.

- Protect employees from retaliation based on complaints of harassment. Any written harassment policy should contain a clear statement that retaliation will not be tolerated.

Employers are not required to terminate alleged harassers in all situations. Employers must address employee harassment complaints and are not excused from acting on the grounds that the complaint was uncorroborated and/or was denied by the harasser.

Age Discrimination

Q. Can employers force workers to retire?

A. Generally speaking, no. The ADEA prohibits mandatory retirement based on age. However, if an employee can no longer perform his or her job duties, the employer is allowed to discharge that person based on nonperformance.

There are some exceptions to the general rules against forced retirement. Executives or high-level policy makers can be forced to retire at age sixty-five if they are entitled to receive retirement benefits of at least $44,000 a year, exclusive of Social Security. Firefighters,

police officers, and prison guards employed by state and local governments can also be forced to retire if required to do so by state or local law and pursuant to a bona fide retirement plan.

Q. Can employers offer voluntary retirement incentives?

A. Yes, so long as they are truly voluntary, and so long as the decision whether to accept the incentives and retire is up to the employee.

Privacy in the Workplace

Q. My employer has a lot of private information about me. What kind of protections does the law provide regarding confidential information?

A. The ADA requires employers to keep any employee medical records confidential and separate from employee personnel files. The law states that the only people who may be informed about an employee's medical conditions are: first aid or safety personnel if the medical condition may require emergency treatment, and government officials investigating compliance with the ADA.

The employer may also inform supervisors and managers about restrictions on work duties or necessary accommodations required by a disability.

The Privacy Act forbids federal government employers from disclosing any information contained in employee files without the written consent of the employee.

Additionally, some state statutes prohibit the disclosure of certain employee information, including medical records or certain other personnel information without the writ-

---

▶ **HOW TO FILE A CHARGE UNDER THE ADEA**

If you believe you have been a victim of age discrimination, you may file a charge with the EEOC. If you are in a state that has a state law prohibiting age discrimination, you may also file a complaint with the appropriate state agency. Before you can bring a lawsuit, you must file a charge with the EEOC and with the applicable state agency, if there is one.

ten consent of the employee. Further, the NLRA imposes a duty on the private employer to disclose to unions information that is necessary and relevant for collective bargaining purposes, which can include employee personnel files.

Unnecessary disclosure of information in which an employee has a reasonable expectation of privacy may result in the employer being liable in tort for invasion of privacy or intentional infliction of emotional distress.

Q. Do employees have a right of access to their personnel files?

A. The Privacy Act allows federal government employees to have access to their records and to make a copy of any portion of the applicable documents. It also establishes a procedure by which federal employees can challenge the information contained in their files.

Several other laws apply to the private sector. These laws require some private employers to maintain medical records when employees are exposed to potentially toxic materials at work, and the Occupational Safety and Health Administration (OSHA) requires that employees have access to these records.

Some states do grant employees access to their personnel files, and may also establish procedures by which employees can challenge information in these files.

Q. Can employers listen to employee telephone calls?

A. The Omnibus Crime Control and Safe Streets Act prohibits employers from eavesdropping on, or wiretapping, telephone calls. There is a large exception allowing employers to listen in on an extension telephone used in the ordinary course of business. A second big exception allows employers to monitor telephone calls where employees have been notified expressly that their telephone conversations will be monitored. Some courts have indicated, however, that once the private nature of a telephone conversation is determined, any continued eavesdropping would not be in the ordinary course of business, and may thus subject the employer to liability. An employer violating the law can be sued for money damages.

Some states have enacted laws that place more restrictions on telephone monitoring—for example, requiring the consent of all parties to the conversation or requiring that employees be notified that their calls may be monitored.

Q. Can employers use video cameras to monitor workers?

A. In general, yes, if the monitoring is for security or antitheft purposes and employees are advised of the surveillance. However, the NLRA prohibits employer surveillance of employee union activity, discussions about unions, or union meetings. In addition, if a union represents employees, then an employer is required to bargain with the union before instituting workplace surveillance.

Some state laws regulate the extent to which an employer can monitor workers. Moreover, state tort law may protect employees against highly offensive intrusions upon privacy in a place where a person has a reasonable expectation of privacy. For example, monitoring an employee bathroom may be considered an invasion of privacy.

Q. Can the employer monitor employee use of the computer at work?

A. Yes. There is currently no federal or state law prohibiting employers from monitoring their own computer systems.

Q. Can the employer read employee e-mail?

A. Although the law is still developing in this area, employers can monitor e-mails sent or received over employer-provided computer equipment. Currently, neither federal nor state law prohibits a private employer's access to e-mails stored in the company computer system. If the employer intercepts e-mail as it is being sent from or to computer equipment owned by the employer, then there may be a violation of the federal Electronic Communications Privacy Act, unless the employer notifies employees that their e-mail may be intercepted. See Chapter 13, "Computer Law," for more about e-mail on the job.

Q. Can employers search workers or their possessions?

A. Yes, generally, if workers have been told in advance that the employer can do so. Within limits, the law usually allows such searches. However, a collective-bargaining agreement might restrict or prohibit such conduct. (For a discussion of the constitutional restrictions on public employers, see "Special Rights of Public Employees" on page 562.)

Q. If I am an employer who wants to search my employees and their possessions, what should I know?

A. In order to avoid tort liability for assault, battery, false arrest, intentional infliction of emotional harm, or invasion of privacy, employers should be extremely careful about the manner in which they conduct searches.

First, employers should have a work-related reason for conducting the search, although they do not have to prove probable cause. Second, any search should be conducted by the least intrusive means possible.

Third, employers should inform employees that searches might be conducted. Fourth, employers should not physically harm employees in the course of the search or threaten employees with physical harm. Fifth, the employer should not attempt to prevent employees from leaving the premises by threat of harm or other coercive means, although they are usually allowed to tell employees that they will be disciplined or discharged if they leave.

Q. Can employers impose dress and grooming codes?

A. Generally speaking, the law allows employers to impose dress and grooming policies. However, such policies may occasionally run afoul of Title VII. For example, if an employer imposes a dress code on female employees but not male employees, this could constitute disparate treatment based on sex in violation of Title VII. Or a grooming code may have a more severe effect on members of a particular protected class, thus having an adverse impact under Title VII. For example, a rule requiring employees to be clean-shaven may particularly affect members of certain religious groups. In that case, the employer would have to show a business necessity in order to enforce the policy.

Q. Can employers require employees to speak only English while at work?

A. The EEOC has interpreted Title VII to prohibit the promulgation of an English-only rule, unless it can be justified by business necessity. Requiring employees to speak only English may have an adverse impact on persons of certain ethnic or national origin. Thus, an employer may be able to justify an English-only rule when its employees are dealing with customers, but could not enforce such a rule in the employee lunchroom.

Q. Can employers prohibit smoking in the workplace?

A. Yes. But if the employees have a union, then the employer must bargain with the union about implementing such a policy.

Q. One of my employees did something when off-duty that isn't criminal, but that I disagree with. Can I take adverse employment-related action against the employee on this basis?

A. It depends. Several states prohibit an employer from taking adverse action against an employee for using lawful products off the employer's premises during nonworking time. In those states, an employer could not fire or refuse to hire a worker who smokes off duty or drinks alcohol. Moreover, most states prohibit employers from firing or refusing to hire employees because they use tobacco products off employer premises during nonworking time.

A collective-bargaining agreement may require the employer to justify employment decisions based on just cause. As a general rule, in order to satisfy a just-cause requirement, the employer would have to show that the employee's off-duty conduct somehow implicated the employer's legitimate business interests.

Q. I have been asked to provide a reference for a former employee. What can I say?

A. This will depend on where you live and what you plan to say. But generally, you should be cautious. Approximately twenty states prohibit employers from engaging in blacklisting. Blacklisting consists of intentionally taking action aimed at preventing someone from obtaining employment. Truthful statements concerning an individual's ability to perform the job in question are not considered to be blacklisting.

The manner in which a reference is made and its content can give rise to employer liability under state tort law relating to defamation, intentional interference with a prospective employment contract, intentional infliction of emotional distress, or negligent misrepresentation. (See Chapter 6, "Personal Injury," for more information on tort law.)

Defamation occurs when one person's false statement injures the reputation of another person. However, most states recognize giving references to prospective employers in good faith as a defense against defamation charges.

Providing false information to a prospective employer with the intent of causing an applicant to lose his or her job constitutes intentional interference with a prospective employment contract.

Disclosure of private personal matters unrelated to work can result in a claim for invasion of privacy or intentional infliction of emotional distress.

Lastly, a false statement that causes a loss of money can be grounds for negligent misrepresentation.

To be safe, an employer should limit the number of people authorized to provide references on its behalf. Second, statements based on hearsay or gossip should be avoided. Third, only items that have a direct bearing on an individual's work performance should be disclosed. Finally, obtaining a release from the former employee before providing any information to third parties can help limit liability.

Q. Must an employer provide a former employee with a reference?

A. Generally speaking, no. However, some states require an employer to provide, upon request, a service letter to the employee. A service letter indicates the nature of the employee's job, the duration of the employment, and the reason for the separation.

Special Rights of Public Employees

Most of the antidiscrimination laws that have been discussed in this chapter apply to public employers as well as private workers. However, in some instances, public employees have different, and sometimes more, protections.

Q. What is a public employee?

A. A public employee is one employed by the government. This would include public school teachers, county clerks, sanitation department employees, and federal prosecutors.

Q. What additional law and protections apply to public employees?

A. Public workers have additional protections not normally available to private employees. These protections are found in civil service laws and the federal and state constitutions.

Q. What are civil service laws?

A. Civil service laws establish employment policies for public employees based on the merit principle. The rationale for establishing civil-service laws was to eliminate political considerations from the public employment process. The elements of a civil service system generally include guidelines for recruiting applicants, testing programs for screening applicants, impartial hiring criteria, job classifications based on duties and responsibilities, and protection against arbitrary discipline and discharge. A commission is usually established to ensure that the public employer is following the civil service rules. The particulars of civil service laws and the role and operation of the commission vary from state to state.

Q. What type of protection does the U.S. Constitution afford public employees?

A. The most important protections afforded by the U.S. Constitution (that are not duplicated by antidiscrimination laws already discussed) are:

- freedom of association;
- freedom of speech;
- freedom from unreasonable searches and seizures; and
- due process protections in the event of discharge from a job.

Q. How does freedom of association protect a public employee?

A. Basically, a public employer cannot base employment decisions on the fact that someone belongs to certain types of clubs or associates with particular people. Thus, a public employer can't refuse to hire applicants just because they are Republicans, or belong to a motorcycle club, or are members of the American Civil Liberties Union.

Q. How does freedom of speech protect a public employee?

A. When public employees speak out on issues of public concern, their employer cannot discipline or discharge them for their comments. For example, if a schoolteacher writes a letter to the newspaper criticizing the curriculum developed by the school board, the school board could not discharge the teacher for making that criticism.

Q. How does freedom from unreasonable search and seizure protect a public employee?

A. An employee may have a reasonable expectation of privacy in certain places at work, such as a desk or a filing cabinet that is not shared with other workers. In those areas, an employer may conduct a work-related non-investigatory search, as well as an investigatory search for work-related misconduct, only if there are "reasonable grounds for suspecting the search will turn up evidence that the employee is guilty of work-related misconduct, or that the search is necessary for a non-investigatory work-related purpose such as to retrieve a needed file."

Although the law on this point is unsettled, public employers would likely need probable cause to suspect workplace misconduct before they could search personal items such as a briefcase, luggage, or a purse that an employee brings into the workplace.

Q. How does due process protect a public employee?

A. The Fifth Amendment to the U.S. Constitution provides that no person shall be "deprived of life, liberty, or property, without due process of law." This means that people accused of crimes have certain protections under the law, as do those whose property the government seeks, as when the government needs to appropriate a homeowner's property in order to widen a road. But when is a job considered "property"?

The courts have held that an employee has a property interest in a job if there is a written or implied contract granting the employee a property interest in that job; if past practice of the employer shows that the employee has a property interest in the job; or if a statute gives the employee a property interest in the job. For example, a teacher with tenure is considered to have a property interest in his or her job, because there is the express or implied understanding that a teacher cannot lose that job without just cause.

If a public employee has a property interest in a job, he or she cannot be discharged without due process. Due process requires that the employee be given notice of the reason for being discharged and a fair hearing at which to contest the decision.

Unions in the Workplace

Unions represent employees. They deal with employers concerning workplace issues. Instead of each worker negotiating separately with his or her employer regarding wages, health insurance coverage, and other employment issues, the union bargains with the employer on behalf of the workers in the bargaining unit.

The National Labor Relations Act (NLRA), which regulates union-employer relations at work, is premised on the notion that individual employees have very little leverage in bargaining with their employers, and that (at least in practice) employers unilaterally set wage and benefit levels without any input from workers. However, if workers pool their individual bargaining power and negotiate collectively through a union, then the result will more likely be the product of true give-and-take, and the workers will have a more effective voice in workplace issues.

Q. What kinds of employees are covered by the NLRA?

A. The NLRA covers private employers engaged in interstate commerce, but excludes railroad, airline, and public employers. (For more information, see "Federal Laws Regulating the Workplace" on page 525.)

However, even if you work for a covered employer, you may not be protected. Certain categories of workers fall outside of the statute: domestic employees of a family, farm workers, persons employed by a parent or a spouse, independent contractors, supervisors, and managers.

Q. Does the NLRA apply to employees in the public sector (i.e., government employees)?

A. No, however other federal and state laws regulate the role of unions in government employment. Title VII of the Civil Service Reform Act (5 U.S.C. Sections 7101–7135) grants federal employees the right to be represented by a union for purposes of collective bargaining, and prohibits employment discrimination based on union activity. This statute also established the Federal Labor Relations Authority and the Federal Services Impasse Panel to enforce the rights and duties contained in the law.

Additionally, many states have comprehensive legislation covering union representation and collective bargaining for all state and municipal employees. Others have authorized collective bargaining for certain categories of employees, including firefighters, police, and schoolteachers. Lastly, a minority of states prohibit collective bargaining for public sector workers. If you are a public worker who would like to look into union representation, it is probably best to contact an attorney in your state with expertise in labor relations.

Q. How does the NLRA regulate the union-employer relationship?

A. First, the NLRA gives employees certain rights and prohibits employers and unions from interfering with those rights. Second, the NLRA sets up a mechanism by which employees can vote by secret ballot on whether

---

▶ EMPLOYEE ACTIVITIES THAT ARE NOT PROTECTED BY THE NLRA

Even if employees are exercising a right under the NLRA, they may not be protected by the law. The law does not protect slowdowns, violence, sabotage, or vandalism of company property.

Also, the NLRA generally protects an activity only if it involves more than one employee. For example, one worker asking the employer to institute health insurance coverage is not engaged in protected conduct. However, if the worker was acting as a spokesperson for other employees, or if the employees went as a group to ask the employer for health insurance coverage, then the law would protect that group. A single employee attempting to organize colleagues would also be protected.

they want a union to represent them in the workplace. Third, it requires employers and unions to engage in collective bargaining, and regulates the type of employer and union tactics that may occur during the course of collective bargaining.

Q. What rights do employees have under the NLRA?

A. The NLRA gives employees the right to

- join unions;
- engage in conduct aimed at promoting or helping unions;
- choose a union to represent them in collective bargaining with their employer; and
- engage in group conduct for collective bargaining or to help each other with workplace issues (this includes the right to strike).

▶ UNION ACTIVITY ON COMPANY PROPERTY AND DURING COMPANY TIME

Employers can prohibit discussions and the distribution of literature during working time, that is, during those periods of the workday when employees are required to work. Thus, an employer could prohibit discussion while employees are working at their machines, but could not prohibit discussions while both parties are on breaks; an employer could prohibit passing out literature on an assembly line, but not passing out literature in non-work areas.

The law also says that employees have the right not to do these things.

Q. What are some examples of how employees might use these rights?

A. Employees might utilize these rights by attending union meetings, talking to co-employees about unions or other workplace issues, passing out union literature, wearing union buttons, campaigning for union office, circulating petitions advocating workplace improvements, or engaging in a work stoppage or picketing.

Q. Must there be a union in the workplace in order for employees to legally exercise their rights?

A. No. Employees have these rights regardless of whether a union represents them in the workplace. For example, a group of workers in a nonunion workplace who circulates a petition asking the employer for a wage increase is engaged in a "protected concerted activity" that is covered by the NLRA.

Q. Can an employer fire employees because they exercise their rights under the NLRA?

A. No. The NLRA prohibits an employer from discharging, disciplining, or otherwise discriminating against employees who exercise their rights under the NLRA. Prohibited discrimination includes demotion, layoff, wage reduction, and denial of a promotion.

Q. What other types of restrictions does the NLRA impose on employer conduct?

A. The NLRA prohibits an employer from interfering with, restraining, or coercing employees in the exercise of their rights. Employers cannot threaten employees with

▶ EXAMPLES OF EMPLOYER CONDUCT PROHIBITED BY THE NLRA

If a group of employees asks the employer for a raise and the employer fires them for asking, then the employer has violated the NLRA, because the employees were engaged in a protected concerted activity. An employer who refuses to promote an employee because that employee spoke with his or her coworkers about union representation has also violated the NLRA. Similarly, an employer who suspends a worker for handing out union leaflets in the locker room during lunch has violated the NLRA.

discipline or other adverse actions because they have exercised their rights. For example, an employer who tells employees that they will lose their jobs if they vote for a union has violated the NLRA.

Neither can an employer promise employees benefits in order to get them to vote against a union, such as promising a wage increase if the employees reject the union.

As a general rule, employers cannot question employees about their union activities, ask them whether other employees support a union, or ask them what happened at a union meeting.

Q. How does a union come to represent a group of employees?

A. A union-organizing campaign can start either because the employees in the workplace have contacted the union or because the union on its own seeks to organize the workers.

The first step in an organizing campaign is to determine whether the employees have any interest in union representation. The union asks the employees to show their interest by signing authorization cards. If at least

▶ FILING A CHARGE UNDER THE NLRA

If workers believe their rights under the NLRA have been violated, they can file an unfair-labor-practice charge with their regional office of the National Labor Relations Board (NLRB). The time limit for filing a charge is six months from the date of the unlawful action. The regional office will investigate the charge and decide whether the law has been violated. If it decides there was no violation, it will dismiss the charge. A worker whose charge has been dismissed may appeal the decision to the NLRB in Washington, D.C., but does not have to the right to file a lawsuit in court.

If the NLRB decides the charge has merit, it will issue a complaint and set a hearing before an administrative law judge, at which evidence will be taken and arguments made. The administrative law judge will then decide whether the law was violated. The decision of the administrative law judge can be appealed to the NLRB. The decision of the NLRB can then be appealed to the federal circuit courts of appeal.

30 percent of the workers sign cards, then the union can ask the NLRB to hold a secret ballot election.

Before the election is held, there is usually time for both the union and the employer to campaign among the workers, discussing the pros and cons of union representation. The election itself usually is held at the employer's place of business so that it is easy for the workers to vote. The NLRB conducts the secret ballot election.

If the union wins the election, it becomes the bargaining agent for the employees and negotiates a collective-bargaining agreement with the employer. The employer must negotiate with the union. If the union loses the election, the status quo prevails.

The key point is that employees may decide whether they want a union; it is their choice to make.

Q. If the union wins the election, which employees does the union represent?

A. Even if the employees vote to be represented by a union, the union doesn't necessarily represent every person employed by the company. The union election is held among those employees who are considered to have a "community of interest" at the workplace. These employees form a **bargaining unit,** which is the group of workers voting in the election who will be represented by the union in the event the union wins the election.

Employees have a community of interest if they share similar working conditions, jobs, hours of work, and supervision. For example, employees who work on an assembly line probably do not have a community of interest with office workers, whereas salespeople in a department store would probably share a community of interest even if they work in different departments and sell different types of goods.

Q. So what happens to those individuals who are not part of the "community of interest?"

A. Their relationship with the employer is the same as it was before the vote.

Q. If a worker votes against the union in the election and the union wins, does the union represent that worker?

A. Yes, if the employee is in the community of interest. The law requires the union to represent all employees in the bargaining unit, fairly and non-discriminatorily, regardless of whether they supported the union.

Q. If a union wins the election, must the workers join the union?

A. No. Just as the NLRA gives employees the right to join unions, it also gives employees the right to refuse to join. The NLRA prohibits both employers and unions from forcing employees to join a union.

However, remember that all employees that are part of the bargaining unit are represented by the union. Therefore, employees can be forced to pay for the work that the union performs on their behalf, even if they do not want to join. Most collective bargaining agreements contain a **union security clause.** In effect, this type of clause requires employees to pay the dues and fees that union members are required to pay. If an employee refuses to pay dues, he or she can be fired.

Because the law requires the union to represent all the employees in the bargaining unit, regardless of whether they are members of the union, the law allows the union to "tax"

▶ RELIGIOUS AND OTHER OBJECTIONS TO UNIONS

If your religion prohibits you from supporting a labor union, you're exempt from paying dues and fees to a union under a union security clause. But the law permits an alternative requirement to be imposed on you: you must pay an amount equivalent to union fees and dues to a nonreligious, non-labor charitable organization. Both the NLRA and Title VII require that such an accommodation be made to your religious beliefs.

If your *personal* views conflict with those of the union, you can object to paying dues or fees used for purposes unrelated to collective bargaining. You are entitled to have the financial obligation imposed by the union security clause reduced. For example, if 20 percent of union dues money is spent on activities unrelated to collective bargaining and representing workers, then you only have to pay 80 percent of your dues. The burden is on you to notify the union of your objection.

the workers for the benefits they receive from union representation. Some states prohibit union security clauses.

Q. What is a collective-bargaining agreement?

A. A collective-bargaining agreement is the contract that the employer and the union negotiate. When a union wins an NLRB election, the law requires the employer to sit down and bargain in good faith with the union about the terms of a contract. This contract will cover the wages, hours, and other terms and conditions of employment for the employees in the bargaining unit. While this contract is in effect (usually a term of three years), the employer, the union, and the employees must comply with its terms. Generally, an employer cannot make any changes in working conditions unless the union agrees to those changes.

Q. What is covered in a collective-bargaining agreement?

A. Most collective-bargaining agreements cover the basic terms and conditions of employment. These include wages, work hours, health insurance, pension benefits, vacations, seniority rights, job assignments, work rules, and procedures for promotions, layoffs, recalls, and transfers. Most contracts also contain a provision allowing the employer to discipline or discharge employees only if there is "just cause," and a provision in which the employer deducts union dues directly from the employees' paychecks and sends them to the union.

Q. What happens if the employer fails to live up to the terms of the collective bargaining agreement?

A. Most union contracts provide for grievance procedures. If the union believes that the employer has violated the contract, then the union can file a complaint using the grievance procedure outlined therein. Such procedures typically include several steps, during which the union and the employer attempt to settle the dispute themselves. If they are unsuccessful, the complaint may be submitted to an arbitrator for an impartial decision. At a hearing, the arbitrator will listen to evidence and arguments from both sides and decide whether the contract was violated. In most instances, the decision of the arbitrator is final.

Q. What is the union's responsibility in representing the employees?

A. The union has two major duties toward the employees in the bargaining unit:

- the union is required to represent the employees in bargaining with the employer; and
- in its dealings with the employer, the union has a duty to represent all employees fairly.

Q. What does "representing employees fairly" mean?

A. In carrying out its responsibilities, the union typically has to make many decisions, for example when seeking wages or benefits. The basis on which the union makes its decision regarding these and other issues affecting the workers cannot be arbitrary, discriminatory, or in bad faith. Unions are allowed considerable discretion in making such judgments. Mere negligence is not a violation of the duty of fair representation. If a union decision is based on arbitrary, discriminatory, or bad-faith reasons, the concerned worker can file a charge with the NLRB alleging a breach of the duty of fair representation. In some circumstances, such a claim can also be the basis for a lawsuit in federal court.

Q. If the union dislikes something the employer is doing, can it call a strike? And if so, what measures can the employer take in response?

A. That depends on the cause of the strike. If the reason for the strike is to protest workplace conditions or to support union bargaining demands, then the strike is called an **economic strike.** The employer can permanently replace the strikers. If the employer replaces them, it's like the employees have been laid off. When the strike ends, if a replacement employee is still employed, then a striker is not entitled to be reinstated to his or her job. However, as soon as a vacancy occurs, then the striking employees may have the right to be reinstated to their jobs.

If the reason for the strike is to protest the fact that the employer has violated the NLRA, then the strike is called an **unfair-labor-practice strike.** Unfair-labor-practice strikers cannot be permanently replaced, and they have the right to be immediately reinstated to their jobs when the strike ends.

In neither event is an employer allowed to discharge, discipline, or otherwise discriminate in terms or conditions of employment because an employee engaged in a strike.

Q. Are all strikes legal?

A. No. Although the NLRA grants employees the right to strike, not all strikes are protected. If a collective-bargaining agreement contains a no-strike clause (i.e., the union agrees not to go on strike while the contract is in effect), then a strike during the life of the contract would not be protected. The strikers could be fired.

The NLRA requires health-care workers to give ten days notice before they go on strike. If these workers strike without giving notice, then they are not protected and can be fired.

Sit-down strikes and intermittent strikes are also unprotected. An example of an intermittent strike is when employees engage in a five-hour work stoppage one day, then two days later engage in another five-hour work stoppage, and then two days later do it again.

Wages and Hours

Q. What laws govern wages and hours?

A. The Fair Labor Standards Act (FLSA) sets the minimum wage that an employer may pay its workers. It also establishes overtime payment requirements. The act only applies to some employers, as explained in "Federal Laws Regulating the Workplace" (see page 525).

Even if an employer and its employees are not covered, many states also have minimum wage and overtime laws that will apply to all employers doing business within the state.

Q. Does the FLSA require employers to offer benefits?

A. No. It deals solely with wage-related issues. It does not require employers to provide any other type of employment benefit, such as health or life insurance or vacation or holiday pay.

Q. What is the minimum wage?

A. Effective July 24, 2007, the federal minimum wage is $5.85 per hour. The majority of states that have minimum wage laws peg theirs to the federal minimum. A few states have set their state minimum wage below the federal limit. About ten states have set minimum wage rates that are higher than the federal rate. A few states have no minimum wage laws.

In states having a minimum wage above the federal rate, all employers—even those covered by the FLSA—must pay the higher state rate. In states where the state minimum rate is below the federal level, those employers covered by the FLSA must pay the higher federal rate.

Q. How is an employee's minimum wage rate determined?

A. The minimum wage is paid for every hour worked in any workweek. Thus, if an employee is entitled to the federal minimum wage of $5.85 per hour and works twenty hours a week, then he or she must be paid at least $117 for that week's work.

Q. What does the law consider to be an "hour worked"?

A. Generally speaking, hours worked includes all the time spent by employees performing their job duties during the workday. When a worker's job requires travel during the workday, as in the case of a service technician who repairs furnaces at customers' homes, then the time spent traveling is considered "hours worked." Preparatory time spent prior to the start of the workday that is required in order to perform the job is also considered hours worked. For example, workers who have to sharpen their knives at a meat-processing plant, or workers who are required to wear special protective clothing at a chemical plant, are compensated for the time spent sharpening their knives or changing their clothes. Mandatory attendance at lectures, meetings, and training programs is also considered hours worked. Also included in hours worked are rest periods and coffee breaks shorter than twenty minutes.

The following activities are generally not considered hours worked for purposes of minimum wage compensation:

- time spent commuting to work;
- lunch or dinner breaks of at least thirty minutes;
- time spent changing clothes, when done for the benefit of the employee;

- on-call time away from the employer's premises that the employee can use for his or her own purposes; and
- holidays or vacations.

Q. Must the minimum wage be paid in money, rather than benefits?

A. Yes. However, if an employer provides certain non-cash benefits to employees, then the employer may credit the cost of these benefits against the amount of minimum wage owed.

Q. What types of credits is an employer allowed to deduct from the wage owed?

A. The employer can credit the reasonable cost of board, lodging, and other facilities customarily provided to employees. In order to credit the cost of such non-cash benefits, they must be furnished for the worker's convenience and must be voluntarily accepted by the worker. Examples include

- meals furnished at the company cafeteria;
- housing furnished by the company for residential purposes; and
- fuel or electricity used by the employee for non-business purposes.

Employers who have a policy of requiring workers to pay for breakage or cash shortages cannot take such amounts as credit toward the minimum wage owed. Nor are employee discounts allowed as credits toward minimum wage.

Q. Can the employer withhold money from an employee's paycheck?

A. The employer is required to withhold from an employee's paycheck any taxes and amounts that have been garnished. (See "Garnishment of Wages" on page 574.)

An employer is allowed to withhold costs for other items from an employee's paycheck if the employee has authorized the withholding. Examples of such items include union dues, charitable contributions, or insurance premiums. These types of withholdings are allowed even if they cause the employee to receive an amount that falls below the minimum wage.

However, costs for other types of items cannot be deducted from employee paychecks if the deduction would cause the pay to fall below the minimum wage. Examples of such costs include the cost of uniforms used for work, the cost of cleaning uniforms used for work, costs incurred due to employee breakage, or the value of cash-shortage debts.

Some states limit the reasons for which an employer can make deductions from wages

---

▶ **EMPLOYER RECORD-KEEPING REQUIREMENTS UNDER THE FLSA**

Employers are required to maintain and preserve certain wage records in order to show FLSA compliance. Employers must keep employee payroll records containing such information as employee names, hours worked each workday and workweek, wages paid, deductions from wages, and straight-time wages and overtime paid for three years. The employer must also keep for at least two years documents supporting the payroll records, such as time cards, work schedules, and order and billing records.

in other ways, or require an employer to follow certain procedures before making deductions.

Q. When is a worker eligible for overtime pay?

A. The general rule is that employees must be paid overtime for all hours worked over forty hours in any workweek.

Q. Are all employees entitled to overtime pay?

A. No. There are several categories of workers who are exempt from the overtime requirements. The most common exemptions are

- certain executive, administrative, and professional employees;
- outside salespeople;
- retail commission salespeople whose regular rate of pay is more than one and a half times the minimum rate and more than half of whose wages come from commissions;

> **► HOW TO ENFORCE YOUR RIGHTS UNDER THE FLSA**
>
> Employees who believe they are not being paid in accordance with the FLSA can file a complaint with the Wage and Hour Division of the U.S. Department of Labor. The division will investigate to determine whether the FLSA has been violated.
>
> Employees can also sue in state or federal court to collect double the back wages and overtime pay owed.

- taxicab drivers; and
- computer system analysts, computer programmers, or software engineers who are paid at least $27.63 an hour.

Q. What is the overtime pay rate?

A. The FLSA requires employers to pay employees one and a half times (150 percent) their regular rate of pay for each hour, or fraction of an hour, over forty hours in any workweek.

Q. How is the overtime pay rate computed?

A. The main issue is to determine the regular hourly rate for the employee in question. When an employee is paid an hourly rate, the employee's regular rate and hourly rate are the same. For example, an employee who is paid $6.00 an hour and who worked 43 hours in the last work week, would be owed $27.00 in overtime pay ($6.00 regular rate × 1.5 = $9.00 overtime rate; $9.00 × 3 [hours worked in excess of 40] = $27.00). The employee's earnings for that week would be $267.00 ($6.00 × 40 hours = $240.00 regular pay; $240.00 regular pay + $27.00 overtime pay = $267.00).

When an employee is paid a salary or commission, the employee's compensation must be converted to an hourly rate. Let's say an employee is paid a fixed salary for a regular workweek of 40 hours. This conversion to an hourly rate is accomplished by dividing the employee's compensation for the week by 40 hours. For example, an employee who is paid $240 a week would be paid $6 an hour. If that employee worked 45 hours in a workweek, he or she would be owed as additional compensation one and a half times the regular rate for the overtime hours worked ($6 an hour × 1.5 = $9 per hour overtime rate; $9 overtime

> ▶ **TIPPED EMPLOYEES AND THE FLSA**
>
> Under certain circumstances, the FLSA allows employers to credit tips received by tipped employees against the minimum wage owed to those employees. In order to qualify for the credit, the tipped employee must be engaged in an occupation in which he or she customarily receives more than $30 per month in tips—for example, waitressing or cosmetology. The employer must pay a tipped employee at least $2.13 an hour. The employer is then allowed to credit all tips received by the employee for the amount of minimum wage owed above $2.13 an hour. However, some states do not allow a tip credit under the minimum wage laws, or have different cash payment levels when a tip credit is allowed.
>
> Of course, the employer can credit only that amount the employee actually receives in tips. Thus, if the employee receives only $2.00 an hour in tips, then the employer would be required to pay any additional amount required to ensure that the employee receives minimum wage. The employee must always receive at least the minimum wage when wages and tips are combined.
>
> Employers may not take the tip credit without informing the workers about it. Employers must also be able to prove that an employee actually receives tips equal to the tip credit taken.

rate × 5 [number of overtime hours worked] = $45). The employee's earnings for that week would be $285 ($240 regular pay + $45 overtime pay).

Workplace Safety

Q. How does the federal government regulate workplace safety?

A. Mostly through the Occupational Safety and Health Act (OSH Act). The OSH Act is a federal law whose purpose is to "assure so far as possible every working man and woman . . . safe and healthful working conditions." The statute is administered and enforced by the Occupational Safety and Health Administration (OSHA).

The OSH Act applies to all private employers engaged in a business affecting commerce. Courts have broadly interpreted the phrase "affecting commerce," such that almost every business with at least one employee is covered. The OSH Act does not apply to public employers.

States may also regulate workplace health and safety in two ways. First, they may have regulations covering workplace conditions that are not dealt with by OSHA standards. Second, they may adopt a state safety and health plan that duplicates the requirements of the OSH Act; if approved by OSHA, the state then would be responsible for enforcing safety and health regulations within its borders. In the absence of OSHA approval, how-

▶ GARNISHMENT OF WAGES

A **garnishment** is a court order that the earnings of a worker be withheld from the worker's paycheck and paid to a third party to whom the worker owes a debt. Employers should take garnishments notices seriously. If they ignore them, they risk being liable for the amount that should have been garnished.

The Consumer Credit Protection Act is a federal law that limits the amount of money that may be garnished. The general rule is that the maximum amount that can be garnished is the lesser of 25 percent of an employee's take-home pay or that part of the take-home pay exceeding thirty times the federal minimum wage. The law permits a larger amount to be deducted when the debt owed is for child support payments, bankruptcy, or back taxes. The Act also prohibits an employer from discharging and employee because his or her wages have been garnished once.

---

ever, a state may not regulate any safety and health issue that is already regulated by the OSH Act.

Q. What does the OSH Act require of employers?

A. The act imposes three obligations on employers:

1. Employers are required to furnish a workplace "free from recognized hazards that are causing or are likely to cause death or serious physical harm" to employees.
2. Employers are required to comply with the safety and health standards promulgated by OSHA.
3. Employers are required to keep records of employee injuries, illnesses, deaths, and exposure to toxic substances, and to preserve employee medical records.

There are some exemptions from some requirements for employers with ten or fewer employees. These companies do not have to maintain certain records, and they are exempt from certain types of penalties and enforcement activities; however, they are still required to provide a safe workplace and comply with OSHA standards.

Q. What types of workplace conditions do the health and safety standards address?

A. The standards regulate such issues as

- the safety of working areas such as ladders, scaffolding, stairs, and floors;
- provision of sufficient entryways and exits;
- exposure to noise, carcinogens, radiation, and other types of harmful substances;
- fire protection systems;
- safety devices for machines and equipment used in the workplace; and
- provision of medical and first-aid services.

There are literally hundreds of standards covering all aspects of the workplace.

▶ WORKING WITH HAZARDOUS CHEMICALS

OSHA requires that employees who work with hazardous chemicals be informed of the types of chemicals they are working with and be trained in their handling. Chemical manufacturers and distributors are required to label containers identifying any hazardous chemicals and give appropriate hazard warnings.

Employers who use such hazardous chemicals in the workplace are required to develop a written hazard communication program. As part of this program, the employer must compile a list of all hazardous chemicals used in the workplace; identify the physical and health hazards associated with these chemicals; state precautions to be used in handling the chemicals; and indicate emergency and first-aid procedures to be used in the event of a problem. This information must be made available to the employees.

Employees must also receive training in detecting the presences of chemicals in the workplace and protecting themselves from hazards.

Q. What should an employee do if he or she thinks there is a safety or health hazard at work?

A. There are two methods of addressing safety and health problems: An employee can notify his or her supervisor or company safety director and discuss the problem; and an employee can also contact OSHA and request a safety inspection.

Q. How does an employee initiate a request for an OSHA inspection?

A. OSHA has regional and area offices throughout the U.S. An employee can either make an oral complaint to OSHA or file a formal written complaint. In either case, the employee should indicate the workplace conditions he or she believes constitute a safety or health hazard. OSHA will decide, based on the information received, whether there are reasonable grounds for believing a violation of the law exists. OSHA will then ei-

ther send the employer a letter regarding the alleged violation that informs the employer how to correct the problem, or send an inspector to the workplace to conduct an on-site safety inspection.

Q. What happens during an OSHA inspection?

A. The OSHA inspector will meet with the employer, explain the nature of the inspection, and review employer documents pertaining to workplace injuries and hazards. Then the inspector will conduct a "walk around," during which he or she will physically inspect the workplace. The employer and a representative of the employees are allowed to accompany the inspector on the walk around. The inspector will also talk with employees and ask questions. At the end of the inspection, the inspector will inform the employer informally of any possible identified violations.

Q. What are the penalties for violating the OSH Act?

A. First, an employer is required to correct any hazards that violate the law. The employer can also be fined, in an amount based on the seriousness of the violation. An employer also faces criminal liability and imprisonment for willfully violating an OSHA standard that results in an employee's death.

Q. If I make a report to OSHA, can my employer retaliate against me?

A. The employer cannot discriminate against an employee because the employee has involved OSHA. In addition, an employee cannot be discharged or disciplined for refusing to perform a job if all the following circumstances apply:

- the reason for the refusal is a good-faith belief that there is a real danger of death or serious injury;
- a reasonable person in the employee's position would conclude there is a real danger of death or serious injury;
- there is insufficient time to eliminate the danger through the regular OSHA channels; and
- the employee has asked the employer unsuccessfully to fix the problem.

In addition, employees acting together concerning safety-related matters are generally engaged in protected concerted activity under the NLRA and cannot be disciplined or discharged because they have acted together.

Workers' Compensation

Q. What are workers' compensation laws?

A. Workers' compensation laws provide money for medical expenses and to replace income lost as a result of injuries or illnesses that arise out of employment. In order to recover under workers' compensation laws, an employee is not required to prove that the injuries were caused by some negligence of the employer. Employees receive compensation even though their own negligence or that of a coworker caused the injury. These laws impose strict liability on employers for injuries suffered at the workplace. (For more on strict liability, see Chapter 6, "Personal Injury.")

Each state has its own law providing workers' compensation benefits. There are separate federal workers' compensation laws covering federal government employees and employees of the railroad and maritime industries.

Q. Who pays for workers' compensation?

A. Employers are solely responsible for the cost of providing workers' compensation, usually through the purchase of a workers' compensation insurance policy. The cost of providing this insurance cannot be deducted from the employees' wages.

Q. Are all employees covered by workers' compensation?

A. Most employees are covered. Some state laws exempt certain categories of workers, such as casual employees, agricultural employees, domestic employees, and independent contractors. Moreover, a few states require coverage only if an employer has a minimum number of employees.

Q. What types of injuries are covered by workers' compensation?

A. Workers' compensation covers injuries and illnesses that "arise out of and in the course of employment." This means that there must be some connection between an employment requirement and the cause of the injury. For example, injuries arising from an automobile accident that occurs on a public street during the commute to work are not compensable, but the injuries of a traveling salesperson involved in an accident while on her way to a sales call would be. Some examples of compensable injuries include injuries caused by defective machinery, fires or explosions at work, repeated lifting of heavy equipment, or slipping on an oily floor surface at work.

Illnesses that are caused by working conditions are also compensable injuries, if the job in question poses a greater-than-normal risk of contracting that illness. Thus, a coal miner who contracts black lung disease would be eligible for compensation.

Q. How much compensation is paid for an injury or illness?

A. Workers receive a fixed weekly benefit based on their regular salary. The percentage of regular salary received varies from state to state, but generally falls between 50 and 66 percent. This payment is made for the period during which the employee is temporarily unable to work due to the injury.

Workers' compensation also pays for all associated medical expenses. Most state laws

---

▶ **CHECKLIST: HOW TO OBTAIN COMPENSATION FOR A WORK-RELATED INJURY**

- If you are injured at work, the first thing you should do is notify the employer as soon as possible. Usually, the employer will have claim forms available for you to fill out. If your employer does not have claim forms, you should contact the state workers' compensation agency.

- The employer then submits the documents to the insurance company and the state workers' compensation agency.

- If the employer does not challenge a claim, the insurance company will pay your medical bills and wages.

- If the employer contests a claim, then a hearing is scheduled. At the hearing, evidence relating to the circumstances of the injury and the extent of the injury is presented. The resulting decision as to whether compensation is owed (and how much) can be appealed by either the employer or the employee.

As a general rule, the only way you can be compensated by your employer for workplace injuries or illnesses is by filing a workers' compensation claim. There are a few exceptions, such as when an employer intentionally injures an employee. In that situation, you may sue in court to collect damages if you can prove that the employer was guilty of intentional wrongdoing. If you or your employer are not covered by the workers' compensation law, then you can file a lawsuit to collect damages if you can prove that the injury was caused by the employer's negligence.

also provide some compensation for the costs associated with medical and vocational rehabilitation.

Employees who suffer a permanent disability, whether partial or total, may also be compensated for any decrease in earnings attributable to the permanent nature of the disability. The amount payable may be determined by a schedule (a list that specifies wage loss for specific disabilities; for example, $8,910 for loss of an index finger), or as a percentage of the weekly wage.

Q. If a workplace injury causes death, is compensation provided to the worker's survivors?

A. Generally, yes. Death benefits generally are provided to an employee's spouse until remarriage, and to the employee's children until they reach the age of majority (usually eighteen). Death benefits consist of a burial allowance and a percentage of the deceased worker's weekly wage. There may be a maximum cap.

Social Security Disability Insurance

Q. How does Social Security Disability Insurance differ from workers' compensation?

A. The Social Security Disability Insurance (SSDI) system differs from workers' compensation in that the cause of the injury is irrelevant for Social Security. To get money under workers' compensation, the employee's injury must arise out of employment. But under Social Security, the main issue is whether the injury prevents the employee from being able to work, regardless of the cause. So, if you're injured in an automobile accident on the commute to work, you probably won't be able to

get workers' compensation, but you may be eligible for Social Security benefits if your injuries prevent you from earning a living.

Q. What requirements must an injured worker meet in order to receive Social Security benefits?

A. An employee must work at a job that is covered by Social Security, and the injury or illness must be considered "disabling."

Q. What types of injuries are considered "disabling"?

A. A **disabling** medical condition is one that can be expected to last at least twelve months, and that causes the employee to be unable to work anywhere in the country. The Social Security Administration has published a list of impairments that are considered disabling, such as severe epilepsy and loss of vision or hearing. A medical condition that is not on the list still may be considered disabling if the worker can show that the condition is the medical equivalent of a listed impairment—that it is equal in severity and duration to a listed impairment.

Q. What if a worker does not suffer from the medical equivalent of a listed impairment?

A. Then the worker would be eligible for benefits only if he or she could prove a disabling medical condition by another means. The employee would have to show that the condition or disease is so severe that it prevents him or her from doing his or her former job or other similar work. This is not easy to prove.

Q. Where can workers apply for Social Security disability benefits?

A. You should file a claim at the local Social Security Administration office. There are offices in most large cities in the United States. With the application, submit documents providing detailed information about

- your medical history, along with a detailed statement from a doctor concerning the cause of the disability;
- your work history; and
- your educational background.

These documents will help the Social Security Administration decide whether your condition is disabling. You can also submit statements from family and friends.

Q. Can a disabled worker's spouse and children receive Social Security benefits for a worker's disability?

A. If the spouse and children meet the requirements for the worker's Social Security retirement benefits, then they should also qualify for disability benefits.

Q. What happens if the Social Security Administration rejects my application for benefits?

A. There is an appeals process for rejected applications. If you are considering undertaking an appeal, you should talk to an attorney or advocate about the process and what will be expected of you.

REMEMBER THIS

- Many laws prohibit discrimination in the workplace. They cover hiring, firing, promotions, job duties, wages, benefits, and reviews. Federal laws prohibit discrimination based on age, disability, race, sex, color, national origin, religion, and union activity. State laws may provide greater protections.

- Antidiscrimination laws protect against discrimination based on race, color, national origin, or gender. The laws prohibit both overt discrimination and policies that don't discriminate directly but have a discriminatory effect.

- Sexual harassment is against the law. It can be either quid pro quo (i.e., tying job benefits to sexual favors), or hostile-environment harassment (in which harassment creates an offensive working environment). Both genders are protected by law from sexual harassment.

- Federal and state laws govern wages and hours, workplace safety, and workplace injuries.

- The federal government and many states have laws that govern unions and union-management relations; employees' right to unionize is protected.

LEAVING A JOB

They say that all good things come to an end, and that's surely true with jobs, whether they're good or not. The law can affect many of these terminations—for example, if you are fired or laid off, or if you choose to retire. This section reviews the legal implications of leaving a job.

Being Fired

Q. Can employers fire employees without worrying about legal consequences?

A. It depends. In the United States, most employees are considered **employees at will.**

This means that they have no written contract that governs the length of their employment or the reasons for which they may be fired. The employer is free to lay off or fire such employees with no notice and for no reason.

However, not all employees are employees at will. Unionized employees covered by a collective-bargaining agreement usually cannot be fired "at will." Their contracts normally provide that they can be terminated only for just cause (that is, for a cause that a person of ordinary intelligence would consider a fair and reasonable justification for dismissal). Moreover, the grievance mechanism contained in most collective bargaining agreements provides a process by which union employees can challenge their firing. (For a fuller discussion of union protections, see "Unions in the Workplace" on page 563.)

Q. What about government workers?

A. Civil-service laws protect public workers. Such laws normally require the employer to have just cause to fire a worker. Civil-service commissions provide a mechanism by which public employees can appeal any decision to discharge them. (For further discussion of civil-service laws, see "Special Rights of Public Employees" on page 562.)

Q. Are there any laws that affect an employer's ability to fire employees at will?

A. Yes, the NLRA, Title VII, the ADEA, and the ADA all prohibit an employer from firing an employee if the reason for the firing is based on the employee's union activity or membership in a protected class—race, sex, religion, ethnicity, national origin, color, age, or disability. Most federal laws regulating the workplace also prohibit employers from retaliating against workers who assert their rights under federal law. (See the "Whistle-blowers" sidebar.)

Moreover, many state antidiscrimination laws protect a broader class of workers from

▶ WHISTLE-BLOWERS

A **whistle-blower** is an employee who reports to a government agency possible violations of the law occurring in the workplace. Whistle-blower statutes prohibit employers from firing a worker who makes reports with reasonable cause to believe that there is a violation. The laws also prohibit employers from firing employees who take part in government investigations and hearings relating to violations of law at the workplace.

Enforcement of employment laws relies heavily on information and help provided by employees. After all, employees are in the best position to know whether their rights have been violated. To stop complaints, employers might try to pressure employees not to make complaints; for example, by threatening layoffs or firings. Because of this potential problem, almost all federal employment laws expressly prohibit employers from taking adverse actions against employees because they have filed a complaint to enforce their rights or cooperated in an investigation conducted by a federal agency enforcing the law.

discrimination in firing. For example, a state could prohibit firings based on weight, height, or sexual orientation. (For further discussion of the antidiscrimination laws, "Discrimination in the Workplace" on page 545.)

Q. Are there any recognized exceptions to an employer's ability to fire at-will employees?

A. Yes. In many states, the courts have held that an employer cannot fire an at-will employee for reasons that conflict with, or undermine, a state's public policy. This is known as the public policy exception to employment at will.

Q. How does firing an employee conflict with public policy?

A. Generally speaking, a state's public policy can be found in its statutes and constitution. Courts have determined that four categories of discharge undermine public policy"

1 Firing employees because they refuse to perform an act that state law prohibits. For example, an employer tells employees to dump toxic waste into the city sewer system. The employees refuse and are fired.
2 Firing employees for reporting a violation of the law. For example, employees report to the state agriculture department that an employer is selling contaminated meat, and the employer fires them.
3 Firing employees for engaging in acts that public policy encourages. For example, employees report to jury duty and the employer fires them for missing work.
4 Firing employees for exercising a statutory right. For example, injured employees file a state workers' compensation claim and the employer fires them.

Q. I have no written contract, but my employer told me that as long as I perform my work well I'll have a job. Can my employer fire me even if I'm performing my job well?

A. It depends. Many state courts will enforce an oral promise from the employer under certain circumstances. Generally speaking, there must be

- evidence that the employer's past practice is to fire employees only for cause; and
- clear, unequivocal evidence that a promise was made; and
- evidence that the employer and employee specifically discussed the issue of job security and reasons for termination.

It also may be helpful to the employee's case if he or she can show

- evidence of the employer's past practice that it fires employees only for cause; and
- evidence that the employee turned down other job offers or left a job in reliance on the promise made.

Other courts, however, will not enforce such an oral promise.

Q. If the employer's handbook states that employees will be fired only for just cause, can the employer still fire someone at will?

A. Not all handbooks or manuals create enforceable contracts. For example, if the manual has clear and express disclaimers informing employees that the information is not meant to create a contract and can be changed or revoked at any time, then courts probably will rule that it does not create an enforceable contract. In order for a handbook to possibly be considered as an enforceable contract, the handbook or manual must have been given to the employee and the language of the manual must also be specific.

Q. Must an employer provide notice to an employee prior to discharge?

A. If the employee has a written contract requiring notice, or if there is a collective-bargaining agreement with a notice requirement, then the employer must provide notice. But generally no notice is required, except in cases where there is a mass layoff or a plant closure.

Q. Is an employer required to pay severance pay when it fires a worker?

A. There is no law requiring employers to pay severance pay. If the employee has a written contract guaranteeing severance pay, or if there is a collective bargaining agreement providing for it, then the employer will be required to pay severance. Otherwise, the employer is under no obligation to pay.

Q. Suppose an employer offers severance pay only if the employee agrees to sign a waiver of rights to sue the company. What is the legal effect of signing such a waiver?

A. Generally, a knowing and voluntary waiver is enforceable and would prevent employees from being able to sue the employer for anything that occurred while they were employed. Whether a waiver is knowing and voluntary depends on the circumstances. The courts usually consider several factors in deciding whether a waiver is knowing and voluntary:

- Is the waiver written in a manner that the employee can understand?

▶ PLANT CLOSING AND MASS LAYOFFS

The Worker Adjustment and Retraining Notification Act (WARN) is a federal law requiring employers to provide workers, their unions, and state and local government officials 60 days' advance notice of a plant closing or mass layoff. The law applies to private employers with 100 or more employees. A mass layoff is defined as a reduction that results in the layoff of a single site of employment or at least 33 percent of the workforce and at least 50 employees, or at least 500 employees. Failure to give 60 days' notice subjects an employer to liability for back pay and benefits under an employee benefit plan for each day that the notice was not given. Employees can enforce the law by filing a lawsuit in federal court.

- In exchange for the waiver, did the employee receive some benefit that he or she was not already entitled to receive?
- Did the employee have a reasonable amount of time to consider the offer?

The ADEA contains a list of specific requirements that must be met in order for a waiver of employee rights under the ADEA to be effective. These include that the employee be advised in writing to consult with a lawyer before signing the waiver and that the employee be given at least 21 days to consider the waiver before signing.

The courts will not enforce a waiver of any claims that arise under the FLSA.

Q. If I feel like I have been unfairly terminated, how is my issue likely to be resolved?

A. Recently, employers have been turning to arbitration as the forum of choice for resolving employment disputes, especially those involving termination. **Arbitration** is a quasi-judicial procedure in which a neutral third party presides over a hearing. At the hearing, the disputing parties present their claims, the evidence in support of their claims, and their arguments. The arbitrator then issues a final and binding decision that resolves the dispute. Many employers believe the process is faster, cheaper, and eliminates the risks associated with a jury deciding a case. Accordingly, some employers are requiring employees to sign arbitration agreements before they are hired, or as a condition of continued employment. By signing an agreement to arbitrate, employees are waiving their right to file a lawsuit in court, and agreeing instead that they will submit the dispute to arbitration.

As a general rule, the courts will enforce an agreement to arbitrate if

- the arbitrator hearing the case is a neutral and impartial third party;
- the hearing is fair, allowing for the opportunity to be heard, to present evidence, and to cross-examine witnesses;
- the remedies available from the arbitrator are the same as those available in court; and
- the cost of the arbitration process is not unduly burdensome to the employee.

Even a valid arbitration agreement cannot, however, prevent an employee from filing a charge with a government agency alleging a violation of the law. Thus, an employee who signed an agreement to arbitrate could still file a charge with the NLRB or the EEOC, though he or she might be precluded from filing a lawsuit.

Unemployment Insurance

The states administer **unemployment insurance (UI)** systems to provide workers and their families with weekly income during periods of unemployment. When unemployed

---

▶ LOSING YOUR JOB DOESN'T MEAN LOSING YOUR HEALTH INSURANCE

The Consolidated Omnibus Budget Reconciliation Act (COBRA) provides that workers who lose their jobs will not lose their health insurance coverage automatically. This federal law requires companies with at least twenty employees carrying group health insurance to offer terminated employees the opportunity to continue participating in the company's health insurance plan for up to eighteen months. The employee may be required to pay no more than 102 percent of the cost of the premium. Usually, 102 percent of the premium cost at the group rate will be less than the premium for an individually purchased policy.

There may be state COBRA laws that apply to smaller employers.

due to circumstances that are not caused by the worker's fault or misconduct, an employee may receive UI benefits.

The system is funded by state and federal taxes that employers pay. Within certain federal guidelines, each state determines the scope, coverage, and eligibility requirements for UI benefits.

Q. Who is covered under the UI system?

A. Most employees are covered, but there are some exceptions. Generally excluded from coverage are self-employed people, independent contractors, casual employees, and agricultural workers.

Q. If employees are covered under UI, are they automatically entitled to receive benefits if unemployed?

A. No. In order to receive benefits, they must meet the eligibility requirements and not be otherwise disqualified from receiving benefits.

Q. What are the eligibility requirements for UI?

A. The eligibility requirements vary by state but most states look at four criteria, all of which have to be met:

- the applicant must have earned a minimum amount of wages within a specified period, and/or worked for a minimum period in the recent past (for example, the applicant must have worked at least twenty weeks at an average weekly wage of at least $200);
- the applicant must have registered for work with the state unemployment office;
- the applicant must be available for work; and

- the applicant must be actively seeking employment.

Q. What will disqualify a worker from receiving UI benefits?

A. As a general rule, employees are disqualified if they voluntarily quit without good cause or were fired for misconduct. In some states, even if workers' conduct disqualifies them, the disqualification will last only for a specific length of time, after which they will be eligible to receive UI benefits.

The meaning of "good cause" varies greatly among the states. Some states consider certain types of personal reasons to be good cause, such as having to care for a sick relative or following a spouse who has found work in another state. Most states, however, require that good cause be due to the employer's actions. For example, working conditions that are so bad that they would cause a reasonable person to quit would be considered good cause in some states.

The meaning of misconduct also varies by state, but incompetence alone generally is not considered misconduct. Violations of known company rules and insubordination are examples of employee behavior normally deemed to be misconduct.

Q. Can an applicant refuse a job offer and still collect UI benefits?

A. It depends on why the applicant refused the offer. If the job is not suitable work, then the refusal is allowed. A job is not suitable if the worker has no experience doing that type of job, if it is more hazardous than the applicant's previous job, or if the physical condition of the applicant prevents him or her from accepting it. States also consider travel costs and time, bad working hours, community wage levels, and compelling personal problems in decid-

---

▶ MOVING OUT OF STATE AND COLLECTING UNEMPLOYMENT

If workers move to another state to look for work, they can still collect UI benefits, because all states belong to the Interstate Reciprocal Benefit Payment Plan. This plan allows workers to register for work and file for UI benefits in a state different from the one in which they previously worked. However, the law of the state in which they employee previously worked, determines the employee's eligibility. The workers must satisfy that state's requirements in order to receive UI benefits in the new state.

---

ing if a job may be rejected. Finally, employees usually cannot lose benefits for refusing a job that is available because the current workforce is on strike.

If the wages and conditions of a new job are below those of the worker's previous employment, he or she may not have to accept it. For example, a skilled craftsperson is permitted to refuse a job as a janitor. After a certain period of time, however, most states require the worker to "lower his sights" and accept a lesser job.

Q. Are employees on strike entitled to collect UI benefits?

A. It depends on the specific state law. A few states allow workers to collect UI if the strike is caused by an employer's violation of the NLRA or an employer's breach of the collective bargaining agreement. Some states allow workers to collect UI if the employer has locked out the workers.

Most states, however, do not permit employees on strike to collect UI benefits for a period of time. The period of disqualification varies—in some states, the disqualification lasts for the duration of the strike; in other states, the disqualification lasts for a fixed period of time. If a striker is permanently replaced, however, the worker may then be eligible.

Q. How does an applicant apply for UI benefits?

A. Applicants file claims for UI benefits at their local state unemployment office. The claim should be filed as soon as possible after unemployment begins, since benefits will not be paid until all the paperwork is processed and eligibility is verified.

Applicants should take the following documents with them to the unemployment office to help verify their eligibility: Social Security card, recent pay stubs, and any documentation relating to the reason for the job loss.

After filing the initial claim, applicants are usually required to report to the unemployment office on a regular basis to verify their continued eligibility for benefits. Failure to report when required can result in a loss of benefits.

Q. How is the amount of UI benefits determined?

A. While the amount varies by state, the general formula is 50 percent of the applicant's weekly wage, not to exceed a specified statutory cap. The cap is based on a percentage of the state's average weekly wages for all workers. Because of the cap on maximum benefits, most workers receive less than 50 percent of their weekly wage.

Q. How long are UI benefits paid?

A. The usual duration for UI benefits is twenty-six weeks. However, in times of extended high unemployment, benefits may be paid for an additional thirteen weeks, and sometimes longer.

Q. Can an unemployed worker receive other benefits or earn extra money while collecting UI benefits?

A. Some states ignore small amounts of money earned. Usually, however, income received is deducted from UI benefits. Some states reduce or stop UI benefits for weeks in which an unemployed worker received disability benefits, severance pay, and other types of income.

Pension Plans

Q. Does the law require employers to provide pensions?

A. No. But if an employer does offer a pension plan, the federal Employee Retirement Income Security Act (ERISA) probably covers it. ERISA applies to private employers whose plans are "qualified" under the federal tax laws. The tax laws provide important advantages to companies whose plans qualify, so most pension plans are regulated by ERISA. (For further information on pensions, see Chapter 16, "The Rights of Older Americans," Chapter 17, "Estate Planning," and Chapter 3, "Family Law.")

REMEMBER THIS

- Most nonunion workers in this country are "employees at will," who may be fired with no notice for any reason.

- Workers protected by a collective-bargaining agreement, as well as government workers, may have more protections.

- Anti-discrimination laws apply to the firing or laying off of workers. Anti-retaliation laws also apply.

- Unemployment compensation provides some income to workers who are laid off or fired for reasons other than misconduct.

- Federal law protects most pension plans, and workers have rights under the law to information about their plan and to appeal if benefits are denied.

CHAPTER SIXTEEN

The Rights of Older Americans

Margaret had a stroke in her fifties, which left her paralyzed down her left side. She is able to walk, but needs to hold on to a bar when she goes up and down stairs. She lives on the ground floor of her apartment block, but there are four steps leading up to the front door. Her landlord won't let her install a bar next to the stairs because he thinks it is unsightly. Margaret is willing to pay for the bar. What can she do?

Before her stroke, Margaret held a full-time job as an accountant. She knows she is eligible to be covered by Medicare, but she doesn't remember signing up for it. Does she have to pay to be covered by Medicare? Will Medicare force her to change doctors? What's the difference between Medicare and Medicaid? Will Margaret's adult children be able to help her at all? What rights do they have when it comes to helping their mother with her affairs?

A generation ago, a chapter on the rights of older Americans would have been unnecessary. But now both the law and society have changed. There's a wide array of laws directly addressing the legal needs of older people, and a growing recognition that the law is crucial to the social and health needs of older persons and their families.

The legal issues discussed in this chapter reflect three realities. First, we are rapidly aging as a society. Far more people are living into their seventh, eighth, ninth, and tenth decades of life than ever before. Thus, the problems and opportunities of aging affect more families than at any time before. Second, the law permeates almost every aspect of our society, especially the programs, protections, and opportunities that benefit older people. This chapter provides a basic knowledge of the law that will help you navigate through such programs as Medicare, Medicaid, and other programs relating to pension benefits. Third, the personal and financial autonomy of older people is at greater risk than that of the greater population, because of the increasing risk of physical and mental impairment. This chapter responds to this risk by offering a variety of planning strategies to help older Americans preserve personal autonomy and financial security.

PENSIONS

When you retire, your financial security will probably depend on pension income, government benefits, and personal savings. The availability of income from a private pension plan can make the critical difference between a comfortable retirement and one plagued by financial worries. This section discusses three basic kinds of employer-sponsored pension plans: traditional defined-contribution and defined-benefit pension plans; Section 401(k) plans; and simplified employee pension plans. It is important to understand your legal rights regarding such plans, so you can ensure that your funds are prudently invested, and that you receive all the benefits to which you are entitled.

TRADITIONAL PENSION PLANS

Q. Is my employer or union required to set up a pension plan?

A. No. The law does not obligate an employer to set up a pension plan. Less than half of American employees in the private sector are covered by traditional defined-contribution and defined-benefit pension plans, although many other employees are covered by employer-sponsored simplified employee pension plans and 401(k) plans. Most pensions are governed by the rules of the Employee Retirement Income Security Act (ERISA), which sets minimum standards for pension plans that already exist and new pension plans that are created.

Q. Does ERISA apply to all pension plans?

A. No. It does not cover pension plans for public employees, nor does it cover church employees unless their employer has elected to have ERISA apply. Most ERISA provisions apply to plan years beginning in or after1976. As a result, ERISA does not protect workers who stopped working or retired before 1976. However, the terms of an employee's pension plan, as well as state law, can offer other protections.

Q. What are the different types of traditional pension plans?

A. There are two major kinds, and they are quite different. One kind, called a **defined-benefit plan,** guarantees you a certain amount of benefits per month upon retirement. For example, a defined benefit plan might pay you $10 a month per year of service. Under that plan, a person who retires after ten years of service would receive $100 per month in pension benefits.

Under the other kind of plan, called a **defined-contribution plan,** the employer and/or the employee contribute a certain amount per month during the years of employment. The amount of the benefit depends on the total amount accumulated in the pension fund at the time of retirement. And that amount depends not only on how much you and your employer contributed, but also on how that money was invested.

Typically, pension trustees invest in stocks, real estate, and other generally safe investments. If those investments do well over the years, the fund grows and your monthly benefits may be relatively high. But if the investments do poorly, the fund may not grow or may even shrink. In that case, your monthly benefits may be far smaller. (See the discussion later in this section of the requirement that plans make prudent investments.)

The choice of defined-benefit or defined-contribution plan is not yours; the employer decides.

Q. I am fifty-five years old and I want to retire now. Can I start collecting my pension at once?

A. Maybe. All pensions set a "normal" retirement age, often sixty-five. They usually set a minimum retirement age as well, perhaps fifty-five, sixty, or sixty-two. Check with your pension plan administrator. You may be able to collect benefits now, or you may have to wait until you are older. Remember that benefits usually are calculated partly on the basis of your age. So the younger you are when you retire, the smaller the benefits, but presumably you will get them for a longer period.

Q. When must I begin to collect my pension?

A. If you choose to retire later, you must begin collecting your pension by April 1st of the year after you turn 70½ years old.

Q. Do I get to choose how my pension will be paid to me?

A. Yes, to some extent.

The most common type of payment is the **joint and survivor annuity benefit.** In a series of equal payments, it pays the full benefit to a married couple until one dies, then pays a fraction of the full benefit to the survivor as long as he or she lives. The amount paid to the survivor must be at least 50 percent of the amount paid to the couple. This kind of disbursement is required unless the worker's spouse signs a waiver. The waiver permits

> ## ▶ AGE DISCRIMINATION AND THE LAW
>
> The Age Discrimination in Employment Act (ADEA) ensures that older workers receive equal and fair treatment in the workplace. It protects most workers forty years of age and older from arbitrary age discrimination in hiring and discharging, in compensation, and with regards to other conditions of employment. The act prohibits employers from doing anything that harms an older worker's status because of his or her age, including offensive age-related jokes and using age as a factor in hiring, firing, layoff, promotion, demotion, establishment of working conditions and hours, training opportunities, compensation, or benefits. ADEA protections include
>
> - A ban on forcing workers who are at least forty years old, and who work for either a private employer with twenty or more employees or a federal or local government, to retire. (Note that there are some exceptions to this rule for government officials and high-level executives.)
>
> - Preventing employers from forcing older employees to take jobs involving less responsibility, or that pay lower salaries.
>
> - Requiring employers to provide employees of all age groups the same benefits—or, alternatively, to provide a benefit that costs the same for all age groups.
>
> - Requiring older and younger employees to receive the same training and promotion considerations.
>
> If you think you have been discriminated against due to your age, you should file a charge of age discrimination in writing with the federal Equal Employment Opportunity Commission (EEOC). If your state has an age discrimination law and enforcement agency (not every state does), you should consider filing the charge with both the EEOC and your state agency. If you have suffered significant loss as a result of age discrimination and you are willing to invest substantial time and money, filing a private lawsuit may also be worthwhile. If you think you have a claim of age discrimination, consider talking to an attorney experienced in employment law.
>
> See Chapter 15, "Law and the Workplace," for a detailed discussion of workplace discrimination.

payment of a higher benefit, but only as long as the retired worker lives. When he or she dies, the benefits end and the surviving spouse gets no more.

The joint and survivor annuity may allow you some options. You might be able to have benefits guaranteed for a certain number of years. For example, if the guarantee is for fifteen years, benefits would be paid as long as one or both spouses are alive. But if both die before fifteen years have passed since retirement, benefits would continue to be paid to their beneficiary until the fifteenth year. Other guarantees might be for longer or shorter periods; the longer the guarantee, the lower the benefit.

There are other kinds of pension disbursements. One pays a fixed amount for a fixed number of years, which means you could outlive your benefits and get nothing in your oldest years. Another pays all your benefits in a single lump sum when you retire.

Q. Will my pension benefits rise over the years?

A. Perhaps. Your union may negotiate cost-of-living increases. Or a nonunion employer may increase benefits voluntarily. But generally, your benefits are frozen at the level where they were when you retired. However, you will probably also be collecting Social Security benefits, and those benefits do rise with the cost of living.

Q. What if I get sick after retiring? Will I still have health insurance?

A. Companies are not required to provide health insurance after retirement. But when they have promised to do so, some courts require them to keep that promise. Under a federal law known as COBRA (short for "Consolidated Omnibus Budget Reconciliation Act"), you must be notified when you retire that you may continue coverage, but your employer may require you to pay the premiums. Coverage generally lasts for eighteen months after you stop working, but may be extended up to twenty-nine months if you are found eligible for Social Security disability or Supplemental Security Income (SSI) disability benefits. You also will be eligible for Medicare at age sixty-five, or possibly earlier.

Q. Can my company's pension plan cover some employees but not others?

A. Yes. Some companies establish pension plans only for certain kinds of workers. A plan might cover assembly line workers, for example, and not file clerks. But a plan cannot discriminate against employees who are not officers or shareholders, or who are not highly compensated. The Internal Revenue Service determines whether a plan is in compliance with these complicated nondiscrimination rules.

Q. When can an employee participate in a pension plan?

A. ERISA requires that employers permit workers to begin earning credit toward pensions if two criteria are met: the worker must be at least twenty-one years old, and he or she must have worked for the employer for at least one year. Under ERISA, a year of employment is equal to 1,000 or more hours of work in a twelve-month period. Once employees satisfy these two requirements, they must be allowed to begin accruing credits toward their pensions.

Of course, as with all ERISA requirements, these are the minimums allowed by law. Employers can have more generous policies.

Q. Once I become a participant, how do I know what my rights are under the plan?

A. ERISA requires that participating employees be given detailed reports and disclosures. Within ninety days of becoming a participant, the employee must receive a summary plan description. This provides details of the employee's rights and obligations, gives information on the trustees and the plan's administration, sets conditions for participation and forfeiture, and outlines the procedure for making a claim and the remedies available to employees who appeal denied claims.

A summary of the plan's annual financial report also must be distributed. If you do not receive one, you should ask the plan's administrators for it. Or you can obtain one by writing to the U.S. Department of Labor (for contact information, see the "World at Your Fingertips" section at the end of this book).

Q. How are years of accrual determined?

A. After you meet the participation requirements, each year you work for an employer counts as a year of accrual time. A year is defined as 1,000 or more hours of work in a twelve-month period. You can work the 1,000 hours at any time during the twelve months; it need not be evenly distributed during the year. Days taken for sick leave or for paid vacation count towards the minimum.

It is important to note that, depending on your company's policy, the first year you work for an employer does not have to count toward your years of accrual. Thus, your years of accrual will not always equal the number of years you've worked.

Q. If I stop working for an employer and later return, do I get credit for my previous years of service?

A. That depends on the length of the break. Generally, a plan must preserve your years of service that count towards vesting if you leave and then return within five years. However, an employer can have more lenient rules. These rules on breaks in service are complex, so you should consult an expert if you think they apply to you.

> ▶ **VESTING**
>
> Your pension is said to **vest** when you have the right to all the benefits you have earned. If your pension has vested, you have a right to the benefits, even when you leave the job for any reason.

Q. Is my right to collect my pension guaranteed?

A. You always have the right to the money you contributed. If you leave a company after only a few years, that money should be paid back to you in a lump sum. If you work for the employer long enough, you will have a vested interest in your pension, meaning that your benefits cannot be denied even if you quit. If the total value of your pension is $3,500 or less, your plan can require that you take it as a lump-sum payment.

Q. When do my pension rights vest?

A. Your pension rights must either vest completely after five years or vest partially after three years of service. Complete vesting after five years is called **cliff vesting.** Under a system of cliff vesting, if you work less than five years, you are not entitled to any pension benefits. But once you hit the five-year mark, you have a right to all your benefits. Partial vesting is called **graded vesting.** Under this system, your rights become 20 percent vested after three years of service, 40 percent vested after four years, and so on. After seven years, your rights are 100 percent vested.

You do not get to choose which vesting method applies; your employer decides.

Q. I want to change jobs. May I take my pension benefits with me to my new job?

A. If you change jobs before your pension has vested, you usually lose all the benefits you built up in your old job, although your employer must refund money you put into the fund. If you change jobs after your benefits have vested, you are entitled to those benefits. You may put (or "roll over") those funds into an individual retirement account (IRA) or some other type of retirement program (to avoid taxes), or transfer the funds to the new employer's pension plan if possible. Some unions allow this, and there are some state and nationwide systems that allow for job changes with continued participation in a unified pension program (such as the Teachers Insurance and Annuity Association, known as TIAA-CREF).

Q. If I retire and begin receiving my pension, can I still work?

A. Under certain circumstances, your benefit payments may be suspended if you continue to work beyond normal retirement age. If you are a retiree and are considering taking a job, you may wish to ask your plan administrator if your benefits would be suspended.

Q. Does the amount of Social Security I collect affect my pension benefits?

A. It might. Some pension plans allow for a reduction of benefits, depending on how much you receive from Social Security. However, federal law places limits on these reductions. These Social Security integration rules are extremely complex and are different for defined-benefit and defined-contribution plans. You should check with your plan's administrators to see whether your pension plan is integrated with Social Security—and, if so, how this will affect you.

Q. Can my employer change an existing pension plan?

A. Yes. ERISA permits an employer to change the way in which future benefits are accumulated. However, the employer may not make changes that result in a reduction in already-accrued benefits. In addition, ERISA specifically prohibits plan amendments that alter vesting schedules to the detriment of employees.

Q. What protection does ERISA offer when my company is sold or taken over?

A. This area of law is not entirely clear. In some cases, **successor liability** is found, and the new company must continue the plan. If such liability is not found, your new employer is under no obligation to continue an existing pension plan. The new employer can go without a plan, or set up a new plan. However, if the new employer decides to continue the plan, then ERISA requires that previous years of service be counted.

And you still have a right to all the benefits earned under the old plan. However, if the new employer abandons the plan, you will not continue to *earn* benefits.

Q. What if the company I work for declares bankruptcy?

A. It depends on what type of bankruptcy. If your employer declares Chapter 11 (reorganization) bankruptcy, this may not have any effect on your plan, and the plan may continue to exist. However, if your employer declares Chapter 7 (final) bankruptcy—in which the company ceases to exist—then the effect on your pension can be very complicated. Because each bankruptcy is unique, you should contact your plan administrator, your union representative, or the bankruptcy trustee and request an explanation of the plan's status.

Q. Do I have a right to know how my pension plan is investing money?

A. Yes. You should receive a summary of the plan's annual financial report. Each year, a report summarizing the plan's financial operations must be made to both the Internal Revenue Service and the secretary of labor. Also, ERISA requires that the people in charge of investing your plan's money use care, skill, and prudence, and invest only in the interest of participants and beneficiaries.

Q. What are ERISA's funding requirements?

A. Generally, the law requires that the employer contribute enough money to cover pension payments when they become due under a defined-benefit plan. Funding provisions are designed to strengthen funds and prevent abuses. The employer and the fund's administrators are obligated to ensure that the funding requirements are met. If the employer or administrators are in violation of these requirements, contact the nearest office of the U.S. Department of Labor for help.

Q. I am worried about my pension plan going broke. Do I have any protection against such a disaster?

A. You might have some protection. ERISA established the Pension Benefit Guaranty Corporation (PBGC), to which your company must pay insurance premiums if it offers a defined-benefit plan. If the plan goes broke, the PBGC will pay vested benefits up to a certain limit, but it may not pay all you are owed. If the pension plan is still functioning but in danger, then the PBGC will step in and take control. It will use the plan's remaining money and the insurance premiums from other plans to keep your benefits flowing.

Certain pension benefits are not covered, particularly for highly paid people and for those who retire before becoming eligible for Social Security.

If your plan is a defined-contribution plan, the PBGC will not get involved. This means that if the plan goes broke, you may be out of luck. You should keep an eye on how the administrators are handling the fund, because ERISA requires that plan trustees act in the best interests of participants. The secretary of labor or plan participants can sue trustees if they act improperly.

Q. If I do not agree with a decision regarding my pension claim, how do I appeal?

A. Claim and appeals processes are regulated by ERISA. The plan summary must also contain information on the appeals process. All plans must give written notice of a decision within ninety days of receiving a claim. If the plan notifies you within ninety days that it needs an extension, then one ninety-day extension is allowed. If you do not receive a written decision by the deadline, consider your claim denied.

If your claim is denied, the decision must state specific reasons for the denial. You then have sixty days in which to file a written appeal. The plan must make available important documents affecting your appeal, and you must be allowed to submit written support for your claim. The plan then has sixty days to review your appeal and give you a written decision, though it may take another sixty days if it notifies you of the need to do so.

After the appeal, if you are still dissatisfied, you have the right to sue in federal court to recover unfairly denied benefits. However, you may not get the opportunity to present additional evidence, so be sure to submit all relevant information and documentation in your appeal to the trustees.

Q. What if I die before retiring? What are my spouse's rights to my pension?

A. If your pension is vested, and if you have been married for at least a year, then your spouse is entitled to your pension benefits. Typically, he or she will receive an immediate annuity for the rest of his or her life. However, if you and your spouse have executed a written waiver of survivor benefits, then your spouse will not be entitled to such benefits.

Q. What are a divorced person's rights to an ex-spouse's pension benefit?

A. In order to be eligible, the divorced person must have been married to the worker for at least one year. State law governs the pension rights of divorced spouses. In most states, these benefits are part of the marital property divided during the divorce. If a divorced spouse is granted a share of pension benefits, either through a property settlement or a court order (called a **qualified domestic-relations order**), then he or she can collect the appropriate sum when the worker retires or dies, or in some cases before (i.e., if a qualified domestic-relations order provides for it).

401(k) Plans and Simplified Employee Pension Plans

Q. My employer offers a Section 401(k) plan. How does this differ from a traditional retirement plan?

A. A **Section 401(k) plan** is another kind of defined-contribution plan. 401(k) plans are very popular, and many companies have elected to set up 401(k) plans rather than provide traditional pension plans.

A 401(k) plan is funded by contributions you elect to make that are deducted from your salary before taxes. A 401(k) plan is therefore often referred to as a **deferred-compensation plan.** Your employer may match all or part of your contributions. There are limits on the amounts that may be contributed, which increase annually. Your employer may create additional limits. For more information on these limits, talk to your employer or financial advisor.

Q. What happens to my contributions after I make them?

A. The contributions are placed in a fund and invested for your benefit. In some 401(k) plans, the employer controls the investment of contributions made by both the employee and the employer. In other plans, employees are given control over the investment of their accounts.

Q. How are retirement benefits paid out of 401(k) plans?

A. Upon retirement, instead of receiving a pension benefit, employees receive distributions from their 401(k) accounts. Your plan may permit the distributions to begin without penalty as early as age 59½, but the participant cannot defer the start of distributions any later than April 1st of the year after you reach age 70½.

Also, unlike with traditional pension plans, you may be permitted access to the funds in the plan before retirement. For example, if you are an active employee, your plan may allow you to borrow from the plan.

Also, your plan may permit you to make a withdrawal on account of hardship, generally from the funds you have contributed. If you make an early withdrawal that is not permitted by the plan, you will be subject to significant tax penalties.

Distributions upon retirement can take the form of periodic payments, installment payments, or even a single distribution of the entire amount in your account. Because deciding on the form of your distribution can have a great effect on your economic security and tax liability, it is a good idea to get professional advice before making this decision.

Q. *Does ERISA apply to 401(k) plans?*

A. In general, the rules that apply to traditional defined-contribution plans also apply to 401(k) plans. Participants in 401(k) plans have the right to receive summary plan descriptions and annual statements that tell them the amount currently in their 401(k) accounts.

Q. *I work for a small company that offers a simplified employee pension plan (SEP). How does a SEP differ from traditional pension plans and 401(k) plans?*

▶ WARNING SIGNS THAT 401(K) CONTRIBUTIONS ARE BEING MISUSED

The Department of Labor urges employees to be alert to the following warning signs that your 401(k) contributions are being misused:

1. Your 401(k) or individual account statement is consistently late or comes at irregular intervals.

2. Your account balance does not appear to be accurate.

3. Your employer failed to transmit your contribution to the plan on a timely basis.

4. There is a significant drop in the account balance that cannot be explained by normal market ups and downs.

5. Your 401(k) or individual account statement shows that your contribution from your paycheck was not made.

6. Unauthorized investments are listed on your statement.

7. Former employees are having trouble getting their benefits paid on time or in the correct amounts.

8. There are unusual transactions, such as a loan to the employer, to a corporate officer, or to one of the plan trustees.

9. There are frequent and unexplained changes in investment managers or consultants.

10. Your employer recently has experienced severe financial difficulty.

A. Simplified employee pension plans (SEPs) are popular with small companies and self-employed workers because they are relatively uncomplicated retirement savings plans. A SEP allows employers to make contributions on a tax-favored basis to **individual retirement accounts (IRAs)** owned by the employees. SEPs are subject to minimal reporting and disclosure requirements. There are contribution limits, and the limit applicable to your plan will depend on the kind of SEP your employer has set up.

Q. Does the form of business organization limit the ability to offer a SEP?

A. No. Any employer, whether a corporation, a partnership, or a sole proprietorship, can offer this employee benefit.

Q. Can an employee have both a SEP and an IRA?

A. Yes. The SEP can function as an additional IRA. The difference is that the employee (and perhaps the employer) makes the contributions to the IRA, while the employer alone makes them to the SEP.

Q. From the employer's perspective, what is the value of a SEP?

A. A SEP is very flexible. You don't have to make a contribution every year—you can lower the contribution in years when business is off, or even skip the contribution entirely. And record-keeping requirements are relatively minor.

Q. From the employee's perspective, what is the value of a SEP?

▶ SOCIAL SECURITY

For most people, Social Security is a major source of financial support during retirement. Social Security is the most extensive program for providing income to older and disabled Americans. It is paid for by a tax on workers and their employers. When you qualify, and how much you qualify for, will be impacted by your birth date, how long you have been working, and whether you take on other part-time or full-time employment during retirement.

When collecting Social Security, you won't get as much money as you did when you were working. Social Security is not meant to be a complete source of retirement income; rather, it is meant to provide a floor of protection. You probably will need other sources of income, such as a pension from your employer or union, a part-time job, or income from your life savings.

Benefits are also available for the spouse and dependents of a retired or disabled worker. When a worker dies, members of the surviving family who qualify can collect the benefits.

Social Security is a complicated area of the law; for a more detailed look at the program and how to apply, consider working with an experienced attorney or advocate, or referring to the *ABA's Legal Guide for Americans Over 50*.

A. The employee has access to the funds immediately, though he or she will face a penalty for early withdrawal. And contributions fully vest immediately, meaning that they belong to the employee as soon as they are made.

REMEMBER THIS

- Pension plans are governed by the rules of the Employee Retirement Income Security Act (ERISA), which provides extensive protection to employees who participate in them.

- ERISA requires that participating employees be provided with detailed reports and disclosures.

- Employees should review these reports carefully to make sure that the plan's assets are being invested prudently.

- Section 401(k) plans allow you to make a defined contribution to your account (often matched, at least in part, by your employer).

- SEPs are very simple retirement plans— essentially, they are employer contributions to an IRA in the employee's name. They provide a great deal of flexibility for both employers and employees.

HEALTH AND LONG-TERM CARE BENEFITS

The federal government provides basic health-care insurance called Medicare for older and disabled individuals. Practically everyone who has a work history and is sixty-five or older is eligible for Medicare— even those who continue to work.

The federal and state governments also work together to provide a comprehensive medical benefits program, called Medicaid, for qualified low-income people. Medicare and Medicaid are not the same, though some older people qualify for both.

This section examines these programs, as well as private Medigap insurance, which is commonly used to supplement Medicare coverage. The section then examines long-term care benefits under public programs, and under private long-term care insurance. Medicare and Medicaid have been revised many times, and more revisions are certain. For more current information on these ever-changing topics, see the resources listed in the "World at Your Fingertips" section at the end of this book.

Medicare

Q. What is the basic structure of the Medicare program?

A. The **Centers for Medicare and Medicaid Services** (**CMS**), a branch of the U.S. Department of Health and Human Services, is the federal agency responsible for administering Medicare.

Original Medicare has two main parts. The hospital insurance part, or **Part A,** covers medically necessary care in a hospital, in a skilled nursing facility, in a psychiatric hospital, through home health care, or through hospice care. **Part B** relates to medical insurance benefits, and covers medically necessary physician's services, no matter where you receive them, as well as outpatient hospital care, many diagnostic tests, rehabilitation services, and a variety of other medical services and supplies not covered by Part A.

The exact coverage rules and limitations are complex. The actual coverage determinations and payments to care providers are handled by insurance companies under contract with Medicare. These insurance companies are referred to as **fiscal intermediaries** under Part A and as **carriers** under Part B. They determine the appropriate fees.

Medicare beneficiaries also have the option of joining a **Medicare Advantage Plan** (or **MA plan**). Collectively, these programs are known as **Medicare Part C.** MA plans are health plans run by private companies. If you choose one, Medicare pays a set amount each month to the plan, and in return, the plan must provide all of your Part A (hospital insurance) and Part B (medical insurance) benefits, and must cover at least the medically necessary services that the Original Medicare Plan covers. These plans may offer extra benefits such as hearing, vision, dental, or wellness programs, and must also provide Part D prescription drug coverage at no extra cost. There are several types of Medicare Advantage Plans: Medicare Health Maintenance Organizations (HMOs), Preferred Provider Organizations (PPOs), Private Fee-for-Service Plans, Medicare Special Needs Plans, and Medical Savings Account Plans.

Finally, the newest benefit under Medicare is **Part D**, the Prescription Drug Benefit Program. Provided through private insurance companies or Medicare Advantage Plans, it is an optional benefits program in which you must choose to enroll. It covers part of the cost of outpatient generic and many brand-name medications. Within certain guidelines established by the government, each plan has significant flexibility to decide what drugs to cover and to set its own premiums, deductibles, coinsurances, and co-payments. Each plan may limit coverage to a specific list of drugs, and the list can change during the year upon sixty days' notice to you and your treating doctor.

▶ **DENIAL OF BENEFITS**

Never accept a denial of benefits without further questioning it. Incorrect denials of Medicare benefits occur often. Medicare beneficiaries who appeal erroneous denials have a substantial likelihood of success on appeal. Your right to an appeal is explained in detail on pages 605–606.

Q. What does Medicare cost me?

A. Part A coverage is provided free to all individuals sixty-five and older who are eligible for Social Security, even if they are still working. If you are not eligible for Social Security, you can enroll in Part A after age sixty-five, but you will have to pay a sizable monthly premium.

Part B is available to all Part A enrollees for a monthly premium that changes yearly. The Social Security Administration can tell you the cost of the current premium. Under both Parts A and B, beneficiaries must pay certain deductibles and coinsurance payments, fixed annually by the federal government, unless they are enrolled in a managed-care organization. **Deductibles** are payments you must make before Medicare coverage begins. **Coinsurance payments** are percentages of covered expenses for which you are responsible. Medicare Advantage Plans may set different deductibles and co-payments.

Costs for Part C vary depending on a number of factors, including whether the plan pays all or part of the monthly Part B premium; whether the plan charges a monthly premium; whether the plan has a yearly or any additional deductibles; how much you pay for each service; the type of services you need and how often you get them; whether you follow the plan's rules; and the types of extra benefits you need and what it charges for them.

Costs for Part D plans also vary. However, each plan will have a monthly premium, annual deductibles, and co-payments for prescriptions. There are numerous plans available, and you can select the one that best covers your needs and budget.

Q. I don't have very much money and am afraid that I won't be able to pay the fees. Is there any way to reduce them?

A. If you meet certain income and resource tests, your state's Medicaid program may assist you in paying Medicare costs. The income and resource tests are more generous than the tests for regular Medicaid eligibility, so even if you are not eligible for Medicaid, you may still be eligible for help with Medicare costs.

Q. I will turn sixty-five soon, but I do not plan to retire then. Am I still going to be able to receive Medicare benefits?

A. Yes, but you must file a written application. This can be done in two different ways. Your initial enrollment period begins three calendar months before your sixty-fifth birthday month, and extends three months beyond your birthday month. You can enroll at any time during this seven-month period. Your benefits will begin on the first day of the month in which you turn sixty-five.

Q. What happens if I don't enroll during that time?

A. If you do not enroll during this time, you can enroll during the general enrollment period, which runs from January 1 to March 31 of each year. However, you may pay a higher monthly premium if you delay enrollment beyond your initial enrollment period.

Q. If I have other health insurance, can I still be covered by Medicare?

A. If you are working and are covered by your employer's health insurance program, or if you are covered by your spouse's plan, then Medicare is usually the secondary payer after the other insurance pays. If you haven't enrolled in Medicare and you lose the other insurance, you may sign up for the Medicare program during a seven-month enrollment period that begins in the month that the other program no longer covers you.

To make sure you receive maximum coverage without penalty, talk to your employer's benefits office, a Center for Medicare and Medicaid Services, or your local Social Security Administration office.

Q. If I am covered by Medicare, will I need any other medical coverage?

A. In most cases, yes. A Medicare Advantage Plan may offer comprehensive coverage, including prescription drugs, but in some of these plans you will only be covered if you see certain doctors or use certain hospitals. Many people opt for coverage by the Original Medicare Plan, for which you need supplemental coverage. Supplemental coverage can be provided by a private Medigap plan (discussed below), by an employer or union plan, or by Medicaid or the Veterans Administration. These supplemental plans may or may not cover prescription drugs, so enrolling in a Medicare prescription drug plan is also important for most people. Finally, you may also benefit from purchasing long-term care insurance if you can afford it and if you qualify, since Medicare does not cover nursing-home care or home care for extended periods of time.

Q. Who qualifies for Medicare?

A. In addition to older Social Security recipients, younger persons who have received Social Security disability benefits for more than twenty-four months are eligible, as well as certain persons with kidney disease. If you are under sixty-five and are receiving disability benefits, your enrollment in Medicare will begin automatically as soon as you have been receiving benefits for twenty-four months.

Q. What does Medicare Part A (hospital insurance) cover?

A. Part A helps pay for medically necessary hospital care, skilled nursing care, home health care, and hospice care as described below.

▶ SIGNING UP FOR MEDICARE

Enrolling in Medicare is no problem for most people. Everyone who is turning sixty-five and applying for Social Security or railroad retirement benefits is automatically enrolled in Medicare Part A. If you are receiving these benefits before turning sixty-five, you should receive a Medicare card prior to the month of your sixty-fifth birthday. Medicare benefits normally begin on the first of the month in which you turn sixty-five.

- **Hospitalization.** This includes
  - a semiprivate room and board;
  - general nursing;
  - the cost of special-care units, such as intensive-care or coronary-care units;
  - drugs furnished by the hospital during your stay;
  - blood transfusions;
  - lab tests, X-rays, and other radiology services;
  - medical supplies and equipment;
  - operating and recovery room costs; and
  - rehabilitation services.
- **Skilled nursing-facility inpatient care following a hospitalization of at least three days.** Your condition must require skilled nursing or skilled rehabilitation services on a daily basis that, as a practical matter, can be provided only in a skilled nursing facility. You must be admitted within a short time (usually thirty days) after you leave the hospital, and the skilled care you receive must be based on a doctor's order. Most nursing-home residents do not require the level of nursing services considered "skilled" by Medicare. Consequently, Medicare pays for relatively little nursing-home care. In addition, not every nursing home participates in Medicare or is a skilled nursing facility. Ask the hospital discharge staff or nursing-home staff if you are unsure of the facility's status.
- **Home health care.** Medicare covers part-time or intermittent skilled nursing care; physical, occupational, and speech therapy services; medical social services; part-time care provided by a home health aide; and medical equipment for use in the home. However, the benefit does not cover general household services.

To be eligible for home health-care services, you must meet four conditions:

1. You must be under the care of a physician who determines you need home health care and sets up a plan.
2. You must be "homebound," although you need not be bedridden. An individual is considered **homebound** if leaving home requires a considerable and taxing effort, and if any absences from the home are either for medical care or to attend adult day care or religious services, or are infrequent or for periods of relatively short duration.
3. The care you need must include intermittent skilled nursing, physical therapy, or speech therapy.
4. Your care must be provided by a Medicare-participating home health-care agency.

- **Hospice care.** A **hospice** is an agency or organization that provides primarily pain relief, palliative care, symptom management, and supportive services to terminally ill people. Hospice services may include physician or visiting-nurse services, individual and family psychological support, inpatient care when needed, home health aide care, medications, medical/social services, counseling, and respite care for family caregivers.

To be eligible for hospice care, a patient must have a doctor certify that he or she is **terminally ill** (defined as having a life expectancy of six months or less); the patient must choose to receive hospice care instead of standard Medicare benefits; and the hospice must be a Medicare-participating program.

Q. What does Medicare Part B (medical insurance) cover?

A. Medicare Part B covers a wide range of outpatient and physician expenses regardless of where they are provided—at home, in a hospital or nursing home, or in a private office. Covered services include:

- doctors' services, including some services by chiropractors, dentists, podiatrists, and optometrists;
- outpatient hospital services, such as emergency room services or outpatient

---

▶ SKILLED CARE OR CUSTODIAL CARE

Medicare helps pay only for "skilled" nursing-home care, it does not pay for "custodial" care. However, the distinction is often fuzzy, and many Medicare denials based on a finding of custodial care can be appealed successfully. Generally, care is considered **custodial** when it is primarily for the purpose of helping the resident with daily needs, such as eating, bathing, walking, getting in and out of bed, and taking medicine. Skilled nursing and rehabilitation services are those that require the skills of professional or skilled personnel such as registered nurses, licensed practical nurses, or therapists. Care that is generally nonskilled may be considered skilled when, for example, medical complications require the skilled management and evaluation of a care plan, observation of a patient's changing condition, or patient education services.

> ▶ **COVERAGE PERIODS**
>
> The various benefits available through Medicare don't necessarily start on the date you will want them to. These coverage periods vary for different types of services and can be rather complex. For more information on these coverage periods, consult with an attorney or advocate experienced in Medicare benefits, or visit Medicare's website.

clinic care, radiology services, and ambulatory surgical services;

- diagnostic tests, including X-rays and other laboratory services, as well as some mammography and Pap smear screenings;
- durable medical equipment, such as oxygen equipment, wheelchairs, and other medically necessary equipment that your doctor prescribes for use in your home;
- kidney dialysis;
- ambulance services to or from a hospital or skilled nursing facility;
- mental-health services, although Medicare generally pays only 50 percent for such services;
- certain services of other practitioners who are not physicians, such as clinical psychologists or social workers;
- certain vaccinations such as those for flu, pneumonia, and hepatitis B;
- prostate cancer screenings;
- pelvic examinations;
- diabetes screening and monitoring;
- colorectal cancer screening;
- bone-mass measurements; and

- many other health services, supplies, and prosthetic devices that are not covered by Medicare Part A (Part B also covers some home health services).

Medicare does not cover

- routine physical examinations;
- most routine foot care and dental care;
- examinations for prescribing or fitting eyeglasses or hearing aids;
- prescription drugs that do not require administration by a physician;
- most cosmetic surgery;
- immunizations, except for certain persons at risk;
- personal comfort items and services; and
- any service not considered "reasonable and necessary."

Q. What is my share of Medicare Part B costs?

A. For Part B benefits, you must pay an annual deductible, which is adjusted every year. Then Medicare generally pays 80 percent of Medicare-approved amounts for covered services for the rest of the year. You pay the other 20 percent of the approved amount. There is no cap on the patient's share of the cost.

If a physician or other provider charges you more than the Medicare-approved amount, then your liability depends on whether the provider accepts assignment. **Accepting assignment** means that the provider agrees to accept the Medicare-approved amount as payment in full. If the provider does not accept assignment, then generally you must pay for any excess charge over the Medicare-approved amount, but only up to certain limits. If you are a Medicaid recipient, then your physician must accept assignment.

The government presently sets the limit on physician's charges at 115 percent of the

Medicare-approved fee schedule. Doctors who charge more than these limits may be fined, and you should get a refund from the doctor.

Here is an example of the difference accepting assignment can make. Mrs. Jones sees Dr. Brown on June 1 for medical care. She has already paid her $100 annual deductible for covered Part B medical care. Dr. Brown charges $230 for the visit. The Medicare-approved amount for such services is $200, and Medicare pays 80 percent, or $160. If Dr. Brown accepts assignment, Mrs. Jones must pay a $40 co-payment (that is, 20 percent of the $200 approved). If Dr. Brown does *not* accept assignment, then Mrs. Jones must pay $40 plus the $30 excess charge. Her total payment is $70. Note that Dr. Brown's actual charge ($230) is within 115 percent of the Medicare-approved amount ($200), and is therefore permissible.

Q. I think I might enroll in Part C. How do I know if it is right for me?

A. Any decision to participate in Medicare Part C must be made under the careful guid-

ance of a professional knowledgeable in Medicare benefits. Selecting the proper Part C program is important. To join, you must have Medicare Part A and Part B. You will have to pay your monthly Medicare Part B premium to Medicare. In addition, you might have to pay a monthly premium to your Medicare Advantage Plan for the extra benefits.

If you decide to join a Medicare Advantage Plan, you will use the health card that you get from your Medicare Advantage Plan provider for your health care. Most of these plans provide more benefits and lower co-payments than the Original Medicare Plan. However, you may have to see doctors that belong to the plan, or go to certain hospitals to receive services. Also, you might have to pay a monthly premium for your Medicare Advantage Plan because of the extra benefits it offers.

Q. What is the enrollment process for Part D?

A. Enrollment in a Part D prescription drug plan is voluntary, although a choice to delay enrollment after your initial eligibility will result in a penalty (i.e., an increased premium). Enrolling in Part D is a separate process from enrolling in Medicare. You can enroll when you first get Medicare, during an annual enrollment period, or (in certain circumstances) during special enrollment periods. Medicare beneficiaries have four enrollment options:

1. Enroll in a stand-alone prescription drug plan (called a PDP).
2. Join or remain in a Medicare Advantage Plan (such as an HMO or PPO) and get all Medicare and prescription drug benefits through the plan.
3. Retain your current coverage from a non-Medicare source, if it is as good as Medicare. For example, if you receive

---

▶ **FINDING A DOCTOR**

Doctors and suppliers who agree to accept assignment under Medicare on all claims are called **Medicare-participating** doctors and suppliers. You can get a directory of Medicare-participating doctors and suppliers from your Medicare carrier or on the Internet. The directory is also available in Social Security Administration offices, state and area agencies on aging, and in most hospitals.

drug coverage from another source, such as an employer, a union, the Veterans Administration, or a Medigap policy, you will be notified by your current plan if its drug coverage is at least as comprehensive as Medicare drug coverage.

4. Decide not to enroll in a Medicare plan at this time, and go without prescription coverage. If your current drug coverage is not at least as comprehensive as Medicare's coverage, and if you wait until a later time to enroll in a Medicare plan, then you will have to pay a permanently higher monthly premium for the coverage.

There are many Medicare drug plans. In most states, you have a confusing array of stand-alone PDPs and Medicare Advantage Plans from which to choose. State Health Insurance Assistance Programs (SHIPs) can help you identify the most important factors to consider in making your selection, including the annual cost of a plan (i.e., the cost of premiums, deductibles, and co-payments), whether the drugs you need are included, and whether your local pharmacy is in the plan network. You can change plans annually, and because plan coverage and prices change yearly, you should review your coverage annually to make sure you have a plan that best fits you.

Q. I have prescription drug coverage now. Do I have to drop it to enroll in Part D?

A. You do not have to remain enrolled in a Medicare Part D prescription plan if you have other prescription drug coverage that is equal to or greater than the Medicare Part D coverage. This is called **creditable prescription drug coverage.** Having creditable prescription drug coverage (and retaining documents

proving that you do) will allow you to join a Medicare Part D plan at a later date and not be subjected to the late enrollment penalties.

Q. How are Medicare claims filed and paid?

A. It differs for each part of Medicare. For Part A benefits, the provider submits the claim directly to the fiscal intermediary (i.e., the insurance company). The provider will charge you for any owed deductible or coinsurance payment. For Part B claims, doctors, suppliers and other providers are required to submit your Medicare claims to the carrier (the insurance company) in most cases, even if they do not take assignment. The provider will charge you (or your private supplemental insurance) directly for any deductible, coinsurance, or excess charge you owe. If you belong to a Medicare Advantage Plan, there are usually no claim forms to be filed, although there may be a co-payment for any covered services. For prescription drugs covered under Medicare Part D, your plan pays the covered portion directly to the pharmacist, while you pay deductibles and co-payments at the time of purchase.

Q. What if I disagree with a Medicare decision? How can I appeal?

A. You have the right to appeal all decisions regarding service coverage or the amount Medicare will pay on a claim. If your claim has been denied in whole or in part, it is usually a good idea to appeal, especially if the basis of denial is unclear. A surprisingly high percentage of denials are reversed on appeal. In any case, the appeal will make clear the reason for the denial.

Medicare Parts A, B, and D have different procedures for appealing, and there are several steps in the appeal process. Procedures also differ somewhat depending on whether you are enrolled in the Original Medicare Plan or in a Medicare Advantage Plan. After the initial levels of review, if your dispute hasn't been resolved, then all parts of Medicare include the option of a hearing before an administrative law judge—and even a review by a federal court if sufficient amounts of money are at stake.

Always be conscious of time limits for filing appeals. You may lose your rights if you wait too long. You may want to get assistance with your appeal from a legal-services office or a private lawyer, particularly if large medical bills are involved. Nonlawyer volunteers and nonlawyer staff members of legal-service programs help a number of people with appeals without charging fees.

Medicaid

Q. What is Medicaid?

A. Medicaid is a medical-assistance program for older or disabled persons who are poor, and for certain children and families whose income and assets fall below certain levels set by federal and state law. Unlike Medicare, which offers the same benefits to all enrollees, Medicaid is managed by individual states, and benefits and eligibility vary by state. The following questions address Medicaid as it applies to older and disabled adults.

Q. Is it possible to receive both Medicare and Medicaid?

A. Yes, if you qualify for both programs. Even if you do not qualify for Medicaid, it still may assist you in paying for all or part of the Medicare premium, deductibles, and coinsurance payments through the Medicare Savings Program, if you pass special income and resource tests.

Q. If I qualify for Medicaid, what sorts of services do I get?

A. Medicaid covers a broad spectrum of services. Certain benefits are mandated by federal law. They include

- inpatient and outpatient hospital services;
- doctors' and nurse practitioners' services;
- inpatient nursing-home care;
- home health-care services; and
- laboratory and X-ray charges.

Other services may include those provided by podiatrists, optometrists, and chiropractors; mental-health services; personal in-home care; dental care; physical therapy and other rehabilitation; dentures; eyeglasses; transportation services; and more. In all cases, you may receive these services only from a Medicaid-participating provider. Providers may choose whether to participate in Medicaid, and they must meet certain standards. Some states have contracted with managed-care organizations to provide comprehensive care to Medicaid-eligible individuals. In these states, you may be limited to using the designated care provider for regular care. For outpatient prescription drugs, you must enroll in a Medicare prescription drug plan, although you will be eligible for a no-cost or low-cost plan.

Q. What does Medicaid cost me?

A. Medicaid does not require you to pay premiums or deductibles. Providers may not charge Medicaid patients additional fees beyond the Medicaid reimbursement amount. However, states are permitted to impose a nominal deductible charge or other form of cost-sharing for certain services. No Medicaid recipient may be denied services by a participating provider because of the patient's inability to pay.

Individuals whose income or assets exceed the state's permissible Medicaid amount may be eligible for Medicaid only after spending down their income or assets to a poverty level by incurring medical expenses. These spend-down amounts can be very high, especially for nursing-home residents whose income far exceeds the Medicaid eligibility level, but who face enormous monthly expenses for care.

Q. Does owning a home disqualify me from Medicaid?

A. No. All states exempt your home as an asset as long as you, your spouse, or certain other qualified individuals live in it. If you must leave your home in order to receive nursing-home care or other long-term care, it is still exempt permanently or for some period of time, but state rules differ and can be complex. Besides your home, all states allow you to keep a very limited amount of cash and personal property.

Q. How do I apply for Medicaid?

A. Contact the state or local agency that handles Medicaid in your area. Its name will vary; it may be called Social Services, Public Aid, Public Welfare, Human Services, or something similar. You can also call your local AAA or senior center for information.

Q. How are Medicaid claims filed and paid?

A. Medicaid providers always bill Medicaid directly.

Q. If I disagree with a decision made by my Medicaid program, what can I do?

A. You have the right to appeal all decisions that affect your Medicaid eligibility or services. When a decision about your Medicaid coverage is made, you should receive prompt written notice of the decision. This will include an explanation of how you can appeal the decision. The appeal process includes a right to a fair hearing before a hearing officer. You may want a lawyer or a public-benefits specialist experienced in Medicaid law to represent you.

Medigap Insurance

Q. Do I need any other insurance coverage besides Medicare?

▶ QUALIFYING FOR MEDICAID

Medicaid programs in each state have different standards for determining whether individuals are eligible. All states require that adults be at least sixty-five years old, blind or disabled, and that they meet income and asset tests. In most states, persons eligible for Supplemental Security Income (SSI) or Temporary Assistance to Needy Families (TANF) are covered automatically. Medicaid eligibility rules are so complicated that it is advisable for older people with low incomes or with high medical expenses to talk with someone with expertise in Medicaid—such as a legal-services lawyer, a paralegal, a social worker, or a private lawyer experienced in handling Medicaid issues.

> ## ▶ YOUR AREA AGENCY ON AGING

One important advocate on behalf of elder Americans is the nationwide network of **area agencies on aging (AAAs)**. Today, every area of the country is served by either an AAA or a state unit on aging. These agencies help local communities develop services specifically for older residents. The AAAs channel funds from the Older Americans Act to local communities.

AAAs also offer information and referral services to older adults. A few provide services directly, but most only coordinate services and provide assistance to designated service agencies in the local communities.

AAAs also provide funding and programming for local senior-citizen centers. Programs include recreation, socialization, meals, and educational programs. Additional funds are generally provided by local and state governments, as well as by organizations such as the United Way, private foundations, corporations, and individual donors.

You can call your AAA with almost any question about services in your neighborhood. You can also go directly to a senior center near you and ask for help. If staff there cannot provide help, they can put you in touch with someone in the AAA who can.

A. Yes. Most older people need to purchase a supplemental, or Medigap, insurance policy to cover some of the costs not covered by Parts A and B. However, there are exceptions, explained in the following answers.

If you can afford it, you may also want to consider purchasing long-term care insurance, because Medicare and Medigap policies do *not* cover long-term care. Long-term care insurance is discussed in the next section, "Paying for Long-Term Care."

Q. What exactly is Medigap?

A. **Medigap** is private, supplemental health insurance that covers some of the expenses not covered by Medicare.

Q. Who doesn't need a Medigap policy?

A. While most people need Medigap coverage, you may already have enough coverage without it if you meet one of these four conditions:

1. If you are already covered by Medicaid, you do not need a Medigap policy. Medicaid covers the gaps in Medicare and more.
2. If you are eligible for help under the Medicare Savings Program. This program pays some or all of Medicare's premiums and may also pay Medicare deductibles and coinsurance for certain people who are not eligible for Medicaid but nevertheless have a limited income and assets.
3. If you have retiree health coverage through a former employer or union, you *may* not need Medigap insurance. This coverage may be comprehensive or, alternatively, may be expressly designed to coordinate its coverage with Medicare. Examine the coverage, costs, and stability

▶ THE APPLICATION PROCESS

When you apply for Medicaid, you will have to document your financial need in detail, as well as your residency. The application form can be lengthy and complex, but the Medicaid agency can help you complete it. However, a better alternative may be to obtain the help of an independent expert, such as a legal-aid attorney or private attorney with expertise in Medicaid. If you are in a hospital or other institution, a staff social worker should be made available to help you apply. Don't let inability to get to the public agency keep you from seeking assistance. Since the start of benefits is linked to your date of application, it is important to apply as soon as you need Medicaid assistance. Almost any written request with your signature may be enough to establish your application date, even if you have not yet completed the full application form. The effective date can be retroactive, up to three months from the date you submit your signed application.

of your coverage to determine whether it is a better option than Medigap.

4. If you belong to a Medicare Advantage Plan, you probably do not need a Medigap policy, since coverage is normally comprehensive. But do not give up your Medigap coverage too quickly if you are joining a Medicare Advantage Plan. If you can afford it, keep it long enough to be sure you are satisfied with the managed-care organization.

Q. How do I find a good Medigap policy?

A. All Medigap insurance conforms to one of twelve standardized benefit plans identified as Plan A through Plan I. Plan A is a core package and is available in all states. The other plans have different combinations of benefits. Check with your state department of insurance for additional information. The federal and many state governments provide buyer's guides.

You should purchase only one Medigap policy. Federal law prohibits the sale of duplicative policies, and multiple policies almost always will provide overlapping coverage for which you pay twice but receive benefits only once. In evaluating policies, decide which features would best meet your health needs and financial situation. New sales of these plans do not include prescription drug coverage, although persons who had Medigap plans before January 2007 may have drug coverage that may or may not be comparable to Medicare Part D drug plans.

Q. What is a Medicare SELECT policy?

A. Medicare SELECT policies, which are available in some states, generally cost less than equivalent Medigap plans. However, with a Medicare SELECT plan, you must use specific hospitals and (in some cases) specific doctors in order to get full insurance benefits (except in an emergency). If you don't, you will have to pay what the original Medicare plan does not pay. The Original Medicare Plan will pay its share of approved charges no matter what hospital or doctor you choose.

Q. When should I get a Medigap policy?

A. Buy a Medigap policy at or near the time your Medicare coverage begins, because during the first six months that you are sixty-five or older and enrolled in Medicare Part B, companies must accept you regardless of any health conditions you have, and they cannot charge you more than they charge others of the same age. After this period, you may be forced to pay much higher premiums for the same policy due to your health status. During this open enrollment period, companies may still exclude preexisting conditions during the first six months of the policy.

Different enrollment rules apply to people under sixty-five who are eligible for Medicare because of disability.

Q. What if I have an old Medigap policy and am considering a replacement? Is that a good idea?

A. If you are considering a replacement policy, be sure you have a good reason and know your options. Beware of illegal sales practices. Both federal and state laws govern the sale of Medigap insurance. These laws prohibit high-pressure sales tactics, fraudulent or misleading statements about coverage or cost, selling a policy that is not one of the approved standard policies, or imposing new waiting periods for replacement policies. If a sales agent offers you a policy that duplicates coverage of your existing policy, the duplication must be disclosed to you in writing. If you feel you have been misled or pressured, contact your state insurance department, your state's health insurance counseling program, or the federal Medicare Hotline at 800-MEDICARE (800-633-4227). TTY users should call 877-486-2048.

Paying for Long-Term Care

Q. What federal programs pay for long-term care in a nursing home?

A. Medicare does not pay for a significant amount of nursing-home care. Coverage of skilled nursing care is narrowly defined and limited to twenty days of full coverage and a maximum of eighty additional days with a large coinsurance payment.

Medicaid, on the other hand, pays a substantial portion of the nation's nursing-home bills (over 40 percent). However, Medicaid pays only when almost all your assets have been depleted. Medicaid will cover nursing-home expenses if your condition requires nursing-home care, if the nursing home is certified by the state Medicaid agency, and if you meet income and other eligibility requirements.

The Department of Veterans Affairs (VA) pays for some nursing-home care for veterans in VA facilities and private facilities, but the benefit is limited to the extent that resources and facilities are available. Priority is given to veterans with medical problems related to their military service, to very old veterans of wartime service, and to very poor veterans. Contact your local VA office for more information.

Q. What if I don't want to live in a nursing home? Are home care services available under Medicare or Medicaid?

A. Yes, but to a limited extent. The home health-care benefit under Medicare focuses mainly on skilled nursing and therapeutic services needed on a part-time or intermittent basis. This benefit is described more fully in the section on Medicare (see page 598).

Medicaid home health care is usually quite limited, too. However, several state Medicaid programs also provide "personal care" services to Medicaid-eligible individuals who need help with normal activities of daily living, such as dressing, bathing, using a toilet, eating, and walking. Many states also offer Medicaid waiver programs that allow the state to use Medicaid dollars for home- and community-based services that normally would not be covered. These waiver programs usually target people who otherwise would have to live in a nursing home. Some of these services include personal care, adult day care, housekeeping services, care coordination and management, and respite care, which enables primary caregivers to take a break from their responsibilities.

Q. What happens if my spouse needs nursing-home care but I am still able to live independently? Will all our income and assets have to be used for his or her support before Medicaid will help pay expenses?

A. If your spouse resides in or may be entering a nursing home, Medicaid has special rules that allow the spouse remaining in the community (the community spouse) to keep

---

> ▶ **SPENDING DOWN TO ELIGIBILITY**
>
> Many people who normally are not eligible for Medicaid become eligible after a period of time spent in a nursing home. This happens because the high cost of nursing-home care forces many individuals to spend down their assets and income to a level that qualifies them for Medicaid. The rules and availability of this option vary by state.

---

more income and assets than is permitted under the regular eligibility rules. The specifics vary, but the general structure is as follows.

The community spouse can keep his or her income up to a set level, and the state may require all or part of joint income to be used to pay nursing-home expenses, depending upon the particular state's rules.

Most of the income of the nursing-home spouse is considered available to pay for nursing-home care. However, a portion of the nursing-home spouse's income may be kept by the community spouse as a "minimum monthly maintenance needs allowance" if the community spouse's income is below a spousal allowance figure set by the state under federal guidelines. States may permit the community spouse to keep a shelter allowance, if shelter costs (i.e., rent, mortgage, taxes, insurance, and utilities) exceed a specified amount.

Assets or resources are treated differently. The state applies a two-step rule. First, Medicaid counts all resources owned by either spouse. This inventory will exclude a few resources, including a home, household goods, personal effects, an automobile, a burial fund of up to $1,500, and in some states additional monies for funeral and burial services (provided the funds are in an irrevocable account).

Second, Medicaid permits the community spouse to keep one-half of the total countable resources, called the **protected resources amount,** as long as this one-half falls between a specified floor and ceiling, adjusted yearly. If the one-half falls below the floor, then the community spouse may keep more of the couple's resources, at least up to the floor amount. If the one-half exceeds the ceiling, then the excess will be considered available to pay for the cost of nursing-home care. Thus, the community spouse is permitted to keep no more than the ceiling amount, even if it equals far less than half of the couple's assets. A more liberal approach in some states permits the community spouse to keep the maximum allowance, even if this is more than one-half of countable assets.

Another special rule applies to your home. Even though your home is normally an excluded resource, the state (in limited circumstances) can place a lien against your home equal to the paid nursing-home expenses. The rules are complicated and vary; the advice of a lawyer experienced in Medicaid law is advisable. Moreover, almost all these rules provide for hardship exceptions in special circumstances.

Q. *If I have assets that exceed my state's Medicaid eligibility requirements, can I transfer these assets to my children or to a trust in order to qualify for Medicaid? After all, these are assets I intend to leave to my children when I die.*

A. The law on transferring assets before making a Medicaid application is complex. Such transfers can result in a period of ineligibility for Medicaid benefits. Some financial avenues may be available to shelter or preserve some of your assets, but there are a number of legal, financial, ethical, and practical consequences to such a transfer. Anyone who may need to rely on Medicaid to pay for nursing-home care should seek advice from an experienced lawyer. Also, Medicaid has the right to "look back" at financial records for the five years prior to your Medicaid application. Medicaid will impose a penalty period of ineligibility based upon the value of gifts made during the look-back period.

Q. *Must children pay for parents in nursing homes?*

A. There is no legal obligation under federal law for children to pay for their parents' care. Only a spouse may be held legally responsible to help pay for the cost of nursing-home care, and as a practical matter, the responsibility is often difficult to enforce against an unwilling spouse. If Medicaid enters the picture, the special rules for spousal responsibility (described earlier) will apply.

Some nursing homes give admission preference to private-pay patients over Medicaid patients, because private-pay rates are often higher than the amount Medicaid pays. While admission priority for private-pay patients is permissible in some states, it is illegal in others. In all states, federal law prohibits nursing homes from requiring a private payment from families, or a period of private payment, prior to applying for Medicaid coverage. Federal law also prohibits nursing homes from requiring patients to waive their rights to Medicare and/or Medicaid, and from caring for Medicaid and private-pay residents differently.

Q. *What is long-term care insurance?*

A. **Long-term care insurance** helps pay for nursing-home care, and usually home care services, for a period of two or more years. Long-term care insurance is still a relatively new type of private insurance, so its features change frequently.

Most individual policies are available for purchase only by people between the ages of fifty and eighty-four, and a medical screening is typically required. Not every older person needs or can afford a long-term care insurance policy. Policies are appropriate for those with substantial income and assets to protect, and those who wish to buy this form of protection against the potential costs of long-term care.

Most long-term care policies are structured as indemnity policies. That is, they pay up to a preset cap for each day of a covered service. Other policies pay a percentage of costs up to a specified cap. The specific provisions should be closely examined before purchasing, since the possible conditions and limitations on coverage can be complex.

Q. How are the costs of a long-term care policy determined?

A. The cost of the premium is determined in part by your age, the extent of coverage you purchase, and your health history. Age is the single greatest factor in determining premium costs, because the risk of needing long-term care increases significantly with age.

Q. Are there any tax implications for long-term care insurance premiums or benefits?

A. Yes. The Health Insurance Portability and Accountability Act of 1996 (HIPAA) clarified the tax treatment of both premiums and benefits to make it the same as for major medical coverage. Under HIPAA, benefits from a policy that meets minimum federal standards are generally not taxable. For taxpayers who itemize their deductions, premiums for long-term care, as well as consumers' out-of-pocket costs for long-term care, can be applied toward meeting the 7.5 percent floor for medical-expense deductions. (Medical expenses are deductible only to the extent that they exceed 7.5 percent of your income). The IRS sets limits, based upon one's age, for the total amount of premiums paid for long-term care insurance that can be applied to the 7.5 percent floor, so check with a tax adviser before taking this deduction.

REMEMBER THIS

- Medicare Parts A and B provide nearly universal basic insurance coverage to older adults, but they have significant limitations in coverage, particularly with respect to prescription drugs and long-term care.

- Most, but not all, older people need to purchase a Medigap policy to cover some of the costs not covered by Medicare.

- Medicaid provides medical assistance for low-income older or disabled persons whose income and assets fall below certain levels.

▶ **HOW MUCH HEALTH INSURANCE DO I NEED?**

Some people covered by Medicare think they need several additional policies to cover Medicare gaps, specific diseases, and long-term care. But that is probably not a good strategy, because the policies would probably duplicate too many benefits to justify the cost. That is why insurance companies are no longer permitted to sell duplicate Medicare supplement policies—you can only purchase one.

The best recommendation for someone on Medicare who is not also on Medicaid is to purchase one good Medigap policy, and possibly one long-term care insurance policy if you can comfortably afford it. Lower-income people are likely to qualify for Medicaid if they need long-term care, so purchasing private long-term care insurance may be a waste of money.

▶ **CHECKLIST: WHAT TO LOOK FOR IN A LONG-TERM CARE POLICY**

- Make sure your policy will pay benefits for all levels of care in a nursing home, including custodial care.

- Buy a federally qualified policy so that you can be certain of its tax advantages.

- A good policy will pay benefits for assisted-living and home care, including in-home personal care. Personal care refers generally to help with activities of daily living, such as dressing, bathing, using a toilet, eating, and walking.

- Consider whether the amount of daily benefits will be adequate now and in the future. Many policies give you a range of daily benefit amounts from which to choose. The right amount depends in part on the amount of assets you have. Make sure the policy has an "inflation adjuster," under which benefits increase by a certain percentage each year to keep pace with inflation.

- Do not assume that more years of coverage are always better. Some policies offer benefit options of six, seven, or more years. It is possible to buy too much coverage.

- Avoid policies that exclude coverage of preexisting conditions for a lengthy period. Six months is considered a reasonable exclusion period.

- Policies should allow payment of nursing-home or home health benefits without requiring a prior period of hospitalization as a condition of coverage.

- Most policies impose waiting periods that restrict benefits until after you have received nursing-home care or home care for a specified period of time—twenty to ninety days is common. First-day coverage will increase your premium.

- Be sure your policy covers Alzheimer's disease and other forms of dementia.

- Be sure that the premium remains constant over the life of the policy, and that the policy is guaranteed renewable for life.

- Buy a policy only from a company that is licensed in your state and has agents physically present in your state. Out-of-state mail-order policies often leave you powerless to remedy any problems.

- Medicare does not provide coverage for most long-term care. Possible alternative sources of coverage include Medicaid, but only when most other resources have been spent, and private long-term care insurance.

HOUSING AND LONG-TERM CARE OPTIONS

The range of housing options available for older people is enormous—from staying in your own home, to home sharing, to moving to a senior housing facility or development. This section explores an important financial option, home equity conversion, that may help you stay in your home, and also describes the wide variety of housing choices that provide shelter plus some combination of recreational and social opportunities or supportive services and health care. In all these areas, older people need to be aware of the personal and financial risks and benefits involved—and, above all, of their legal rights.

Home Equity Conversion

Q. I own my home and do not want to move, but I'm having trouble making ends meet. What can I do?

A. **Home equity conversion** plans can add to your monthly income without you having to leave your home. These plans fall into two broad categories: loans and sales. Sales that permit the individual to lease back the residence or retain a life estate are less common, and need to be carefully worked out with the benefit of legal advice. Loan plans permit you to borrow against the equity in your home. They include reverse mortgages and special-purpose loans on which repayment is deferred until you sell your house, move out, or die. They should not be confused with home equity loans and home equity lines of credit, which require you to make monthly payments immediately or risk losing your house.

Q. How does a reverse mortgage work?

A. A **reverse mortgage** lets you borrow against the equity in your home, receiving a lump sum or monthly installments, or drawing on a line of credit. The amount you will

receive is based on your age, the value of your home and your equity in the home, the interest rate, the term of the loan, and other factors. Except for some special-purpose state- or local-government-sponsored plans, like those designed to pay for home repairs, there are no restrictions on how you use the money.

The loan usually does not have to be repaid until you die, or sell or move from your home. When the loan does come due, the amount to be repaid cannot exceed the appraised value of the property.

Q. Who is eligible for a reverse mortgage?

A. A borrower must be at least sixty-two years of age, and must own and occupy the home as a principal place of residence. The property should be free of liens or mortgages, except for those that can be paid off at closing. Unlike traditional loans or home equity lines of credit, the borrower's income is not considered. Mobile homes and cooperatives are not eligible for reverse mortgages.

Q. How will a reverse mortgage affect my other benefits?

A. The income from a reverse mortgage will not affect eligibility for Social Security, Medicare, or other retirement benefits or pensions that are not based on need. However, without careful planning, the income from a reverse mortgage could affect eligibility for Supplemental Security Income, Medicaid, food stamps, and some state benefit programs.

In general, reverse mortgage payments are considered to be a loan and will not affect benefits if the money is spent during the month in which it is received. But if the money is not spent during that month, it will be counted as a resource and may lead to loss of benefit eligibility. Be aware that payments received under an annuity mortgage plan will be considered income, even if they are spent in the month in which they are received.

Q. Is a regular home equity loan the same as a reverse mortgage?

A. No. A traditional home equity loan is very different from a reverse mortgage, and can be a risk for an older person on a fixed income. With a reverse mortgage, you borrow against the equity you have built up in your home. But in a home equity loan, you must make regular monthly payments of principal and interest, or you may lose your home.

Q. What other kinds of home equity conversion are available?

A. In addition to loan plans, you can generate income from the equity that you have acquired in your home through sale plans. Sale plans include sale-leasebacks, life estates, and charitable annuities.

Q. Can I sell my house to a new owner who will let me live in it?

A. Yes. In a **life estate,** or **sale of a remainder interest,** you sell your home to a buyer, but retain the right to live there during your lifetime. The buyer pays you a lump sum, or monthly payments, or both. You are usually responsible for taxes and repairs, but you pay no rent. At your death, full ownership passes automatically to the buyer. This arrangement is most common within families, as part of an estate plan, and should be pursued only with legal advice.

Q. Is home equity conversion the only way to increase my monthly income?

A. Not necessarily. If you find that your monthly income does not meet your expenses,

> ▶ **SALE-LEASEBACKS**

In a sale-leaseback, you sell the equity in your home, but retain the right to live there, often paying a monthly rent. The buyer usually makes a substantial down payment to you. You act as a lender by granting the buyer a mortgage. You receive the buyer's mortgage payments, and the buyer receives your rent payments, which are set lower than the mortgage payments, so you gain a positive net monthly income. You remain in the home, and can use the down payment and the mortgage payments as income. The buyer can deduct the mortgage interest payment from his or her income, and the buyer also will benefit if the value of the property increases.

However, be aware that the IRS requires both the sale price and the rental payments to be fair. Today, there are few tax advantages to sale-leasebacks, so finding an investor may be difficult.

you may be eligible for government benefits, such as Supplemental Security Income, food stamps, or Medicaid. Some states also have property tax credit or deferral programs for which you may be eligible. To find out more about these programs, call your local AAA. You should consider all of the available options before you make a decision.

Q. I am not sure that I can continue to live in my own home, but I would like to stay in my community. What other choices do I have?

A. You have several choices, depending on your current and future health needs, your financial circumstances, and your personal preferences, although not all may be available in your community. There are home-sharing programs, in which homeowners are matched with individuals seeking housing in exchange for rent or services; accessory units that provide private living in (or next to) single-family homes; or assisted living (described below), which combines a homelike setting with services designed to meet individual needs. For more information on programs available in your area, contact your local agency on aging.

Retirement Communities

Q. I have heard a lot about retirement communities that offer all kinds of services and amenities. What types of retirement communities are available?

A. Between the extremes of independent living and nursing-home care, a variety of alternatives offer endless combinations of shelter plus services or amenities. Physically, facilities may range from single-family-type housing, to high-rise or garden apartment buildings, to campus-like developments.

Facility definitions differ among states and sometimes even within states. For simplicity's sake, it is useful to distinguish three levels based on the services provided. At one end of the continuum are **independent-living communities.** These offer little or no health and supportive services, although they may have recreational and social programs. At the opposite end are **continuing-care retirement communities** (**CCRCs**). These provide a wide range of housing options, care, and services, including nursing-home services. In

between are facilities that offer a wide variety of housing and health or supportive services, but not nursing-home care. Today, these are often referred to as **assisted-living communities,** but they include facilities variously called "housing with supportive services," "congregate-care homes," "board-and-care homes," and "personal-care homes."

Q. What purchase or payment arrangements do retirement communities offer?

A. Conventional independent-living communities without health services typically involve home ownership or rental arrangements that are similar to standard real estate purchases or rentals. These transactions are governed by local real estate and landlord-tenant law. Residents pay the costs of their mortgage or lease, as well as condominium or association fees. In facilities that provide additional services, accommodations, or health care, there are three basic types of contracts, typically categorized

---

▶ **WHO SPONSORS AND WHO REGULATES RETIREMENT COMMUNITIES?**

Most retirement communities are developed privately, although many are sponsored by nonprofit groups and agencies, including churches and charitable organizations. All states regulate one or more types of assisted-living community, and most states regulate continuing-care communities, but the extent of regulations varies considerably among states.

▶ CHECKLIST: WHAT TO CONSIDER BEFORE SELECTING A CONTINUING-CARE RETIREMENT COMMUNITY

Solvency and Expertise of the Provider

- What is the provider's background and experience? The provider is the legally and financially responsible person or entity. Some facilities may advertise that they are "sponsored" by nonprofit groups or churches that in reality may have no legal control or financial responsibility. Be wary if such illusory sponsorship is trumpeted in sales literature.

- Is the provider financially sound? Ask a professional to review the facility's financial, actuarial, and operating statements. Determine whether the facility has sufficient financial reserves.

- Are all levels of care licensed or certified under applicable state statutes regulating continuing-care, assisted-living, and nursing-home care?

- How does the facility ensure the quality of care and services provided? Is the facility accredited by any recognized private accrediting organization?

Fees

- What is the entrance fee, and when can you get all or part of it back? The facility should provide a formula for a pro rata refund of the entrance fee based on the resident's length of stay, regardless of whether the facility or the resident initiates the termination.

- What is the monthly fee? When and how much can it be increased? What happens if fee increases exceed your ability to pay? Some facilities have a program that grants financial assistance to residents whose income becomes inadequate to pay increasing monthly fees and personal expenses.

- Will fees change when the resident's living arrangements or level-of-care needs change (for example, in the event of transfers from independent living to assisted living or nursing care)?

- If I own my unit, are there limits on who I can sell my property to? What happens to my residence and financial obligations if I move from my residence?

Services and Health Care

- Exactly what services are included in the regular fees? Especially inquire about coverage, limitations, and costs of the following:

  ### Housing/Social/Recreational

  - meal services
  - special diets/tray service

- utilities
- cable television
- furnishings
- unit maintenance
- linens/personal laundry
- housekeeping
- recreational/cultural activities
- transportation

Health and Personal Care

- physician services
- nursing services outside a nursing unit (for example, assistance with medications)
- private-duty nursing
- dental and eye care
- personal-care services (that is, assistance with eating, dressing, bathing, and using bathroom facilities)
- homemaker/companion services
- drugs
- medication
- medical equipment/supplies
- facility services

- If the facility provides a nursing unit, what happens if a bed is not available when you need it?

- To what extent does the facility have the right to cut back, change, or eliminate services, or change the fees?

- Does the facility limit its responsibility for certain health conditions or preexisting conditions? When are you considered too sick or impaired to be cared for by the facility?

- Can you receive Medicare and Medicaid coverage while in the facility?

- Does the facility require residents to buy private insurance or participate in a special group insurance program?

- What are the criteria and procedures for determining when a resident needs to be transferred from independent living to assisted living, or to a nursing-care unit, or to an entirely different facility? Who is involved in these decisions?

Residents' Rights

• What does my living unit consist of, and to what extent can I change or redecorate it?

• What happens if I marry, divorce, become widowed, or wish to have a friend or family member move in?

• What rights do residents have to participate in facility management and decision making? How are complaints handled?

• On what grounds can residents' contracts or leases be terminated against their wishes?

• What other rules and policies cover the day-to-day operation of the facility?

• Does the contract release the facility from any liability for injury to a resident or guest resulting from negligence by the facility or third parties? (Such waivers should be avoided.)

according to payment arrangement (though keep in mind that state regulations may categorize facilities differently):

1. **Entrance-fee-plus-monthly-fee contracts.** Entrance fees, ranging from $20,000 to over $400,000, are charged by most continuing-care retirement facilities. An entrance fee may represent a partial prepayment for future services. It normally does not buy an interest in the real estate. Increasingly, CCRCs are providing greater refundability of entrance fees, even 100 percent, although this usually results in higher monthly fees. Residency rights and obligations are governed by a long-term lease or occupancy agreement. Monthly fees are subject to periodic inflation adjustments and, possibly, adjustments when the resident's level-of-care needs change.

2. **Pay-as-you-go contracts.** With no entrance fee, these contracts are essentially straight rental arrangements with a defined set of services included in the fee (or available when needed for an additional charge). Most assisted-living facilities and an increasing number of continuing-care facilities offer this arrangement. This type of contract involves no initial investment, but it is subject to greater changes in monthly fees, since the resident assumes most or all of the financial risk for services.

3. **Condominiums or cooperatives with continuing-care contracts.** Some retirement communities offer an ownership interest to residents under a condominium or cooperative arrangement with a service package included. These ownership/contractual arrangements are unavoidably complex and bring with them special ad-

vantages and risks that need to be weighed carefully.

Nursing-Home Care

Q. What is a nursing home?

A. A **nursing home** is a facility that provides skilled nursing care and related services for residents who require medical or nursing care; rehabilitation services for injured, disabled, or sick persons; and health-related care and services, above the level of room and board, that can be made available only through institutional facilities.

Often, nursing facilities make distinctions between levels of care—skilled and custodial—for purposes of Medicare, Medicaid, or private insurance coverage. The distinction between "skilled" and "custodial" care is discussed on page 602.

Q. How does living in a nursing home affect my personal rights and privileges?

A. You do not check your rights and privileges at the door when you enter a nursing home. Although institutional care, by its very nature, substantially limits one's lifestyle and scope of privacy, one should nevertheless expect high-quality, compassionate, and dignified care from nursing facilities.

Residents in nearly all nursing facilities are protected by the federal Nursing Home Reform Amendments of 1987, by federal regulations, and by corresponding state laws. For residents who lack decision-making capacity, the resident's agent under a health-care power of attorney (or another legal surrogate recognized by state law, typically a family member) may exercise the resident's rights. Federal law requires that nursing homes meet strong basic standards for the quality of life of each resident and for the provision of services and activities. Specific rights guaranteed by federal and state law include the following:

- **Information rights.** Nursing homes must provide
  - written information about residents' rights;
  - written information about the services available under the basic rate, and any extra charges for extra services;
  - advance notice of changes in roommate or room assignment;
  - upon request, the latest facility inspection results and any correction plan submitted to state officials;
  - an explanation of the resident's right to draft a health-care advance directive—that is, a power of attorney for health care, or a living will—and facility policies on complying with advance directives (see the discussion of advance directives under "Health-Care Decision-Making Issues" on page 638); and
  - information about eligibility for Medicare and Medicaid and the services these programs cover.
- **Self-determination rights.** Each resident has the right to
  - participate in an individualized assessment and care-planning process that accommodates the resident's personal needs and preferences;
  - choose a personal physician;
  - voice complaints without fear of reprisal and receive a prompt response; and
  - organize and participate in resident groups (such as a resident council) and family groups.
- **Personal and privacy rights.** Residents have the right to

- participate in social, religious, and community activities as they choose;
- privacy in medical treatment, accommodations, personal visits, written and telephone communications, and meetings of resident and family groups;
- confidentiality of personal and clinical records;
- access to the long-term care ombudsman, their physician, and family members, and reasonable access to other visitors, all subject to the resident's consent;
- freedom from physical or mental abuse, corporal punishment, and involuntary seclusion;
- freedom from any physical restraint or medication used for purposes of discipline or convenience, and not required to treat the resident's medical symptoms; and
- protection of resident's funds held by the facility, including the right to a quarterly accounting.
- **Transfer and discharge rights.** Residents may be transferred or discharged only if
  - the health, safety, or welfare of the resident or other residents requires it;
  - the resident fails to make necessary payments;
  - the resident's health improves so that he or she no longer needs nursing-home care; or
  - the facility closes.

Normally, residents must receive at least thirty days' advance notice, with information about appealing the transfer and how to contact the state long-term care ombudsman program. The facility must prepare a discharge plan and orient residents to ensure safe and orderly transfer from the facility.

- **Protection against Medicaid discrimination.** Nursing homes must
  - have identical policies and practices regarding services, regardless of the payment source (however, be aware that not all facilities participate in Medicaid);
  - provide information on how to apply for Medicaid;
  - explain the Medicaid "bed-hold" policy—that is, how many days Medicaid will hold the resident's bed, or ensure priority readmission, after temporary absences;
  - not request, require, or encourage residents to waive their rights to Medicaid;
  - not require a family member to guarantee payment as a condition of a resident's admission or continued stay; and
  - not "charge, solicit, accept, or receive gifts, money, donations, or other considerations" as a precondition for admission or continued stay for persons eligible for Medicaid.

Q. What can I do to ensure that I will receive quality care and that my needs will be met?

A. The key to ensuring that you receive individualized care that adequately addresses your medical and personal needs is active participation in the care-planning process. Federal law requires that a resident assessment and a written plan of care be prepared with the resident or the resident's family or legal representative. This process should occur just after admission and then yearly, or after any significant change in physical or mental condition.

Q. What can I do if I think a nursing home is not providing adequate care or respecting my rights?

A. Different problems require different responses. The following steps should help resolve most problems. The order may vary depending on the problem.

1. Keep a log of the relevant details, including dates and personnel involved.
2. Try to resolve the problem informally by talking to supervising staff.
3. Many facilities have active resident councils or family councils. Bring the problem before these groups.
4. Contact your long-term care ombudsman.
5. Contact the state regulatory agencies that license, certify, and survey nursing homes. Usually, the state department of health has this responsibility.
6. Contact a community legal-assistance

▶ **THE BASIC QUALITY-OF-LIFE STANDARD FOR NURSING HOMES**

Federal law requires each nursing facility to "care for its residents in such a manner and in such an environment as will promote maintenance or an enhancement of the quality of life of each resident." Federal law further requires each nursing facility to "provide services and activities to attain or maintain the highest practicable physical, mental, and psychosocial well-being of each resident in accordance with a written plan of care that . . . is initially prepared, with participation to the extent practicable of the resident or the resident's family or legal representative."

---

program, other advocacy organization, or private lawyer experienced in long-term care issues.

Q. Is there someone in the nursing home to advocate on my behalf?

A. Yes. The federal Older Americans Act requires every state to operate a long-term care ombudsman program. The **ombudsman** is responsible for advocating on behalf of nursing-home residents and residents of other long-term care facilities, such as assisted-living or board-and-care facilities. The ombudsman provides education on long-term care options and residents' rights, and investigates and resolves complaints made by or on behalf of residents.

Most states operate local or regional programs with paid or volunteer ombudsmen. Residents and family members often find ombudsman staff to be helpful partners in resolving problems. Federal law requires nursing homes to allow the ombudsman access to residents and their records. In addition, the ombudsman usually has special authority under state law to inspect records and take other steps necessary to respond to complaints.

REMEMBER THIS

- Home equity conversion plans, such as reverse mortgages, can help you add to your monthly income without having to leave your home. But you should carefully examine the costs, risks, and benefits of these plans before choosing one.

- Continuing-care retirement communities are a major investment, so you should seek professional advice from a lawyer or a financial adviser before you sign a contract.

▶ THE OLDER AMERICANS ACT AND SERVICES

The Older Americans Act is the main federal law that provides funding for services to the elderly. The act provides funding for a wide variety of services, such as education, social services, recreation, personal assistance, and counseling. It also makes available transportation, legal and financial assistance, career and retirement counseling, advocacy, long-term care ombudsman services, services for the disabled, crime prevention, elder abuse prevention, and volunteer services. In addition, your local area agency on aging (AAA) can provide information and guide you to services in your community. These might include home helpers, money management agencies, or special discounts available to seniors.

To find out about programs in your areas, start at your local or state agency on aging, or call Eldercare Locator at 800-677-1116. This toll-free service helps to identify community resources nationwide.

- Federal law guarantees the rights of nursing-home residents, including information rights, privacy rights, self-determination rights, and the right to a personalized care plan.
- Each state has a long-term care ombudsman who is responsible for investigating problems at nursing homes.

RIGHTS OF PEOPLE WITH DISABILITIES

Many older people are unable to manage their daily activities as well as they once did. Others have disabilities that have worsened with age. Two major federal laws, the Americans with Disabilities Act and the Fair Housing Act, protect people with physical or mental disabilities from discrimination in virtually every aspect of their lives. In addition, these laws require employers and service providers to modify their rules and policies, as well as the physical environments under their control, to meet the needs of persons with disabilities. A third law, Section 504 of the Rehabilitation Act of 1973, provides the same protections against discrimination by organizations that receive federal contracts.

Q. Who do these laws protect?

A. These laws protect people with mental or physical impairments that limit their ability to perform one or more major life activities. Major life activities include walking, seeing, hearing, taking care of personal or health needs, or performing everyday chores. These laws also protect people who are perceived to have a disability, or whose family members or friends are disabled.

They do not protect people who threaten the safety or health of others, or whose behavior would result in substantial damage to the property of others. Nor do they protect current users of illegal drugs.

Q. What situations does the Americans with Disabilities Act cover?

A. The Americans with Disabilities Act (ADA) protects people with disabilities against discrimination in employment, public transit, and public accommodation—for example, in hotels, restaurants, stores, banks, schools, and senior centers. It generally does not cover housing (though the Fair Housing Act does; see below for more information), although it does cover some non-housing activities that are based in housing facilities, such as meals or activity programs open to the public.

Q. What laws cover housing?

A. The Fair Housing Act (FHA) applies to almost all housing transactions. Most important for the purposes of this chapter, the law prohibits landlords from refusing to rent to older people, or asking them to move, simply because they need certain assistance. The law does not apply to rental buildings that contain fewer than four units, where the owner also lives in the building. Examples of prohibited discrimination include

- refusing to rent to a family because a family member has a mental illness;
- requiring applicants for senior housing to provide a doctor's letter stating that they are in good health and can live on their own;
- denying a resident who uses a wheelchair or a walker access to a communal dining room; and
- evicting a tenant because he or she is receiving homemaking help or other services.

Section 504 of the Rehabilitation Act offers similar protections to residents of federally subsidized housing.

Q. If I need changes made to my home so that I can get in and out in my wheelchair, does the law allow me to make them?

A. Usually, yes. In most circumstances, the law allows for reasonable accommodations

and modifications so that disabled people can have equal access to programs and buildings.

Q. What does "reasonable accommodation" mean?

A. Reasonable accommodations are changes in rules or procedures that are reasonable under the circumstances, and that provide a disabled person with equal opportunity to participate in a specific activity, program, job, or housing situation. They are very individualized and often can be worked out informally. Examples include

- giving a job or housing applicant more time to fill out an application;
- providing large-print notices, leases, or other written materials;
- waiving a no-pets rule for a tenant with a mental disability who is emotionally dependent on his or her pet, or waiving a no-guest rule for a tenant who needs a live-in aide; and
- assisting a customer who needs help with packages, opening and closing doors, or dialing a telephone.

Q. What are reasonable modifications?

A. Reasonable modifications are changes to the physical structure of a building or property, which are reasonable under the circumstances, and which give a disabled person equal access to the premises. Examples include

- widening doorways and installing ramps;
- replacing doorknobs with lever handles; and
- installing grab bars in bathrooms.

Q. Who pays for these alterations?

A. In an apartment or other privately owned housing, the tenant is responsible for the cost of alterations. Modifications of public facilities, hotels, public meeting rooms, rental offices, and other sites covered by the ADA are paid for by the owner of the facility. In buildings that are federally subsidized, the owner is responsible for modifications to individual apartments as well as public areas.

Q. Must housing meet certain accessibility standards?

A. For buildings first occupied after March 1991 that have four or more units, federal law requires that at least the ground floor meet the following requirements:

- public and common areas must be accessible to persons with disabilities;
- doors and hallways must be wide enough for wheelchairs; and
- units must have
  - an accessible route into and through the unit;
  - accessible light switches, electrical outlets, thermostats, and other environmental controls;
  - reinforced bathroom walls to allow later installation of grab bars; and
  - kitchens and bathrooms that can be used by people in wheelchairs.

If the building with four or more units has an elevator, then these standards apply to all units. State or local laws may require more stringent standards.

Q. How do I go about getting changes made in my apartment?

A. Although many housing providers are familiar with the FHA and work to make sure that their buildings are accessible, they may not be aware of accommodations that would make life easier for individual tenants. All you need to do is request changes in writing; if they are related to your disability, and if they are reasonable, then they should be honored. Remember that you are responsible for the cost of physical alterations inside your own apartment, unless the alternation is mandatory under the above standards. Also, the landlord may require you to return the premises to their original condition when you move.

Q. What do I do if I believe I am being discriminated against?

A. The ADA, the FHA, and Section 504 of the Rehabilitation Act can be enforced through court action or by filing a complaint with an administrative agency. The U.S. Department of Justice oversees enforcement of the ADA, and the U.S. Department of Housing and Urban Development oversees enforcement of the Fair Housing Act. See the "World at Your Fingertips" section for applicable contact information.

REMEMBER THIS

- The American with Disabilities Act protects people with disabilities against discrimination in employment, public transit, and public accommodations.

- The Fair Housing Act prohibits landlords from refusing to rent to older people, or from asking them to move, simply because they need assistance with certain activities or modifications of their residence.

- Federal law requires landlords to allow tenants to make reasonable modifications to an apartment to improve accessibility, but the tenant may have to pay for those changes unless the building is federally subsidized or otherwise subject to minimum accessibility standards.

A RIGHT TO CONTROL YOUR OWN AFFAIRS

As we grow older, we all face the possibility that one day we may become mentally incapacitated. The time may come when we are no longer able to make our own health-care decisions, manage our own financial affairs, or act on our own behalf.

If that happens, you hope that your property will be protected and people will honor your wishes. This section addresses the critical legal issues regarding your right to control your own affairs. How and where do you want to live? What decisions can you make? What decisions should you leave to someone else? Whom do you want to make decisions for you? Several alternative methods of advance planning can ensure that people respect your wishes and values whenever possible. Through planning, the decisions made on your behalf can be those you would have made yourself.

Durable Power of Attorney

Q. What may I do to make sure that people consider my wishes if I become incapacitated?

A. You should make plans now, while you have capacity. Several planning tools can help guarantee you a voice in your future. The first priority is to make sure that, in the event of incapacity, someone of your choice is authorized to act on your behalf, and/or to tell other people how to care for you and your property.

There are different types of planning tools that can help you accomplish this goal. Some tools, including the power of attorney, joint property arrangements, and living trusts, can help you to manage your property and financial affairs. Others, including advance-directives for health care, can help you to address your health-care concerns, including decisions to be made near the end of life.

The details of creating these documents vary by state; however, some general principles apply.

Q. What is a power of attorney?

A. A **power of attorney** is a document in which you (the **principal**) grant certain authority to another person (the **agent** or **attorney in fact**) to act on your behalf. A power of attorney may be very specific—for example, authorizing a person to sell a car for you, and nothing more. Or it can be very broad, allowing the agent to do almost anything on your behalf. A **general power of attorney** grants a person broad authority to handle all types of financial matters. Note that the Social Security Administration will not permit your agent to cash or deposit your Social Security check. To deal with this problem, you may want to designate a representative payee (discussed on pages 633–634).

Q. Will a power of attorney be valid if I become mentally incapacitated or incompetent?

A. In most states, a power of attorney is not valid if you become incapacitated, unless it's a durable power of attorney. A **durable power of attorney** clearly states that you intend the power to continue if you become disabled or incapacitated. It generally remains in effect until you deliberately revoke it or you die. In some states, your durable power of attorney is terminated if a guardian is appointed for you (although appointment of a guardian is usually unnecessary, because the durable power of attorney takes care of the management of your affairs).

Q. Do I need a lawyer to write a durable power of attorney?

A. While not required, it is advisable to contact a lawyer to draft your durable power of attorney. A lawyer should make sure that your document meets your state's requirements, and that the powers you wish to give your agent are actually spelled out in language that will be effective and will protect your interests.

Some powers need to be very clearly spelled out—for example, the power to make gifts or loans or file tax returns. Some states require a specific format or specific wording in the document. Certain states offer do-it-yourself, short-form durable powers of attorney. These documents allow you to simply mark off the powers to be granted to the agent, with state law providing an in-depth definition of what each power means. However, even if you're using these simplified forms, legal consultation is advisable.

Q. Whom should I name as my agent under a durable power of attorney? Does the person have to be a lawyer?

A. Your agent does not have to be a lawyer. In most states, it can be any adult or an institution. However, it should be someone who knows you well and whom you trust completely to manage your affairs. After all, decisions made by your agent can have tremendous consequences. Your agent has to carry out your wishes and should always act as you would choose or with your best interests in mind. If there is no one whom you trust with this power, other planning tools may suit you better.

Q. Can I have more than one agent?

A. Yes. You may name multiple agents who exercise all or some of the powers jointly (i.e., all the agents must agree in order to exercise the power) or separately (i.e., any one of the agents may act alone). Note that disputes among agents can become a significant obstacle. With multiple agents, some process for handling disagreements among agents should be considered. In all cases, it is a good idea to name an alternate to serve as your agent in case your first choice becomes unavailable.

Q. What if I do not want a power of attorney to take effect now, but only if I become disabled or incapacitated?

A. In general, a durable power of attorney becomes effective when you sign it. But even while effective, the agent cannot override your wishes or directions, and you may revoke the durable power of attorney at any time while you still have capacity. It is also possible to write your durable power of attorney so that it becomes effective only if you become incapacitated. This is called a **springing power of attorney.** Most states allow you to write this type of durable power of attorney. Consult a knowledgeable lawyer to find out what is possible in your state.

Q. How may I ensure that my agent under my power of attorney will manage my affairs properly after I become incapacitated?

A. Your power of attorney should contain specific guidance for what is expected, including your agent's particular duties, responsibilities, and limitations. You can also build in some oversight by requiring annual accountings to other family members, or requiring co-signatures for large transactions.

Q. My father has Alzheimer's disease. I would like him to appoint me to act

for him under a durable power of attorney, since he can no longer manage on his own. May he do this now, or is it too late?

A. It is up to your father to decide whether he wants to grant you power of attorney. And it may or may not be too late. Durable powers of attorney and other planning tools must be made while a person still has mental capacity. However, just because doctors diagnose someone as having a specific disease does not mean that the person is necessarily incapacitated. Also, incapacity does not affect all functions in the same way. Thus, people in the early stages of a disease such as Alzheimer's usually have the capacity to make some decisions. They may have more capacity at certain times of the day than at others, or their capacity may be affected by medication.

Capacity must be assessed on a case-by-case basis. If your father is willing to see a lawyer about writing a durable power of attor-ney, the lawyer can help assess whether your father understands the purpose and conse-quences of the durable power. Sometimes a medical assessment will be recommended be-fore signing legal documents.

Q. Who decides whether I'm incapaci-tated?

A. You can specify how you wish to have your incapacity and mental status determined if the need should arise. For example, in your durable power of attorney, you can name a doctor or particular mental health profes-sional who will be responsible for making this determination, or you could say that if two doctors certify in writing that you lack capac-ity, then your power of attorney becomes ef-fective. Any doctor or clinical psychologist who makes evaluations of capacity should have experience in this area. If you provide no instructions, then a court may ultimately have to decide the issue, guided by generally ac-cepted standards.

▶ A LEGAL TEST OF CAPACITY

There is no universal legal test of mental capacity or incapacity. Laws vary from state to state, but some general principles apply everywhere.

Incapacity is always evaluated in connection with specific tasks. The relevant ques-tion is always, "Incapacity to do what?" Different legal standards of capacity may apply to different tasks, such as capacity to make a will, to drive, to enter into contracts, to manage money, or to make medical decisions. In a typical guardianship proceeding, most (but not all) states use a two-part test to determine **incapacity** (sometimes called **incompetency**). First, some type of disability must be verified—for example, mental illness, mental retardation, and/or Alzheimer's disease. Second, there must be a finding that the disability prevents the person from performing activities essential to taking care of his or her personal needs or property. Before appointing a guardian, most courts also will insist that all feasible alternatives to guardianship have been explored.

Living Trusts

Q. What is a "living trust"?

A. A **living trust** (also called an **inter vivos trust**) is an arrangement under which you transfer ownership of all or part of your property to the trust during your lifetime. As the person establishing the trust, you are called the **grantor** or **settlor.** You name a **trustee,** who manages the property according to the terms of your written trust document. The trustee may be an individual or an institution or yourself. A trust operates for the benefit of one or more persons (including yourself) called the **beneficiaries.**

Frequently, a will is used to set up a trust (called a **testamentary trust**) that becomes effective after the death of the person establishing the trust. A **living trust** is effective during the lifetime of the settlor, although it may be written to continue after his or her death. In a living trust, the settlor and/or members of his or her family are usually the beneficiaries of the trust. A living trust is usually revocable, but also can be drafted to be irrevocable.

Q. What is a living trust useful for?

A. Living trusts are one way to ensure that someone (a trustee) has the legal authority to manage your assets properly if you become incapacitated or simply do not wish to manage your own estate anymore. Living trusts also may enable your loved ones to avoid probate proceedings after your death. They are especially useful in cases involving a substantial amount of property, where professional management is desired. Like the durable power of attorney, a living trust may make it unnecessary to appoint a guardian or conservator to manage your financial affairs. However, a trust is generally more expensive to create and to manage than a durable power of attorney.

Q. How may I use a living trust to plan for possible incapacity?

A. You may design a living trust so that you and only you manage the assets in the trust, unless you become incapacitated. At that point, the **successor trustee** (whom you have named in the trust) takes control. Alternatively, the trust can be written so that it becomes operational only when and if you become incapacitated. Either way, you control your affairs until incapacity. As with a durable power of attorney, the means of determining incapacity should be spelled out in the document.

To make the trust effective, you must transfer assets into it. The trust will only control the assets and property that have actually been transferred into the trust.

▶ REVOKING A POWER OF ATTORNEY

To revoke a power of attorney, simply notify the person you have named to act as your agent. For your protection, it is best to do this in writing. You also should destroy all copies of the power of attorney and notify in writing any third parties with whom your agent might have done business. Where substantial assets are at stake, you may also want to file a document called a **revocation of power of attorney** in the public records where you live or own real estate, and maybe even in the local newspaper if business interests are at stake.

Q. I thought a trust simply paid an allowance to someone. Can a trust help me manage my own finances?

A. Some trust arrangements do simply pay a periodic sum to the beneficiary. However, you may design a living trust in which the trustee handles many of the daily tasks of managing the estate, including paying bills and taxes. You may state in the trust agreement exactly what you want the trustee to do, how you want your assets managed, and how much discretion you want to give your trustee, including the discretion to use up the assets for your benefit if needed.

Q. My father has a lot of money in his estate, but he is becoming increasingly forgetful every week. May he still write a living trust?

A. Like the durable power of attorney, people must have capacity to prepare a living trust. First of all, your father must want to make a trust. If he does, his lawyer may determine his ability to do so. Sometimes, this is done by having him examined by his physician or other mental health professional. His lawyer will know what standard of capacity must be met. If your father does not have that capacity, he cannot make and sign a living trust.

Q. How may I ensure that my trustee will manage my affairs properly after I become incapacitated?

A. Your trust instrument should contain specific instructions. You should include a precise statement of what the trustee should do on your behalf, and specify the trustee's particular duties, responsibilities, and limitations.

Q. My wife and I hold most of our assets in common. May I still draft a living trust to protect my share of the estate?

A. Yes, but it can be complicated by the rights and interests of your wife in her portion of the estate. Sound legal advice and careful drafting is needed. You and your wife may need separate counseling and planning advice, as your interests may conflict. In states that allow property to be held as community property or as marital property, there may be additional complications to the drafting process. (See the "Home Ownership" and "Family Law" chapters for more information on different types of property ownership.)

If their interests are united, some couples find it helpful to draft joint trusts. It is important to note that drafting these trusts properly can be a complicated process; if you are considering such a trust, you should likely consult an experienced attorney.

Q. It sounds as though a living trust is a very complex. Who can help me decide if one is right for me?

A. A living trust is a complicated document; it is best to consult with a lawyer or a trust officer familiar with living trusts to determine if one is right for you. Do not rely solely on mail-order or do-it-yourself trust kits, as they may contain information that is misleading or

---

▶ **DETAILS**

For more information on the tax implications of living trusts, and on changing or revoking a living trust, see Chapter 17, "Estate Planning."

inappropriate for your circumstances or your state's law. For more information on living trusts, see Chapter 17, "Estate Planning."

Joint Ownership

Q. I have most of my property and bank accounts held jointly with my spouse and my adult child. Isn't this good enough to ensure management of my property if I become incapacitated?

A. No. Joint ownership, or joint tenancy with right of survivorship, is a common and simple form of property ownership for homes, cars, securities, and bank accounts. The **right of survivorship** means that when one joint owner dies, the surviving owner or owners own 100 percent of the property. It is a convenient way to allow another person to access your assets or deposit or write checks on your behalf.

However, joint ownership is not a substitute for other planning tools, because it has serious disadvantages. For example, an untrustworthy joint owner may withdraw all the money in a bank account and leave you with nothing. And while it is possible to challenge a co-owner's improper use of your money, it may be difficult. In some states, creditors of a co-owner may be able to reach your account, even though the co-owner is only listed on your account to help you manage your money. In addition, being listed as a co-owner of a bank account could affect a co-owner's eligibility for public-benefit programs such as Medicaid. Finally, transfers of a home, a car, or securities normally require the signature of all owners. The loss of capacity of one owner may prevent a needed sale or transfer of the property.

Q. Is there a way that I can give someone access to my bank account without giving that person ownership of my money?

A. Some states have laws allowing persons to create an **agency bank account** (or **convenience account**), although this is really nothing more than a power of attorney over a particular bank account. You name an agent on your bank account, who then has the authority to make deposits or withdrawals and manage the account. The authority remains effective if you become incapacitated or disabled, unless you indicate otherwise. The agent has no right of ownership in the money in the account before or after your death, unless you indicate that the agent is to receive the money when you die. This may be a useful tool if you do not want to give someone authority over your other financial affairs through a durable power of attorney. It also may be useful as a supplement to your durable power of attorney, because some banks prefer that you use their forms and procedures rather than a general durable power of attorney.

Representative Payees

Q. I have no income other than my Social Security check. Would a living trust or a power of attorney help me manage my money?

A. A living trust is far too costly and complicated for this kind of situation. A durable power of attorney could be helpful. However, if the primary need is to take care of government benefits, a representative payee may be the simplest way to help you take care of your daily expenses and manage your income.

Q. What is a representative payee?

A. A **representative payee** is a person or an organization appointed by a government agency, such as the Social Security Administration (SSA) or the Department of Veterans Affairs (VA), to receive and manage public benefits on behalf of someone who is incapable of doing so. The payee actually receives your government benefits on your behalf, and is responsible for managing them and making sure that they are spent for your welfare.

Q. What types of income may a representative payee manage?

A. He or she may manage only the income paid by government programs (usually federal programs such as Social Security and Supplemental Security Income, veterans' benefits, and Black Lung benefits). The representative payee has *no* authority over any other income or property that you might receive. If you have additional income from other sources, you may need other assistance (such as help from an agent under your durable power of attorney or from a money management program, discussed on page 634) in addition to the help of a representative payee.

Q. How is a representative payee appointed?

A. You, or someone on your behalf, must ask the Social Security Administration (or other program) to appoint a representative payee. Generally, you must have a physical or mental disability that prevents you from managing your own financial affairs, and you must provide documentation of the disability. The government agency that provides the benefits must decide that you need help managing them. Although the decision is made by the agency and not by a court, you have the right to contest the appointment of a representative payee if you disagree with the decision, including the right to a hearing and all the appeals rights that apply to any claim before the applicable agency.

Q. How can I be sure a representative payee will manage my money properly?

A. Oversight of representative payees is minimal. In principle, the payee must provide a detailed accounting to the agency paying the benefits. An annual report must be filed with Social Security. However, some exceptions exist. For example, if you live certain types of mental-health institutions, an annual accounting is not required, though the Social Security Administration will audit the institution once every three years. Under some benefits programs, such as those administered by the VA, reporting requirements vary with the size of the benefit. There is not much you can do to protect yourself, except to plan for incapacity through other methods that allow someone else of your choice to manage your income.

Q. If I regain my ability to control my own finances, may I dismiss a representative payee?

A. Yes. First you need to file a form with the Social Security Administration asking to resume control of your own financial affairs. You must then notify the government agency of your wish to dismiss the representative payee, and the agency must determine that you have regained the capacity to manage your own benefits.

Money Management Services

Q. I don't really have anyone I can name as an agent to manage my financial affairs, but I have heard of some organizations offering "money management" services. What are these?

A. Money management programs, also known as **daily money management** programs or **voluntary money management** programs, offer a broad group of services designed to help older people or disabled people who need assistance managing their financial affairs. These services might include check depositing, check writing, checkbook balancing, bill paying, insurance claim preparation and filing, tax preparation and counseling, investment counseling, and public-benefit applications and counseling.

Q. Who provides money management services?

A. An individual or an organization may provide this type of service. An organization may provide services on a for-profit or not-for-profit basis. Services may be provided for free, on a sliding-scale basis (where you pay according to your income), or for a flat rate.

Q. How can money management programs help me?

A. A money management program may be able to help you by providing the financial management assistance you need in the way that you want it. It may also help you avoid the need for guardianship. Money management services work on a voluntary basis, so you must be able to ask for help or accept an offer of help. Money management services may be particularly useful if you have no fam-

---

▶ **PROTECTING YOUR MONEY**

If you receive or are considering money management services, make sure that the service has a system of cash controls to prevent (or at least minimize) the risk of embezzlement of client funds. The service providers should also be bonded and insured to protect clients from theft or loss of funds.

---

ily or friends who are able (or whom you trust) to act as your agent or trustee.

Guardianship

Q. What exactly is a guardian?

A. Guardian is a general term for a court-appointed surrogate (i.e., substitute) decision maker. More specifically, a guardian is someone appointed by a court to make personal and/or financial decisions on your behalf. Your state may use other terms to refer to a person in this role, such as "conservator." In a growing number of states, the term "guardian" refers to someone who makes decisions about health care and personal affairs, while the term "conservator" refers to someone who makes decisions about finances. If there is no appropriate family member or friend to serve as guardian, then the court may appoint a public or private agency. A person who has a guardian may be called a **ward,** an **incapacitated person,** or something else.

Q. When is the appointment of a guardian appropriate?

A. People need a guardian when

1. they can no longer manage their affairs because of serious mental incapacity;
2. no voluntary arrangements for decision making and management have been made ahead of time (or, if they have been set up, they are not working well); and
3. serious harm will come to the individual if no legally authorized decision maker is appointed.

Q. Are there any disadvantages to a guardianship?

A. Yes. Although a guardianship may be necessary to protect the welfare of an incapacitated person, it may also result in the loss of individual rights. Depending on state law and the judge's order, the ward may lose several civil rights: the right to marry, the right to vote, the right to hold a driver's license, the right to make a will, or the right to enter into a contract. Because of these consequences, guardianship should be considered as a last resort.

In addition, the court proceedings themselves can be costly, time-consuming, and emotionally trying. Moreover, a guardian has less flexibility in management of the estate than a trustee or an agent under advance-planning tools such as durable powers of attorney or living trusts. Guardians must operate within strict fiduciary limitations and normally must file annual accountings and personal status reports with the court. On the positive side, these requirements ensure at least some oversight and accountability.

Q. Who appoints a guardian?

A. Procedures vary by state, but generally a court appoints a guardian after hearing evidence that a person is incapable of making decisions, and after deciding that the person needs a surrogate decision maker.

In most states, the law requires some form of due process to help protect a person from inappropriately being declared incapacitated. Due process rights include the right to be notified of the date and place of the applicable hearing, the right to be present at the hearing, the right to present evidence and cross-examine witnesses, and the right to be represented by a lawyer.

Q. My elderly mother is often confused. I think she needs a guardian to look after her interests. What do I do?

A. First, you may want to contact your local AAA to see if there are any programs or services that might help your mother manage, and thus render guardianship unnecessary. It also will help to have her examined by a doctor or a psychologist experienced in geriatric-capacity evaluation. This may involve assessments by multiple specialists from different disciplines, such as medicine, nursing, and social work. Often, a person's decision making may be impaired because of physical or other causes that are temporary and can be corrected (such as depression or the effects of medication). If the evaluation shows that your mother still retains the capacity to execute a financial or health-care power of attorney, then a guardianship may not be necessary or may be necessary only to a limited extent.

If the evaluation supports the need for a guardianship, check with a lawyer to learn the specifics of your state's laws and procedures, as they vary substantially. The appointment of a guardian normally requires the filing of a court petition, notice to the ward and to other interested parties (such as close relatives),

▸ GUARDIANSHIP

Guardianship is a serious step, and should be taken only when a person displays serious inability to make or understand the consequences of decisions. The decision to create a guardianship should not based on stereotypical notions about old age, mental illness, or disability. A person has a right to make foolish or risky decisions; these decisions by themselves do not indicate a need for guardianship.

and a court hearing. You probably will need a lawyer to help you through it.

The court also may appoint an investigator, or visitor (often referred to as a **guardian ad litem**) to interview your mother and make a report, or a lawyer to represent your mother and protect her interests. At the hearing, a judge will review the petition, the investigator's report, any medical reports or evaluations, and the lawyer's statement.

The judge may ask the person filing the petition why the guardianship is needed. The judge also may question the alleged incapacitated person. The hearings are usually fairly informal. If there is disagreement, the judge may set the case for a more extended hearing with witnesses, cross-examination, and argument by counsel.

Q. What if someone thinks I need a guardian and I do not want one?

A. Every state gives the alleged incapacitated person a chance to fight the guardianship petition. If you do not think you need a

guardian, you must notify the court. Usually you do this by appearing in court at the hearing, or by asking someone to represent you at the hearing.

It is best to get your own lawyer to represent you. If you cannot afford one, many states require that the court appoint one. Some free legal-services programs for older people may help you fight. If you cannot get to court or hire a lawyer, you should write to the court about your objections.

Q. Who pays for a guardianship?

A. Guardianships can be expensive. There are court charges and lawyer's fees, and fees for the doctor or other persons conducting examinations. If the court appoints a guardian, the estate of the incapacitated person usually pays the guardian's fees. Older people who are either seeking guardianship over a family member or challenging a guardianship may be able to get free legal help through legal-services programs or through lawyers who volunteer their services pro bono.

Q. If I need a guardian, may I specify whom I want (and do not want) to play this role?

A. Yes. The court will consider your preference, and in some states must honor your preference unless there is good cause not to do so. You should nominate a guardian as part of your general planning for incapacity. Because sometimes even the best plans for incapacity fail (for example, if your agent under your durable power of attorney dies after you become incapacitated), it is a good idea to name in your planning documents one or two people whom you want to serve as your guardian if necessary.

> ## ▶ WHO MAY BE A GUARDIAN?
>
> Laws vary by state. In most states, the courts may appoint almost anyone as a guardian if the person meets legal requirements. Often, the court appoints the person filing the petition. Most courts like to appoint a relative who knows the person and is most likely to act in his or her best interests. However, the court may appoint a friend or a lawyer, especially if no family members are available. The courts also may appoint co-guardians, either with shared or split responsibilities. If there are no friends or family willing or able to serve, many states permit public or private agencies to act as the guardian and to charge fees for that service if the estate of the incapacitated person is unable to pay.

Q. May the court remove a guardian?

A. Yes. A guardian may be removed if the incapacitated person can prove that he or she has regained capacity to make decisions. But this can be difficult to prove. Therefore, if someone's incapacity may be temporary, consider whether some other arrangement (such as money management or a representative payee) will meet the person's needs, and thus render guardianship unnecessary.

A court also may remove a guardian who is not properly carrying out his or her responsibilities. Usually, a new guardian will replace the person who is removed.

Q. My elderly aunt needs some help with her affairs, but she is not totally incapable. Might a guardianship meet her needs?

A. Your aunt still may have the capacity to execute a financial and a health-care power of attorney. Additionally, in most states, if a person has limited ability, a guardian may be given only partial control. This is generally called a **limited guardianship.** In your aunt's case, the court's guardianship order would identify the specific matters over which the guardian has authority. Your aunt would retain legal authority over all other areas.

In all states, the courts try to ensure that a guardianship is the **least restrictive alternative.** This means that a guardianship restricts the individual as little as possible, letting the person do whatever he or she still has the ability to do. Some states may require annual evaluations to ensure that the guardianship remains the least restrictive alternative.

Even when a limited guardianship is not feasible, the guardian should try to involve the person in making decisions whenever possible, and should make decisions consistent with his or her values. The guardian is said to "step into the shoes" of the incapacitated person, making decisions as he or she would have made them.

Q. What if I have complaints about what the guardian is doing or not doing?

A. If you believe a guardian is not carrying out his or her responsibilities, let the court know. You should not be intimidated about contacting the judge's office or the clerk. In addition, if you think an incapacitated person is being neglected or abused, you should call adult protective services in your area.

Health-Care Decision-Making Issues

Q. To what extent can I control decisions about my health care?

A. With few exceptions, the law recognizes the right of capable individuals to control what happens to their bodies. This includes the right to refuse suggested medical treatment. We normally exercise this right by talking to our doctors and other health-care providers. You have a right to

- know all the relevant facts about your medical condition;
- know the pros and cons of different treatments;
- talk to other doctors and get their opinions;
- say "yes" to treatment or care that you want, and "no" to treatment or care that you don't want; and
- have your pain and symptoms managed effectively, so that you can function in reasonable comfort.

Your doctor is an expert in medicine, but you are the expert in defining and applying your personal values and preferences.

Q. What happens to my right to make medical decisions if I am too sick to decide?

A. In an emergency, the law presumes consent. In all other instances, someone else must make decisions for you. The best way to ensure that decisions are made the way you would want, and by the person you would want, is to create an advance-directive for health care before you become incapacitated.

Q. What is an advance directive for health care?

A. An **advance directive** is generally a written statement, which you complete in advance of serious illness, about how you want medical decisions made. The two most common forms of advance directive are a **living will** and a **durable power of attorney for health care,** or a combination of the two.

An advance directive allows you to state your choices regarding health care, or to name someone to make those choices for you, if you become unable to make decisions about your medical treatment. In short, an advance directive enables you to have some control over your future medical care.

Q. What is a living will?

A. A living will, also called a **medical directive** or **medical declaration,** is simply a written instruction regarding any treatments you want or don't want if you become unable to speak for yourself and are terminally ill or permanently unconscious. A living will simply says, "Whoever is deciding, please follow these instructions." It is called a living will because it takes effect while you are still alive.

Q. What is a durable power of attorney for health care?

A. A durable power of attorney for health care (sometimes called a **health-care proxy**) is a document that appoints someone of your choice to be your authorized agent (or attorney-in-fact or by proxy) for purposes of health-care decisions. You can give your agent as much or as little authority as you wish to make some or all health-care decisions for you when you are unable to do so on your own. You can also include the same kind of instructions that you would put in a living will.

Q. Which is better, a living will or a durable power of attorney for health care?

A. On its own, a living will is a very limited document because, in most states, living wills apply only to terminal illness or permanent unconsciousness. They address only life-sustaining medical treatments and not other treatment decisions, and they provide fairly general instructions that may be difficult to interpret or apply to complicated medical situations.

The durable power of attorney for health care is a more comprehensive and practical document. It may cover any health-care decision, and is not limited to terminal illness or permanent coma. More important, it authorizes someone of your choice to weigh all the facts at the time a decision needs to be made, and to speak for you legally according to any guidelines you provide.

Q. What happens if I do not have an advance-directive?

A. Many states have family consent (or health surrogate) statutes that authorize someone else, typically family members in the order of kinship, to make some or all health-care decisions for you. Even in the absence of such statutes, doctors and health facilities will take one of two routes. They will either rely on the consent of family members, as long as they are close family members and no controversial decisions need to be made, or they will exercise all available treatment options, unless a temporary or permanent guardian can be appointed to make decisions.

However, without an advance directive, decisions may not be made the way you would want them to be made, or by the person you would want to make them. And any disagreement among family members may undermine the process and require court involvement to resolve. In addition to benefiting you, making an advance directive benefits your family members, because it spares them the agony of having to guess what you would really want.

If no close family member or other surrogate is available to make decisions for you, a court-appointed guardian may be necessary. This is an option of last resort.

Q. How do I make an advance directive?

A. Requirements differ by state. Most states provide suggested forms. A few dictate specific language or provisions that must be included. Most states have witnessing or notary requirements. Follow these requirements closely. Commonly, two witnesses are required; and often, several categories of persons are disqualified from serving as witnesses, such as relatives, heirs, or health-care providers.

Q. What should my advance directive say?

A. No one can tell you exactly what to say in your advance directive. However, the most important task to accomplish is to name someone you trust to act as your agent for healthcare decisions.

Also consider addressing these points:

- **Alternate proxies.** Whenever possible, name one or more alternate or successor agents in case your primary agent is unavailable.
- **Life-sustaining treatments.** Are there any specific types of treatment you want or don't want? Be careful about what you

instruct, because you don't know the future and the medical complexities it may bring.

- **Artificial nutrition and hydration.** Some states will presume that you want nutrition and hydration in all circumstances, unless you instruct otherwise.
- **Organ donation.** In many states, you can include instructions about donating organs.
- **The Health Insurance Portability and Accountability Act of 1996 (HIPAA).** Including language that ensures compliance with HIPAA will permit your agent to review prior medical records and bills.

Q. Can I change or terminate my advance directive?

A. Yes. You always have the right to change or revoke your advance directive while you have the mental capacity to do so. Normally, you can revoke it orally or in writing in any way that indicates your intent. Your intent should be communicated to your agent, your family, and your doctor.

If you want to change the document, it is best to execute a new document. The same formalities are required for changes as are required for signing and witnessing.

▶ TELLING YOUR DOCTOR IS NOT SUFFICIENT

Telling your doctor and others what you want provides important evidence of your wishes if you later become incapacitated, especially if your doctor writes your wishes down in your medical record. However, written advance directives are more likely to carry weight and be followed.

Q. Whom should I select as my agent or proxy for health decisions?

A. The choice of agent is the most important decision you may make in doing an advance directive. Your agent will have great power over your health and personal care if you become incapacitated. Name a person whom you trust fully and with whom you are comfortable talking about end-of-life decisions. If no such person is available, it may be best not to name a health-care agent; instead, only include instructions about what is most important to you if you face a serious and eventually fatal illness.

▶ DISCUSSING YOUR OPTIONS

The most important point to remember about forms is that they are supposed to aid, and not take the place of, discussion and dialogue. Therefore, a form ought to be a starting point—not an end point—for making your wishes known. There is no ideal form. Any form you use should be personalized to reflect your values and preferences. Before drafting an advance-directive, talk with your doctor, family members, and advisers. This will help you to understand the medical possibilities you may face, and to clarify your values and choices.

Before you appoint a person, speak to him or her beforehand. Explain your intentions and obtain his or her agreement. Consider naming alternate or successor agents, in case the primary agent is unavailable. If there is anyone whom you absolutely want to keep from playing any role in your health-care decisions, you may expressly disqualify that person. Also, make sure you find out who can and cannot be your agent under state law.

Q. What do I do with my advance directive after completing it?

A. Make sure someone close to you knows where it is located. If you have named an agent, give your agent a copy. Also give your physician a copy, and ask that it be made part of your permanent medical record. You may also want to make a small card for your purse or wallet stating that you have an advance directive and providing the name, phone number, and address of your agent or a person who can provide a copy of it. But remember: if you change your directive, you will need to notify everyone who has a copy of the original. There are also an increasing number of electronic registers for advance directives.

Q. What if my doctor or hospital refuses to follow my advance directive?

A. It is best to find out ahead of time your doctor's views about advance directives and your specific wishes. If he or she disagrees, you may wish to find a new doctor.

Under federal law, most hospitals, nursing homes, and home health agencies must inform you at the time of admission about their policies regarding advance directives. Most will respect advance directives, but some may have restrictive policies. No facility can require you to have, or not have, an advance directive as an admission requirement.

If you are in a condition to which your advance directive applies, and if your providers will not honor your directive, then state law spells out their obligations. Usually, the provider must make a reasonable effort to transfer the patient to another provider who will respect the advance directive.

Q. Is a lawyer needed to do an advance directive?

A. No. A lawyer is not necessary, but one experienced in doing advance directives may be helpful. A lawyer can draft a personalized document that reflects your particular wishes and ensures that all legal formalities are followed. A lawyer is especially helpful if there are potential conflicts or special legal or medical concerns.

Abuse and Exploitation

Q. What is elder abuse?

A. In its most general sense, **elder abuse** is an act (or failure to act by a person required to act) that results in harm to an older person. Definitions of elder abuse vary by state, but generally include

- physical abuse—use of physical force that may result in bodily injury, physical pain, or impairment;
- sexual abuse—nonconsensual sexual contact of any kind;
- emotional and psychological abuse—infliction of anguish, pain, or distress through verbal or nonverbal acts;
- neglect—the refusal or failure to fulfill any part of a person's obligation or duties to an older person;
- abandonment—the desertion of an elderly person by an individual who has

▶ OUT-OF-STATE DIRECTIVES

Many people want to know whether, if they make an advance directive in one state, it will be recognized in others. In many states, the law expressly honors out-of-state directives. But in some states, the law is unclear. Realistically, providers will normally try to follow your stated wishes, regardless of the form you use or where you executed it. However, if you spend a great deal of time in more than one state (for example, summers in Wisconsin, winters in Arizona), then you may want to consider executing an advance directive for each state. Or, it may be advisable to find out whether a single document could meet the formal requirements of each state. As a practical matter, you may want different health-care agents if the same agent is not easily available in each location.

physical custody or by a person who has assumed responsibility for providing care;

- self-neglect—behavior of an older person that threatens his or her health or safety; and
- financial exploitation—illegal or improper use of an older person's funds, property, or assets.

Every state has specific elder abuse laws. You can find details on local laws and programs from your local or state AAA or your state adult protective services program.

Q. Is elder abuse a problem that only affects very frail old people who live in nursing homes?

A. No. Elder abuse is a real problem for many older people, regardless of where they live. Some victims are very frail and are unable to seek help on their own. Other victims are physically or mentally capable of seeking help, but cannot or do not do so for a variety of reasons—including fear that they will not be believed, love or concern for the person abusing them, fear that they will lose their independence, embarrassment at

being victimized, or a belief that nothing can be done.

Elder abuse affects older people of all races, ethnic groups, social classes, and economic levels.

Q. My son is using all my money to buy illegal drugs. He is also running up large charges on my credit cards. (His name is on my credit card accounts and my bank accounts.) Since he is a co-owner of

▶ VICTIMS' SERVICES

Your local AAA can provide a valuable resource when confronting issues of elder abuse or neglect. If you are being victimized, know someone who is, or know someone who needs some extra help and support, contact your local AAA. They can help you contact the correct authorities or social-service program.

my home, I am afraid he will mortgage it or possibly even sell it. What can I do?

A. Even if he has the legal right to reach your funds, you can protect yourself from this type of financial exploitation. Ask your bank to help you transfer funds to new accounts that your son may not access. Write all your credit card companies and ask them to remove your son's name from your accounts. Have them issue new credit cards to you.

Contact a lawyer to see what you must do to protect your home. A free legal-services program for older or poor persons may be able to help you. Your local AAA can help you find the appropriate resources.

Finally, local social-services agencies may be able to help you and your son. Many agencies have experience in dealing with family difficulties of this sort. And if you are in physical danger, court protective orders are available. You do not have to allow your son's problems to threaten your own well-being and financial security.

Q. My son and daughter-in-law live with me in my home. They are living rent free and give me no money for household bills or food. I feel like they are taking advantage of me. Can someone help me?

A. Yes. The situation you describe is surprisingly common. You can get help from a local adult protective services program, community program, or legal-services program for older or poor people.

Q. My neighbor is very old and sick. She depends on her daughter for shopping, cooking, and cleaning. However, her daughter often leaves her mom without food and clean

clothes. Is there anything I can do to help?

A. Yes. You may report this neglect to your local adult protective services program. This may be your state or local AAA or some other human services agency. You may even report abuse and neglect to the police. To find the adult protective services program serving your community, you can call your AAA or call the Eldercare Locator. Adult protective services programs are responsible for investigating reports of suspected abuse, neglect, or exploitation. If the program determines that abuse is

---

▶ **DOMESTIC VIOLENCE**

Suppose your spouse or partner sometimes hits you or pushes you around. You are both over sixty-five. This may have been going on for a long time, or it may be a new problem. Because of your age or limited resources, it is harder for you to run away. Is there anything you can do?

You don't have to live with abuse, no matter what your age. Domestic violence is against the law. It is no more legal for your spouse or partner to hit you than for a stranger to hit you. A domestic violence or adult protective services program may be able to help you. Additionally, more and more police departments and courts are sensitive to domestic violence and are able to help victims. See page 104 of the "Family Law" chapter for a more detailed discussion of domestic violence and your options.

occurring, they can provide or arrange a variety of services to help the victim.

You should not worry about being sued for reporting suspected abuse. Almost all states protect people who make such reports in good faith. You may even make an anonymous report.

REMEMBER THIS

- Advance planning for financial and health-care decision making is the most effective means of ensuring that your wishes will be followed if you become incapacitated.

- Tools for dealing with financial incapacity or difficulties in managing finances include a durable power of attorney, a living trust, joint ownership, representative payees for government benefits, and money management services.

- You can use health-care advance directives, such as a living will and a durable power of attorney for health care, to provide instructions about your medical care in the event you are incapacitated.

- In the absence of advance planning for financial management or health-care decision making, a petition for guardianship may be necessary in cases of serious incapacity.

- Elder abuse includes physical and sexual abuse, emotional and psychological abuse, neglect, abandonment, financial exploitation, and self-neglect. It occurs more frequently than many realize. But it can be prevented or stopped if suspected abuse is reported early.

Estate Planning

Mary is a widow, without children or close relatives. She is no longer able to live alone in her home or to handle her finances. At her death, Mary wants most of her estate to go to organizations that protect the environment. And she wants to leave some of her assets to her close friend, Maggie, who has been helping Mary as she's become more disabled.

Mary's lawyer advises her to establish a living trust and to transfer her property and other assets to its trustee. The trustee will sell Mary's home and invest the proceeds, along with the other assets, to provide for Mary's support during her lifetime. After she dies, will Mary's estate be administered according to her wishes? What if she changes her mind? Can Mary change the trust arrangements?

Estate planning is, in a sense, planning for death. We're all a little squeamish about death, especially when we're the ones involved. This discomfort can lead to procrastination—which might account for the fact that only about two out of every five Americans have a will. Most of us fail to plan our estates. But an estate plan is the one thing that's essential to ensure that those we care about receive the fruits of our labor.

This chapter answers commonly asked questions about estate planning. The rules governing estate planning, wills, and trusts are determined by state law, which means that some of the principles discussed in this chapter may not apply in your state. As you begin to plan your estate, consult with one or more lawyers with experience in estate planning. After a consultation, a lawyer can give you a good idea of the cost involved with ensuring that your estate is in order for today and tomorrow.

ESTATE-PLANNING BASICS

This section covers the basics of estate planning, including the value of writing a will and the logistics of getting started.

Q. *Why should I go to the trouble of planning my estate and writing a will?*

A. Estate planning pays real dividends—in results achieved, in dollars saved, and, most importantly, in security and peace of mind. And it doesn't have to be expensive, traumatic, or even especially time consuming.

An **estate plan** is your blueprint for where you want your property to go after you die. Estate planning allows you to:

- **Determine what happens to your property.** It enables you to coordinate gifts during your lifetime with bequests in your will or trust. You can apportion property among your family members, your friends, and worthy charities. If you don't have an estate plan, then state law will dictate how to dispose of your property.

- **Determine who will be in charge of carrying out your wishes.** Your executor carries out your wishes if you have a will, and your trustee carries out your wishes if you have a trust.

- **Save money.** An estate plan allows you to save on probate, taxes, and other expenses typically associated with settling a person's affairs after death.

- **Be in control of your own life.** A living trust can provide a way to manage your property should you become disabled. A living will or a health-care advance directive can set up a plan for your medical care, should you no longer be able to make decisions for yourself.

- **Coordinate estate planning with other financial planning.** Tax laws provide significant incentives to save for education, making estate planning an ideal opportunity to plan for the education of children and grandchildren.

- **Decide whether your business will be sold or stay in the family.** If you'd like a family business to stay within the family, your estate plan can specify who will run it.

Q. *Isn't a will all I need?*

A. Not necessarily. While a will is usually an important part of an estate plan, it's not the only part. These days, it's common (and often beneficial) for a person to have up to a dozen **will substitutes**—that is, various ways of distributing property regardless of whether the person has a formal will. Pensions, life insurance, gifts, joint ownership, and trusts are just a few of the ways you can transfer property at or before death quickly and inexpensively.

Q. *How can an estate plan make things easier on my family after I die?*

> ▶ **WHAT IS AN ESTATE?**
>
> Your **estate** consists of all your property, including
>
> - your home and other real estate;
> - tangible personal property such as cars and furniture; and
> - intangible property like insurance, bank accounts, stocks and bonds, and pension and Social Security benefits.

A. You want your beneficiaries to receive promptly the property you've left them as part of your estate plan. Options include

- gifts made before you die;
- insurance or pension benefits paid directly to them as the named beneficiaries;
- a living trust;
- using expedited probate for wills, which is available in many states, especially for smaller estates; and
- taking advantage of laws in certain states that provide partial payments to beneficiaries while the estate is in probate.

Estate planning can also minimize expenses by keeping the cost of transferring property as low as possible. For example, choosing a competent executor and giving the executor the necessary authority to carry out your directives can simplify the administration of your estate, which may save time and money in the long run.

If you have minor children, an estate plan enables you to designate the best available person to care for them after your death. Through a will, you can nominate a legal guardian for your children and name an executor to handle the distribution of your estate to your designated beneficiaries.

Q. How can we ensure that the guardians we've named for our children have the resources to raise them well?

A. Just as you have a named a legal guardian to raise your children, you may also name a guardian of property left to your children, who may or may not be the same person as the legal guardian—it's up to you. The trust or will should contain instructions for the distribution of funds for the financial well-being of the children in a way that is consistent with your wishes.

Whether you have a will-based or trust-based plan, it is important that your documents enable your trustees/property guardians and personal guardians to act in the best interest of your children in ways that are consistent with your wishes, directions, and values.

Q. Can an estate plan help reduce taxes on my estate?

A. Yes. A good estate plan gives the maximum amount allowed by law to your beneficiaries, and the minimum possible amount to the tax collector. This becomes especially important as your estate approaches the so-called estate tax exemption amount, which is currently $2 million and increasing to $3.5 million in 2009.

Q. Isn't an estate plan just for old people?

A. Emphatically not. Many young and middle-aged people die suddenly or become mentally or physically incapacitated. An estate plan can be tailored to anticipate both of these contingencies.

Q. When should I plan my estate?

A. The time to plan for death or disability is when you're healthy. As a general rule, people tend to make worse decisions when coping with mental or physical stress, strain, or illness. Moreover, a so-called deathbed will, or one made by someone whose mental competence is questionable, may invite a legal challenge.

It's also important not to procrastinate. Don't put off making your estate plan until your estate reaches a certain level or value. Even if you don't have as many assets now as you expect to have someday, it's easy to update the plan every few years as your assets and life circumstances change. If you put in a few hours now learning the basics and setting up your plan, you'll know you're covered in case of an unexpected event.

▶ INFORMATION YOU NEED TO PLAN YOUR ESTATE

When planning your estate, it's helpful to have as much of the following information on hand as possible including:

- The names, addresses, and birth dates of all people, whether or not related to you, that you expect to name in your will;
- The name, address, and telephone number of the person (or people) you expect to name as the executor of your will;
- If you have minor children, the names, addresses, and telephone numbers of possible guardians;
- The amount and source of your principal income and other income, such as interest and dividends;
- The amount, source, and beneficiaries (if any) of your retirement benefits, including IRAs, pensions, Keogh accounts, government benefits, and profit-sharing plans;
- The amount, source, and beneficiaries (if any) of other financial assets such as bank accounts, annuities, and loans owed to you;
- The amount of your debts, including mortgages, installment loans, and business debts, if any;
- A list (with approximate values) of valuable property you own, including real estate, jewelry, furniture, collections, heirlooms, and other assets;
- A list and description of jointly owned property and the names of any co-owners;
- Any documents that might affect your estate plan, including prenuptial agreements, marriage certificates, divorce decrees, recent tax returns, existing wills and trust documents, property deeds, and so on; and
- The location of any safe-deposit boxes and an inventory of the contents of each.

Q. My spouse doesn't like to talk about finances or estate planning. What should I do?

A. You can't plan your estate if you don't know all the facts about your family's assets. Yet many people don't have basic information about their spouse's income—how much he or she earns, benefits to which he or she is entitled, his or her assets and debts, and where assets are invested.

It's especially important to know who holds title to real estate and to **titled personal property**—for example, automobiles, boats, and recreational vehicles. It is also important for you to know the beneficiaries of your spouse's insurance policies, pension plans, retirement accounts, and other similar assets.

Q. What can I do to minimize the costs of estate planning?

A. Ask about fees at your first legal or professional consultation, and inquire about how much your total plan might cost. If your legal adviser charges by the hour, the more time you invest in locating relevant documents and putting your wishes in writing, the less preparatory work your adviser will have to do. This should go a long way toward reducing final costs.

Working with a Lawyer

Q. Should I consult a lawyer as I plan my estate?

A. As a general rule, the larger your estate, the more important it is for you to consult a lawyer. You should most certainly use a lawyer if you own a business, if your estate nears or exceeds $2 million, or if you anticipate a challenge to the will from a disgruntled relative or anyone else.

If your estate is relatively small and your objectives straightforward, then you might plan your estate mostly on your own, with the help of the ABA's *Guide to Wills and Estates* and other resource materials. However, a caveat is in order. "How-to" guides can assist you as you start the estate-planning process. But before finalizing anything, consult with an experienced estate lawyer to make sure that your property goes where you want it to; that your family is protected fully; and that you are assured of proper care in the case of incapacity.

Q. Why can't I just use a book, or one of those computerized "will kits" and do it myself?

A. You might be able to. For some people—those with very small or otherwise uncomplicated estates (e.g., no real estate)—such alternatives might be sufficient. But if you choose this route, make sure that the book or kit is up-to-date and thorough, especially since probate laws vary from state to state.

And remember: these alternatives don't provide you with a legal expert to review your work. Although many people might be able to plan their estates using a standard form, many more have unique situations that can benefit from custom-tailored advice. Once you begin totaling up all your assets, you may be surprised to find that your estate is larger than you thought, meaning that a simple will isn't enough. In addition, family relationships are becoming more complicated these days.

What's more, most do-it-yourself alternatives can't tell you what strategies might help you save money or make sure your wishes are accomplished. Estate planning for most people should consist of more than just a will: IRAs, insurance, living trusts, and other elements can also be valuable tools. The precise mix that's best for you is unique to your circumstances. And because they are not allowed to give legal advice, many alternative estate providers will fail to inform you when there might be a better (and cheaper) way to accomplish your goals.

In light of these factors, consulting with a lawyer might be a good idea after all. Lawyers generally charge smaller fees for less-complicated estates, so the benefits and flexibility of real legal advice could be yours for little more than the cost of a computerized will kit.

Q. How can I find a lawyer to help me plan my estate and draft any necessary documents?

A. Ask for recommendations from friends who have hired lawyers to draw up their wills. Or you can use any of the Internet resources listed in the appendix. Or you can see if you are (or can be) covered by a **legal service plan,** a type of plan for which many Americans are eligible. In many such programs, simple wills are either free or cost far less

than the going rate; lawyers will also provide more comprehensive estate planning and preparation of other documents at a reduced hourly rate. About 80 percent of plans are available to members of certain organizations (like AARP, the military, or a union), or to employees of certain companies as a result of collective-bargaining agreements or adoption of a plan by the employer. Plans also may be available to credit card holders and bank customers or through individual sales agents. Some of these plans have no fee at all to the participant; others may require payment of a monthly fee.

Legal clinics are another low-cost alternative. At a legal clinic, legal assistants do much of the work under a lawyer's guidance, generally by adapting standard computerized forms to fit the needs of individual clients. If you have a small, simple estate, the cost for this type of service may be modest, and you will receive professional advice and reassurance that your will meets your state's standards. You may be able to find a law school clinic or other type of clinic by looking in the yellow pages or online.

Q. How will I work with my lawyer to plan my estate?

A. Don't just expect to pile some papers on your lawyer's desk and have a will or trust magically appear. Preparing these documents is seldom as simple as filling in blanks on a form. Most people will meet with their lawyer several times, with more extensive estates requiring more meetings.

At the first meeting, be prepared to tell your lawyer about some rather intimate details of your life: how much money you have; how many children you plan to have; which relatives, friends, or other associates you want to receive more or less of your estate. Bring as

---

▸ FEEL COMFORTABLE WITH YOUR LAWYER

An essential: Be comfortable with the lawyer you choose! A good estate lawyer will have to ask questions about many private matters, and you need to feel free to discuss these personal considerations. If you don't feel comfortable, you should find another lawyer who's willing to explain the options to you—and who'll help you do it right.

much information and as many relevant documents as you can to the meeting (see "Information You Need to Plan Your Estate" on page 648).

After talking with you, your lawyer will explain the options the law provides for accomplishing your estate-planning goals. Your lawyer can then draft a will or trust or both, depending on your circumstances.

It's a good idea to ask your lawyer to send you a draft of the will or trust document for your review. After examining the draft, ask for any needed clarification and provide any necessary changes. This information will assist your lawyer in preparing the finalized will or trust document that, upon signing, will become legally effective to distribute your estate.

You should review your estate plan periodically, so you'll want to stay in touch with your lawyer. Don't think of estate planning as a one-time transaction; think of it as a process that works best when you have an ongoing relationship with your advisers.

REMEMBER THIS

- Estate planning is not just for the elderly—it's a wise precaution at any stage of life.

- Estate planning puts you in control by letting you determine exactly how you want your property distributed.

- You may be able to save money in taxes and fees through intelligent and thorough estate planning.

- Estate planning can provide a way for you to plan for any possible incapacity, letting you determine how you will be cared for when you're too ill to make decisions for yourself.

WILLS

This section details the steps involved in preparing a will, including working with a lawyer or estate planner, deciding what to include in your will, choosing your beneficiaries and executor, and making the will legal.

Q. Do I have to have a lawyer write my will?

A. No. If your will meets the legal requirements established by your state's law, it is valid, whether you wrote it with a lawyer or by yourself. However, a lawyer can help ensure that your will is valid and that it does what you really want it to do.

Q. Does my will have to be written?

A. The best rule to follow in creating a will is to put it in writing. By writing your will, you are ensuring that your intentions are clear and that you have a degree of certainty about the exact distribution of your estate upon your death.

As with all general rules, there are exceptions. Some states recognize oral wills or holographic wills—handwritten, unwitnessed wills—but only under extremely limited circumstances.

A few states have **statutory wills** that are created by law and allow people to fill in the blanks on a standard form. However, these wills are designed for simple estates and provide little flexibility. They will not be useful if you have a large or complicated estate.

Q. What happens if I die without a will?

A. If you die without a will, you die **intestate.** Your property still must be distributed, and will be done so according to your state's laws of **intestacy.** The probate court in your area will appoint someone (who may or may not be

▶ THE VIDEO WILL

Some people may choose to prepare a **video will,** which is a video recording that shows them reading the will aloud, perhaps explaining why certain gifts were made and others not. The video recording might also show the execution of the will. Should a disgruntled relative decide to challenge the will, the video can provide compelling proof that the **testator**—the person making the will—really intended to make a will, was mentally competent to do so, and observed the formalities of execution. Consult a lawyer before making such a video.

the person you would have wanted to comb through your affairs) as the administrator of your estate. He or she will be responsible for distributing your property in accordance with state law.

The probate court will supervise the administrator's work closely, and may require the administrator to post bond to ensure that your estate will not be charged for any errors made by the administrator. Of course, all this involvement may be much more expensive than administration under a will—and these costs come out of your estate before it is distributed. Some of your property may have to be sold to pay these costs, instead of going to family or friends.

Q. Who gets my property if I die without a will?

A. By not leaving a valid will or trust, or by not transferring your property in some other way before death, you've left it to the law of

your state to write your "will." In the absence of a will, the law of your state has made certain judgments about who should receive your property. Those judgments may or may not bear any relationship to the judgments you would have made if you had prepared a will or executed a trust.

As a general rule, state law gives your property to the people most closely related to you by blood, marriage, or adoption. As a result, your hard-earned money might end up with relatives who don't need it, while others are passed over who (related to you or not) might be in greater need or more deserving. In the unlikely event that you have no relatives or that your relatives cannot be located after diligent efforts, your property will go to the state—a big reason to have a will or a trust.

Q. Does a will cover all my property?

A. Probably not. It is easy to think that a will covers all of your property. But because property can be passed to others by gift, contract, joint tenancy, life insurance, or other methods, a will might best be viewed as just one of many ways of determining how and to whom your estate will be distributed at your death.

Many of the various methods of distributing your estate are discussed in this chapter. Be sure to keep in mind the kinds of property that a will may not cover, and include them in your estate planning.

Q. Are there any special legal formalities required to make my will legal?

A. After you've drawn up your will, there remains one step: the formal legal procedure called **executing** the will. This requires witnesses to your signing of the will. In almost all states, the signature of at least two witnesses is required. In some states, a will is not deemed legally valid unless the witnesses ap-

> ▶ **KINDS OF WILLS**

Here's a brief list of terms used to describe the various kinds of wills under the law:

- **Simple will:** A will that provides for the distribution of the entire estate to one or more people or entities, known as **beneficiaries,** so that no part of the estate remains undistributed.

- **Testamentary-trust will:** A will that sets up one or more trusts into which designated portions of your estate are placed after you die.

- **Pourover will:** A will that leaves your estate to a trust established before your death.

- **Holographic will:** A will that is unwitnessed, and written in the handwriting of the will maker. Some states recognize the validity of such wills.

- **Oral will** (also called a **noncupative will**): A will that is spoken, not written down. A few states permit these.

- **Joint will:** A single document consisting of two wills: a wife's and a husband's.

- **Living will:** Not really a will at all—since it has force while you are still alive and doesn't dispose of property. A living will often is executed at the same time you make your true will. It tells doctors and hospitals which treatments (e.g., life support) you do and do not want in the event that you are terminally ill or, as a result of accident or illness, cannot be restored to consciousness. (A power-of-appointment for health care or a **durable power of attorney for health care** can also be used to address this concern. For more on such advance directives, see Chapter 16, "The Rights of Older Americans."

pear in court and testify about witnessing the will. However, in a growing number of states, a will can be "self-proved"—that is, the will is accepted as valid and the witnesses will not be required to appear and testify if, at the time the will was executed, the witnesses' signatures were notarized and the witnesses submit affidavits attesting to the fact that they witnessed the signing of the will.

Q. Does it matter who my witnesses are?

A. Yes. The witnesses should have no potential conflicts of interest—that is, they should

not be people who receive anything under the will or who might benefit from your death. Thus, in some states, a will is invalid if witnessed by a beneficiary. In other states, a beneficiary can serve as a witness but, in doing so, might lose whatever property or interest is left to him or her in your will.

Q. In my will, can I leave my property to anyone I wish?

A. In general, you can pick the people you want your property to go to and leave it to them in whatever proportions you want, but there are a few exceptions. For example, a

▶ UNMARRIED COUPLES

It is especially important for unmarried couples to write a will or trust, since these tools allow you to leave your property to anyone (or any organization) you wish. A will or a trust also lets you name an executor or trustee for your estate to supervise distribution of your assets, and can allow you to appoint your partner as the person responsible for carrying out your funeral arrangements. Remember that your will likely will not be admitted to court until after your funeral, so you should make sure your partner is aware of its contents and of your wishes regarding your funeral. The mention of your wishes in a will and a signed statement of funeral instructions should go a long way toward convincing funeral directors of your partner's authority in the event of a dispute between the partner and other family members.

Additionally, some unmarried people create cohabitation agreements to cover the rights and responsibilities of each partner. These agreements cover such contingencies as each partner's disability and division of property in case the relationship ends. They often are coordinated with wills and trusts. You'll want a lawyer who's experienced in non-spousal domestic partnerships to help you write yours.

A word of caution is in order, however. In some states, cohabitation, regardless of the sex of the parties, may be thought to be against sound public policy. In these states, the courts might not enforce cohabitation agreements.

---

surviving husband or wife may have the right to take a fixed share of the estate, regardless of the will. Some states limit how much you can leave to a charity if you have a surviving spouse or children, or if you die soon after making the provision.

Some people try to make their influence felt beyond the grave by attaching bizarre or excessive conditions to a gift made in a will. Most lawyers will advise you not to try this. Courts don't like such conditions, and you're inviting a will contest if you try to tie multiple, unreasonable conditions to a gift. For the most part, though, it's your call.

Q. Can I disinherit my spouse and children?

A. Absent express provisions to the contrary in a valid premarital agreement, you usually can't disinherit your spouse. State laws generally entitle a surviving spouse to take a portion of the deceased spouse's estate—regardless of the deceased spouse's will or estate plan.

The situation with children is dramatically the opposite. Except for Louisiana, every state permits you to disinherit your children. However, to be effective, it is better if your intent to disinherit is "express," which usually means it has to be stated in writing.

Q. What share will my spouse receive under state law?

A. If a husband or wife dies with a will that makes no provision for the surviving spouse,

▶ **PROBATE**

Probate is the court-supervised legal procedure that determines the validity of a will. Probate affects some, but not all, of your assets. Non-probate assets include things like a life insurance policy paid directly to a beneficiary. During probate, the main players are the probate court and your personal representative (either your executor or the administrator appointed by the court). Once the court determines the will is valid, all property, debts, and claims of the estate are inventoried and appraised, all valid claims of the estate are collected, and the remainder of the estate is distributed to beneficiaries according to the will.

The average estate completes the probate process in six to nine months, depending on the state's probate laws. The reformed probate procedures present in many states now make it possible for your survivors to obtain funds to live on while your estate is being probated, without waiting for the entire estate to clear probate. The expenses of probate (which can include court and appraiser fees) depend on the state in which you live and the size of your estate. If there are complications—for example, an invalid will or a will contest—then naturally the costs will go up. Contrary to popular belief, today probate is seldom as costly and time consuming as it was in the past.

Although many think they should try to avoid probate, in many states, it may well not be worth the trouble to do so. But if your lawyer thinks probate is apt to be costly or time consuming for your estate, then good estate planning can minimize expenses. Passing most of your property through a living trust or by joint tenancy or some other means that avoids probate leaves very little property to be distributed through your will. The smaller the size of the probate estate, the lower the costs, especially if your estate is small enough to qualify for expedited processing.

or conveys to the spouse less than a certain percentage of the deceased spouse's assets, then the surviving spouse can take a statutorily defined **elective share** of the estate. This means that he or she can choose to accept the amount allowed by law, usually one-third or one-half of the estate.

The surviving spouse doesn't have to take an elective share of the estate—it's his or her choice. If he or she doesn't exercise the choice, the will stands and the property is distributed as stated in the will.

Elective-share provisions are troubling to many people entering into second marriages, particularly late in life, because the surviving spouse of only a few years would be eligible to take up to one-half of the deceased spouse's property, even if the deceased spouse wanted it to go to his or her own children. Recent revisions to the Uniform Probate Code provide a sliding scale for surviving spouses who take against the will. Under this approach, the longer the marriage, the greater the elective share. If the marriage lasted only a few years,

▶ WHICH LAW APPLIES?

If you own property in more than one state when you die, the laws of the state where your primary home is located determine what happens to your personal property—car, stocks, and cash. The laws of the state in which any other real estate is located govern its distribution. If you do own homes or land in different states, it's a good idea to make sure that the provisions of your estate-planning documents comply with the laws of the appropriate states.

then the percentage could be quite low, which minimizes one source of worry for older couples.

Q. What does it mean when a will is contested?

A. Human nature being what it is, some people who don't receive what they consider a fair share from a dead relative's will may want to challenge—that is, **contest**—the will.

Common grounds for contesting a will include: that the will was not executed properly; that the testator lacked **testamentary capacity** (i.e., the ability to make a will)—for example, that he was senile when he left his estate to the named beneficiary; undue influence (e.g., the evil sister hypnotized her dying brother into leaving her the whole estate); fraud (e.g., the evil brother retyped a page of the will to give himself the Porsche collection); or mistake (e.g., you leave your million-dollar summer home to "my cousin John," and it turns out you have three cousins named John).

Q. How can I plan to avoid a will contest?

A. There's an old saying that you never really know someone until a will is read. However, if your will conforms to legal requirements, a challenge is unlikely to be successful. This is another reason to consult with an experienced estate-planning lawyer and to update your will periodically.

There are other concrete steps you can take to reduce the chances of a will contest. One is called a **no-contest clause,** which in some states allows you to disinherit a beneficiary who unsuccessfully contests the will. Of course, be aware that any heir can always challenge a trust or will by claiming that the person who executed the document did not have the legal capacity to do so, or did so as a result of fraud or undue influence. But if you exercise care and obtain good legal advice, these challenges will generally be defeated and your intentions will generally be carried out.

The Executor

Q. Whom should I make the executor of my will?

A. There's no consensus about who makes the best executor. It all depends on individual circumstances.

One approach is to appoint someone with no potential conflict of interest—that is, someone who doesn't stand to gain from the will. Under this approach, you can minimize the likelihood of a will contest from a disgruntled beneficiary who might be tempted to accuse the executor of taking undue advantage of the role to the detriment of others named in the will. On the other hand, if you believe that there is little possibility of a will contest, you could choose a beneficiary as ex-

▶ **LEGAL PROTECTIONS FOR SURVIVING SPOUSES**

Depending on the state, a surviving spouse may have the protection of homestead laws, exempt property laws, and family allowance laws. Typically, these protections are in addition to whatever the spouse receives under the will, the elective share that the spouse can choose to take against the will, or the statutory share that he or she receives if there is no will.

Homestead laws protect certain property from the deceased spouse's creditors. Typically, they permit the surviving spouse to shelter a certain value of the family home and some personal property from creditors. In some states, the homestead exemption protects a statutorily specified sum of money from creditors, rather than the deceased's real or personal property. As a general rule, the protection is temporary, extending for the lifetime of the surviving spouse or until any minor children reach legal adulthood. However, in a few states, homestead laws permanently shelter specified property.

Exempt property laws give the surviving spouse certain specified property, provide protection from creditors, and protect against disinheritance.

Family allowance laws make probate less of a burden on family members. Under these laws, the family is entitled to a certain amount of the estate's money during probate, regardless of the claims of creditors.

ecutor. Since an executor who is a beneficiary usually waives the executor's fee, your estate will save money.

For most people whose assets amount to less than a million dollars, a good choice is your spouse or the person who will be the main beneficiary of your will. This person naturally will be interested in making sure the probate process goes efficiently and with minimal expense. For larger estates and those that involve running a business, it may be advisable to use the estate-planning department of your bank, your accountant, or your lawyer.

Q. Are paid executors preferable?

A. There are sometimes reasons for choosing a paid executor—usually a lawyer—instead of a family member. Your family may be incapacitated by grief, illness, or disability. Since the executor must gather all the estate assets, your family member may be faced with the odious duty of retrieving money or property you lent to other family members or friends.

Nonetheless, your executor will be personally liable for unpaid estate taxes and fines for late filings, even if he or she has delegated such tasks to a lawyer. If you think your family member may not be up to the job, you might choose a lawyer or other professional, even if it means paying a fee. Remember, this is a job that (primarily because of tax procedures) can last more than three years, though most last far less.

Q. What if the executor I choose can't serve when the time comes, or doesn't want to?

A. Whomever you choose as executor, be sure to provide in your will for a successor executor in case the first named executor dies or

▶ THE ESSENTIALS OF A VALID WILL

In order to be valid, your will doesn't have to conform to a specific formula. However, there are certain elements that usually must be present.

- **Legal age.** You must be of legal age to make a will. This is eighteen in most states, but may be several years older or younger in some places.

- **Sound mind.** You must be of sound mind, which means that you should know you're executing a will, know the general nature and extent of your property, and know the objects of your bounty—that is, your spouse, descendants, and other relatives who ordinarily would be expected to share in your estate. The law presumes that a will maker was of sound mind, and the standard for proving otherwise is very high—much more than mere absentmindedness or forgetfulness.

- **Intent to transfer property.** The will must have a substantive provision that disposes of property, and it must indicate your intent to make the document your final word on what happens to your property—that is, it must state that you really intend it to be a will.

- **Written.** Although oral wills, if witnessed, are permitted in limited circumstances in some states, wills usually must be written and witnessed.

- **Properly signed.** You must voluntarily sign your will, unless illness or accident or illiteracy prevents it, in which case you can direct that your lawyer or one of the witnesses sign for you. This requires a lawyer's guidance, or at least knowledge of your state's law, since an invalid signature could void a will.

- **Properly witnessed.** In almost all states, the signing of a formal will must be witnessed by at least two adults who understand what they are witnessing and are competent to testify in court. In most states, the witnesses have to be disinterested (i.e., not getting anything in your will). If they aren't, you run the risk of voiding certain provisions in the will, opening it to challenge, or invalidating the entire will.

- **Properly executed.** At the end, your will should contain a statement attesting that it is your will, the date and place of signing, and the fact that you signed it before witnesses, who then also signed it in your presence—and watched each other signing it. Most states allow so-called self-proving affidavits, which eliminate the necessity of having the witnesses go to court to testify that they witnessed the signing.

If your will doesn't meet these conditions, it might be disallowed by a court, and your estate would then be distributed according to a previous will or under your state's intestacy laws.

▶ WHAT TO INCLUDE IN YOUR FINAL INSTRUCTIONS

Your will should include

- Funeral arrangements—information about any funeral plan you've bought or account you've set up to pay burial expenses, location of cemetery and burial plot, choice of funeral director and services, and so on;

- Disposition of your body—directions specifying burial, cremation, or donation to science;

- A provision for donating certain specified organs for transplants;

- The name of any charity or cause to which you wish contributions sent in your name;

- The location of your will and the identity and telephone number of the executor and your lawyer;

- The location of any trust document and the identity of any cotrustee or successor trustee;

- The location of your safe-deposit box, the key to it, and any important records not located in the box—e.g., birth certificates; marriage, divorce, and prenuptial documents; military discharge records and your service number; important business, insurance, and financial records; and pension and benefit agreements;

- An inventory of assets, including documents relating to debts owed and loans outstanding, credit card information, any post office boxes and keys, information on any investments, household contents, bank accounts, list of expected death benefits, and so on;

- Important information: names, addresses, and dates and places of birth for you and your spouse, family members and other heirs, and ex-spouses, if any; Social Security numbers for you and your spouse and dependent children, along with the location of Social Security cards; policy numbers and telephone numbers and addresses of insurance companies and agencies that control your death benefits (employer, union, Veterans Affairs office, etc.); and

- Any information you want included in your obituary.

---

is unable or unwilling to perform. Without a backup executor, the probate court will have to appoint someone, and that person may not be to your liking.

One final caution: don't name someone as your executor unless you have spoken to that person and he or she agrees. This will ensure that the person of your choice—and not the court's—administers your estate.

Q. Can I appoint more than one executor?

A. Yes. Naming coexecutors is popular with small-business owners who name a spouse or

▶ WHAT EXECUTORS DO

The law requires an executor to be responsible for

- collecting the assets of the estate;
- protecting the estate property;
- preparing an inventory of the property;
- representing the estate in claims against others;
- paying valid claims against the estate (including taxes); and
- distributing the estate property to the beneficiaries.

These last two functions may require liquidating assets—that is, selling items like stocks, bonds, and even furniture or a car to have enough cash to pay taxes, creditors, or beneficiaries.

The will can impose additional duties on the executor that are not required by law. These include planning post-death tax strategies, choosing which specific property goes to which beneficiaries, and even investing funds.

It can be a lot of work and some of it can be complicated. However, the executor doesn't necessarily have to shoulder the entire burden. He or she can pay a professional out of the estate assets to take care of most of these functions, especially those requiring legal or financial expertise. However, this will reduce the amount that goes to the beneficiaries. Therefore, handling an estate is often a matter of balancing expertise, convenience, and cost.

relative to oversee the personal side, and a second person with business expertise to oversee the management of the business.

Naming coexecutors may be a good idea if the main beneficiary lives in a different state and is unable to make the trips necessary to handle the many details involved in administering an estate. While this person could be a coexecutor, another coexecutor living in the state in which the estate is being administered could be named to handle the day-to-day administration. Finally, don't forget to name one or more successor executors so that if a coexecutor dies or declines the position, someone else of your choice will be available.

Q. Is there anyone whom I shouldn't appoint as executor?

A. As a general rule, the executor can't be a minor, a convicted felon, or a non-U.S. citizen (although in some states a non-U.S. citizen can serve as a coexecutor with a U.S. citizen). In addition, while all states allow an out-of-state resident to act as executor, some require that the nonresident executor be a primary beneficiary or a close relative. Some states require that a nonresident executor obtain a bond or engage a resident to act as the nonresident executor's representative. For these reasons, and because handling an estate can take months and require several court appearances, it's a good idea to pick at least one executor who is a legal resident of the state where your estate will be administered.

Q. What is an "independent executor"?

A. About a dozen states permit the appointment of an **independent executor** who, after appraising the estate's assets and filing an inventory of assets with the probate court, is free to administer the estate without court intervention. This generally saves time and money. However, a court could become involved if someone challenges the independent executor's administration of the estate.

The independent executor has the power to do just about anything necessary to administer the estate. He or she can sue and be sued; settle claims made by others against your estate; deny or pay claims made by others against your estate; pay debts, taxes, and administration expenses; run a business if it is part of the estate; and distribute the assets of your estate to your beneficiaries as spelled out in your will. In some states, the independent executor can sell your property without first securing a court order to do so.

Q. How much does an executor charge for his or her services?

A. If the executor is a beneficiary—for example, a family member—he or she may choose to forgo the statutory executor's fee, but you can expect any executor who is not a beneficiary, such as a bank or a lawyer, to charge a fee. Fees vary by state and usually are set as a percentage of the estate's value. For small and mid-sized estates—estates under $200,000, for example—expect a fee of 1 to 4 percent of the total estate. Probate courts and state laws usually regulate fees.

Setting Up a Will

Q. Isn't there a set formula that dictates what goes into a will?

A. Not really. All of us have unique circumstances that resist easy, one-size-fits-all solutions. However, most wills do include clauses that address the following topics.

- **Funeral expenses and payment of debts.** Your debts don't die with you; your estate is still liable for them, and your executor has the authority to pay them off if they are valid and binding. You can also forgive any debts someone owes you by saying so in this clause. As for funeral directions and your wishes regarding anatomical donations, while you can include them in your will, be aware that the will might not be found or admitted to probate until after you're buried. It's best to put these in a separate document.

- **Gifts of personal property.** It's important to identify carefully all recipients of gifts, including their addresses and relationships to you. There are too many cases of people leaving property to "my cousin John," not realizing that more than one person might fit that description. Also remember that personal property can include intangible assets like insurance policies (e.g., if you own a policy on your spouse's life, that policy and the cash value of the premiums paid into it can be passed on through your will), bank accounts, certain employee benefits, and stock options. Finally, if you have several people whom you want to share in a gift, be careful to specify what percentage of ownership each will have. If you don't, then the court probably will presume that you intended the beneficiaries to share equally. You can save on taxes by using gifts wisely. This section of your will can also be used to give gifts to institutions and charities.

- **Executors.** By giving the executor authority to act efficiently, by saying that a surety bond will not be required, and by directing that the involvement of the probate court be kept to a minimum, you can save your family money. It helps to spell out certain powers the executor can have in dealing with your estate: to buy, lease, sell, and mortgage real estate; to borrow and lend money; and to exercise various tax options. If you run a business, be sure to give your executor specific power to continue the business—or to enter into new business arrangements.

- **Gifts of real estate.** Most people prefer that their spouses receive the family home. If the home isn't held in joint tenancy, then your will should include instructions about what will happen to it. If you die before you've paid off the mortgage on your house, then your estate normally will have to pay it off. If you're afraid this will drain the estate too much, or if you want the recipient of the house to keep paying the mortgage, you must specify that in your will. If you haven't paid off the family house, and if you're afraid your survivors can't afford to do so, then you may be able to buy mortgage-canceling insurance.

- **Residuary clause.** This is one of the most crucial parts of a will, covering all assets not specifically disposed of by other parts of the will. You probably will accumulate assets after you write your will, and if you haven't specifically given an asset to someone, it won't pass through the will—unless you have a **residuary clause** that covers everything. (If your will omits a residuary clause, the assets not left specifically to anyone would pass on through intestate succession laws; in technical terms, your estate would be **partially intestate,** with some portions passing as you specified in your will and some according to state law.) No matter how

---

▶ **WHAT IF?**

In writing your will, you should always ask, "What if?" In other words, try to figure out where a gift would go if something unexpected happened—and then account for that possibility in your will. What if a beneficiary dies before you? In that event, the gift you made to the dead person is said to **lapse** (be cancelled), and the gift goes back into your residuary estate, to be distributed to your residuary beneficiary. (See the discussion of residuary clauses above.)

However, most states have **antilapse statutes.** These statutes provide that if a beneficiary related to you predeceases you, then that beneficiary's descendants would receive the gift (particularly gifts of real and personal property). So if you left your shoe collection to your daughter Imelda, and she died before you did, in a state with an antilapse statute the shoes would go to Imelda's descendants. In a state without an antilapse statute, it would go to whomever you had named to receive your residuary estate. If Imelda were your best friend and not your daughter, then the antilapse statute would not apply.

small your residuary estate seems, you should almost always leave it to the person you most care about.

- **Trusts.** In a trust clause, you can set up a testamentary trust in your will, or have your will direct funds from your estate into a trust you had previously established (which would make your will a pourover will).

Q. How do I make gifts of personal property in a will?

A. A **tangible personal property memorandum** (**TPPM**) (or tangible personal property direction) is a separate handwritten document that is incorporated into the will by reference, is dated, and contains lists of tangible personal property (e.g., jewelry, artwork, furniture) and the people to whom you want the property to go.

This means that the will says something like, "This will incorporates the provisions of a separate Tangible Personal Property Memorandum . . ." Then the TPPM is regarded as part of the will. Some states recognize the validity of such a signed instrument. Some require it to be in existence when the will is signed, and will not give effect to changes made after the will is signed. If you use a TPPM, it's important to remember to make provisions for what happens to any of the property listed if the person who is in line to receive it should die before you, and if you neglect to adjust the TPPM accordingly before your death. Often, the reference in the will

---

▶ **GENERAL OR SPECIFIC? IT DEPENDS**

In making gifts of specific property, you should be certain to identify the property carefully to avoid disputes about which items you meant. For example, specify "my grandmother's three-carat diamond engagement ring" or "the portrait of my grandfather." Such language is advisable when the item is valuable or a dispute about the property is expected.

Generally speaking, however, it is preferable to make gifts of broad categories of property. For example, a category can be used if the meaning is clear—"all my jewelry." Similarly, "all my tangible personal property" has a reasonably clear legal meaning. This covers the possibility that you dispose of some items and acquire others between the time you write the will and the time you die. Another example of this kind of general bequest would be to leave your son not "my 1986 Yugo" but "the car I own when I die." The same applies to stocks or bank accounts—the bank may be taken over by another bank, or the stock may be sold. Better to include a general description or leave a dollar amount or fractional share.

And if you're trying to leave your children equal values of different kinds of property that's liable to fluctuate in value (say, a stock portfolio or real estate), then you might add a clause to the will that specifies that if one asset turns out to be worth more than the other, the difference will be made up between the children.

specifies that the gifts should go to still-living recipients.

In addition, the reference in the will often states that if no TPPM is found within sixty days of the will maker's death, that is conclusive evidence that the TPPM does not exist. This provision means that the estate can be settled in a timely manner, without waiting indefinitely for something that may never turn up.

Q. Where should I keep my will?

A. Keep it in a safe place, such as your lawyer's office, a fireproof safe at home, or a safe-deposit box. If you do keep your will in a safe-deposit box, make sure to provide that the executor can access the will when you die. Also, keep in mind that some jurisdictions require a decedent's safe-deposit box to be sealed immediately after death until certain legal requirements have been satisfied.

Q. What other estate documents should I keep with the will?

A. You should keep a record of other estate-planning documents with your will, such as trust documents, IRAs, insurance policies, income savings plans such as 401(k) plans, stocks and bonds, and retirement plans.

REMEMBER THIS

- Even though you may not have a lot of assets, or even if you plan to use a living trust or other means of transferring your property to others after you die, you still need a will.

- Most of the time, you can leave your property to whomever you want under whatever conditions you desire. However, the law does impose some limits on this freedom. Your lawyer can inform you about these limits before you write your will.

▶ PROPERTY THAT DOES NOT PASS VIA A WILL

- Property held in joint tenancy
- Life insurance payable to a named beneficiary
- Property held in a trust
- Retirement plans payable to named beneficiaries, including IRAs, Keogh accounts, and pensions
- Bank accounts payable to named beneficiaries upon the death of the depositor
- Transfer-on-death stock accounts payable to a named beneficiary
- Some community property
- Income savings plans

- To be valid, a will generally has to meet a number of criteria. It has to be made by someone of legal age and sound mind. It has to be intended to transfer property. And it has to be written, properly signed, witnessed, and executed.

- Take care in the selection of your executor, since that person will be charged with carrying out the directions you give in the will. For most estates, you may want to consider making the primary beneficiary the executor.

- There is no set formula that dictates what goes into a will. Key clauses typically cover the payment of debts, gifts of property, the naming of an executor, and the disposal of assets that you may acquire after the will is written. Also, your will should give directions for what will happen if one or more of your beneficiaries dies before you do.

TRUSTS AND LIVING TRUSTS

This section covers trusts and living trusts, their advantages, their requirements, and your options among different types of trusts.

Q. What is a trust?

A. A **trust** is a legal relationship in which one person or qualified trust company (the **trustee**) holds property for the benefit of another (the **beneficiary**). The property can be any kind of real or personal property—money, real estate, stocks, collections, business interests, or personal possessions.

A trust generally involves at least three people: the **grantor** (the person who creates the trust, also known as the **settlor** or the **donor**), the trustee (who holds and manages the property for the benefit of the grantor and others), and one or more beneficiaries (who are entitled to the benefits).

Putting property in trust transfers it from your personal ownership to that of the trustee who holds the property for you. The trustee has **legal title** to the trust property. For most purposes, the law looks at these assets as if the trustee now owned them. For example, many (but not all) trusts have their own taxpayer identification numbers.

But trustees are not the full owners of the property. Trustees have a legal duty to use the property as provided in the trust agreement and as permitted by law. The beneficiaries retain what is known as **equitable title** or **beneficial title,** meaning the right to benefit from the property as specified in the trust.

Q. When are trusts set up?

A. Many trusts are set up in wills—these are called **testamentary trusts**—and take effect upon death. Others can be established while you are still alive (see below).

Q. If I create a trust, I no longer own the property—the trustee does. This is profoundly unsettling to me. How can I be sure that the property won't be misappropriated?

A. The trust instrument itself, together with hundreds of years of legal cases and the current law in your state, provide rules for how the trustee must act. In legal terms, this spells out the trustee's duties with respect to the trust property. To assuage your doubts, you might ask your lawyer to explain the trustee's duties and your legal rights.

Q. Why do people use trusts?

A. The reasons vary. For example, parents might use a trust to manage assets for the benefit of minor children in the event the parents die before the children reach the age of legal adulthood. The trustee can decide how best to carry out the parents' wishes that the money be used for education, support, and health care.

A trust is a good idea for anyone who is unable to manage money and assets prudently. For someone who is unable to manage his or her estate because of mental or physical incapacity, a trust is an effective way to avoid the expense and undesirable aspects of a court-appointed guardian.

Q. Should I consider setting up a trust?

A. It depends on the size of your estate and what you want to do with it. For example, if

> ▶ **SPENDTHRIFT TRUSTS**

Trusts are handy tools if you aren't certain that a beneficiary can handle the money he or she will receive. They can be written to prevent a beneficiary from squandering the money, typically by limiting the income the beneficiary receives and by making it difficult or impossible for the beneficiary to access the assets contained in the trust. A trust written with these protections and established for such a beneficiary is sometimes known as a **spendthrift trust.**

you are primarily interested in protecting yourself in the event you become unable to manage your estate, then a living trust is a good option. If you want to provide for minor children, grandchildren, or a disabled relative, then a trust might be appropriate. Before making a decision, consult an estate lawyer.

Q. What are some of the possible downsides of trusts?

A. There are several possible disadvantages to trusts.

- **Hassle.** Besides the hassle of preparing the trust document itself, if the trust is a living trust, you will have to transfer all of the assets specified in the trust document to the trustee. This can require executing deeds or bills of sale, submitting tax forms, re-titling assets, and other registration procedures. You have to be sure to keep transactions involving your trust separate from those involving property owned in your own name. After creating the trust, each time you buy, inherit, or otherwise acquire an asset that you don't want subject to probate, you have to remember to buy it in the name of the trustee or transfer it to the trustee.

- **Cost.** While a lawyer isn't required for setting up a trust, it's usually a good idea to work with one. A trust generally costs more than a will to prepare. In addition, there may be an annual management fee, particularly if the trustee is a bank or a trust company. (However, if all of your property is in trust so that there is no estate to probate at your death, these higher initial costs may be offset later.) Depending on the state in which the property is located, putting your home in a living trust might jeopardize a homestead exemption, require a transfer fee, or cause your property to be reassessed for property tax purposes. Moreover, a revocable living trust will not reduce estate taxes.

- **Unresponsiveness to family changes.** In some states, a revocable living trust, unlike a will, is not automatically revoked or amended in the event of divorce. This means that, if you don't amend the trust, your ex-spouse could end up being the beneficiary.

- **Conflicts.** Beneficiaries often prefer riskier, higher-income investments than trustees, who have a duty to preserve the original assets of the trust as well as the duty to invest the assets prudently. Conflict of this sort is especially likely to occur if the trust is designed for the benefit of more than one generation. Conflicts also might arise among different classes of beneficiaries. For example, your child may be the current beneficiary, with your grandchildren becoming beneficiaries after your child dies. In this situation, your child and grandchildren may have conflicting interests in the trust. As the creator of the trust, you can minimize any conflict by clearly stating in the trust document whose interests are paramount.

Living Trusts

Q. What is a living trust?

A. A **living trust** (also known as an **inter vivos trust**) is simply a trust established while you are still alive. It can serve as a partial will substitute. Upon the death of the person creating the trust, property is distributed as specified in the trust document to the beneficiaries, who are also specified in the document.

As in other kinds of trusts, there are potentially three parties to a living trust (creator, trustee, and beneficiary, though in many living trusts all three are the same person). If you set up a **revocable living trust** (see the sidebar definition of this term on the next page) with yourself as trustee, you retain the rights of ownership you'd have if the assets were still in your name. You can buy anything and add it to the trust, sell anything out of the trust, and give trust property to whomever you wish.

Q. How do I know whether a living trust is right for me and my estate?

A. A trust is likely to help if

- Your estate has substantial property or assets that are difficult or costly to dispose of using a will.
- You don't want the task of managing your property (e.g., because you rent out a number of condos). A living trust allows you to transfer those duties to your trustee

while you continue to receive the income, minus the trustee's fee (if any).

- You want your estate administered by someone who doesn't live in your state. A living trust might be better than a will because the trustee probably won't have to meet the residency requirements that some states impose upon executors.
- You own property in another state. Many lawyers recommend setting up a living trust to hold the title to that property. This helps you avoid additional probate procedures in another state, called **ancillary probate** procedures, which can be complicated.

Q. What exactly can a living trust do for me?

A. The flexibility of trusts makes them useful for many different people with all kinds of needs. In addition, trusts can do a number of things wills can't do, such as

- manage assets efficiently if you should die while your beneficiaries are minors;
- protect your privacy (unlike a will, trusts are confidential);
- provide a way to care for you if you should become disabled;
- avoid probate on assets held in the trust;
- speed transfer of your assets to beneficiaries after your death; and
- provide more options than a simple will (living trusts give you wide flexibility in distributing your property).

In addition, depending on how they're written and depending on state law, trusts can serve asset protection needs—for example, by protecting your assets from creditors—and, with proper planning, may reduce taxes. However, this usually requires the trust to be irrevocable, unlike most living trusts, and may require special steps.

Q. *What can't a living trust do for me?*

A. A living trust is a very important estate-planning tool. But it can't do everything. Here's a summary of what a living trust can't do.

- **It won't necessarily help you avoid taxes.** A revocable living trust doesn't save any income or estate taxes that couldn't also be saved by a properly prepared will. Trust property still is counted

---

> ▶ **REVOCABLE AND IRREVOCABLE TRUSTS**

A trust can be **revocable**—that is, subject to change or termination; or **irrevocable**—that is, difficult to change or terminate. Most living trusts are revocable, but you have the option of making yours irrevocable.

A revocable trust gives the creator great flexibility but no tax advantages. An irrevocable trust is the other side of the coin—it has less flexibility but considerable tax benefits, as such trusts often minimize federal and state taxation. In addition, an irrevocable trust may protect trust property from the creditors of the trust creator. However, an irrevocable trust often doesn't avoid taxes entirely. Because it can be difficult to balance the costs and benefits of an irrevocable trust, it's wise to consult with an estate-planning lawyer before you proceed.

---

as part of your estate for the purposes of federal and state income and estate taxes. Your successor trustee still has to pay income taxes generated by trust property and owed at your death. (Your executor would have to pay such taxes out of your estate if the property was controlled by a will.) And if the estate is large enough to trigger federal or state estate or inheritance taxes, then your trustee will be required to file the appropriate tax returns. These and other duties can make the cost of administering an estate distributed by a revocable living trust almost as high as traditional estate administration, at least in some states.

- **It won't make a will unnecessary.** You still need a will to take care of assets not included in the trust. If you have minor children, you also need a will to suggest or nominate a guardian for them. While only a court can appoint a guardian, courts strive to implement your wishes in this regard if you have stated them.
- **It won't affect nonprobate assets.** Like a will, a living trust won't control the disposition of jointly owned property, life insurance, pension benefits or retirement plans payable to a beneficiary, or other nonprobate property.
- **It won't necessarily protect your assets from creditors.** Creditors can attach the assets of a revocable living trust. In fact, since the assets you place in a living trust don't have to be probated, they could lose the protection of the statute of limitations, which means that your creditors will have longer to get at them.
- **It won't necessarily protect your assets from disgruntled relatives.** While it is sometimes harder to challenge a living

trust than a will, a relative can still bring suit to challenge the trust on grounds of fraud, undue influence, or duress.

- **It won't entirely eliminate delays.** A living trust might well lessen the time it takes to distribute your assets after you die, but it won't completely eliminate delays. Many states impose a waiting period that must expire before creditors can file claims against the estates of people with living trusts. The trustee still has to collect any debts owed to your estate after you die, prepare tax returns, pay bills, and distribute assets, just as would the executor of a will. All this takes time.

Q. Why doesn't a revocable living trust save taxes?

A. When you put property in a revocable living trust, the trustee becomes its owner. But you retain the right to use and enjoy the property and, because you do, the tax law deems the property in the trust to be yours for tax purposes. Thus, if the trust receives income from the assets, you must report the income from the trust on your individual income tax return.

Q. Can a living trust help if I become disabled?

A. Yes. You can set up a living trust, name a reliable co- or successor trustee to manage the property in the trust should you become ill, and fund the trust adequately by transferring title of assets to the trustee (or give someone you trust the power of attorney to do so in the event of your incapacity). This avoids the delay and red tape of expensive, court-ordered guardianship. And, at the same time, the trustee can take over any duties you had to provide for other family members. (For more information, see Chapter 16, "The Rights of Older Americans.")

▶ **YOU MAY NOT BENEFIT FROM A LIVING TRUST IF . . .**

1. Your state's probate system has simple and easy procedures for administering estates your size.
2. You're young and healthy and don't have a lot of money. A will can usually take care of the immediate needs of a young family. You can think about a trust when you have children and your assets have grown.
3. You are not rich, but re-registering all of your assets would cost more than it's worth. For example, you might own a number of properties, none particularly valuable, but all of the property would require re-titling if placed into a trust.

Q. Once I put my property in a revocable living trust, can I still manage it or sell it?

A. Yes. In a revocable living trust, you retain the right to manage the trust property. This right includes the right to sell any of the property you placed into the trust.

Other Kinds of Trusts

Q. What other kinds of trusts are there?

A. There are many other kinds of trusts that serve particular needs. Here's a brief rundown of some of the most popular types of trusts. Your lawyer can help you decide if they're right for you—and, if so, can help you set one up.

- **Support trusts** direct the trustee to spend only as much income and principal as may be needed for the education, health care, and general support of the beneficiary.
- **Discretionary trusts** permit the trustee to distribute income and principal among various beneficiaries as he or she sees fit.
- **Charitable trusts** support a charitable purpose. Often, these trusts will make an annual gift to a worthy cause of your choosing.
- **Dynasty trusts** (also sometimes called **wealth trusts**) can last for a number of generations, and sometimes can last forever. They can help those with great fortunes control the distribution of their wealth over a very long period.
- **Generation-skipping trusts** are tax-saving trusts that benefit several generations of your descendants.
- **Insurance trusts** are used to avoid (or at least minimize) federal and state estate taxes on the proceeds of life insurance. Here, trust assets are used to buy a life insurance policy whose proceeds benefit the creator's beneficiaries.
- **Special-needs trusts** are for people with disabilities who want to keep their government benefits. **Medicaid trusts** are a particular kind of special-needs trust. They help you qualify for federal Medicaid benefits. This device is mostly used when family members are concerned with paying the costs of nursing-home care.

Setting Up and Maintaining a Trust

Q. Who can advise me about setting up a living trust?

A. Your lawyer may be the obvious choice, but that's not your only option. Most banks provide trust services. Of course, the bank's setup and management fees can add up, and could exceed the cost of probating your estate. In addition, the bank may insist on managing the trust, which means that you won't be in control. Be sure to weigh these factors before deciding to use a bank as your trustee.

For people with more assets or people who don't want the uncertainty and work of writing and funding their own trust, it's definitely wise to work with a lawyer. It's especially good to have a lawyer's assistance in determining which assets to put into the trust and which to dispose of through a will.

Q. How do I choose a lawyer to help me set up a trust?

A. First, make sure the lawyer you select has expertise in trust-and-estate law in your state, and is willing to work with you to tailor the trust to your particular needs; otherwise, the primary benefit of a trust—its flexibility—might be lost. A knowledgeable lawyer will provide you with the expertise necessary to ensure that the trust property is preserved and, where possible, is invested wisely to ensure that the assets placed in the trust actually grow in value.

Second, because trusts have tax consequences and are scrutinized closely by the IRS, choose a lawyer who understands the interplay between various types of trusts and their tax obligations.

Q. I just received a call from someone claiming to sell living trusts. Should I buy one?

A. No. A number of dubious companies, playing on people's fears of probate and suspicions about lawyers, have taken to selling living-trust kits door-to-door, by mail, or through seminars. Often, they exaggerate the costs and difficulties of the probate process, even though probate procedures and fees in many states, especially for simple estates, are increasingly manageable. Authorities in several states have filed consumer fraud suits against these promoters for deceiving consumers.

Most lawyers and financial advisers urge you to avoid such pitches. The products seldom live up to their touts and often cost $2,500 or more—far above what you'd typically pay to get a good personalized trust prepared by a lawyer. Because living trusts should be crafted to fit your particular situation, it's next to impossible to find a prepackaged one that will suit your needs as well as one prepared by your lawyer.

Q. What are the requirements for setting up a living trust?

A. Requirements for setting up a living trust vary with each state. In general, you execute a document saying that you're creating a trust to hold property for your benefit and that of any other designated beneficiary. Some trust declarations list the major assets (home, investments, and so on) that you're putting into trust; others refer to another document (a **schedule**) in which you list the exact property that will be in the trust. In either case, you can add and subtract property whenever you want. You will have to change ownership registration on all property put into the trust— deeds, brokerage accounts, stocks or bonds, bank accounts, and so on—from your own name to the name of the trustee (for example, "Brett Campbell, Trustee of the John A. Smith Trust"). If you make yourself the trustee, you will have to transfer the ownership registrations to yourself as trustee, and

remember to sign yourself in trust transactions as "John A. Smith, Trustee," instead of using only your name.

Q. How do I put money and other assets in a living trust?

A. Setting up the trust is actually the easy part. The harder part is putting something into the trust—i.e., funding the trust. This includes not just depositing money in the trust account, but also transferring title of the assets to the name of the trustee.

Living trusts can be funded while you're living or after you're dead. If you want to fund a living trust before you die (a funded trust), you transfer title of your assets to the trustee, and make the trustee the owner of any newly acquired assets you want to include in the trust.

Many people choose to fund their trusts through a will. To do this, you set up a revocable trust and a pourover will, which transfers the assets to the trustee upon your death. You can transfer some assets to the trustee before you die, but generally, the will specifies that all estate property "pours over" into the trust, including any life insurance and other death benefits.

Obviously, you can't avoid probate this way. But funding a trust with a will is an option for people who don't want to go through the hassle of funding a living trust while they're alive, but also don't want their after-death gifts to be a matter of public record. These people can give their estate to a trust via their wills, and specify named beneficiaries through the privacy of the trust.

Q. How do I transfer titles to the trust?

A. Take a copy of the trust agreement to your bank, stockbroker, mortgage and title insurance companies, and anyone else who controls title to your assets. Then request a transfer of ownership to the trustee. Make sure you keep a record of these transfers; it will make your successor trustee's job much easier.

Q. Are there any assets I should leave out of my trust?

A. Likely, yes. The special tax treatment given to individual retirement accounts (IRAs) might encourage you to leave them in your own name. Similarly, the fees your state charges to transfer title of a mortgage or other property could make the cost of that transfer prohibitive. You might want to hold off on transferring your home to the trust until the mortgage is paid off or one spouse dies. Some people worry about taking the family home out of the husband and wife's names in joint tenancy and putting it into a living trust in the name of one of the spouses. In such cases, a lawyer may suggest putting the living trust in both your names—for example, "The Stephen and Diana Hogg Trust," with both spouses as cotrustees.

If the trust is in one name only, and the other spouse is not a cotrustee or successor trustee, then many lawyers recommend leaving some property—for example, a sizable bank account—outside the trust. If you use a bank account, it should be in the names of both spouses so that if one should die, the other will have access to the funds. However, a word of caution is in order. The law in some states will freeze such accounts for a specified period of time after the death of the cosignatory. Consult your lawyer to get the specifics.

Finally, keeping a few assets out of the living trust can help protect against creditors' claims down the line. When your estate contains some property and goes through pro-

bate, it triggers the running of the statute of limitations on claims against your entire estate. Creditors are put on notice that you have died and, once the statutory period expires, the estate is safe from most creditors' claims.

The important point: Be sure to go through each of your assets with your lawyer to determine whether it's wise to transfer that asset to the trust.

Q. Whom should I pick as trustee?

A. A trustee's duties can continue for generations and, in many cases, require expertise in collecting estate assets, investing money, paying bills, filing periodic accountings, and managing money for beneficiaries.

The biggest decision to make in designating a trustee is whether to use a family member, a professional trustee, or both. Many trust creators choose a family member as a trustee. A family member usually won't charge a fee and, generally, has a personal stake in the trust's success. If the family member is competent to handle the financial matters involved, has the time and interest to do so, and if you're not afraid of family conflicts, then naming a family member as trustee may be a good move, particularly for a small or medium-sized estate.

A professional trustee, such as a bank, will charge a management fee. In some cases, such fees can be substantial. Professional trustees also have been criticized for being impersonal in their dealings with beneficiaries who require, or at least desire, more personal attention. On the other hand, a professional trustee is immortal, unlikely to take sides in family conflicts, and commands the kind of investment and money-management expertise that a lay trustee may not. Particularly if you have a large estate, give serious consideration to a professional trustee.

Q. Can I name more than one trustee?

A. Yes. Many trust creators name cotrustees. For example, when a married couple decides to establish a trust, the spouse creating the trust often names himself or herself as one cotrustee and the spouse as the second cotrustee. As a further protection, the creator can name a successor trustee who would manage the trust in the event that one or both of the cotrustees dies or resigns as trustee.

Q. How can I reduce the costs of a revocable living trust?

A. By doing some preparation, you can minimize the time a lawyer spends setting up the trust, and thus reduce your legal costs. As with making a will, ask your lawyer what doc-

---

▶ SOME RESPONSIBILITIES OF THE SUCCESSOR TRUSTEE

If you have become the successor trustee because of the death of the original trustee

- obtain a copy of the deceased trustee's death certificate, as well a copy of the trust creator's death certificate if the creator has died;

- inform the trust creator's family that you are the successor trustee;

- ensure that each trust beneficiary has a copy of the trust document;

- inform all financial institutions holding trust assets that you are the new trustee;

- collect and pay all taxes and other debts;

- monitor all income;

- make sure there is an accurate inventory of all trust property;

- ensure that the trust property has been or will be distributed to beneficiaries;

- prepare and file all appropriate tax returns; and

- prepare a final accounting and distribute the assets from the trust to all beneficiaries.

If you become a successor trustee because the creator of the trust, who was also the trustee, has become incapacitated

- obtain a medical opinion confirming the creator-trustee's incapacity;

- inform the family of the trust creator that you are his or her successor trustee;

- provide each beneficiary with a copy of the trust document;

- inform all financial institutions holding trust property that you are the successor trustee;

- pay all taxes and debts; and

- monitor all income.

uments are important. After collecting the necessary records, deeds, bank statements, and so on, make a list of your assets and where you want them to go when you die. If you take over the task of transferring assets, that will save the lawyer time—and you money.

Q. What happens to the property in the trust when I die?

A. When you die, your trustee distributes the property according to the terms of the trust.

Q. How does a trust end?

A. A trust often terminates when the principal is distributed to the beneficiaries, at the time stated in the trust agreement. For example, you might provide that a trust for the benefit of your children would end when the youngest child reaches a certain age. At that time, the trustee would distribute the assets to the beneficiaries according to your instructions. The law generally allows a "windup phase" to complete the administration of trust duties (e.g., filing tax returns) after the trust has officially terminated.

You can also give your trustees the discretion to distribute the trust assets and terminate the trust when they think it's a good idea, or place some restrictions on their ability to do so. For example, you could allow the trustees to terminate the trust at their discretion, provided that your child has completed his or her education.

Q. What about irrevocable trusts? How do they end?

A. Your trust should have a termination provision even if it is an irrevocable trust. **Irrevocability** means that you, the donor, can't change your mind about how you want the trust to terminate. It doesn't mean that you can't set up termination procedures in the first place.

If you have an irrevocable trust and don't have a termination provision, then the trust can usually terminate only if all beneficiaries consent and if no material purpose of the trust is defeated. However, an irrevocable trust can also be terminated if there was fraud, duress, undue influence, or other problems when the trust was set up; if the operation of the trust becomes impracticable or illegal; or if the period of time specified by state law expires. We're obviously into technical territory here, but the basic rule is this: Don't set up an irrevocable trust unless you're prepared to live—and die—by its terms.

REMEMBER THIS

- Trusts come in many different forms. Some help with reducing estate taxes; others fund the education of children and grandchildren, or help provide for people with disabilities or those who might have trouble managing their own affairs; still others fund charities.

- Trusts can also provide protection from your beneficiaries' creditors.

- If a trust is right for you, be sure it's funded properly and complies with all legal requirements in your state.

- A living trust can be a useful device—but it doesn't work automatically and all by itself. You have to make sure that it's funded, which probably entails re-titling assets and adding newly acquired assets to the trust. You also should name one or more successor trustees, who can take over for you in the event of your incapacity or death.

- Be sure to coordinate your living trust with the rest of your estate plan—i.e., with your will, insurance policies, pensions, IRAs, and other instruments for transferring property.

- A trust must be maintained after it's set up—that is, by making sure the beneficiary designations are up-to-date.

OTHER ESTATE-PLANNING ASSETS AND TOOLS

Too many people don't understand that there's more to estate planning than writing a will. This section will tell you what else you might need to do in order to plan your estate effectively.

Q. Isn't a will enough to cover my estate-planning needs?

A. A will is usually the most important document in your estate plan, but it doesn't cover everything. In the community property states (see the community property discussion on page 677), your will can only control half of most marital assets. Other benefits not controlled by a will (or by a trust being used as a will substitute) include IRAs, insurance policies, income savings plans, retirement plans, and property held in joint tenancy.

A good estate plan must coordinate these benefits with your will. Use them well, and you can give money to your beneficiaries much more efficiently than you can with a will. Use them poorly, and you can negate your estate plan and frustrate your wishes.

Q. My wife and I own our house in joint tenancy. Can I use joint tenancy to pass property without having to draw up a will?

A. Yes. Joint tenancy is a form of co-ownership. If you and your wife buy a house or a car in both your names and as joint tenants, then each of you is a co-owner. When one of the co-owners dies, joint ownership usually gives the other co-owner instant access to the jointly held property.

For more information on joint tenancy and other forms of ownership, such as tenancy in common, see Chapter 8, "Home Ownership."

Q. Besides using a will or trust, are there other ways to give money to minor children?

A. Yes. The most common way is through the Uniform Gift to Minors Act (UGMA) or the Uniform Transfers to Minors Act (UTMA), which are straightforward enough that you may be able to make a gift without consulting a lawyer. These statutes allow you to open an account in a child's name and deposit money or property in it. If the child is over age thirteen, the income is taxed at his or her tax rate, which almost certainly will be lower than yours. For younger children, the government taxes the income at your tax rate.

Q. How can I use life insurance in my estate plan?

A. Life insurance can be a very good estate-planning tool, because you pay relatively little up front, and your beneficiaries can get much more when you die. When you name beneficiaries other than your estate, the money passes to them directly, without probate.

Life insurance often is used to pay the im-

▶ TEN SITUATIONS IN WHICH YOU DON'T WANT TO USE A JOINT TENANCY

1. When you don't want to lose control. By giving someone co-ownership, you give him or her co-control. If you make your son co-owner of your house, then you can't sell or mortgage it unless he agrees.

2. When the co-owner's creditors might come after the money. Your co-owner's creditors may be able to get part of the house or any bank account held in joint tenancy.

3. When you can't be sure of your co-owner. You and your co-owner could have a falling-out, and he or she would still have rights to any property held jointly.

4. When you're using co-ownership to substitute for a will. Often, parents with several children will put one child's name on an account, assuming that child will divide the money equally among the other children. But this method provides no control. The surviving joint tenant can do with it as he or she pleases.

5. When it might cause confusion after your death. Unplanned ownership of property often leads to unwanted results—especially for people unable to manage assets.

6. When it won't speed the transfer of assets. Some states automatically freeze jointly owned accounts upon the death of one of the owners until the tax authorities can examine it. As a result, the surviving owner can't count on getting to the money immediately.

7. When it compromises tax planning. Careful planning to minimize taxes on an estate can be completely thwarted by an inadvertently created joint tenancy that passes property outright to the surviving tenant.

8. When you're in a shaky marriage. Your individual property may become marital property once it's transferred into joint tenancy.

9. When one of the joint tenants could become incompetent. If this happens, part of the property may go into a conservatorship, making it cumbersome at best if the other joint tenant wants to sell some or all of the jointly held property.

10. When you don't want to transfer assets all at once. Joint tenancies deprive you of the flexibility of a will or trust, in which you can use gifts and asset shifts to minimize taxes or pay out money over time to beneficiaries instead of giving it to them all at once.

If the value of your estate falls below the federal estate tax level, joint tenancy might not be such a bad idea. However, keep in mind that most of the advantages of joint tenancy can also be achieved using a revocable living trust.

mediate costs of death (e.g., funeral or hospital expenses), set up a fund to support the deceased's family so they won't have to return to work immediately after the death, replace the deceased's lost income, pay for the deceased's children's education, and so on.

You can use life insurance to distribute assets among children from different marriages. And you can set up an irrevocable trust for your children that's funded with the life insurance policy. You pay the premiums, but the trust actually owns the policy. When you die, your children receive the benefits from the trust, while your spouse gets the rest of your estate.

Q. How do retirement benefits affect my estate plan?

A. Many of us are entitled to retirement benefits from an employer. Typically, a retirement plan will pay benefits to beneficiaries if they die before reaching retirement age. After retirement, you can usually pick an option that will continue payments to a beneficiary after your death. In most cases, the law requires that some portion of these retirement benefits be paid to your spouse. This right may be waived only with your spouse's properly witnessed, signed consent.

IRAs (individual retirement accounts) provide a ready means of cash when one spouse dies. If your spouse is named as the beneficiary, then the proceeds immediately will become his or her property when you die. Like retirement benefits (and unlike assets covered by a will), they will pass to the named beneficiary without having to go through probate. As the rules governing IRAs can and do change, check with a lawyer to see how such plans can best be coordinated with your estate plan.

Q. Do prenuptial agreements play a role in estate planning?

A. Any couple in a situation where one partner has a lot more money or property than the other, or where one partner is substantially older than the other, should consider entering into a prenuptial agreement as part of their estate planning.

Older people with grown children from another marriage may want their property to go to their own children after they die, rather than to the new spouse and his or her children. A prenuptial agreement can accomplish this purpose. See Chapter 3, "Family Law," for more information about prenuptial agreements.

Q. I live in a community property state. How does this affect my estate plan?

A. In community property states, most property acquired during the marriage by either spouse is held equally by both as community property—that is, as property belonging to both spouses. The major exceptions are property acquired during the marriage by inheritance or gift. In a community property state, when one spouse dies, his or her half of the property passes either by will or operation of law; the other half of the property belongs to the surviving spouse.

If you live in a community property state, you can only dispose of your half of the community property via a will or a trust. If you and your spouse have the same estate-planning objectives, there's no problem. But if you don't, living in a community property state could make it more difficult to meet your estate-planning goals.

Q. I live in a separate-property state, but own property in a community property state. Which law applies?

A. If the property is real estate, state laws may treat that real estate as community property for estate-planning purposes. Thus, if you live in Arkansas (a separate-property state) but own land in Texas (a community property state), an Arkansas court probating your will would treat the Texas property just as Texas would—as community property. But not every state would extend the same treatment.

This property division can get complicated—and this is only one example of how state laws differ. If you own property in more than one state, consult an estate-planning lawyer who is conversant in the estate laws of each state.

Q. Should I give some of my property away before I die?

A. Making gifts during your lifetime can be a good idea, especially if you have a large estate. Such gifts can help you avoid high estate and inheritance taxes. In some states, they might enable you to reduce your estate to one that is small enough to avoid formal probate. Another advantage of giving property away before you die is that you get to see the recipient's appreciation of your generosity.

But watch out for pitfalls. Such gifts will be subject to gift taxes if they're larger than the amount allowed by law. Current law allows you to give away up to $12,000 per person per year ($24,000, if a couple makes the gift) before the gift tax applies. You can make gifts to any number of people, whether related to you or not. You can also make gifts to trusts, but keep in mind that not all trust gifts qualify for this exclusion.

Your will should clearly state that any gifts made before you die are not to be considered advances—if that is your intent. Without such a clear statement, the probate courts in some states may subtract the amount of any gifts from the amount left to a person in your will.

When Circumstances Change

Q. Once I've planned my estate, do I have to worry about it again?

A. Most definitely, yes. Life does not stand still. After you've crafted your initial estate plan, your circumstances are likely to change—you may have more children or grandchildren, acquire more assets, or have a falling-out with your spouse, other relatives, or friends you've named as beneficiaries. Other major changes in your life or in your financial situation might include the purchase of a new house, divorce or remarriage, moving to another state, a variation in income, death of relatives, and so on. Life changes like this may occasion changes in your estate plan.

Every three or four years, it's a good idea to review your will or trust document, along with your inventory of assets and list of beneficiaries, to make sure your past decisions continue to meet your current needs. Think of estate planning not as a one-time transaction, but as a process that works best if periodically reviewed.

Q. How do I change my will after it has been executed?

A. You can change, add to, or even revoke your will at any time before your death, as long as you are physically and mentally com-

> ▶ **STEPFAMILIES**

If you're part of an older couple in which both of you have children from previous marriages, then you might want to arrange things so your own money goes to your children and your spouse's money goes to his or her children. The versatility of a revocable living trust makes it a useful instrument for allocating assets among different families. You can set up a separate trust for the children of different marriages, or even for each family member. Some families use **qualified terminable-interest property trusts** (known as **QTIP trusts**) to address the special concerns of stepfamilies. This type of trust allows you to do several things: (1) leave your property in trust for your spouse during your spouse's lifetime; (2) give the trust property to another person (or persons) of your choice after your spouse's death; and (3) reduce estate taxes. Talk to your lawyer about the details of such a trust.

petent to make the change. An amendment to a will is called a **codicil.**

However, if you want such changes to be effective, you can't simply cross out old provisions in your will and scribble in new ones. You have to formally execute a codicil, using the same procedures that were used when you executed the will itself. The codicil should be dated and kept with the will. It's a good idea to check with your lawyer before signing a codicil or revoking your will.

Q. When and how should I revoke my will entirely?

A. Sometimes when you have a major life change, such as a divorce or a remarriage, winning the lottery, having more children, or getting the last child out of the house, it's a good idea to rewrite your will from scratch rather than making a lot of small changes. You can do this by executing a formal statement of revocation and executing a new will that revokes the old.

If you write a new will, be sure to include the date it's signed and executed and include a sentence to the effect that the new will revokes all previous wills. Otherwise, a court might rule that the new will only revokes the old one to the extent that the two documents conflict.

Q. What happens if I fail to keep my will up-to-date?

A. Some life changes may be accommodated by the law, regardless of what your will says. For example, if you have a new child, and if your will doesn't explicitly say that you don't want him or her to inherit anything, then the law generally will put that child in the same position as the children included in your will. So if you split your estate evenly between two children and don't provide for a child born after the will was made, then the court could give each child a third of the estate.

If you don't include your new spouse in the will (or the spouse you've had for years, for that matter), then he or she has the right to take a share of the estate. This typically varies from between 33 to 50 percent, depending on state law. If the spouse does not elect to take a

▶ DIVORCE AND YOUR ESTATE PLAN

Depending on your state's law, a divorce may revoke your will in its entirety, or those provisions of your will that favored your former spouse. Either way, be sure to revise your will or write a new one after the divorce, changing the provisions that relate to your former spouse and his or her family. Also be sure to modify other related documents such as living wills, survivorships, and insurance policies.

Trusts may need to be specifically amended, and names of trustees changed if they were members of your ex-spouse's family. Settlement negotiations at the time of the divorce should address all of these issues.

---

share of the estate, then the property is distributed as specified in your will.

Q. What about property that I acquire after I write my will?

A. If you come into property that is not accounted for by the will, it becomes part of your **residuary estate.** If you have a residuary clause in your will, you can specify which person or institution should get everything not specifically identified in the will.

But even if you have a residuary clause, it's best to modify your will periodically to account for life changes or "after-acquired assets." If you don't, you run the risk of paying higher taxes, giving certain property to people you don't want to have it, or creating confusion (and possibly probate delays or even litigation).

Q. Besides my will, are there other documents I should update?

A. Yes. Other estate-planning documents you should keep up-to-date include IRAs, insurance policies, income savings plans such as 401(k) plans, government savings bonds (if payable to another person), and retirement plans. You should keep a record of these documents with your will, and update them whenever you update your will.

Q. What if I set up a revocable living trust, then change my mind about it?

A. You can modify a trust through a procedure called **amendment.** You should amend your trust when you want to change or add beneficiaries, take assets from the trust, or change trustees. You amend a trust by adding a new page for every change, specifying the new additions. To avoid a legal challenge from a disgruntled nonbeneficiary, you should not detach a page from the trust document, retype it to include the new information, and put it back in its original place.

Q. How do I add property to the trust?

A. You don't have to write a formal amendment to add property to the trust, because a properly drafted trust will contain language giving you the right to include property acquired after the trust is drafted. Just make sure the title to the new property indicates that it is owned by the trustee, and be sure to list it on the schedule of the trust's assets. You do have to amend the trust if the newly acquired property is going to a different beneficiary than the one already named in the trust.

Q. I want to make some very sweeping changes to my trust. How do I do this?

A. When making major changes, you should completely restate or revoke your trust—not amend it. You revoke a trust by destroying all copies of it or writing "revoked" on each page and signing them. When you create a new trust to replace a revoked one, give the new trust a different name, usually one containing the date the new document was executed.

▶ DO I NEED TO UPDATE MY ESTATE PLAN?

Ask yourself if any of these changes has occurred in your life since you executed your will or trust.

- Have you married or divorced?
- Have your children married or been divorced?
- Do your children or any other beneficiaries need protection from creditors?
- Have relatives or other beneficiaries or the executor died, or has your relationship with them changed substantially?
- Has the mental or physical condition of any of your relatives or other beneficiaries, or your trustee or executor, changed substantially?
- Have you had more children or grandchildren, or have children gone to college or moved out of (or into) your home?
- Have you moved to another state?
- Have you bought, sold, or mortgaged a business or real estate?
- Have you acquired major assets (e.g., a car, home, or bank account)?
- Have you inherited significant property?
- Have your business or financial circumstances changed significantly (e.g., estate size, stock portfolio value, pension, salary, or asset ownership)?
- Has your state law (or federal laws) changed in a way that might affect your tax and estate planning?
- Have you changed your mind about what to do with any of your assets?
- Have you decided to do more (or less) charitable giving?
- Have you made gifts that should be taken into account, such as by reducing bequests that were to occur under the will?

When you do update your estate plan, you should also update your final instructions and will with the addresses and phone numbers of beneficiaries, trustees, executors, and others mentioned in estate-planning documents. It will make settling the estate much easier.

▶ ARE YOUR AFFAIRS IN ORDER?

Ask yourself the following questions to see whether you've really done everything you can to prepare for your death:

- Where are your bank accounts?
- Where is the deed to your home and other real estate records?
- Who is your lawyer? Your broker? Your executor? Your accountant?
- What credit cards do you have? What are their numbers?
- Where is your will? Who drew it up?
- What insurance do you have? Where is the documentation?
- What other funds will be paid to your family after your death?
- Do you have a retirement account such as an IRA, or a pension fund? Where are the relevant documents?
- Where is your safe-deposit box?
- Where are your other valuables stored?
- What stocks, securities, bonds, annuities, and the like do you own? Where are the relevant documents?
- Have you provided for the guardianship of your minor children?
- What funeral arrangements have you made? Where are they written down?

REMEMBER THIS

- A will isn't the only document in your estate plan. Talk to your lawyer about your retirement plans, your bank accounts, and any property you hold in joint tenancy.
- Changes in your life often necessitate a change in your estate plan, so it's important to schedule a regular review of your plan—and, if necessary, to update it.
- Make sure to revise your estate plan if you've experienced major life or financial changes since it was prepared or updated.

DEATH AND TAXES

Ever since Caesar Augustus imposed an estate levy to pay for imperial Roman exploits, death and taxes have walked hand in hand. No one really likes paying taxes, but they pay for many of the things we value in modern society.

Death taxes also have been a traditional way of redistributing wealth. During the difficult days of the Great Depression, Franklin Roosevelt used the estate and gift tax system to transfer money from those with wealth to those who were more unfortunate. This section explains the basics of modern federal and state estate taxes.

Q. I'm not rich. Do I have to worry about federal estate taxes?

A. Your estate isn't liable for federal estate taxation unless it exceeds the available exemption amount. The Economic Growth and Tax Relief Reconciliation Act of 2001 (EGTRRA) provides for a gradual increase in the amount of the exemption. It is now $2 million, and will rise to $3.5 million in 2009.

In addition, you can pass your entire estate, without any estate taxes, to your spouse. (This is called the **unlimited marital deduction.**) If you simply leave your estate to your spouse and don't create an appropriate trust to take advantage of the exemption detailed above, then your spouse's estate will pay taxes on any amount over the exemption amount when he or she dies (unless he or she leaves it to a new spouse).

If your estate is likely to exceed the current threshold, then good estate planning can sharply reduce the amount of money that goes to the government instead of to your beneficiaries.

Q. The law allows me to leave everything to my spouse tax free, right? How can we use this fact to our children's maximum advantage?

A. From the taxpayer's perspective, the best provision of federal estate tax law is the **unified credit,** which gives each person a $2 million total exemption from estate taxation in 2007–2008 (the amount will go up in later years). But what do you do if your wealth exceeds that amount?

One of the most basic tax-planning devices is the unlimited marital deduction. It allows one spouse to pass his or her entire estate, regardless of size, to the other—and not pay federal estate taxes. No matter how large the estate, no taxes are due when it is passed to the spouse.

If you only cared about leaving your property to your spouse, that would end your tax worries. However, most people want to leave property to their families after the death of the surviving spouse—and this is where tax planning comes into play.

To take full advantage of the unified credit and the unlimited marital deduction,

married taxpayers with assets above the exemption amount probably will be advised to use a trust. Trusts are one of the main ways to minimize taxes upon death. By using a trust properly, you should be able to transfer at least double the exemption amount free of estate taxes to your children or other beneficiaries, no matter which spouse dies first or who accumulated the wealth.

Q. Can the state where I live also tax my estate?

A. Yes. Some states charge an additional estate tax similar to (but less than) the federal tax; other states impose an inheritance tax. (**Inheritance taxes** are charged to beneficiaries; **estate taxes** are charged to the deceased person's estate.)

What is taxed (and at what rate) depends on state law—not only of the state in which you live, but also of the state where the property is located. Unless your state has an inheritance tax, your beneficiaries don't pay tax when they receive money or other property from your estate. But they will have to pay income tax on any earnings after they invest the property. In addition, death itself may produce numerous tax consequences.

Q. I'm the owner of a business, and I understand that my estate would have to pay taxes on the value of the business if I don't do any estate planning—but what can I do to lighten the tax load?

A. Congress is sympathetic to the plight of business owners, and has created several breaks in the tax code for you. The most commonly used provision allows your estate to pay the estate tax on the business over as long as fifteen years, while paying only a 2 percent interest rate on the deferred tax. These tax breaks

▶ SUBJECT TO INCOME TAX

Most of us won't have to pay estate taxes. But what about income taxes that result from a death? Although bequests in a will usually pass to the beneficiaries free of income tax, some income is still subject to income tax when received by the estate or its beneficiaries, including:

- wages, bonuses, and fringe benefits;
- deferred compensation;
- stock options;
- qualified retirement plans;
- some IRAs (other than Roth IRAs);
- medical savings accounts;
- insurance renewal commissions;
- professional fees;
- interest earned before death;
- dividends declared before death;
- crop shares;
- royalties;
- proceeds of a sale entered into before death; and
- alimony arrearages.

have complex requirements, and you should not assume that you will qualify automatically.

There are also a number of other tested estate-planning techniques—such as annual gifting and placing your business in a family partnership—that can have the effect of reducing the value of the business for purposes of your estate. The successful implementation of these techniques will require the services of an experienced estate-planning lawyer.

Q. What if I receive a bequest and don't want it?

A. Because of taxes or other reasons, those named as will or trust beneficiaries may not always want the property left to them. For example, if you go bankrupt and then your father dies, your creditors may be entitled to first shot at the property he left to you. You might want to give up this property so that it will go, for example, to your sister instead of to your creditors. Or you may receive property that is subject to liens and mortgages greater than its market value, so it may be a burden you would rather not have.

Most states permit beneficiaries to **disclaim** (i.e., refuse) an inheritance or benefit. The Internal Revenue Code describes how a beneficiary may disclaim an interest in an estate for estate tax purposes. See a knowledgeable tax lawyer if you intend to disclaim any gift or bequest.

REMEMBER THIS

- Your estate isn't liable for federal estate taxation unless it exceeds the available exemption amount. This is currently $2 million, and will rise to $3.5 million in 2009 (the estate tax will have a brief period of repeal in 2010, although further congressional action to change this is likely).

- If you're married, when your estate gets over the $4 million mark in 2008 ($7 million in 2009), trusts may be the way to save as much money in taxes as possible.

- By using the unlimited marital exemption and unified credit, you can shelter much of your money from taxation. But the laws and accounting in this area are so complicated that you should certainly rely on the advice of a good tax lawyer.

Appendix

GLOSSARY

A

acceptance—Consent to the terms of an **offer,** creating a **contract.**

accomplice—A person who assists in a crime.

acquittal—A trial verdict indicating that the defendant in a criminal case has not been found guilty of the crime charged. Note that "acquittal" and "not guilty" are not the same as "innocent," a term that is not actually used in criminal law.

action—A legal dispute brought to court for trial and settlement (see also **case, lawsuit**). In a case that has already been filed, an **action to implead** is a request to the court to name defendants who were not originally named, but who are allegedly responsible, in whole or in part, for the injuries or losses.

actual damages—See **compensatory damages.**

actus reus—A Latin term meaning "the guilty act." The actus reus is the wrongful act that is the physical component of a crime; the other component of a crime is the **mens rea,** or guilty intention.

addendum—See **rider.**

ademption—Failure of a gift because the will maker, by the time of death, no longer owns the property that he or she attempted to grant in the will.

adhesion contract—A contract between two parties of unequal bargaining power. It is not negotiated, and usually is embodied in a standardized form prepared by the dominant party. Also called a **contract of adhesion.**

adjudication—Giving or pronouncing a judgment or decree; also the term for the judgment that is given.

adjustable-rate mortgage (ARM)—A loan typically offered at a lower-than-market interest rate for the first year or first few years, with future interest rates adjusted annually.

administration—The process of collecting an estate's assets; paying its debts, taxes, expenses, and other obligations; and distributing the remainder as directed by the will.

administrator—Appointed by a probate court, a personal representative who administers the estate of someone who dies without a will, or who leaves a will naming an executor who dies before the will maker, or who refuses to serve.

admissible evidence—Evidence that can be legally and properly introduced in a trial.

adoption—When an adult becomes the legal parent of a child. An **agency adoption** is conducted by a state-licensed agency. **Private adoption** bypasses the use of agencies, and usually is coordinated by a lawyer or adoption specialist. A **related adoption** is one in which a child's relatives, such as grandparents or an aunt and uncle, formally adopt the child as their own. An **open adoption** is one in which the adoptive parents agree to let the biological parent or parents have some continued contact with the child after adoption.

advance directive—A document in which a person expresses his or her wishes regarding medical treatment in the event of incapacitation. The two most common forms of advance directive are a **living will** and a **durable power of attorney for health care.** In the latter, a person can appoint a health-care agent to make decisions on his or her behalf.

adversary system—The system of trial practice in the United States and some other countries, which is based on the belief that truth can best be determined by giving opposing parties a full opportunity to present and establish their evidence, and to test by cross-examination the evidence presented by their adversaries, under established rules of procedure before an impartial judge and/or jury. An adversary proceeding is contested because it features opposing parties (i.e., it differs from an **ex parte** proceeding).

adverse possession—When a trespasser who occupies land for a substantial period of time (usually over twenty years) is able to legally claim ownership right over the land.

affidavit—A written statement of fact given voluntarily and under oath. In criminal cases, affidavits often are used by police officers seeking to convince courts to grant a **warrant** to make an arrest or perform a search. In civil cases, affidavits of witnesses often are used to support motions for **summary judgment.**

affirmative action plan (AAP)—Guidelines for recruiting, hiring, and promoting women and minorities in order to eliminate the present effects of past employment discrimination.

affirmative defense—A defense in which, without denying the charge, the defendant raises extenuating or mitigating circumstances, such as insanity, self-defense, or entrapment, in order to avoid civil or criminal responsibility. The defendant must prove any affirmative defense he or she raises.

affirmed—In the practice of appellate courts, this term means that the decision or order at issue is declared valid and will stand as rendered in the lower court.

age of majority—The age at which a person is considered to be legally responsible for all of his or her actions and is granted by law the rights of an adult. In most states the age of majority is eighteen.

agency bank account—A bank account on which a person has named an agent, who then has the authority to make deposits or withdrawals and manage the account. Similar to a **power of attorney.**

agent—A person authorized to act on behalf of and under the control of another person, called the **principal.** The agent is a **fiduciary.** A **health-care agent** is one who makes health-care decisions for the principal.

aggravating factors—Factors relating to a crime or defendant that suggest a tougher sentence might be warranted.

alimony—A court-ordered payment for the support of one's estranged spouse in the case of divorce or separation. Alimony also is known as **maintenance** or **spousal support.**

allegation—In a **pleading,** the statement of what a party expects to prove. For example, an indictment contains allegations of crime against the defendant.

alternative dispute resolution (ADR)—A means of settling a dispute without a formal trial. **Mediation** and **arbitration** are forms of ADR.

alternative sentences—A sentence, other than confinement, that a judge can issue when there is no mandatory sentence of incarceration. Examples include the offender making some sort of payment; supervision; and enrollment in a residential program or attendance in a day program.

amicus brief—A document filed by an **amicus curiae** in support of a party in a lawsuit.

amicus curiae—A Latin term meaning "friend of the court." A party who volunteers information on some aspect of a case or law to assist the court in its deliberation.

amortization schedule—A table showing how much of each loan payment will be applied toward principal and how much toward interest over the life of the loan, including the gradual decrease of the principal until it reaches zero.

ancillary bill or **suit**—A cause of action growing out of and supported by another action or suit, such as a proceeding for the enforcement of a judgment.

annual goals—Part of an Individual Education Plan: those goals that a special-needs child can accomplish in one year.

annulment—A court ruling that a marriage was never valid.

answer—A **pleading** by which a defendant resists or otherwise responds to the plaintiff's **allegation** of facts.

antenuptial agreement—see **premarital agreement.**

antilapse statutes—State laws providing that if a beneficiary related to you predeceases you, then that beneficiary's descendants will receive any gifts in your will intended for the deceased beneficiary (particularly gifts of real and personal property).

appeal—A request by the losing party in a lawsuit for higher court review of a lower court decision.

appearance—The formal proceeding by which a defendant submits himself or herself to the jurisdiction of the court. A **first appearance** is the first time a criminal defendant is brought before a judge or magistrate, and must occur within a reasonable time after arrest.

appellant—The party appealing a decision or judgment to a higher court. Sometimes called a **petitioner.**

appellate court—A court having jurisdiction to review a **trial court's** decisions on procedure and law.

appellee—The party against whom an **appeal** is filed. Sometimes called a **respondent.**

appraisal—A professional's opinion of the fair market value of an item or piece of real estate.

arbitration—Dispute settlement conducted outside the courts by a neutral third party. May or may not be binding.

arraignment—The proceeding in criminal cases where an accused individual is brought before a judge to hear the charges filed against him or her, and to file a plea of "guilty," "not guilty," or "no contest." Also called an **initial appearance** or a **first appearance.**

arrest—The act of being taken into custody by legal authority.

articles of incorporation—The document that legally establishes a corporation, association, or other organization and outlines the name, address, and purpose; the aggregate number of shares permitted; whether cumulative voting or other special voting or assessment rights are provided; and, in general, the power of the board to make, alter, and repeal bylaws.

assault—An attempt or threat by a person to inflict immediate offensive physical contact or bodily harm, which the person has the present ability to inflict. An assault need not result in actual touching, but the victim must have reasonable fear of harm or contact. An assault can be a **crime** or a **tort.** Often combined with **battery.**

assignment—The transfer of one's interest in a right or property to another person or entity.

assisted-living communities—Retirement communities that offer a wide variety of housing and health or supportive services, but not nursing-home care.

assumption of the risk—A defense that may be raised in personal injury cases, alleging that the plaintiff agreed to face a known danger and accepted the risk that some harm might result.

at issue—The contested points in a lawsuit are said to be "at issue."

attempt—A crime that consists of intending to commit the crime, and taking some step toward committing the crime, but for some reason not completing it.

attorney-at-law—A lawyer licensed to provide legal advice and to prepare, manage, and try cases.

attorney-in-fact—The **agent** named in a **power of attorney.**

automatic stay—Imposed when bankruptcy proceedings are filed. An automatic stay prevents creditors from attempting to collect from the debtor for debts incurred before the filing.

automobile guest statutes—State statutes that make drivers liable for injuries to nonpaying or guest passengers only if the drivers were "grossly negligent" by failing to use even slight care in their driving.

B

bail (also called **bail bond**)—Money or other security given to secure the release of a criminal defendant or witness from legal custody. The money or security can be forfeited if he or she subsequently should fail to appear before the court on the day and time appointed. An **unsecured bond** is one that does not have to be posted for the defendant to be released—the financial liability will only be attached if the defendant fails to return to court when ordered.

bailiff—A court attendant whose duties are to keep order in the courtroom and to have custody of the jury.

bait and switch—A widely illegal practice in which a customer is encouraged to come into a store by an ad for a product or service, is then told that the specific item is no longer available, and is instead encouraged to purchase a more expensive alternative.

balance of powers—The theory behind the U.S. system of government that requires each branch of the government to keep an eye on the others.

balloon loan—A type of loan where the buyer is expected to pay off the unpaid balance completely within a fixed period of time, usually in three, five, or seven years, instead of making regular payments to completely pay off the loan.

bankruptcy—Refers to statutes and judicial proceedings involving persons or businesses that cannot pay their debts and seek the assistance of the court in getting a fresh start. Under the protection of the bankruptcy court, debtors may **discharge** their debts (no longer be liable for them), in some cases by paying a portion of each debt, and in some cases, where the debtor has no assets, by paying no portion of them.

bargaining unit—The group of workers voting in a unionization election who will be represented by the union in the event the union wins the election.

battery—Intentionally or recklessly causing offensive physical contact or bodily harm that is not consented to by the victim. Battery can be a crime or a tort. It is the component of actual touching found in "assault and battery."

bench trial—A trial heard by a judge without a jury.

bench warrant—An order issued by a judge for the arrest of an individual.

beneficiary—Someone named to receive property or benefits in a will. In a trust, a person who is to receive benefits from the trust.

beneficiary designations—The persons one selects to receive benefits of a life insurance policy, retirement savings plan, pension, or the like. Normally these forms of property do not pass through a will, but rather through the beneficiary designations of the policies and plans, and so they avoid **probate.**

bequeath—To give a gift to someone through a will.

bequest—A gift made in a will. Also called a **legacy.**

best evidence—Primary evidence; the best evidence available. Evidence short of this is "secondary"; for example, an original letter is the "best evidence," a photocopy is "secondary evidence."

best interest of the child—The standard applied by courts when making custody and visitation determinations. Determining the best interest of the child involves consideration of many factors, which may include the health and sex of the child, the primary caregiver prior to the divorce, parenting skills and willingness to care for the child, the emotional ties between child and parent, willingness to facilitate visitation by the other parent, and each parent's moral fitness.

better-judgment rule—A theory applied to decisions made by corporate and association directors. It states that if a decision was arrived at honestly and with no fraudulent intent, then the board's decision will be upheld even if it was foolish or if reasonable persons may disagree with it.

beyond a reasonable doubt—The standard in a criminal case requiring that the jury be satisfied to a moral certainty that every element of a crime has been proven by the prosecution. This **standard of proof** does not require that the state establish absolute certainty by eliminating all doubt, but it does require that the evidence be so conclusive that all reasonable doubts are removed from the mind of the ordinary person.

bifurcated trial—A trial in which the judge or jury will determine liability and outcome (damages or sentencing) in two different phases.

billing error—An error on a bill that represents a charge for something that you didn't buy, or for a purchase made by someone not authorized to use your account; that is not properly identified on your monthly statement, or that is for an amount different from the actual purchase price; or for something that you refused to accept on delivery because it was unsatisfactory, or that the supplier did not deliver according to your agreement.

bill of sale—A document that is often required during automobile sales, typically detailing: the date of the sale; the year, make, and model of the car; the vehicle identification number; the odometer reading; the amount paid for the car, and the form in which payment was made (cash, check, etc.); and the buyer's and seller's names, addresses, and phone numbers.

bind over—To hold a person for trial on bond (**bail**) or in jail. If the judicial official conducting a preliminary hearing finds **probable cause** to believe the accused committed a crime, he or she will "bind over" the accused, normally by setting bail for his or her appearance at trial.

binding instruction—An **instruction** in which a jury is told that if it finds certain conditions to be true, it must decide in favor of the plaintiff, or defendant, as the case might be.

bona fide occupational qualification (BFOQ)—A very limited exception to the prohibition on discrimination in hiring. An employer must show both that all persons of the excluded class would be unable to perform the requirements of the job, and that the requirements of the job directly relate to the essence of the employer's business.

boundary fence—A fence that sits directly on the property line of two neighbors.

breach of contract—A legally inexcusable failure to perform a contractual obligation.

breach of peace—Any act likely to produce disorder or violence, such as an unauthorized entry into your home.

brief—A written statement prepared by each side in a lawsuit to explain to the court its view of the facts in a case and the applicable law.

building code—Municipal construction standards.

burden of proof—In the law of evidence, the duty of proving the facts in dispute in a lawsuit. The burden of proof is not the same as the standard of proof. Burden of proof deals with which side must establish a point or points; **standard of proof** indicates the degree to which those points must be proven.

burglary—Entry into, or remaining in, any residence, building or vehicle without consent, with the intent to commit a **felony** or **larceny** within.

business interruption policy—An insurance policy that offsets losses if the business is forced to shut down for a substantial period because of a fire, flood, or some other catastrophe.

business owner's policy (BOP)—An insurance policy for business owners that covers risks like fire and other hazards, and lawsuits if someone is injured on the property, as well as other risks that are unique to the business situation.

bylaws—The rules and regulations dictating how the managing board of a corporation, association, or other organization defines its duties and powers.

C

calendar—The clerk of court's list of cases, which lists dates and times set for hearings, trials, and/or arguments.

calling the docket—The public calling of the docket or list of cases, for the purpose of setting a time for trial or entering orders.

capitalized cost reduction—A down payment made when you lease a car.

case—A legal dispute.

case law—Law based on published judicial decisions; similar to **common law.** Law made by the legislature is **statutory law.**

cause—A lawsuit, litigation, or legal action.

cause of action—Facts giving rise to a lawsuit.

caveat emptor—A Latin term meaning "let the buyer beware."

censure—When a lawyer is publicly criticized for acting unethically.

certiorari—A Latin term meaning "to be informed of." A **writ of certiorari** is a request to a higher court to review a case. An order of certiorari is an order to a lower court to deliver the record of a case to an appellate court.

challenge—An objection, such as when a lawyer objects at a **voir dire** hearing to the seating of a particular person on a civil or criminal jury; a challenge may be a **challenge for cause** or a **peremptory challenge.**

challenge for cause—Objection to the seating of a particular juror for a stated reason (usually bias or prejudice for or against one of the parties in the case); the judge has discretion to deny such a challenge (differs from **peremptory challenge**).

change of venue—Moving a trial to a new location, generally because pretrial publicity has made it difficult to select an impartial jury.

charge—In an accusation or **indictment,** a description of an offense made in order to bring the accused person to trial. In an age discrimination case before the Equal Employment Opportunity Commission, a charge is a written statement alleging discrimination signed by the alleged victim (different from a **complaint**).

charge account—A credit account that usually requires payment in full within thirty days. Travel and entertainment cards, such as American Express and Diners Club, operate this way, as do most charge accounts with local businesses, especially service providers like doctors and plumbers.

charge to the jury—The judge's **instructions** to the jury before it begins deliberations. The instructions deal with the law in the case and the jury's authority to determine the facts and to draw inferences from the facts in order to reach a verdict. Instructions often include the questions the jury must answer.

charitable trust—A trust set up to benefit one or more charities.

chattel—Personal property.

child support—Court-ordered financial support for children.

circuit courts—In the federal system, the courts of appeal beneath the U.S. Supreme Court. In several states, the name given to a tribunal, the territorial jurisdiction of which may comprise several counties or districts.

circumstantial evidence—Evidence that suggests something by implication. Circumstantial evidence is indirect, as opposed to eyewitness testimony, which is **direct evidence.** For example, fingerprints at the scene of a crime are circumstantial evidence.

citation—A citation is the charging document issued for the least serious criminal offenses. It commands the appearance of a party in a proceeding. A citation is also a reference to a source of legal authority—for example, a case citation.

civil actions—Noncriminal cases in which one private individual or business sues another to protect, enforce, or redress private or civil rights. Also called a **civil suit.**

civil service laws—Employment policies for public employees based on the merit principle.

civil union—A voluntary union that affords same-sex couples similar to benefits and protections heterosexual couples who enter into marriage.

claim—An assertion of a right to money or property made by the party that is suing.

clear and convincing evidence—A **standard of proof** requiring the truth of the facts asserted to be highly probable. This standard is commonly applied in civil lawsuits and in regulatory agency cases. It requires more than a **preponderance of the evidence** but less than **beyond a reasonable doubt.**

clerk of the court—A court employee who is responsible for maintaining permanent records of all court proceedings and exhibits, and administering the oath to jurors and witnesses.

client security fund—A fund that may reimburse clients if a court has found that their lawyer has defrauded them. May also be called a **client indemnity fund** or **client assistance fund.**

closed-end lease contract—A car lease for which the car's value when you return it does not matter, unless you have put excessive mileage or extreme wear on the car. Sometimes called a **walk-away lease.**

closing—The final stage in the process of buying real estate, consisting of a meeting at which the buyer and the seller, usually accompanied by their respective lawyers and real estate agents, complete the sale.

closing arguments—The summaries of the evidence presented to the jury at the end of a trial by the lawyers for each side.

codicil—An amendment to a will.

coinsurance payments—Payments (for health care, a home, or auto repair) equal to a percentage of the applicable expense. Your insurance plan covers the remaining percentage.

collective-bargaining agreement—A contract between a union and employer outlining the terms and conditions of employment for those employees covered by the agreement.

collision damage waiver (CDW)—A policy in a rental car agreement providing that the rental company will cover damages to the rental car.

common carriers—Bus lines, air lines, and railroads. Common carriers are expected to exercise the highest degree of care and have a special responsibility to protect their passengers.

common law—Law arising from judicial decisions rather than laws passed by the legislature. Similar to **case law.**

common-law action—A case in which the issues are determined by common law legal principles established by courts, as opposed to statutes.

community property—Community property is generally the property and income acquired during a marriage; see also **marital property.**

community property states—States that adhere to the doctrine that each spouse shares equally in the income earned and the property acquired during a marriage. In these states, it is more difficult for a spouse to hold property separately from the other spouse.

community service—A relatively lenient sentence in which the court requires you to spend a certain number of hours (usually hundreds or thousands) doing service work.

comparative negligence—A legal doctrine providing that the responsibility for damages incurred between the plaintiff and the defendant is allocated according to their relative negligence. Comparative negligence largely has replaced the doctrine of **contributory negligence.**

compensatory damages—Money paid to an injured party to compensate for losses sustained as a direct result of the injury suffered. Also called **actual damages.**

complainant—The individual who initiates a lawsuit; synonymous with **plaintiff.**

complaint (civil)—The initial document filed by the plaintiff in a civil case stating the claims against the defendant. In an age discrimination case before the Equal Employment Opportunity Commission, a complaint is a written statement alleging discrimination that is not signed by the alleged victim.

complaint (criminal)—A formal accusation or charge against someone alleging that he or she has committed a criminal offense.

concurring opinion—An appellate court opinion by one or more judges that agrees with the majority opinion in the case; it often agrees with the result reached by the majority, but offers different reasoning.

condition—An event that must occur if a contract is to be performed. For example, in real estate contracts the sale is often conditional on the buyers obtaining financing, or selling their current home, or on an acceptable home-inspection report.

conditional release—A release from custody, without the payment of bail, which imposes restrictions on the activities and associations of the defendant.

condominium—A common-interest community in which the owner has exclusive title to his or her own unit, from the interior walls in, and ownership of an individual interest in the common elements of the condominium, such as hallways, exteriors, and any land surrounding the building.

condominium declaration—The document that describes the land, building, and other improvements for an entire condominium development; the location of each unit; percentage of ownership; the common elements; and the intended use of each unit.

confidential informant—Someone who provides information to the police on the condition that his or her identity will not be disclosed.

confidentiality—Secrecy.

consent judgment—A **judgment** in which the provisions and terms of the judgment are agreed on by the parties and submitted to the court for its sanction and approval. This is often the result of bargaining between the parties and formalizes their **settlement** of the case.

conservator—One appointed by a court to manage the property and financial affairs of someone deemed incapable of doing so for himself or herself. Similar to a **guardian,** except that a guardian usually has duties beyond the financial, such as responsibility for minor children.

consequential damages—A form of **compensatory damages** ordered to be paid when the injury done resulted from the other side's wrong, but was not a natural or necessary consequence of that wrong. Also called **special damages.** Special damages must be specifically pleaded and proven.

consideration—Something of value, including a promise to do (or not do) something, given in return for another's performance or promise to perform. Consideration is one of the requirements of a **contract,** and distinguishes a contract from a mere gift.

conspiracy—A crime consisting of an agreement between two or more people to commit a separate crime, followed by any activity aimed at carrying out that agreement.

constructive eviction—A legal doctrine providing that a tenant may be able to move out of a rental property before a lease ends without penalty when the property is in such poor condition that the tenant reasonably cannot live there.

contempt of court—Any act calculated to embarrass, hinder, or obstruct a court. Contempts are of two kinds: direct and indirect. **Direct contempts** are those committed in the immediate presence of the court; **indirect** is the term mostly used with reference to the failure or refusal to obey a court order. The penalty for contempt of court may be a fine or imprisonment.

contest—To challenge a will or estate document. A will can include a **no-contest clause** that will disinherit a beneficiary who unsuccessfully challenges the will.

contingency clause—A clause that makes a contract dependent on some particular event or circumstance. For example, contracts for the sale of land often contain a contingency clause stating that if the buyer is unable to obtain satisfactory financing within a certain period, the buyer may be released from his or her obligation.

contingent fee—A legal fee that is payable only if a case is successful.

continuance—The postponement of a proceeding to a later date.

continuing-care retirement communities (CCRCs)—Retirement communities that provide a fairly extensive range of housing options, care, and services, including nursing-home services.

contract—An agreement between two or more parties that the law will enforce, made either orally or in writing. To form a contract, the parties must be of the requisite age and mental capacity; there must be **consideration;** and the subject of the promise cannot be illegal.

contract of adhesion—See **adhesion contract.**

contributory negligence—Legal doctrine providing that a plaintiff cannot recover damages in a civil action for negligence if the plaintiff was also negligent. Most states have overcome the harshness of this rule by adopting a **comparative negligence** rule.

conversion—Converting someone else's property into your own.

convertible ARM—An adjustable-rate mortgage that allows the borrower to convert to a fixed-rate loan after a specified period of time.

conviction—A trial verdict or judgment finding that a criminal defendant is guilty of a crime.

cookies—Small bits of information on your computer hard drive that track your Web usage.

co-operative—A common-interest community in which buyers purchase shares of stock in a corporation that owns an entire building, and then enter into a lease to occupy a particular apartment. Stockholders don't actually own any real estate.

copyright—The right to literary property, giving authors, composers, and other creators the sole right to reproduce and distribute their work for a limited period of time. Copyright is a form of **intellectual property.**

corroborating evidence—Supplementary evidence that supports the evidence already given.

cosign—See **surety.**

counsel—Legal advice; also a term used to refer to lawyers in a case.

count—Separate issues or claims brought in a complaint or charge.

counterclaim—A claim by a defendant in a civil case that he or she has been injured by the plaintiff.

court costs—In addition to legal fees, the expenses associated with prosecuting or defending a lawsuit.

court of last resort—The final court that decides a case on appeal (for example, the Supreme Court of the United States or the supreme court of any state).

court reporter—A person who records, transcribes, or stenographically takes down testimony, motions, orders, and other proceedings during trials, hearings, and other court proceedings.

covenant—A private restriction designed to maintain quality control over a neighborhood. Also called a **condition.**

credit bureau—An organization that maintains computer files of your financial payment histories, public-record data, and personal identifying data. Sometimes called **credit reporting agencies** or **consumer reporting agencies.**

credit counseling—Individual or group counseling that outlines the opportunities and options available for people in debt, and assists such people in analyzing their budgets.

crime—Conduct that is prohibited by law and has a specific punishment (for example, incarceration or a fine).

criminal case—A case brought by the government against an individual accused of committing a crime.

cross-claim—See **counterclaim.**

cross-examination—The questioning of a witness by the other side's lawyers.

custody—Care and control over a person or property. **Child custody** refers to the right and duty to care for a minor child on a day-to-day basis and to make major decisions about the child.

cyberlaw—A developing area of law relating to computers, electronic commerce, **intellectual property** on the Internet, and the like.

cybersquatting—Illegally attempting to profit by reserving a domain name that is or contains a trademark, and then attempting to resell or license the domain name to the trademark owner.

D

D.A.—Abbreviation of **District Attorney.**

damages—Money awarded by a court to a person injured by the unlawful act or negligence of another person. Damages can be **compensatory, punitive, consequential,** and even **nominal.** A **damages cap** is a statutory limit on the amount of punitive damages that may be awarded, and on noneconomic damages such as pain and suffering.

dealer—Someone who makes it his or her business to sell a specific product. For example, in the case of used cars, a dealer is

someone who sells six or more used cars in a twelve-month period.

debt collector—Someone, other than a creditor, who regularly collects debts on behalf of others.

decision—The judgment reached or given by a court of law.

declaratory judgment—A judgment that declares the rights of the parties or expresses the opinion of the court on a question of law, without ordering anything to be done.

decree—A decision or order of the court. A **final decree** is one that disposes of the litigation; an **interlocutory decree** is a provisional or preliminary decree that is not final.

deductibles—Payments you must make before insurance (including private health, Medicare, and homeowners) coverage begins.

deed—A written document that transfers ownership of **real property** from one person to another. A **deed of trust** is a type of mortgage.

defamation—That which tends to injure a person's reputation. See **libel** and **slander.** A **retraction statute** may allow a defendant in a defamation suit to take back the defamatory statement and thus avoid or limit liability.

default—Failure to discharge a duty. For example, people default on a mortgage if they fail to repay their home loan, and default on a contract if they fail to perform it.

default judgment—A judgment against a defendant who does not file the proper response within the time allowed, or who fails to appear at the trial.

defendant—In a civil case, the person being sued. In a criminal case, the person accused of committing the crime.

defined-benefit plan—An employer-provided pension plan that guarantees you a certain amount of benefits per month upon retirement.

defined-contribution plan—An employer-provided pension plan where the employer and/or the employee contribute a certain amount per month during the years of employment. The amount of the benefit depends on the total amount accumulated in the pension fund at the time of retirement.

deliberation—The process by which a jury reaches a verdict at the close of a trial.

delinquent acts—Acts committed by juvenile offenders that would constitute crimes if committed by an adult.

demand letter—A carefully thought-out letter to a person with whom you have a disagreement, including an accurate summary of the history of the problem and a date by which you would like a response or settlement.

demur—In some state courts, to file a pleading (called a **demurrer**) admitting the truth of the facts in the complaint or answer, and contending they do not make out a cause of action.

de novo—Latin term for "anew." A "trial de novo" is the retrial of a case. A "de novo" standard of review permits an appellate court to substitute its judgment for that of a trial judge.

deposition—The testimony of a witness taken under oath in preparation for a trial. Such statements often are taken to examine potential witnesses and to obtain information.

descent-and-distribution statutes—See **intestacy laws.**

direct evidence—Proof of facts by witnesses who saw acts done or heard words spoken, as distinguished from **circumstantial** (i.e., indirect) evidence.

direct examination—The first questioning of witnesses by the party on whose behalf they are called.

directed verdict—An instruction by the judge to the jury to return a specific verdict, because one of the parties failed to meet its burden of proof.

disability—Under the law, a person who is disabled is one who has a physical or mental impairment that substantially limits a major life activity; has a record of having such a physical or mental impairment; or is regarded as having such an impairment.

disbar—To remove a lawyer's license to practice law as a result of the lawyer's unethical or illegal practices. Lawyers may also be censured or reprimanded (i.e., publicly or privately criticized), or suspended (i.e., have their license to practice law taken away for a certain time).

discharge—To release from an obligation; for example, when a bankruptcy is discharged a person is relieved from the liability to pay debts.

disclaim—To voluntarily give up a right or claim. For example, to refuse a gift under a will.

disclaimer—A denial of responsibility for a thing or act. Many contracts and warranties disclaim liability for some events, and will not cover you if, for example, your new car breaks down because you tried to fix it yourself instead of taking it to an approved dealer.

discovery—The pretrial process by which each party ascertains evidence upon which the other party will rely at trial.

discriminatory effect—When conduct has the effect of discriminating against people in a protected class, even if the employer's reason for the different treatment is not based on protected class. Also called **disparate impact.**

dismissal—A court order terminating a case. May be voluntary (at the request of the parties) or involuntary.

disposable income—Whatever is left over from your total income after you have paid for taxes and reasonable and necessary living expenses.

dispute resolution centers—Centers, which may be known as **neighborhood justice centers** or **citizens' dispute settlement programs,** that specialize in helping people who have common problems and disputes.

dissent—An appellate court opinion setting forth the minority view and outlining the disagreement of one or more judges with the decision of the majority.

dissolution of marriage—See **divorce.**

district attorney—A state government lawyer who prosecutes criminal cases. Also referred to as a **prosecutor.**

district courts—U.S. district courts are federal trial courts. State district courts are also often trial courts of general jurisdiction.

diversion—The process of removing some minor criminal, traffic, or juvenile cases from the full judicial process, on the condition that the accused undergo some sort of rehabilitation or make **restitution** for damages. Diversion may take place before the trial or its equivalent, as when a juvenile accused of a crime consents to probation without an admission of guilt. If the juvenile completes probation successfully (takes a course or makes amends for the crime), then the entire matter may be **expunged** (erased) from the record.

divorce—The dissolution of the legal bonds of marriage. A **no-fault divorce** is one in which neither person blames the other for the breakdown of the marriage. A **fault-based divorce** is still allowed in some states and is usually based on adultery, physical cruelty, mental cruelty, attempted murder, desertion, habitual drunkenness, use of addictive drugs, insanity, impotence, or infection of one's spouse with venereal disease.

docket—A list of cases to be heard by the court.

domain name—A unique Web address, which is used by the Internet's infrastructure to allow other computers to find you on the Internet.

domestic partnership—Partnership of homosexual couples, and of heterosexual couples in some states, who are living together without being married. To become domestic partners, the couple must register their relationship at a government office and declare that they are in a "committed" relationship.

domicile—The place where a person has his or her true and permanent home. A person may have several residences, but only one domicile.

donor—The person who sets up a trust. Also known as its **grantor** or **settlor.**

double jeopardy—Putting a person on trial more than once for the same crime; forbidden by the Fifth Amendment to the U.S. Constitution.

dramshop acts—Statutes that allow people injured by drunk drivers to recover against the owner of the bar that served the driver.

due-on-sale clause—A mortgage clause that requires the seller to pay off the entire mortgage loan when the property is sold or transferred in any way.

due process—U.S. law in its regular course of administration through the courts. The constitutional guarantee of due process requires that everyone receive such constitutional protections as a fair trial, assistance of counsel, and the rights to remain silent, to a speedy and public trial, to an impartial jury, and to confront and secure witnesses.

duress—Refers to conduct that has the effect of compelling another person to do what he or she would not otherwise do. Being under duress is a recognized defense to any act, such as a crime, contractual breach, or tort, all of which must be voluntary to create liability or responsibility.

E

easement—The right of a person to make lawful use of the land of another in accordance with an express or implied agreement. For example, easements often give a person the right to cross another's land.

economic strike—A strike to protest workplace conditions or to support union bargaining demands.

elder abuse—An act or failure to act by a person required to act, that results in harm to an older person, including physical and sexual abuse, emotional and psychological abuse, abandonment, or financial exploitation.

elective share—The statutorily mandated minimum that a surviving spouse may elect to receive from a deceased spouse's estate.

ejectment action—A legal action to determine who has superior title to a property.

emancipated—When a minor is completely living on his or her own and no longer considered a child in the eyes of the law.

emergency medical condition—When symptoms are so severe that any delay in medical treatment could reasonably be expected to seriously harm a patient. At this point, the law requires that a hospital stabilize a patient before transfer, regardless of ability to pay or government coverage.

eminent domain—The right of the government to take property from a private owner for public use, without the owner's consent. The Fifth Amendment to the U.S. Constitution requires the government to compensate the owner of property taken by eminent domain. State constitutions contain similar provisions.

employee at will—Employees who have no written contract governing the length of their employment or the reasons for which they may be fired.

employer identification number (EIN)—A number that identifies businesses for tax purposes. Also referred to as a **federal tax identification** number.

en banc—French term meaning "by the full court." Refers to a situation in which all the judges of an appellate court sit together to hear oral arguments in a case of unusual significance and to decide the case.

encroachment—Occurs when one neighbor's property stands partially on that of another.

encrypt—To encode emails and computer files for security purposes.

enjoin—To require a person, through the issuance of an **injunction,** to perform or to abstain from some specific act.

entrapment—An affirmative defense claiming that the defendant was improperly induced by the government to commit the crime.

equal protection of the law—A guarantee under the Fourteenth Amendment of the U.S. Constitution that all persons receive equal treatment under the law.

equitable action—An action brought to restrain the threatened infliction of wrongs or injuries, and to prevent threatened illegal action, through a court order known as an **injunction.**

equitable distribution—During a divorce proceeding, when a court divides marital property as it thinks is valid, just, and equitable.

equity—The value of your unencumbered interest in your home. An ownership interest in something.

escalator clause—A clause in a premarital agreement that will increase the amount of assets or support given to the less-wealthy spouse based on the length of the marriage or an increase in the wealthier party's assets or income after the agreement was made. Also called a **phase-in provision.**

escheat—The process by which a deceased person's property reverts to the state if no heir can be found.

escrow—Money or a written instrument such as a deed that, by agreement between two parties, is held by a neutral third party (i.e., held in escrow) until all conditions of the agreement are met.

estate—All that a person owns. An estate consists of **personal property** (e.g., a car, household items, and other tangible items), **real property,** and **intangible property,** such as stock certificates and bank accounts owned in the individual person's name.

estate planning—A process by which a person determines what will happen to his or her property after death.

estate tax—A tax imposed on the transfer of property at death, charged to the person's estate.

estop—To stop or prevent.

evaluation procedures—Part of an Individual Education Plan: The specific procedures used by a teacher to determine whether a child has met his or her goals.

eviction—The physical expulsion of a tenant from property, by force or by legal process.

evidence—Any form of proof presented by a party for the purpose of supporting its factual allegations or arguments before the court.

exclusionary rule—A judge-made rule that prevents unconstitutionally obtained evidence from being used in court to build a case against a criminal defendant.

execute—To complete the legal requirements (such as signing before witnesses) that make a will or other document valid. Also, to execute a judgment or decree means to put the final judgment of the court into effect.

executive branch—In the federal government, the branch consisting of the office of the U.S. President and most government agencies.

executor—A personal representative, named in a will, who administers an **estate.**

exemplary damages—See **punitive damages.**

exempt assets—During a bankruptcy proceeding, assets that may be protected from unsecured creditors.

exhibit—A document or other article introduced as evidence during a trial or hearing.

ex parte—Latin term meaning "for one party." An **ex parte proceeding** is one in which only one side is represented, without any notice to any other party (as opposed to an **adversary proceeding**). For example, a request for a search warrant is an ex parte proceeding, since the person subject to the search is not notified of the proceeding and is not present during the hearing.

expert witness—A witness with special knowledge, skill, training, or experience on the subject on which he or she gives evidence. An expert witness is the only kind of witness whose opinion on that subject is admissible as evidence.

ex post facto—Latin term meaning "after the fact." The Constitution prohibits the enactment of ex post facto laws—laws that make acts committed before the passing of the law, and that were not criminal at the time they were committed, punishable as a crime.

expungement—The official and formal elimination of part of a record.

extradition—The process by which one jurisdiction (state or nation) surrenders a person to another jurisdiction who is accused or convicted of a crime in that other jurisdiction.

F

fair housing—The legal term applied to federal, state, and municipal laws that prohibit landlords from refusing to rent property because the prospective tenant falls into one or more protected classes.

false advertising—An unfair method of competition that is usually illegal. It involves misleading a consumer about a product's place of origin, nature or quality, or maker.

family purpose doctrine—A legal theory under which the "head" of the family who maintains a car for general family use may be held liable for the negligent driving of a family member who was authorized to use the vehicle.

fee simple ownership—Ownership of real property free from any conditions, limitations, or restrictions.

felony—A serious criminal offense, generally punishable by imprisonment of one year or more.

fidelity bond—See **surety bond.**

fiduciary—A person with a duty to act primarily for another's benefit—for example, a guardian, trustee, or executor. A fiduciary has a duty to act with loyalty and honesty and in the best interests of the beneficiary.

finding—A formal conclusion by a trial judge or jury regarding the facts of a case.

first appearance—See **arraignment.**

fixed fee—A set fee that will be charged for routine legal work.

fixed-rate loan—A loan for which the interest rate cannot be increased during the term of the loan, typically 15, 20, or 30 years.

fixture—An object that is bolted or otherwise attached to the property.

foreclosure—A legal action in which a lender takes ownership of the property used to secure the loan, because the owner failed to make the required payments.

franchise agreement—The contract between a franchisee and franchisor outlining responsibilities and rights.

fraud—Intentional deception designed to deprive another person of property or to injure him or her in some other way.

free appropriate public education (FAPE)—A publicly funded education at the preschool, elementary, and secondary levels, provided to a special-needs student in conformity with the student's Individualized Education Program.

freeware—Computer programs, software, and media that programmers make available for free through online bulletin boards and user groups.

frustration of purpose—When a contract is voidable because a change in conditions makes performance of the contract meaningless. The frustration must be substantial, not reasonably foreseeable, and must not have been the fault of one of the contract parties.

funeral rule—A federal law that requires funeral homes to quote customers prices and other requested information over the telephone in order to prevent operators from taking advantage of customers.

G

garnishment—A legal proceeding in which a debtor's money, in the possession of another (called the **garnishee**), is applied to the debts of the debtor. An example is when a creditor garnishes a debtor's wages.

Good Samaritan laws—Statutes that protect rescuers from ordinary negligence, but still allow them to be sued for so-called gross (extreme) negligence.

government tort liability acts—Statutes that sharply limit suits against government bodies.

graduated-payment mortgage—A type of loan, typically sought by young buyers who expect their incomes to rise, where the payments are low in the first couple of years and gradually rise for five to ten years.

grand jury—A group of citizens assembled in secret to hear or investigate allegations of criminal behavior. A grand jury has authority to conduct criminal investigations and to charge a person with a crime through an **indictment.**

grantor—The person who sets up a trust. Also called a **settlor** or **donor.**

gray-market goods—Goods that were never intended for sale in the U.S.

guaranty—An agreement or promise to be responsible for another's debt in the event that the person defaults and does not make the required payments. A person who gives a guaranty is called a **guarantor.** The term **surety** is sometimes used interchangeably with "guarantor."

guardian—A person appointed by will or by law to assume responsibility for incompetent adults or minor children.

guardian ad litem (GAL)—An adult legal representative who brings a suit on behalf of a minor. Also referred to as a **next friend.**

guardianship—A legal right given to a person to be responsible for the food, housing, health care, and other necessities of a person deemed incapable of providing these necessities for himself or herself. A guardian's responsibilities can also include financial affairs, which would also make him or her a **conservator.** A **limited guardianship** is when the guardian has only partial control over the ward's affairs.

guilty—The verdict of a jury or judge who believes that a defendant committed the crime with which he or she is charged, or some lesser crime. Defendants may also plead guilty or **nolo contendere** if they do not want to contest the charges.

H

habeas corpus—Latin for "you have the body." One of the oldest protections in English (and now American) law, it is a procedure for obtaining a judicial determination of the legality of a person's custody. Generally, a writ of habeas corpus forces law enforcement authorities to produce a prisoner they are holding and to legally justify his or her detention. A federal writ of habeas corpus is used to test the constitutionality of a state criminal conviction and imprisonment.

harmless error—An error committed by a trial court that the appellate court finds not serious enough to have affected the outcome of a trial, and therefore not sufficiently harmful to justify reversing the lower court's judgment.

health-care proxy—A power of attorney for health-care issues.

health maintenance organizations (HMOs)—Private health service plans that promise to provide care, not merely pay for it.

hearing—Any form of judicial, quasi-judicial or legislative proceeding at which issues are heard, or testimony taken.

hearing on the merits—A hearing before a court on the legal questions at issue, as opposed to procedural questions.

hearsay—Statements by a witness who did not see or hear the incident in question, but instead heard about it from someone else. Hearsay is usually not admissible as evidence in court.

holdover tenant—A tenant who remains on a premises after the expiration of the lease. Also called a **tenant at sufferance.**

holographic will—A handwritten will.

home equity conversion—A plan that uses the equity in your home to help you add to your monthly income without having to leave your home. Such plans include reverse mortgages, special-purpose loans, and sale-leasebacks.

hostile witness—A witness who is subject to cross-examination by the party who called him or her to testify, because he or she exhibited antagonism towards that party in direct examination.

housing code—A municipal ordinance or state statute that sets standards for the construction, rehabilitation, and maintenance of residential buildings.

hung jury—A jury that is unable to reach a verdict.

I

identity theft—When one person takes another's personal information in order to commit fraud or theft.

illegal lease—A lease for property that is in defective condition and violates applicable building codes.

illegality—A defense to a contract on the basis that it involves illegal subject matter.

immunity—A grant that a court gives someone to protect him or her against prosecution, in return for providing criminal evidence against another person or party. **Use immunity** means the prosecutor is not permitted to use what you say, or evidence derived from what you say, to help prosecute you later. **Transactional immunity** provides far greater protection. It means the prosecution will never prosecute you for the crime, even based on evidence independent of your testimony.

impaneling—The process for selecting jurors and swearing them in.

impeachment of witness—An attack on the **credibility** (believability) of a witness through the testimony of other witnesses or other evidence.

implied contract—A contract that is not explicitly written or stated, and is determined by deduction from known facts or from the circumstances or conduct of the parties.

impossibility of performance—When a contract is set aside because it is impossible to perform it, such as when a specific product is no longer available, a house burns down, or an earthquake hits. Also know as **impracticability of performance.**

inadmissible evidence—Evidence that cannot under the rules of evidence be admitted in court.

in camera—Latin for "in chambers" or "in private." A hearing or inspection of documents in camera takes place in the judge's office, outside of the presence of the jury and public.

incompetent—Refers to a defendant who cannot comprehend the nature of the charges against him or her, and thus cannot assist properly in his or her own defense.

independent contractor—A worker who is not considered an "employee" because the employer merely specifies the result to be achieved, and the worker uses personal judgment and discretion in achieving that result. The law treats independent contractors and employees differently.

independent-living community—A type of retirement community that offers little or no health and supportive services, although some may offer recreational and social programs.

indictment—The formal charge issued by a **grand jury** stating that there is enough evidence that the defendant committed the crime to justify having a trial; used primarily in cases involving **felonies.**

indigent—Meeting certain standards of poverty, thereby qualifying a criminal defendant for representation by a public defender.

Individualized Education Program (IEP)—A written document, developed annually for a special-needs student by a multidisciplinary team, outlining the student's needs, present level of performance, goals, and needed services.

inferior courts—Courts of limited jurisdiction.

in forma pauperis—Latin for "in the manner of a pauper." By claiming indigence or poverty, someone may receive permission from the court to sue in forma pauperis and proceed without paying court fees.

information—A formal accusation by a prosecutor that the defendant committed a crime. An information is an alternative to an **indictment** as a means of charging a criminal.

informed consent—A patient's voluntary and knowledgeable acceptance of medical treatment; doctors are not allowed to treat a patient until they have informed consent.

infraction—A violation of law not punishable by imprisonment. Minor traffic offenses generally are considered infractions.

inheritance tax—A state tax on property that an heir or beneficiary receives from a deceased person's estate. The heir or beneficiary pays this tax. In contrast, the deceased person's estate pays the **estate tax.**

initial appearance—See **arraignment.**

injunction—An order of the court prohibiting (or compelling) the performance of a specific act to prevent irreparable damage or injury.

insanity—An affirmative defense to some criminal charges, claiming that the defendant's state of mind was such that it was impossible for him or her to have had the required intent.

instructions—See **charge to the jury.**

intangible assets—Nonphysical items—such as stock certificates, bonds, bank accounts, and pension benefits—that have value.

intellectual property—Property that derives from the work of the mind or intellect. Trade secrets, patents, copyrights, and trademarks are all forms of intellectual property.

intentional discrimination—When an employee is treated differently because of his or her protected status. Also called **disparate treatment.**

intentional tort—A **tort** that the wrongdoer intended to commit. Some common intentional torts against a person include **assault, battery, defamation, false imprisonment** and **intentional infliction of emotional distress.** Intentional torts against property include **trespass to land, trespass to chattel** (personal property) and **conversion** (converting someone else's property into your own). Intentional torts may also be crimes.

interest of justice—A theory that allows a prosecutor to drop a criminal case when he or she feels the case is not significant enough to pursue (for example, a case involving minor damage to property).

interlocutory—Provisional; temporary; not final. Refers to orders and decrees of a court.

interrogatories—Written questions asked by one party of an opposing party, who must answer them in writing under oath; a **discovery** device in a lawsuit.

intervention—A proceeding in which a court permits a third person to become a party to a lawsuit already in progress.

inter vivos—Latin term meaning "between the living." An inter vivos gift is one made during the giver's life.

inter vivos trust—Another name for a **living trust.**

intestacy laws—State laws that provide for the distribution of estate property of a person who dies without a will. Also called **descent and distribution statutes.**

intestate—Dying without a will.

intestate succession—The process by which the property of a person who has died without a will passes on to others according to the state's intestacy laws.

irrevocable trust—A trust that, once established, the grantor may not revoke.

issue—The disputed point in a disagreement between parties in a lawsuit.

installment credit—An arrangement in which the consumer agrees to repay the amount owed in two or more equal installments over a definite period of time. Automobile loans and personal loans are examples of this type of consumer credit. Also referred to as **closed-end credit.**

J

joint and survivor annuity benefit—The most common type of pension payment. It pays the full benefit to a married couple until one dies, then pays a fraction of the full benefit to the survivor as long as he or she lives

joint custody—A custody agreement that can involve joint legal custody or joint physical custody, or both. **Joint legal custody** may mean that both parents share in major decisions affecting the child, or it may mean that each parent may make such decisions when the child is in that parent's care. **Joint physical custody** means that the child spends time with each parent.

joint tenancy—A form of legal co-ownership of property that gives the parties an equal right to enjoy the property, and a right of **survivorship.** At the death of one co-owner, the surviving co-owner or co-owners become sole owners of the property.

jointly and severally—A theory that when more than one defendant has caused damage, any one of the defendants can be held liable for the entire amount of damages. Also called **joint and several liability.**

judgment—The decision of a court regarding the outcome of a dispute, which determines the rights of the parties to the lawsuit. See also **consent judgment, default judgment, summary judgment,** and **judgment notwithstanding the verdict.**

judgment notwithstanding the verdict—A judge's decision to rule in a case contrary to the jury's verdict.

judgment proof—Having no property, or having no property in the jurisdiction where an adverse judgment was obtained, or having property that is protected by statute from the execution of a judgment. A judgment for money cannot be enforced against a debtor who is judgment proof.

judicial branch—In the U.S. system of government, the branch made up of the courts.

judicial bypass—A legal requirement that, if a state law requires a minor to get parental consent before an abortion, the minor must have the option of going to court for a judicial hearing. The hearing then decides whether the abortion may take place without parental consent, either because the minor is mature, or because the abortion would be in the minor's best interest.

judicial review—The review by a court of the official actions of other branches of government; the authority to declare **unconstitutional** the actions of other branches.

judicial safeguards—The required approval of a judge in order for certain activities to take place.

jurisdiction—The power, right, or authority to apply the law. A court's authority to hear cases. Also, the territory from which a court is authorized to hear cases. **General jurisdiction** is when a court has authority over all types of cases. **Specific jurisdiction** limits courts to hearing only certain types of cases. **Concurrent jurisdiction** refers to both the federal and state court having jurisdiction over the same case, and **diversity jurisdiction** refers to federal court jurisdiction based on the fact that the dispute involves citizens from two different states.

jury—A certain number of persons—usually selected from lists of registered voters or licensed drivers—sworn to decide on the facts in issue at a trial. An **alternate juror** is an extra juror selected to guard against the possibility that some of the jurors will become ill or otherwise be unable to complete the trial.

jury panel—See **venire.**

justiciable claim—A claim that is capable of being resolved in the courts.

juvenile court—A court specifically established to hear cases concerning minors.

L

laches—Means "long delay." Under the doctrine of laches, an innocent party who finds out about a wrong, but then delays bringing suit for a substantial period of time, may be barred from bringing the suit altogether.

larceny—Larceny or **theft** is the unlawful taking or attempted taking of property from the possession of another, without force and without deceit, with intent to permanently deprive the owner of the property.

lawsuit—An action brought in court, in which an individual seeks a legal remedy for an alleged wrong.

lawyer—A licensed professional who advises and represents others in legal matters. Also called an **attorney, counsel,** or **counselor.**

leading question—A question that instructs a witness how to answer or suggests which answer is desired. Such questions usually are prohibited on direct examination, but can be asked to hostile witnesses or on cross-examination.

lease—An agreement by which an owner of property gives exclusive possession of the property to another person for a period of time, usually in exchange for rent. At the end of the lease, the owner may take possession of the property again. A lease may be **month by month** (in which case rent is payable monthly, and the lease can be changed or terminated by either party after provision of notice), or for a **fixed term** (in which case neither party can end or modify the lease before the end of the term without the permission of the other).

legacy—See **bequest.**

legalese—The "legal speak" used by lawyers and legal professionals.

legal separation—An arrangement in which a husband and wife live separately, and formalize the arrangement through a court order or written agreement.

legislative branch—The branch of the government that drafts laws and statutes; in the federal government, the branch of government that is made up of the Congress.

legislative courts—Courts authorized by Congress to serve U.S. territories.

lemon—A car that continues to have a defect that substantially restricts its use, safety, or value, even after reasonable efforts have been made to repair it.

lessee—Someone who leases something from another person.

lessor—Someone who leases something to another person.

liability insurance—A portion of a homeowner's insurance policy designed to cover unintentional injuries on the premises and unintentional damage to other people's property. An **umbrella liability policy** is designed to protect a homeowner in case of a big judgment that would not be covered by a regular policy.

liable—Legally responsible.

libel—Published words or pictures that falsely and maliciously defame a person—that is, injure his or her reputation. Libel is published defamation; **slander** is spoken defamation.

license—Permission to use specific software, or—in the case of rental property—permission to use some property that can be revoked by the landlord, and is not a guarantee of continued right to use that property. Can also include permission to practice a certain profession (medicine or law) or to exercise a privilege (driving).

license cancellation—Voluntary relinquishment of one's driving privilege without penalty. Cancellation allows you to reapply for a license immediately.

lien—A legal claim against another person's property as security for a debt. A lien does not convey ownership of the property, but gives

the lienholder a right to have his or her debt satisfied out of the proceeds of the property if the debt is not otherwise paid. A **mechanic's lien** is one placed on a home, and is created by law for the purpose of securing payment for work performed or materials furnished in construction.

liquidated damages—A sum of money specified in advance by a contract or agreement, which must be paid if the agreement's terms are violated.

litigant—A participant in a lawsuit—i.e., a **plaintiff** or a **defendant.**

litigation—A civil case or lawsuit.

listing agreement—A contract between the seller of real property and the listing real estate agency. The listing agreement outlines their relationship, including the length of the listing period, the commission rate, the responsibilities of the firm and its agents, and who will pay for the cost of advertising and other associated costs.

living trust—A trust set up and in effect during the lifetime of the grantor. Also called an **inter vivos trust.**

living will—See **advance directive.**

local education agency (LEA)—The term used by federal law to refer to a local public board of education or other authority that is charged with administering, controlling, and directing the public elementary and secondary schools in a city, district, or county.

loss of consortium—Refers to the loss of companionship and sexual relationship with one's spouse.

M

magistrate judges—Judicial officers who assist U.S. district judges in getting cases ready for trial. They may decide some criminal and civil trials when both parties agree to have the case heard by a magistrate judge instead of a judge.

maintenance—See **alimony.**

malpractice—Negligence, misconduct, lack of ordinary skill, or a breach of duty in the performance of a professional service, resulting in injury or loss. Examples include **medical malpractice** and **legal malpractice.**

mandate—A judicial command directing the proper officer to enforce a judgment, sentence, or decree.

manslaughter—The unlawful killing of another without premeditation. This can be voluntary and upon a sudden impulse—for example, if a quarrel erupts into a fistfight in which one of the participants is killed. Or it can be involuntary—for example, during the commission of an unlawful act not ordinarily expected to result in great bodily harm, or during the commission of a lawful act without proper caution, such as driving an automobile at excessive speed resulting in a fatal collision.

marital property—See **community property.**

material misrepresentation—An important untruth, made with the intent to deceive, that another party reasonably relies on to his or her disadvantage.

material noncompliance—Substantial noncompliance.

mediation—A form of alternative dispute resolution in which the parties bring their dispute to a neutral third party, who helps them agree on a settlement.

Medicaid—A medical assistance program for older or disabled persons who are poor, and for certain children and families whose income and assets fall below certain levels set by federal and state law.

medical directive—See **living will.**

Medicare—A federally funded health-care insurance program for older disabled individuals.

Medigap—Supplemental health insurance that covers some of the expenses not covered by Medicare.

mens rea—Latin term meaning "guilty mind." Mens rea is the mental component of a crime: the intent necessary to establish criminal responsibility; the physical component of a crime is the **actus reus.**

merits—Issues of legal substance at stake in a case, as opposed to procedural considerations.

metatags—Programming codes that Web creators use to enable search engines to find their websites.

Miranda warning—The warning police must give suspects regarding their constitutional right to remain silent and their right to a lawyer.

misdemeanor—A less serious criminal offense than a **felony,** usually punishable by a sentence of one year in jail or less.

mistake—An act or omission arising from ignorance or misconception. A **mutual mistake** is one made by both parties to a contract, and a court may set the contract aside on the basis that there has been no mutual assent. A **unilateral mistake** is a mistake on the part of one party to a contract. A unilateral mistake is not usually grounds for setting aside the contract, unless one party stands to profit or benefit improperly from the mistake.

mistrial—An erroneous or invalid trial; a trial that cannot stand in law because of lack of jurisdiction, incorrect procedure with respect to jury selection, or disregard of some other fundamental requisite; a trial that is invalid because of the inability of a jury to reach a verdict.

mitigating factors—Factors relating to a crime or defendant that suggest a shorter sentence might be warranted.

mortgage—A loan secured by property. Usually the loan is for the purchase price of the property, minus the amount of a down payment. If the borrower (called the **mortgagor**) defaults on the loan, then the lender (called the **mortgagee**) has the right to **foreclose** on the property to pay the debt. A mortgage can also be called a **deed of trust.** A **reverse mortgage** is one that lets you borrow against the equity in your home—receiving a lump sum or monthly installments, or drawing on a line of credit—and does not have to be paid off until you die or sell your home.

motion—An application to a court or judge for a ruling or order. For example, a **motion to suppress** is an application to the court to exclude evidence that was obtained illegally; a **motion to dismiss** is a formal request for the court to dismiss a complaint because of insufficiency of evidence or because the law does not recognize the injury or harm claimed. A **motion to quash** is a claim to throw a case out because service was improper.

multiplicity of actions—Several lawsuits against the same defendant seeking to litigate the same right.

municipal courts—In the judicial organization of some states, courts whose territorial authority is confined to a city or community.

murder—The unlawful killing of a human being with malice aforethought (i.e., deliberate intent to kill). Murder in the first degree is characterized by premeditation; murder in the second degree is characterized by a sudden and instantaneous intent to kill or to cause injury without caring whether the injury kills or not.

mutuality of obligation—Under contract law, the theory that binds both parties to a contract; each party to a contract must give some form of **consideration** in order for the agreement to count as a valid contract.

mutual mistake—See **mistake.**

N

nail-and-mail summons—When a court summons is nailed to a person's front door, and a copy is also sent to the person by mail. Can be used for eviction notices in some jurisdictions.

necessaries—Those items that you cannot live without, such as food and basic clothing.

Under basic contract law, when a minor makes a contract for necessaries, his or her parents may be responsible for the fair market value of the necessaries, even if the minor would normally be able to void the contract.

necessity—An affirmative defense claiming that natural forces outside of the defendant's control forced him or her to commit the crime in order to prevent greater injury.

neglect—When someone with guardianship or responsibility over another person fails to provide for the other's basic needs, including food, shelter, clothing, medical treatment, and supervision. Also referred to as **endangerment;** neglect often involves children or the elderly.

negligence—Failure to exercise ordinary care; the basis for many **tort** (personal injury) lawsuits. The doctrine of **negligent supervision** applies to parents whose children engage in certain acts (such as drinking and driving).

nolo contendere—Latin for "I do not wish to contend." Has the same effect as a plea of guilty as far as the criminal sentence is concerned, but may not be considered an admission of guilt for any other purpose.

nominal damages—A trivial sum of damages (e.g., $10) awarded in cases in which a party has been injured but no loss resulted from the injury, or in which the injured party failed to prove that loss resulted from the injury. Often awarded in intentional tort cases.

nominal party—One who is joined as a party or defendant merely because the technical rules of pleading require his or her presence in the record.

not guilty—Pleaded by a defendant who intends to contest the charges; also, the verdict of a jury who finds that the prosecution has not proven the defendant's guilt beyond a reasonable doubt.

notice—A formal notification to the party being sued that a lawsuit has been initiated.

notice to produce—A notice in writing requiring the opposite party to yield a certain de-scribed paper or document in advance or at the trial.

nuisance—In **tort** law, the legal term for a person's unreasonable action that interferes with your enjoyment of your property. Any-thing from noxious gases to annoying wind chimes may constitute grounds for a nui-sance suit.

nuncupative will—An oral (unwritten) will.

nursing home—A facility that provides skilled nursing care and related services for residents who require medical or nursing care; rehabili-tation services for injured, disabled, or sick persons; and health-related care and services, above the level of room and board, that can be made available only through institutional facilities.

O

objection—The act of taking exception to some statement or procedure in a trial. Used to call the court's attention to improper evidence or procedure.

objection overruled—A judge's rejection of an objection as invalid. The statement or proce-dure objected to will stand.

objection sustained—A judge's support or agreement with an objection. The statement or procedure objected to will have to be rephrased or changed.

of counsel—A phrase commonly applied to a lawyer employed to help prepare or manage a case, but who is not the principal attorney of record. Also, a senior member of a law firm who may be retired or semi-retired.

offer—An act of willingness to enter into a purchase agreement that justifies another person in understanding that his assent to that purchase agreement is invited and will establish a contract. The person who makes the offer is called the **offeror;** the person to whom the offer is made is called the **offeree.**

ombudsman—A government official whose job is to mediate and resolve minor landlord-tenant, consumer, or employment issues.

one day—one trial jury service—System used in many jurisdictions in which potential jurors either serve for the length of a trial (if assigned to a jury), or complete their service in one day (if not assigned to a jury).

opening statements—The outlines of the evidence that each side expects to prove, presented to the jury or judge by the lawyers at the start of a trial.

opinion—A trial court's written explanation of its decision, or the written decision of judges of an appellate court.

option—A contract that gives the holder a right or option to buy or sell specified property, such as stock or real estate, at a fixed price for a limited period of time. The option holder is called the **optionee.** An **option to renew** is a lease clause that enables the lessee to renew the lease at the end of the lease term for an additional term.

oral argument—An opportunity for lawyers to summarize their positions before the court, and also to answer the judges' questions.

order—A command from the court directing or forbidding an action.

organ donation—The procedure by which any part of a person's anatomy (including organs, tissues and bones) is given to another person in need or for scientific study. Also called an **anatomical gift.**

original jurisdiction—A court's authority to hear a case in the first instance (i.e., to be the first court to hear it).

overrule—To not allow an objection in a trial; also, to declare that a lower court decision was in error.

P

paralegals—Nonlawyers who receive training that enables them to assist lawyers in a num-ber of tasks; they typically cannot represent clients in court.

parole—The supervised, conditional release of a prisoner.

parol evidence—Any evidence of an agreement outside of what appears in a contract.

parties—The persons who are actively involved with the prosecution or defense of a legal proceeding. **Plaintiffs** and **defendants** are parties to **lawsuits; appellants** and **appellees** are parties in **appeals.** (They may also be known as **petitioners** and **respondents.**)

patent—The exclusive right granted to an inventor to make or sell his or her invention for a term of years.

peremptory challenge—A **motion** by a party to reject a juror for an unspecified race-neutral reason. May only be used a limited number of times. Differs from **challenge for cause.**

perjury—The criminal offense of making a false statement under oath.

personal injury—See **tort.**

personal property—Tangible physical property (such as cars, clothing, furniture, and jewelry) and **intangible personal property,** but not **real property**—that is, not land or rights in land.

personal recognizance—When a person is released from custody before trial based on his or her promise to return for further proceedings. Also known as **release on own recognizance.**

petit jury—The twelve (or fewer) jurors selected to sit in the trial of a civil or criminal case. Compare to **grand jury.**

petitioner—See **appellant.**

placement offer—A written offer, completed by a local education agency after the completion of an Individualized Education program, outlining the specific services to be offered to a special-needs student and the location where those services will be offered.

plaintiff—A person who begins a civil lawsuit.

planned community—A hybrid subdivision combining certain aspects of cooperatives and condominiums.

plea—The defendant's declaration of "guilty" or "not guilty" in response to criminal charges.

plea bargain—The process by which an accused person agrees to plead guilty to some charges in return for the government's promise to drop other charges or recommend leniency in sentencing.

pleadings—Written statements of fact and law filed by the parties to a lawsuit. Pleadings are comprised of complaints, answers, and replies.

points—Interest charges paid up front when a borrower closes a loan, or fees imposed by a lender to cover certain expenses of making a real estate loan.

polling the jury—A practice whereby the jurors are asked individually whether they agree, and still agree, to the verdict.

pourover will—A will that leaves some or all estate assets to a trust established before the will maker's death.

power of attorney—A document in which one person (called the **principal**) authorizes another (called the **agent**) to act on his or her behalf. A general power of attorney covers all financial matters. A springing power of attorney only becomes effective once you are incapacitated.

precedent—A previously decided case that guides subsequent decisions.

preexisting condition clause—A clauses in an insurance policy that disallows coverage for medical conditions that someone had before applying for the new policy.

prejudicial error—Synonymous with **reversible error;** an error that warrants the appellate court's reversal of the judgment before it.

preliminary hearing—A criminal hearing held after the **first appearance,** at which a judge determines whether **probable cause** exists to believe the suspect committed the crime with which he or she is charged.

premarital agreement—A contract entered into by a man and woman before they marry. The agreement usually describes what each party's rights will be if they divorce or when one of them dies. Premarital agreements usually set forth who is entitled to what property, and how much support, if any, will be paid in the event of divorce. Also known as **prenuptial agreements** or **antenuptial agreements.** If such an agreement is entered into after a marriage, it is a **postnuptial agreement.**

premises liability—Legal responsibility arising from injuries or losses occurring on one's property.

prenuptial agreement—See **premarital agreement.**

prepetition debts—Debts incurred before filing for bankruptcy.

preponderance of evidence—The greater weight of evidence, or evidence that is more credible and convincing, but not necessarily offered by the greater number of witnesses. This is the common standard of proof in civil cases.

pre-sentence investigation—An inquiry conducted at the request of the court after a person has been found guilty of a criminal offense. Provides the court with extensive background information so that it can determine an appropriate sentence.

present level of performance—A clear, descriptive statement of how a disabled child is performing in a specific area of need.

presumption—An assumption of a fact that is not certainly known, which can be drawn from the known or proven existence of some other fact.

pretrial conference—A meeting in which lawyers for both sides meet the judge in advance of a trial to seek to clarify or narrow the issues.

prima facie case—Latin term meaning "at first sight." A case supported by at least the minimum amount of evidence and free from obvious defects. A party is entitled to have a case heard by a jury if he or she has a prima facie case.

principal—In criminal law, one who commits an offense, or an accomplice who is present during the commission of a crime. In commercial law, the amount received in loan, or the amount upon which interest is charged. In the law of agency, one who has permitted or engaged another (the **agent**) to act for his or her benefit.

privacy rule—Part of the Health Insurance Portability and Accountability Act of 1996 (HIPAA), the rule gives you some control over how your personal health information is used and disclosed.

private mortgage insurance (PMI)—Insurance that is required when a down payment on a property is not equal to 20 percent of the purchase price. PMI insures the lender against nonpayment of the difference between the customary down payment and the down payment actually paid.

privilege—Arises in confidential relationships, and grants the parties in the relationship an exemption from the legal requirement to disclose information at trial. For example, **attorney-client privilege** means that lawyers cannot give evidence about legal advice they gave to their clients. This privilege can be waived by the client but not by the lawyer. The **doctor-patient privilege** means that the doctor cannot disclose the patient's personal information during a legal proceeding without the patient's consent.

probable cause—Sufficient facts and circumstances to justify the belief that certain circumstances exist (for example, that a crime has been committed).

probate—The judicial process of determining whether a will is valid; also, the process of settling an estate (e.g., gathering assets, paying claims, distributing bequests) under the supervision of the **probate court. Ancillary probate** is an additional probate procedure occurring in another state.

probate court—The court with authority to

determine the validity of wills and supervise estate **administration.**

probate estate—Estate property that may be disposed of by a will.

probation—A sentencing alternative to imprisonment in which the court releases convicted defendants under supervision as long as certain conditions are observed.

pro bono publico—Latin term meaning "for the public good or welfare." When lawyers work for clients without pay, they are said to be working pro bono.

procedural law—Law regulating the procedure of the courts and the legal system, including pleadings and evidence. Compare to **substantive law.**

product liability insurance—Insurance that protects a business from damage claims filed by third parties who are injured by a product produced by that business.

pro hac vice—A Latin phrase meaning "for this one particular occasion." Refers to situations in which lawyers are allowed to participate in specific cases in states where they are not licensed.

promissory note—A note containing a promise to pay a sum of money to a specified person or the bearer at a specified future time.

promissory reliance—Reasonable reliance by one party on the promise of another. Promissory reliance can create a contract.

pro se—A Latin term meaning "on one's own behalf." In courts, it refers to persons who present their own cases without lawyers.

prosecution—The act of pursuing a lawsuit or criminal trial. In a criminal suit, the prosecution is the state.

prosecutor—A government lawyer who tries criminal cases. See **district attorney.**

pro tanto award—An offer made by the government to purchase land from a private owner.

protected status—An individual's race, religion, national origin, sex, age, disability, or union activity. Under federal law, you cannot be

discriminated against because of your protected status.

protective order—See **restraining order.**

provision—See **term.**

public defender—A lawyer employed by the government to represent individuals accused of crimes who cannot afford to hire their own private lawyers.

punitive damages—An order to pay money for an error that has caused legal injury, as a form of punishment and of deterrence from future commissions of the same error; also known as **exemplary damages.**

putative-spouse doctrine—A legal theory allows a putative (i.e., supposed) spouse to claim the same benefits and rights as a legal spouse for as long as she or he reasonably believed an invalid marriage to be valid.

Q

quash—To overthrow; to vacate; to annul or void a summons or indictment.

question of fact—A disputed contention of fact that is usually decided by a jury, and may not be reconsidered in an appeal.

question of law—A disputed legal contention that depends on an examination of the law. Questions of law are decided by a judge, and may be reexamined in an appeal.

quiet title—A lawsuit that determines which claimant has the right to certain real property or portions of such property.

R

rape—See **sexual assault.**

reaffirming debt—During a bankruptcy proceeding, this is the process by which a debtor can keep certain property after promising to the pay the creditor the amount owed.

real estate owned by the lender (REO)—Foreclosed property owned by the lending institution or government agency that backed the mortgage.

real property—Land, buildings, and other improvements affixed to land, as opposed to **personal property.**

reasonable accommodation—Changes in rules or procedures that are reasonable under the circumstances, and that give a disabled person equal opportunity to participate in a specific activity, program, job, or housing situation.

reasonable doubt—Uncertainty that might exist in the mind of a reasonable person applying reason to the evidence introduced. See **beyond a reasonable doubt.**

reasonable modifications—Changes to the physical structure of a building or property that are reasonable under the circumstances, and that give a person with disabilities equal access to the premises.

reasonable person—A hypothetical person used in the law as an objective standard. The reasonable person has an ordinary degree of care, foresight, intelligence, and judgment. Negligence stems from careless or thoughtless conduct under the reasonable-person standard, or from a failure to act when a reasonable person would have acted.

rebuttal—The introduction of contrary evidence; the showing that statements of witnesses as to what occurred are not true; the stage of a trial at which such evidence may be introduced.

recall—A request by a manufacturer that consumers return a defective product.

reckless driving—Driving with "willful or wanton disregard for the safety of persons or property."

record—A written account of all the acts, proceedings and testimony in a lawsuit.

redeem—To buy back certain property. Can occur during a bankruptcy proceeding.

redirect examination—Follows **cross-examination,** and is exercised by the party who called and questioned the witness first. Redirect examination must only extend to those matters brought up in cross-examination, and is not another chance for **direct examination.**

referral—A written request for a child to begin special education and related services.

reform—When a court rewrites a contract that is voidable for some reason, such as fraud. This process brings the contract in line with the law and protects the wronged party.

rehabilitative support—A type of spousal support or maintenance that is intended to provide a chance for education or job training so that a spouse who was financially dependent or disadvantaged during marriage can become self-supporting.

related services—Any services that are necessary to assist a child in benefiting from special education services.

release on own recognizance—See **personal recognizance.**

reletting—When a landlord signs a completely new lease with a replacement tenant, and releases the original tenant from the obligation to pay rent.

reliance—Confidence or dependence upon what is deemed sufficient authority (for example, a warranty that provides a written guarantee of the integrity of a product).

remand—To send a dispute back to the court where it was originally heard. This often occurs when an appellate court sends a case back to a lower court for further proceedings.

remedy—The means by which a right can be enforced or a wrong can be redressed; also the relief that a court may order. For example, a court may order specific performance as a remedy for a breach of contract.

removal, order of—An order by a court directing the transfer of a case to another court.

rent control—Limits on the amount of rent that landlords can charge, or on the rent increases they can impose.

repair and deduct—A legal theory that permits a tenant to hire someone to make repairs and then to deduct the cost of those repairs from the rent.

repair order—A repair contract describing the work to be done and, once signed, authorizing the person doing the repairs to perform the described work.

reply—A plaintiff's response to a plea, allegation, or counterclaim in the defendant's **answer.** The purpose of a reply is to respond to new matters raised in the answer.

repossess—To take back—as in a seizure or **foreclosure**—to satisfy the obligation to the seller, bank, or finance company after the debtor defaults on his or her payments.

representative payee—A person or an organization appointed by a government agency, such as the Social Security Administration (SSA) or the Department of Veterans Affairs (VA), to receive and manage public benefits on behalf of someone who is incapable of doing so.

reprimand—When a lawyer is privately criticized for acting unethically.

repudiation—An act or declaration by a party to a contract that he or she will not perform the contract.

resale tax certificate—A certificate from the state tax authority saying that the materials you buy from a wholesaler will be sold to the public as part of a product, at which time a sales tax will be collected. This prevents you from having to pay sales tax when you purchase the raw materials.

rescission—The cancellation of a contract, which returns the parties to the position they would have been in if the contract had never been made. The **right of rescission** gives customers three business days to cancel any contract that was signed in their homes (or any location other than the seller's place of business) and that involves any financial claim to the home.

reserve—When the court postpones ruling on a motion until after the trial, or until after the jury has rendered a verdict.

residential placement—A special education service that includes programs where children are cared for at locations outside of their family homes, including medical and non-medical care, room, and board.

residuary estate—In situations where a will exists, any property that is left out of the will.

respondeat superior—See **vicarious liability.**

respondent—See **appellee.**

rest—A party is said to "rest" or "rest its case" when it has presented all the evidence it intends to offer.

restatement—In the law of **trusts,** a new trust that replaces an existing trust; rather than modify an existing trust with many changes, it is often simpler to restate the trust—i.e., create a new trust.

restitution—The making good of an injury, often by payment of money. A criminal may have to pay restitution to the victim of a crime.

restraining order—An order intended to protect one individual from violence, abuse, harassment, or stalking by another, by prohibiting or restricting access or proximity to the protected party.

retainer—When a client pays a lawyer a set amount of money regularly to make sure that the lawyer will be available for any necessary legal services. Not a **retainer fee.**

retainer fee—In effect, a down payment on legal fees that will be applied toward the total fee billed.

retroactive rent abatement—When a tenant paid full rent but the premises were defective, a rent reduction sought by the tenant for rent paid in previous months.

reverse—To set aside the decision of a lower court because of an error. A reversal is often accompanied by a **remand** to the lower court that heard the case.

reverse mortgage—See **mortgage.**

reversible error—An error sufficiently prejudicial (harmful) to justify reversing the judgment of a lower court; compare to **harmless error.**

revocable trust—A trust that the grantor may change or revoke.

revoke—To cancel or nullify a legal document. To revoke someone's driver's license means that the state has terminated that person's driving privileges.

revolving credit—An arrangement in which the consumer has the option of drawing on a preapproved open-end credit line from time to time, and then paying off the entire outstanding balance, paying only a specified minimum, or paying something in between. With this type of credit, the consumer may use the credit, make a payment, and use the credit again. Credit cards such as Discover, MasterCard, and Visa, and those issued by major retail establishments, are examples of revolving credit. Also referred to as **open-end credit.**

rider—A page or several pages containing an addition or change to the main body of a contract. Often it's simpler to put changes in a rider, which supersedes any contradictory parts of the contract.

right of survivorship—A form of property ownership in which, when one joint owner dies, the surviving owner or owners own 100 percent of the property.

right to counsel—The right to have a lawyer's advice.

robbery—The unlawful taking or attempted taking of property that is in the immediate possession of another, by force or by threat of force.

rule of court—An order made by a court having jurisdiction. Rules of court are either general or special: the former are the regulations by which the practice of the court is governed; the latter are special orders made in particular cases.

rules of evidence—Standards governing whether evidence in a civil or criminal case is **admissible.**

S

safety inspection sticker law—A state law that creates certain legal rights if a recently purchased used car fails a safety inspection.

search warrant—See **warrant.**

section 401(k) plan—A defined-contribution plan funded by contributions that the employee elects to make, and that are deducted from his or her salary before taxes.

security—Property that can be sold to pay a debt if the borrower cannot pay. For example, a mortgage is a secured debt, because if the borrower defaults on the mortgage, then the lender can foreclose on the house to pay the debt.

security of tenure—The legal theory that a tenant has the right to continue the tenancy indefinitely, unless the tenant violates certain rules or regulations or the landlord has a compelling reason to reclaim possession of the premises.

self-proving will—A will whose validity does not have to be testified to in court by witnesses, since the witnesses executed an affidavit reflecting proper execution of the will prior to the will maker's death.

sentence—The punishment ordered by a court for a defendant convicted of a crime.

separate property—Property of a spouse that is not community or marital property. Also called **nonmarital property.**

separation of powers—In the U.S. system of government, the theory that no single branch of the government should unduly influence the others or have too much power.

separation of witnesses—An order of the court requiring all witnesses to remain outside the courtroom until each is called to testify, except the plaintiff or defendant.

sequester—To separate. Sometimes juries are sequestered from outside influences during their deliberations.

serve—To deliver a legal document, such as a complaint, summons, or subpoena.

service—The delivery of a legal document—such as a complaint, summons, or subpoena—notifying a person of a lawsuit or other legal action taken against him or her. Service constitutes formal legal notice.

service contract—A contract for repair services and maintenance for a set period of time.

settlement—An agreement resolving a dispute between parties in a lawsuit without trial. Settlements often involve the payment of compensation by one party in satisfaction of the other party's claims.

settlor—The person who sets up a trust. Also called the **grantor** or **donor.**

sexual assault—Forced sexual conduct or penetration without the victim's consent or when the victim is underage. Such crimes are often called **rape, sexual conduct,** or **sexual battery,** and may include special designations when the victim is a child.

sexual harassment—Harassment of an individual because of his or her sex. Can include **quid pro quo harassment,** where submission to harassment is used as the basis for employment decisions; and **hostile-environment harassment,** which creates an offensive working environment.

shared-appreciation mortgage—A type of loan that offers lower-than-market rates of interest and low payments in exchange for a lender's share in appreciation of the property. Usually the lender will require that its share of equity be turned over when the home is sold, or at a specified date set forth in the loan agreement.

shareware—Computer software, programs, and media that are protected by copyright, but which the copyright holder permits to be freely copied and distributed. The new user is usually requested, on the honor system, to remit a relatively small payment for costs and to register as a user.

sheriff—An officer of a county, often chosen by popular election, whose principal duties are to aid the courts. The sheriff serves processes, summons juries, executes judgments, and holds judicial sales.

short-term objectives—Part of an Individual Education Plan: specific, sequential steps aimed at helping a child progress from his or her present level of functioning to achievement of the annual goal.

sidebar conference—Confidential discussion between judge and attorneys to resolve legal matters, which could be prejudicial if aired before the jury.

simplified employee pension plan (SEP)—A relatively uncomplicated type of retirement savings plan that is particularly popular with small companies. A SEP allows employers to make contributions on a tax-favored basis to individual retirement accounts owned by the employees.

slander—False and defamatory spoken words tending to harm another's reputation, business, or means of livelihood. Slander is spoken defamation; **libel** is published defamation.

small-claims court—A court that handles civil claims for small amounts of money. In small-claims court, people often represent themselves rather than hire a lawyer. Also called **magistrate court, justice of the peace court,** or **pro se court.**

special damages—See **consequential damages.**

specific performance—Where damages would be inadequate compensation for the breach of a contract, the requirement that the party who breached the contract perform what he or she originally agreed to do.

spendthrift trust—A trust set up for the benefit of someone who the grantor believes would be incapable of managing his or her own financial affairs.

spite fence—A fence that is excessively high, has no reasonable use, and was clearly constructed to annoy a neighbor.

spousal support—See **alimony. Permanent spousal support** is alimony that provides money for a spouse who cannot become economically independent or maintain a lifestyle that the court considers appropriate given the resources of the parties.

stand mute—A type of criminal plea allowed in some jurisdictions when the defendant refuses to admit to the correctness of the proceedings against him or her at that point.

standard of proof—The degree to which a point in dispute between the parties must be proven. For example, in a civil case the **burden of proof** rests with the plaintiff, who must establish his or her case by such standards of proof as a **preponderance of evidence** or **clear and convincing evidence.** In a criminal case, the standard of proof is much higher—the prosecution must prove guilt **beyond a reasonable doubt.**

standing—The legal right to sue or enter a lawsuit on a particular matter. Only a person with something at stake has standing to bring a lawsuit.

stare decisis—Latin term meaning "to stand by that which was decided." When a court has once laid down a principle of law as applicable to a certain set of facts, it will adhere to that principle and apply it to future cases where the facts are substantially the same.

statute—A law enacted by legislatures or executive officers.

statute of limitations—A law that sets the time within which parties must take action to enforce their rights.

stay—A court order halting a judicial proceeding.

steering—The practice of showing potential buyers of a certain race, religion, gender, color, or national origin homes located only in certain neighborhoods.

stipulation—An agreement by lawyers on opposite sides of a case as to any matter pertaining to the proceedings or trial, such as an agreement to admit certain facts at the trial. A stipulation is not binding unless agreed to by the parties.

strict liability—Liability that is imposed on a party who is not negligent. Strict liability is often imposed in the context of ultrahazardous activities. For example, a person who uses explosives may be strictly liable for any injuries caused to a bystander, even if the bystander was standing too close to the explosives and the person using them did nothing wrong.

strike—To remove improperly offered evidence from the court record.

subleasing—When an original tenant rents to a new tenant.

subpoena—A document issued by the court to compel a witness to appear and give testimony or to procure documentary evidence in a proceeding.

subpoena duces tecum—Latin for "under penalty you shall bring with you." A process by which the court commands a witness to produce certain documents or records in a trial.

substantive law—Law dealing with rights, duties and liabilities, as distinguished from law that regulates procedure.

summary judgment—A court order that decides a case in favor of one side on the basis of affidavits or other evidence, before the trial commences. It is used when there is no dispute as to the facts of the case, and one party is entitled to judgment as a matter of law.

summons—Legal notice informing an individual of a lawsuit and the date and location of the court where the case will be heard.

support trust—A trust that instructs the trustee to spend only as much income and principal (the assets held in the trust) as is needed for the beneficiary's support.

surety—See **guaranty.** Traditionally, a surety can be distinguished from a **guarantor** because the guarantor is liable only if the principal defaults on the contract. The surety is directly and immediately liable for another person's debt and other obligations. Also sometimes called a **cosigner.**

surety bond—A bond purchased at the expense of the estate to insure the executor's proper performance. Often called a **fidelity bond.**

surrogacy—When one woman carries a child for another couple that will become the child's legal parents. Surrogacy can include **traditional surrogacy,** in which a woman (the surrogate) undergoes intrauterine insemination with sperm from the man who wants to be the legal father, or **gestational carrier surrogacy,** in which the baby ends up with no genetic connection to the surrogate because the fertilized embryo was transferred to the surrogate who carried the baby.

survey—An accurate depiction of property.

survivorship—The right of a person who holds property with another as a joint tenant or tenant by the entirety to take the interest of the other person when he or she dies.

suspended—When a lawyer's license to practice law is taken away for a certain time. Can also apply to driver's licenses.

sustain—To issue a court order allowing an objection or motion to prevail.

T

tangible personal property memorandum (TPPM)—A separate handwritten document that is incorporated into a will by reference, is dated, and contains lists of tangible personal property (e.g., jewelry, artwork, furniture) and the people who should receive that property.

temporary restraining order (TRO)—Prohibits a person from an action that is likely to cause irreparable harm. This differs from an **injunction** in that it may be granted immediately, without notice to the opposing party, and without a hearing. It is intended to last only until a hearing can be held.

tenancy by the entirety—A form of property ownership in which husband and wife own the property together. If either spouse dies, the surviving spouse is entitled to the whole property; a divorce usually ends the tenancy by the entirety and converts it into a **tenancy in common.**

tenancy in common—A form of property ownership in which each tenant is entitled to equal use and possession of the property, but neither party has any right to the other's interest when one person dies.

tender of delivery—When the seller actually delivers goods to the buyer. This is the point at which certain rights and obligations transfer between the parties.

term—A period of time—for example, a court term or a prison term; also, a clause or **provision** of a contract.

testamentary capacity—The legal ability to make a will.

testamentary trust—A trust set up by a will.

testator—A person who makes a will.

testatrix—A female testator.

testimony—Evidence given by a competent witness, under oath, as distinguished from evidence derived from writings and other sources.

theft—See **larceny.**

third-party claim—An action by the defendant that brings a third party into a lawsuit.

title—Legal ownership of property, usually real property or automobiles. An **abstract of title** outlines the results of a title search indicating whether title is free of exceptions or encumbrances. **Title insurance** is insurance from a company that agrees to defend against and pay losses involved in any claim resulting from a problem with title.

tort—A civil wrong or breach of a duty to another person, as outlined by law. A very common type of tort is negligent operation of a motor vehicle that results in an automobile collision and subsequent property damage and personal injury. A tort lawsuit is often called a **personal injury** case. A **tortfeasor** is someone who commits a tort.

trademark—Any word or words; name; symbol or picture; or device that a company or business uses to distinguish its goods from someone else's. The use of trademarks is protected by common law; trademarks can also be registered to provide the owner with greater protection. Trademarks are a kind of **intellectual property.**

trade name—A name that identifies a business, and that gives the owner the right to conduct business under that name in advertising, applying for permits, billing customers, paying taxes, and so on.

transcript—The official record of proceedings in a trial or hearing.

transferred intent—A legal doctrine that allows the intent to commit a tort to transfer between the intended victim and the actual victim. For example, if your neighbor fired his shotgun to scare a solicitor, but one of his bullets grazed a passerby, then the neighbor's intent is said to be transferred—i.e., he intended to commit the crime in the eyes of the law, even though he intended to commit it against a different victim.

transition services—A coordinated set of activities for a special-needs student that promote movement from school to post-school activities, including post-secondary education, vocational training, employment, continuing and adult education, and independent living.

transitory—A lawsuit is transitory when it can be brought wherever the defendant may be found and served with a summons, and when the jurisdiction has sufficient contact with one of the parties and the incident that gave rise to the suit. A lawsuit is **local** if it can only be brought in the county where the subject of the suit is located—for example, the property being foreclosed on.

traverse—In **pleading,** to traverse means to deny. When a defendant denies any material allegation of fact in the plaintiff's declaration, then he or she is said to traverse it.

trial—The examination of fact and law before a court.

trial court—The court that first tries and determines issues of fact and law. Compare to **appellate court.**

trust—A legal device used to manage property—real or personal—established by one person (the **donor, grantor,** or **settlor**) for the benefit of another (the **beneficiary**). A third person or the grantor manages the trust. This person is known as the **trustee.**

trust agreement or declaration—The legal document that sets up a trust.

trustee—The person or institution that manages the property put in trust.

U

unauthorized practice of medicine—When an unlicensed person does something covered by the legal definition of "medicine." The unauthorized practice of medicine can result in criminal prosecution.

unconscionable—Unreasonably unfair to one party. For example, one-sided contracts signed by a party with little bargaining power may be so unfair and commercially unreasonable as to be unconscionable, and a court may set such contracts aside.

unconstitutional—Conflicting with some provision of a constitution. A statute that is found to be unconstitutional—that is, conflicting with the U.S. Constitution—is considered **void,** or as if it had never existed.

unemployment insurance—State-administered systems to provide workers and their families with weekly income during periods of unemployment.

undue influence—Influence of another that destroys the freedom of a testator or donor and creates a ground for nullifying a will or invalidating a future gift. The exercise of undue influence is suggested by excessive insistence, superiority of will or mind, the relationship of the parties, or pressure on the donor or testator by any other means to do what he is unable, practically speaking, to refuse.

unfair labor practice strike—A strike to protest the fact that the employer has violated the NLRA.

unilateral mistake—See **mistake.**

union security clause—A clause in a collective-bargaining agreement that requires all employees to pay the dues and fees that union members are required to pay.

used-car rule—A rule that forbids used car dealers from misrepresenting the mechanical condition of a used car or any warranty terms.

V

variance—Permission from a governing body to deviate from zoning laws.

venire—Latin for "to come." A writ summoning persons to court to act as jurors. More popularly, the panel of citizens called for jury service from which a jury will be selected.

venue—The particular county, city, or geographical area in which a court with jurisdiction may hear and determine a case. A **change of venue** is a request to the court to move a case to a different jurisdiction in order to ensure that justice is served.

verdict—A formal decision made by a jury, read before a court, and accepted by the judge. A **general verdict** is one where the jury decides which side won on an all-or-nothing basis. A **special verdict** requires the jury to enter separate written findings on each of several issues.

vesting—Refers to the point after which an employee's accrued benefits cannot be taken away—i.e., they must be paid to the employee upon retirement or the switching of jobs. **Cliff vesting** requires complete vesting after five years, and **graded vesting** is partial vesting over the course of five years.

viable—Able to live outside the womb; used in reference to a fetus. When a fetus becomes viable, this is the point at which laws can start to regulate abortions.

vicarious liability—Liability that is imposed on one person for the actions of another, in situations where the law judges that such liability is appropriate. One specific kind of vicarious liability is that of an employer for the actions of an employee (this is the doctrine of **respondeat superior,** from the Latin for "let the superior reply").

void—Of no force or legal effect. For example, if a contract is declared void, it is unenforceable between the parties. A **voidable** contract is one that isn't automatically void, but was written in such a manner and under certain circumstances that one of the parties may choose to ask a court to void it. For example, usually when a minor enters into a contract, the contract is voidable, and the minor or his or her family may petition a court to void it.

voir dire—French for "to speak the truth." Voir dire is a process in which prospective jurors are questioned to determine whether they can perform their duties in an impartial manner.

W

waive—To voluntarily give up a right or a claim.

ward—A person who is under the control of a guardian or under the protection of the court because of incapacity (for example, because the person is a minor).

warrant—A court order authorizing a law enforcement officer to perform a specified act required for the administration of justice. For example, an **arrest warrant** authorizes a police officer to make an arrest; a **search warrant** authorizes police officers to make a search and seize evidence.

warranty—A written or oral statement by one party to a contract that a fact is or will be as it is expressly declared or promised to be. Warranties can be implied, express, and limited.

waste—When a tenant unreasonably and permanently damages a rental property.

weight of evidence—The balance or **preponderance of evidence;** the inclination of the greater amount of credible evidence, offered in a trial, to support one side of the issue rather than the other.

whistle-blower—An employee who reports to a government agency possible violations of state or federal law occurring in the workplace. Whistle-blowers are usually protected by law from being fired after making such reports.

will—A legal declaration that disposes of a person's property when that person dies.

with prejudice—As applied to a judgment of dismissal, the term refers to the adjudication of a case on its merits, barring the right to bring or maintain another action on the same claim.

without prejudice—A dismissal "without prejudice" allows a new suit to be brought on the same cause of action.

witness—One who testifies under oath as to what she or he has seen, heard or otherwise observed.

workers' compensation—Money for medical expenses and to replace income lost as a result of injuries or illnesses that arise out of employment.

workers' compensation insurance—Insurance that protects a business from damages that arise under the state's workers' compensation system.

writ—An order issued from a court requiring the performance of a specified act, or giving authority and commission to perform such an act.

Z

zoning ordinances—Municipal regulations that limit what types of businesses are permitted in certain areas.

THE WORLD AT YOUR FINGERTIPS

This section aims to provide you with up-to-date, relevant information and resources to assist you with legal issues that may confront you or your family.

GENERAL RESOURCES

Legal Services and Information

- Various bar associations provide excellent information on legal topics generally, on finding a lawyer in your area, and on where to find additional information and resources:
  - American Bar Association (*www.abanet.org*).
  - Your state or local bar association: Every state and most communities have their own bar associations. The ABA has a searchable database that you can use to find your local bar association (*www.abanet.org/barserv/stlobar.html*).
- *Legal services:* The ABA has compiled a state-by-state listing of the websites and contact information for various local legal services that can be a helpful starting point (*www.findlegalhelp.org*).
  - Pine Tree Legal Assistance provides information on various (low-cost or free) legal services and legal-aid providers across the country (*www.ptla.org/links.htm*).
  - The Legal Services Corporation provides links to federally funded legal-service programs (www.lsc.gov).
- *Lawyer Referral Programs:*
  - For your local lawyer referral program, call your local or state bar association, look in the yellow pages, or access *www.abanet.org/lawyerlocator/searchlawyer.html* to find a listing of the lawyers practicing in your area.
- *Areas of the Law:* FindLaw's public information website provides information on many different areas of law (*www.public.findlaw.com*).

- *Information on the Law and Courts:*
  - The ABA's Division for Public Education provides information on various issues relating to the law and the courts, including consumer legal issues, the U.S. Supreme Court, and the rule of law (*www.abanet.org/publiced*).
  - The Legal Information Institute at Cornell Law School is a great starting point for more in-depth research into the substance of the law; *visit www.law.cornell.edu/.*

Government Agencies and Departments

- *Better Business Bureau* (*BBB*): Allows you to search for customer complaints filed against businesses, and provides an online complaint form that you can use if you have problems with a business (*www.bbb.com*).
- *Department of Housing and Urban Development* (*HUD*) (*www.hud.gov*): Provides information on buying and selling a home, home foreclosure, fair housing laws, and mortgages and lending practices.
- *Department of Justice* (*DOJ*) (*www.usdoj.gov*): 950 Pennsylvania Avenue NW, Washington, DC 20530-0001, AskDOJ@usdoj.gov, (202) 514-2000.
- *Department of Labor* (*DOL*) (*www.dol.gov*): Provides information on the Family Medical Leave Act, employment practices, and other work-related issues. The main office can be contacted at Employment Standards Administration, U.S. Department of Labor, 200 Constitution Avenue NW, Washington, DC 20210. The Department of Labor can be contacted by phone at 1-866-4-USA-DOL.
- *Equal Employment Opportunity Commission* (*EECO*) (*www.eeoc.gov*): Handles workplace discrimination and equal opportunity in hiring and in all aspects of employment. 1801 L Street NW, Washington, DC 20507. You can also contact the EEOC by phone at 202-663-4900.

- *Federal Courts:* The main access points for the various levels of the federal court system, including district and bankruptcy courts (*www.uscourts.gov*).
- *Federal Government:* A comprehensive listing of U.S. government links (*www.USA.gov*).
- *Federal Trade Commission* (*www.ftc.gov*): Provides valuable information on a variety of consumer issues, including contractors and credit-lending practices.
- *Internal Revenue Service* (IRS): The basic resource for information about federal income taxes is the IRS. You can find your regional office in the phone book under "U.S. Offices," or go to the IRS website at *www.irs.gov.* The website features many comprehensive publications and information sheets that can help you in your tax planning and answer your tax questions. IRS publications can be downloaded directly from the IRS website.
- *Social Security Administration* (SSA) (*www.ssa.gov*): Provides information on Social Security benefits, disability benefits, and your Social Security number. The main office for the Social Security Administration is located at Social Security Administration, Office of Public Inquiries, Windsor Park Building, 6401 Security Blvd., Baltimore, MD 21235. The Social Security Administration can be contacted by phone at 800-772-1213.
- *State Courts:* A website hosted by the National Center for State Courts links to each state's individual court system. (*www.ncsconline.org/D_KIS/info_court_web_sites.html#State*).
- *U.S. Supreme Court:* The website of the U.S. Supreme Court features information about the Supreme Court and the full text of Supreme Court opinions; visit *www.supremecourtus.gov.*
- *Veteran's Affairs* (*www.va.gov* and *www.homeloans.va.gov*): Offers information on services for veterans, including home loans, medical services, and legal services.

RESOURCES LISTED CHAPTER-BY-CHAPTER

Chapter 1—When and How to Use a Lawyer

- *Finding a Lawyer:* Martindale-Hubbell, a leading source for information on lawyers practicing in the United States and abroad, offers a free website for the public. The site provides profiles of more than 440,000 lawyers and law firms, tips on selecting a lawyer, and a "Find a Lawyer" service that locates lawyers by areas of specialization and geographic location: www.lawyers.com.
- *Bar Admissions:* If you are hiring a lawyer and want to make sure he or she is licensed to practice law, go to the directory of state bar admission offices (*http://www.abanet.org/legaled/baradmissions/barcont.html*).
- *Certifications and Specializations:* To find out which types of law are certified in which states, access *www.abanet.org/legalservices/specialization/directory/*.
- *Lawyer Discipline:* The ABA has compiled a directory of state lawyer discipline agencies that you can contact for more information (*www.abanet.org/cpr/regulation/scpd/disciplinary.html*).
- *Alternative Dispute Resolution:*
  - Check the listings in the yellow pages, or contact your bar association or court system for information about mediation in your community.
  - The National Center for Community Mediation provides information about community mediation organizations, and some links; visit *www.nacfcm.org/index.*
  - The ABA's Section of Dispute Resolution offers resources and information on dispute resolution across the country. Visit *www.abanet.org/dispute* and click on "Resources."

Chapter 2—How the Legal System Works

- *Federal Courts:*
  - The Federal Judicial Center website features many downloadable publications concerning recent issues facing the judiciary, as well as some judicial history; visit *www.fjc.gov.*
  - The Federal Judiciary Homepage (*www.uscourts.gov*) features useful information on court structure and function, and links to the websites of all the federal courts.
  - The Supreme Court History website provides a history of the Supreme Court, as well as a description of the decisions made by the Court; visit *www.supremecourthistory.org.*
- *State Courts:*
  - The National Center for State Courts is an excellent first stop for research on state courts. The site contains information on alternative dispute resolution, criminal procedure, juries, and judges, among other topics; visit *www.ncsconline.org.*
  - The ABA's Division for Public Education publishes an inexpensive booklet for the public about courts and their work, *Law and the Courts: Volume II—Court Procedures.* The book includes a detailed step-by-step guide to trials, both civil and criminal. It is available from the ABA's Web Store at *www.abanet.org/abastore.* Enter Product Code 2350041.
- *Criminal Justice:*
  - The ABA's Criminal Justice Section links to some good criminal justice websites at *www.abanet.org/crimjust/ infosvcs/home.html.*
  - The American Civil Liberties Union website has information on recent criminal justice issues, and links to relevant legal documents and legislation at *www.aclu.org/crimjustice/index.html.*

- A good starting point for finding more information on criminal law is FindLaw's website at *public.findlaw.com/criminal.*
  - Nolo provides some excellent information for the public on various aspects of criminal law and procedure. Click on "criminal laws" at *www.nolo.com.*
- *Juvenile Justice:*
  - Information on criminal law relating to juveniles can be found, in question-and-answer format, at *criminal-law .freeadvice.com/juvenile_law/.*
  - The National Center for Juvenile Justice provides information on juvenile justice reforms across the country (*http://ncjj.servehttp.com/ NCJJWebsite/main.htm*).
- *The Police and Your Rights:*
  - A huge amount of information on warrants, searches, and arrests can be found at *http://criminal-law.freeadvice .com/arrests_and_searches/.*
  - The National Association of Criminal Defense Lawyers can put you in touch with associations of criminal justice lawyers in your state, and also provides links to state information on public defenders at *www.nacdl.org* (click on "Links").
- *Witnesses:* Findlaw offers an overview of the do's and don'ts of being a witness (*http://public.findlaw.com/litigation_appeals/ le17_2dos.html*).
- *Juries:*
  - An example of a handbook for trial jurors serving in the federal district courts can be found at *www.nysd .uscourts.gov* (click on "Jury Duty" and then "Jury Handbook"). The handbook provides information on what a juror can expect and will need to know while serving.
  - The National Center for State Courts provides a listing of links to information

on jury duty in various states (*www
.ncsconline.org/WC/CourTopics/
StateLinks.asp?id=48*).
- ○ The Federal Judiciary's website provides
  an FAQ on serving on a federal jury
  (*www.uscourts.gov/faq.html#juror*).
- *Victims:*
  - ○ The U.S. Department of Justice's Office
    for Victims of Crime helps victims in
    the United States. Visit their website at
    www.ojp.usdoj.gov/ovc.
  - ○ The National Center for Victims of
    Crime is a private, not-for-profit agency
    that can help you find local resources;
    its website is *www.ncvc.org,* and its
    phone number is 1-800-FYI-CALL.

Chapter 3—Family Law
- *General Information:*
  - ○ The ABA Section of Family Law has a
    General Public Resources section that
    provides answers to some frequently
    asked questions, and has charts
    summarizing the laws in each state,
    at *www.abanet.org/family/resources/
    home.shtml.*
- *Marriage:*
  - ○ The requirements of each state regard-
    ing blood tests for marriage licenses, as
    well as answers to other questions about
    marriage, can be found at the Nolo
    Press website by clicking on the "Mar-
    riage and Living Together" heading
    under "Family Law" at *www.nolo.com.*
  - ○ Information on how to obtain records
    from each state regarding marriage,
    birth, and death records can be found at
    the National Center for Health Statis-
    tics website at *www.cdc.gov/nchs/.*
- *Adoption:*
  - ○ For information about agency adop-
    tions, contact the Child Welfare League
    of America, 2345 Crystal Drive, Suite
    250, Arlington, VA 22202. Its telephone
    number is (703) 412-2400, or you can

access its website at *www.cwla.org.*
Search for "adoption."
- ○ The website of the National Council for
  Adoption (*www.ncfa-usa.org*) provides
  information on adoption regulations
  throughout the country for parents
  thinking of adopting and for parents
  thinking of giving up a child for adoption.
- ○ For information on independent adoption, check with your state or city bar
  association. Ask if independent adoptions
  are legal in your state. Also ask if the bar
  association will refer you to lawyers who
  handle independent adoptions.
- *Divorce:*
  - ○ For a variety of materials on divorce law
    and policy, visit the website of the
    American Academy of Matrimonial
    Lawyers: *www.aaml.org.*
  - ○ The ABA publishes a *Guide to Marriage,
    Divorce, and Families* that can be pur-
    chased from the ABA Web Store
    (*www.abanet.org/abastore*), Product
    Code 2350223. It is also available in
    bookstores across the country.
  - ○ The site of *Divorce* magazine has
    many articles on the legal side of di-
    vorce at *www.divorcemagazine.com.*
    The Divorce Online website
    (*www.divorceonline.com*) also
    contains useful information.
  - ○ The Cornell Legal Information
    Institute site includes basic legal
    information about divorce, as well
    as a state-by-state listing of the law, at
    www.law.cornell.edu/topics/divorce.html.
  - ○ Many gay rights groups offer publica-
    tions and other information about
    the legal rights and needs of people
    who are in nontraditional relationships.
    A good place to start is the Lambda
    Legal Foundation website at
    www.lambdalegal.org/.
  - ○ Search for "cohabitation agreements"
    on the Internet to find many sources of

information. A particularly useful site is the Equality in Marriage Institute website at *www.equalityinmarriage.org.*

- *Child Support:*
  - Information about child support, including links to the support guidelines of each state, can be found at *www.supportguidelines.com.*
  - The Federal Office of Child Support Enforcement can be contacted at *www.acf.hhs.gov.*
  - Every state has child support enforcement units that help custodial parents establish and enforce child support orders and locate absent parents. (These offices are sometimes called IV-D Offices because they are required by Chapter IV-D of the Social Security Act.) You can locate these offices by looking under county or state government listings in the telephone book or by asking the state government switchboard.
- *Domestic Violence:*
  - Many communities offer shelters for battered spouses and their children. Details on these shelters are available from the police, crisis intervention services, hospitals, churches, family or conciliation courts, local newspapers, or women's organizations. The National Coalition Against Domestic Violence is a national information and referral center. It can be contacted at P.O. Box 18749, Denver, CO 80218; by phone at 303-839-1852; by fax at 303-831-9251; or online at *www.ncadv.org.* You can also call the National Domestic Violence Hotline at 800-799-7233, or visit the website at *www.ndvh.org.*
  - The local or state chapter of the National Organization for Women (NOW) can also provide information to help battered spouses. You can contact NOW via its website at *www.now.org.*
  - Womenslaw.org provides information

on each state's domestic violence resources (*www.womenslaw.org*).

Chapter 4—Health-Care Law

- *Patients' Rights:*
  - You can find more information about filing a complaint for violations of HIPAA at the Office of Civil Rights website at *www.hhs.gov/ocr/hipaa,* or by calling the HIPAA toll-free number, 866-627-7748.
  - An excellent and detailed guide to the privacy rule can be found at the Health and Human Resources website at *www.hhs.gov/ocr/hipaa/guidelines/ guidanceallsections.pdf.*
  - The American College of Emergency Physicians offers a comprehensive site discussing all aspects of emergency care at *www.acep.org.*
- *Health-Care Options*
  - Health insurance companies and plans are required to establish rules and procedures for handling complaints and grievances internally. Utilizing these procedures is an important first step in seeking resolution of a dispute. You can start an internal review with a phone call to a complaints hotline. You may need to follow it up with a complaints form or a written complaint. Some sample letters that demonstrate how to seek review can be found at *www.healthcarerights.org/letters/ lettersindex.html.*
  - Most health maintence organizations are accredited with nongovernmental groups such as the National Committee for Quality Assurance (*www.ncqa.org*), the American Accreditation HealthCare Commission/URAC (*www.urac.org*), and the Joint Commission on Accreditation of Health Care Organizations (*www.jcaho.org*). HMOs rely on their accreditation by these organizations in

their marketing to employers and unions. Therefore, making a well-documented complaint to the relevant organization and sending a copy to your HMO might get results.

- You can find more information on Medicare at *www.medicare.gov.* Chapter 16, "The Rights of Older Americans," also provides more detailed information.
- You can find more information about Medicaid at *cms.hhs.gov/medicaid/consumer.asp.*
- To find more information about the Children's Health Insurance Program that applies to kids in your state, visit the Insure Kids Now website, sponsored by the Department of Health and Human Services, at *www.insurekidsnow.gov/states.asp.*
- *Regulating Health Care Professionals:* The American Medical Association offers the Doctor Finder online. This service provides information on more than 650,000 licensed doctors in the United States. Use this site to get background information on your doctor. The site, *www.ama-assn.org/aps/amahg.htm,* does not provide information on disciplinary actions or malpractice suits.
- *Assisted Reproduction:*
  - The Fertile Thoughts website contains helpful information about infertility, assisted reproductive technology, and adoption. It also has links to other useful sites. Visit *www.fertilethoughts.com.*
  - The American Society for Reproductive Medicine is a nonprofit group that studies infertility issues. Here you can research state insurance laws to find out what level of coverage is required for infertility treatments and obtain patient education booklets. Visit *www.asrm.org.*
  - To learn about state laws regarding surrogacy, access *www.surrogacy.com/legals/states.html.*

- *Organ Donation:*
  - To find out more about organ donations, search for "organ donation" in your favorite search engine. Among the many good resources are a federal government site (*www.organdonor.gov*) and several sites maintained by private organizations (*www.transweb.org* and *www.shareyourlife.org*).

Chapter 5—Children With Special Needs: Special Education

- *General Information:*
  - About.com offers an overview of special education topics and laws (*specialed.about.com*).
  - Internet Special Education Resources (*www.iser.com*) provides a listing of various special education resources, professionals, and organizations.
  - Your local and state bar associations can provide you with information on finding an education lawyer in your area.
  - The Office of Special Education and Rehabilitative Services (*www.ed.gov/about/offices/list/osers/index.html*) is the federal government office providing services for disabled Americans. The website also provides links to the various federal special education laws.
  - Wrightslaw offers a comprehensive online resource for parents, advocates, and attorneys (*www.wrightslaw.com*). Their website also allows you to purchase various publications focusing on special education advocacy and understanding the law.
  - Parent Training and Information Centers and Community Parent Resource Centers offer the parents of disabled children various resources and training opportunities. Each state has at least one center. To find the one closest to you, access their website at *www.taalliance.org/Centers/index.htm.*

Chapter 6—Personal Injury

- *General Information:*
  - For FAQs on slip-and-fall cases, see *accident-law.freeadvice.com/slips_falls/*.
  - The Lectric Law Library on Medical Malpractice offers much practical litigation information; visit the website at *www.lectlaw.com/tmed.html.*
  - MegaLaw provides many links to pages on breast implant litigation and related areas at *www.megalaw .com/top/breast.php.*
  - There is a forum about toxic tort law at *www.toxlaw.com.*
- *Privacy Torts:*
  - For information on privacy torts, see *www.privacilla.org/releases/ Torts_Report.html.*
  - For more information on defamation law, see the Media Law Resource Center website at *www.medialaw.org.*
- *Product Liability:*
  - Several government agencies provide helpful background material on their websites. For example, the federal Consumer Product Safety Commission—*www.cpsc.gov*—regulates many products put into commerce, including toys, and its website could be helpful if you believe a product is defective. The federal Food and Drug Administration—*www.fda.gov*—regulates drugs and other items, like breast implants, that have been subject to recent litigation.
  - Cornell Law School, as part of its Legal Information Institute, offers a product liability overview and links to the applicable legislation at *www.law.cornell.edu/ topics/products_liability.html.*

Chapter 7—Buying and Selling a Home

- *General Information:*
  - The ABA publishes a Guide to Home Ownership that can be purchased from the ABA Web Store (*www.abanet.org/abastore*), Product Code 2350028. It is also available in bookstores across the country.
  - There are many readily accessible publications that will give you some basic information on buying a home. A good place to start is FindLaw's website for the public. The real estate link will give you access to articles and information about home ownership. Visit *http:// realestate.findlaw.com/homeownership/.*
  - Various nonprofit agencies, such as the Better Business Bureau, can help you get more information on your legal rights and obligations in buying and selling a home.
  - Sites such as HomeGain (*www .homegain.com*) offer screening services that enable you to compare brokers to help you get the best home purchase or sale help. In addition, all large brokerage firms have websites that enable you to see online profiles of brokers, their listings, and other information.
- *Finding and Listing Properties:*
  - An Internet search will produce dozens of results for services that provide MLS listings. Some of these will provide an MLS listing for a smaller-than-usual commission; for example, *www .forsalebyowner.com.* Other sites will provide a listing on the MLS for a flat fee; for example, *www.flatraterealty .usa.com.*
  - If you are using the Internet to find foreclosed properties, a good starting point is the HUD website, which offers links to homes owned by various government agencies and lenders (*www.hud.gov/homes/homesforsale.cfm*). Other sites such as *www.1stforeclosure .com* and *www.foreclosurefreesearch.com* may provide a free trial period, but will charge a fee for full foreclosure searches.

- *Discrimination:* If you suspect that someone has discriminated against you in home buying, you can request a complaint form by calling the federal Department of Housing and Urban Development at 800-424-8590, or by visiting the agency's website at *www.hud.gov/hdiscrim.html.*
- *Financing a Home:*
  - Working out how much home you can afford involves a lot of number crunching. There are dozens of free loan calculators available on the Internet that can do some of the hard work for you. Loan calculators of varying complexity can be found at *www.bankrate .com/gooword/rate/calc_home.asp, www.pine-grove.com/pi03000.htm,* or by typing "loan calculator" into your favorite search engine.
  - The ABA's website can provide you with some consumer information and advice about mortgages and loans, in easy-to-understand language. Visit *www.abanet.org/buslaw/safeborrowing.*
  - If you think you might qualify for a special government-insured loan offered through the Federal Housing Administration (FHA) or the Veterans Administration (VA), you should seek more information at *www.hud.gov/buying/ loans.cfm* and *www.homeloans.va.gov.*
- *Home Value:* There are some great websites that can help you set a price for your property by providing you with a list of homes sold through the local multiple listing service within the last year. Try *realestate.yahoo.com/re/homevalues* and *www.domania.com.*

Chapter 8—Home Ownership

- *Fair Housing:* You can learn more about the federal Fair Housing Act at the Department of Housing website at *www.hud.gov/offices/fheo/FHLaws.*
- *Closings:* Information on what to expect

when closing a home purchase is available from the American Land Title Association. Its website includes links to state land title associations; visit *www.alta.org* and click on "Consumer Information."
- *Community Property:* You can find more information on community property states and what this form of ownership means at *www.fairmark.com/spousal/comprop.htm.*
- *Home Safety and Insurance:*
  - Rating services study insurance companies' financial stability and ability to pay claims. You can find out more about your insurance company at A.M. Best (*www.ambest.com*); at Moody's Investor Services (*www.moodys.com*); or at Standard & Poor's (*www .standardandpoors.com*). If you're dissatisfied with the way your insurance company handles your claim, you can call the National Insurance Consumer Helpline (telephone: 800-942-4242; fax: 212-791-1807), which might be able to suggest a course of action.
  - You can find more information about arbitration at the website of the American Arbitration Association at *www.adr.org.*
  - You can find more information about the lead-based paint disclosure rule, and sample disclosure forms, at the Housing and Urban Development site: *www.hud.gov/offices/lead.*
  - The federal government has created resources to help you prepare and to stay informed, including *www.ready.gov* and 1-800-BE-READY.
- *Pets and Neighbors:* Nolo.com has lots of free information on neighbor law and pet law (*www.nolo.com*—search "pets" or "neighbors"). You can also purchase books on each of these topics online.
- *Remodeling:* The National Association of the Remodeling Industry website includes a national directory of remodeling contrac-

tors; visit *www.nari.org* (click on "Home-owners").

- *Common-Interest Communities:* MegaLaw offers a listing of links to various federal and state laws on condominiums (*www.megalaw .com/top/condo.php*), as does *http:// condolawyers.com/nationalaw.htm.*

Chapter 9—Renting Residential Property

- *General Information:*
  - ○ Many states and cities have departments of housing, departments of fair housing, departments of consumer affairs, or departments of human relations. Employees there can usually answer questions and accept complaints. Check government listings in the local telephone directory. Additionally, HUD can provide valuable information on regulations governing public housing, publicly subsidized housing, and fair housing, and can answer questions and accept complaints about housing discrimination.
  - ○ A good source of general landlord-tenant information, with many links, is provided on the website of Cornell Law School's Legal Information Institute (*www.law.cornell.edu/wex/index.php/ Landlord-tenant*).
  - ○ State and local bar associations may provide referrals to local lawyers who are familiar with landlord-tenant law, consumer protection law, or fair housing law in the community.
  - ○ You can find the entire text of the Uniform Residential Landlord and Tenant Act (URLTA), with annotations, at *www.lectlaw.com/files/lat03.htm.*
  - ○ The National Fair Housing Center (*www.fairhousing.com*) offers a terrific website, with recent developments, a legal research section, and many links.
- *Tenant Resources:*
  - ○ Tenants may seek the assistance of the National Housing Institute, which provides information and referral to local tenant organizations. NHI is located at 439 Main Street, Suite 311, Orange, NJ 07050. You can also reach NHI by telephone at 973-678-9060, by fax at 973-678-8437, or online at *www.nhi.org.*
  - ○ The Tenants Union of Illinois provides information and FAQs on tenant rights in Illinois that can serve as a helpful guide for tenants nationwide (*www.tenant.org*).
- *Landlord Resources:*
  - ○ Landlords can check the credit records of prospective tenants at various credit bureaus, including *www.accuratecredit .com* and *firstcreditbureau.com/ landlord.htm.*
  - ○ Landlords may seek the assistance of local real estate or building management organizations. A good website, *www .landlord.com,* provides legal information, downloadable forms, and much more.
- *Housing Codes:*
  - ○ Information on local housing codes is available from the local code enforcement department—such as the building inspectors' office, the health department, or the fire department.
  - ○ The International Code Council has developed a set of eleven comprehensive national model housing codes. These codes create standards for new construction, rehabilitation work, and property maintenance. See the council's website at *www.iccsafe.org/index.html.*

Chapter 10—Consumer Credit

- *General Information:*
  - ○ You can find the addresses and telephone numbers for consumer protection offices in your local telephone directory. You also can find them in the Consumers Resource Handbook, by

calling 1-888-878-3256; or by accessing *www.pueblo.gsa.gov.*

○ The FTC also has many publications on credit and consumer protections available on their website at *www.ftc.gov.*

○ The U.S. Financial Literacy and Education Commission's website at *www.mymoney.gov* provides information about credit and other matters.

○ The Federal Reserve has many publications related to credit available on its website at *www.federalreserve.gov* (click on "Consumer Information"). These publications include information on adjustable-rate mortgages, credit protection laws, mortgage refinancing, vehicle leasing, and many other topics.

○ On its website, the Legal Information Institute provides a brief overview of consumer credit, and provides links to relevant legislation and to other consumer credit sites; visit *www.law.cornell.edu/topics/consumer_credit.html.*

○ MsMoney.com has a section on credit, which provides some good practical information, at *www.msmoney.com/mm/banking/credit/crupdown_intro.htm.*

• *Credit Cards:*

○ There are several places online where consumers can get information that will help them choose a credit card. These include:

  ▪ Cardweb—*www.cardweb.com*
  ▪ Bankrate—*www.bankrate.com*
  ▪ CreditCardSearchEngine—*www.creditcardsearchengine.com*

○ The Federal Trade Commission provides a fact sheet for consumers called "Choosing and Using Credit Cards." This is another useful source of information. You can download it at *www.ftc.gov/bcp/conline/pubs/credit/choose.htm.*

○ The American Bankers Association offers a Credit Card Guide that explains credit card basics and how to choose a card at *aba.com/ABAEF/.*

○ Cardtrak is a resource that provides information—APRs, annual fees, and so on—about different credit cards, and is a useful tool when shopping for a credit card; it can accessed by visiting *www.cardweb.com.* Other websites like *www.kiplinger.com* provide similar information. In addition, many large banks offer information on their websites about the cards they offer.

• *Credit Record and Reports:*

○ To obtain your free annual credit report, visit *www.annualcreditreport.com.*

○ To learn more about your own credit and credit score, contact one of these credit reporting agencies:

  ▪ Equifax: *www.equifax.com*
  ▪ Experian: *www.experian.com*
  ▪ TransUnion: *www.transunion.com*

○ The text of the Fair Credit Reporting Act is available online at *www.ftc.gov/os/statutes/031224fcra.pdf.*

○ The Federal Trade Commission publishes a useful summary of your rights under the Fair Credit Reporting Act, which includes information on whom to contact in the event of a complaint, at *www.ftc.gov/bcp/conline/pubs/credit/fcrasummary.pdf.*

○ The Federal Reserve Board has a section on credit histories and records in its Consumer Handbook to Credit Protection Laws, which is available online at *www.federalreserve.gov/pubs/consumerhdbk/histories.htm.*

○ You may also access the "Consumer Info" section of the website of the Consumer Data Industry Association at *www.cdiaonline.org/ConsumerInfo/index.cfm?pnItemNumber=510.*

○ For information on credit scoring, access the Federal Trade Commission

(FTC) website at *www.ftc.gov/bcp/edu/pubs/consumer/credit/cre24.shtm,* or the CreditInfo Center site at *www.creditinfocenter.com/creditreports/scoring.*

- ○ The Federal Trade Commission provides more information on the Equal Credit Opportunity Act at *www.ftc.gov/bcp/conline/pubs/credit/ecoa.htm.*

- *Leasing:* The Consumer Justice Center provides more information about leasing and the Consumer Leasing Act at *www.consumerjusticecenter.com* (click on "Legal Information").

- *Credit and Divorce:* The Federal Trade Commission has a short report entitled *Credit and Divorce* that appears at *www.ftc.gov/bcp/conline/pubs/credit/divorce.htm.*

- *Billing Problems:* The Federal Trade Commission website at *www.ftc.gov/bcp/conline/pubs/credit/fcb.htm* also provides information on the Fair Credit Billing Act, and includes a sample letter that could be copied and sent to a creditor.

- *Debt Collection:*
  - ○ The Federal Trade Commission provides simple information on the Fair Debt Collection Practices Act, and what debt collectors can and cannot do, at *www.ftc.gov/bcp/conline/pubs/credit/fdc.htm.*
  - ○ If you have a complaint about a debt collector or a consumer credit reporting agency, you can mail it to the Federal Trade Commission, Consumer Response Center, 6th Street and Pennsylvania Avenue NW, Washington, DC 20580. Alternatively, you can call the FTC's toll-free number, 877-FTC-HELP (877-382-4357); or you can use the online complaint form on the FTC website at *www.ftc.gov/ftc/cmplanding.shtm.*

- *Credit Counseling:*
  - ○ To find a credit counselor in your area, check the yellow pages of your phone book for "Credit & Debt Counseling Services" or call this toll-free number: 800-388-2227. Or find a CCCS on the website of the National Foundation for Credit Counseling at *www.nfcc.org.*
  - ○ You can find nonprofit credit counseling services online at *www.cccsintl.org.*

- *ID Theft:*
  - ○ If you believe that you have been the victim of identity thief, call the Federal Trade Commission's Identity Theft Hotline toll-free number, 877-IDTHEFT (877-438-4338). The FTC has also developed a so-called ID Theft Affidavit, which is a form you can fill out to track where an ID thief has struck.
  - ○ The Identity Theft Resource Center (*www.idtheftcenter.org*) offers information on ID theft statistics, as well as ways to protect yourself and what to do if you are a victim.

Chapter 11—Consumer Bankruptcy

- *General Information:*
  - ○ The American Bankruptcy Institute (*www.abiworld.org*) provides a variety of information on bankruptcy, including the applicable laws, a schedule of fees, and help in finding a qualified bankruptcy attorney.
  - ○ To understand more about bankruptcy, access the U.S. Bankruptcy Code and bankruptcy rules at *www.thebankruptcysite.com/bankruptcy_law.htm.*
  - ○ To find a certified bankruptcy lawyer, access the American Board of Certification website at *www.abcworld.org/abchome.html.*
  - ○ For bankruptcy basics and forms, access the site of the U.S. Bankruptcy Courts: *www.uscourts.gov/bankruptcycourts.html.*

- *Alternatives to Bankruptcy and Money Management:*
  - As noted in Chapter 7, "Consumer Credit," you can find the nearest CCCS by calling 800-388-2227 or going online at *www.nfcc.org.* Some of these centers charge a small monthly service fee.
  - Myvesta.org offers an interactive website focusing on nonbankruptcy remedies such as debt consolidation; access *www.myvesta.org.*
  - Debt Advice is a major nonprofit site, affiliated with the National Foundation for Credit Counseling and offering much information for consumers; access *www.debtadvice.org/index.html.*
  - Another nonprofit site is the website of American Consumer Credit Counseling; visit *www.consumercredit.com.*
  - DebtReliefUSA.net is a for-profit site that can help you reduce your debt; visit *www.debtreliefusa.net.*
- *Steps to Bankruptcy:*
  - You can download official bankruptcy forms for all types of bankruptcy from the U.S. Courts website at *www.uscourts.gov/bankruptcycourts.html.* If you are filing for Chapter 13 bankruptcy, note that each judicial district has its own form of Chapter 13 plan. You should use the Chapter 13 plan form that applies in your district.
  - To obtain statement-of-financial-affairs forms, access *www.uscourts.gov/rules/comment2002/b7.pdf.*
  - For a list of exemptions in different states, visit Bankruptcy Site.com at *www.thebankruptcysite.com/what_do_i_keep.htm.*
  - The Nolo website features information on the steps to bankruptcy, as well as information on states with large homestead exemptions. Visit *www.nolo.com* and click on the "Property and Money" heading.

  - The ABA publishes a Guide to Credit and Bankruptcy that can be purchased from the ABA Web Store (*www.abanet.org/abastore*), Product Code 2350044. It is also available in bookstores across the country.

Chapter 12—Contracts and Consumer Law

- *General Information:*
  - Cornell University Law School provides an overview of contract law on its website at *www.law.cornell.edu/topics/contracts.html.*
  - To investigate whether a company has a record for not living up to its end of a contract, contact the Better Business Bureau at *www.bbb.org.*
  - The Federal Trade Commission provides tips for consumers on its website; to access the site, visit *www.ftc.gov.*
  - Your state's attorney general can help with many consumer protection issues. The National Association of Attorneys General can help you find the contact information for your state (*www.naag.org*).
  - The most comprehensive government website on the topic of consumer protection is *www.consumer.gov.* This site is a project of numerous federal agencies and is updated on a regular basis.
- *Do-Not-Call Registry:*
  - To register, all you have to do is contact the FTC either online (*www.donotcall.gov*) or at a toll-free number (888-382-1222 [TTY: 866-290-4236]) and tell the agency that you want to be added to the list. Placing your number on the National Do-Not-Call Registry will stop most telemarketing calls, including those from overseas. However, you may still receive calls from political organizations, charities, people taking surveys, and companies with which you have an existing business relationship.

- ○ The Electronic Privacy Information Center has a website explaining how consumers can block, or at least reduce the number of, telemarketing calls; access *www.epic.org/privacy/ telemarketing/#reduce.*
- *Protections for Travelers:* The U.S. Department of Transportation's Aviation Consumer Protection Division provides travel tips, rules, and guidelines. Visit the website at *airconsumer.ost.dot.gov.*
- *Automobile Consumer Protections:* See the resources provided in connection with Chapter 14.

Chapter 13—Computer Law

- *General Information:*
  - ○ The Better Bureau Business website is a great place to find both qualified computer and technology stores as well as places to shop online safely.
  - ○ The Computer Law Association helps link Internet users with legal experts. Visit the CLA's site at *www.cla.org.*
- *Protecting Your Information and Family:*
  - ○ The Federal Trade Commission offers consumers tips on avoiding what the agency calls "dot cons." Visit *www.ftc.gov/bcp/conline/pubs/online/ dotcons.htm.*
  - ○ The Securities and Exchange Commission provides investors with tips on avoiding fraud. Visit its website at *www .sec.gov/investor/pubs/cyberfraud.htm.*
  - ○ Though they might not take action against spam that is merely unwanted, it might be worthwhile to send a copy of spam e-mail to the FTC at *uce@ftc.gov.*
  - ○ Try to educate yourself about new viruses. There are many good sites you can visit to check for up-to-date information on viruses, including Symantec (*www.symantec.com*) and McAfee (*www.mcafee.com*). Urban Legends (*www.snopes.com*) contains useful

information regarding chain e-mails and other Internet and computer hoaxes. Your Internet service provider can also inform you about new viruses that are infecting computers.

- ○ Emailabuse.org, an ad hoc group, provides advice on combating spam. Visit the group's website at *www.emailabuse.org.*
- ○ MSNBC provides news on antivirus efforts on its website at *www.msnbc .com/news/TECHCRIMES_Front.asp.*
- ○ You can search for shareware and freeware at many websites, including *www.shareware.com, www.nonags.com,* and *www.tucows.com.*
- ○ The U.S. Justice Department has a website devoted to the discussion of Internet crime at *www.usdoj.gov/ criminal/cybercrime.* It also has a website devoted to teaching children how to act ethically online; you can access it at *www.usdoj.gov/criminal/ cybercrime/rules/kidinternet.htm.*
- ○ Most ISPs, such as MSN.com and AOL.com, have parental permission restrictions that you can activate, as do some browsers, such as Internet Explorer.
- ○ The Federal Bureau of Investigation has made its publication "A Parent's Guide to Internet Safety" available online at *www.fbi.gov/publications/pguide/pguide .htm.*
- ○ If you think your child has been the victim of an online predator, the FBI advises you to turn off your computer to preserve any evidence for law enforcement, and then call the police, the FBI, and the National Center for Missing and Exploited Children. The center's website is online at *www.missingkids.com.*
- ○ To learn more about online plagiarism, visit the website run by the creators of Turnitin.com at *www.plagiarism.org.*

- *Online Purchases:*
  - The ABA's Section of Business Law has developed a website outlining tips for shopping safely online. You can visit the site at *www.safeshopping.org.*
  - You can access shopping information— and pricing data, too—at *www.CNET.com.*
  - For prices, check out *www.shopper.com, www.pricegrabber.com,* and *www .pricescan.com.*
  - The TRUSTe website (*www.truste.org*) provides information on protecting your privacy when shopping online.
  - The FDA website (*www.fda.gov*) provides information on the safety of online pharmacies. Consumers who suspect that a site is illegal can report it to the FDA at *www.fda.gov/oc/ buyonline/buyonlineform.htm.*
  - Before buying from an online pharamcy, check with the National Association of Boards of Pharmacy (*www.nabp.net;* 847-698-6227) to determine whether a website is a licensed pharmacy in good standing. Click on "Accreditation Programs" and then select "VIPPS" (for "Verified Internet Pharmacy Practice Sites").
- *Copyright and Trademark Issues:*
  - If you want the definitive word on whether a domain name is registered, you can check the "Whois" database of registered names by using a search service such as *www.whois.net* or *www.geektools.com* (click on "Whois").
  - For more information on domain names and the new dots, visit the Internet Corporation for Assigned Names and Numbers' website at *www.icann.org.*
  - To determine whether a name has been trademarked, check with the U.S. Patent and Trademark Office at *www.uspto.gov* or have a lawyer perform the check for you.
  - For a good overview of trademarks and copyright, access Nolo's legal encyclopedia (*www.nolo.com*) and click on "trademarks and copyright."
  - The San Francisco-based Electronic Frontier Foundation, which promotes "digital rights," opposes a number of the new laws protecting intellectual property. To learn more, visit its website at *www.eff.org.*
  - You can also find reports of phishing and other email-based schemes by visiting web sites such as the Anti-Phishing Work Group (www.antiphishing.org)

Chapter 14—Automobiles

- *General Information*
  - Websites such as *www.autocheck.com* and *www.carfax.com* make it easy to find services that will provide you with detailed repair histories and odometer readings for many used cars on the market.
  - Many state government websites provide consumer information about buying a car. You can access your state government website, and various agencies and departments, at *www.statelocalgov.net.*
  - The National Automobile Dealers Association provides consumers with purchase information on a wide variety of vehicles at *www.nadaguides.com.*
  - The Better Business Bureau offers great information about automobile-related complaints, particularly regarding warranties.
  - The Consumer Federation of America provides online and printed material dealing with auto safety, consumer protection for motorists, and insurance. Contact them at *www.consumerfed.org.*
  - If your state's department of motor vehicles sponsors a website, this might

be an excellent resource for more information about warranties, repairs, odometer disclosure, lemon laws, and other topics. The California DMV website is a good example; check it out at *www.dmv.ca.gov.*

○ The National Highway Traffic Safety Administration (NHTSA) provides much useful online and printed information on auto safety, car recalls, and defect investigations. You also can report safety-related defects. The home page also has a link to a search engine for vehicles subject to recalls at *www.nhtsa.dot.gov.*

○ The Center for Auto Safety (*www.autosafety.org*), provides online information on automobile defects for various models of cars, warranties, secret warranties, and many other topics.

• *Leases:* You can find more information for consumers on vehicle leases at *www.leaseguide.com.*

• *Lemon Laws:*

○ FindLaw provides links to several different sources of information on lemon laws, car repair, and what to expect when making a claim at *public.findlaw.com/lemon.*

○ You can find a private website with extensive information about lemon laws, including a state-by-state listing of such laws, at *www.autopedia.com/html/HotLinks_Lemon.html.*

• *Inspections and Repairs:* For online information about using certified car technicians for repairs, contact the National Institute for Automotive Service Excellence at *www.asecert.org.*

• *Your Automobile and the Police:*

○ Mothers Against Drunk Driving (MADD) is the definitive source for information on drunk driving. There are many local chapters, which can easily be located at the MADD website at *www.madd.org.*

○ Nolo sponsors several Web pages with information about the police and your car. The link "Cars & Tickets" under the heading "Rights and Disputes" contains FAQs regarding traffic accidents, police stops, and drunk driving. You can access the website at *www.nolo.com.*

○ For driver's license requirements in all states, including special provisions for older and younger drivers, access the Insurance Information Institute site at *www.iii.org/individuals/auto/a/stateautolaws.*

• *Accidents:*

○ Several online legal advice pages feature information about the law relating to auto accidents. Check out *http://accident-law.freeadvice.com/auto/* and *www.lawguru.com/faq/1.html.* But remember that general online legal information, even if it seems appropriate to your own circumstances, is no replacement for the specific advice of a lawyer who is fully informed about all the circumstances of your case and has done up-to-the-minute research on the latest developments in the law.

○ You can find more information about insurance at the Autopedia website at *autopedia.com/html/Insure.html.*

Chapter 15—Law and the Workplace

• *General Information:*

○ Agencies of the federal government are a good source of information about your rights and duties on the job. We list the main office addresses in Washington, D.C., below, but most agencies also have regional offices located in major cities throughout the United States. To find a federal agency, look in your local phone directory under "United States Government."

○ The Legal Information Institute (LII) at Cornell University maintains a website on topics relating to many aspects of workplace law. You can access the list of topics at *www.law.cornell.edu/wex/index.php/Employment*. The LII website also contains the full text of all the legislation referred to in this section. You'll find sections covering such topics as collective bargaining; employment discrimination; employment law; labor law; pension law; unemployment compensation; workers' compensation; and workplace safety. By clicking on the relevant topic, you can access information providing a general overview of that topic and links to source materials and other references discussing it.

  ○ LII also offers an index on unemployment compensation. The site, *www.law.cornell.edu/topics/unemployment_compensation.html*, provides an overview of unemployment compensation and has links to source materials and references discussing unemployment compensation issues.

- *Civil Rights and the Workplace:*
  ○ The EEOC website provides information on workplace discrimination and equal opportunity in hiring and in all aspects of employment (see *www.eeoc.gov*).
  ○ Your state may also have its own civil-rights agency that handles employment discrimination. The EEOC website provides information on state agencies.
- *Fair Labor Standards:* You can find some general information on the FLSA on the DOL website at *www.dol.gov/esa/regs/compliance/whd/mwposter.htm*. The site provides links to the law, the regulations, and useful fact sheets.
- *Immigration Issues:* Regarding the IRCA, a good source of information is the home page of the Office of Special Counsel for Immigration-Related Unfair Employment Practices (*www.usdoj.gov/crt/osc*) and the FAQ page of this same agency (*www.usdoj.gov/crt/osc/htm/facts.htm*).

- *NLRA:* You can find information regarding your rights and responsibilities under the National Labor Relations Act (NLRA) by contacting the National Labor Relations Board, 1099 Fourteenth Street NW, Washington, DC 20570. You can phone the NLRB at 1-866-667-6572, or access its website at *www.nlrb.gov.*
- *Job Safety:* You can direct inquiries concerning job-related safety issues to the Occupational Safety and Health Administration (OSHA). The staff can answer your questions and send literature about the OSH Act. You can contact them at U.S. Department of Labor (OSHA), Office of Public Affairs, Room N-3649, 200 Constitution Avenue NW, Washington, DC, 20210. You can also contact OSHA by phone at 1-800-321-6742, or access its website at *www.osha.gov.*
- For specific workers' compensation information in your state, write to your state department of labor.
- *Social Security:* Your local Social Security Administration office can provide details and literature about your Social Security Disability Insurance benefits. Look in your local phone book under "U.S. government," or visit *www.ssa.gov.*
- For information about unemployment compensation, contact the local office of your state's employment security or unemployment department or the state job service.
- *Pension Information:* For information about ERISA and your rights under a pension plan, contact the Employee Benefits Security Administration (EBSA) at the U.S. Department of Labor, 200 Constitution Avenue NW, Washington, DC 20210. You can phone EBSA at 202-219-8776 or 800-998-7542 (to order publications toll free), or access its website at *www.dol.gov/ebsa.*
- *Small Businesses:*
  ○ Quicken, at *www.quicken.com*, has a good small-business site that includes

much useful information, including small-business forums where you can ask questions and exchange ideas.

○ The website for the Service Corps of Retired Executives at *www.score.org* gives you the opportunity to obtain free, confidential advice via e-mail. You can also seek business counseling face-to-face at one of their local chapters.

○ You can access *www.sba.gov/sbdc* for a state-by-state list of over nine hundred Small Business Development Centers.

○ Your local Chamber of Commerce probably has a package containing all the information and forms you'll need to get started in your community.

○ The American Express small-business site has much useful information on buying a business. Access *www.americanexpress.com*.

○ The Business Owner's Toolkit is a very useful site for small businesses. It contains much useful information on starting corporations and other practical legal matters. Access the material on corporations at *www.toolkit.cch.com/ text/P01_4770.asp*.

• *Franchising:*
  ○ The FTC (*www.ftc.gov*) provides a package of information about the FTC Franchise and Business Opportunity Rule. The website has many resources relating to franchising, including commentary about the federal rule, state rules, and FAQs.
  ○ The Small Business Administration has a pamphlet titled "Understanding the Franchise Contract." Get it from a local office or the SBA website (*www.sba.gov*).
  ○ Franchise-oriented websites include Franchise Handbook Online (*www .franchise1.com*), BetheBoss (*www .betheboss.com*), the International Franchise Association (*www*

.franchise.org), and the American Franchisee Association (*www.franchisee.org*). In addition, articles on franchising and small business issues are available online at *www.ltbn.com*.

• *Business Scams:*
  ○ The National Fraud Information Center provides much information on small-business scams at *www.fraud.org*.
  ○ Additionally, both the FTC (*www.ftc.gov*) and Better Business Bureau (*www.bbb.com*) can be helpful resources for ensuring your business doesn't become the victim of a scam.

• *Bankruptcy:* Check out *www.bankrupt.com* for the "Internet Bankruptcy Library," largely intended for bankruptcy professionals, but also of interest to businesspeople seeking information about various alternatives.

Chapter 16—The Rights of Older Americans

• *General Information:*
  ○ The AARP's website (*www.aarp.com*) provides information on many topics and issues affecting older Americans, including health care, discrimination, estate planning, and reverse mortgages, just to name a few.
  ○ The Eldercare Locator is a toll-free number, 800-677-1116, with operators who will connect you to information about state and area agencies and private organizations serving older persons in communities anywhere in the country. It is a public service of the U.S. Administration on Aging, administered by the National Association of Area Agencies on Aging and the National Association of State Units on Aging. An online version of the Eldercare Locator is available at *www .eldercare.gov*.
  ○ The ABA publishes a Legal Guide for Americans Over 50 that can be purchased from the ABA Web Store

(*www.abanet.org/abastore*), Product Code 2350226. It is also available in bookstores across the country.

- *Age Discrimination:*
  - The EEOC's website provides a great deal of information on age discrimination in employment (see *www.eeoc.gov*).
- *Pension Plans:*
  - The Pension Rights Center (*www .pensionrights.org*) offers information regarding retirement plans and your rights under ERISA, as well as contact information for legal organizations and lawyers with expertise in legal issues relating to pension claims.
  - The Department of Labor website (*www.dol.gov*) is another valuable resource for information on pension rights.
- *Social Security and Other Benefits:*
  - Contact your local office of the Social Security Administration (SSA) for literature about Social Security benefits, or to ask specific questions about your own case (*www.ssa.gov*).
  - The National Organization of Social Security Claims Representatives (NOSSCR) is an association of more than 3,300 attorneys and paralegals who represent Social Security claimants. Its Web page at *www.nosscr.org* contains information about Social Security benefits, federal policy issues, and legal resources for claimants. Its telephone lawyer referral number is 800-431-2804.
- *Health Care Insurance, Medicaid, and Medicare:*
  - The ABA's Commission on Law and Aging has a consumer tool kit for health-care advance planning available at *www.abanet.org/aging*.
  - The Centers for Medicare and Medicaid Services maintains a website at *www.cms.gov* that contains comprehen-

sive information regarding Medicare and Medicaid. The website includes features such as detailed explanations of coverage under the two programs, frequently asked questions, and a list of publications, many of which can be accessed online. The Centers for Medicare and Medicaid Services can also be contacted at 7500 Security Boulevard, Baltimore, MD, 21244-1850, and by telephone at 410-786-3000 or 800-MEDICARE.
  - Medicare also maintains a consumer website at *www.medicare.gov*, which provides a wealth of information about Medicare, Medigap, Medicaid, and nursing homes. The website also has a Medigap Compare feature. This is an interactive tool for Medicare beneficiaries to help find the insurance companies in each state that sell Medigap plans.
  - Also see the website of Medicare Access for Patients-Rx (MAPRx), a coalition of patient, family caregiver, and health professional organizations: *http://MAPRx.info*.
  - Visit the website of the National Clearinghouse for Long-Term Care at *www.longtermcare.gov*. The U.S. Department of Health and Human Services developed this site to provide information on both public and private resources available to help in planning and paying for future long-term care needs.
- *Housing Options:*
  - Information regarding not-for-profit retirement communities is available from the American Association of Homes and Services for the Aging (AAHSA)(*www.aahsa.org*) and from its affiliated organization, the Continuing Care Accreditation Commission (CCAC)(*www.carf.org*).
  - The National Citizens' Coalition for Nursing Home Reform can provide you

with information regarding the rights of nursing-home residents, including how to contact the state long-term care ombudsman. It also publishes an excellent resource to help you with the care-planning process, entitled Nursing Homes: Getting Good Care There. It is available by writing to the organization at 1424 Sixteenth Street NW, Suite 202, Washington, DC 20036, or by calling 202-332-2275 or visiting its website at *www.nccnhr.org*.

○ State or local agencies on aging frequently prepare directories or guides on housing options for older persons and persons with disabilities. You can find your local agency's number in your local telephone book.

• *Controlling Your Affairs:*

○ Information about advance directives for health care is available from most state area agencies on aging and from many state bar associations and medical societies.

○ State-specific information and forms are also available from Partnership in Caring (formerly Partnership in Dying), an organization concerned with excellent end-of-life care, at *www .partnershipforcaring.org*.

○ Americans for Better Care of the Dying, at *www.abcd-caring.org*, publishes "Handbook for Mortals," an excellent guide for dealing with serious and eventually fatal illness.

○ Last Acts provides a wealth of similar information on its website, *www .lastacts.org*.

○ Information on elder abuse, including telephone numbers for state ombudsmen and adult protective services offices, is available at the website of the National Center on Elder Abuse, *www.elderabusecenter.org*. You can also find a local adult protective services

program by calling Eldercare Locator at 800-677-1116.

○ Another good source of information on elder abuse is the website of the National Committee for the Prevention of Elder Abuse, *www.preventelderabuse.org*.

○ If you are a victim of domestic violence, call the National Domestic Violence Hotline for assistance and information at 800-799-7233. See the discussion of domestic violence in Chapter 3, "Family Law," for more helpful information.

• *Services for Older Americans:*

○ National Council on the Aging, which can be contacted at 1901 L Street NW, Washington, DC 20036 (telephone: 800-479-1200; website: *www.ncoa.org*).

○ Older Women's League (*www .owl-national.org*).

○ Alliance of Retired Americans (*www .retiredamericans.org*).

○ You can get more information about Alzheimer's disease at your local Alzheimer's Association. Visit the national website at *www.alz.org*.

○ For more information about studying and traveling, contact your local agency on aging or write to Elderhostel at 11 Avenue de Lafayette, Boston, MA 02111 (toll-free telephone: 800-454-5768; website: *www.elderhostel.org*).

○ If you need help finding a lawyer who specializes in elder law, the NAELA website includes a geographical directory of its members and specifies those who are certified elder law lawyers. In addition, NAELA can provide consumer information about what questions to ask a lawyer to make sure he or she can meet your legal needs. You can contact NAELA through its website: *www.naela.org*.

○ Your state or local agency on aging can refer you to publicly funded legal programs. These programs, along with other possible sources of legal assistance, are listed on the website of the American Bar Association's Commission on Law and Aging, at *www.abanet.org/aging* (click on "Law and Aging Resource Guide," and then select your state).

Chapter 17—Estate Planning

- *General Information:*
  - The American Bar Association's Section of Real Property, Trust, and Estate Law offers useful information for the public on its website at *www.abanet.org/rpte/public.*
  - Nolo.com provides detailed information on planning your estate. Visit *www.nolo.com* and click on "Wills and Estate Planning."
  - FindLaw is another excellent site for the public, with plenty of information on wills and estates available at *consumer.pub.findlaw.com/wills.*
  - The Internet Law Library contains a long list of links to estate-planning articles at *www.lawmoose.com/internet-lawlib/112.htm.*
  - The National Association of Financial and Estate Planning website contains good information, especially for those with large estates, at *www.nafep.com.*
  - The ABA publishes a Guide to Wills and Estates that can be purchased from the ABA Web Store (*www.abanet.org/abastore*), Product Code 2350210. It is also available in bookstores across the country.
- *Finding an Estates Attorney:*
  - The ABA and your local and state bar association can be good starting points for finding an attorney experienced in estate planning.
  - Sites on the Web that enable you to find

more information, and sometimes the names of lawyers in your area, include the Senior Law website, *www.senior-law.com,* and the National Network of Estate Planning Attorneys website, *www.netplanning.com.*
  - The American College of Trust & Estate Counsel offers a membership listing of lawyers by state whose practices concentrate in estate planning. You can visit their website at *www.actec.org.*
  - The National Association of Estate Planners & Councils (*www.naepc.org*) can provide a listing of lawyers certified in estate planning through experience, education, and examination.
  - The National Academy of Elder Law Attorneys publishes a directory of elder law lawyer members, including those certified in elder law by the National Elder Law Foundation. Their website can be accessed at *www.naela.com.*
  - The American Academy of Estate Planning Attorneys website, *www.aaepa.com/consumers.aspx,* and the National Association of Financial and Estate Planning website, *www.nafep.com,* may also be useful if you are trying to find an estate-planning lawyer.
- *Information for Executors:*
  - IRS Publication 559 provides tax information for executors and survivors. You can access it online at *www.irs.gov/pub/irs-pdf/p559.pdf.*
  - Insurance company websites often feature useful information for executors and family members. For example, the United Services Automobile Association site provides information about the duties of an executor, the probate process, and suggestions for coping with grief; you can access it at *www.usaaedfoundation.org/family/cp01.asp.*

ABOUT THE AUTHORS AND EDITORS

This book benefited from the advice and careful review of numerous ABA members and other experts from all over the country. All of them generously gave their time to assure that this book is accurate, up-to-date, and complete. The various drafts of this book were the work of many writers and editors. Catherine Hawke of the staff of the Division for Public Education of the American Bar Association served as lead editor for the project. She was assisted by Charles Williams and other members of the Division staff.

Ms. Hawke is as an Editor/Program Manager and Associate Editor of *Preview of United States Supreme Court Cases*. Ms. Hawke manages and edits the Division's series of legal guides published by Random House. Additionally, she helps facilitate and edit the YourLaw newsletter and *Preview*. She received her BA in History and Political Science from the University of Michigan in 1999 and her J.D., summa cum laude, from Loyola University Chicago School of Law in 2006.

Mr. Williams is an associate director of the Division for Public Education and the editor of *Preview of United States Supreme Court Cases*. He is a graduate of the University of Maryland School of Law, where he served as Articles Editor for the *Maryland Law Review*.

Various authors and editors were responsible for each chapter. "Authors" of chapters wrote the chapter for this edition. "Editors" of chapters brought the chapters up-to-date, but did not write the original version.

Catherine Hawke served as the primary editor on the following chapters: "When and How to Use a Lawyer," "How the Legal System Works," "Con-

tracts and Consumer Law," "Automobiles," and "Health-Care Law." She revised and updated material from previous editions of this book.

Dianna J. Gould-Saltman, editor of the chapter on family law, is a principal in the Los Angeles firm of Gould-Saltman Law Office, LLP, specializing in mediation and litigation of family law issues. A certified family law specialist (The State Bar of California, Board of Legal Specialization) and a fellow of the American Academy of Matrimonial Lawyers and International Academy of Matrimonial Lawyers, Ms. Gould-Saltman received her B.A. in psychology from the University of California, Irvine and her J.D. from Southwestern University School of Law.

Eric Fish contributed the sections on international family law issues. Mr. Fish is a legislative counsel with the Uniform Law Commission. In this capacity, Mr. Fish covers uniform acts on family and procedural law. Mr. Fish received his A.B with Honors from the University of Chicago. He received his J.D. from the Loyola University of Chicago School of Law, where he also served as Editor in Chief of the Loyola *International Law Review*.

Rick Hackett edited the finances sections of the chapter on buying and selling a home. Mr. Hackett is a partner with Pierce Atwood, LLP, in Portland, Maine. His practice involves all aspects of state and federal regulation of retail financial products origination and marketing, e-payments, regulation of financial service entities, and lending, deposit, and insurance transactions. Mr. Hackett is a member of the faculty of the Morin Center for Banking Law at Boston University School of Law. From 1978 to 1979, he served as

Law Clerk to the Honorable Frank M. Coffin, then Chief Judge of the U.S. Court of Appeals to the First Circuit. Mr. Hackett holds an A.B. degree, Phi Beta Kappa, magna cum laude, from Dartmouth College (1972) and a J.D., summa cum laude, from Cornell University Law School (1978).

Marjorie Bradwell edited the chapter on home ownership. Ms. Bradwell is Vice President and Senior Staff Underwriting Counsel for the Fidelity National Title Group. A member of the Wisconsin State Bar, the Illinois State Bar and the American Bar Association, she has spent over thirty years in the title industry. In addition, Ms. Bradwell is the Chair of the Residential, Multi-Family and Special Use Group of the Real Property Probate and Trust section of the ABA, author of the ABA's new Web-based training module on the 2006 ALTA Policies, and a frequent speaker on title insurance and real estate-related topics.

Brian Smith, editor of the chapter on renting residential property, is an associate in the Real Estate Practice Group of Arnall Golden Gregory. Mr. Smith's practice focuses on commercial leasing. Mr. Smith is experienced in the representation of both landlords and tenants in the negotiation and leasing of retail, office and warehouse property. Mr. Smith also represents franchisors and franchisees in their negotiation of letters of intent, seeing the leasing process through to lease execution. Mr. Smith is a 2003 graduate of the University of Texas at Austin and a 2006 graduate of Mercer University, Walter F. George School of Law.

Wendy Nutt and Howard Rosen edited the chapter on law and the workplace. Ms. Nutt is Vice President of Labor Relations for MGM MIRAGE in Las Vegas, Nevada. Ms. Nutt is the Management Publications Co-Chair of the American Bar Association Section of Labor and Employment Law and serves as a Chapter Editor for the Section's Developing Labor Law publication.

When he is not practicing Ashtanga yoga, Mr. Rosen is a union and employee attorney with the firm of Posner & Rosen LLP. Mr. Rosen is the Union and Employee Publications Co-Chair of the American Bar Association Section of Labor and Employment Law and a member of the College of Labor and Employment Lawyers.

Amie Martinez and Dave Barber edited the chapter on personal injury law. Ms. Martinez is a shareholder in Anderson, Creager & Wittstruck, P.C. in Lincoln, Nebraska. Her practice includes civil litigation and family law. She is presently Chair of the Solo & Small Firm Committee within ABA TIPS, where she also participates on the Ethics and Professionalism Committee, Law in Public Service Committee and the Task Force on Outreach to Young Lawyers. She is active in her local and state bar associations, and she is a member of the ABA House of Delegates.

Mr. Barber is a plaintiff's trial lawyer in a three-attorney firm in Louisville, KY, practicing in state and federal courts. His past speaking and writing has included publications for new lawyers on mediation and civil trial practice, and continuing legal education on issues relating to personal injury litigation. He also enjoys coaching Little League baseball.

The consumer credit chapter was edited by Nessa Feddis, Catherine Brennan, and Michael Goodman.

Ms. Feddis is vice president and senior counsel to the ABA's Government Relations Division. She focuses on consumer banking, fraud, and payment system issues in the federal, legislative, and regulatory arenas. Ms. Feddis received her law degree from Catholic University and is a member of the Washington, D.C. Bar. She is also a fellow of the American College of Consumer Financial Services Lawyers and former Chair of the Subcommittee on Electronic Fund Transfers of the American Bar Association's Consumer Financial

Services Committee. Her articles discussing regulatory and legislative developments in consumer banking matters have appeared in *ABA Banking Journal* and *ABA Bank Compliance.*

Ms. Brennan is a partner with the law firm of Hudson Cook, LLP. She assists national and state banks, investment banks, commercial finance companies, savings associations, mortgage bankers and other licensed lenders in the development and maintenance of nationwide consumer mortgage and motor vehicle finance programs. Ms. Brennan received her B.A. from Fordham University in 1992 and her J.D. from State University of New York at Buffalo, Amherst in 1995.

Mr. Goodman is also a partner with the law firm of Hudson Cook, LLP. He works with retailers, mortgage bankers, automobile finance companies, and credit card companies in the development and maintenance of consumer credit programs. Prior to joining Hudson Cook, Mr. Goodman was a staff attorney with the Federal Trade Commission, Bureau of Consumer Protection. He has a B.A. from Wesleyan University and a J.D. from the University of Colorado School of Law.

Ralph Anzivino, editor of the chapter on bankruptcy, began teaching at Marquette University Law School in 1976, after five years of practicing law. He teaches contracts, creditor/debtor law, business bankruptcy, sales, and secured transactions. In addition to numerous law review articles and bar journal publications, Professor Anzivino is the author of the book *Partner and Partnership Bankruptcy.* He is also coauthor of the four-volume treatise *Uniform Commercial Code Transactions Guide,* and coauthor of the multi-volume set *Uniform Commercial Code Series.*

The chapter on computer law was edited by William B. Baker, Jose E. Guzman Jr., Mary P. Kirwan, and Michael Hawes.

William B. Baker is a partner in the Washington, D.C., law firm of Wiley Rein LLP. He has practiced for more than twenty years in the areas of technology, communications, and postal law, with particular interest in privacy, electronic commerce, and telecommunications. He is a frequent author and lecturer on privacy, Internet, and postal matters. A graduate of the University of Virginia's College of Arts and Sciences and School of Law, he lives in Arlington, Virginia, with his wife and two children.

Jose E. Guzman Jr. is a partner in the San Francisco office of Nossaman, Guthner, Knox & Elliott LLP specializing in telecommunications and other regulated public utilities. Mr. Guzman's practice is concentrated on regulatory and administrative law and business transactions involving utility and other infrastructure clients. He represents public utility, telecommunications, energy, water, and transportation companies in business transactions and before the California Public Utilities Commission, the California legislature, and other state and federal regulatory agencies. He also advises municipalities and other public agencies on telecommunications, cable television, water and transportation issues.

Mary P. Kirwan has practiced commercial litigation in Toronto, Canada, for several years, where she worked on a number of high-profile commercial and international white-collar crime and fraud cases. She was also a Senior Federal Crown Attorney in the wiretap and money laundering division at the Department of Justice in Toronto. Ms. Kirwan is a regular contributor to the *Globe and Mail* newspaper in Canada, and has written extensively about data security, risk management, corporate governance, and public policy issues.

Michael Hawes is a partner with Baker Botts LLP in Houston, Texas. He assists companies seeking to resolve technology disputes, handling cases concerning claims of patent and trademark infringement, antitrust violations, trade secret misappropriation, and violation of the intellectual property provisions of employment agreements.

Elizabeth Huber edited the finance sections of the automobile chapter. Ms. Huber is a partner in the Maryland firm Hudson Cook, LLP, and manages the firm's Los Angeles office. Her practice includes the counseling of financial institutions and financial services companies in the areas of consumer lending and retail financial services, including federal and state regulation of consumer lending and leasing and state licensing issues. Prior to joining Hudson Cook in January 1997, Ms. Huber served for nine years as in-house counsel with Toyota Financial Services, the finance subsidiary of Toyota Motor Sales USA, Inc. Prior to her tenure at Toyota Financial Services, Ms. Huber was in-house counsel with Mitsui Manufacturers Bank in Los Angeles. Ms. Huber was admitted to the California Bar in 1980 and the District of Columbia Bar in 1997. She graduated from Western State University College of Law in Orange County in 1980.

Jay Grenig authored the chapter on special needs and education. Professor Grenig is a professor of law at Marquette University Law School in Milwaukee, Wisconsin. He received his B.A. from Willamette University and his J.D. from the University of California, Hastings College of Law. He currently teaches administrative law, alternative dispute resolution, civil procedure, education law, and labor law. Professor Grenig has authored numerous books and articles and is the author of *Alternative Dispute Resolution* (3d ed., West Group).

Charlie Sabatino originally authored the chapter on the Rights of Older Americans and updated and edited the chapter for this edition. Walter Burke, JulieAnn Calareso, John Huffaker, Hunter Patrick, and Margadette Demet also edited the chapter for this edition.

Mr. Sabatino is the Director of the ABA Commission on Law and Aging and an Adjunct Professor at Georgetown University Law Center.

Mr. Burke has practiced in the areas of tax, estate planning, and financial planning. He currently practices in elder law (and did so before it was considered a viable practice area for attorneys). Mr. Burke is involved with the New York State Bar Association, the New York State Elder Law Executive Committee, the ABA's Senior Lawyers Division, and is a former Chair of the Elder Law Section in New York State. He currently practices at the law firm of Burke and Casserly, P.C.

Ms. Calareso is an associate attorney with the Albany, New York law firm of Burke & Casserly, P.C. A graduate of Fordham University and Albany Law School, she focuses her practice on elder law, trusts and estates, and business planning. She serves on the Board of Directors of the Northeastern New York Chapter of the Alzheimer's Association, and is a member of the New York State Bar Association's Elder Law and Trusts and Estates sections.

Mr. Huffaker was a legislative attorney on the staff of the Joint Committee on Taxation from 1953 to 1956, having graduated from UVA Law in 1948. His assignment included responsibility for the transition of the Estate and Gift Tax Chapters from the 1939 Code to the 1954 Code. He returned to private practice and ultimately became chair of the tax department at Pepper, Hamilton & Scheetz in Philadelphia. Mr. Huffaker is a former chairman of the Committee on Income Taxation of Trusts and Estates of the Tax Section of the ABA, and coauthor of the handbook on Taxation of Fiduciaries published by the Tax Section some years ago. He is currently coeditor of the Estates, Trusts & Gifts Department of the Journal of Taxation, and is active in the ABA Tax Section.

A principal in the firm of Demet & Demet, S.C., Ms. Demet's current practice is concentrated in estate planning, probate, trust work, and family law, including guardianships. She works extensively with the elderly and handicapped. She is a past officer and member of the Board of Governors of the State Bar of Wisconsin, and a Fellow of the Wisconsin Bar Foundation. Ms. Demet is a Life Fellow of the American Bar Foundation. She is Vice President and President-Elect of the Board of the Senior Lawyers Division of the State Bar of Wisconsin.

Mr. Patrick retired after thirty-seven years on the bench—nineteen in a part-time limited jurisdiction court, and then eighteen in a general jurisdiction state trial court—and decided to go back to practicing law. Currently, he practices primar-

ily elder law, focusing on estate planning and probate, in Powell, Wyoming.

Karin Prangley, editor of the chapter on estate planning, is an associate at the law firm of Winston & Strawn LLP in Chicago, Illinois. She advises individuals and families on a range of trust and estate-planning matters. She received a B.A. in Business, summa cum laude, from Mount St. Mary's University, and her J.D. from the University of Virginia School of Law, where she was elected to the Order of the Coif. Ms. Prangley is currently serving as a Fellow for the American Bar Association's Section on Real Property, Trust and Estate Law, and is also a member of several local and state bar associations.

ACKNOWLEDGMENTS

This book would not have been possible without the assistance of more than 150 American Bar Association members and other experts from all over the country. Law professors, judges, and practicing attorneys—as well as staff members of the American Bar Association and other bar associations—reviewed the material in the various chapters, assuring that the information was accurate, up-to-date, and expressed clearly, in laypersons' terms.

These experts generously donated their time to this effort. Many of them serve on American Bar Association committees in their areas of expertise. Others serve as writers and editors of American Bar Association scholarly and professional publications. They represent some of the finest minds in the association, and we are deeply grateful for their generosity with their time and their willingness to read drafts repeatedly as part of the process of making them accurate, clear, and helpful.

The reviewers are listed for each chapter to which they contributed.

CHAPTER ONE:
WHEN AND HOW TO USE A LAWYER

Arthur Garwin, Director of Publications and Conference Planning, Center for Professional Responsibility, American Bar Association, Chicago, Illinois;

William Hornsby, Staff Counsel, Division for Legal Services, American Bar Association, Chicago, Illinois;

Frances Johansen, Unauthorized Practice of Law Counsel, State Bar of Arizona, Phoenix, Arizona;

George Kuhlman, Associate Director and Ethics Counsel, Center for Professional Discipline, American Bar Association, Chicago, Illinois;

Marian P. McCulloch, Attorney, Allen Dell, P.A., Attorneys-at-Law, Tampa, Florida;

James Bernard McLindon, Chair, American Bar Association Standing Committee on Lawyer Referral and Information Service, and Attorney-at-Law, Northampton, Massachusetts;

Karma S. Rodgers, President, America Prepaid Legal Institute; Member, American Bar Association Task Force on Lawyers Center for Personal Legal Services; and Member, Butler Rodgers & Johnson LLC, Attorneys-at-Law, Milwaukee, Wisconsin;

Alec M. Schwartz, Associate Director, Division for Legal Services, American Bar Association, Chicago, Illinois;

Leopold Sher, Co-Chair, Standing Committee on Continuing Legal Education, American Bar Association Section of Real Property and Probate, and Attorney, Sher Garner Cahill et al., Attorneys-at-Law, New Orleans, Louisiana;

Sheree Swetin, Executive Director, San Diego County Bar Association, San Diego, California.

CHAPTER TWO: HOW THE LEGAL SYSTEM WORKS

Honorable Rebecca Albrecht, Past Chair, Lawyer's Conference of the Judicial Administration Division, American Bar Association, and Judge, Superior Court of Arizona, Maricopa County, Phoenix, Arizona;

Seth S. Andersen, Project Manager, Standing Committee on Judicial Independence, American Bar Association, Chicago, Illinois;

Honorable Louraine Arkfeld, Member, Coalition for Justice, American Bar Association, and Judge, Tempe Municipal Court, Tempe, Arizona;

Honorable Lorenzo Arredondo, Former Member,

Standing Committee on Public Education, American Bar Association, and Circuit Court Judge, Lake Circuit Court, Crown Point, Indiana;

Honorable Thomas Barland, Reserve Judge, Eau Claire County, Wisconsin;

Mary Lou Boland, Chair, Victims Committee, American Bar Association Criminal Justice Section, and Attorney, Cook County State's Attorney's Office, Chicago, Illinois;

Stephen J. Bronis, Co-Chair, Defense Function/Services Committee, American Bar Association Criminal Justice Section, and Partner, Zuckerman Spaeder LLP, Attorneys-at-Law, Miami, Florida;

Vincent A. Citro, Chair, Criminal and Juvenile Justice Committee, American Bar Association Young Lawyers Section, and Attorney, Lowndes Drosdick Doster et al., Attorneys-at-Law, Orlando, Florida;

Amie L. Clifford, Member, American Bar Association Standing Committee on Substance Abuse, and Assistant Director, National College of District Attorneys, University of South Carolina, Columbia, South Carolina;

Honorable B. Michael Dann, Judge (ret.), Superior Court of Arizona, Maricopa County, Phoenix, Arizona, and Visiting Fellow, National Center for State Courts, Williamsburg, Virginia;

David Durfee, Executive Director of Legal Affairs, Administrative Office of the Courts, Maryland Judicial Center, Annapolis, Maryland;

Robert D. Evans, Director, Governmental Affairs Office, American Bar Association, Washington, D.C.;

Eileen Gallagher, Staff Director, ABA Standing Committee on Federal Judicial Improvements, American Bar Association, Chicago, Illinois;

Michael F. Garrahan, Trial Court Services, Special Programs Unit, Administrative Office of the Courts, State of New Jersey, Trenton, New Jersey;

Gerald T. Giaimo, Co-Coordinator, Special Projects, American Bar Association Young Lawyers Division, and Attorney, Tyler Cooper & Alcorn LLP, Attorneys-at-Law, New Haven, Connecticut;

Honorable Janice Gradwohl, Former Presiding Judge, County Court, Third Judicial District of Nebraska, and Adjunct Professor of Law, University of Nebraska College of Law, Lincoln, Nebraska;

Jolanta Juszkiewicz, Deputy Director, Pretrial Services Resource Center, Washington, D.C.;

Steven M. Kowal, Chair, Criminal Practice and Procedure Committee, American Bar Association Section of Antitrust Law, and Member, Bell, Boyd & Lloyd LLC, Attorneys-at-Law, Chicago, Illinois;

Honorable Gary Lumpkin, Presiding Judge, Oklahoma Court of Criminal Appeals, Oklahoma City, Oklahoma;

Jack B. Middleton, Past Secretary, American Bar Association; Member, House of Delegates, American Bar Association; and President, McLane, Graf, Raulerson & Middleton PA, Attorneys-at-Law, Manchester, New Hampshire;

Laura Ariane Miller, Co-Chair, Criminal Litigation Committee, American Bar Association; Past Chair, Health Litigation Committee, American Bar Association; and Partner, Nixon Peabody LLP, Attorneys-at-Law, Washington, D.C.;

Wallace John Mlyniec, Associate Dean (Clinical Education and Public Service Programs), Lupo-Ricci Professor of Clinical Legal Studies, and Director, Juvenile Justice Clinic, Georgetown University Law Center, Washington, D.C.;

Honorable Gayle A. Nachtigal, Circuit Court Judge, Washington County Circuit Court, Hillsboro, Oregon;

Paula Nessel, Staff Director, Coalition for Justice, American Bar Association, Chicago, Illinois;

Honorable James A. Noe, Past Chair, American

Bar Association National Conference of State Trial Judges; Past Chair, American Bar Association Judicial Division; Past Judiciary Member, ABA Board of Governors; and Judge (Ret.), King County Superior Court, Seattle, Washington;

Robert O'Neil, Director, Thomas Jefferson Center, Charlottesville, Virginia;

Barry Pollack, Chair, Subcommittee on Federal Rules and Jury Instructions, American Bar Association Section of Litigation Criminal Litigation Committee, and Partner, Nixon Peabody LLP, Attorneys-at-Law, Washington, D.C.;

Alan Raphael, Associate Professor of Law, Loyola University Chicago School of Law, Chicago, Illinois;

David A. Sellers, Assistant Director for Public Affairs, Administrative Office of the United States Courts, Washington, D.C.;

Honorable Norma L. Shapiro, Chair, Coordinating Council of the Justice Center, American Bar Association, and Judge, U.S. District Court, Philadelphia, Pennsylvania;

Honorable James Scott Sledge, Chair, American Bar Association Judicial Division, and United States Bankruptcy Judge, Northern District of Alabama, Anniston, Alabama;

Kathy Swedlow, Assistant Professor of Law and Deputy Director, Cooley Innocence Project, Thomas M. Cooley Law School, Lansing, Michigan;

Honorable Daniel E. Wathen, Former Chief Justice, Maine Supreme Judicial Court, now Of Counsel to Pierce Atwood, Attorneys-at-Law, Portland, Maine.

Pauline Weaver, Member, Board of Governors, American Bar Association; Member, General Practice, Solo and Small Firm Council, American Bar Association; and Public Defender, Alameda County, California.

CHAPTER THREE: FAMILY LAW

Willard DaSilva, Member, Council of the Section of Family Law, American Bar Association, and Partner, DaSilva, Hilowitz & McEvily LLP, Attorneys-at-Law, Garden City, New York;

Howard Davidson, Director, Center on Children and the Law, American Bar Association, Washington, D.C.;

Linda Elrod, Past Chair, Family Law Section, American Bar Association, and Professor of Law, Washburn University School of Law, Topeka, Kansas;

Diane Geraghty, Professor of Law, Loyola University Chicago School of Law, Chicago, Illinois;

Honorable Debra Lehrmann, Judge, 360th District Court, Fort Worth, Texas;

Ira Harold Lurvey, Past Chair, American Bar Association Family Law Section, and Partner, Lurvey & Shapiro, Attorneys-at-Law, Los Angeles, California;

Laura W. Morgan, Vice-Chair, Conference of State and Local Bar Family Law Leaders, American Bar Association Family Law Section, and Owner, Family Law Consulting, Charlottesville, Virginia;

Ronald W. Nelson, Member, Council of the American Bar Association Family Law Section, and Partner, Nelson & Booth, Attorneys-at-Law, Overland Park, Kansas;

Arnold Rutkin, Attorney-at-Law, Westport, Connecticut;

Carolyn J. Stevens, Chair, Family Law Committee, American Bar Association General Practice Section, and Attorney-at-Law, Lolo, Montana.

CHAPTER FOUR: HEALTH-CARE LAW

Lawrence Gostin, Professor of Law, Georgetown University; Professor of Public Health, the Johns Hopkins University; and Director, Center for Law & the Public's Health, Washington, D.C.;

Ami S. Jaeger, Chair, Subcommittee on Genetic Research, Committee on Regulation of Research, American Bar Association; Co-Chair, Assisted Reproductive Technology and

Genetics Committee, American Bar Association; and Principal, BioLaw Group LLC, Santa Fe, New Mexico;

Timothy Jost, Robert L. Willett Family Professor, Washington and Lee University School of Law, Lexington, Virginia;

Joan Polacheck, Partner, McDermott, Will & Emery, Attorneys-at-Law, Chicago, Illinois;

Salvatore J. Russo, Past Chair, Health Law Section, New York State Bar Association, and Executive Senior Counsel, New York City Health & Hospitals Corporation, New York, New York;

Bethany J. Spielman, Member, Planning Board, *Health Lawyer*, American Bar Association, and Associate Professor, Department of Medical Humanities, SIU School of Medicine, Springfield, Illinois.

CHAPTER SIX: PERSONAL INJURY

William Ryan Acomb, Vice-Chair, Self Insurers and Risk Managers Committee, and Immediate Past Chair and Current Website Coordinator, Automobile Law Committee, American Bar Association Section of Tort and Insurance Practice, and Member, Porteous Hainkel et al. LLP, Attorneys-at-Law, New Orleans, Louisiana;

Stanley Jerome Cohn, Attorney, Lugenbuhl Wheaton Peck et al., Attorneys-at-Law, New Orleans, Louisiana;

Peter Kochanski, Attorney-at-Law, Baltimore, Maryland;

William R. Levasseur, Attorney-at-Law, Baltimore, Maryland;

Stephen I. Richman, Partner, Richman & Smith LLP, Attorneys-at-Law, Washington, Pennsylvania;

Mark L. Sklan, Attorney, Law Office of Linda Libertucci, Orange, California;

Michelle Tilton, Revenue Officer, Tort and Insurance Practice Section, American Bar Association; Former Director and Special Projects Chair, Young Lawyers Division,

American Bar Association; and Executive Vice-President, First Media Insurance Specialists, Inc., Kansas City, Missouri.

CHAPTER SEVEN: BUYING AND SELLING A HOME; AND CHAPTER EIGHT: HOME OWNERSHIP

Gurdon Buck, Former Member, Council of the Real Property, Probate and Trust Law Section, American Bar Association, and Counsel, Robinson and Cole, Attorneys-at-Law, Hartford, Connecticut;

Sally H. Foote, Partner, Thompson and Foote, P.A., Attorneys-at-Law, Clearwater, Florida;

Richard M. Frome, Vice-Chair, Committee on Assigning and Subleasing, American Bar Association Section of Real Property, Probate, and Trust Law, and Attorney-at-Law, New York, New York;

David Haron, Principal, Frank, Stefani, Haron & Weiner, Attorneys-at-Law, Troy, Michigan;

Jonathan Hoyt, Past Chair, Purchase and Sale of Residential Real Estate Committee, American Bar Association, and Attorney-at-Law, Clinton, Connecticut;

Jack S. Levey, Past Vice-Chair, Title Insurance Committee, American Bar Association; Member, Commercial Leasing Group, American Bar Association; and Attorney-at-Law, Columbus, Ohio;

Ronald J. Maas, General Counsel, Century/Intercounty Title Agency, Inc., Pine Brook, New Jersey;

Frank A. Melchior, Vice-President & Senior Underwriting Counsel, New Jersey Title Insurance Company, Parsippany, New Jersey;

Ellen G. Pollack, Council Member-at-Large, General Practice, Solo and Small Firm Section, American Bar Association, and Attorney, Fentin & Goldman LLP, White Plains, New York;

Julius Zschau, Partner, Pennington, Moore, Wilkinson, Bell & Dunbar, P.A., Attorneys-at-Law, Tampa, Florida.

CHAPTER NINE: RENTING RESIDENTIAL PROPERTY

Allison Gould, Vice-Chair, Committee on Affordable Housing, American Bar Association Section of Real Property, Probate, and Trust Law, and Attorney in Atlanta, Georgia;

Myron Moskovitz, Professor of Law, Golden Gate University School of Law, San Francisco, California;

Tracie R. Porter, Vice-Chair, Public Education Committee, American Bar Association Section of Real Property, Probate, and Trust Law, and Attorney, Brown Udell & Pomerantz, Attorneys-at-Law, Chicago, Illinois;

Frederic White, Jr., Professor of Law, Cleveland Marshall College of Law, Cleveland State University, Cleveland, Ohio.

CHAPTER TEN: CONSUMER CREDIT

James C. Conboy, President and Chief Operating Officer, Citizens National Bank, Cheboygan, Michigan;

John L. Culhane, Jr., Former Member, Consumer Financial Services Committee, American Bar Association Business Law Section, and Partner, Ballard Spahr et al., Attorneys-at-Law, Philadelphia, Pennsylvania;

Marianne B. Culhane, Professor of Law, Creighton University School of Law, Omaha, Nebraska;

Michael M. Greenfield, Walter D. Coles Professor of Law, Washington University School of Law, St. Louis, Missouri;

Thomas B. Hudson, Member, Consumer Financial Services Committee, American Bar Association Business Law Section, and Member, Hudson Cook LLP, Attorneys-at-Law, Linchicum, Maryland;

Robert W. Johnson, Former Director, Credit Research Center, Krannert Graduate School of Management, Purdue University, and Member, Consumer Credit Intelligence LLC, Greenwich, Connecticut.

CHAPTER ELEVEN: CONSUMER BANKRUPTCY

Sara A. Austin, Attorney, Blakey, Yost, Bupp & Rausch LLP, Attorneys-at-Law, York, Pennsylvania;

Honorable Bernice Donald, Judge, U.S. District Court, Memphis, Tennessee;

David A. Greer, Vice-Chair, Consumer Bankruptcy Committee, American Bar Association Business Law Section, and Principal, Hofeimer Nusbaum, P.C., Attorneys-at-Law, Norfolk, Virginia;

John P. Hennigan, Jr., Professor of Law, St. John's University School of Law, Jamaica, New York;

Shayna Michele Steinfeld, Co-Chair, Bankruptcy Committee, American Bar Association Family Law Section, and Partner, Steinfeld & Steinfeld, P.C., Attorneys-at-Law, Atlanta, Georgia.

CHAPTER TWELVE: CONTRACTS AND CONSUMER LAW

Michael M. Greenfield, Walter D. Coles Professor of Law, Washington University School of Law, St. Louis, Missouri;

Robert M. Langer, Chair, Consumer Protection Committee, American Bar Association Antitrust Section, and Attorney, Wiggin & Dana LLP, Attorneys-at-Law, Hartford, Connecticut;

Frederick H. Miller, Professor of Law, University of Oklahoma Law Center, Norman, Oklahoma.

CHAPTER THIRTEEN: COMPUTER LAW

Jeffrey Allen, Vice-Chair, Committee on Communications and Technology, American Bar Association Senior Lawyers Division, and Partner, Graves & Allen, Attorneys-at-Law, Oakland, California;

Elizabeth W. Benet, Chair, Emerging Issues Committee, American Bar Association Tort and Insurance Practice Section, and Second

Vice-President and New Product Development Specialist, GeneralCologne Re, Stamford, Connecticut;

Katherine Catlos, Partner, Lewis Brisbois Bisgaard & Smith, Attorneys-at-Law, San Francisco, California;

Debbie Chong, CEO, Virtual Boardwalk/Lenos, San Francisco, California;

William Sloan Coats, Division Chair, Computer Law Division, American Bar Association Section of Science and Technology Law, and Partner, Orrick Herrington & Sutcliffe, Attorneys-at-Law, Menlo Park, California;

Daniel A. Cotter, Member, E-Commerce Committee, American Bar Association Section of Tort and Insurance Practice, and Counsel, Unitrin, Inc., Chicago, Illinois;

Richard Field, Secretary, American Bar Association Section of Science and Technology Law, and Attorney-at-Law, Cliffside Park, New Jersey;

Ivan K. Fong, Vice-Chair, American Bar Association Section of Science and Technology Law, and Senior Counsel, E-Commerce & Information Technology, General Electric Company, Fairfield, Connecticut;

Rolland E. Grefe, Liaison from American Bar Association Senior Lawyers Section to the Standing Committee on Technology and Information Systems and Co-Founder, Grefe & Sidney PLC, Attorneys-at-Law, Des Moines, Iowa;

Shannon B. Hartsfield, Vice-Chair, Committee on eHealth and Privacy, American Bar Association Health Law Section, and Partner, Holland & Knight LLP, Attorneys-at-Law, Tallahassee, Florida;

Lester L. Hewitt, Partner, Akin Gump Strauss et al., Attorneys-at-Law, Houston, Texas;

Jonathan S. Jennings, Chair, Federal Trademark Legislation Committee, American Bar Association Section of Intellectual Property Law, and Attorney, Pattishall McAuliffe et al., Attorneys-at-Law, Chicago, Illinois;

Armando Lasa-Ferrer, Member, American Bar Association Board of Governors, and Partner, Lasa Monroig & Veve, Attorneys-at-Law, Guaynabo, Puerto Rico;

William Joseph Luddy, Jr., Vice-Chair, Computer Law Division, American Bar Association Section of Science and Technology Law, and Clinical Professor, Lally School of Management & Technology, Rensselaer Polytechnic Institute, Hartford, Connecticut;

David W. Maher, Chair, Committee on Internet Governance, American Bar Association Section of Science and Technology Law, and Partner, Sonnenschein Nath & Rosenthal, Attorneys-at-Law, Chicago, Illinois;

Joseph I. Rosenbaum, Partner, Reed Smith LLP, Attorneys-at-Law, New York, New York;

Randy V. Sabett, Vice-Chair, Committee on Information Security, American Bar Association Section of Science and Technology Law, and Attorney, Cooley Godward LLP, Attorneys-at-Law, Reston, Virginia;

Ruven Schwartz, Vice-Chair, Electronic Commerce Division, American Bar Association Section of Science and Technology Law, and Business Systems Consultant, Wells Fargo Cryptography Services, Minneapolis, Minnesota;

Thomas J. Smedinghoff, Past Chair, American Bar Association Section of Science and Technology Law, and Partner, Baker & McKenzie, Attorneys-at-Law, Chicago, Illinois;

Sandra P. Thompson, Chair, Special Committee on Patents and the Internet, American Bar Association Section of Intellectual Property Law, and Attorney, Rutan & Tucker LLP, Attorneys-at-Law, Costa Mesa, California;

Jonathan B. Wilson, Chair, Internet Industry Committee, American Bar Association Section of Public Utility Law, and Assistant General Counsel, Interland, Inc., Atlanta, Georgia;

Stephen S. Wu, Co-Chair, Committee on Information Security, American Bar Association Section of Science and Technology Law, and

President and CEO, InfoSec Law Group, PC, Los Altos, California.

CHAPTER FOURTEEN: AUTOMOBILES

James J. Ahern, Partner, Ahern, Maloney & Moran LLC, Attorneys-at-Law, Chicago, Illinois.

CHAPTER FIFTEEN: LAW AND THE WORKPLACE

Tom Allison, Partner, Allison, Slutsky & Kennedy, P.C., Attorneys-at-Law, Chicago, Illinois;

Alan Blanco, Attorney, Rothman Gordon, P.C., Attorneys-at-Law, Pittsburgh, Pennsylvania;

Donald W. Cohen, Arbitrator and Mediator, Glenview, Illinois;

Jay Grenig, Professor of Law, Marquette University Law School, Milwaukee, Wisconsin;

Peggy Hillman, Attorney, Macey Macey & Swanson, Attorneys-at-Law, Indianapolis, Indiana;

Kenneth D. Kleinman, Co-Chair (Management), Occupational Safety and Health Law Committee, American Bar Association Section of Employment and Labor Law, and Shareholder, Stevens & Lee, Attorneys-at-Law, Wayne, Pennsylvania;

Louis B. Kushner, Co-Chair (Union), Employment Rights and Responsibilities Committee, American Bar Association Section of Labor and Employment Law, and Attorney, Rothman Gordon, P.C., Attorneys-at-Law, Pittsburgh, Pennsylvania;

Adrienne Mazura, Partner, Piper, Marbury, Rudnick, et al., Attorneys-at-Law, Chicago, Illinois;

Susan Potter Norton, Co-Chair, Employment and Labor Relations Committee, American Bar Association Section of Litigation, and Partner, Allen Norton & Blue, P.A., Attorneys-at-Law, Coral Gables, Florida;

Steven F. Pockrass, Attorney, Ice Miller, Attorneys-at-Law, Indianapolis, Indiana;

Theodore St. Antoine, Degan Professor of Law, University of Michigan Law School, Ann Arbor, Michigan;

Darlene A. Vorachek, Co-Chair (Plaintiff), Employment Rights and Responsibilities Committee, American Bar Association Section of Labor and Employment Law, and Partner, Abrahamson Vorachek & Mikva, Attorneys-at-Law, Chicago, Illinois;

Paul Wyler, California Unemployment Insurance Appeals Board, Los Angeles, California.

CHAPTER SIXTEEN: THE RIGHTS OF OLDER AMERICANS

The Center for Law and Aging of the American Bar Association is a nationally recognized source of information on law for older Americans. Its mission is to strengthen and secure the legal rights, dignity, autonomy, quality of life, and quality of care of elders. It carries out this mission through research, policy development, technical assistance, advocacy, education, and training.

Five lawyers on the staff of the Center reviewed this chapter. In addition to the team leader Charles P. Sabatino, Assistant Director of the Commission on Law and Aging and Adjunct Professor at Georgetown University Law Center, they were:

Stephanie Edelstein, Associate Staff Director, who specializes in housing, economic security, and legal-services delivery issues;

Naomi Karp, Associate Staff Director, who specializes in grandparent visitation, kinship care, health care, nursing homes, and dispute resolution;

Lori Stiegel, Associate Staff Director, who specializes in elder abuse, alternatives to guardianship, consumer fraud, and legal-services delivery; and

Erica Wood, Associate Staff Director, who specializes in issues concerning guardianship, long-term care, dispute resolution, court access, and legal services delivery.

CHAPTER SEVENTEEN: ESTATE PLANNING

Lena Barnett, Attorney-at-Law, Silver Spring, Maryland;

Michael G. Cumming, Member, Dykema Gossett PLLC, Attorneys-at-Law, Bloomfield Hills, Michigan;

Edgar T. Farmer, Of Counsel, Husch & Eppenberger, Attorneys-at-Law, St. Louis, Missouri;

Thomas M. Featherston, Council Member and Probate Editor of *Probate and Property Magazine,* American Bar Association Section of Real Property, Probate and Property Magazine, American Bar Association Section of Real Property, Probate and Trust Law, and Mills Cox Professor of Law, Baylor Law School, Waco, Texas;

Susan N. Gary, Associate Articles Editor for Probate and Trust of *Probate and Property Magazine,* American Bar Association Section of Real Property, Probate and Trust Law, and Associate Professor of Law, School of Law, University of Oregon, Eugene, Oregon;

Rik Huhtanen, Attorney-at-Law, Eugene, Oregon;

John Laster, Co-Chair, Committee on Estate Planning for Individuals with Multi-State Property or Contacts, American Bar Association Section of Real Property, Probate and Trust Law, and Attorney-at-Law, Falls Church, Virginia;

Rebecca C. Morgan, Vice-Chair, Health Care Decisions Committee, American Bar Association Section of Real Property, Probate and Trust Law, and Boston Asset Management Distinguished Professor of Law and Director, Center for Excellence in Elder Law, Stetson University College of Law, Gulfport, Florida;

Harold Pskowski, Acquisitions Editor for Probate and Trust, Media/Book Products, American Bar Association Section of Real Property, Probate and Trust Law, and Attorney, BNA Tax Management, Washington, D.C.;

Douglas J. Rasmussen, Member, Clark Hill PLC, Attorneys-at-Law, Detroit, Michigan;

Pamela L. Rollins, Partner, Simpson Thacher & Bartlett, Attorneys-at-Law, New York, New York;

Charles P. Sabatino, Associate Director, American Bar Association Commission on Law and Aging, Washington, D.C.;

Michael D. Whitty, Co-Chair, Committee on Estate Planning and Administration for Business Owners, American Bar Association Section of Real Property, Probate and Trust Law, and Partner, Winston & Strawn, Attorneys-at-Law, Chicago, Illinois.

INDEX